POPULAR STORIES OF
ANCIENT EGYPT

ॐ

ABC-CLIO CLASSIC FOLK AND FAIRY TALES

Jack Zipes, Series Editor

Collectors in the nineteenth and early twentieth centuries unearthed a wealth of stories from around the world and published them in English translations for the delight of general readers, young and old. Most of these anthologies have been long out of print.

The ABC-CLIO Classic Folk and Fairy Tales series brings back to life these key anthologies of traditional tales from the golden age of folklore discovery. Each volume provides a freshly typeset but otherwise virtually unaltered edition of a classic work and each is enhanced by an authoritative introduction by a top scholar. These insightful essays discuss the significance of the collection and its original collector; the original collector's methodology and translation practices; and the original period context according to region or genre.

Certain to be of interest to folklorists, these classic collections are also meant to serve as sources for storytellers and for sheer reading pleasure, reviving as they do hundreds of folk stories, both reassuringly familiar and excitingly strange.

OTHER TITLES IN THIS SERIES:

Creation Myths of Primitive America, by Jeremiah Curtin;
Introduction by Karl Kroeber

English Fairy Tales and More English Fairy Tales, by Joseph Jacobs;
Introduction by Donald Haase

Italian Popular Tales, by Thomas Frederick Crane;
Introduction by Jack Zipes

Folktales from Northern India, by William Crooke and
Pandit Ram Gharib Chaube;
Introduction by Sadhana Naithani

Old Deccan Days or Hindoo Fairy Legends, by Mary Frere;
Introduction by Kirin Narayan

Popular Tales and Fictions, by William Alexander Clouston;
Introduction by Christine Goldberg

POPULAR STORIES

OF

ANCIENT EGYPT

SIR G. MASPERO

EDITED AND WITH AN INTRODUCTION
BY HASAN EL-SHAMY

Santa Barbara, California
Denver, Colorado   Oxford, England

Copyright © 2002 by ABC-CLIO, Inc.

Library of Congress Cataloging-in-Publication Data

Maspero, G. (Gaston), 1846–1916.
  Popular stories of ancient Egypt / by Sir G. Maspero; edited and with an introduction by Hasan El Shamy.
      p. cm. — (ABC-CLIO classic folk and fairy tales)
Includes index.
  ISBN 1-57607-639-3 (hardcover: alk. paper)
  1. Tales—Egypt. 2. Legends—Egypt. 3. Egypt—Civilization—To 332 B. C. I. El-Shamy, Hasan M., 1938– II. Title. III. Series.
  GR355.M37 2002
  398.2'0932—dc21

                              2002008009

        06 05 04 03 02   10 9 8 7 6 5 4 3 2 1 (cloth)

This edition reprints in its entirety and retains the original chapter sequence of Popular Stories of Ancient Egypt, *collected and edited by Gaston Maspero, translated by Mrs. C. H. W. Johns, published in New York by G. P. Putnam's Sons and in London by H. Grevel & Co., 1915. The text of this edition has been altered only to fit an increased page dimension and to reflect contemporary typographical conventions.*

ABC-CLIO, Inc.
130 Cremona Drive, P.O. Box 1911
Santa Barbara, California 93116–1911

This book is also available on the World Wide Web as an e-book. Visit www.abc-clio.com for details.

Contents

*Introduction to This Edition and Classification
  by Tale-Type and Motif*   VII

Preface to English Edition   XCI

Introduction   XCIII

Complete Stories

1   The Story of the Two Brothers   1

2   The King Khufuî and the Magicians   17

3   The Lamentations of the Fellah   35

4   The Memoirs of Sinuhît   55

5   The Shipwrecked Sailor   81

6   How Thutîyi Took the City of Joppa   89

   The Cycle of Satni-Khamoîs:

7   I. The Adventure of Satni-Khamoîs with
       the Mummies   95

8   II. The Veritable History of Satni-Khamoîs
        and His Son Senosiris   118

9   III. How Satni-Khamoîs Triumphed over
         the Assyrians   137

   The Cycle of Ramses II:

10 I. The Daughter of the Prince of Bakhtan
       and the Possessing Spirit   141

Contents

11   II. The Exploits of Sesôstris   147

12   III. The Exploits of Osimandyas   150

13   The Doomed Prince   153

14   The Story of Rhampsinitus   163

15   The Voyage of Unamunu to the Coasts of Syria   169

The Cycle of Petubastis:

16   I. The High Emprise for the Cuirass   181

17   II. The High Emprise for the Throne of Amon   201

Fragments

Introductory Note   217

18   Fragment of a Fantastic Story, Anterior to the Eighteenth Dynasty   219

19   The Quarrel of Apôpi and Saqnûnrîya   223

20   Fragments of a Ghost Story   229

21   Story of a Mariner   233

22   The Adventure of the Sculptor Petêsis and King Nectonabo   239

23   Fragments of the Theban-Coptic Version of the Romance of Alexander   243

24   Epigraph: On Those Who Caused Alexander to Drink the Death Potion   255

Index of Proper Names   257

Index of General Subjects   269

About the Volume Editor   277

꣠

Introduction to This Edition
and
Classification by Tale-Type and Motif
of Maspero's
Popular Stories of Ancient Egypt
Hasan El-Shamy

The Author

Sir Gaston Camille Charles Maspero is one of the towering figures in the fields of Egyptology and archaeology. He was born in France on June 23, 1846, to a French mother and an Italian father; he died on June 30, 1916.

Maspero's interest in ancient Egypt and classical cultures emerged while he was still a teenager. He was introduced to the study of hieroglyphs by Auguste Mariette (1821–1881), founder and director of the service des antiquités de l'Égypte and the musée de Boulaq in Cairo (currently the Egyptian Museum). He was educated at the Lycée Louis-le-Grand and the École Normale. Shortly afterward, he became professor of Egyptology at the École des Hautes Études, and he was appointed professor of Egyptian Philology and Archaeology at the Collège de France in 1874.

The opportunity to visit Egypt came in 1880; he went as part of a French mission, an organization that later became known as the Institute Français d'Archaeologie Orientale. He worked closely with Auguste Mariette, his mentor, and when Mariette died one year later, Maspero succeeded him to the directorship of the Service and the Boulaq Museum. His tenure in that position of leadership was for a period of some twenty years, in two intervals: from 1881 to 1886, and again from 1899 to 1914.

Maspero organized the Service into inspectorates throughout Egypt, and traveled extensively up and down the Nile on board a private houseboat, often accompanied by friends. Thus, he came into close contact with the Egyptian population, especially laborers who worked on excavation sites, and observed their traditional activities, especially singing, which he tried to collect (see pp. xxviii–xxxi, below). Also, in between those trips to investigate archaeological sites, he carried out his own work at Giza and arranged for the recording of the tombs in the Valley of the Kings. Many discoveries are credited to him. In 1881, the appearance of small royal objects on the antiquities market alerted officials to the possibility of an ongoing grave robbery. In a manner reminiscent of the "The Story of Rhampsinitus,"[1] the investigation of the source and the search for the grave robber led to a major discovery of royal mummies in Deir el-Bahari, which were quickly moved to the museum in Cairo.

Maspero proved to be a meticulous scholar with vast knowledge in a variety of fields, and a prolific author. More than one thousand books and articles on Egyptology, the history of civilization, and affiliated subjects bear his name. Among his chief works is the editing of the fifty-volume Cairo Catalogue of Antiquities and the Nubian Temple volumes.

Biographers describe Maspero as having been "sociable," "diplomatic," "shrewd," and "portly." These personal characteristics were advantageous traits for running the Service, since archaeological activities often revolved around social life and interaction with foremen and laborers. Also, being "portly" may be presumed to have given him an aura of kindness among Egyptian and other Arabic-speaking assistants.[2] (See "…. Fieldwork Factor in Maspero's Work," pp. xxviii–xxx, below).

Through his international contacts, Maspero won support for his projects from a wide circle of influential persons in the West. He was also helpful to fellow authors, such as Sir William Matthew Flinders Petrie, whose illustrated *Egyptian Tales* was published in 1895.[3]

Maspero returned to France in 1914 as permanent secretary of the Académie des inscriptions et belles lettres. He died two years later, at age 70, as he was about to address a meeting of the Académie in Paris.[4]

---

1. See tale No. 14, pp. 196–201, in Maspero's *Popular Stories.*

2. Mot. W256.8.2.3§, "Fat persons are good hearted." See: H. El-Shamy, *Folk Traditions of the Arab World: A Guide to Motif Classification,* 2 vols. (Indiana University Press, Bloomington, Ind., 1995).

3. Petrie acknowledged his indebtedness to Maspero's *Contes,* and described his own *Tales* as the first book that presents in the English language "the oldest literature and fiction of the world." Petrie, Series I, p. 2.

4. Some sources describe Maspero's life as "marred by tragedy" (perhaps a hyperbole): he lost his first wife early in their married life, then he lost a beloved son in World War I. It is

The Book

Popular Stories of Ancient Egypt is an anthology of narratives gleaned from various ancient written sources. When first published in 1882, under the title *Contes populaires de l'Égypte ancienne*,[5] it was the first anthology of ancient Egyptian narratives in book form.

The link between ancient Egyptian narrative accounts and folktales (*contes populaires*) was established in 1852 when Emmanuel de Rougé announced the discovery of the "Tale of Two Brothers." The tale came to be viewed as a work of pure fantasy, a category of narrative not beforehand encountered in Egyptian records. Previously known narratives belonged to the realms of belief (myths, religious legends) and of the factual (historical legends, personal experiences, and business reports).

A flurry of studies of that tale and debates about its nature ensued. In 1859 W. Mannhardt designated the tale as "the oldest Märchen" in the world—a viewpoint cited by Maspero and recently confirmed in an exhaustive monographic study of that tale.[6] Maspero contributed to the debates with studies focused on the story.[7] His interest in the folktale peaked with the publication of the present anthology, which assembled scattered texts of ancient Egyptian stories and in which "The Tale of the Two Brothers" was the lead text as *the* celebrated ancient folktale.

In response to demands by a readership that was broad and diverse, three more editions of the anthology were published.[8] The edition in English appeared in 1915.[9] The translator, Mrs. C. H. W. Johns, states

suspected that Maspero's sudden death might have been due to a "broken heart." Another son was killed in World War II (but that loss couldn't have affected Maspero). A grandson established the Maspéro Publishing House in commemoration of his august grandfather and his distinguished services to the world of knowledge.

5. A volume in Les littératures populaires de toutes les nations, IV. Paris: Maisonneuve et Cie.

6. See Maspero, *Popular Stories,* p. 1. Also see Susan T. Hollis, *The Ancient Egyptian "Tale of Two Brothers," The Oldest Fairy Tale in the World.* University of Oklahoma Press: Norman and London 1990.

7. E.g., Gaston Maspero. "Le Conte des deux frères: récit égyptien d'il y à trois mille ans," in *Revue de Cours Littéraires,* 7 (Feb. 28, 1871): 780–84; and "Conte des deux frères," in *Revue Archéologique*, XXXV (March 1878). 164–79.

8. In 1889, 1906, 1911; more recently a reprint of the first edition was issued in 1998, Maisonneuve et Larose.

9. Offered here by ABC-CLIO in the new series. Also it was reprinted in 1967: New Hyde Park, N.Y.: University Books.

that the translated work received additional scrutiny and significant augmentations from Maspero himself. Thus, the 1915 English edition may be viewed as Maspero's last major undertaking before his death in 1916.

The original work contained thirteen (13) texts[10] divided into two groups: the first, which was not labeled, consisted of seven (7) presumably "nonfragmentary" texts; the second, labeled "fragments," consisted of six (6) texts.[11] Subsequently, eleven texts were added to the original work as it went through the various editions.[12]

The present English edition contains a total of twenty-four (24) narratives, divided into five groups:

Complete Stories (9 units [Nos. 1–6; 13–15])
The Cycle of Satni-Khamoîs: (3 units [Nos. 7–9])
The Cycle of Ramses II: (3 units [Nos. 10–12])
The Cycle of Petubastis: (2 units [Nos. 16–17])

10. The stories are not numbered in either the French or the English edition; a numerical identification is provided in the present ABC-CLIO edition parenthetically.

11. List of text correspondences

1882 (French)*	1915 (English)
[1], pp. 1–32. The Story of the Two Brothers	= 1–20 [No. 1]
[2], pp. 33–42. The Doomed Prince	= 185–201 [No. 13]
[3], pp. 43–82] I. The Adventure of Satni-Khamoïs with the Mummies	= 115–43 [No. 7]
[4], pp. 83–96. How Thutîyi Took the City of Joppa	= 108–14 [No. 6]
[5], pp. 97–134. The Memoirs of Sinuhît	= 68–97 [No. 4]
[6], pp. 135–48. The Shipwrecked Sailor	= 98–107 [No. 5]
[7], pp. 149–60. The Story of Rhampsinitus	= 196–201 [No. 14]

Fragments

[8], pp. 165–72. Fragment of a Fantastic Story, Anterior to the XVIIIth Dynasty	= 265–68 [No. 18]
[9], pp. 173–84. The Lamentations of the Fellah	= 43–67 [No. 3]
[10], pp. 185–96. The Quarrel of Apôpi and Saqnûnrîya	= 269–74 [No. 19]
[11], pp. 197–204. Fragments of a Ghost Story	= 275–79 [No. 20]
[12], pp. 205–14. Story of a Mariner	= 280–84 [No. 21]
[13], pp. 215–22. The Adventure of the Sculptor Petêsis and King Nectonabo	= 285–89 [No. 22]

*There are some discrepancies in pagination between the table of contents (p. 223) and the actual page on which a story begins.

12. The added texts are as follows:

Complete Stories

[02]. The King Khufuî and the Magicians ... pp. 21–42
[15]. The Voyage of Unamunu to the Coasts of Syria ... pp. 202–16

The Cycle of Satni-Khamoîs:

[08]. II. The Veritable History of Satni-Khamoîs and his Son Senosiris ... pp. 144–70
[09]. III. How Satni-Khamoîs Triumphed over the Assyrians ... pp. 170–71

Fragments (7 units [Nos. 18–24])[13]

Maspero as Folklorist

Tools for Text Analysis

Maspero approached his texts from the perspective of an Egyptologist and a literary scholar, rather than from that of a folklorist or anthropologist-archaeologist. The term "folk-lore" (or "folklore") was not used in his

The Cycle of Ramses II:
[10]. I. The Daughter of the Prince of Bakhtan and the Possessing Spirit ... pp. 172–79
[11]. II. The Exploits of Sesôstris ... pp. 180–82
[12]. III. The Exploits of Osimandyas ... pp. 183–84

The Cycle of Petubastis: (2 units [16–17])
[16]. I. The High Emprise for the Cuirass ... pp. 217–42
[17]. II. The High Emprise for the Throne of Amon ... pp. 243–62

Fragments (7 units [18–24])
[23]. Fragments of the Theban-Coptic Version of the Romance of Alexander ... pp. 290–303
[24]. Epigraph ["On Those Who Caused Alexander to Drink the Death Potion"] ... p. 304.

---

13. Table of contents (an asterisk * indicates location in the 1882 edition):

1915	*1882
Complete Stories (nine units [1–6; 13–15])	
[1]. *= [1] The Story of the Two Brothers	1–20
[2]. The King Khufuî and the Magicians	21–42
[3]. *= [9] The Lamentations of the Fellah	43–67
[4]. *= [5] The Memoirs of Sinuhît	68–97
[5]. *= [6] The Shipwrecked Sailor	98–107
[6]. *= [4] How Thutîyi Took the City of Joppa	108–14
[13]. *= [2] The Doomed Prince	185–201
[14]. *= [7] The Story of Rhampsinitus	196–201
[15]. The Voyage of Unamunu to the Coasts of Syria	202–16
The Cycle of Satni-khamoîs: (3 units [7–9])	
[7]. *= [3] I. The Adventure of Satni-Khamoîs with the Mummies	115–43
[8]. II. The Veritable History of Satni-Khamoîs and his Son Senosiris	144–70
[9]. III. How Satni-Khamoîs Triumphed over the Assyrians	170–71
The Cycle of Ramses II: (3 units [10–12])	
[10]. I. The Daughter of the Prince of Bakhtan and the Possessing Spirit	172–79
[11]. II. The Exploits of Sesôstris	180–82
[12]. III. The Exploits of Osimandyas	183–84
The Cycle of Petubastis: (2 units [16–17])	
[16]. I. The High Emprise for the Cuirass	217–42
[17]. II. The High Emprise for the Throne of Amon	243–62
Fragments (7 units [18–24])	
Introductory Note ... 263–64	
[18]. *= [8] Fragment of a Fantastic Story, Anterior to the XVIIIth Dynasty	265–68

anthology;[14] similarly, other labels for the discipline such as "Volskunde," or "ethnography," do not appear at all. Although the word "folk" does occur, its use is confined to referring to social groups (e.g., peasants, lower class, etc.).[15] Basic folkloristic terms such as "tale-type" and "subtype" do not appear in his work, since these analytical devices were introduced during the first part of the twentieth century. Yet his treatment of the texts reveals awareness of the conceptual principles underlying these analytical tools. He consistently used a number of terms that prove to be in accordance with modern folkloristic usage. For example, he applied the term "plot" to a narrative to denote a complete story in a manner that coincides with the folkloristic term "tale-type";[16] other labels referring to a narrative's plot, or tale-type, such as "scheme" and "framework," appear sporadically.[17] He also used the term "episode," basically in the same sense that it is used by folktale scholars today.[18] Meanwhile, he used the term "motif" (though infrequently)[19] and the term "theme" to designate narrative data that correspond essentially to those designated by the current term "motif" as defined in Stith Thompson's *Motif-Index of Folk Literature*.[20]

Theoretical Orientation

The latter part of the nineteenth century witnessed the emergence and spread of numerous theories and hypotheses concerning the age, origins,

[19]. *= [10] The Quarrel of Apôpi and Saqnûnrîya   269–74
[20]. *= [11] Fragments of a Ghost Story   275–79
[21]. *= [12] Story of a Mariner   280–84
[22]. *= [13] The Adventure of the Sculptor Petêsis and King Nectonabo   285–89
[23]. Fragments of the Theban-Coptic Version of the Romance of Alexander   290–303
[24]. Epigraph ["On Those who Caused Alexander to Drink the Death Potion"]   304

14. The word "Folklore" appears only once in the entire work (p. 2), but only as part of the title of a journal.

15. See Maspero, *Popular Stories*, pp. xlviii, l, lvi, 45, 110 n. 2. Also see H. El-Shamy "Folk Group," in *Folklore: An Encyclopedia of Forms, Methods, and History*. Thomas A. Green, Gen. Ed., ABC-CLIO, 1997.

16. Antti Aarne and Stith Thompson's *The Types of the Folktale, FF Communications* No. 184, Helsinki: Academia Scientartum Fennica, 1961; first published by Aarne in 1910. Cf. Maspero, *Popular Stories*, pp. xx, lviii, 78, 289.

17. See Maspero, *Popular Stories*, p. xiii and 283, respectively.

18. See examples on pp. xii, xiii, xiv, xxx, xxxix, xlvi, liv, 42, 104, 108, 135, 180, 182, 192, 196, 208, 256, 268, 281, 283, 290, 291, 293, 294, 301.

19. See pp. xv, xvii.

20. 6 vols. Bloomington: Indiana University Press, 1955–1958. For examples see: pp. iii, xix, xxiii, xxvii ("universal"), xxix, xlvii, lxv, 146, 170, 173, 180, 214, 215, 243, 267, 278.

birthplace, and national ownership of folklore materials, especially the *Märchen* (fairy tale). These are labeled: historical-reconstructional, philological, evolutionary, romantic-nationalistic, ritualistic, etc.[21] Maspero's annotations of the texts seem to be free of preconceived theoretical assumptions. Yet he addressed numerous theoretical issues, especially concerning the origin of the tales, and reached specific conclusions on the basis of careful analysis of the texts and related social and historical records.[22] His theoretical orientation may be viewed as belonging to the historical-reconstruction approach.[23]

Although Maspero pointed out scores of cultural practices that the modern Egyptian has in common with the ancient, he made no attempt to explore the possibility of the presence of any of his ancient stories in the oral traditions of modern Egypt. The unique exception is when an *oral* rendition of one of the stories in his book, Rhampsinitus, told by a schoolboy, was brought to his attention by a third party.[24]

In accordance with a comparative folklorist's approach, Maspero placed considerable emphasis on locating "versions" of his ancient texts in modern tale collections, especially from European and Asian cultures.[25] Yet he did not try to relate the ancient texts to counterparts in modern tale collections from the geographic areas in which ancient Egyptian culture once existed and thrived.[26] The sole work[27] for his com-

21. For a succinct presentation of these "theories," see R. M. Dorson's "Current Theories of Folklore," *Folklore and Folklife*, pp. 7–47; also see Dorson's "Current Folklore Theories," in: *Current Anthropology*, Vol. 4, No. 1 (1963), 93–112.

22. When exercised on a living text, connected to specific narrator, within a given social environment, etc., such an approach would be labeled "contextual." See: H. El-Shamy, "Context," in *Folklore*, T. Green, Ed.

23. For a brief description of the "historical reconstructional," see: R. M. Dorson, *Folklore and Folklife*, pp. 12–15.

24. See the field text, p. xxxi, below.

25. See for example his introduction to the "The Story of the Two Brothers," pp. 1–3; and "How Thutîyi Took the City of Joppa," pp. 108–9.

26. E.g., Artin, Yacoub [Artîn, Yaʒqûb]. *Contes populaires inédits de la vallée du Nil.* Paris, 1893 (Reprint, Paris, 1968); Spitta, Wilhelm. *Grammatik des arabischen Vulgärdialektes von Ägypten.* Leipzig, 1880; Spitta, Wilhelm. *Contes arabes modernes.* Leiden, 1883; Reinisch, Leo. *Die Somali-Sprache, Südarabische Expedition,* Vol. 1. Vienna, 1900; Rhodokanakis, Nikolaus. *Der vulgärarabische Dialekt im Dofârzfâr), Südarabische Expedition,* Vol. 8. Wien, 1908; Littmann, Enno. *Modern Arabic Tales* [from al-Quds, in Arabic]. Leyden, 1905; Müller, David H. *Die Mehri-und Soqutri-Sprache,* pt. I *texte, Südarabische Expedition,* Vol. 4. Vienna, 1902; Müller, David H. *Mehri-und Soqutri-Sprache* pt. II *Soqutri Texte, Südarabische Expedition,* Vol. 6, Wien, 1905; Müller, David H. *Die Mehri-und Soqutri-Sprache* pt. III *Shhauri Texte, Südarabische Expedition,* Vol. 7. Wien, 1907.

27. In addition to the citing of biblical materials.

parisons with modern Egyptian and Arabic cultures is *The Arabian Nights*. This choice will be shown to be more representative of the nature of materials contained in the two anthologies—the ancient Egyptian and the recent Arabic—than Maspero may have suspected. (See "Authorship of the Stories" and "Written and Oral Traditions," pp. xxiii–xxviii, below).

Maspero's Contes populaires
in Folklore Indexes

There are two basic indexes for folk narratives: Antti Aarne and Stith Thompson's *The Types of the Folktale*,[28] and Stith Thompson's *Motif-Index of Folk Literature*.[29] Both reference works pay negligible attention to sources addressing ancient Egyptian materials. Maspero's anthology does not appear at all in *The Types of the Folktale*. Only an allusion to the ancient text of the "Tale of the Two Brothers" is given in connection with Type 318, which carries the title "*The Faithless Wife*. Batu: the Egyptian 'Two Brothers' Tale." Still, no bibliographic reference was cited to link Tale-type 318 to an ancient Egyptian text.[30] Actually, no "Egyptian" texts are cited in relation to other tale-types that were known to exist in ancient Egyptian literature. These include Types 934A, *Predestined Death,* or 934A¹, *Three-fold Death* (Maspero No. 13: "The Doomed Prince"); Type 950, *Rhampsinitus* (Maspero No. 14); Type 954, *The Forty Thieves*—represented by Motif K754.1, "Trojan wooden horse" (Maspero No. 6: "How Thutîyi Took the City of Joppa").[31] Thus, the absence of Maspero's work from the Aarne-Thompson tale-type index is total.

Similarly, Thompson's *Motif-Index of Folk Literature*[32] contains only two peripheral motifs from Maspero's *Contes*.[33] Two additional "Mythological"

28. See n. 16, above.

29. As in n. 20, above.

30. The link is: Von Sydow "Den fornegyptiska Sagan om de tv Brderna" *Yearbook of the New Society of Letters of Lund,* 1930, 53ff. (as given by Thompson).

31. See: Stith Thompson, *The Folktale* (New York, 1946), p. 276. Also see n. 71, below.

32. Second "Revised and enlarged" edition, Bloomington, Ind.: 1955–1958; first published in Helsinki, 1932–1936.

33. These are: F943, "Sinking into mud in duel"; and K753, "Capture by hiding in disguised object." Cited as "Egyptian: Maspero Contes populaire de l'Égypte ancienne (Paris, 1882)."

motifs were cited from another work by Maspero.[34] Yet in discussing "The Folktale in Ancient Literature" some ten years before the appearance of the revised edition of the *Motif-Index*, Thompson[35] had listed more than a dozen motifs that are identifiable in ancient Egyptian texts, mostly from the "The Tale of Two Brothers" (Type 318).[36] Surprisingly, the *Motif-Index*'s new edition relates none of these motifs to ancient Egyptian lore.

Consequently, ancient Egyptian narrative traditions remained outside folklore indexes. The rich data and constructive thoughts that Maspero's work offered played no significant role in the development or the testing of folklore theories.[37]

The Sources of the Narratives

The texts come from a variety of historical periods (kingdoms, dynasties) spanning millennia.[38] Several languages and writing systems are involved: hieroglyphic, hieratic, and demotic; a few texts are in Coptic or Greek.

34. These are: A12, "Hermaphroditic creator"; and A240, "Moon-god," attributed to "Maspéro Histoire ancienne des peuples de l'Orient classique."

Likewise, the Motif-Index cites only two motifs from Petri's anthology: E465, "Revenant rewards its conqueror"; attributed to "Egypt (ancient): Petrie II 87";* and S401, "Unsuccessful attempts to kill person in successive reincarnations (transformations)", cited as "Egyptian: Petrie Egyptian Tales (London, 1895) I 36ff.," which corresponds to Maspero's tale no. 1.

----

*This reference designates "Tales of The Magicians: Hordedef's Tale" No. 1, which is not present in Maspero's "Contes" (1882), and appears as no. 2, in Maspero's "Popular Stories" (1915).

It is worth noting that closer examination of these two motifs reveals that neither citation seems to correspond to narrative data at the specified pages in Petrie's work.

35. *The Folktale*, pp. 272–82; esp. pp. 274–76.

36. These motifs are: B211, "Animal uses human speech"; B741.2, "Neighing of stallion in Assyria impregnates mares in Egypt"; D672, "Obstacle flight . . ."; E30, "Resuscitation by arrangement of members"; E607.2, "Person transforms self, is swallowed and reborn in new form"; E670, "Repeated reincarnation"; E710, "External soul"; E761.6.4, "Life token: beer foams"; K754.1, "Trojan wooden horse. [Smuggling soldiers into city]"; K2111, "Potiphar's wife [and Joseph]"; K2213.4, "Betrayal of husband's secret by his wife"; M340, "Unfavorable prophecies"; M372, "Confinement in tower to avoid fulfillment of prophecy"; and T11.4.1, "Love through sight of hair of unknown princess."

37. This serious deficiency is also reflected in the treatment of Middle Eastern materials, especially Arabic; see "The Aarne-Thompson Type Index and Egyptian Folktales," in H. El-Shamy, *Folktales of Egypt*, pp. 237–39.

38. Some anthologies group texts according to the historical period or dynasty: e.g., "Narratives and Tales of Middle Egyptian Literature," "Late Egyptian Stories" (see: William K. Simpson, ed., *The Literature of Ancient Egypt*. New Haven: 1972). Others group texts according to theme or subject matter: e.g., "Tales of the Gods," "Tales of Magic," "Tales of Adventure" (see: Roger Lancelyn Green, *Tales of Ancient Egypt, Selected and Retold* (New York: 1967/1968).

All texts contained in this volume are of "literary" nature. They were committed to the written form, or copied from written documents, by male scribes who were mostly clerics (priests). A few stories seem to have been learned from oral sources and then committed to writing, but mostly by non-Egyptians.[39]

Only rarely is the text truly complete: "King Khufuî and the Magicians" ([No. 2], pp. 21–42), which is listed under "Complete Stories," has many component stories missing; Maspero noted that "[i]t ends in the middle of a phrase, and we cannot conjecture with any certainty what is required to render it complete."[40] In most cases, considerable efforts to reconstruct missing components had to be exerted. Irrespective of whether complete or fragmentary, a folk narrative is in essence a description of life and living—real or fictitious,[41] that relies for its meaningfulness on understanding the sociocultural system to which it belongs. The reconstructing of the extinct Egyptian language, and attempting to reconstitute related social and cultural systems, is a challenging and ongoing undertaking. Consequently, in the absence of the actual social behavior described in these texts, treating written portrayals of life and living in ancient Egypt must rely on a great deal of reconstruction, inferences, and conjecture.

Each text is prefaced by an introductory note presenting a succinct life history of that text, and a comprehensive list of scholars who treated it and the contributions by each. Clearly, Maspero strove to present as accurate a translation of each ancient text as possible under the circumstances—a standard continued by Mrs. Johns in her outstanding English translation. Yet an exception to this rule is the exclusion of an "obscene" section from one text ("The Adventure of Satni-Khamoîs with the

---

39. E.g., Herodotus, who transmitted to us "The Story of Rhampsinitus," (Type: 950; see: Maspero, *Popular Stories*, pp. 196–201); and the "fable" of the "Pharaoh who had become blind ..." (Type: 844C§, *Search for a Chaste Woman (Virgin)*. None is readily found; see: Maspero, *Popular Stories*, p. xlviii); and the Roman historian Strabo, who transmitted to us an early version of Cinderella (Type: cf. 510, *Cinderella and Cap o' Rushes;* see: H. El-Shamy, *Tales Arab Women Tell: and the Behavioral Patterns They Portray.* Collected, translated, edited, and interpreted. Indiana University Press, 1999; No. 34, pp. 271–72. Not included in Maspero's anthology.)

Maspero (p. xxxii) attributes the Egyptian fables and legends in Herodotus's writings to "The interpreters and priests of the lower class, who acted as guides to foreigners."

Compare the role of lower clerics, as interpreters of Islamic dogma, in generating fantasy narratives as part of religious creed; see: El-Shamy, *Tales Arab Women Tell*, pp. 11–12.

40. Maspero, *Popular Stories*, p. 22. For similar cases of incomplete texts see: No. 4 pp. 69, 71; No. 6 pp. 108, 109, 112 n. 1; No. 7 pp. 116, 121 n. 1; No. 8 pp. 158 n. 1, 163 n. 1; No. 16 p. 242 n. 1; No. 19 p. 270.

41. For details of this definition, see: El-Shamy, *Folk Traditions of the Arab World*, Vol. 1, p. xiii.

Mummies," [No. 7]). This was done in spite of the evident instrumentality of the untranslated portion in the negative portrayal of the character of Tbubui, one of the tale's cardinal female personae. Maspero noted:

> An obscene detail, which occurs several lines farther on, and *which I have not translated,* proves that here, as in all tales of the kind, Tbubui was forced to yield herself entirely in order to get her enemy into her power.[42]

Hundreds of comments are made in the form of introductory notes to each story, and as explanatory footnotes to specific issues in the texts of narratives. The placement of the notes at the foot of the page allows the reader easy access to valuable data necessary for understanding the nature of action inscribed on the lifeless scrolls or rocks. The explanatory notes may be grouped into three main categories: (1) dealing with language, (2) providing context, and (3) comparative.

Language

Since the written words (signs) had to be deciphered, their meanings were not always definite. Also, allegorical usage of words and phrases rendered meanings indefinite. Recent translations benefit from advances in Egyptology and new discoveries of records. For example, in Maspero's work "giant" ("géant") is cited as helper of the Doomed Prince. A recent translation identifies this being as a "water spirit."[43]

The Degree of Certainty of the Accuracy of the Translation

Maspero meant to address the general reader; he specified his approach as follows:

> I have been forced to paraphrase rigorously those passages that a modern, unversed in Egyptology, would not have understood had I transcribed them literally. The general meaning is there; it remains for others to scrutinize the several phrases minutely and extract

42. Maspero, *Popular Stories,* p. 140 n. 1. Emphasis added. Motifs T455.6, "Woman sells [(sexual)] favors for large sums of money (property)"; cf. T9.1§, "The power of sex: female's influence", and T370§, "Satanic (diabolic) beauty: an utterly wicked (evil) person with extraordinary good looks." On the presumed symbolic significance of an adult male in "a place of furnace without any clothes on his back," (p. 115 n. 65) compare Mot. Z186.8.2.1§, "Symbolism: oven (furnace)=vagina, womb."

43. Maspero, *Popular Stories,* p. 190; *Contes* (1882), p. 41. See Edward F. Wente, in Simpson, *The Literature,* p. 90. For other examples see: "son," Maspero, *Popular Stories,* p. 94, n. 3; also cf. "milk," p. 91, vrs. Wente: "beer," p. 90.

from them the subtle shades of thought and of language by which they charmed the Egyptians.[44]

Congruence between a restored passage and the central values (ethos) of the social group to which the passage belongs is another facet of accuracy. Maspero provides cases that describe the conditions under which conjecture may not be undertaken. Commenting on a conclusion to "The Doomed Prince" [No. 13] postulated by a modern author, Maspero noted:

> In his conclusion, [Georg] Ebers relates that the prince reveals to the daughter of the chief of Naharinna his real origin, and that he returns to Egypt, where his father receives him with joy. He speedily returns to Naharinna, defeats his murderers, and replaces the old chief on his throne. On his return, he consecrates the booty to Amonrâ, and passes the remainder of his days in complete happiness.

Maspero then gives this "diplomatic" comment:

> Nothing could be better conceived than this ending; I do not, however, believe that the ancient Egyptian writer had the compassion for his heroes that is so ingeniously shown by the modern author. Destiny does not allow itself to be set aside in the ancient East, and does not permit its decrees to be evaded. At times it suspends their execution, but never annuls them.[45]

Contextual

The notes supply information on cultural and social practices constituting aspects of "common knowledge" that the ancient scribe (writer-narrator) deemed needless to commit to writing or inscription. This information, already known to the ancient Egyptian but not to the modern reader, is

44. Maspero, *Popular Stories*, pp. 67, 260 n. 2. For additional examples see Maspero's comment on M. de Rougé's approach to translation, p. ix, n. 1. Also see his note on the restoration of a passage omitted by the scribe who wrote "The King Khufuî and the Magicians," p. 34 n. 4. Compare Maspero's assessments of Spiegelberg's restorations of "context," p. 225 n. 1; and of Ebers' restoration of "The prophecy of the crocodile …," pp. 191–92.

Another salient case portraying Maspero's emphasis on exactness of the text addresses Brugsch's translation of a hieroglyphic word as "the temple of Bastît" instead of simply "Bubastis" (now Tell Basta, near Zagazig); Maspero asserts that "the orthography of the Egyptian text does not admit of this interpretation," p. 137 n. 1.

45. Maspero, *Popular Stories*, p. 195. This theme is expressed in Mot. A196.2, "Decree of gods irrevocable." It also constitutes a basic contemporary practice that marks a "true" believer: new Motifs: V318.1§, "Submission to fate (God's prejudgment: *qaḍâ', qadar*) a mark of true

necessary for the understanding of the verbal text. The following are examples:

The Nature of Action

The women's apartment is on an upper floor. [Thus,] the servant had to go downstairs to fetch the corn.

   Or:

> The roof of Egyptian houses is flat, and like that of the temples, formed terraces on which the open air could be enjoyed. Slight kiosks were built on them, and sometimes, as at the temple of Denderah, actual ediculæ of worked stone, which served as chapels and observatories.[46]

The Stage and Time for Action

Southern Thebes is the modern Luxor; it was therefore the patronal festival of the temple of Luxor that the king was celebrating when the arrival of the Syrian messenger was announced to him, and during which the statue of Amon and its bark were transported from Luxor to Karnak, and then taken back to Luxor, three weeks later.[47]

Social Practice

Lit. "he kissed him many hours"—one of those exaggerated formulæ. . . . The kiss on the mouth had replaced the ancient greeting of placing the noses together . . . perhaps under Greek influence, at least in official ceremonies.[48]

The Role Material Culture Plays in the Process of Reconstructing Verbal Lore[49]

Elaborating on the scene of birth assisted by deities, in the narrative of "The King Khufuî and the Magicians," Maspero observed:

---

faith"; and V318.1.1§, "Suppliant pleads not that God revoke His prejudgment but only that He lighten its impact."

46. Maspero, *Popular Stories,* p. 40 n. 3; and p. 187 n. 1 respectively. Motifs: P604.1§, "House-top (flat roof) as terrace or living quarters"; P605.9.2.1§, "'Upper floor' for intimate living," and F773.5§, "Private-chapel: mosque, church, temple, etc. at private residence."

47. Maspero, *Popular Stories,* p. 175 n. 6.

48. Maspero, *Popular Stories,* p. 261 n. 2.

49. For additional examples, see: the comment on the location of women's apartment within a home: p. 32 n. 55; herders' customs: p. 4 n. 7; fishing tools: p. 47 n. 38; drinking vessels: p. 166.

Even to the most intimate events of private life, such as births, there is nothing which cannot be explained and illustrated by scenes taken from the temples. . . . [W]e have pictures before our eyes from which we can exactly realise what happened when Rudîtdidît gave birth to the three sons of Râ. . . . The patient is crouched on her chair or on her bed, one of the midwives clasps her from behind, and another, crouched in front of her, receives the child as it is born. She hands it to the nurses, who wash it, hold it in their arms, caress, and give it suck.[50]

Compatibility between Verbal and Material Aspects of Culture

An examination of the monuments shows that the same [drawing] is the case with those stories of which we possess the original hieratic; and I have proved it also for the greater number of those we possess only in a foreign language. It is the case with Rhampsinitus. I do not intend to repeat the text word for word, in order to show that it is substantially Egyptian, notwithstanding the Greek dress with which Herodotus has clothed it; I will content myself with discussing two of the points which have been objected to as indicating a foreign origin.[51]

Comparative

The anthology provides valuable comparisons between how a theme or a practice occurs in two different cultures (ethnological), or within the same culture at different time periods or in different segments of the population (ethnographic).

Ethnological

Ethnological examples of such cross-cultural comparisons may be seen in the following:

The fact that adult males in certain nations are typically either bearded or beardless, and the significance of this theme in attributing a tale—where it plays a role—to a specific nation.[52]

---

50. Maspero, *Popular Stories*, p. xliv-l, 37 n. 3.

51. Maspero, *Popular Stories*, p. l. Also cf. the comment on being bearded or beardless: p. cxxvii, below; drinking vessels: p. 166 n. 5.

52. Mot. P717.1.1§, "Bearded nations." See: Maspero, *Popular Stories*, p. xlv-xlvi, 199, 274.

Or, the observation by an author that the Egyptian theme of the creation of a female by Khnumu for Baîti (Batu), and the Greek theme of the creation of Pandora fashioned by Hephaestion share certain similarities.[53]

Or, the fact that the Seven Hâthors who appear in the stories "play the same rôle as the fairy godmothers of our [European] fairy tales."[54]

Ethnographic (within the Same Culture)

The anthology offers a multitude of insightful remarks on Egyptian social and cultural processes, values, and practices.

Commenting on the injustice that triggered "The Lamentations of the Fellah" Maspero noted:

> The man who had robbed him belonged to one in high position, and had friends, relations, and a *master*. The peasant was merely a *masterless man*. The author takes care to point this out, and to have no master was an unpardonable error in feudal Egypt. A single individual was defenceless against the great lords who shared the country between them, and the officials who exploited it on behalf of Pharaoh.[55]

In contemporary Egyptian society, this very idea is expressed in the proverbial saying: "He who has no senior (elder, leader) should buy himself one."[56]

Other valuable observations correlate ancient narrative themes to modern practices. These include spinning while driving flocks;[57] daubing the face and head with lumps of dust and of mud to express grief;[58] women expressing joy by uttering "zaggarit";[59] and belief in the existence of an immortal serpent that is "supposed to live in the Nile, and of which the fellahîn tell strange stories."[60]

---

53. Maspero, *Popular Stories*, p. xvii n. 4. Cf. Mot. F34, "Temptress sent from upper world by deity (Pandora)."

54. Maspero, *Popular Stories*, p. lv n. 6, lvi, 12, 186. Mot. A471.1.1§, "Seven (nine) Hathors prophecy for mortal."

55. Maspero, *Popular Stories*, p. xliii.

56. Designated as new Mot. P741.1§. Also, for this aspect of social organization compare Mot. P743§, "Fealty (*walâ'*), and partisanship."

57. Maspero, *Popular Stories*, p. 3 n. 4.

58. Maspero, *Popular Stories*, p. 10–11 n. 3.

59. I.e. *zaghârît:* Mot. P790.1.2.1§; see Maspero, *Popular Stories*, p. 40, n. 4.

60. Maspero, *Popular Stories*, p. 125 n. 4.

On the Genres of the "Stories"

It is significant that Mrs. Johns, presumably with Maspero's approval, translated the book's title ("Contes populaires de . . ."), as "Popular Stories of . . .," rather than "Folktales of . . . ." Whether this translation was a deliberate eschewing of the term "folktale" or not, it is actually more representative of the anthology's contents than the original French title. The majority of narratives are referred to with the nondescript label "romance" ("*roman*").

The fairy tale (*conte de fée, Zaubermärchen*) is absent from the anthology.[61] As pointed out above, a major portion of the stories belong to the historical legend, and to the personal experience narrative (memorate, labor reminiscences).[62] Also, although "The Tale of the Two Brothers" (Type 318) is perceived as an "Ordinary Tale," listed in the Aarne-Thompson *Type-Index* under "Tales of Magic," this characterization of the Egyptian text is not universally accepted. The fact that the two brothers may also be seen as representing gods lends some support to the argument that the story is actually a myth rather than a *Märchen*/fairy tale. "Baîti and Anupu, belong either to religion or to legend," Maspero stated; other Egyptologists concur.[63]

A label that is frequently applied is "fable," which Maspero seems to use to designate the unreal or the fantastic. Assessing the nature of the stage of action in "The Shipwrecked Sailor," he states:

> [W]e can see clearly how the hero passed without any intermediate stages from the domain of reality into that of fable.[64]

He also used "fable" to designate the historical legend as well as the belief legend.[65]

---

61. This label occurs only once ("our fairy tales") to refer to European tales, see: Maspero, *Popular Stories*, p. 12, n. 3. Meanwhile, "folk tales" is used in a general manner on pages lxxv, and 263.

62. Such personal narratives are labeled "Memorates." See: T. A. Green, pp. 533–55. Also see: Laurits Bødker, *Folk Literature (Germanic)*, Vol. 2: *International Dictionary of Regional European Ethnology and Folklore* (Copenhagen, 1965), pp. 195–97.

63. Maspero, *Popular Stories*, p. xxiv, cf. p. 3 n. 4. Also see: E. F. Wente, in Simpson, *The Literature*, pp. 92–93; E. Brunner-Traut, *Altägyptische Märchen*, p. 259; Hollis, *The Ancient Egyptian "Tale of Two Brothers*," pp. 3, 43.

64. Maspero, *Popular Stories*, p. xxxii. For other examples of the use of the label, see: p. cxxi ("High Emprise for the Cuirass"); p. xlviii (account of the story of the blind king by Herodotus); p. 182 (the fable of Sesôstris).

65. E.g., The fable of Sesôstris, see: Maspero *Popular Stories*, p. 182.

The Märchen among Non-Aryans

Folkloristic circles in Europe had accorded the *Märchen*/fairy tale and its presumed creators a privileged status. This assumption formed the basis of such theories as Wilhelm Grimm's,[66] which attributed the origins of folk narratives to Indo-European (Aryan) peoples. This claim acquired powerful impetus at the beginning of the twentieth century through the assertion that true *Märchen* existed only within Indo-Germanic linguistic boundaries, and that non-Aryans distorted the *Märchen*, which they copied from the Indo-Germanic groups.[67] Similarly, the "Indianist" theory, suggested by A. Loiseleur-Deslongchamp[68] in 1838, and developed by Theodor Benfey[69] and E. Cosquin,[70] was based on the principle of citing India as the original source for *all* folktales except Aesop's fables, and that other nations copied their tales from Indian sources.

Authorship of the Stories

Maspero reported that his examination of the stories raised many "questions which are difficult to answer." The primary issues for him were "How were they composed?" and whether they were "entirely invented by their author, or did he borrow the substance of preexistent works and rearrange or alter them to form a new romance?"

He attributed to individual authorship a number of texts:

> Several of them certainly emanated from one sole source and constitute original work—the *Memoirs of Sinuhît,* the *Shipwrecked Sailor,* the *Stratagem of Thutiyî against Joppa,* the *Story of the Doomed Prince.*[71]

The criterion was the unity of action in that "A continuous action is carried through from the first line to the last." Whereas "the main

---

66. Wilhelm Grimm, *Kinder- und Hausmärchen,* Vol. 3 (Leipzig, 1856), pp. 427–429.

67. See: C. W. Von Sydow, "Das Märchen als indogermanische Tradition (Auszug) übertragen von Lily Weiser." In: *Neiderdeutsche Zeitschrift für Volkskunde,* Vol. 4 (1926), 207–215. For an evaluation of that hypothesis see: Archer Taylor, "A Theory of Indo-European Märchen," *Journal of American Folklore,* Vol. 44, pp. 54–60.

68. Deslongchamps, *Essai sur les fables indiennes et sur leur introduction en Europe* (Paris, 1838).

69. *Panchatantra: fünf Bücher indischer Fablen, Märchen, und Erzählungen,* 2 vols. (Leipzig, 1859).

70. *Les contes indiens et l'occident* (Paris, 1922).

71. Maspero, *Popular Stories,* p. xii–xiii.

scheme" in other tales could be viewed as composite of a number of semi-independent units; the most obvious example of such "an artificial composition . . . is that afforded by the story of Khufuî and the magicians."[72] This criterion, though useful in assessing the quality of the structure of a narrative, need not necessarily be indicative of how that narrative originated. Many individualistic compositions manifest this quality of being a "composite text"—which links serially a number of independent stories, or a "frame story"—which incorporates several stories within the frame—without undergoing re-creation at the hands of several tellers.

Irrespective of how each of these narratives originated, Maspero concluded:

> Everything in them is Egyptian from beginning to end, and even the details that have been pointed out as being of foreign provenance appear to us to be entirely indigenous when closely examined. Not only the living, but also the dead, have the peculiar characteristics of the people of the Nile, and could not in any way be mistaken for the living or the dead of another nation. From these facts I consider that Egypt must be regarded, if not as the original home of folk tales, at least as one of those countries in which they were earliest naturalised, and where they earliest assumed the form of actual literature. I am convinced that those entitled to speak with most authority will agree with this conclusion.[73]

Stith Thompson, perhaps influenced by Maspero's views, arrived at a similar conclusion:

> The tales are given a definitely Egyptian setting and are closely related not only to the known history and geography of Egypt but to its religious conceptions and practices as well.[74]

Maspero accounted for some of the similarities between Egyptian narratives and those of other nations in terms of what may be seen as *Elementargedanke,* which he labeled "primitive theme." Thus, the similarities between the "Potiphar's wife" theme (motif) in the "Tale of Two Brothers"

---

72. Maspero, *Popular Stories,* p. xiii.
73. Maspero, *Popular Stories,* p. lxxiv-lxxv.
74. *The Folktale,* p. 273.

and its biblical counterpart would be a matter of independent development of each (polygenesis, or multiple origins).[75]

Whether originated in Egypt or imported from other lands, the texts that survived the ravages of time and reached us in modern times are mostly the work of scribes; some came from Greek or Latin sources. A significant portion of the records containing narratives proved to be products (or drafts) of classroom exercises in writing or creative rhetoric.[76] Maspero suggested that ancient scribes injected (or dwelt on) certain themes that allowed the writer to parade his rhetorical prowess; one of these themes is "the wiles of women." Thus, he argued that all the women of a scribe's time period may have been virtuous, but the scribes "may have invented vices for them in order to give scope to their eloquence."[77]

The negative effects of such stylistic excesses can be clearly seen in the story of "The Lamentations of the Fellah." Drawing on his personal experiences as a European official in the countryside of British-occupied Egypt, Maspero compared the ancient Egyptian's style with the "modern's." He noted:

> The difficulties presented by his speeches no doubt arose from the same cause which prevents a European understanding a fellah when he lodges a complaint. The incoherence of his ideas and the obscurity of his language were due to the desire to speak well, and his want of practice in using fine language. It seems to me that the author of this story has *succeeded only too well for our comprehension,* in reproducing this somewhat comic and satirical side of the national character.[78]

Today, this writing style is still highly valued in the entire Arab world, and constitutes standard practice in Egyptian schools. Typically, it is referred to as *'inshâ*-style, which relies on addressing *"formula-serviceable environment* (i.e., [a topic] with a stock of available formulae)."[79] In this

75. Maspero, *Popular Stories,* p. xix, cf. xv. On the *Elementargedanke* and its relation to "Archetype," see: El-Shamy, "Archetype," In: T. Green, pp. 36–39.

76. See Maspero, *Popular Stories,* p. lxv, cf. lxv n. 2; Budge, *Egyptian Tales and Romances: Pagan, Christian and Muslim,* pp. 22–23, 35, 67; Simpson, *The Literature,* p. 57.

77. Maspero, *Popular Stories,* p. xlvii; also cf. p. 248 ("Egyptian scribes waxed eloquent ...."). Motifs W47§, "Eloquence." Also see n. 79, below.

78. Maspero, *Popular Stories,* pp. 45–46. Emphasis added.

79. Motif Z1.0.1§, "*'inshâ*-style literary composition: constituted mainly from copied (memorized) famous quotations." On this stylistic device, see: El-Shamy, *Tales Arab Women Tell,* pp. 22–23 n. 35.

respect, the form and style of a literary expression are deemed more important than the message or contents of that expression.[80]

The example, par excellence, of this style in modern folk-literature is *'alf laylah wa laylah* (*A Thousand Nights and a Night*—abbreviated as *The Nights*), or as it is commonly referred to in the west: *The Arabian Nights*. Verbal embellishments—such as *saj̆ǧ* (rhymed-prose) and "tropes," paronomasia, and short verses—dominate; they are found in every individual text of the "*The Nights*."[81] By contrast, "No oral folktale is phrased in such a manner."[82]

Written and Oral Traditions

As postulated by the present writer, oral and written traditions belong to separate cognitive systems. Folk groups do not consider stories that come from books "folktales," and the elite/educated do not consider oral tales to be worthy of *any* recognition or attention.[83] The scarcity of the true fairy tale (Märchen) in Arabic written records is, like its ancient Egyptian counterpart, due largely to this factor. Significantly, with the exception of materials added by European translators and editors,[84] women's folktales are not found in the Arabic editions of *The Nights*. This absence of female-bound tales, in addition to the dominance of male-bound themes, values, and stylistic features, lead us to conclude that *'alf laylah wa laylah* is a product of male scribes, and is predominantly an illustration of a male's world.[85]

For centuries, *The Nights* was looked down upon by Arab literary scholars. Viewing it with some favor occurred only in the middle of the

80. See the comments of Salîm Ḥassan, n. 91, below.

81. See "The Language and other Stylistic Features," in El-Shamy, "Oral Traditional Tales and the Thousand Nights and a Night: The Demographic Factor." In: *The Telling of Stories: Approaches to a Traditional Craft*. Morton Nøjgaard *et. al*, eds. (Odense University Press, Odense, Denmark, 1990) pp. 63–117; pp. 77–79. (Henceforth: "The Demographic Factor".)

82. El-Shamy, "The Demographic Factor," p. 79. The present writer knows of only one situation where this style was encountered in oral traditions. However, the narrator—an illiterate, itinerant tinsmith—was trying to emulate the style of *'alf laylah (The Arabian Nights)*.

83. See: El-Shamy Folktales of Egypt, p. lxviii–xlix. Also, A. H. Sayce noted the absence of *'alf laylah* stories from oral traditions. See: *Folk-Lore*, 31:3 (London, 1920): 173–203, p. 197.

84. For a list of added materials, see: El-Shamy, "The Demographic Factor," pp. 84–85, and notes no. 106–108.

85. El-Shamy, "The Demographic Factor," pp. 63–117, pp. 83–84. For the criteria applied in assessing the degree to which a tale pertains to women's circles, and in terms of the "ratio of f:m narrators," see El-Shamy, *Tales Arab Women Tell*, pp. 9–10, 413–58.

twentieth century, as an outcome of nationalistic ideologies, and the fact that it was admired in the West. Thus, it has been stated that

> with the élite and other groups of the "educated," this anthology of tales has been perceived as *the model* for the folktale. . . . The recent surge of interest in the folktale has come mainly from these and other literature-bound circles, . . . which viewed oral folktales as rudimentary artistic cultural expressions to be elevated to the level of literary works through re-fashioning into the formal and stylistic mold provided by the *'alf laylah wa laylah*.[86]

Maspero's anthology manifests the same male-bound qualities. These include emphasis on classical Arabic, literary semantic embellishments, and the absence of women's tales that illustrate a woman's worldview. Hence, the comparisons he draws between the ancient tales and the *Arabian Nights* are quite relevant. It is also worth noting that the style of the English translation of Maspero's anthology is decidedly *Arabian Nights*–like, especially concerning the use of archaic ("classical") English.[87]

The reactions of two eminent scholars—an American and an Egyptian—to the same ancient Egyptian story may shed some light on the value of the stylistic features for each. For Folklorist Stith Thompson, "The Shipwrecked Sailor" is a story that is "so confused that it seems hardly possible that the man who wrote it in its present form understood its motivation."[88] For Egyptologist Salîm Ḥassan, it is a story "told in a lucid manner, and sweet (*ʒadhbah* [i.e., mellow]) language."[89]

Conversely, reacting to "The Contendings of Horus and Seth,"[90] a mythological account of considerable narrative significance, Ḥassan found it to be characterized by "simplicity of style that degenerated to the

---

86. El-Shamy, "The Demographic Factor," p. 71.

87. Mot. Z1.1.1§, "Scriptural (scripture-like) formulas . . ."; e.g. "thou shalt," "If thou desirest," "If I am vanquished, when thou drinkest or when thou eatest, the water will become the colour of blood before thee," etc.

88. *The Folktale*, p. 273.

89. Salîm Ḥassan,* *mawsûʒat Miṣr al-Qadimah* (*Encyclopedia of Ancient Egypt*). Vol. 17, al-'adab al-miṣri al-qadim (*Ancient Egyptian Literature*), (al-Hay'ah: Cairo, 2000, first published in two volumes in 1945), p. 30.

*The correct Arabic spelling of this name is: Ḥasan; "Ḥassan" is a common error that occurs only in Latinized transcriptions.

90. It is not part of Maspero's anthology.

level of lewdness (*'ibtidhâl*) and the adoption of the speech of commoners [i.e., vernacular, or folk-speech]. . . ."[91]

The "Folk"/Fieldwork Factor
in Maspero's Work

THE FOLLOWING account of a personal experience by Maspero told in the first person reveals the negative attitudes of "educated" Egyptians—even when having received minimum schooling—toward folklore materials and their typical medium of expression: vernacular Arabic.[92] In daily life, vernacular Arabic is the normal medium of communication at all levels of society—high and low; classical language is used mostly by the educated only when required by religious or governmental institutions. Folk songs, folktales, folk proverbs, etc. are known and enjoyed; yet they are not tolerated in the context of written elite "literature."

Being in the field and in close proximity to Egyptian laborers at work gave Maspero the opportunity to experience firsthand some aspects of their oral traditions in action. Clearly, he was impressed with what was possible for him to observe of the overt behaviors of native Egyptians around him. We may infer that he did not hear fantasy tales told, but he certainly listened to folk singing often, especially work songs by laboring groups and individuals. He opened his collection of *Chansons populaires recueillies dans la Haute-Égypte de 1900 à 1914 pendant les inspections du Service des antiquités*[93] with the statement: "Le peuble chant beacoup en Égypte . . . (People sing much in Egypt . . .)."[94]

Maspero reported that during his first stay in Egypt (1881–1886), he heard much singing by workers and other natives. He wished to understand the words of those songs but he was unable to grasp their words or the meaning as they were being performed. He left Egypt without

91. Salîm Hassan, *mawsû̲at Miṣr*, pp. 141–42. Certain aspects of this viewpoint are also expressed by literary-oriented Egyptologists. Also see: "Attitudes toward Narration," in El-Shamy, *Folktales of Egypt*, pp. xlvi-lxviii.

92. The account also shows some of the problems encountered by many non-native speakers of Arabic in acquiring the text of an oral folk tradition.

93. Le Caire: Service des antiquités de l'Égypte: Impr. de l'Institut français d'archéologie orientale, 1914. A secondary title: "Extrait des *Annales du Service des Antiquités,* T. XIV, pp. 97–290."

94. Maspero, *Chansons,* p. 98/[1]. The pagination is dual: the main figure refers to the page in *Annales du Service des Antiquités,* the second, provided parenthetically, refers to page in the book. The book begins with page 97/[1].

achieving his goal. Upon his return in 1900, and during the first trip for inspection of monuments, his interest in those folk songs was revived, but still he was unable to collect them on his own. Due to the shortness of the stay in each location, it was impossible for him to get peasants or the professional singers themselves to chant or sing slowly enough for him to catch the words.

Maspero tried to get his Egyptian office secretary to assist him in collecting texts in the field, but he encountered "problems that couldn't have been expected." At first, the secretary agreed to repeat what he had heard and understood. However, he did so only in part; and "*refused to commit it to writing.*" When Maspero obliged him with a formal order to do so, the secretary yielded; but he distorted the data that he collected. He claimed that the reasons for not giving Maspero an accurate text were as follows: presence of repugnant themes ("motifs"), the vulgarity of the [colloquial] language; his own lack of knowledge of rules of grammar; and the coarseness of certain ideas (images), in addition to errors in the prosody (meter) of the songs. After two or three failing attempts to get the man to change his stand, Maspero dismissed him.[95]

Then, Maspero tried to get some of the performers themselves to enable him to write down the texts. Still, the attempts were not successful. He reported that, among other things, "Some refused due to poor judgment and contrived sense of shame, for they suspected that I was *trying to ridicule them.*"[96] Similarly, native inspectors who were in the employ of the Department of Antiquities, to whom Maspero explained his desire, seem to have developed no interest in responding. Only after years of persuasion was Maspero able to enlist the aid of a few employees in the collecting project.

In other words, a modern educated Egyptian, holding what must have been seen as a desirable and lucrative position as secretary (scribe) to an influential European, would rather be dismissed from his job than allow himself to "descend" to the levels of the true oral lore and vernacular Arabic. It is this attitude on the part of the Arab "elite" that has been responsible, until recently, for the near total absence of true folktales and other folklore genres from the records of Arabic literature.

The thesis being advanced here is that this attitude on the part of the "learned" ancient Egyptian scribes could have been a reason for the vir-

95. Maspero referred to the secretary as "mon homme." See: Maspero, *Chansons,* p. 89/[1]. Emphasis added.

96. Maspero, *Chansons,* p. 98/[2]. Emphasis added.

tually total absence of true folktales from their recorded literature. The narratives retold by Greek historians traveling in ancient Egypt and reported to have been learned from ordinary non-learned Egyptians, such as travel guides, indicate the existence of an active repertoire of orally transmitted folktales among the masses. Like their counterparts in modern Egypt that remained outside Arabic literary anthologies, these ancient folktales seem to have been excluded from ancient literature recorded by Egyptian scribes. Also like their modern counterparts, reported from the field by European students of language,[97] the ancient folktales were retold by European students of history and by other travelers.

We may also wonder what the outcome might have been had Maspero asked his secretary to collect folktales for him from modern Egyptians. Would he have agreed to "stoop" to the task? Would the harvest of field-texts have yielded modern variants currently told in Egypt of such ancient tales as "The Two Brothers,"[98] "The Blinding of Truth by Falsehood,"[99] "The Contendings of Horus and Seth,"[100] or "The Veritable History of Satni-Khamoîs and his Son Senosiris"?[101]

97. See note 26, above.

98. Type 318. For a contemporary text of this tale as it appears in Nubia, see: "The Man Who Severed His Own Thing," in El-Shamy, *Tales Arab Women Tell,* No. 25, pp. 208–15, 434–35. This modern version is classified as Type 318A§, *The Man who Lost his Organ and then Regained it.* The ungrateful wife.

99. Type: 613, *The Two Travelers (Truth and Falsehood);* see: "The Noble and the Vile," in *Folktales of Egypt,* No. 14, pp. 95, 261–62, cf. p. xlix.

The narrative also appears in *The Arabian Nights* under the distorted title of "Abu-Qîr and Abu-Sîr," i.e., The Evil and the Good (Type 980*, *The Painter and the Architect.* [The vile dyer and the noble barber...]). For detailed treatments of the names involved see H. El-Shamy, "Oral Traditional Tales and the Thousand Nights and a Night: The Demographic Factor," pp. 85–92; and El-Shamy, "'Noble and Vile' or 'Genuine and False'? Some Linguistic and Typological Comments on *Folktales of Egypt.*" In: *Fabula,* vol. 24 (1983) nos. 3–4, pp. 341–46.

The arguments that this narrative is connected to Type 613, and that one of the two names (Abu-Sîr) denoted a noble character are substantiated by the fact that Osiris was referred to as "the lord of Bû-Sîr": Bû-Sîr (Abu-Sîr) being a site in the Eastern Nile Delta that was a center for the veneration of Osiris. (See: Ḥassan, *mawsûᶾat Miṣr,* pp. 161, 380, n. 2; and E. F. Wente, in Simpson, *The Literature,* p. 126, where the name appears as "Busiris."

100. Type 325, *The Magician and His Pupil.* See: "The *Maghrabî's* Apprentice," in *Folktales of Egypt,* No. 6, p. 248.

101. Type: cf. 801, *Master Pfriem* [Man expelled from heaven for interfering]; or 470, *Friends in Life and Death,* pt. II, *The Journey.* See: "It Serves me Right!," In: El-Shamy *Folktales of Egypt,* No. 12, pp. 259–60. Designated as new Type: 470C§, *Man in Utopian Otherworld Cannot Resist Interfering: He is Expelled.*

For other tales that seem to harken to ancient Egyptian antiquity, see: H. El-Shamy, "Belief and Non-Belief in Arab, Middle Eastern and sub-Saharan Tales: the Religious-

Maspero's Hope for His Book

PRESUMABLY under the impression that the ancient stories are not to be found in modern Egypt, Maspero seems to have made no attempt to find out whether any of them still "live" in contemporary local traditions. He, however, had a different reverse plan: that the stories in his anthology be reintroduced or transplanted into current Egyptian culture, and thus they would "live anew in their right home."[102]

In February 1885, a European resident of Luxor informed Maspero that he had heard the story of Rhampsinitus told in Arabic in a neighboring village. A written text of the rendition was mailed to Maspero. The writer-narrator, a boy of about 14 years of age, had heard it from his Italian teacher. The teacher, in recognition of services rendered to Maspero, had received from him a copy of his *Contes* as a gift.[103] The Italian teacher had told the story of Rhampsinitus in the classroom; the young pupils learned it and told it orally on their own. The text that Maspero received did not include the episode in which Rhampsinitus prostitutes his daughter in order to catch the thief.[104] He explained the deviation from the original in terms of cultural values that prevent an educator from including such a risqué theme in a story told to young pupils in a conservative community.

Thus Maspero, albeit inadvertently, touched upon the theoretical issues involved in the debate on the factors contributing to stability and change in oral traditions, and the role of written-down texts ("books") in the learning of *Märchen* (magic tales).[105] Although Maspero's contribution may seem marginal when compared to those made by such stalwarts of "experimental folklore" as Walter Anderson and Albert Wesselski, his attempt had the distinction of primacy in time.

Maspero had hoped that additional narratives from his anthology would be encountered in oral traditions, first in Luxor and its environs and subsequently in wider areas. Alas! None of the tales seem to have

Non-Religious Continuum. A Case Study." In: *al-Ma-thûrât al-Shaʿbiyyah*. vol. 3, no. 9 (Doha, January 1988), pp. 7–21.

102. "... *revivre dan leur propre pays.*" See: M. G. Maspero, "Sur une version Arab du conte de Rhampsinite," in *Journal Asiatique,* 1885, vol. vi, pp. 149–159; p. 159.

103. Maspero published the text with comments: "Sur une version Arab du conte de Rhampsinite." See n. 102, above.

104. Mot.: K425, "King's daughter put into brothel to catch thief"; and T455.9§, "Maiden (woman) gives sexual favor for story (personal adventure, confession)."

105. On the Anderson-Wesselski exchange, see: H. El-Shamy, "Behaviorism and the Text." In: *Folklore Today: A Festschrift for Richard M. Dorson,* Linda Dégh, Henry Glassie, and Felix Oinas, eds. (Bloomington, Ind., 1976), pp. 145–60; esp. pp. 152–54.

caught on! This fact was revealed by intensive collecting undertaken recently in southern Egypt and Nubia. Even the Rhampsinitus rendition cited above seems to have vanished. A similar fate of another ancient tale learned by pupils from a schoolbook was reported in 1893:

> In his *Contes populaires de la vallée du Nil,* Yacob Artin reported a situation in which the ancient Egyptian story of "The Lost Sailor" seemed to be catching on in oral tradition. As of today [1970s], almost a century later, not a trace of the story has been found in Egyptian oral tradition.[106]

Concluding Remarks

Maspero's *Popular Stories of Ancient Egypt* is an invaluable work, made accessible to readers of the English language by the outstanding translation of Mrs. C. H. W. Johns. Its excellence is due not only to the intriguing nature of the ancient narratives it brings back to life but also to the meticulous scholarship that accompanies the ancient texts.

As demonstrated in El-Shamy's *Folktales of Egypt,* the assessment of the types of relationships between Ancient Egyptian narratives and their counterparts elsewhere, especially in sub-Saharan Africa, still awaits more objective research. Toward that goal, selections of newly developed, culture-specific tale-types and motifs have been applied to the tales in the present work as more precise means of data identification.[107]

The reissuing of the present work by Maspero as a part of "The ABC-CLIO Series of Classic Folk and Fairy Tales," Professor Jack Zipes Series Editor, will place it within a broader context and bring it to the attention of contemporary scholars in the various fields it so competently addresses.

—Hasan El-Shamy
Indiana University
August 2001

106. El-Shamy, *Folktales of Egypt,* p. 1.

107. Some 768 motifs, of which 544 are newly developed and culture specific, were used to identify data in the present (partial) anthology. A more inclusive treatment of the data will be found in Hasan El-Shamy, *A Demographically Oriented Type-Index for Tales of the Arab World.* Indiana University Press, 2002 (forthcoming).

Tale-Types and Motifs

Register of Tale-Types

All *new* tale-types added to the Aarne-Thompson tale-type system, and new motifs added to the Thompson motif system are marked by the sign (§) at the end of the number.

A double dagger sign ("‡") indicates a *newer* tale-type or motif, added or developed after the publication of El-Shamy's *Folk Traditions of the Arab World: A Guide to Motif Classification* in 1995. (See Vol. 1, Appendix I, "Locations of Tale-types in the Arab World," pp. 415–42.)

Intro., pp. cxxix–cxxx. The "Pharaoh who had become blind ...."

> Type: 844C§, *Search for a Virgin (Chaste Woman)*. None is found readily.
> Intro. pp. cxxix–cxxx;
> Introduction to This Edition, p. xvi n. 39.

[No. 1]. The Story of the Two Brothers:

> Type: 318, *The Faithless Wife*. Batu: the Egyptian "Two Brothers" Tale;
> + 917§, ‡*Innocent (Chaste) Man Slandered as Seducer (Rapist): Subsequently Vindicated*. (Batu and Anubis, Joseph and Pharaoh's wife, etc.);
> + 516B, *The Abducted Princess* (Love through Sight of Floating Hair);
> + Cf. 315, *The Faithless Sister*. [Treacherous sister conspires with paramour against her brother];
> 590A, *The Treacherous Wife*. [Faithless wife conspires with paramour against her husband].

[No. 2]. King Khufuî and the Magicians:

> Type: cf. 1920, *Contest in Lying;*
> 1920E1§, *Contest: Strangest (Most Bizarre) Story Awarded Prize.*

No. 2 pt. I, Khâfrîya's story (pp. 20–22):
Type: 1359, *Husband Outwits Adulteress and Paramour.*
No. 2 pt. IV Dadûfhoru's-Didi's story (pp. 27–33):
Type: 930E§, ‡*Prophecy: Unborn Child (Infant) Predestined to Replace King.* (Attempts to get rid of child follow him.)

[No. 4]. The Memoirs of Sinuhît:
Type: cf. 922A, *Achikar.* Falsely accused minister reinstates himself by cleverness.
Cf. 938, *Placidas (Eustacius).* [Loses all, then regains all.]

[No. 5]. The Shipwrecked Sailor:
Type: cf. 936A§, *Voyages (Adventures) of an Entrepreneur.* (Sindbâd the sailor.) (Focus.)

[No. 6]. How Thutîyi Took the City of Joppa:
Type: 954A§, ‡*Enemy's Defences Overcome by Smuggling Concealed Warriors Past Fortifications (Garrison, Moat, Wall, etc.).*
Cf. 954, *The Forty Thieves.*
Introduction to This Edition, p. xiv.

[No. 7 I]. The Adventure of Satni-Khamoîs with the Mummies:
Type: 1645D§, *Perilous Journey in Search of Treasure Trove;*
+ 792§, ‡*Resuscitation in Order to Learn Truth (Get Information about Past Events).* The tell-tale corpse (mummy);
+ 1469§, *Foolish Person Tricked into a Humiliating (Disgraceful) Position,* (pp. 111–14);
+ cf. 681, *King in the Bath; Years of Experience in a Moment.* (Conclusion of story, pp. 115–18).

[No. 8 II]. The Veritable History of Satni-Khamoîs and His Son Senosiris:
8 II. (pp. 120–25):
Type: 471B§, *Enigmatic (Eccentric) Occurrences in Another World Explained to Hero.*
8 II. (pp. 125–37)
Type: 325A§, *Contest in Magic between Two Master Magicians.*

[No. 10]. The Daughter of the Prince of Bakhtan and the Possessing Spirit:
Type: 817*, *Devil Leaves at Mention of God's Name.*

[No. 13]. The Doomed Prince:
Type: 934A1, *Three-fold Death.*

+ As intro.:

870D§, ‡*Youth Raised in Solitary Confinement Gains Access to Outside World.* Adventures follow.

(Cf. 870, *The Princess Confined in the Mound.* [Digs her way out, and eventually marries her sweetheart to whom she had been betrothed]);

+ cf. 530: II–III, =*The Princess on the Glass Mountain.*

[No. 14]. The Story of Rhampsinitus:

Type: 950, *Rhampsinitus.* [Series of skillful thefts by a master thief and assistant];

Introduction to This Edition, p. xvi n. 39;

Intro. pp. cxxix–cxxx.

[No. 19]. The Quarrel of Apôpi and Saqnûnrîya:

Type: cf. 875B, *The Clever Girl and the King.* For each impossible task she gives countertasks. [Also told of clever boy.]

[No. 20]. Fragments of a Ghost Story:

Type: 760B§, ‡*Restless Souls:* Deceased cannot rest because of worldly concerns; his soul contacts the living to make wishes known.

Cf. 506**, *The Grateful Saint.* The hero redeems a saint's maltreated picture and is afterwards rewarded by the grateful saint.

Other Tale-Types Cited—(passim)

325, *The Magician and His Pupil.*
Introduction to This Edition p. xxx n. 100.

801, *Master Pfriem* [Man expelled from heaven for interfering].
Introduction to This Edition p. xxx n. 101.

470, *Friends in Life and Death,* pt. II, *The Journey.*
Introduction to This Edition p. xxx n. 101.

470C§, *Man in Utopian Otherworld Cannot Resist Interfering: He Is Expelled.* ("It Serves me Right!")
Introduction to This Edition p. xxx n. 101.

510, *Cinderella and Cap o' Rushes.*
Introduction to This Edition, p. xvi n. 39.

613, *The Two Travelers (Truth and Falsehood).*
Introduction to This Edition p. xxx n. 99.

980*, *The Painter and the Architect* [The noble barber and the vile dyer ...].
Introduction to This Edition p. xxx n. 99.

꒿

REGISTER OF MOTIFS

A. Mythological [and Related Beliefs] Motifs

A6.3§, ‡Reason for creation of woman.
    No. 1 p. 10

A6.3.1.1§, ‡Mate (house-companion, wife, etc.) molded for hero so that he would not live alone (the gods grant Batu female companionship).
    No. 1 p. 10

A12, Hermaphroditic creator.
    Introduction to This Edition p. xv n. 34.

A14.1§, ‡Lesser deity as maker (modeler) of men—(Khnum).
    No. 1 p. 10 n. 28;
    No. 2 p. 30–31.

A100.5.1§, ‡Groups of deities (gods, goddesses).
    Intro. p. cxxxvi;
    No. 2 p. 29

A102, Characteristics of deity.
    No. 10 pp. 143–44,—(Horus).

A102.13.1§, ‡God as shepherd for flock (of believers).
    No. 2 p. 27 n. 30.

A105.1§, ‡Deity's energy derives from mystical fluid (elixir, nectar)—("*sa*").
    No. 10 p. 146 n. 12.

A106, Opposition of good and evil gods.
    Intro. p. cxxxiv,—("Sîtu" and Osiris).

A109.3§, ‡Deity with multiple souls.
    No. 10 p. 144 n. 3,—(Horus).

A109.3.1§, ‡Deity with seven souls.
    No. 5 p. 86 n. 18,—(Ra).

A120.5§, ‡Deity with ability to disintegrate into infinite number of secondary forms.
    No. 1 p. 9 n. 25.

A125.6§, ‡Deity disguised as human.
    No. 2 p. 29

A131.3.5.1§, ‡Goddess with viper's (serpent's) head.
    No. 7 p. 105 n. 32,—(Maruîtsakro.)
A132.17.1§, ‡Goddess in form of frog. (Heket.)
    No. 2 p. 30 n. 42.
A154.1, ‡Magic drink gives immortality to gods.
    No. 10 p. 146 n. 12, cf.
A161.3.1§, ‡Isis as "queen of the gods."
    No. 22 pp. 240–41,—("goddess of the gods").
A164.1, Brother-sister marriage of the gods.
    No. 7 p. 100 n. 12.
A164.1.1, Mother-son marriage of the gods.
    No. 10 pp. 143–44, cf. Horus.)
A165.2.5.1§, ‡"Amon of the Road" as divine ambassador of Amon.
    Intro. p. cx;
    No. 15 pp. 170, 173, 177 n. 19, 179.
A165.6, Scribe of the gods.
    No. 2 p. 25 n. 20,—(Thoth.)
A166.7.1§, ‡Praiser of the gods.
    No. 7 p. 113 n. 58.
A167.1.1§, ‡Council of the nine gods.
    No. 1 p. 9 n. 25.
A168.2.2§, ‡Daughter of the gods.
    Intro. pp. c, civ;
    No. 1 pp. 11, 22;
    No. 2 p. 29;
    No. 10 p. 155 n. 6.
A169.2§, ‡Bringing suit to law court of the gods.
    No. 7 p. 106, cf. (of Ra);
    No. 22 pp. 240–41.
A170.1§, ‡Miracle. Supernatural deed or manifestation by God.
    No. 8 p. 120;
    No. 9 p. 137.
A182.0.3.1§, ‡God reveals himself in human form to mortal.
    No. 7 p. 115 n. 66.
A185.1, ‡God helps mortal in battle.
    No. 9 p. 138.
A185.12, ‡Deity provides man with soul.
    No. 1 p. 10 n. 28.

A189.7.0.1§, ‡Goddess of human destiny. (Maskhonuît/Meshkent).
> No. 2 p. 29 n. 37;
> No. 2 p. 30 n. 46.

A196.2, ‡Decree of gods irrevocable.
> Introduction to This Edition pp. xviii–xix n. 45.

A225, ‡Son of the sun.
> Intro. p. cxl;
> No. 4 p. 69;
> No. 7 p. 110 n. 47;
> No. 10 pp. 143, 144 n. 3.

A240, Moon-god.
> Introduction to This Edition p. xv n. 34.

A281, Storm-god.
> No. 15 p. 177,—(Sutekhu);
> No. 19 pp. 224–25,—(Sutekhu).

A310.1, ‡Goddess of the world of the dead.
> No. 4 p. 68 n. 34.

A310.1.1§, ‡Goddess as guardian to the entrance of the world of the dead (crypt, tomb).
> No. 7 p. 105 n. 32,—(Maruîtsakro).

A454.3.1§, ‡Deity heals from spirit-possession.
> No. 10 p. 146.

A464.5§, 'The balance' of Judgment Day: for weighing religious exercise (soul, heart, etc.).
> No. 8 p. 130.

A471.1.1§, ‡Seven (nine) Hathors prophecy for mortal.
> Introduction to This Edition p. xxi n. 54;
> Intro. p.cxxxvi n. 176;
> Intro. p. cxxxvii;
> No. 1 p. 10;
> No. 2 pp. 30–31 cf.;
> No. 13 p. 154.

A477.3§, ‡Goddess as midwife: presides at childbirth.
> No. 2 pp. 29–30.

A477.3.1§, ‡Goddess presides over births of kings and queens. (Heket.)
> No. 2 p. 30 n. 42.

A483.1.1§, ‡"Lady of Heaven" as goddess of clemency.
> No. 4 pp. 76–77 n. 79.

A485, ‡God of war.
    No. 19 p. 227.
A485.0.3§, ‡Montu (Mont) as god of war.
    No. 4 pp. 67, 74;
    No. 10 pp. 143–44,—(Horus/simile);
    No. 19 p. 227.
A485.7§, ‡War deity thanked for victory.
    No. 4 pp. 67, 74;
    No. 19 p. 227.
A491, ‡God of travelers.
    No. 15 p. 173, cf.
A499.9§, ‡God (lord) of the desert. (Min/Minn).
    No. 4 p. 72 n. 58.
A501.1.1§, ‡Seven demigoddesses.
    Intro. p. cxxxvi, cf.,—(seven goddesses);
    No. 2 p. 29, cf.,—(seven goddesses).
A517§, ‡Culture-hero as rulers of the entire world (cosmocrator)—
    (Alexander, Solomon, etc.).
    No. 23 pp. 252–53.
A527.1, Culture-hero precocious.
    No. 10 pp. 143–44,—(Horus).
A604.3§, *maktûb, muqaddar, qismah* (written, predestined, kismet)—one's
    fated lot.
    No. 13 p. 158.
A659.3.1§, ‡River's source in heaven. (Nile.)
    No. 1 pp. 7–8 n. 19.
A698.6.1.1§, ‡The highest strata in paradise are those closest to God.
    No. 8 pp. 122–23,—(to Osiris).
A721.2.1.2§, ‡Darkness due to goddess (Nut, sky) swallowing sun.
    No. 1 p. 15 n. 48.
A722.3.1§, ‡Sun's night journey: in lower world ("Lower Hemi-
    sphere").
    Intro. p. cxli n. 196.
A726.5§, ‡Place (location) where sun rises and sets. (The horizons of
    sunrise and sunset.)
    No. 20 p. 230, cf.
A726.6§, ‡Shafts (holes, passages) for sunrise and sunset. (They lead
    from earth to sky, for sun or moon to traverse.)
    Intro. p. cxli n. 195.

A762.2.1§, Serpent marries star-girl.
> No. 5 p. 86.

A872.0.1§, ‡Names given rivers and ('The Salty') seas.
> No. 1 p. 10 n. 31;
> No. 7 p. 103 n. 20.

A876, Midgard Serpent. A serpent surrounds the earth.
> No. 7 p. 103 n. 23, cf., (surrounds coffer, book).

A872.2§, ‡River (sea) that leads to the land (island) of the dead.
> No. 5 pp. cli–cliii.

A1170.1§, ‡Night and day caused by the daily swallowing and rebirth of the sun.
> No. 1 p. 15 n. 48.

A1242§, ‡Deity fashions man on potter's wheel—(Khnum).
> No. 1 p. 10 n. 28;
> No. 2 p. 31.

A1278.4.1.1§, ‡Deity (Khnum) molds beautiful mate for unjustly treated man (Batu/Bata).
> No. 1 p. 10 n. 28.

A1336.1.1.1.1§, ‡Set murders his brother Osiris.
> Intro. p. cxxxiv.

B. Animals

B14.1.1§, ‡Ammut (Amemt). Combination of lion, hippopotamus, and crocodile. Devours hearts of sinners.
> No. 8 p. 130,—("Amaît").

B15.1.2.1.5§, ‡Two-headed calf (bull).
> Intro. pp. civ–cvi;
> No. 1 p. 13 n. 39.

B108.1, Serpent as patron of wealth.
> No. 7 p. 103 n. 23.

B143.3.1, ‡Dog warns of coming.
> No. 13 p. 159.

B176.1, Magic serpent.
> No. 7 p. 103 n. 23.

B211, Animal uses human speech.
> Introduction to This Edition p. xv n. 36.

B211.1.5, ‡Speaking cow.
> No. 1 p. 4.

B211.6.1, Speaking snake (serpent).
>   No. 5 p. 85.

B216, Knowledge of animal language.
>   No. 1 p. 4 n. 8.

B225.1.2§, Island ruled by serpent as its king.
>   No. 5 p. 85.

B244.1, ‡King of serpents (snakes).
>   No. 5 p. 85.

B263.3, War between crows and owls.
>   No. 6 pp. 90–94, cf.

B335.3.2§, ‡Predator (crocodile) tries in vain to get hero to kill his human (giant) helper.
>   No. 13 pp. 158–59.

B411, Helpful cow.
>   No. 1 p. 4.

B421, ‡Helpful dog.
>   No. 13 pp. 158–60.

B437.2, Helpful mouse.
>   No. 9 p. 139, cf.

B491.1, Helpful serpent ([snake]).
>   No. 5 p. 85.

B521, Animal warns of mortal danger.
>   No. 1 p. 4.

B521.3.6§, ‡Cow warns against attack (murder).
>   No. 1 p. 4.

B763.1.1§, ‡Snake attracted to milk.
>   No. 13 p. 158 n. 14, cf.

B741.2, Neighing of stallion in Assyria impregnates mares in Egypt.
>   Introduction to This Edition p. xv n. 36.

B811.3.2.1§, ‡Sacred bull with special markings: Apis.
>   No. 1 p. 13 n. 39,—(after Mariette).

B811.3.4, ‡Sacred cat.
>   Intro. p. cii.

C. Tabu

C60.1.1§, ‡Ritual polluter: sexual intercourse (being *junub,* in a state of *janâbah*).
>   No. 7 p. 115 n. 67.

C221.1.3.1, Tabu: eating certain fish.
>No. 1 p. 8 n. 20, cf.

C423.3, ‡Tabu: revealing experiences in otherworld.
>No. 8 p. 125.

C423.5, ‡Tabu: revealing sacred mysteries.
>No. 8 p. 125.

C433.3§, ‡Animals committing offense against deity (holy man) not to be named.
>No. 1 p. 8 n. 20.

C433.3.1§, ‡Tabu: mention of catfish: it ate Osiris's phallus.
>No. 1 p. 8 n. 20.

C637§, ‡Tabu: certain acts on unlucky day ("cross-day").
>Intro. p. cxxxiv.

C637.1§, ‡Tabu: business transaction on unlucky day.
>Intro. p. cxxxiv.

C867.2.2.1§, ‡"Let it not be a human being (that is used for the cruel demonstration)!"
>Intro. p. xcvii;
>No. 2 p. 27.

C867.3§, ‡Tabu: cruelty to animals.
>Intro. p. cii—(cat).

C898.1§, Tabu: indignities to corpse (beating, cremation, etc.).
>No. 14 p. 166 n. 5.

C898.1.2§, ‡Tabu: publication of slaying (execution). Public display of corpse or a part thereof.
>No. 14 p. 166 n. 5.

D. Magic [and Similar Supernatural Occurrences]

D12, Transformation: man to woman.
>No. 7 p. 115 n. 67.

D445.5.1§, ‡Transformation: statue of crocodile comes to life.
>No. 2 pp. 19, 21.

D445.5.1.1§, ‡Statue of crocodile comes to life and kills person.
>No. 2 p. 21.

D610.3§, Self-transformation by saint (magician, holy man, etc.).
>No. 1 p. 13

D612.2§, ‡Animal sold (given) proves to be enchanted (transformed).
>No. 1 p. 13.

D651.1.1, ‡Transformation of magic object to animal which kills enemy.
    No. 2 p. 21.
D659.8, ‡Transformation to test fidelity.
    No. 7 p. 115 n. 67.
D672, Obstacle flight. . . .
    Introduction to This Edition p. xv n. 36.
D936, ‡Magic island.
    No. 5 pp. cli–clii, cf.
D1101.0.1§, ‡Armor endowed with animal's magic (totemistic) characteristics (e.g., bull's, lion's, eagle's, etc.).
    No. 17 p. 206 n. 52.
D1101.2, ‡Magic cuirass.
    No. 16 p. 183, cf.,—(talisman).
D1101.4, ‡Magic helmet.
    No. 17 p. 206 n. 52, cf.
D1266, Magic book.
    No. 7 p. 102.
D1266.1, Magic writings (gramerye [gramarye], runes).
    No. 7 p. 111 n. 51.
D1273, Magic formula (charm).
    No. 18 p. 220.
D1273.0.6§, 'raqwah'/ruqwah: charm containing sacred words renders invulnerable (protects).
    No. 18 p. 220.
D1380.22.1§, ‡Feather of ibis protects against predator (crocodile).
    Intro. p. cxxix.
D1380.28§, ‡Sacred (magic) book protects.
    No. 7 p. 108 n. 40.
D1402.19.1, ‡Magic statue of animal kills.
    No. 2 p. 21.
D1536§, ‡Statue animated by a spiritual component ('double') from the entity (deity, person) it represents.
    No. 10 p. 145 n. 10.
D1551, Waters magically divide and close. [Parting of the sea.]
    No. 2 p. 24.
D1551.9.1§, ‡Magic formula causes waters to divide (part).
    No. 2 p. 24;
    No. 7 p. 98.

D1555.5§, ‡Magic formula (charm) causes ground (earth) to open.
  No. 7 p. 98.
D1621.1§, ‡Statue of deity renders judgments vocally or by movement.
  No. 10 pp. 145–46 n. 11.
D1645.12§, ‡Book emits light.
  No. 7 p. 99.
D1705§, *barakah* (blessedness): supernatural [positive] power residing in object, act, or person.
  No. 10 p. 146 n. 12, cf.
D1707§, ‡Blessed objects.
  No. 10 p. 146 n. 12.
D1711.4.1§, ‡Teta (Didi), the Egyptian, as master magician (sorcerer).
  No. 2 p. 25 n. 18.
D1712.0.1, ‡Astrologer-magician.
  No. 22 p. 240.
D1714.1.2§, ‡Magic healing by chaste virgin (woman).
  Intro. pp. cxxix–cxxx.
D1719.1.5.1§, ‡Contest in magic writing between scribes (magicians).
  No. 7 p. 190 n. 43.
D1720.0.1§, ‡Means of learning magic.
  No. 2 p. 25 n. 20.
D1720.0.1.1§, ‡Magic learned from books.
  No. 2 p. 25 n. 20.
D1735.5§, ‡Magic powers from soaking supernatural charm (written) in water and drinking (swallowing) brew.
  Intro. p. cxliii n. 208.
D1741.6.2§, ‡Magic (supernatural) power lost through erotic activity.
  No. 7 p. 115 n. 67.
D1789§, Contagious magic. Magic results obtained by contact or touch.
  No. 1 p. 11 n. 34.
D1789.0.1§, *'athar* ("trace") object carrying identifying residuals of target for magic ritual.
  No. 1 p. 11 n. 34.
D1812.3.2.2§, Fortune told by reading coffee (tea) residuals in cup.
  Intro. pp. cxxvi–cxxxii.
D1812.3.3.3, Prophetic dream induced by incantation [(*'istikhârah*)].
  No. 22 p. 240.
D1812.5, Future learned through omens.
  Intro. pp. cxxxiv–cxxxviii.

D1816.7§, ‡Jewel (ornament) retrieved from bottom of lake (river) supernaturally (by magic).
>   No. 2 pp. 23–24

D1825.3.6.1§, ‡Magic power to learn contents of sealed letter (envelope).
>   No. 8 pp. 126–27.

D2012, Moments thought years. In a moment a person seems to experience events of many years.
>   No. 7 p. 115 n. 67, cf.

D2012.3§, Person given the illusion that he (she) has undergone a tragic life experience (e.g., family destroyed, children murdered, or the like).
>   No. 7 p. 115.

D2065.1, Madness from demonic possession.
>   No. 10 p. 146, cf.

D2065.1.1§, Epilepsy from possession by jinn.
>   No. 18 p. 221, cf.

D2161.3.1, Blindness magically cured.
>   Intro. p. cxxx.

D2157.4, ‡Miraculous speedy growth of a tree.
>   No. 1 p. 14.

D2176.3.5, ‡Evil spirit exorcised by deity.
>   No. 10 p. 146.

D2188.4§, ‡Island vanishes (supernaturally).
>   Intro. p. clii;
>   No. 5 p. 87 n. 21.

E. The Dead

E30, Resuscitation by arrangement of members.
>   Introduction to This Edition p. xv n. 36.

E52, ‡Resuscitation by magic charm.
>   No. 2 p. 27.

E125.3.1§, ‡Brother resuscitates brother.
>   No. 1 pp. 12–13.

E193.0.1§, ‡Togetherness in death: burial in same grave insures that souls remain together.
>   No. 7 p. 116 n. 71,—("doubles").

E193.1§, ‡Corpse(s) buried away brought 'home' and reunited with other deceased members of family (in same grave).
>   No. 7 p. 116.

E200, Malevolent return from the dead.
 No. 7 p. 117, n. 74.

E235.2, ‡Ghost returns to demand proper burial.
 No. 7 p. 117, n. 74, cf.

E235.4, Return from dead to punish theft of part of corpse.
 Intro. p. cxliv;
 No. 7 p. 111.

E235.6, ‡Return from dead to punish disturber of grave.
 Intro. p. cxliv;
 No. 7 p. 111.

E236, ‡Return from dead to demand stolen property.
 Intro. p. cxliv
 No. 7 p. 111.

E236.9§, ‡Return from dead to demand magic book (scroll, formula, charm, etc.) stolen from grave.
 Intro. p. cxliii;
 Intro. p. cxliv;
 No. 7 p. 111 n. 52.

E261, Wandering ghost makes attack. Unprovoked and usually unmotivated.
 No. 7 p. 117, n. 74, cf. (motivated).

E419.1, ‡Soul wanders and demands that a temple be built for him.
 No. 20 p. 230.

E419.8, Ghost returns to enforce burial wishes or to protest disregard of them.
 No. 7 p. 117, n. 74.

E465, Revenant rewards its conqueror.
 Introduction to This Edition p. xv n. 34.

E473§, ‡Revenant seeking revenge at the hands of the living.
 Intro. p. cxliv, cf.

E541.6§, ‡Fields of the dead: land next to burial grounds dedicated to providing the deceased with food. ("Fields of the funerary domain.")
 No. 4 p. 79 n. 92.

E577, ‡Dead persons play games.
 No. 7 p. 109 n. 44.

E577.0.1§, ‡Dead person challenges living to game (wager).
 No. 7 p. 109.

E577.4§, ‡Dead persons play the game of draughts (checkers, or the like).
 No. 7 p. 109 n. 44.

E577.4.1§, ‡Play draughts with a dead person (mummy, ghost).
No. 7 p. 109.

E607.2, Person transforms self, is swallowed and reborn in new form.
Introduction to This Edition p. xv n. 36.

E607.7§, ‡Dead visits (returns) to world of living in any form he chooses.
No. 7 p. 112.

E611.2.1, ‡Reincarnation as bull.
No. 1 p. 15.

E631, ‡Reincarnation in plant (tree) growing from grave.
No. 1 p. 14.

E631.0.7§, ‡Tree (plant) from blood of slain animal.
No. 1 p. 15.

E670, Repeated reincarnation.
Introduction to This Edition p. xv n. 36.

E710, External soul.
Introduction to This Edition p. xv n. 36.

E717§, Multiple souls: a being with more than one soul.
No. 5 pp. 86–87.

E721.1.0.1§, The dead 'come to' (communicate with) the living in dreams
(visions).
No. 20 pp. 230–31.

E721.1.2.3.2§, Body cremated so soul cannot return to it.
No. 2 p. 22 n. 11.

E724.0.1§, ‡The *Ka* as a person's counter-spirit ('Double').
No. 5 p. 85 n. 12;
No. 7 pp. 99, 116 n. 71.

E728.0.1§, ‡Soul (double) possesses living person.
No. 7 p. 117, n. 74.

E750.0.2§, ‡Destroying tomb deprives the deceased of burial rituals and
angers the soul (double).
No. 7 p. 117 n. 74.

E753§, ‡Homeless soul (or 'double').
No. 2 p. 22 n. 11
No. 7 p. 117, n. 74.

E753.1§, ‡Homeless soul: soul without the body to which it belonged.
No. 2 p. 22 n. 11.

E753.2§, ‡Homeless soul: soul without tomb for burial of body to which
it belonged.
No. 7 p. 117 n. 74.

E755.0.4.3.1§, ‡Souls reside with deity in west.
    Intro. pp. clii, cliii, cf.
E755.0.4.4.1.1§, ‡"The Island of the Double" (Island of the *Ka*) as the
    abode of humans' souls.
    No. 5 pp. clii, cliii.
E761.6.4, ‡Life token: beer foams.
    Introduction to This Edition p. xv n. 36;
    No. 1 p. 9.
E789.3.1§, ‡Severed head rejoins body.
    No. 2 p. 27.

F. Marvels

F34, ‡Temptress sent from upper world by deity (Pandora).
    Introduction to This Edition p. xxi n. 53;
    Intro. p. c n. 31, cf.
F69.1§, Saint takes person (mother) on tour of paradise and hell.
    No. 8 pp. 121–22, cf.
F72§, ‡Beings (creatures) from other planets 'descend' to earth on flying
    object (spaceship, meteor, falling star, etc.).
    No. 5 p. 86 n. 15.
F81, ‡Descent to lower world of dead (Hell, Hades).
    No. 8 pp. 123–25.
F110.3§, Perilous sea voyage.
    No. 5 pp. 84–85;
    No. 15 p. 172.
F129.4.4, ‡Voyage to island of the dead.
    No. 5 pp. clii, cf.
F150.2.2.1§, ‡Entrance to world of the dead (crypt, tomb) guarded by
    deity (goddess).
    No. 7 p. 105 n. 32,—(Maruîtsakro).
F162.6.3§, ‡Reservoir of nectar of energy (vitality) in otherworld.
    No. 10 p. 146 n. 12.
F171.0.1, Enigmatic happenings in otherworld which are later explained.
    No. 8 p. 123.
F171.6.0.1§, Futile behavior (efforts) in otherworld.
    No. 8 pp. 123–24.
F215, ‡Fairies live in star-world.
    No. 5 p. 86, cf.

F282.4§, ‡Jinn (fairies) came to earth on falling star.
>   No. 5 p. 86 n. 15.

F311.1, ‡Fairy godmother. Attendant good fairy.
>   Intro. pp. cxxxvi–cxxxvii;
>   No. 1 p. 10 n. 29;
>   No. 13 p. 154 n. 2.

F362.2, Fairies cause insanity.
>   No. 18 p. 221, cf.

F364.2, ‡Fairies wrestles with mortals.
>   No. 18 pp. 221–22.

F364.2.1§, ‡Fairy wrestles with man for prize.
>   No. 18 pp. 221–22.

F385.2.2§, Possessing *zâr*-jinn (*asyâd*) placated by sacrifice.
>   No. 10 pp. 146–47, cf.

F415.1§, Invisible spirit negotiates terms of departure with healer (shaman, exorcist, holy man, etc.): healing psychodrama.
>   No. 10 pp. 146–47.

F420.1.4.10, Water-spirit with extraordinarily long hair.
>   No. 18 p. 219, cf.

F420.1.6.8§, ‡Female water-spirit exhibits figure (appears in the nude).
>   No. 18 p. 220.

F420.5.2.1.1, ‡Water-maiden enamors man and draws him under water.
>   No. 18 pp. 221–22, cf.

F420.6.1.5, Water-maidens make conditions for lovers.
>   No. 18 p. 220, cf.

F471.2.1, Succubus. Female incubus.
>   No. 7 pp. 114–15 n. 64.

F491.10§, *en-Naddâhah* ('the she-Caller'): female spirit who calls people by name and then leads them astray.
>   No. 18 p. 220.

F499.3.5.3§, ‡Jinn dwell in old ruins (temples, monuments).
>   No. 18 p. 221.

F531, Giant. A person of enormous size.
>   No. 13 p. 157.

F531.6.17.5.1§, ‡Fear-evoking herdsman.
>   No. 17 p. 202.

F555.0.1§, ‡Remarkable hairstyle (hairdressing, hairdo).
>   No. 1 p. 5 n. 10.

F555.0.3.1§, ‡Remarkable black (blue) hair.
>   No. 2 p. 30.

F569.9§, ‡Lifestyles in conflict (rural-urban, nomadic-settler, modern-conventional/traditional, etc.)—each is unusual for the other(s).
>   No. 4 p. 66, 76–78.

F571, ‡Extremely old person.
>   No. 2 p. 25 n. 18.

F571.7, Person hundreds of years old.
>   No. 2 p. 25, cf.

F575.1.6§, ‡Beauty that disorients (dazzles) the beholder.
>   No. 2 p. 20,—(man's).

F611.4, ‡Precocious son saves kingdom.
>   No. 8 pp. 125–37.

F628.2.1, Strong man kills many men at once.
>   No. 1 p. 11.

F628.2.1.1§, ‡Hero kills all attackers except one: survivor is to report news of battle.
>   No. 1 p. 11.

F632, Mighty eater. Eats whole ox at a time, or the like.
>   No. 2 pp. 24–25.

F633, Mighty drinker. Drinks whole pools of water, or the like.
>   No. 2 p. 25.

F670§, ‡Skillful storyteller (bard, reporter, etc.).
>   No. 2 p. 19.

F676, Skillful thief.
>   No. 14 pp. 163–67.

F701.0.1§, ‡Island of plenty. Every sort of food is found.
>   No. 5 p. 84.

F706, Land of darkness.
>   No. 23 p. 252.

F732.4§, ‡Island of incense (fragrant herbs, perfume).
>   No. 5 pp. 86–87.

F773, ‡Remarkable church (chapel, temple).
>   No. 12 p. 151.

F773.5§, ‡Private chapel: mosque, church, temple, etc. at private residence.
>   Introduction to This Edition p. xix n. 46;
>   No. 13 p. 154, n. 3.

F782.7§, ‡Undetectable door (secret door or passage) to palace (castle, house).

No. 14 p. 164.

F821.1.8§, ‡Garment of see-through material (e.g., net, thin textile, etc.).

Intro. p. cxxix;

No. 2 p. 23;

No. 7 p. 114 n. 62.

F827.9.1§, ‡Extraordinary glazed-earthenware ornament (amulet).

Intro. pp. cxlii–cxliii;

No. 2 p. 23 n. 13.

F840.0.1.2.3.1§, ‡Courageous person (warrior) horrified by unexpected sight of small animal (mouse, rat, bird, etc.).

Intro. p. cxxxvi n. 172.

F849.1§, ‡Loved meat (mammals, fowl, fish, insects) dishes.

No. 1 p. 14,—(liver).

F849.9.1§, ‡Brewed cereal (barley, bread)—labeled: *bûẓah* (native Egyptian beer).

No. 2 p. 32 n. 54;

No. 3 p. 38, n. 4.

F853.1.1§, ‡Book kept in extraordinary strong box of stone (iron).

No. 2 p. 25 n. 20.

F853.2§, ‡Series of enclosed boxes (chests) one within the other.

No. 7 p. 103.

F855.9.1.1§, ‡Waxen statue.

No. 2 p. 21.

F879.1§, ‡Poison so potent that it corrodes metal (glass).

No. 23 p. 253.

F888§, ‡Extraordinary (marvelous) craftsmanship (non-magical).

No. 14 p. 164.

F943, Sinking into mud in duel.

Introduction to This Edition p. xiv n. 33.

F944.3, ‡Island sinks into sea.

No. 5 p. 87 n. 21, cf.

F961.2.10§, ‡Star falls to earth: shooting (falling) star.

No. 5 p. 86.

F962.1.1§, Storm wrecks (sinks) ship.

No. 5 p. 84.

F962.1.2§, ‡Storm throws ship off course—sailors lost.

No. 15 p. 171.

F966, Voices from heaven (or from the air). [*hâtif/ munâdî*.]
　　No. 8 pp. 120–21.

F1012.1.1§, ‡Long search for a chaste woman (girl).
　　Intro. pp. cxxix–cxxx.

F1013.2.1§, ‡Sudden quivering of ground indicates arrival of supernatural
　　creature (giant, ogre, etc.).
　　No. 5 p. 84.

F1034.5.2.1§, ‡Magic formula swallowed so as to protect (hide) it.
　　No. 8 p. 134 n. 112.

F1041.1.11.2.1§, ‡Paralysis from fear of spirits (demons).
　　No. 10 p. 147.

F1041.2, Horripilation. Hair rises on end in extraordinary fashion from
　　joy, anger, or love.
　　No. 18 p. 219.

F1041.9.1, Going to bed for sorrow.
　　No. 8 p. 126 n. 94.

F1041.9.9.1§, Dumbness from horror.
　　No. 5 p. 84 n. 9.

F1041.16.1.1§, ‡Man's eyes flash sparks when enraged.
　　No. 17 p. 205

F1041.16.6, ‡Extraordinary physical reactions of angry warriors in
　　battle.
　　No. 19 p. 227.

F1041.17.3§, ‡Fainting away from fear (horror).
　　No. 10 p. 147, cf.

F1041.25§, ‡Uncontrollable physical reactions to joy.
　　No. 4 p. 72.

G. Ogres [and Satan]

G308.1, ‡Fight with sea (lake) monster.
　　No. 13 p. 159, cf.

G308.2, ‡Sea monster.
　　No. 13 p. 159, cf.

H. Tests

H51.2§, ‡Recognition of supernatural (sacred) animal by its markings
　　(physical attributes).
　　No. 1 p. 13 n. 39,—(after Mariette).

H58, Tell-tale hand-mark. Clandestine lover is identified by paint marks left on his skin by mistress.
>   No. 14 pp. 163–67, cf.

H70.3§, ‡Sign of piety: sincerity of voice: 'truthfulness of tongue,' being 'true of voice.' (Usually denoted by narrator through performance.)
>   No. 4 p. 69 n. 37.

H71.2.1, ‡Golden body of boy as sign of royalty.
>   No. 2 p. 30.

H71.2.2§, ‡Hair with blue radiance (color of precious stone, lapis lazuli, etc.) as sign of royalty.
>   No. 2 p. 30.

H270§, Storytelling contest.
>   No. 2 p. 23.

H271§, Contest in telling the strangest (most bizarre) life experience (story).
>   No. 2 p. 19.

H331, Suitor contest: bride offered as prize.
>   No. 13 p. 156.

H331.2.2.1§, ‡Suitor contest: reaching maiden (princess) in tower.
>   No. 13 p. 156.

H400, Chastity test.
>   Intro. pp. cxxix–cxxx.

H413, ‡Special powers of chaste woman.
>   Intro pp. cxxix.

H515, Guessing contest between kings.
>   Intro. pp. cxi–cxii;
>   No. 8 p. 119, 125.

H518.1§, ‡Test: guessing the contents of sealed letter.
>   No. 8 p. 125.

H572, Reductio ad absurdum of riddle: stallions of Babylon. . . .
>   Intro. p. cxi.

H591, Extraordinary actions explained.
>   No. 8 p. 124

H614, Explanation of enigmatic phenomenon.
>   No. 8 p. 124.

H904.1§, ‡Task: conquer city (nation).
>   No. 6 pp. 90–94.

H904.2§, ‡Task: put down rebellion (insurrection).
    No. 6 pp. 90–94.
H1024.10, ‡Task: silencing wild animals (birds).
    No. 19 p. 226.
H1054.1, Task: coming neither naked nor clad. (Comes wrapped in a net or the like.)
    No. 2 p. 23, cf.
H1132.1.8§, ‡Task: recovering lost ornament (jewel) from river (lake, sea, etc.).
    No. 2 p. 24.
H1199.9.2§, Task: discovering money thief.
    No. 15 p. 173.
H1238§, ‡Failure on assigned quest or mission.
    No. 5 p. 88.
H1356.1§, ‡Quest for wood for building seaworthy ship.
    No. 15 pp. 172–80.
H1445§, Fearless youth (hero) frightened by a harmless experience (event).
    Intro. p. cxxvi n. 172;
    No. 10 p. 147, cf.

J. The Wise and the Foolish

J39§, ‡Knowledge acquired from inferences from proverb—how proverbs (parables) work.
    No. 5 p. 88.
J80, Wisdom (knowledge) taught by parable.
    No. 21 p. 235.
J149§, ‡The value of education (schooling).
    No. 2 p. 25 n. 20.
J152.7§, Wisdom from old man who has a book in hand.
    Intro. pp. cxvi–cxvii;
    No. 7 p. 97, cf.
J157, Wisdom (knowledge) from dream. [Instructive dream.]
    No. 8 p. 131 n. 108;
    No. 9 p. 138.
J169§, *sīrah/siyar:* personal life history (biography, vita).
    No. 20 pp. 229–30.
J169.0.1§, Personal experience narrative by story's character.
    No. 5 p. 83.

J169.5§, Epitaph: inscription on grave sums up owner's accomplishments in life.

No. 20 p. 230, cf.

J170.2§, ‡King orders story recorded as history (and parable).

No. 16 p. 200.

J227.9.1§, ‡Death-wish: person in misery wishes to die.

No. 13 p. 161.

J2233.3§, ‡Victim of injustice (aggression) tries to get even by committing the same act (crime) against another (who is innocent).

No. 15 p. 173.

J2233.3.1§, ‡Thief defends his act by saying that he had been robbed.

No. 15 p. 173.

J234§, ‡Choice between kingship (political power) and health (longevity, physical strength).

No. 23 p. 252.

J234.1§, ‡Kingship (power) chosen over health (longevity).

No. 23 p. 252.

J570.1.2§, ‡A speeding horse stumbles.

No. 23 p. 252.

J581, ‡Foolishness of noise-making when enemies overhear.

No. 13 p. 160, cf.,—(dog barking).

J582, ‡Foolishness of premature coming out of hiding.

No. 13 p. 160.

J708.8§, ‡'Planting a kindness (jamîl/'gimîl,' maᵹrûf): harvesting a kindness.

No. 3 p. 39 n. 13, cf.

J760.0.1§, ‡Living person prepares for own burial.

No. 4 p. 68;

No. 7 p. 102 n. 19.

J760.1§, ‡Burial plot (grave) prepared (along with other accompaniments —coffin, shrouds, prayers, etc.).

No. 7 p. 102 n. 19;

No. 20 pp. 230–31.

J1074.3§, Silence saves, talkativeness brings about trouble (is regretted).

No. 13 p. 160, cf.

J1077§, ‡Merits of distant travel.

Intro. p. cxlv.

J1115.6.1§, Clever eloquent peasant.

No. 3 pp. 35–54.

J1142.4, Thief's corpse carried through street to see who will weep.
No. 14 p. 165.

J1320, Repartee concerning drunkenness [and similar states of altered consciousness].
No. 21 pp. 234–35.

J1321, The unrepentant ["unrepentent"] drunkard.
No. 21 pp. 236–37.

J1514.5§, ‡'He who would dig a pit for another will [himself] fall in it.'
No. 17 p. 211.

J1536.3§, ‡Absurdity of accusation of impossible crime (violation) rebuked.
Intro. p. xix,-(cat).

J1847.8.1§, ‡Person blamed for wild beast's (natural) behavior.
Intro. pp. cv–cvi;
No. 19 p. 227.

J1876§, ‡Absurd kindness to animal (bird) before cruel treatment.
No. 5 p. 88.

J1876.1§, ‡Relieving bird's (animal's) thirst before slaughtering it.
No. 5 p. 88.

K. Deceptions

K231.2.2.2§, ‡Payment for sexual service made (by client), but service withheld (deferred).
No. 7 p. 112.

K303.2.3§, ‡Theft from grave (tomb).
No. 14 p. 164.

K303.2.3.1§, ‡Corpse (cadaver) stolen or borrowed.
No. 14 p. 166.

K312, Thieves hidden in oil casks. [Ali-Baba and the forty thieves.]
No. 6 pp. 90–94, cf.

K315, ‡Thief enters treasury through secret passage.
No. 14 p. 164.

K315.1, Thief enters treasury through passage made by him as architect of the building.
Intro. p. cxxvi;
No. 14 p. 164.

K332.1, ‡Theft by giving narcotic to guardian of goods.
No. 13 p. 163,—(wine).

K332.1.1§, ‡Guards of corpse induced to drink much wine: when drunk corpse stolen.
No. 13 p. 163.

K407, ‡Severed limb prevents detection.
No. 14 p. 164.

K407.1, Thief has his companion cut off his head so that he may escape detection.
No. 14 p. 166.

K407.2.1, ‡Thief's confederate cuts off own arm to furnish alibi for family's grief. (Previously he had severed father's or brother's head to escape detection.)
No. 14 p. 166.

K407.2.2§, ‡Companion's head cut off so as to prevent identification.
No. 14 p. 164.

K425, King's daughter put into brothel to catch thief.
Introduction to This Edition p. xxx n. 101;
No. 14 p. 166.

K539.1§, ‡Escapes by use of artificial limb (arm, leg)—pursuer seizes the limb: fugitive escapes leaving it behind.
No. 14 p. 166.

K539.1.1§, ‡Captor given cadaver arm to seize: captive escapes.
No. 14 p. 166

K632, ‡Mice gnaw enemies' bow strings and prevent pursuit.
No. 9 pp. 137–39, cf.,—(if a deliberate war tactic).

K712.0.2.1§, ‡Enemy (rebel) invited to inspect king's baton (staff, scepter) and then struck with it.
No. 6 pp. 90–94.

K741.2§, ‡Capture by tar-pit (or vessel, caldron).
No. 14 p. 164.

K753, Capture by hiding in disguised object.
Introduction to This Edition p. xiv n. 33.

K754.1, Trojan wooden horse. [Smuggling soldiers into city.]
Introduction to This Edition p. xiv, p. xv n. 36;
Intro. p. xcv,—("Ali Baba");
No. 6 pp. 90–94, cf.

K758, ‡Capture by hiding in baskets of food.
No. 6 pp. 90–94.

K776, Capture by intoxication (or narcotics).
No. 13 pp. 158, 163, cf.

K871.3.2§, ‡Person intoxicated (drugged, etc.) and then disfigured (mutilated).
  No. 14 p. 166.
K961, Flesh of certain animal alleged to be only cure for disease: animal to be killed. (The sick lion.)
  No. 1 p. 14, cf.
K1214.1.1, Importunate lover is induced to undergo a series of humiliations.
  No. 7 p. 112.
K1226§, ‡Promise of sexual liaison with beautiful woman induces man to undergo series of spiraling (ascending) humiliations (slapping, shaving of beard and eyebrows, nakedness, etc.).
  No. 7 pp. 113–16.
K1817.1.2§, ‡Disguise as runaway (fugitive).
  No. 13 p. 156.
K1817.3.2§, ‡Disguise as wandering musician (singer, bard, etc.).
  No. 2 p. 29.
K1817.4, ‡Disguise as merchant.
  No. 6 pp. 90–94.
K1872.9.1§, ‡Passage to treasury (tomb) covered with movable stone.
  Intro. p. cxxvi;
  No. 14 p. 164.
K1886.1.3§, ‡Aiming toward illusory island in the sea (marshes).
  Intro. p. clii.
K2040.1.1§, ‡Partisan (patriot, spy, soldier, etc.) leads enemy to believe that he is switching sides: enemy betrayed and defeated.
  No. 6 pp. 90–94.
K2105.1.5.1§, ‡The hippopotami of the Nile: their neighing said to awaken sleeper at great distance. King of land held responsible.
  Introduction to This Edition p. xv n. 36;
  Intro. p. cvi;
  No. 19 p. 227.
K2111, Potiphar's wife [and Joseph].
  Intro. pp. ci–cii.
K2201.1§, ‡Secret betrayed out of spite (or for revenge).
  No. 2 p. 33.
K2213.4, Betrayal of husband's secret by his wife.
  Introduction to This Edition p. xv n. 36.
K2215§, ‡Treacherous father.
  No. 11 p. 149.

K2218.3§, Treacherous stepmother.

>No. 13 p. 157, cf.

K2350, Military strategy.

>No. 6 pp. 90–94.

K2351, Animals help in military victory.

>No. 12 pp. 150–51.

K2357.15, ‡Capture by hiding warriors in baskets on back of oxen driven into enemy's camp on pretense that food is being brought.

>No. 6 pp. 90–94, cf.

K2357.16§, ‡Strategy to get into enemy city: fighters smuggled past defenses (gate).

>No. 6 pp. 90–94.

K2378, Temporary advantage by pretending to yield in combat.

>No. 4 p. 67.

K2378.4, ‡Ammunition saved till enemy has used his.

>No. 4 p. 67.

K2400§, ‡Deception for deception (tit for tat): deceived person gets even in a like manner (same ruse, strategy, trick, etc.).

>No. 15 p. 173.

L. Reversal of Fortune

L167§, ‡Robber (thief) becomes policeman (lawman).

>No. 14 pp. 163–67, cf.

L311, Weak (small) hero overcomes large fighter.

>No. 4 p. 67.

L407§, ‡Invincible adversary (warrior, ogre, etc.) killed with his own weapon.

>No. 4 p. 67.

L413, Proud inscriptions sole remains [(relic)] of powerful king. [="Ozymandias"].

>No. 12 p. 151, cf.

L490.1.2§, ‡Fugitive (prisoner) made nobleman (king's courtier, advisor, or the like).

>No. 4 p. 67.

M. Ordaining the Future

M117.0.1§, *nadhr/'nadr'*: conditional vow: pledge to perform certain (good) act if prayer is answered (request is granted).

>No. 8 pp. 127 cf.

M117.1.2§, ‡"If the gods were to protect me, I would do ..."
No. 8 p. 128.

M119.0.1§, Swearing by God.
No. 1 p. 14;
No. 16 pp. 193, 200 n. 36.

M177, Vow to change religion [(to convert)].
No. 19 p. 226,—(adopt another god).

M223, ‡Blind promise (rash boon). Person grants wish before hearing it.
No. 1 p. 14.

M302.0.3§, 'istikhârah: prophesying by asking God to indicate right choice (through: dream, opening Holy Book, rosary).
No. 9 p. 138, cf.;
No. 10 p. 143;
No. 22 p. 240, cf.,—(by prayer and sacrifice).

M302.4.3§, ‡Sign of the Zodiac indicates (determines) future.
No. 13 p. 157 n. 13.

M311, Prophecy: future greatness of unborn child.
No. 8 p. 121.

M311.4, ‡Prophecy: unborn child to become king.
No. 2 p. 28.

M314, ‡Prophecy: Man (child) will become king.
No. 2 p. 28, cf.

M340, Unfavorable prophecies.
Introduction to This Edition p. xv n. 36;
No. 13 p. 154.

M341, Death prophesied.
No. 13 p. 154.

M341.0.7§, ‡Prophecy: death by one of a limited number of means (agents).
No. 13 p. 154

M341.0.7.1§, ‡Prophecy: child to die by snake, crocodile, or dog. It so happens.
No. 13 p. 154.

M341.2.4, ‡Prophecy: three-fold death. Child to die from hunger, fire, and water. It so happens.
No. 13 p. 154.

M341.2.6.1§, ‡Prophecy: death by dog.
No. 13 p. 154.

M341.2.21, ‡Prophecy: death by snake bite.
    No. 13 p. 154, cf.
M341.2.24, ‡Prophecy: death by alligator (crocodile).
    No. 13 p. 154.
M342, ‡Prophecy: downfall of kingdom.
    No. 2 p. 28.
M356.1.6§, ‡Prophecy: country (island) will vanish.
    No. 5 p. 87 n. 21.
M361.3§, ‡Prophecy: yet unborn hero will achieve task (exploit).
    No. 2 pp. 27–28.
M370.1, Prophecy of death fulfilled.
    No. 1 p. 16;
    No. 13 p. 161.
M372, Confinement in tower to avoid fulfillment of prophecy.
    Introduction to This Edition p. xv n. 36;
    No. 13 pp. 154–55.
M405§, ‡Curse of total ruin for violator(s) of object or site ('curse of the Pharaohs').
    No. 7 p. 111.
M411.25§, ‡Curse by scribe (author, writer).
    No. 1 p. 16 n. 53.

N. Chance and Fate

N1.8§, ‡Betting between man and supernatural being (jinni, devil, ogre,etc.).
    No. 18 pp. 221–22.
N2.0.4§, ‡Own beliefs (faith, religion) as wager.
    No. 19 p. 226.
N2.0.5§, ‡Wagers with uneven stakes (e.g., "If I win you pay me one, if you win I pay you two").
    No. 18 p. 222.
N2.1.1§, ‡Woman's body as stake: winner to do with it as he pleases.
    No. 18 p. 222.
N3.0.1§, Gambling with a goddess.
    No. 14 p. 163.
N3.6§, ‡Gambling (wager) with the dead (corpse, mummy, ghost, soul, etc.).
    No. 7 p. 109.

N110, Luck and fate personified.
>   No. 2 p. 31.

N112.4.1§, ‡Agent of man's doom speaks to him (declares self).
>   No. 13 p. 158, (crocodile).

N120.1.1§, ‡Entity (animal, human, object, time-period, etc.) associated with certain events becomes harbinger of omen.
>   Intro. p. cxxxiv.

N127, The auspicious (lucky) day (days).
>   Intro. p. cxxxvii.

N128, Unlucky days ("cross-days").
>   Intro. p. cxxxvii.

N128.0.2§, ‡Time (hour, day, year) when tragic event occurred is inauspicious.
>   Intro. pp. cxxxiv–cxxxviii.

N128.6§, ‡Evil occurrence (event) marks unlucky (inauspicious) time.
>   Intro. pp. cxxxiv.

N190.0.1.4§, ‡Deities prevent mortals from finding food (wealth) by placing obstacles in their way.
>   No. 8 p. 124.

N301.2.1§, ‡Shipwreck. Ship (ferry-boat) sinks: many drown.
>   No. 5 p. 84.

N335.5.1§, ‡Hound (dog) defending master against attacker (crocodile) inflicts mortal wound on master.
>   No. 13 p. 163.

N335.6.1, ‡Attacking animal is killed by another in ambush.
>   No. 13 p. 159, cf.

N337, Accidental death through misdirected weapon.
>   No. 13 p. 160.

N430.2§, Efficacious exorciser requested abroad.
>   No. 10 p. 144.

N456, Enigmatical smile (laugh) reveals secret knowledge.
>   No. 7 p. 97.

N485.1§, ‡Natural phenomenon destroys army's weapons (equipment).
>   No. 9 p. 139.

N485.1.1§, ‡Field mice destroy army's equipment.
>   No. 9 p. 139.

N512, ‡Treasure in underground chamber (cavern).
>   No. 14 p. 164.

N520§, ‡Treasure (riches) hidden in tomb (grave, cemetery).
No. 14 p. 164.

N582, Serpent guards treasure.
No. 7 pp. 103 n. 23, 105 n. 32.

N582.1§, ‡Viper guards treasure.
No. 7 p. 105.

N659.6§, ‡Criminal's plan accidentally foiled.
No. 1 pp. 4–5.

N659.6.1§, ‡Would-be murderer's plan accidentally foiled (interrupted).
No. 1 pp. 4–5.

N812, Giant or ogre as helper.
No. 13 p. 157, cf.

N815.0.2, Helpful water-spirit.
No. 13 p. 157, cf.

N840§, ‡Nomad (Bedouin) as helper.
Intro. p. cxlvii;
No. 4 p. 64.

N841.1§, ‡Shepherd as helper.
No. 16 p. cxxiii.

N848.1, ‡Hero ransoms maltreated picture of a saint. As reward he gets help from the grateful saint.
No. 20 p. 230, cf.

N859§, Fisher as helper.
No. 16 p. cxxiii.

N769.1§, ‡Person(s) given up for dead found alive.
No. 5 pp. 87–88 n. 22;
No. 7 p. 115 n. 67.

P. Society

P5.3.5§, ‡Having servants (slaves) as 'status symbol'.
No. 4 p. 68.

P5.4.1§, ‡Formal (state) badge as indicator of social status. (E.g., medal, ribbon, baton, or the like).
No. 4 p. 77 n. 80.

P5.5.1§, ‡Emblems (tools) of the trade as status symbol.
No. 16 p. 183 (cuirass).

P12.2.1.1§, 'Pharaoh' as tyrant.
No. 1 p. 11, n. 33, cf.

P12.6.0.1§, ‡Just king (ruler).
No. 3 pp. 35–54.
P12.15.3§, ‡Present to king must be commensurate with his high rank.
No. 15 p. 179 n. 24.
P12.16§, ‡Negligent king.
No. 21 pp. 234–35.
P13.9.3.1§, ‡King's scepter (baton).
No. 4 p. 76 n. 77–78.
P14.15.2.1.1§, ‡Mistreatment of a state's envoy is an offense against that state.
No. 15 pp. 175 n. 10, 180.
P14.15.3.1§, ‡Court singer (musician).
No. 15 p. 180.
P17.4.2§, ‡Brother succeeds his brother to the throne.
No. 1 p. 16.
P14.25.0.1§, ‡Audience with king.
No. 2 p. 27;
No. 4 pp. 72 n. 53, 75 n. 74, 76 n. 77;
No. 8 pp. 125, 134–35;
No. 16 p. 184;
No. 17 p. 205;
No. 22 p. 241.
P14.25.0.2§, ‡Accompaniments of being before the sovereign.
No. 4 p. 72 n. 53;
No. 17 p. 215 n. 77.
P14.25.1§, ‡Ranks (classes) of courtiers.
No. 4 pp. 61 n. 1, 77;
No. 7 p. 108 n. 39;
No. 8 p. 125.
P14.25.2.0.1§, ‡Master of ceremonies (maintainer of protocol, "chief lector").
No. 2 pp. 19 n. 2, 20 n. 5.
P14.25.2.1§, ‡Courtier must seek king's permission to travel.
No. 4 p. 74.
P17.15§, Conflict over kingship.
No. 16 p. cxxiii.
P18.3§, ‡King (prince) marries foreign princess.
No. 13 p. 155 n. 4.
P29.0.1§, ‡Titles given queens (royal consorts).
No. 1 p. 15;
No. 10 p. 144 n. 7.

P30, Princes.
    No. 21 p. 235 n. 4.

P50.0.1, ‡King and vassals: obligations of vassals to king.
    No. 2 p. 19, cf.

P91§, ‡Formal title (medal) bestowed by ruler (state).
    No. 1 p. 12.

P97§, ‡Royal children paraded before the king.
    No. 4 p. 76.

P112§, Trusted vizier (royal minister).
    No. 2 p. 19.
    No. 19 p. 226, cf.

P112.0.1§, ‡Council of royal ministers (cabinet)—advises sovereign.
    No. 19 p. 226.

P116, ‡Minister acts as stepping-stone in midst of flame-filled trench so that king can step across from one side to the other.
    No. 11 p. 149, cf.

P140.0.3§, Favor (pardon) won through intercession of person of influence.
    No. 4 p. 70.

P141.1§, Corrupt mayor.
    No. 3 pp. 35–54.

P150.0.1§, Feudal landlord.
    Intro. p. cxxv;
    No. 3 p. 51 n. 61.

P169.1.1§, ‡Poor peasant.
    No. 3 pp. 35–54.

P191.1.5.1§, ‡Stranger pities self—(usually in poem or song).
    No. 4 p. 68.

P196.1.2§, ‡Drunkard loses control over his social conduct.
    No. 21 pp. 235–37.

P196.1.2.5§, ‡Drunkard fails at work (cannot fulfill terms of contracts).
    No. 22 pp. 240–42.

P196.2§, ‡Lazy (dull, impotent) drunkard.
    No. 21 pp. 236–37.

P208.2§, ‡Matrilineal descent: child identified by mother's line.
    No. 1 p. 3 n. 1.

P208.3§, Bilineal descent (double descent): child identified by both father's and mother's lines.
    No. 20 p. 232.

P208.7.0.1§, ‡Child's name received from supernatural source—by means of prophetic dream (or the like).
No. 8 p. 121.

P208.7.7§, ‡Child remains unnamed till reaching certain age (stage of life).
No. 1 p. 16 n. 50.

P230.0.1.1§, Misery of childlessness (person weeps).
No. 8 p. 120;
No. 13 p. 154.

P230.0.2.2.1§, ‡Importance of having a son(s)—(male children).
No. 13 pp. 154–55.

P233.0.1§, ‡Father-love for son.
No. 8 p. 121.

P234.0.3§, ‡Only daughter(s), no son(s).
No. 13 p. 155.

P249.2.1§, ‡Loving parent should be affectionate toward family members (his child and his wife).
No. 5 p. 86.

P250.0.3§, ‡Full siblings: "from same loins (father)" and "from same womb (mother)."
No. 1 p. 3.

P251.5, Two brothers.
No. 1 p. 3;
No. 14 pp. 163–67.

P282, Stepmother.
No. 13 p. 157.

P282.0.2§, ‡Stepmother unjustly blamed (accused).
No. 13 p. 157.

P282.3, Stepmother in love with stepson.
Intro. p. cii.

P317.1, ‡Refusal to believe that a friend will harm one. Alexander drinks cup said to have been poisoned by his friend.
No. 23 p. 253, cf.

P318.2§, ‡Foreign land (country) as place of refuge.
No. 4 p. 63;
No. 17 p. 202.

P322.0.2§, ‡Refugee (guest) protected by host as long as he is within host's domain (country).
No. 15 p. 180.

P324.0.2§, ‡Providing welcome (conversation, entertainment, 'greetings')
is host's responsibility.
No. 15 p. 180, (singer).

P401, Son insists on following father's trade.
No. 14 pp. 163–67.

P401.1§, ‡Thief's son takes up thievery as occupation (trade).
No. 14 p. 164.

P411, Peasant.
No. 3 pp. 35–54.

P411.0.1§, ‡Peasant's work (farming) is arduous and unprofitable.
No. 3 p. 35–54.

P424.7§, Midwife (dâyah, qâbilah).
No. 2 p. 30 n. 42.

P425, Scribe.
No. 8 p. 119.

P425.0.1§, ‡Scribe as hero (sage).
No. 2 p. 25 n. 21;
No. 8 p. 119.

P427.7.5.1§, munshid (chanter of spirituals, religious balladeer).
No. 7 p. 107 n. 37, cf.

P427.7.5.2§, maddâḥah ('praiser', female religious balladeer, bard).
No. 2 p. 32 n. 53;
No. 16 pp. 196–97 (seen in dream).

P431.5.2.1§, ‡Traveling merchant's wife becomes unfaithful.
No. 21 p. 235.

P448, Butcher.
No. 1 p. 14.

P449§, Seaman (sailor, mariner).
No. 5 p. 83;
No. 21 p. 234.

P449.0.1§, Sindbad the sailor (seaman, mariner).
No. 13 pp. 160–61, passim.

P455, Mason (bricklayer [builder]).
No. 14 p. 163.

P455.1.1§, ‡Skillful architect.
No. 22 p. 242 n. 10.

P461.0.2§,‡Un-soldierly behavior—(deeds unbecoming a soldier).
No. 17 p. 211 n. 64.

P470.0.1§, ‡Tale-teller needed (required)—so as to tell story.
No. 2 p. 19;
No. 21 pp. 234–35.
P475.0.1§, Grave robber ('nabbâsh').
No. 14 pp. 163–67.
P482.0.1§, ‡Sculptor (artist).
No. 22 pp. 241–42.
P486.1§, ‡Embalmer.
Intro. pp. cxl–cxliii.
P500.0.3.1§, ‡Ruler as shepherd. Ruler's responsibilities towards subjects (citizens).
No. 3 p. 46 n. 37, cf.
P503§, Bureaucracy and bureaucrats.
No. 3 pp. 35–54.
P503.0.1§, ‡Formal documents required for bureaucratic (formal) procedures.
No. 15 p. 175.
P503.1.2§, ‡Bureaucracy: endless prerequisites (requirements) before task may be tended (considered).
No. 3 p. 37.
P503.2.1§, Proving one's identity.
No. 15 p. 175.
P503.4§, Corrupt bureaucrats (officials, officers, etc.).
No. 3 pp. 35–54.
P505§, Rule by disbelievers (infidels, sinners).
No. 19 p. 224 n. 11.
P506.3§, Rebellion against government.
Intro. pp. cxii–cxiii;
No. 16 p. cxxiii.
P506.3.0.1§, ‡Civil war.
No. 4 p. 62.
P507§, Divine (ecclesiastical) government (ecclesia). A theocracy.
No. 9 pp. 137–38.
P522.0.1.3§, ‡Legal persecution of the weak (powerless): politically (legally) sanctioned injustice.
No. 3 pp. 35–54.
P522.2§, Vendetta: a life for a life, of equal (or higher) social rank.
Intro. p. cxv.

P525.8§, ‡Mercy killing.
        No. 14 pp. 164–65, cf.
P527.1§, Legal will deprives heir of birthright (inheritance).
        No. 7 p. 114, cf.
P528.2§, ‡Mercy killing by relative (e.g., husband, wife, father, brother,
        etc.).
        No. 14 pp. 164-65, cf.
P528.7§, ‡Killing (suicide) to avoid capture (enslavement).
        No. 14 pp. 164-65 cf.
P529.9.2§, ‡Legal rights of a concubine (consort, common-law wife).
        No. 7 p. 113 n. 60.
P531.1.1, Tribute required of conquered foreigners.
        Intro. pp. cxii–cxiii;
        No. 19 pp. 224–25.
P532.1§, Heavy taxes.
        No. 3 pp. 35–54.
P550.1§, ‡War.
        No. 6 pp. 90–94
P550.1.0.5§, ‡Preparations (readiness) for war.
        No. 16 p. 184.
P550.1.0.5.3.1§, ‡Troops refuse to fight.
        No. 9 pp. 138–39.
P550.1.1§, ‡Declaration of war.
        No. 17 p. 210.
P550.1.1.2§, ‡Call to arms ('istinfâr).
        No. 9 pp. 138–39;
        No. 17 p. 210.
P550.1.1.4§, ‡War declared (waged) in order to retrieve usurped national
        property (land, treasure, etc.).
        No. 16;
        No. 17 p. 201–16.
P551.0.1.1§, ‡Band of herdsmen (tribesmen) warriors.
        Intro. p. cxxiii;
        No. 17 p. 202.
P551.0.3§, Army of volunteers.
        No. 9 pp. 138–39.
P551.10§, ‡Army leader (general).
        No. 6 pp. 90–94;
        No. 17 p. 208.

P551.10.0.1§, ‡Characteristics of military leader (army general).
No. 6 pp. 90–94.

P551.2.1§, ‡Mercenary army (band of warriors).
No. 17 p. 211 n. 64.

P552, Battle formations.
No. 12 pp. 150–51;
No. 16 p. 190;
No. 17 p. 207.

P552.4, War-machines.
No. 12 pp. 150–51.

P553.5.2§, ‡Feline (lion, leopard, etc.) used as weapon.
No. 12 pp. 150–51.

P553.5.3§, ‡Canine (dog) used as weapon.
No. 16 p. 199 n. 35.

P554, ‡Formal title (e.g., Lord, Chevalier, Pasha, Bey, Prince, etc.) as indicator of social status.
No. 21 p. 235 n. 4.

P555.2.1.1, "Publication of slaying." Heads of slain enemies displayed.
No. 12 p. 151;
No. 14 p. 166 n. 5.

P556.7§, ‡Challenge to duel: weapon ready (open, drawn, unfolded, etc.).
No. 4 p. 67.

P557.4.5.1§, ‡Duelers salute king before putting on armor for duel.
No. 17 p. 205.

P557.8§, ‡Truce: respite from combat (duel).
No. 16 pp. 194 n. 27, 198.

P559.1.2§, ‡Slain (defeated) warrior's possessions.
No. 4 p. 67.

P559.2.2§, ‡Merchants (traders) follow army (into conquered lands).
Intro. p. cxlv.

P570§, ‡Fortifications of cities.
No. 6 pp. 90–94.

P570.1§, ‡Wall around city.
No. 6 pp. 90–94.

P571§, ‡Siege: city (castle, troops, etc.) surrounded by enemy troops.
No. 6 pp. 90–94.

P604§, ‡"Layout of a residence (floor-plan of house, palace, hut, etc.)."
Introduction to This Edition p. xix n. 46;
No. 13 p. 154 n. 3.

P604.1§, ‡House-top (flat roof) as terrace or living quarters.
Introduction to This Edition p. xix n. 46;
No. 13 p. 154, n. 3.

P604.9.1§, ‡Annexes (accessories) to a household (e.g., servants' quarters,
guest-house, tunnels, fields, garden, etc.).
No. 2 p. 20 (kiosk, garden);
No. 4 pp. 77–78 n. 84.

P605.9.2.1§, ‡"Upper floor" for intimate living.
Introduction to This Edition p. xix n. 46;
No. 2 p. 32 n. 55.

P634.0.8.1§, ‡Customs connected with drinking vessels (i.e., glass, cup,
mug, water skin, etc.).
No. 14 p. 165 n. 4.

P672.1§, ‡Shaving a man's beard as an insult.
No. 14 pp. 163–67.

P678.1, Tearing garment as sign of grief.
No. 13 p. 159.

P681.1.1.2.1.2§, ‡Mourning: dancing ('nadb'-[dance]).
No. 4 p. 71 n. 48.

P681.1.1.2.3.1§, ‡Mourning: putting dust (dirt) on own head.
No. 1 p. 9 n. 23.

P682.7.1§, ‡Greeting by placing tip of one's nose against another's.
No. 5 p. 86;
No. 17 p. 215 n. 78.

P682.7.2§, ‡Greeting by a kiss (use of lips).
No. 17 p. 215 n. 78.

P710.0.1.1§, ‡Contest between nations (kings) to prove which nation is
superior.
No. 8 pp. 119–20, 125.

P711.3, Common citizen saves the honor of his country.
No. 8 pp. 125–37 (child).

P711.8, ‡Aversion to burial in foreign soil.
No. 4 p. 68 n. 35.

P712§, ‡Homesickness: yearning for homeland.
No. 4 p. 68.

P712.0.2§, ‡Kissing earth (ground) of homeland to show love (reverence,
gratitude, etc.).
No. 4 p. 75.

P713.1§, ‡Secession: one segment of nation (tribe) breaks away from rest.
No. 8 p. 127.

P717.1.1§, ‡Bearded nations.
Introduction to This Edition p. xx n. 52;
Intro. p. cxxvii;
No. 14 p. 166;
No. 19 p. 227, cf.

P717.1.2.1§, ‡Egyptians (ancient) as shaven people.
Intro. p. cxxvii;
No. 14 p. 166 n. 5;
No. 19 p. 227, cf.

P717.2.1.1§, ‡Egyptians (ancient) as people who attended call of nature at home.
No. 8 p. 120, n. 80, passim.

P723.1§, Characteristic behavior of peasants (farmers, countrymen).
No. 3 pp. 35–54.

P731§, Characteristic behavior of Bedouins.
Intro. p. cxlvii.

P731.0.1§, Bedouin behavior ('Arab'-ways) as 'The ideal.'
No. 16 p. cxxiii.

P731.3.1§, ‡Nomad mocks (despises) sedentary (urban, rural) lifestyle (people).
No. 4 pp. 66–67.

P731.3.2§, ‡Sedentary person mocks (despises) nomad's lifestyle (people).
No. 4 pp. 76–78.

P738.1.1§, ‡Parlance of foreigners ('ruṭân') not understood.
No. 15 p. 171.

P741.1§, 'He who has no senior (elder, leader) should buy himself one.'
Introduction to This Edition p. xxi n. 56.

P741.1.1§, ‡Being masterless.
Intro. p. cxxv.

P741.1.1.1§, ‡"He who has no 'back' will be struck on the 'belly' [where more damage can be done]"—(i.e., In the absence of a protector, one will be abused frequently and severely).
Intro. p. cxxv, cf.

P743§, Fealty (walâ'), and partisanship.
Introduction to This Edition p. xxi n. 56.

P743.2§, ‡Publication of homage to ruler—(usually in the form of public praise).
    No. 4 pp. 62-63.
P760.0.1§, ‡Property in the hands of only a few. (Feudalism.)
    Intro. p. cxxv.
P760.5.3.4§, ‡Copyrights: author's ownership.
    No. 1 p. 16.
P760.5.3.4.1§, ‡Theft of contents of written book punished—(intellectual piracy).
    No. 1 p. 16.
P761§, ‡Inheritance.
    Intro. p. cxxiv.
P761.0.1§, ‡All children inherit equal shares.
    Intro. p. cxxiv.
P761.0.1.1§, ‡Illegitimate children (children of concubine, slave-woman, etc.) have right to inheritance.
    Intro. p. cxxiv.
P762§, Owner (landlord) and tenant.
    No. 3 p. 51 n. 61.
P762.1§, Hardhearted (greedy) landlord.
    No. 3 p. 51 n. 61.
P715.9.1§, ‡The uncivilized (barbarian, cannibals, savages, etc.).
    Intro. p. cxxvii;
    No. 4 pp. 64–65, 75;
    No. 10 p. 143.
P770§, ‡Markets: buying, selling, trading.
    No. 3 p. 38.
P770.0.3§, ‡Marketplace (location for buying and selling).
    No. 3 p. 38.
P771§, ‡Barter: payment in kind (exchange of goods or services).
    No. 15 p. 171.
P771.1§, ‡Goods exchanged.
    No. 15 p. 171.
P771.3.1§, ‡Food for a service (e.g., ear of corn for a shave, an egg for knife sharpening, and the like).
    No. 2 p. 19 (story/tale).
P775.2.1§, ‡Grants (gratuities, tips), and acts of generosity (philanthropy).
    No. 4 p. 68.

P779.1§, ‡Imported finery (expertness, craftsmanship, or goods of higher quality from abroad).
No. 15 p. 180 (singer).

P779.1.5§, ‡Imported raw materials (wood, metal, etc.).
No. 15 p. 171.

P790.1.2.1§, ‡Trellis (ululation) of joy (ˈzaghrûṭahʾ/zaghrûdah). (Typically voiced by women at a joyous occasion such as a wedding, pilgrimage, winning at lawcourt, release from prison, etc.)
Introduction to This Edition p. xxi n. 59;
No. 2 p. 32 n. 56.

P806.7.1§, ‡Hunting with help of animals or birds (dogs, leopards, falcons, etc.).
No. 13 p. 158 (hound).

P807.1.2§, ‡Listening to stories (tales) as hobby (for relaxation).
Intro. p. cxix;
No. 2 p. 19.

P807.3.2§, ‡Boating (sailing, rowing) as recreation.
No. 2 p. 23.

P807.3.3§, ‡Watching rhythmic body movements (sport-dancing) as recreation.
No. 2 p. 23.

P807.4§, ‡Watching dancing as pastime.
No. 2 p. 23.

P986§, ‡Commemoration of victory in war (battle).
No. 12 pp. 150-51.

Q. Rewards and Punishments

Q69§, ‡Eloquence rewarded.
No. 3 pp. 35-54.

Q73§, ‡Bravery (valor, courage) rewarded.
No. 4 p. 66;
No. 6 p. 90 n. 3.

Q83.1, ‡Reward for wife's fidelity.
No. 13 p. 160.

Q91.1, Princess given in marriage to clever thief.
No. 14 p. 167, cf.

Q111.8, ‡Large quantity of land as reward—[(ˈiqṭâ̧ˈ)].
No. 4 p. 66.

Q136.1.1§, ‡Secular title as reward (e.g., "Pasha," "Bey," "Lord," "Knight," "Lady," etc.).

No. 1 p. 12.

Q151.9, ‡Resurrection as reward.

No. 13 p. 160.

Q151.9.1§, ‡Resuscitation as reward for fidelity (faithfulness).

No. 13 p. 160.

Q156, ‡Victory as reward for piety.

No. 9 p. 138.

Q220.2.1§, ‡Depriving of funeral (burial) rites as punishment for impiety.

No. 2 p. 25 n. 21.

Q225.5§, ‡Practice of nether magic (sorcery, witchcraft) punished as *kufr* (disbelief).

Intro. p. cxxix, cf.

Q222.7§, ‡Punishment for violating sanctity of tomb (grave, cemetery).

No. 7 p. 117, n. 74.

Q407§, ‡Annihilation for eternity as punishment.

No. 2 p. 22 n. 11.

Q407.1§, ‡Depriving of resurrection (afterlife, life after death) as punishment.

No. 2 p. 22 n. 11.

Q407.1.1§, ‡Body destroyed so that soul cannot return to it: resurrection impossible.

No. 2 p. 2 n. 11.

Q414, Punishment: burning alive.

No. 2 p. 2 n. 11.

Q414.0.2, ‡Burning as punishment for adultery.

No. 2 pp. 21–22.

Q414.0.2.1§, ‡Burning alive as punishment for unchastity.

Intro. p. cxxx.

Q414.3, ‡Punishment: burning and scattering ashes.

No. 2 pp. 21–22.

Q415.10.1§, ‡Crocodile devours the wicked.

No. 2 p. 33 n. 59.

Q436.0.1§, ‡Spiritual punishments.

No. 2 p. 25 n. 21.

Q451.7.0.2.7§, ‡Miraculous blindness as punishment for impiety.

Intro. p. cxxxix.

Q491.6.2§, ‡Corpse of slain person thrown to carnivorous animals (dogs, wolves, etc.).
No. 1 p. 9 n. 24,
No. 7 p. 114 n. 63.

R. Captives and Refugees

R152, ‡Wife rescues husband.
No. 13 pp. 157–58.
R215.5.2.1§, ‡Escape from fire by using another person as stepping-stone.
No. 11 p. 149 (steps on sons).
R217§, ‡Escape by sea: (captive, fugitive) escapes by sea.
No. 5 p. 88.
R226§, Flight from home so as to escape wrath of patriarch (father, husband, master).
No. 4 p. 62 n. 5, cf.
R270.2§, ‡Hider's own animal (dog, horse, etc.) betrays his presence.
No. 13 p. 160.
R270.2.1§, ‡Dog's barking betrays presence of hiders and brings about their destruction by enemy.
No. 13 p. 160.
R346§, ‡Refuge in the wilderness (swamps, marshlands, prairies, etc.).
No. 17 pp. 201–2.
R347.3§, Runaway becomes successful.
No. 4 p. 67.

S. Unnatural Cruelty

S11.3.10§, ‡Cruel father escapes from harm by exposing (sacrificing) own children.
No. 11 p. 149.
S73.1, Fratricide.
No. 1 pp. 6–7, cf.;
No. 14 pp. 164–65.
S73.1.4, Fratricide motivated by love-jealousy.
No. 1 pp. 6–7, cf.
S110.9.1§, ‡Attempted murder: unsuccessful attempt to murder person (intended victim escapes).
No. 1 pp. 6–7.

S401, Unsuccessful attempts to kill person in successive reincarnations (transformations).

Introduction to This Edition p. xv n. 34.

T. Sex

T5.1.3.2§, ‡Girl (woman) attracted to man because of his physical strength.

No. 1 p. 5.

T9.1§, The power of sex: female's influence.

Introduction to This Edition p. xvii n. 42;

No. 1 p. 14;

No. 7 pp. 111–17.

T9.1.3.1§, ‡Father agrees to kill (expose, cast out) own child(ren) in return for sexual intercourse (love).

No. 7 p. 114.

T11.4.1, Love through sight of hair of unknown princess.

Introduction to This Edition p. xv n. 36.

T11.4.8§, ‡Love through smelling object emitting aromatic scent (fragrance, perfume).

No. 1 p. 11.

T35.5, ‡Lover goes to see his beloved in her husband's (or her father's) house, defiant of the danger.

No. 2 p. 20.

T35.9.2§, ‡Lovers meet in garden (park, woods, etc.).

No. 2 p. 20.

T55, Girl as wooer. Forthputting woman.

No. 2 p. 20.

T55.6.4§, ‡Fashion display (fashion show): body exhibited in various complimentary dresses (costumes).

No. 2 p. 23;

No. 7 p. 114 n. 62 cf. (artist's).

T59.1.0.1§, ‡Lovers' kiss.

No. 5 p. 86, cf.

T131.11§, Lower social class as obstacle to marriage.

No. 4 p. 76

No. 13 p. 156.

T135.0.1§, ‡Marriage contract written (and signed).

No. 7 p. 113.

T145.0.1, Polygyny.
> No. 1 p. 3 n. 1.

T148.1.2§, ‡"Set son of Nut."
> No. 10 p. 144 n. 1.

T188§, Practices believed to insure birth of sons (male offspring).
> No. 8 p. 120.

T211.1.6§, ‡Wife shields her husband from attackers with her own body.
> No. 13 p. 160.

T230.3§, ‡Love relations between man and his friend's wife.
> No. 21 p. 235.

T277.2§, ‡Wife steals from her husband.
> No. 8 p. 124, cf.

T306§, Wife's nakedness or exposure.
> Intro. p. cxxix, cf.

T332, Man tempted by fiend [(devil)] in woman's shape. (Or woman by fiend in man's shape.)
> No. 7 pp. 114–115 n. 64, cf.

T370§, Satanic (diabolic) beauty: an utterly wicked (evil) person with extraordinary good looks.
> Introduction to This Edition p. xvii.

T370.0.1§, Diabolic beautiful woman.
> Intro. p. c n. 31;
> No. 7 pp. 113–14.

T380.0.1§, Harem: place of female seclusion.
> No. 1 p. 13.

T380.3.2§, ‡Trusted males allowed in women's quarters: e.g., cleric, instructor, teacher, healer-shaman (and the like).
> No. 4 p. 69

T405§, Casual (accidental) illicit exposure of body of one relative to another.
> Intro. p. cxxix.

T405.3§, Sister's nakedness or exposure.
> Intro. p. cxxix.

T409.3.1§, ‡Stepmother's incestuous desire for stepson masked as maternal affection (love).
> Intro. p. cii.

T415.5, Brother-sister marriage.
> No. 7 p. 100 n. 12.

T415.5.1§, ‡Parents approve (arrange) marriage between their son and daughter (brother-sister).

No. 7 p. 100.

T455.6, Woman sells [(sexual)] favors for large sums of money (property).

Introduction to This Edition p. xvii n. 42;

No. 7 p. 112.

T455.9§, ‡Maiden (woman) gives sexual favor for story (personal adventure, confession).

Introduction to This Edition p. xxx n. 101;

No. 14 p. 166, cf.

T479§, ‡Eunuch's sexual activities.

No. 1 p. 9 n. 27.

T510.1§, ‡Procreation without male element (semen).

No. 1 p. 9 n. 27.

T511.1.3.4§, ‡Conception from eating colocasia ('taro').

No. 8 p. 120.

T511.8.7§, ‡Woman impregnated after accidental swallowing of wood splinters.

No. 1 p. 15.

T548.1, Child born in answer to prayer. [('ṭulbah')].

No. 8 p. 121;

No. 13 p. 154.

T583.0.1§, ‡Parturition posture—(position assumed by woman in labor so as to facilitate childbirth).

Intro. p. cxxv–cxxvi;

No. 2 p. 30 n. 42.

T583.0.1.1§, ‡Birth stool posture—(crouching position for childbirth).

No. 2 p. 30 n. 42.

T584.0.4, Childbirth assisted by angel.

No. 2 pp. 29–30, cf.

T584.0.4.1§, ‡Childbirth assisted by deity (god, goddess).

No. 2 p. 30 n. 42.

T596.0.1§, ‡Name makes child complete.

No. 1 p. 16 n. 50.

T603.0.1§, ‡Pampered (spoiled) only-child ("el-ḥîlah").

No. 13 p. 155.

T603.2§, ‡Pampered daughter(s).

No. 13 p. 155.

T617, Boy reared in ignorance of the world.
>No. 13 p. 154.

U. The Nature of Life

U10.5.1§, ‡Victim of theft becomes a thief.
>No. 15 p. 173.

U86.1§, ‡In its homeland a valuable herb (incense) is only a weed—(because of plenitude).
>No. 5 pp. 86–87.

U86.1.1§, ‡Visitor to the 'island of incense' promises a native gifts of fragrant herbs and perfume: only the manufactured item (perfume) is of value to the native.
>No. 5 pp. 86–87.

U304.5§, ‡Perceiving morality-immorality, propriety-impropriety.
>Intro. p. cxxix.

V. Religion [and Religious Services]

V1.1.3.1§, ‡Spiritually advantageous death.
>No. 6 p. 107 n. 37 (euphemism: drowning/praise Râ).

V1.7.1.6§, ‡Sacred sycamore-tree.
>No. 4 p. 59.

V1.7.1.7§, ‡Sacred persea-tree.
>No. 1 p. 15.

V1.7.1.8§, ‡Sacred acacia-tree (cedar-tree).
>No. 1 p. 12, cf.

V1.12§, ‡Cat worship.
>Intro. p. cii.

V4.5.12.1§, ‡Pious (saintly) offspring as intercessor.
>No. 8 p. 124 n. 90.

V5.4§, ‡Negligence in building (maintaining) houses of worship (temple).
>No. 22 pp. 240–42.

V17.5.2§, ‡Sacrifice to learn deity's choice.
>No. 22 p. 240 (by prayer and sacrifice).

V61.0.1.1§, ‡Burial in pyramid (for person of distinction).
>No. 4 p. 78.

V61.0.3.0.1§, ‡Accessories of a family's burial yard (tomb garden, attendant's living quarters, etc.).
>No. 4 p. 78 n. 90.

V61.0.4.2§, ‡Person of distinction buried within series of coffins.
No. 7 p. 102 n. 19.

V65.0.5§, ‡Commemoration of martyrdom.
Intro. p. cxxxiv (Osiris's).

V65.9.1.1§, ‡Sacred-drama: commemoration of death of holy personage by re-enactment of tragic scene—"Passion Play."
Intro. p. cxxxiv (passim).

V67.3.2§, ‡Precious book (scroll) buried with dead cleric (monk, scribe, author, etc.).
Intro. p. xciv.

V67.9§, ‡Accompaniments of burial—miscellaneous.
No. 4 p. 79 n. 92.

V67.9.1§, ‡Property of the dead: certain objects buried with the corpse.
No. 4 p. 79 n. 92;
No. 7 p. 102 (book).

V68, Preparations for burial.
No. 4 p. 68;
No. 7 p. 102 n. 19.
No. 20 p. 231.

V68.0.1§, ‡Dead embalmed (mummified).
No. 4 pp. 70–71 n. 47.

V93.1§, Ecstasy (trance) through religious dancing (*dhikr, zikr'*).
No. 15 p. 174 n. 9, cf.

V140.0.1.2§, ‡Weapon (sword, shield, cuirass, etc.) as sacred relic.
No. 16 p. 184 n. 4.

V140.0.1.4§, ‡Temple accessory (chalice, grail, throne, alter, etc.) as sacred relic.
No. 17 pp. 201–16.

V144.1, ‡Sacred relics carried in battle to aid victory.
No. 17 p. 205 n. 50, 208.

V147.1§, ‡War waged to restore usurped sacred relic.
No. 16 pp. 181–200;
No. 17 pp. 201–16.

V311.5§, Visiting graveyards—as reminder of death and the life to come—is recommended.
No. 7 p. 97, cf.

V318.1§, ‡Submission to fate (God's prejudgment: *qaḍâ', qadar*) a mark of true faith.
Introduction to This Edition pp. xviii–xix n. 45.

V318.1.1§, ‡Suppliant pleads not that God revoke His prejudgment but only that He lighten its impact.

Introduction to This Edition pp. xviii–xix n. 45.

V320.3.1§, ‡Heretic punishes deity by closing (destroying) his temple(s).

No. 2 p. 33.

V462.8.0.3§, *ʾingidhâb*: madness (dissociation) from ascetic immersion.

No. 15 p. 174 n. 9.

V462.8.0.3.1§, ‡Epileptic ecstasy (convulsions).

No. 15 p. 174 n. 9.

V463.7.5§, ‡Martyrdom: dying accidental, unnatural (violent) death (e.g., drowning, burning, etc.).

No. 6 p. 107 n. 37, cf. (drowning like Osiris).

V510.1, God speaks in vision to devotees.

No. 9 p. 138;

No. 10 pp. 146-47, cf.

V511, Visions of the other world.

No. 8 p. 130, cf.

V512, Vision of judgment. Man sees his own soul being judged.

No. 8 pp. 122–23, 130, cf.

V517§, Instructive sleeper's-vision or dream (*ruʿyah, manâm*).

No. 9 p. 138.

W. Traits of Character

W47§, Eloquence.

Introduction to This Edition p. xxv n. 77;

No. 3 pp. 35–54.

W47.1§, The power of the spoken word.

No. 3 pp. 35–54.

W47.4§, ‡The power (authority) of the written word.

No. 7 p. 109 n. 43.

W50§, ‡Humility as trait of character.

No. 17 p. 215 n. 77.

W111.2.10§, Procrastinating craftsmen (hirelings, workers): "Tomorrow!"

No. 22 p. 242.

W116.7, Use of strange language to show one's high education [(*taḥadhluq*)].

No. 3 pp. 37–38, cf.;

No. 20 p. 232.

W117.3§, ‡Skillful professional (craftsman) boasts of own ability.
No. 22 p. 242 n. 8.
W131.4§, ‡Wasteful wife (woman).
No. 8 p. 124.
W181, Jealousy.
No. 4 p. 66.
W195, Envy.
No. 4 p. 66.
W195.4§, Wealth (material possessions) envied.
No. 4 pp. 66–67.
W195.6§, Social status (influence, authority) envied.
No. 4 pp. 66–67.
W256.1§, Stereotyping: ethnic and national traits.
No. 3 pp. 37–38, cf. (national character).
W256.6§, Stereotyping: gender (sex) traits.
Intro. p. cxxix.
W256.6.0.1§, ‡Females stereotyped—general.
Intro. p. cxxix.
W256.6.1.1§, ‡Stereotyping: women surrender instantly to sexual temptation.
Intro. p. cxxix.
W256.6.5§, ‡Wastefulness of women—(as compared to men).
No. 8 p. 123.
W256.8.2.3§, Fat persons are good hearted.
Introduction to This Edition p. viii n. 2.

X. Humor

X52, Ridiculous nakedness or exposure
No. 14 p. 165.
X800, Humor based on drunkenness.
No. 14 pp. 165–66.

Z. Miscellaneous Groups of Motifs

Z1§, ‡Formulistic language (speech, parlance).
No. 3 pp. 35–54.
Z1.0.1§, ‡'inshâ-style literary composition: constituted mainly from copied (memorized) famous quotations.
Introduction to This Edition p. xxv n. 79;
No. 3 pp. 35–54.

Z1.1.1§, ‡Scriptural (scripture-like) formulas: (e.g., *yâ 'ayyuhâ* ... ('O ye who ...'), *'inna 'Allâha* ... (Verily, the Lord ....), etc.

Introduction to This Edition p. xxvii n. 87.

Z1.1.3§, ‡Oracle's (augurer's, magician's) rhymed prose (*sajǧ kuhhân*).

No. 2 p. 28 n. 35.

Z10.2.4§, ‡Contentious (threatening) end formula.

No. 1 p. 16 n. 53.

Z61.2.2§, ‡Living forever.

No. 10 p. 146.

Z64, Proverbs.

No. 5 p. 88.

Z88§, ‡Sarcasm.

No. 3 pp. 35-54.

Z92.8.3§, ‡Formulas for immense (large) volume (size).

No. 7 p. 103 n. 23 (serpent's).

Z93.1.2§, ‡Incalculable: like sand (dust, pebbles, etc.).

Intro. p. cxlvi.

Z95§, ‡Puns (homophony).

Intro. p. cxxxvii;

No. 2 pp. 30 n. 43, 30 n. 45,—("*nubu*") p. 31 n. 47,—("*sâhû*"), p. 31 n. 48,—("Kakuaî").

Z95.0.1§, ‡Double-meaning: word or phrase that denotes more than one meaning.

No. 1 p. 10 n. 31;

No. 6 p. 107 n. 37,—(euphemism: drowning/praise Râ).

No. 7 p. 103 n. 20,—(river/sea).

Z105.1.1§, ‡Shape symbolism: circle or halo—power.

No. 4 p. 77 n. 82.

Z105.2§, ‡Shape symbolism: square(c)

No. 7 p. 108 n. 39, cf.

Z108§, ‡Sound (name) symbolism: association based on sound similarities (homophony).

No. 2 p. 30 n. 45.

Z112.2§, ‡The plague personified.

No. 8 p. 125.

Z122.9.1§, ‡Formulas signifying passage of time (moments, nights, days, years, etc.).

No. 1 p. 4 n. 6.

Z124.2§, ‡Valor personified as deity (culture-hero).
  No. 10 p. 144 n. 1,—(Set).
Z139.11§, ‡Balance (scales) as symbol of justice.
  No. 3 pp. 43, 45–46, 51 n. 63, 52.
Z152.6.4§, ‡Corner(s) of a building (*rukn/'arkân*): strength.
  No. 4 p. 77 n. 82.
Z159.4.1§, ‡Sign of the Zodiac personified.
  No. 13 p. 83 n. 4.
Z179.1.2.1.1.1§, ‡Submission: kissing ground (before a certain person).
  No. 4 p. 72 n. 53.
Z179.2§, ‡Kissing allegorically interpreted.
  No. 5 p. 86.
Z183.0.1§, Meaning of a name.
  Intro. p. cvi n. 57, cf.;
  No. 1 p. 9 n. 27, 11 n. 33,—(Pharaoh).
Z183.4§, ‡Naming person after location: country, region, city, etc. (e.g., el-Maghrabî, the-Northern, el-Shâmî, el-Baghdâdî, etc.).
  No. 4 p. 76.
Z183.6.1§, "Daughter-of-..." (*Bint-.../'Bit-...'*).
  Intro. p. cx;
  No. 10 p. 144 n. 7.
Z183.9.1§, Variation(s) on a name.
  No. 8 p. 119 n. 76,—(Satni/Satmi).
Z186.8.2.1§, ‡Symbolism: oven (furnace)—vagina, womb.
  Introduction to This Edition p. xvii n. 42.
Z183.9.2§, ‡Names given a game's play-pieces (e.g., chess' king, queen, knight, elephant, dog, pawn, etc.).
  No. 7 p. 110 n. 45.
Z194.1.8§, ‡Bull (ox) symbolism.
  No. 17 p. 206 n. 53,—(helmet).
Z194.1.8.1§, ‡Bull: strength (brute force).
  No. 10 pp. 143–44,—(Horus).
Z194.1.8.1.1§, ‡Bull: maleness, sexual stamina.
  Intro. p. cvi n. 57, cf.;
  No. 1 p. 9 n. 27.
Z194.2.1§, ‡Lion—courage.
  No. 12 pp. 150–51.

Z199.2.1§, ‡Symbolic number four: power.

    No. 4 p. 77 n. 82;

    No. 7 p. 108 n. 39.

Z356.2.1§, ‡Sole survivor of (military) battle.

    No. 1 p. 11, cf.

Z356.3§, ‡Sole survivor of tragic accident (calamity: shipwreck, fire, earthquake, etc.).

    No. 5 p. 86 n. 15.

References Cited

(in Introduction to This Edition)

Aarne, Antti, and Stith Thompson. *The Types of the Folktale. FF Communications* No. 184. Helsinki: Academia Scientartum Fennica, 1961; first published by Aarne in 1910.

Artin, Yacoub [Artîn, Ya¿qûb]. *Contes populaires inédits de la vallée du Nil.* Paris, 1893 (Reprint: Paris, 1968).

Benfey, Theodor. *Panchatantra: fünf Bücher indischer Fablen, Märchen, und Erzählungen.* 2 vols. Leipzig, 1859.

Bødker, Laurits. *Folk Literature (Germanic).* Vol. 2: *International Dictionary of Regional European Ethnology and Folklore.* Copenhagen, 1965, pp. 195–97.

Brunner-Traut, Emma. *Altägyptische Märchen.* Düsseldorf, 1965.

Budge, Ernest A. W., ed. and trans. *Egyptian Tales and Romances: Pagan, Christian and Muslim.* London: T. Butterworth, 1931.

The Columbia Encyclopedia. Sixth Edition.

Cosquin, Emmanuel. *Les contes indiens et l'occident.* Paris, 1922.

Dorson, R. M. "Current Folklore Theories." *Current Anthropology* 4, no. 1 (1963): 93–112.

Dorson, R. M., ed. *Folklore and Folklife: An Introduction.* Chicago, 1972.

Encyclopædia Britannica Online. http://www.eb.com/.

Gran-Aymerich, Evelyne, and Jean Gran-Aymerich. "Gaston Maspero." *Archéologia* 192/193 (1984): 109–113.

Green, Roger Lancelyn. *Tales of Ancient Egypt, Selected and Retold.* New York: Henry Walack, 1967/1968.

Grimm, Jacob, and Wilhelm Grimm. *Kinder- und Hausmärchen.* Vol. 3. Leipzig, 1856.

Ḥassan, Salîm. *mawsûẓat Miṣral-Qadîmah* (*Encyclopedia of Ancient Egypt*). Vol. 17, *al-'adab al-miṣrî al-qadîm* (*Ancient Egyptian Literature*). al-Hay'ah: Cairo, 2000, first published in two volumes in 1945.

Hollis, Susan T. *The Ancient Egyptian "Tale of Two Brothers," The Oldest Fairy Tale in the World.* University of Oklahoma Press: Norman and London, 1990.

Littmann, Enno. *Modern Arabic Tales* [from al-Quds, in Arabic]. Leyden, 1905. (German translation and annotation: *Arabische Märchen.* Leipzig, 1935.)

Loiseleur-Deslongchamp, A. *Essai sur les fables indiennes et sur leur introduction en Europe.* Paris, 1838.

Maspero, Gaston. *Chansons populaires recueillies dans la Haute-égypte de 1900 à 1914 pendant les inspections du Service des antiquités.* Le Caire: Service des antiquités de l'Égypte: Impr. de l'Institut français d'archéologie orientale, 1914. (A secondary title: "Extrait des *Annales du Service des Antiquités,* T. XIV, pp. 97–290.")

———. "Le Conte des deux frères: récit égyptien d'il y à trois mille ans." *Revue de Cours Littéraires* 7 (Feb. 28, 1871): 780–84.

———. "Conte des deux frères." *Revue Archéologique* 35 (March 1878): 164–79.

———. *Contes populaires de l'égypte ancienne.* Les littératures populaires de toutes les nations, IV. Paris: Maisonneuve et Cie.

Müller, David H. *Die Mehri-und Soqutri-Sprache,* pt. I *texte, Südarabische Expedition.* Vol. 4. Vienna, 1902.

———. *Mehri-und Soqutri-Sprache* pt. II *Soqotri Texte, Südarabische Expedition.* Vol. 6. Wien, 1905.

———. *Die Mehri-und Soqutri-Sprache* pt. III *Shḥauri Texte, Südarabische Expedition.* Vol. 7. Wien, 1907.

Petrie, William Matthew Flinders, trans. and ed. *Egyptian Tales.* 2 vols. London: Methuen, 1895.

Rhodokanakis, Nikolaus. *Der vulg ärarabische Dialekt im Dofâr (ẓfâr).* *Südarabische Expedition.* Vol. 8. Wien, 1908.

Sayce, A. H. "Cairene and Upper Egyptian Folklore." *Folk-Lore* 31, no. 3 (1920): 173–203.

El-Shamy, Hasan. "Behaviorism and the Text." In: *Folklore Today: A Festschrift for Richard M. Dorson.* Linda Dégh, Henry Glassie, and

Felix Oinas, eds. Bloomington, Ind., 1976, pp. 145–160.

———. "Belief and Non-Belief in Arab, Middle Eastern and sub-Saharan Tales: the Religious-Non-Religious Continuum. A Case Study." *al-Ma'thûrât al-Sha'biyyah* 3, no 9 (January, 1988): 7–21.

———. "Context." In: *Folklore: An Encyclopedia of Forms, Methods, and History.* Thomas A. Green, gen. ed. Santa Barbara, Calif.: ABC-CLIO, 1997.

———. *A Demographically Oriented Type-Index for Tales of the Arab World.* Indiana University Press, 2002 (forthcoming).

———. "Folk Group." In: *Folklore.* T. A. Green, gen. ed. Santa Barbara, Calif.: ABC-CLIO, 1997.

———. *Folk Traditions of the Arab World: A Guide to Motif Classification.* 2 vols. Bloomington: Indiana University Press, 1995.

———. *Folktales of Egypt: Collected, Translated and Edited with Middle Eastern and African Parallels.* Chicago: University of Chicago Press, 1980.

———. "'Noble and Vile' or 'Genuine and False'? Some Linguistic and Typological Comments on *Folktales of Egypt*." *Fabula* 24, nos. 3–4 (1983): 341–46.

———. "Oral Traditional Tales and the Thousand Nights and a Night: The Demographic Factor." In: *The Telling of Stories: Approaches to a Traditional Craft.* Morton Nøjgaard et al., eds. Odense University Press, Odense, Denmark, 1990, pp. 63–117.

———. *Tales Arab Women Tell: and the Behavioral Patterns They Portray.* Collected, translated, edited, and interpreted. Indiana University Press, 1999.

Simpson, William K., ed. *The Literature of Ancient Egypt.* New Haven: Yale Univ. Press, 1972.

Spitta, Wilhelm. *Contes arabes modernes.* Leiden, 1883.

———. *Grammatik des arabischen Vulgärdialektes von ägypten.* Leipzig, 1880.

Reinisch, Leo. *Die Somali-Sprache, Südarabische Expedition.* Vol. 1. Vienna, 1900.

Taylor, Archer. "A Theory of Indo-European Märchen." *Journal of American Folklore* 44: 54–60.

Theban Mapping Project, American University in Cairo. 1997–2000. Website.

Thompson, Stith. *The Folktale.* New York, 1946.

———. *Motif Index of Folk-Literature.* 6 vols. Bloomington, 1955–1958.

Von Sydow, C. W. "Das Märchen als indogermanische Tradition (Auszug) übertragen von Lily Weiser." *Neiderdeutsche Zeitschrift für Volkskunde* 4 (1926): 207–15.

———. "Den fornegyptiska Sagan om de tv Brderna." *Yearbook of the New Society of Letters of Lund* (1930): 53ff. (as given by Thompson).

Preface to English Edition

This volume is not merely an exact translation of the published French edition. Sir Gaston Maspero has revised the work throughout, furnishing in places new renderings of the Egyptian texts and new readings of Egyptian names and titles. An index of proper names has been added as well as one of general subjects.

A. S. Johns
Cambridge 1915

~~

Introduction

WHEN a story of the Pharaonic period analogous to the stories of *The Arabian Nights* was discovered in 1852 by M. de Rougé, it occasioned great surprise even among the scholars who were supposed to know most about Ancient Egypt. The solemnity of the exalted personages whose mummies repose in our museums was so well established by renown, that no one suspected them of having been amused by such frivolities at the time when they were mummies only in expectation. The story existed nevertheless; the manuscript had belonged to a prince, a king's son who himself became King Setuî II, son of Mînephtah, grandson of Sesôstris. An Englishwoman, Madame Elizabeth d'Orbiney, bought it in Italy, and on her way home through Paris M. de Rougé explained the contents to her. They concern two brothers, the younger of whom, falsely accused by the wife of the other and forced to take to flight, changed into a bull, then into a tree, and finally was re-born in the person of a king. M. de Rougé made a paraphrase of the text rather than a translation;[1] several portions were simply analysed, others were broken at short intervals by numerous lacunæ, caused either by the bad condition of the papyrus or due to the difficulty encountered in deciphering certain groups of signs, or in disentangling the subtleties of the syntax, even the name of the hero is incorrectly transcribed.[2] Since that time no specimen of Egyptian literature has been more minutely studied, or with greater profit. The unceasing industry of scholars has corrected the errors and filled in the gaps. Today the *Story of the Two Brothers* can be read consecutively, with the exception of a few words.[3]

---

1. In the *Revue archéologique*, 1852, vol. viii, pp. 30 *et seq.*, and in the *Athénæum français*, vol. i, 1852, pp. 280–284; cf. *Œuvres diverses*, vol. ii, pp. 303–319.
2. *Satu* instead of Baîti. It was M. de Rougé himself who later on corrected this error.
3. This is the first story given in this volume, pp. 1–16.

For twelve years it remained unique of its kind. A thousand relics of the past were brought to light—lists of conquered provinces, catalogues of royal names, funerary inscriptions, songs of victory, private letters, books of accounts, formulæ of magic incantations, and judicial documents, as well as treatises on medicine and geometry—but nothing resembling a romance. In 1864, near Deîr-el-Medineh and in the tomb of a Coptic monk, illicit explorations brought to light a wooden coffer, which besides the cartulary of a neighbouring convent contained manuscripts which had nothing monastic about them—the moral advice of a scribe to his son,[4] prayers for the twelve hours of the night, and a story yet more strange than that of the *Two Brothers.* The hero is called Satni-Khamoîs, and he holds debates with a band of talking mummies, sorcerers and magicians, ambiguous beings of whom one is doubtful whether they are living or dead. It is not easy to see what could justify the presence of a pagan romance beside the body of a monk. We may conjecture that the possessor of the papyri must have been one of the last of the Egyptians who had known anything of the ancient writings, and that at his death his devout companions enclosed in his grave the magic books of which they understood nothing, and which they regarded as some unfathomable snare of the evil one. However that may have been, the romance was then incomplete at the beginning, but sufficiently complete further on to be made out without difficulty by a scholar accustomed to demotic.[5] Up to that time the study of demotic writing had not been very popular among Egyptologists; the tenuity and indecision of the characters that compose it, the novelty of the grammatical forms, and the dullness or feebleness of the subjects dealt with, alarmed or repelled them. That which Emmanuel de Rougé did for the d'Orbiney papyrus, Brugsch alone was then capable of attempting for the Boulaq papyrus; the translation published by him, in 1867, in the *Revue arahéologique,* is so correct that at the present time few changes have been made in it.[6]

---

4. Analysed by Maspero in *The Academy* (August 1871), and by Brugsch, *Altägyptische Lebensregeln in einem hieratischen Papyrus des viceköniglichen Museums zu Bulaq,* in the *Zeitschrift,* 1872, pp. 49-51, completely translated by E. de Rougé, *Étude sur la Papyrus du Musée de Boulaq, lue à la séance du 25 août,* 1872, 8vo, 12 pp. (Extrait des *Comptes rendus d l'Académie des Inscriptions et Belles-Lettres,* 2ᵉ Série, vol. vii, pp. 340–351), by Chabas, *L'Égyptologie,* vols. i-ii, *Les maximes du scribe Ani,* 4to, 1876–1877, and by Amélineau, *La Morale Égyptienne,* 8vo, 1890.

5. The writing in use for the civil and religious life at the commencement of the XXVIth dynasty was called *demotic.* It was derived from the ancient cursive writing known as *hieratic.*

6. It is the *Adventure of Satni-Khamoîs with the mummies,* pp. 95–118 of this volume.

Since then successive discoveries have been made. In 1874 Goodwin, ferreting haphazard in the Harris collection, just acquired by the British Museum, came upon the *Adventures of the Doomed Prince*[7] and on the conclusion of a tale which he regarded as possessing historic value, notwithstanding some similarity with the story of Ali Baba.[8] Several weeks later Chabas observed at Turin what he thought to be disconnected portions of a kind of licentious rhapsody,[9] and at Boulaq the remains of a love story.[10] Immediately afterwards, at Petrograd, Golénischeff deciphered three romances, of which the texts are not yet fully edited.[11] Then Erman published a long story about Cheops and the magicians, the manuscript of which formerly belonged to Lepsius and is now in the Berlin Museum.[12] Krall researched in the fine collection of the Archduke Régnier, and patiently readjusted the fragments of *The High Emprise for the Cuirass*.[13] From the stores of the British Museum Griffith extracted a second episode of the cycle of Satni-Khamoîs,[14] and Spiegelberg acquired for the University of Strasburg a Theban version of the *Chronicle of King Petubastis*.[15] Finally, in one of the Berlin papyri there was discovered the commencement of a fantastic romance that was so much mutilated as to make it difficult to be sure of the subject,[16] and on a series of ostraca scattered among the

7. *Transactions of the Society of Biblical Archæology*, vol. iii, pp. 349–356, announced by M. Chabas at the Académie des Inscriptions et Belles-Lettres during the session of April 17, 1874; cf. *Comptes rendus*, 1874, pp. 92, 117–120, and pp. 153–161 of this volume.

8. *Transactions of the Society of Biblical Archæology*, vol. iii, pp. 340–348. It is published in this volume under the title of *How Thutîyi took the town of Joppa*, pp. 89–94.

9. Announced by M. Chabas at the Académie des Inscriptions et Belles-Lettres during the session of April 17, 1875, and published under the title *L'Episode du Jardin des Fleurs*, in *Comptes rendus*, 1875, pp. 92, 120–124. The careful examination I have made of the original has convinced me that the fragments have been badly put together, and that they should be placed in a very different arrangement from that known to M. Chabas. They do not contain a licentious story, but love songs similar to those of the Papyrus Harris, No. 500 (Maspero, *Études égyptiennes*, vol. i, pp. 219–220).

10. *Comptes rendus de l'Académie des Inscriptions et Belles-Lettres*, 1874, p. 124. These fragments have not yet been translated nor even studied.

11. *Zeitschrift für Ægyptische Sprache und Alterthumskunde*, 1876, pp. 107–111, under the title *Le Papyrus No. 1 de Saint-Pétersbourg*, and *Sur un ancien conte égyptien. Notice lue au Congres des Orientalistes à Berlin*, 1881, 8vo, 21 pp.; cf. pp. 81–88 of the present volume.

12. For the bibliography and the story itself see pp. 17–33 of the present volume.

13. The discovery was announced at the Congress of Orientalists at Geneva in 1894; for the bibliography see pp. 181–183 of the present volume.

14. It is the story printed in pp. 118–137 of the present volume.

15. For the story see pp. 201–216 of the present volume.

16. Lepsius, *Denkmäler*, Part VI, pl. 112, and pp. 219–242 of this volume.

European museums, fragments of a ghost story.[17] We may add that certain works, which at first were regarded as serious documents—the *Memoirs of Sinuhît,*[18] the *Lamentations of the Fellah*[19] the negotiations between King Apôpi and King Saqnûnrîya,[20] the *Stela of the Princess of Bakhtan,*[21] the *Voyage of Unamunu*[22]—are in reality purely works of imagination. Even after twenty centuries of ruin and oblivion, Ancient Egypt possesses almost as many tales as lyric poems or hymns addressed to the deity.

I

EXAMINATION of these stories raises a variety of questions which are difficult of solution. How were they composed? Were they entirely invented by their author, or did he borrow the substance of pre-existent works and rearrange or alter them to form a new romance? Several of them certainly emanated from one sole source and constitute original work—the *Memoirs of Sinuhît,* the *Shipwrecked Sailor,* the *Stratagem of Thutiyî against Joppa,* the *Story of the Doomed Prince.* A continuous action is carried through from the first line to the last, and where episodes are introduced they are only necessary developments of the main scheme, mediums without which it could not arrive safely at the denouement. Others, on the contrary, divide almost naturally into two, three or more parts, which originally were independent, and between which the author has often established an arbitrary connection in order to include them within the same story. For instance, each of those which treat of Satni-Khamoîs contains the subject-matter of two romances—that of Nenoferkephtah and that of Tbubui in the first, that of the descent into the Inferno and that of the Ethiopian magicians in the second. The most obvious example, however, of an artificial composition that we possess up to the present time is that afforded by the story of Khufuî and the magicians.[23]

17. Two in the Florence Museum (Golénischeff, *Notice sur un ostracon hiératique,* in the *Recueil,* vol. iii, pp. 3–7), one in the Louvre (*Recueil,* vol. iii, p. 7), one in the Vienna Museum (Bergmann, *Hieratische und Hieratisch-demotische Texte der Sammlung Ægyptischer Alterthümer des Allerhöchsten Kaiserhauses,* pl. iv, p. vi); cf. pp. 230–232 of this volume.

18. Lepsius, *Denkmäler,* Part VI, pl. 104–106, and pp. 55–79 of this volume.

19. *Ibid.,* pl. 108–110, 113–114; for the bibliography see pp. 35–38 of this volume.

20. *Papyrus Sallier* I, pl. 1–3; pl. 2 *verso;* see pp. 223–227 of this volume.

21. See pp. 141–147 of this volume.

22. Published in pp. 169 *et seq.* of this volume.

23. See pp. 17–33 of the present volume.

From the first it resolves itself into two elements: the glorification of several magicians, living or dead, and a miraculous version of the events that led to the downfall of the IVth and the rise of the Vth dynasty. We should perhaps understand better what caused the author to combine them if we possessed the first pages of the manuscript; in its present condition conjecture is dangerous. It appears, however, that it was not compiled all at one time, but was formed as it were in two stages. At some period which we cannot now determine, there were perhaps half a dozen stories circulating in Memphis or the neighbourhood, which had for their heroes sorcerers of a long past time. An unknown rhapsodist decided to compile a collection of these in chronological order, and in order to effect this successfully he had recourse to a method which was one of those held in highest honour in Oriental literature. He set forth that Cheops, one of the popular Pharaohs, once was struck with the idea of demanding something from his sons to distract the ennui with which he was beset. The sons rose up one after another in his presence, and boasted in turn of the prowess of various sorcerers of bygone times; Dadûfhoru alone, the last of them, chose as his subject the praise of a living man. On considering this part more closely we see that the sages were all *chief men of the book, or of the roll, to Pharaoh,* that is to say, men with an official standing, who possessed their rank in the hierarchy, while the contemporary Didu bore no title. He was a mere provincial who had attained to extreme old age without having enjoyed court favours; that the prince knew him was owing to his being himself an adept and having travelled over the whole of Egypt in search of ancient writings or of men of learning capable of interpreting them.[24] He thereupon journeyed to the house of his protégé and brought him to his father, that he might perform some miracle even more amazing than those of his predecessors; Didu refused to meddle with a man, but he restored a goose and a bull to life, and then returned home full of honours. The first collection of stories undoubtedly ended here, and formed a work complete in itself. But at the same period and in the same locality there was a story of three children, triplets, sons of the sun and of a priestess of Râ. They eventually become the first kings of the Vth dynasty. Did Didu originally play some part here? At any rate the author to whom we are indebted for this present redaction selected him as the link in the transition between the two chronicles. He set forth that, having been present at the resurrection of the goose and the bull, Cheops afterwards requested Didu to procure

24. Cf. p. 20, n. 5, p. 26, n. 29, p. 97, n. 3, and p. 121 of the present volume.

him the books of Thoth. Didu did not deny that he knew them, but he declared that there was only one man who was capable of ensuring their possession to the king—the eldest of the three boys who at that time were in the womb of a priestess of Râ, and who were destined to reign at the end of four generations. Cheops was perturbed by this disclosure, as was only natural, and he inquired at what date the children should be born. Didu told him and then returned to his village. The author left him at this point, and turned immediately to the destinies of the priestess and her family.

The author did not worry himself long as to the method of making this transition; and he was right, for his auditors or his readers were not difficult to please in the matter of literary composition. They asked to be amused, and provided that it was done, they did not trouble themselves as to the means by which it was accomplished. The Egyptian romancers therefore felt no scruples in appropriating the stories that were current in their neighbourhood and arranging them as they would, complicating them when necessary with episodes that were absent from the first redaction or reducing them to the position of secondary episodes in a different cycle from that to which they originally belonged. Many of the elements which they combine are essentially Egyptian, but they also utilised others which are found in the literature of neighbouring peoples, and which they had perhaps borrowed from abroad. We remember in the *Gospel according to St. Luke* the rich man, clothed in purple and fine linen, who feasted sumptuously every day, while at his gate lay Lazarus full of sores and desiring in vain to be fed with the crumbs that fell from the rich man's table. "And it came to pass that the beggar died and was carried by the angels into Abraham's bosom, and the rich man also died and was buried; and in hell he lift up his eyes, being in torments, and seeth Abraham afar off and Lazarus in his bosom."[25] In the second romance of Satni-Khamoîs, we read an Egyptian version of this parable of the Evangelist, but there it is dramatised and amalgamated with another popular conception, that of the descent of a living man into hell.[26] Without insisting on this subject for the moment, I would remark that many of the motifs developed by Egyptian writers are held by them in common with story tellers of foreign nations, both ancient and modern. If you will

25. *Gospel according to St. Luke,* xvi, 19–23.

26. Maspero, *Contes relatifs aux grand-prêtres de Memphis,* in the *Journal des Savants,* 1901, p. 496.

analyse the *Tale of the Two Brothers* and endeavour to define its internal structure, you will be amazed to find to what extent it resembles, in its general bearing and in its details, certain stories which are in circulation among other nations.

At the first glance we see that it is double: the story teller, too idle or too devoid of imagination to invent a tale, chose two from among those transmitted to him by his predecessors and has, more or less awkwardly, placed them one at the end of the other, contenting himself with introducing various small incidents that in some measure facilitated their contact. The veracious history of Satni-Khamoîs is in the same way a junction of two romances, the descent into hell, and the adventure of King Siamânu. The redactor has united them by supposing Senosiris of the first to be reincarnated in Horus, who was the hero of the second part.[27]

The *Story of the Two Brothers* first brings on the scene two brothers, one married, the other single, who lived together and followed the same occupation. The wife of the elder brother fell in love with the younger one on observing his unusual strength, and took advantage of the absence of her husband to give way to a sudden access of untamed passion. Baîti refused her advances with anger; she accused him of assaulting her, and did this with so much skill that her husband decided to kill his brother by treachery. The cattle that he was bringing back to the stable having warned him of the peril, the younger brother fled and escaped his pursuer, thanks to the protection afforded him by the Sun; he mutilated himself, and exculpated himself, but he refused to return to their mutual home, and exiled himself to the Vale of the Acacia. Anupu returned home deeply grieved; he put his calumniating wife to death, and then "dwelt mourning for his younger brother."[28]

So far the marvellous does not occupy too large a place; with the exception of some remarks made by the cattle, and a piece of water full of crocodiles that suddenly arose between the two brothers, the narrator employs incidents borrowed from ordinary life. The remainder is nothing but marvels from beginning to end.[29] Baîti has returned to the Valley to live in solitude, and he has placed his heart on a flower of the Acacia. This is a most natural precaution, to enchant one's heart, and put it in a safe place such as

27. The first story is to be found on pp. 119–125 of this volume, the second on pp. 128–137, and the transition on pp. 125–128.

28. This first story occupies pp. 3–10 of the present volume.

29. It extends from pp. 9–16 of the present volume.

a tree-top; so long as it remained there, no force could prevail against the body that it animated even in that position.[30] The gods, however, come down to visit the earth, pity Baîti in his solitude, and fashion a wife for him.[31] As he loves her to distraction, he confides his secret to her, and he commands her not to leave the house, as the Nile that waters the valley is enamoured of her beauty and will certainly wish to carry her off. This confidence imparted, he goes off to hunt, and she immediately disobeys him. The Nile pursues her and would have taken possession of her, if the Acacia, who in some way not entirely explained acts the part of protector, had not saved her by throwing a lock of her hair into the water. This, carried as flotsam into Egypt, was taken to Pharaoh, and he on the advice of the magicians sent in search of the daughter of the gods. Force miscarried the first time, but on a second attempt treachery was successful, the Acacia was cut down, and as soon as it fell Baîti died. For three years he remained inanimate; during the fourth he revived with the help of Anupu, and determined to avenge himself for the crime of which he had been the victim. Henceforth there is a struggle of magic power and malicious spite between the injured husband and the faithless wife. Baîti changes into a bull; the daughter of the gods contrives that the bull's throat shall be cut. When the blood touches the ground two persea trees spring up, that find words to denounce the perfidious woman; the daughter of the gods contrives that the trees shall be cut down, to be made into furniture, and in order to taste the joys of vengeance, she is present while it is done. A chip sent flying by the carpenter's adze enters her mouth, she conceives, and bears a son who succeeds Pharaoh, and who is Baîti reincarnated. As soon as he ascends the throne he assembles the counsellors of state, and states his wrongs. He then sends to execution the woman who after being his wife had, without desiring it, become his mother. Thus in this tale there is the material of two distinct romances, of which the first presents the idea of a servant accused by the mistress whom he has scorned, while the second depicts the metamor-

30. This is the idea of *the body without a soul*, which occurs frequently in popular literature. Le Page Renouf has collected a number of examples of it in *Zeitschrift* (1871, pp. 136 *et seq.*) and in the *Proceedings of the Society of Biblical Archæology* (vol. xi, pp. 177 *et seq.* reproduced in Le Page Renouf's *Life-Work*, vol. i, pp. 442 *et seq.*, and vol. ii, pp. 311 *et seq.*).

31. Hyacinthe Husson, who has studied *The Tale of the Two Brothers* fairly closely (*La Chaîne traditionnelle, Contes et Legéndes au point de vue mythique*, Paris 1874, p. 91), has aptly compared the creation of this female by Khnumu, and the creation of Pandora, fashioned by Hephœstion by order of Zeus. "Both these women are endowed with all the gifts of beauty; nevertheless both are fatal, one to her husband, the other to the entire human race." In the part played by the river there seems to be an allusion to the custom of making a *Bride of the Nile*.

phoses of the husband betrayed by his wife. Popular imagination has united the two by a third motif—that of the man or demon who conceals his
heart, and dies when an enemy discovers it. Before expatriating himself
Baîti had asserted that a misfortune would shortly overtake him, and
described the marvels that would announce the bad tidings to his brother.
These occurred at the moment that the Acacia fell, and Anupu departed
with speed to search for the heart. The help given by him at this juncture
compensates for his previous attempt to murder his brother, and forms the
link between the two stories.

Greek tradition also possessed stories where the hero is slain or menaced with death for having refused the favours of unfaithful wives, Hippolytus, Peleus, and Phineus. Bellerophon, the son of Glaucus, "to whom
the gods gave beauty and a kindly vigour," repelled the advances of the
divine Anteia, who, furious, spoke thus to King Proetus: "Die, Proetus, or
slay Bellerophon, who wished to unite in love with me, who did not desire
it." Proetus despatched the hero to Lycia, where he imagined the
Chimæra would rid him of him.[32] The Bible records in detail an incident
similar to that in the Egyptian tale. Joseph dwelt in Potiphar's house, as
Baîti did in that of Anupu. "Joseph was a goodly person and well favoured;
and it came to pass after these things that his master's wife cast her eyes
upon Joseph; and she said, 'Lie with me.' But he refused, and said unto his
master's wife, 'Behold, my master wotteth not what is with me in the
house, and he hath committed all that he hath to my hand, there is none
greater in this house than I; neither hath he kept back anything from me
but thee, because thou art his wife: how, then, can I do this great wickedness, and sin against God?' And it came to pass, as she spake to Joseph day
by day, that he hearkened not unto her, to lie by her, or to be with her. And
it came to pass about this time, that Joseph went into the house to do his
business, and there was none of the men of the house there within; and
she caught him by his garment, saying, 'Lie with me'; and he left his garment in her hand, and fled, and got him out. And it came to pass, when
she saw that he had left his garment in her hand, and was fled forth, that
she called unto the men of her house, and spake unto them, saying, 'See,
he hath brought in a Hebrew unto us to mock us; he came in unto me to
lie with me, and I cried with a loud voice: and it came to pass, when he
heard that I lifted up my voice and cried, that he left his garment with me,

---

32. *Iliad*, Z., 155–210. Hyacinthe Husson has already made this comparison (*La Chaîne traditionelle*, p. 87).

and fled, and got him out. And she laid up his garment by her, until his lord came home; and she spake unto him according to these words, saying, 'The Hebrew servant, which thou hast brought unto us, came in unto me to mock me: and it came to pass, as I lifted up my voice and cried, that he left his garment with me, and fled out.' And it came to pass, when his master heard the words of his wife which she spake unto him, saying, 'After this manner did thy servant unto me'; that his wrath was kindled. And Joseph's master took him, and put him into the prison, a place where the king's prisoners were bound, and he was there in the prison."[33] Comparison of this with the *Tale of the Two Brothers* is so natural, that it was made by M. de Rougé as early as 1852.[34] But the attempted seduction, the guilty fears of the temptress, her shame, her meditated revenge, are simple ideas that might occur independently to the teller of popular stories in many quarters of the globe at the same time.[35] We need not regard Joseph's adventure as the variant of a story of which the *d'Orbiney Papyrus* gives the version current in Thebes towards the end of the XIXth dynasty.

It may perhaps be well to treat with the same caution a story of the *Arabian Nights* which has some analogy with the *Two Brothers*. The primitive theme is here duplicated and aggravated in a singular manner: instead of a sister-in-law, who offers herself to her brother-in-law, there are two step-mothers who attempt to debauch the sons of their common husband. Prince Kamaralzaman had Amgiâd by the Princess Badiûr, and Assad by the Princess Haïat-en-nefûs. Amgiâd and Assad were so beautiful that from infancy they inspired the sultanas with inconceivable affection. As the years passed, that which had appeared to be maternal affection developed into violent passion; instead of struggling against their criminal longings, Badûr and Haïât-en-Nefûs concerted together and declared their love in letters very unequivocal in style. Repelled with horror, they feared denunciation and, like the wife of Anupu, they pretended that violence had been attempted. They wept, they cried, together they flung themselves on the same bed, as if their strength were exhausted by resistance. The next morning, Kamaralzaman, returned from hunting, found them bathed in tears, and inquired of them the cause of their sorrow. The reply may be guessed. "My lord, the grief that overpowers us is of such a nature that we can no longer endure the light of day after the outrage which the two princes, your children, have been guilty of

---

33. Genesis xxxix, 6–20.

34. *Notice sur un manuscrit égyptien*, p. 7, note 5 (cf. *Œuvres diverses*, vol. ii, p. 308, note 2), but without insisting on the points of resemblance.

35. Ebers, *Ægypten und die Bücher Moses*, 1868, vol. i, p. 316.

towards us. During your absence they have had the audacity to attempt our honour." Then follows the wrath of the father, and sentence of death against the sons; the aged emir charged with their execution did not execute them, as otherwise there would have been an end of the story. Kamaralzaman shortly afterwards recognised the innocence of Amgiâd and Assad, but instead of killing his two wives he contented himself with imprisoning them for the remainder of their lives.[36] It is the plot of the *Story of the Two Brothers,* but adapted to the requirements of Mohammedan polygamy. Modified in this manner, it has gained nothing either in interest or morality.[37]

The versions of the second story are more numerous and more strange.[38] One meets with them everywhere—in France,[39] in Italy,[40] in different parts of Germany,[41] in Transylvania,[42] in Hungary,[43] in Russia and in the Slavonic countries,[44] among the Roumanians,[45] in the Peloponnesus,[46] in Asia Minor,[47] in Abyssinia,[48] and in India.[49]

36. *Arabian Nights:* "The History of Prince Amgiâd and Prince Assâd."

37. A Pahlavî version of this first of the two stories embodied in the *Orbiney Papyrus* has been observed by Nöldeke, *Geschichte des Artachschîr î Papakân,* in the *Beiträge zur Kunde der indogermanischen Sprachen,* vol. iv, 1879.

38. They have been collected and discussed by M. Emmanuel Cosquin, in his article *Un problème historique à propos du conte égyptien des deux Frères* (*Extrait de la Revue des Questions historiques,* Oct. 1877, Tirage à part, 8vo, 15 p.); I have most scrupulously indicated on each occasion the references borrowed by me from this fine memoir. Le Page Renouf has introduced the greater part of these stories into the article of the *Proceedings* indicated by me above, p. c, note 30 of the present volume.

39. *Cabinet des Fées,* vol. xxxi, pp. 233 *et seq.,* after E. Cosquin.

40. Giambattista Basile, *Il Pentamerone,* No. 49, after E. Cosquin.

41. In Hesse, J. W. Wolff, *Deutsche Hausmärchen,* Gottingen, 1851, pp. 494 *et seq.*

42. In Transylvania, J. Haltdrich, *Deutsche Volksmärchen aus dem Sachsenlande in Siebenbürgen,* Berlin, 1856, No. 1, after E. Cosquin; cf. Le Page Renouf, *Life-work,* vol. iii, p. 319–321.

43. O. L. B. Wolff, *Die schönsten Märchen und Sagen aller Zeiten und Völker,* Leipzig, 1850, vol. i, p. 229 *seq;* Gaal and Stier, *Ungarische Volksmärchen,* Pest, 1857, No. 7, after E. Cosquin; Majlath, *Magyarische Sagen,* vol. ii, p. 195; cf. Le Page Renouf, *Life Work,* vol. iii, p. 321.

44. In Lithuania, Alex. Chodzko, Paris, 1864, p. 368, after E. Cosquin; in Russia the work of Alfred Rambaud, *La Russie épique,* Paris, 1876, pp. 377–380.

45. Franz Obert, *Romänische Märchen und Sagen aus Siebenbürgen,* in *Ausland,* 1858, p. 118; Arthur and Albert Schott, *Walachische Märchen,* Stuttgart, 1845, No. 8, p. 322, after E. Cosquin; cf. Lepage-Renouf, *Life-Work,* vol. iii, p. 319.

46. P. d'Estournelles de Constant, *La vie de province en Grèce,* Paris, 1878, pp. 260–292, and the *Bulletin, de l'Association pour l'encouragement des Études grecques en France,* 1878, pp. 118–123.

47. J. G. von Hahn. *Griechische und Albanesische Märchen,* Leipzig, 1864, No. 49, after E. Cosquin.

48. Leo Reinisch, *Das volk der Saho,* in the *Osterreichische Monatschrift für den Orient,* 1877, No. 5.

49. M. Frere, *Old Deccan Days, or Hindoo Fairy Legends,* London, 1868, No. 6, after E. Cosquin.

In Germany, Baîti is a shepherd, possessor of an invincible sword. A princess deprives him of his talisman; he is conquered, slain, cut in pieces, and then brought to life again by enchanters who grant him the power to "assume all the forms that please him." He changes into a horse. Sold to the king who is his enemy and recognised by the princess, who insists that he shall be decapitated, he secures on his behalf the assistance of the cook of the castle. "When my head is cut off, three drops of my blood will fall on thy apron; thou shalt put them in the ground for love of me." The next day a superb cherry-tree has grown on the very spot where the three drops had been buried. The princess cuts down the cherry-tree; the cook collects three chips and throws them into the pool, where they change into so many golden drakes. The princess kills two of them with arrows, seizes the third and imprisons it in her chamber; during the night the drake regains possession of the sword and disappears.[50]

In Russia Baîti is named Ivan son of Germain the sacristan. He finds a magic sword in a bush, he goes off to fight the Turks who have invaded the country of Arinar, and slays eighty thousand of them; as the reward of his exploits he is given the hand of Cleopatra, the king's daughter. His father-in-law dies, and he is king in his turn, but his wife betrays him and gives over the sword to the Turks; when Ivan, thus disarmed, perishes in battle, she abandons herself to the Sultan, as the daughter of the gods does to Pharaoh. Nevertheless Germain the sacristan, warned by a flow of blood that spouted out in the middle of the stable, sets off and recovers the body. "If thou desirest to restore him to life," says the horse, "open my body, take out my entrails, rub the dead man with my blood, then when the ravens come to devour my body, take one of them and force it to bring to thee the marvellous water of life." Ivan revives and dismisses his father: "Return to thy house; I take upon myself to settle my account with the foe." On the way he perceives a peasant: "I will change myself for thee into a marvellous horse with a mane of gold; thou shalt lead it in front of the palace of the Sultan." The Sultan sees the horse, shuts it up in the stable and goes to admire it continually. "Why, my lord," says Cleopatra, "are you continually in the stables?" "I have bought a horse that has a golden mane." "That is not a horse—that is Ivan, the son of the sacristan: command that he shall be slain." An ox with a golden coat is born of the blood of the horse; Cleopatra has its throat cut. From the head of the ox springs an apple tree with golden apples; Cleopatra has it cut down. The first chip that the axe

50. J. W. Wolff, *Deutsche Hasumärchen*, Göttingen, 1851, 8vo, p. 394, after E. Cosquin.

sends flying from the trunk changes into a magnificent drake. The Sultan gives orders that it shall be chased, and he himself jumps into the water to catch it, but the drake escapes to the other side. He there assumes once more the form of Ivan, with the garments of the Sultan; he throws Cleopatra and her lover on to a funeral pyre and then reigns in their place.[51]

Here, after an interval of more than three thousand years, are unmistakably the main outlines of the Egyptian version. If we take the trouble to examine the details, analogies equally striking can be found everywhere. The lock of hair intoxicates Pharaoh with its perfume; in a Breton story, the luminous lock of hair belonging to the princess of Tréménéazour causes the King of Paris to fall in love.[52] Baîti places his heart on the Acacia flower; in the Pantchatantra, an ape remarks that he never leaves his forest without leaving his heart concealed in the hollow of a tree.[53] Anupu is informed of the death of Baîti by a sign arranged beforehand, the disturbance of the wine and beer; in several European stories a brother starting on a journey informs his brother that on the day when the water in a certain vial is troubled, they will know that he is dead.[54] And it is not only the popular literature that has the equivalent of these incidents; the religions of Greece and of Western Asia include legends that may be compared with them at almost every point. Merely to quote the Phrygian myth, Atys disdained the love of the goddess Cybele, as Baîti did that of the wife of Anupu, and, like Baîti, he mutilated himself [55]; and as Baîti, by a series of changes, was transformed into a persea tree, Atys became a pine.[56] Neither Anupu nor Baîti, however, as they appear in this tale, are unknown heroes or gods. The first is closely allied with the dog deity of the Egyptians,

51. Rambaud, *La Russie épique,* pp. 377–380. A Hungarian legend, quoted by Cosquin, p. 5, presents only slight variations from the German and Russian stories.

52. F. M. Luzel, *Troisième rapport sur une mission en Bretagne,* in the *Archives des Missions scienteifiques,* 2nd series, vol. vii, pp. 192 *et seq.*

53. Benfey, *Pantschatantra,* 1, p. 426; cf. Hyacinthe Husson, *La Chaîne traditionelle,* pp. 88–90.

54. See the examples of identical or analogous signs brought together by Cosquin, in pp. 10–12 of his memoir, and by Le Page Renouf, *Life-Work,* vol. iii, pp. 321–323.

55. Cf. in *De Deâ, Syriâ,* pp. 19–27, the *Story of Combabos,* where the theme of mutilation is more intelligently developed than in the *Story of the Two Brothers.* Baiti mutilates himself *after* the accusation, which proves nothing; Combabos mutilates himself *before,* which enables him to prove his innocence.

56. The mythological side of the question has been brought into prominence, with some exaggeration, by Fr. Lenormant in *Les Premières Civilizations,* vol. i (8vo edition), pp. 375–401; cf. H. da Charencey, *Les Traditions relatives au fils de la Vierge* (extract from the *Annales de Philosophie chrétienne*), 8vo, Paris, 1881, pp. 12 *et seq.*

and the second bears the name of one of the most ancient divinities of archaic Egypt—that Baîti of the double bull's bust and head,[57] of which the cult was established very early in Middle Egypt, at Saka in the Cynopolite nome,[58] beside that of Anubis[59]: later it was considered to be one of the kings anterior to Menes,[60] and his individuality and mythical rôle confounded with those of Osiris.[61] Others have made or will make those necessary comparisons better than I have done. I have said enough to show that the two principal elements existed elsewhere than in Egypt, and at periods other than the Pharaonic time.

In all this is there sufficient proof to allow us to assert that they are or are not original? One point alone appears to me to be beyond doubt: the Egyptian version is by far the earliest in date that we possess. It has, in fact, come down to us in a manuscript of the thirteenth century B.C., many years before the period at which we can begin to recover the trace of others. If the people of Egypt borrowed the ideas, or if they transmitted them to foreign countries, it was done by them at a period yet more remote than that to which the redaction carries us back. Who can say today how or by whom it was done?

II

WHETHER the groundwork was foreign, or whether it was not, the form is invariably indigenous; if by chance the subject were borrowed it was at any rate completely assimilated. The names must first be considered. Some of them, Baîti and Anupu, belong either to religion or to legend;

57. This Baîti was remarked on for the first time by Naville, who collected the instances where his name occurs in the Pyramid texts (*Pepi* II, 1. 1246; *Mirniri*, 1. 480 = *Pepi* I, 1. 267; *Unas*, 1. 538 = *Pepi* I, 1. 229), and also the representations of the god with the double bull's head found on Thinite remains (Petrie, *Royal Tombs*, vol. i, pl. xi, I. 13, and vol. ii, pl. x).

58. The correlation was recognised by Alan Gardiner (*The Hero of the Papyrus d'Orbiney*, in the *Proceedings of the Society of Biblical Archæology*, 1905, vol. xxvii, pp. 185–186) from an ostracon at Edinburgh.

59. Dümichen, *Recueil de Monuments*, vol. iii, pl. 2, 1. 57; cf. Brugsch, *Dictionnaire géographique*, p. 863. Spiegelberg has come to the conclusion that the two brothers Anupu and Baîti are the two gods of Cynopolis, and consequently that the *tale* belongs to a cycle of Cynopolite legends (*Der Gott Bata*, in *Zeitschrift*, vol. xliv, 1907, pp. 98, 99). Cf. Reitzenstein, *Hellenistische Wundererzählungen*, pp. 13 *et seq.*

60. It was Lauth who first recognised the identity of the name Baîti with that of Butes or Bytis (*Ægyptische Chronologie*, 1877, pp. 30–31).

61. Virey, in an article of *Revue des Questions historiques*, 1893, pp. 337–343, and in *La Religion de l'Ancienne Égypte*, 1910, pp. 193 *et seq.*, has interpreted the *Tale of the Two Brothers* by the Osirian myth.

Anupu,[62] as I have said, is connected with Anubis, and his brother Baîti with Baîti the double bull.

Others are derived from history, and recall the memory of some of the more celebrated of the Pharaohs. The instinct that leads story tellers of all countries and all periods to choose a king or personage of high rank as hero is associated in Egypt with very keen patriotic sentiment. A townsman of Memphis, born at the foot of the temple of Ptah, who had grown up, as we may say, under the shadow of the Pyramids, was familiar with Khufuî and his successors: the bas-reliefs displayed their authentic portraits before his eyes, the inscriptions enumerated their titles and proclaimed their glory. Although Thebes does not extend back as far into the past as Memphis, she was no less rich in monuments, on the right bank of the Nile as well as on the left, at Karnak and at Luxor, as well as at Gurneh and at Medinet Habu, the walls spoke to her children of victories won over the nations of Asia and Africa, and of distant expeditions beyond the seas. When the story teller placed a king on the scene, the image he evoked was not merely that of a mannikin decked out in gorgeous attire; his audience and he himself recalled those ever-triumphant princes whose forms and memory were perpetuated among them as in life. It was not sufficient to state that the hero was a sovereign and was called Pharaoh, he must make it clear of which glorious Pharaoh he was speaking—if it was Pharaoh Ramses or Pharaoh Khufuî, a builder of pyramids or a conqueror of the warlike dynasties. Truth frequently suffered. However familiar they might be with the monuments, the Egyptians who had not made a careful study of their annals were inclined to mangle the names and confuse the different epochs. As early as the XIIth dynasty Sinuhît relates his adventures to a certain Khopirkerîya Amenemhaît, who combines with the proper name Amenemhaifc the prenomen of the first Sanuosrît, and who may be sought in vain in the official lists.[63] In the romance now at Petrograd Sanafruî of the IVth dynasty is introduced in company with Amoni of the XIth[64]; Khufuî, Khâfrîya, and the first three Pharaohs of the Vth dynasty play important

62. I have good reasons for believing that the personal name ordinarily read Anupu should be Anupuî, *he who belongs to Anubis*. However, as I have not yet stated them anywhere, I shall preserve the old reading for the present.

63. It is perhaps a mistake of the copyist, as Borchardt would regard it (in *Zeitschrift*, 1890, vol. xxviii, p. 102), also perhaps a combination suggested to the author by some recollection of the combined reign of Sanuosrît I and of Amenemhaît II. Cf. in this volume *The Adventures of Sinuhît*, pp. 55 *et seq.*

64. W. Golénischeff in *Zeitschrift*, 1876, pp. 109–111.

parts in the stories of the Westcar papyrus[65]; Nabkaiûrîya of the IXth appears in one of the Berlin papyri[66]; Uasimarîya and Minibphtah of the XIXth,[67] and Siamânu of the XXIst, with a prenomen Manakhphrê, which recalls that of Thûtmôsis III [68] in the two *Tales of Satni;* Petubastis of the XXVIth,[69] Rahotpu and Manhapurîya in a fragment of a ghost story[70]; and an anonymous king of Egypt in the *Tale of the Doomed Prince.* The names of former times lent an air of reality to a story which it would not otherwise have possessed; a marvellous incident ascribed to a Ramses would appear more probable than it would have done if attributed to some worthy but undistinguished commoner.

In this way, in addition to the official annals, there arose a popular chronicle, occasionally comic and always amusing. The characters of the Pharaohs and even their renown suffered from it. As in Europe in the middle ages there was the cycle of Charlemagne, in which the character and doings of Charlemagne were completely misrepresented, in Egypt there were the cycles of Sesôstris and of Osimandûas, the cycles of Thûtmôsis II, of Thûtmôsis III, of Cheops, so much altered as to be frequently unrecognisable. Entire periods were presented in the guise of romantic epics, and the age of the great Assyrian and Ethiopian invasions furnished inexhaustible material for the rhapsodists; in accordance with fashion, or in harmony with their own birthplace, they grouped the incidents which that warlike period afforded with such prodigality round the Saïte monarchs Bocchoris and Psammetichus,[71] around the Tanite

65. Cf. pp. 17–33 of this volume.

66. He is the king to whom the fellah complains of the theft of his goods by Thotnakhuîti; cf. pp. 42, 53 of this volume.

67. See pp. 96, 98, 99–109, 112–119 *et seq.,* 125 *et seq.,* of this volume.

68. See pp. 128, 129, 130 *et seq.* of this volume. M. Legrain, during our campaign of 1904-5, discovered at Karnak a monument of a Thûtmôsis Manakhphrê, who appears to me to be Thûtmôsis III; the monument is of the late Saïte period or the commencement of the Ptolemaic period.

69. Cf. in pp. 181–216 of this volume the narratives entitled *High Emprise for the Cuirass* and *High Emprise for the Throne.*

70. Cf. pp. 229–232 of the present volume.

71. See *Herodotus,* II, cxlvii-clii, xxx, part of the romance of Psammetichus, the Dodecarchy, the arrival of the men of iron, the flight of the soldiery. Herodotus was inspired by an informant who had the highest respect for the oracle of Bûto, and who related the narratives or the explanation of events furnished by this oracle. Other compatriots were adherents of the Oracle of Jupiter Ammon, and they upheld the versions of the same events that issued thence; in the story of Temanthes and the Carian cocks we have one of the Ammonian traditions of the Dodecarchy.

Petubastis, or round the Beduîn Pakrûr, the great Eastern chieftain.[72] Nevertheless Khufuî is perhaps the most striking example we have of this degeneration. The monuments give a most favourable impression of him. He was a warrior, and he was able to restrain the Nomads who menaced the mining establishments of Sinai. He was a builder, and within a short period, and without injury to the prosperity of the country, he built the highest and most massive of the Pyramids. He was pious, and enriched the gods with statues of gold or other valuable materials; he restored the ancient temples and he built new ones. In short, he belonged to the finest type of the Memphite Pharaoh. This is the evidence of contemporary documents; but when we turn to that of later generations, as it was collected by Greek historians, we are told that Cheops was an impious tyrant, who oppressed his people, and prostituted his daughter in order to complete his pyramid. He banished the priests, he plundered the temples and kept them closed for fifty years. The transition from Khufuî to Cheops cannot have been effected in a day, and were we in possession of more Egyptian literature we might mark out the stages across the centuries, as we are able to do with those between Charlemagne of the annalists and Charlemagne of the troubadours. In the story of the Westcar Papyrus[73] we can detect one moment of the metamorphosis. There already Khufuî is no longer the Pharaoh religiously submissive to the wishes of the gods. When Râ shows himself in opposition to him and upholding the three princes who dethroned his family, Khufuî enters into a conspiracy with a magician to counteract the projects of the god, or to postpone their execution; one sees that he would not hesitate to treat the temples of Sakhîbu as badly as the Cheops of Herodotus treated all the temples of Egypt.

Here, at least, the romance does not follow the lead of historical evidence; on the *Stela of the princess of Bakhtan*[74] romance is surrounded by names and dates so cleverly combined that it has acquired an appearance of reality. The fundamental theme shows nothing that is essentially Egyptian; it is the universal one of a princess possessed by a ghost or a demon, and delivered by a magician, a god, or a saint. The Egyptian variant, when appropriating it, has brought into action the inevitable Ramses II, and has

72. See pp. 181–216 of the present volume, *High Emprise for the Cuirass* and the *High Emprise for the Throne*, and the preponderant part played by Pakrûr in conjunction with and almost above that of the Pharaoh.

73. See pp. 17–33 of this volume.

74. See pp. 141–147 of this volume.

made use of the marriage made by him in the xxxivth year of his reign with the eldest daughter of Khattuîl II, the king of the Khâti, to place the principal scene of action in Asia. It marries him to the princess almost a quarter of a century before the time of the real marriage, and as early as his xvth year she sends an ambassador to tell him that her sister-in-law Bintrashît is obsessed by a spirit, from which she can only be delivered by expert magicians. He sends the best of his, Thotemhabi, but he fails in his exorcisms and returns crestfallen. Ten years pass, during which the spirit remains master of the situation, but in the xxvith year another ambassador is sent. This time one of the figures, one of the *doubles* of Khonsu, consents to exert itself, and travelling in state to the foreign country, chases away the evil one in the presence of the people of Bakhtan.[75] The prince, delighted, plans to keep the deliverer, but a dream followed by illness promptly revenges this untoward project, and in the xxxiiird year Khonsu returns to Thebes loaded with honours and gifts. There is reason for the romance adopting the semblance of history. Khonsu had long remained obscure and little honoured. His popularity, which scarcely began before the end of the XIXth dynasty, grew rapidly under the later Ramessides: at the time of the Tanites and Bubastites it almost equalled that of Amon himself. This could not happen without exciting the jealousy of the ancient god and his partisans, the priests of Khonsu and his devotees must naturally have searched into the past for traditions of a nature to raise their prestige. I do not believe that they invented the whole of our narrative. It existed before they thought of making use of it, and the Asiatic conquests of Ramses, as well as his exotic marriage, necessarily pointed him out as the hero of an incident in which a Syrian princess was the heroine. So much for the name of the king; that of the healing god was above all a matter of fashion or of personal piety. Khonsu was the fashion at the time when the story was written, and to his statue was attributed the glory of having wrought this miraculous cure. The priests confined themselves to recovering this romance which was so in favour of their god, they gave it the semblance of an actual fact, and proclaimed it in the temple.[76]

75. The journey of Unamunu affords a second example of a secondary form of the divinity commissioned by the divinity himself to represent him in a foreign country; the *Amon of the Road* is there the divine ambassador of Amon, as Unamunu is the human ambassador (cf. p. 177, note 19, of the present volume).

76. Erman, *Die Bentreschstele* in *Zeitschrift*, 1884, pp. 59–60. A series of analogous documents should exist of a deified minister of Amenothes III, Amenothes, son of Hapuî, of whom an oracle and funerary temple is known at Thebes. One only has come down to us in original form, the so-called foundation stela of the funerary temple at Deîr el Medineh, first

It is comprehensible that Egyptologists should regard seriously, facts thus stated on a monument with every appearance of authenticity. They were victims of a pious fraud, as our archivists have been when confronted with falsified abbey charters. But it is less comprehensible that they should have allowed themselves to be misled by the romances of Apôpi or of Thutîyi. In the first, which is much mutilated, the shepherd king Apôpi sends message after message to the Theban Saqnûnrîya and summons him to hunt the hippopotami on the Theban lake, which prevented his sleeping. We should scarcely suspect that this strange demand served as a pretext for a religious propaganda, but it is nevertheless the case. If the prince of Thebes refused to obey, he would be forced to relinquish the worship of Râ for that of Sutekhu.[77] The quarrel between Apôpi and Saqnûnrîya also appears to be no other than the local variant of a theme which was popular throughout the East. "The kings of that time sent problems on all sorts of subjects from one to another to be solved, on condition of payment of a sort of tribute or reward according to whether they answered well or ill." It was thus that Hiram of Tyre with the aid of a certain Abdemon unravelled the enigmas propounded to him by Solomon.[78] Without examining in this place the diverse fictions that have been founded on this idea, I will quote one that will render intelligible what exists of the Egyptian narrative. The Pharaoh Nectanebo sent an ambassador to Lycerus, king of Babylon, and to his minister Æsop. "I have mares in Egypt that conceive by the neighing of the horses that are about Babylon: what have you to answer as to this?" The Phrygian took back his reply the next day, and when he arrived at his lodging he ordered children to take a cat and to whip it along the streets. The Egyptians, who adore that animal, were extremely scandalised at the treatment it received; they rescued it from the hands of the children, and went to complain to the king. The Phrygian was brought into his presence. "Do you not know," said the king to him, "that this animal is one of our gods? Why then have you caused it to be treated in this manner?" "It is by reason of the crime that it has committed against Lycerus, for last night it strangled a cock of his that was very industrious, and crowed at all hours."

translated by Birch (Chabas, *Mélanges égyptologiques,* 2nd series, pp. 324–343); others have reached us in a Greek dress.

77. Maspero, *Études égyptiennes,* vol. i, pp. 195–216; cf. the complete translation of the fragments of the romance, pp. 223, 227–228 of this volume.

78. Ælius Dius, fragm. 2, in Müller-Didot, *Fragmenta Historicorum Græcorum,* vol. iv, p. 398; cf. *Ménadre d'Ephèse,* fragm. 1, in Müller-Didot, *op. cit.* vol. iv, p. 446.

"You are a liar," replied the king; "how is it possible for a cat to make so long a journey in so short a time?" "And how is it possible," said Æsop, "for your mares to hear our horses neigh at so great a distance, and to conceive by hearing them?"[79] A challenge carried by the king of the country of the negroes to Pharaoh Usimares leads up to the crisis of the second romance of Satni, but there it concerns a closed letter the contents of which had to be guessed,[80] and not prodigious animals that the two rivals might possess. In the *Quarrel* the hippopotami of the Lake of Thebes which the king of the South was to hunt down, in order that the king of the North might sleep in peace, are relations of the horses whose neighing carried as far as Egypt, and of the cat who accomplished the journey to Assyria, there and back, in one night.[81] I have no doubt that, after having received the second message from Apôpi, Saqnûnrîya found among his councillors a sage as far-seeing as Æsop, whose prudence rescued him safe and sound. Did the romance go farther, and did it describe the war that broke out between the North and the South, and then the deliverance of Egypt from the yoke of the Shepherd kings? The manuscript does not take us far enough to enable us to guess the dénouement arrived at by the author.

Although the romance of Thutîyi is incomplete at the commencement, the narrative does not suffer much from the loss. The lord of Joppa, having revolted against Thûtmôsis III, Thutîyi attracts him to the Egyptian camp under pretext of showing him the great staff of Pharaoh, and kills him. But to get rid of the man was not enough if the town still held out. He therefore encloses five hundred men in immense jars and transports them to the foot of the walls, and there he forces the chief equerry to announce that the Egyptians have been beaten and that their general is being brought a prisoner. This is believed, the gates are opened, the soldiers come out of their jars and seize the place. Is this an account of a real episode in Egyptian warfare? Joppa was one of the first places in Syria that was occupied by the Egyptians. Thûtmôsis I had subdued it, and it figures in the list of conquests of Thûtmôsis III. Its position under its new masters was not particularly unpleasant; it paid tribute, but it kept its own laws and its hereditary chieftain. The *vanquished of Jôpu*—as *vanquished* is the title of Syrian princes in the language of the Egyptian gov-

79. *La vie d'Ésope le Phrygien,* translated by La Fontaine (*Fables de La Fontaine,* edit. Lemerre, vol. i, pp. 41–42, 45).

80. See pp. 125 *et seq.* of this volume.

81. See pp. 225, 276–227 of this volume.

ernment—were bound to act frequently in the same manner as the *vanquished of Tunipu,* the *vanquished of Kodshu* and many others, who constantly revolted and brought down the wrath of Pharaoh upon their people. That the lord of Joppa should be rebelling against his suzerain is by no means unlikely in itself—even when it is against a Pharaoh so powerful and stern in repression as Thûtmôsis III. The officer Thutîyi is also not entirely a fictitious person. A Thutîyi is known who also lived under Thûtmôsis and was entrusted with large commands in Syria and Phœnecia. His titles were "Hereditary Prince, Delegate of the king in all foreign countries situated on the Mediterranean, Royal scribe, General of the army, Governor of the countries of the North."[82] There is no reason why in one of his campaigns he should not have had to encounter the lord of Joppa.

The principal actors may thus be historical people, but do the deeds attributed to them bear the impress of historical facts, or do they belong to the realm of fancy? Thutîyi insinuates himself as a turncoat into the confidence of the principal foe and then assassinates him. He disguises himself as a prisoner of war in order to gain an entrance into the town. With him he took soldiers dressed as slaves, who carried other soldiers concealed in earthen jars. Among the greater number of classical authors we find examples that sufficiently justify the use of the first two tricks. I fully agree that they may have been employed by the Egyptian generals as well as by those of Greece and Rome. The third includes an element that is not only probable but real—the introduction into a fortress of soldiers dressed as slaves or in the guise of prisoners of war. Polyænus relates how Nearchus the Cretan took Telmissus by pretending to confide a troop of female slaves to Antipatridas the governor. Children wearing chains accompanied the women with the outfit of musicians and the whole guarded by an escort of armed men. Once entered into the citadel, each opened his flute case, which contained a dagger in place of a musical instrument; they then fell upon the garrison and seized the town.[83] If Thutîyi had confined himself to lading his people with ordinary jars or boxes enclosing well-sharpened blades, I should have no objection to

---

82. Cf. Birch, *Mémoire sur une patère égyptienne,* in Chabas, *Œuvres diverses,* vol. i, pp. 225–274, and the supplement of the memoir of Birch in Th. Deveria, *Mémoires et Fragments,* vol. i, pp. 35-53.

83. Polyænus, *Strat.* v, xi. Cf. analogous events that occurred in 1037 at Edessa (G. Schlumberger, *l'Épopée Byzantine,* vol. iii, pp. 198–199), and with the Turks of Asia Minor, Casanova, *Numismatique des Danichmendites,* p. 25.

make as to the authenticity of the incident. But he crushed them under the weight of huge tuns of earthenware, each of which contained an armed soldier or chains in lieu of weapons. To find the equivalent of this stratagem we must come down to the veracious stories of the *Arabian Nights*. The captain of the forty thieves, in order to lead his troop unrecognised to Ali Baba, could think of nothing better than to hide them in jars, one man in each, and to represent himself as an oil-merchant who under stress of circumstances desired to place his merchandise in safety. Here again the Arab romancer was more concerned than the Egyptian to give his story a semblance of probability, and he places the pots on the backs of animals and not on those of men. The setting of the story is historic, the groundwork is pure imagination.

If modern Egyptologists were thus misled, the ancients must have been still more completely duped by similar inventions. The interpreters and priests of the lower class, who acted as guides to foreigners, knew fairly well what the edifice was that they were showing, its founder, who had restored or enlarged it, and which part bore the cartouche of which sovereign, but as soon as they were questioned as to details they stopped short, or could only recount fables. The Greeks had dealings with them, and one has only to read the second book of Herodotus to see what sort of information he received as to the past history of Egypt. Some of the legends accepted by him included a collection of facts more or less distorted, such as the history of the XXVIth Dynasty, or of ancient times, that of Sesostris. The greater part of the stories told by him anterior to the accession of Psammatichus I are absolute romances, in which there is no shade of truth. The subject of Rhampsinitus and the ingenious thief exists in other places besides Egypt.[84] The legendary life of the kings who built the pyramids has nothing in common with their real life. The chapter devoted to Pheron contains an abbreviated version of a humorous satire on women.[85] The meeting of Proteus with Helen and Menelaus is the Egyptian adaptation of a Greek tradition.[86] Formerly one might have wondered whether the guides had drawn on their own imaginations; the discovery of Egyptian romances has shown that there as elsewhere, their imagination failed. Like parrots they were contented to repeat the fables that were current among the people, and their task was rendered more

---

84. The variants have been collected by Schiefner, in the *Bulletin de l'Académie de Saint-Pétersbourg*, vol. xiv, cols. 299–316.

85. *Herodotus*, Bk. II, chap. cxi.

86. Id., *ibid.*, chap. cxvi.

easy by the fact that the greater number of the heroes were invested with authentic names and titles. Thus the dynasties given by those historians who gathered their knowledge from them are a mixture of authentic names. Menes, Sabaco, Cheops, Chephren, Mykerinus, or distorted by the addition of a parasitic element intended to differentiate tham from their homonyms, Rhampsinitus by the side of Rhamses, and Psammeni-tos with Psammis or Psammetichus, the prenomens altered by pronunci-ation, Osimanduas for Uasimarîya;[87] popular nicknames, Sesûsrîya, Sesôstris-Sesoôsis; titles, Pherô, Pruîti, turned into proper names; and finally names which were entirely fictitious, such as Asychis, Uchoreus, Anysis.

The passion for historical romance did not disappear with the national dynasties. As early as the Ptolemies, Nectanebo, the last king of the indigenous race, had become the centre of an important cycle. He had been metamorphosed into a skilful magician, a consummate maker of tal-ismans; he figured as the father of Alexander the Macedonian. When we pass on to the Roman period we find the Byzantine and Coptic literature derived from it had also the exploits of Cambyses and Alexander, the lat-ter copied from the writings of the Pseudo-Callisthenes[88]; and there is no need to scan the Arab chronicles attentively in order to discover in them an imaginary history of Egypt borrowed from Coptic books.[89] Whether the works that deal with this jumble be Latin, Greek, or Arabic, it is easy to imagine how chronology has been treated amidst these productions of popular imagination. Herodotus and, following his example, almost all writers ancient and modern up to our times, have placed Moiris, Sesôstris, and Rhampsinitus before the Pharaohs who built the pyramids. The names of Sesôstris and of Rhampsinitus are relics of the XIXth and XXth dynasties, those of the pyramid builders—Cheops, Chephren, Mykeri-nus—carry us back to the IVth dynasty. It is as though a French histo-rian placed Charlemagne after Bonaparte, but the cavalier fashion in which Egyptian romancers treat the sequence of reigns shows us how it was that Herodotus made the same mistake. One of the stories of which we have the original in a papyrus, that of Satni, introduces two kings and

87. The same phenomenon of the transcription of an Egyptian r-l by the combination of nd is found in Mandulis, the Greek form of the name of the Nubian god Maruri, Maruli, Maluli.

88. See pp. 243–255 of this volume. The fragments of the romance of Cambyses were dis-covered and published by H. Schäfer, in the *Sitzungsberichte* of the Berlin Academy of Sciences.

89. See Maspero, *Le Livre des Merveilles*, in the *Journal des Savants*, 1899, pp. 69–86, 154–172.

a prince royal. The kings were named Uasimarîya and Mînibphtah, the prince royal, Satni Khamoîs. Uasimarîya is one of the prenomens of Ramses II, one that he bore in his youth while he was still associated with his father. Mînibphtah is an alteration, perhaps a voluntary one, of the name of Mînephtah, son and successor of Ramses II. Khamoîs, also a son of Ramses II, administered the empire over twenty years for his aged father. If there was a sovereign in Ancient Egypt whose memory was retained by the fellahîn, it was certainly Ramses II. Tradition had placed to his credit all the great deeds that had been wrought by the whole succession of Pharaohs during long centuries. One might therefore hope that the romancer would respect the verities at least so far as they concerned this popular idol, and that he would not interfere with his genealogy:

UASIMARÎYA RAMSES II

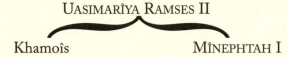

Khamoîs   MÎNEPHTAH I

He has, however, ignored it. Khamoîs is there, as in history, the son of Uasimarîya, but Mînibphtah, the other son, is displaced. He is represented as being so much anterior to Uasimarîya, that an old man consulted by Satni-Khamoîs as to certain events that happened in the time of Mînibphtah, is forced to invoke the testimony of a far-off ancestor: "The father of the father of my father spake to the father of my father, saying, 'The father of the father of my father said to the father of my father: The tombs of Ahuri and of Maîhêt are below the northern corner of the house

MÎNIBPHTAH

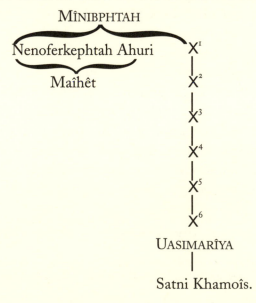

Nenoferkephtah Ahuri   X[1]

Maîhêt   X[2]

                              X[3]

                              X[4]

                              X[5]

                              X[6]

UASIMARÎYA

Satni Khamoîs.

of the priest."'[90] Thus there appear to be at least six generations between the Mînibphtah of the romance and Uasimarîya.

The son Mînibphtah has become an ancestor and remote predecessor of Uasimarîya, his own father, and to make the confusion complete, the foster-brother of Satni bears a name of the Persian period, Eiernharerôu, Inarôs.[91] Satni, on the contrary, now become the contemporary of the Assyrian Sennacherib,[92] is represented as living and active six hundred years after his death. In a third story[93] he, with his father Ramses II, is placed fifteen hundred years after a Pharaoh who appears to be a duplicate of Thûtmôsis III.

Let us suppose a traveller as ready to set down the miracles of Satni as Herodotus was to believe in the wealth of Rhampsinitus. Would he not have fallen into the same error with regard to Mînibphtah and Ramses II that Herodotus committed with regard to Rhampsinitus and Cheops? He would have inverted the order of the reigns and placed the fourth king of the XIXth dynasty long before the third. The dragoman who showed the temple of Ptah and the pyramids of Gizeh to visitors had apparently inherited some story which set forth, no doubt like many others, how a Ramses called Rhampsinitus, the wealthiest of kings, had been succeeded by Cheops, the most impious of mankind. He held forth in this manner to Herodotus, and the worthy Herodotus inserted it in his book. As Cheops, Chephrên, and Mykerinus form a well-defined group, and their pyramids stand together, the guides had no occasion to break the order of their succession, and having displaced Cheops, it was necessary to treat Chephrên, Mykerinus, and the prince named Asychis, *the rich*,[94] in the same manner. To-day, when we can check the statements of the Greek traveller by the evidence of the inscriptions, it matters little that he was mistaken; he did not write a history of Egypt. Even had he been better informed, he would not have developed that part of his writings more fully which relates to Egypt. All the dynasties would have been crowded into a few pages, and he would have taught us nothing that we do not learn to-day from the

90. See p. 116 of this volume.

91. On the identity of the name Eiernharerôu and the Greek form Inarôs cf. Spiegelberg, *Demotische Miscellen*, in the *Recueil de Travaux*, 1906, vol. xxviii, pp. 19, 599.

92. Herodotus, Bk. II., chap. cxli., cf. pp. 137, 138 of this volume.

93. *The Veritable History of Satni-Khamoîs*, p. 136.

94. Asûkhis, Asychis, is the Hellenised form of a name Ashukhî[tu], which signifies "the rich one," and which is not met with before the Saite and Greek periods.

monuments themselves. On the other hand, we should have lost most
of the strange and often comic stories that he has told so delightfully
on the authority of his guides. We should not be familiar with Pheron,
nor with Proteus, Sethôn nor Rhampsinitus, and I consider that would
have been a great loss. The hieroglyphs tell us, or they will tell us one
day, what was done by the Cheops, Ramses, and Thûtmôsis of the real
world, Herodotus tells us what was said of them in the streets of Memphis. That part of his second book which is filled with their doings is
far better for our purpose than a course of history. It is a chapter of the
history of literature, and the romances we read there are as completely
Egyptian as the romances we find in the papyri. No doubt it would be
better to possess them in their original language, but the Greek dress in
which they are clothed is not sufficiently opaque to disguise them;
modified as they are in detail, they preserve sufficient of their primitive
physiognomy to be able without too great disparity to figure side by
side with the *Tale of the Two Brothers* or the *Memoirs of Sinuhît*.

III

So much for the names: the setting is purely Egyptian, and so accurate
that a complete picture of morals and of society might be drawn from the
romances alone. Pharaoh is here depicted as less divine than we should
be disposed to consider him if we judged him solely by the haughty
demeanour accorded him by his sculptors in triumphal and religious
scenes. The romancer does not shrink at times from depicting him as
ridiculous and placing him in situations that contrast with the superhuman dignity of his appearance. He is deceived by his wife like an ordinary mortal,[95] robbed and then duped at every turn by thieves,[96] snatched
away by a magician from the midst of his palace, and severely thrashed
before an obscure negro king.[97] It was the revenge taken by the despoiled
and beaten inferior classes, against the tyrant who oppressed them. The
fellah who had just smarted under the rod for having refused to pay taxes,
consoled himself for his empty pockets and bleeding wounds by hearing

95. Thus the Pheron of Herodotus, II, cxi.
96. Cf. *The Tale of Rhampsinitus,* pp. 163–167 of this volume.
97. Manakhphrê Siamânu in *The Veritable History of Satni,* pp. 128–130 of the present
volume.

how Manakhphrê Siamânu had received three hundred strokes in one night, and how he had piteously exhibited his bruises to the courtiers. These were but passing incidents, and generally his paramount authority remained intact in fiction as in history. Etiquette was very strictly maintained between him and his subjects, but ceremonial ones satisfied, if the man pleased as in the case of Sinuhît[98] he would condescend to become human and the *good god* would show himself a good fellow[99]; he is even jovial and jokes about the rustic appearance of the hero, royal jests that rouse the mirth of those around him, but of which the salt must have lost its savour in the course of ages, as we cannot appreciate them.[100] He goes even farther with his intimates, and without shame gets drunk before them and in spite of them.[101] He is also a prey to that overwhelming ennui that oriental despots have experienced at all periods, and that ordinary pleasures are not sufficient to dispel.[102] Like Harûn-ar-rashid of the *Arabian Nights,* Khufuî and Sanafruî attempted to gain relief by listening to marvellous stories, or being present at magic séances, but only with moderate success. Occasionally, however, some minister more alert than the rest would invent some diversion that by its novelty would enable him to spend a day or two almost joyfully. Sanafruî must have been almost as wearied as Harûn of the delights of his harem; his sorcerer nevertheless discovered a means of arousing his interest by making a crew of young girls row in front of him, barely veiled by nets with wide meshes.[103] Civilisations have disappeared and religions have changed, but the spirit of the East remains the same under all masks, and Mohammed Ali in this century found nothing better than Sanafruî found in his. At Shubra we can still visit baths constructed on a peculiar plan. "There is," says Gérard de Nerval, "a white marble basin, surrounded by columns, Byzantine in style, with a fountain in the centre, from which the water emerges through crocodiles' mouths. The whole enclosure is lighted with gas, and on summer nights the Pasha was rowed by the women of his harem on the basin in a gilded *cange* or pleasure boat. These fair dames also bathed before the eyes of their lord, but in dressing gowns of *crêpe de*

98. See pp. 75 *et seq.* of this volume.

99. Good God, the Good God, is one of the formulæ with which the protocol of the Pharaohs commences, and one of the titles most frequently given to them in the texts.

100. See p. 76 of this volume.

101. See the *Story of a Mariner,* pp. 233–237 of this volume.

102. See p. 19 of this volume.

103. See *King Khufuî and the Magicians,* p. 23.

soie, as the Koran forbids nudities." No doubt! but the crêpe of Mohammed Ali was scarcely less transparent than the net of Sanafruî.

Sanafruî was a Pharaoh of one of the mighty dynasties, who wielded undisputed authority over the whole of Egypt, and under whom the barons were merely subjects, slightly superior to the rest in rank. But after centuries of absolute power royalty became weakened, and no longer commanded the respect of the feudal lords. These obtained the upper hand with new characteristics adapted to the various periods, and the most powerful chieftains gained their independence, or very nearly so, each in his hereditary fief. Pharaoh was then no more than an over-lord, scarcely more wealthy or more powerful than the others, who was obeyed according to traditional usage, and with whom the great barons would join in alliance against their rivals, to prevent their usurping the throne and replacing a merely nominal sovereignty by an effective domination. Such is Petubastis in the *High Emprise for the Cuirass* and *for the Throne.*[104] There is no longer the imperious ruler such as other romances portray in Cheops, Thûtmôsis, or Ramses II. He is still by divine right the so-called possessor of the two Egypts; he alone wears the double diadem, he alone is the son of Râ, he alone has the right to enclose his names in cartouch-es, and it is according to the years of his reign that the official dating of the events that occurred during his lifetime is reckoned. He is before all things peaceable, pious, submissive to all the demands of religion, the prototype of that being, without free will or power of initiative that the Greeks of the Macedonian period represent as an ideal prince.[105] The power does not rest in his hands. Of the ancient Pharaonic domain noth-ing now remains to him except a small part, the nomes of Tanis and Memphis, and perhaps two or three others in that neighbourhood. Fam-ilies, mostly akin to his own, have appropriated the greater part of the territory, and press him closely, Pakrûr on the east in the Wady Tumilât, the great lord of Amon at Diospolis in the north at Mendes and Busiris, Petekhonsu and Pemu on the south, one at Athribis and the other at Heliopolis, not to mention the lords of Sebennytos, of Sais, of Meîtum, of far-away Elephantine, and a dozen or more of less importance. In the-ory all of these owe him homage, tribute, implicit obedience, service at court, and militia, but they do not always fulfil their obligations with

104. See pp. 184, 195, 198 *et seq.* of the present volume.

105. Cf. Diodorus of Sicily (I, lxx-lxxii), who borrowed the description of the life of the kings from the work of Hecatiæus of Abdera on Egypt.

good grace, and peace very rarely reigns among them. Each has his army and his fleet, in which Libyan, Syrian, Ethiopian, and even Asiatic mercenaries were largely employed on occasions. They had their vassals, their court, their finances, their gods by whom they swore, their colleges of priests or of magicians; they formed alliances, they quarrelled, they fought, they chased each other from one bank of the Nile to the other, they coalesced against Pharaoh to deprive him of fragments of his domain, and then, when one of them rose too high and obtained the ascendancy, they would temporarily combine against him, or call in Ethiopians from outside to compel him to return to the ranks. It was a feudal system almost similar to that of France, and the same conditions gave rise to conditions analogous with those that obtained there during the Middle Ages.

See, for instance, what happens in the *High Emprise for the Cuirass*, the fable that Krall has reconstructed with so much ingenuity. The lord of Heliopolis, one Inarôs, possessed a cuirass of which his rivals were envious. He dies, and during the days of mourning that precede the funeral the Great Lord of Diospolis carries it off in some way unknown to us. The son of Inarôs, Pemu the Small, claims it, and when it is refused he declares loudly that he will recover it by force. This would mean war, clan against clan, town against town, nome against nome, and god against god, if Petubastis did not intervene. But the vassals would hardly have listened to him had not the great chieftain of the East, Pakrûr, joined with him, and the two together force the mass of smaller lordlings to obey them.[106] They insist that instead of commencing a destructive campaign the adversaries and their partisans shall fight in the lists according to the regulations that governed that sort of encounter, and which apparently were very complicated. They have platforms erected on which they sit as judges. They assign a particular post to each champion, Pakrûr matches them one against another, and if one is left out when the pairing is complete he is held in reserve for any unforeseen occasion that may arise.[107] Everything is regulated as in a tourney, and we may presume that the weapons are blunted. But the treachery of the lord of Diospolis upsets all the measures taken. He attacks Pemu before the arrival of his allies, and although the intervention of Pakrûr prevents his carrying his advantage

---

106. See pp. 184, 195, 196–197, 198–199 of this volume, the reiterated advice of Petubastis, and the efforts of the different lords concerned to prevent the struggle developing into a serious war.

107. See the episode of Montubaal, pp. 195 *et seq.* of this volume.

too far, his felony leaves an angry impression on the minds of his adversaries. The longer the engagement lasts the hotter grow the tempers, and the combatants forget the moderation enjoined on them by the master of the joust. They provoke and insult one another, attacking out of order, and the victor, forgetting that he is taking part in a peaceful passage of arms, prepares to slay the vanquished as he would do in battle. The king and Pakrûr hasten to the spot, and it is with difficulty that they prevent the catastrophe by their injunctions or entreaties. When a truce is proclaimed after several hours of this fighting it appears, however, that neither party has suffered greatly, and that they have escaped with a few wounds. We may compare this with one of the encounters of the eleventh century between French and Anglo-Normans, when after a whole day of exchange of blows the two armies would part, full of admiration for each other's prowess, and leaving three knights on the field stifled by their armour. The Bedûin of Arabia do the same thing to-day, and their customs enable us to understand why Petubastis and Pakrûr strove so hard to avoid the death of any prince; if a chief were killed it was obligatory on his clan to avenge him, and the vendetta would survive for numberless years. Petubastis did not wish that Egypt should be desolated by war in his time, and as his wish was in accord with the popular interests it prevailed in this instance.

The exploits of the Pharaohs were at times presented in different ways, according to whether they were composed by the Memphites or the Thebans. The provinces of the north and of the south of Egypt differed greatly, not only in language, but in character and political tendencies. Misunderstandings frequently occurred between them, and these easily degenerated into bad feeling and civil war. Those kings who were popular with one were little liked by the other, or were not known by the same name. In the Memphite temple of Ptah, Ramses II was mentioned on the monuments by his name Sesusi or Sesusrîya, from which the legend of Sesôstris arose.[108] At Thebes his prenomen of Uasimarîya predominated, and from this he became the Usimarês of the romance of Satni, and the Osimanduas whose victories were celebrated and whose palace was

108. E. de Rougé demonstrated that Sesôstris was no other than Ramses II (*le Véritable Sesôstris*, in the *Œuvres diverses*, vol. iii, pp. 11–14). Sethe has tried to prove that he was Sanûosrit III (*Sesôstris*, 1900, p. 24). I have tried to show that de Rougé was right, and that Manetho was mistaken in identifying the Sesôstris of Herodotus with a Pharaoh of the XIIth dynasty. (*La Geste de Sesôstris* in the *Journal des Savants*, 1901, pp. 599–609, 665–683.)

described by the writers copied by Diodorus of Sicily. The discovery by Spiegelberg of a new romance shows that Petubastis shared the same fate. Some of the personages by whom he was surrounded in Krall's romance reappear in the other, but the object of the quarrel is different. It is a throne or pulpit, and I suspect that here it concerns a form of the divinity in frequent use at the Græco-Roman period in the Theban nome, an indeterminate emblem of nature, perhaps the image of a sacred stone placed on a chair of state. Probably Amon manifested himself thus to his son Alexander of Macedonia, when he came to consult him in his oasis.[109] The legitimate heir, as in the *High Emprise for the Cuirass,* was the child of the first owner, a prophet of Horus of Bûto, but it devolved on the son of the king Ankhhoru, and the refusal to give it up was the origin of the conflict. Elsewhere[110] we shall observe the vicissitudes of the combats fought at Thebes by the champions of the two parties in the presence of the sovereign; here we must point out that the prophet of Horus is assisted in his demands by thirteen sturdy herdsmen, whose prowess at first assures him victory over the Egyptian army. The clans, half of them fishermen and half of them shepherds, that inhabited the marshy plains of the northern Delta, the Bucolics, submitted very unwillingly to the yoke of regularly constituted authority, whether Greek or Roman. They seized the slightest occasion to declare war against it, and were usually only subdued at the price of lengthy and expensive efforts. The most bloody of their revolts was in the year 172 A.D,[111] but there were others under the Ptolemies of which the remembrance lingered long in the valley of the Nile. If Heliodorus, a Greek romancer of the late empire, was pleased to describe their pillaging habits,[112] we cannot be surprised that an indigenous author should have chosen them as types of brutal courage.

In contrast with the *Exploits of the Pharaohs,* full of movement and the noise of battle, the first pages of the *Tale of the Two Brothers*[113] presents an admirable picture of the life and habitual occupations of the ordinary fellah. Anupu, the elder, has his house and wife; Baîti, the younger, has nothing, and he lives with his brother, but not like a relative with a relative, nor a guest with his host. He takes charge of the cattle, he leads

---

109. Cf. on this point Daressy, in the *Annales du Service des Antiquités,* vol. ix, pp. 66–69.
110. See pp. 202–216 of the present volume.
111. A summary account has come down to us from Dio Cassius, lxxi, 4.
112. Heliodorus, *Ethiopios* I.
113. pp. 3–6 of this volume.

them to the fields and brings them back to the stable, he guides the plough, he mows, he binds the hay, he beats out the corn, and brings in the hay. Every evening before going to bed, he puts the household bread into the oven, and he rises early to take it out baked. During the season for field work, it is he who runs to the farm to fetch the seed, and carries a load sufficient for several men on his back. He spins the linen or wool as he leads his animals to pastures of good grass, and when the inundation confines men and beasts within doors, he seats himself at the loom and weaves. In short he is a servant, a servant united by blood relationship to his master, but still a servant. We must not conclude from this the existence of the law of primogeniture in Egypt, nor yet that custom in default of law placed the younger in the power of the elder. All the children of one father inherited his goods in equal shares, whatever might be their order of birth. The law was explicit in this respect, and the benefit extended not only to the legitimate children, but to those born out of wedlock; the sons and daughters of a concubine inherited by the same title and in the same proportion as the sons or daughters of the regularly married wife.[114] Anupu and Baîti, if they had been children of different mothers, would have been equal, according both to law and custom. How much more so when, as the story particularly states, they were children of the same father and the same mother. The obvious inequality of their position was therefore not due to the law, and we must seek for some other cause. Supposing that after the death of their parents, instead of remaining with Anupu, Baîti had taken the half which was his share of the inheritance and gone to seek his fortune in the world, to what extortions and annoyances he would be exposed. The fellah whose story is told in the *Berlin papyrus* No. II, and who traded between Egypt and the Plain of Salt,[115] was robbed by the liege-man of a great lord through whose territory he passed.[116] He brought a complaint, and inquiry proved the justice of his claim; it would be supposed that his due would immediately be rendered him. Not at all! The man who had robbed him belonged to one in high position, and had friends, relations, and a *mas-*

114. Wilkinson, *Manners and Customs of the Ancient Egyptians,* first series, vol. iii, p. 320.

115. The name of the Oasis that surrounds the natron lakes, the *Scythiaoa regio* of classical geography (Dümichen, *Die Oasen der Libyschen Wüste,* p. 29 *et seq.*; Brugsch, *Reise nach der Grossen Oase,* pp. 74 *et seq.*)

116. Cf. *The Lamentations of the Fellah,* pp. 38–54 of this volume. A stela of Harmhabi, unfortunately damaged, shows the misfortunes to which peasants were exposed who left home, even those who merely undertook a journey to pay taxes to Pharaoh.

ter. The peasant was merely a *masterless man*. The author takes care to point this out, and to have no master was an unpardonable error in feudal Egypt. A single individual was defenceless against the great lords who shared the country between them, and the officials who exploited it on behalf of Pharaoh. The poor wretch wept, implored, and repeatedly urged his piteous plea. As after all he was in the right, Pharaoh commanded that his wife should be cared for, and that he should not be allowed to die of hunger; but whether the matter was to be adjudged and sentence delivered was a matter to be decided later. We now know that he obtained justice in the end, but only after having delivered eloquent harangues for the entertainment of Pharaoh. The distress and delays to which he was subjected appear to afford sufficient explanations of the reason why Baîti remained with his brother. The elder brother, become master as a means of precaution, was a protector for the younger one, who guarded him and his property, until the time when a wealthy marriage, the caprice of the sovereign, a sudden rise in position, an unexpected inheritance, or merely admission among the scribes, should insure him a more powerful protector, when possibly he himself would in turn become protector to some one in need of such aid.

Thus in considering each tale in detail we see that on the material side the civilisation it describes is purely Egyptian. The scenes at the beginning of the *Tale of Two Brothers* might easily be illustrated by scenes from the paintings in the rock tombs of Thebes; the expressions used by the author are found almost word for word in the texts that explain the pictures.[117] Even to the most intimate events of private life, such as births, there is nothing which cannot be explained and illustrated by scenes taken from the temples. Whether at Luxor,[118] at Deîr-el-Baharî,[119] or at Erment,[120] whether they concern Mutemua, Ahmasi, or Cleopatra, we have pictures before our eyes from which we can exactly realise what happened when Ruditdidît gave birth to the three sons of Râ.[121] The patient is crouched on her chair or on her bed, one of the midwives clasps her from behind, and another, crouched in front of her, receives the child as

117. Maspero, *Notes sur quelques points de Grammaire et d'Histoire*, in *Zeitschrift*, 1879, pp. 58–63 (cf. *Mélanges de Mythologie*, vol. iv, pp. 66–73).

118. Gayet, *Le Temple de Louxor*, pl. lxiii-lxvii.

119. E. Naville, *Deîr el Bahari*, vol. ii, pl. xlii-li.

120. The scenes in the temple of Erment, now destroyed, have been preserved by Champollion, *Monuments de l'Égypte*, pl. cxlv, 6, 7, cxlviii, *ter;* by Rosellini, *Monumenti del Culto*, pl. lii-liii; and by Lepsius, *Denkm*. iv, pl, 59c, 60a.

121. See pp. 29–31 of this volume.

it is born. She hands it to the nurses, who wash it, hold it in their arms, caress, and give it suck. An examination of the monuments shows that the same is the case with those stories of which we possess the original hieratic; and I have proved it also for the greater number of those we possess only in a foreign language. It is the case with Rhampsinitus. I do not intend to repeat the text word for word, in order to show that it is substantially Egyptian, notwithstanding the Greek dress with which Herodotus has clothed it; I will content myself with discussing two of the points which have been objected to as indicating a foreign origin.

The architect commissioned to construct a treasury for Pharaoh shaped and laid a stone so perfectly that two men, nay! even one alone could move it from its place.[122] It has been said that the movable stone was not an Egyptian invention. In Egypt the public edifices were built with stones of immense size; and not all the skill in the world would enable an architect to dispose of a block in the manner described by Herodotus. Strabo, however, was aware that the entrance to the Great Pyramid was by a passage the mouth of which was concealed by a movable stone[123]; and in addition to the Pyramid, we have proved that the same method was employed for the hiding-places that abounded in the temples. At Denderah, for instance, there are a dozen crypts concealed in the foundations or thickness of the walls. They communicate with the temple by narrow passages which open into the chambers in the form of holes which to day are open and vacant. But formerly they were closed by a stone *ad hoc,* of which the front turned outwards was carved like the rest of the wall.[124] A passage in the *Tale of Khufuî* appears to state that the crypt at Heliopolis, where the god Thoth concealed his library, was closed by a block similar to those of Mariette.[125] The inscriptions also show that when a secret chamber was made all possible precautions were taken to prevent its being known not only to visitors, but also to the inferior priesthood. "The door is unknown to the profane; if they seek for it, no one finds it except the prophets of the

---

122. *Herodotus*, II, cxxi, and p. 164 of this volume. Cf. *Nouveau fragment d'un commentaire sur le second livre d'Hérodote*, in Maspero, *Mélanges de Mythologie et d'Archéologie*, vol. iii, pp. 416–416.

123. Strabo, xvii, p. 508: cf, L. Borchardt, *Der λιθοδ εξαιρεσιμοδ*, in *Zeitschrift*, vol. xxxv, pp. 87–89. Flinders Petrie has likewise shown that the great pyramid of Dahchûr was closed by means of a pivoted stone (*The Pyramids and Temples of Gizeh*, pp. 145, 167–169, and pl. xi).

124. Mariette, *Dendérah*, texte, pp. 227–228. Jomard had already remarked on a movable stone of this kind in the temple of Deîr el Medineh (*Description spéciale de Memphis et des Pyramides* in the *Description de l'Égypte*, 2nd edition, vol. v, p. 444).

125. See the story with the title *King Khufuî and the Magicians*, pp. 17–33 of this volume.

goddess."[126] Like the architect of Rhampsinitus and his sons, those prophets of Denderah knew the entrance to a secret chamber crowded with metals and precious objects, and they alone possessed the knowledge. By raising a stone, of which nothing was known by the vulgar, they disclosed the opening of a passage; into this they crawled, and in a few moments arrived at the treasury. When the block was replaced, the most experienced eye could not distinguish the precise spot where the passage opened.[127]

Later on, the son of the architect who had escaped death, contrived to make the guards who were watching over the corpse of his brother intoxicated, and shaved them on the right side.[128] Wilkinson, I think, was the first to remark that in Egypt the soldiers are represented without beards, that all classes of society shaved habitually, and that the only bearded personages must have been barbarians.[129] Since then his assertion has been continually repeated as a proof of the foreign origin of the story. But here, as in many other instances that occur in his work, the assertion is the result of a too hasty study of the monuments. The pure race of Egyptians could wear a beard, and those who wished did wear one, as is fully proved by the monuments of all periods. Moreover, the police were not all natives; they were recruited principally from a tribe of Libyan origin, the *Mazaiu*, and since, as Wilkinson himself remarks, foreigners were exempted from the ordinary usage, why should not the officers whom Rhampsinitus put in charge of the corpse be wearing hair on their chin or cheeks? The soldiers who composed the Egyptian army, as it was in the time of the Saites and Persians, as it was in fact when Herodotus knew about it, were some of them Libyans, and some Semitic mercenaries, Carians or Greeks, while others formed part of the Persian garrison, and were all of them bearded as a rule.[130] It must therefore be conceded that for contemporary Egyptians there was nothing unusual in seeing bearded police, whether they were born in the country or brought in from abroad; the episode of the shaved beard is no proof against the indigenous origin of the story.

We will now turn from the material details. The moral side of the civilisation is no less accurately reproduced in our narratives. No doubt we

126. Mariette, *Dendérah*, Plates, vol. iii, pl. 30, c.

127. See Mariette, *Dendérah*, vol. v, *Supplément;* the plate in which the plan and the method of opening are shown.

128. Herodotus, II, cxxi; cf. pp. 165–166 of this volume.

129. Cf. Rawlinson's *Herodotus*, vol. ii, p. 165, note 4.

130. A stela of the XVIIIth dynasty provides us with the portrait of an Asiatic mercenary, who died in Egypt; he is completely bearded (Spiegelberg, in *Zeitschrift*, vol. xxxvi, pp. 126–127).

must be on our guard against accepting as absolute fact all that they appear to tell us of the private life of the Egyptians. Like modern authors, the writers of those times sought to develop those sentiments and characters which were exceptional among the great mass of the nation. If we were forced to judge the Egyptian women by the portraits we find in these stories, our opinion of their chastity would be a very low one. The daughter of Rhampsinitus throws open her chamber and yields herself to any who will pay her; it may be that she is a victim for reasons of state, but she is a resigned victim.[131] Tbubui greets Satni, and at the first interview declares herself ready to share her couch with him. If she appears undecided at the decisive moment, and several times causes delays, it is no feeling of shame that makes her hesitate; it is only the determination to make him pay as highly as possible for what she intends to sell, and not to yield to him until the price is paid.[132] The sight of Baîti, young and vigorous, kindles an irresistible desire in the breast of the wife of Anupu,[133] and the wife of Ubaû-anir is equally susceptible to the attractions of a young man.[134] The divine wife of Baîti consents to betray her husband in exchange for some jewels, and to become the favourite of the King.[135] Princesses, girls of the sacerdotal caste, of the middle class, and of the peasantry, are all alike in the matter of virtue. I find none of them respectable except Ahuri,[136] Mahîtu-askhît,[137] and a stranger, the daughter of the chief of Naharinna; and the passion with which the latter flings herself into the arms of a man whom chance has made her husband, affords food for reflection.[138]

A satire on feminine morals in the writings of a professional moralist has little value for history. It is a common theme, that varies according to the period and the country, but which proves nothing decisive against the period or the country. It is of no importance that Phtahhotpu should define the vicious woman as a bundle of all kinds of wickedness, a sack full of all kinds of malice,[139] or that Ani, resuming the same theme after an interval of three thousand years, describes her as a deep river of which no one

131. *Herodotus,* II, cxxi; cf. p. 166 of this volume.
132. See the whole episode in pp. 112–115 of this volume.
133. See p. 5 of this volume.
134. See p. 20 of this volume.
135. See p. 12 of the present volume.
136. In the *Adventure of Satni-Khamoîs,* pp. 99 *et seq.* of this volume.
137. In the *Veritable History of Satni-Khamoîs,* pp. 119 *et seq.* of this volume.
138. In the *Tale of the Doomed Prince,* pp. 153 *et seq.* of this volume.
139. In the moral treatise of the *Prisse Papyrus,* pl. x, 1. 1–4. Cf. Virey, *Études sur la Papyrus Prisse,* pp. 64–66.

knows the windings.[140] All the women of their time may have been virtuous, and they may have invented vices for them in order to give scope to
their eloquence. But the story tellers did not set out to preach propriety,
they did not undertake to satirise the women; they described them as they
were for their contemporaries—perhaps as they themselves had found
them. I doubt whether they had ever in the course of their fortunes
encountered a princess of the royal harem, but Tbubui wandered daily
through the streets of Memphis, the hierodules did not reserve their
favours entirely for princes of the blood royal, Baîti's companion was not
alone in her love of ornaments, and there was more than one brother-in-
law who, without any pangs of conscience, knew the whereabouts of the
abode of the wife of Anupu. In Egypt morals were lax. Ripened to a precocious maturity, the Egyptian women lived in a world where the laws and
customs seem to conspire to develop her native ardour. As a child she
played unclothed with her unclothed brothers, as a woman fashion left her
chest uncovered, clothed her in transparent materials, and left her nude
before the eyes of men. In the towns the servants by whom she was surrounded, and who swarmed round her husband and his guests, were only
clothed in a girdle drawn tightly round the loins; in the country, the peasants on her property cast aside their loin-cloth to work in the fields. Both
religion and the cult ceremonies drew her attention to the obscene figures
of the deity, and the very writing displayed indecent figures before her eyes.
When love was spoken of, she bethought herself of no ideal love such as
the modern maiden dreams of, but actually and precisely of physical love.
With all this it is not surprising that the sight of a robust man aroused the
wife of Anupu to such a point as to make her lose all self-control. For an
Egyptian woman to conceive the idea of adultery was almost enough to
make her immediately attempt to gratify the desire. But were there more
women in Egypt than elsewhere who would entertain the idea?

Herodotus was told by the guides, and in his turn tells us with all the
gravity of an historian, that a certain Pharaoh who had become blind
owing to his impiety was condemned by the gods in a merry mood not
to recover his sight . . . Herodotus is at times impossible to translate! In
short, it was necessary to find a woman who had been faithful to her husband. The queen was put to the proof, and then the ladies of the court,
then those of the town, the provincials, the country folk, and finally the

140. In the philosophical dialogue between Ani and his son Khonshotpu. (Mariette,
Papyrus de Boulaq, vol. i, pl. xvi, 1. 13–17. Cf. Chabas, *L'Égyptologie*, vol. i, pp. 65 *et seq.*)

slaves. None availed, and the worthy king remained blind. After much searching the woman was found who could confer the remedy, and he married her. As for the others, he shut them up in a city and burnt them. Such things were done in those days.[141] This fable, related by a story teller at some street corner, or read at leisure after drinking, would be sure to meet with the success that a scandalous story always obtains among men; but even while jesting at his neighbour, each Egyptian would bethink himself that in such circumstances his good wife would be able to effect a cure, and did not trouble himself. These broad stories from Memphis mean no more than those of other nations; they arise from that quality of general rancour that men have always possessed, and more especially against women. The loose women of our Middle Ages and the uncontrolled Egyptian women of the Memphis stories are alike undesirable, but what is related of them in the stories proves nothing against the morals of their times.

Within these restrictions, the particulars of the incidents are Egyptian. Read once more the passage where Satni meets Tbubui, and crudely confesses his desire. With the names changed, we have here an exact representation of what occurred in Thebes or Memphis in a similar case. The preliminaries arranged by the manservant and the maid, the meeting, the festivities, and the elaborate supper, and then the bargaining before the final yielding. The lovers of the *Arabian Nights* acted in the same way, even the inevitable cadi who is called in to celebrate the marriage of the Zobeïde with the Ahmed or Noureddin of the particular story is already foreshadowed by the scribe of the School who draws up the contracts intended to transfer the property of Satni-Khamoîs to Tbubui.[142] As to the events that precipitate or retard the *dénouement*, they are most frequently incidents of the life of that period.

IV

I SAY ALL incidents without exception, even those which appear most improbable in our eyes, because we must not judge the conditions of Egyptian life by those of our own. For the purposes of romance we do not commonly employ apparitions of divinities, dreams, men transformed into beasts, animals that talk, magic boats or litters, those who

141. *Herodotus* II, cxi.
142. See p. 113 of this volume.

believe in such marvels regard them as extremely rare, and they are not made use of in ordinary romance.

This was not the case in Egypt, and what we term the supernatural was there of daily occurrence. Dreams played a decisive part in the lives of the sovereign and distinguished personages, whether they were caused by the voluntary intervention of a god, or whether they were sought by sleeping for a night in certain temples.[143] The belief in signs reigned everywhere supreme, and it was not only in romance that the bubbling up of a jug of beer or the deposit of dregs in a bottle of wine warned a man of the death of his brother.[144] So many people had received these mysterious warnings that no one would be inclined to dispute their probability when they met with them in a romance. Sorcery had its recognised place in ordinary existence, as much as war, commerce, literature, business, amusements, and pleasure; not every one had witnessed its power, but every one was connected with some one who had seen its results and had profited or lost by it. It was, in fact, regarded as a science, and of a very high order. If we consider, we realise that the priest was a magician; the ceremonies he performed, the prayers he recited, were so many methods by which he forced the gods to act for him in the way he desired, and to accord him such and such a favour in this world or the next. The priests—*bearers of the roll* or *of the book* (khri-habi), who possessed the secrets of the divinity, in heaven, on earth, and in hell—could perform all the prodigies demanded of them; Pharaoh had some around him whom he called chief khri-habi, and who were his official sorcerers. He consulted them, he stimulated their researches, and when they had invented some fresh miracle for him, he loaded them with gifts and honours. One of them could reunite a severed head to its body, another made a crocodile that devoured his enemies, a third cleft the water, raised it and piled it up at will.[145] The great folk themselves, Satni-Khamoîs and his foster-brother, were convinced adepts, and they read eagerly the collections of mystic formulæ; Satni even acquired so

143. Cf. *the incubation* of Mahîtuaskhît and Horus, the son of Panishi, in the *Veritable History of Satni*, pp. 119–121, 130–132 of this volume.

144. This is what happens to the brother of Baîti in the *Tale of Two Brothers*, pp. 8–9 of the present volume. Cf. pp. 133, 158, similar intersigns in the *Veritable History of Satni*, and in the *Doomed Prince.*

145. See the story entitled *Khufuî and the Magicians*, p. 17 *et seq.* Jewish and Arab tradition have retained the recollection of these powerful magicians, as is shown in the history of Moses, and the description that Makrizî, for instance (Malan, *A Short Story of the Copts and of their Church* pp. 13–15), gives of a meeting between Egyptian sages.

great renown in this class of studies that a complete cycle of stories was grouped round his name.[146] A prince of magic in our days would gain very moderate esteem; in Egypt magic was not incompatible with royalty, and the magicians of Pharaoh often had Pharaoh himself for a pupil.[147]

Many of our personages were therefore either amateur or professional sorcerers: Tbubui,[148] Nenoferkephtah,[149] Ubaû-anir and Zazamankhu,[150] Didi,[151] Senosiris,[152] and Horus the son of the negress.[153] Baîti "enchants his heart," takes it out of his breast without ceasing to live, and changes himself first into a bull and then a tree.[154] Khamoîs and his foster-brother learn by chance of the existence of a book written by Thoth with his own hand, and which was endowed with marvellous qualities. It was supposed to contain two formulæ, and two only; but what formulæ! "If thou recite the first, thou shalt charm the heaven, the earth, the moon of the night, the mountains, the water; thou shalt understand what is said by the birds and the reptiles, as many as there are; thou shalt behold the fish of the lowest depths, for a divine power shall cause them to rise to the surface of the water. If thou recite the second formulæ, even when thou art in the tomb, thou shalt regain the form that thou hadst on earth; thou shalt see the sun rising in the heavens and his cycle of the gods, the moon and the form that she hath when she appears."[155] Satni Khamoîs was determined to procure, in addition to the inestimable delight of producing a rising of the moon at will, the certainty of never losing the form that he had on earth; his desire to possess the marvellous book is the principal motive of the romance. The

146. See the three stories or summaries of stories relating to Satni on pp. 95–139 of this volume.

147. Even as late as the time of the Renaissance a prince was more highly regarded because he was a sorcerer. For example, in the *Weisskunig* one finds the young Maximilian of Austria instructed by his ecclesiastical preceptors not only in the secrets of white magic, but of black.

148. The heroine of the second part of the *Adventure of Satni-Khamoîs,* pp. 118 *et seq.* of this volume.

149. See p. 101 of this volume for what is said by the author of the *Adventure* as to the magical studies of Nenoferkephtah.

150. Their exploits are recorded in full at the beginning of the part that is preserved of the *Story of Khufuî,* pp. 20–24.

151. See p. 24 *et seq.,* the description of this personage and the marvels wrought by him.

152. He is the hero of the *Veritable History,* pp. 118–137 of this volume.

153. He is an Ethiopian instructed in the learning of Egypt by Horus, the son of Panishi, and in that of the Soudan by his mother, Tnahsît, the negress. Cf. p. 129 of the present volume.

154. See pp. 8–9, 13, 14–15 of the present volume.

155. Cf. pp. 97, 98, 102, 103 of this volume.

science to which he devotes himself is otherwise exacting, and imposes abstinence, chastity, and other virtues on its devotees which they could not always maintain to the end.[156] And yet the study is so attractive to them that they become absorbed and neglect all else for it. They no longer see, they no longer drink, they no longer eat; they permit themselves only one occupation—that of reading their book of magic without relaxation and exercising the authority gained thereby on people and things.[157] This absorption is not without peril; the gods and the dead, whom the sorcerer has deprived of their talismans, attempt to recover them, and all methods are regarded by them as permissible. They hover around them and profit by their passions or weaknesses to get them into their power; love is their great ally, and it is by means of a woman that they most frequently succeed in winning back their lost treasure.[158]

The power of magic art did not cease with life. Whether he wished it or not, every Egyptian after his death was as fatally subject to charms and incantations as he was during life. It was in fact believed that the existence of mankind was attached by unavoidable bonds to that of the universe and the gods. The gods had not always manifested that contemptuous indifference towards humanity which they appeared to have entertained from the time of Menes. At first they descended into the newly created world, they mixed familiarly with the newly born nations, and assuming a fleshly body, they were subject to fleshly passions and weaknesses. The people of those times beheld them in turn loving and fighting, reigning and succeeding, victorious and defeated. Jealousy, anger and hatred then stirred their divine breasts, as though they had been simple human breasts. Isis, a widow and miserable, wept the helpless tears of a wife over her assassinated husband,[159] and her divine nature did not save her from the pangs of child-birth. Râ narrowly escaped perishing by the bite of a serpent,[160] and in an access of fury destroyed those reptiles; he became old, and in his decrepitude he experienced the trials of second childhood, his head shook and he drib-

---

156. Cf. p. III, note 51, and p. 115, note 67, of this volume.

157. Thus Satni Khamoîs; cf. p. III of this volume.

158. See p. 109 *et seq.;* the struggle between Nenoferkeptah and Satni, and the victory won by Nenoferkeptah owing to the interposition of Tbubui.

159. The book of the *Lamentations d'Isis et de Nephthys* has been published by M. de Horrack, *Œvres diverses,* pp. 33–53.

160. E. Lefébure, *un Chapitre de la Chronique solaire,* in *Zeitschrift,* 1883, pp. 27–38; cf. *Œvres diverses,* vol. i. pp. 203–213.

bled like an ordinary old man.[161] Horus, the child, conquered the throne of Egypt by the use of weapons.[162] But later on, the gods retired to the heavens, and just as formerly they had rejoiced in appearing with men below, so now they assiduously concealed themselves in the mysteries of their eternity. Who was there among the living who could boast of having beheld their face?

Moreover the incidents of their corporal life, whether happy or the contrary, determined from afar the happiness or misfortune of each generation, and in each generation, of each individual. On the 17th of Athyr in some year so completely lost in the remote past that it was unknown how many centuries had elapsed since that time, Situ entrapped his brother Osiris and slew him by treachery at a banquet.[163] Each year on the corresponding day the tragedy that was enacted in the terrestrial palace of the god appears to have been resumed in the depths of the firmament, as at the time of the death of the God, the power of good was weakened, the sovereignty of evil prevailed, and the whole of nature, abandoned to the powers of darkness, recoiled on mankind. A devotee was careful to undertake nothing on that day; anything he was desirous to do must be avoided. If he went down to the edge of the river he would be attacked by a crocodile, as the crocodile sent by Situ attacked Osiris. If he started on a journey, he might say farewell for ever to his wife and household—he was certain never to return. It was better to remain shut up indoors and to wait trembling and inactive while the hours of peril passed one by one, until the sun of the following day dispelled the powers of evil. On the 9th of Khoïak Thoth had encountered Situ, and gained a signal victory over him. Each year on the 9th of Khoïak there was a festival on earth among mankind, festival in heaven among the gods, and security in commencing all things.[164] Days were lucky or unlucky, according to the events that occurred on them during the time of the divine dynasties.

"Tybi 4.—Good, good, good.[165] Whatever thou shall behold on this day, it is of lucky presage for thee. He who is born on this day shall die

161. E. Naville, *La Destruction des Hommes par les Dieux,* in *Transactions of the Society of Biblical Archæology,* vol. iv, pp. 1–19, vol. viii, pp. 412–420.

162. E. Naville, *Le Mythe d'Horus,* folio, Geneva, 1870; Brugsch, *Die Sage der geflügelten Sonne,* 4to, 1871, Göttingen.

163. *De Iside et Osiride,* ch. 13. Confirmation of Plutarch's text is found in several passages or the magic or religious texts (*Papyrus magique Harris,* édition Chabas, Pl. ix. 1. 2 *et seq.*) etc.

164. *Sallier papyrus* iv, pl. x, ll. 8–10.

165. The Egyptians divided the twelve hours of the day, from sunrise to sunset, into three parts or, as they said, into three seasons, *tori,* of four hours each. Each of the three adjectives

at the greatest age of all the people of his house; he will have long life in succession to his father.

"Tybi 5.—Evil, evil, evil.—It is the day when the chieftains were burnt by the goddess Sokhît who dwells in the white abode, when they rage, transform themselves and come.[166] Offerings of cakes for Shu, Ptah, Thoth; incense on the fire for Râ and the gods who attend on him, for Ptah, Thoth, Hu-Sau on this day. What thou seest on this day shall be lucky.[167]

"Tybi 7.—Evil, evil, evil.—Do not unite with women before the eye of Horus.[168] The fire that burns in thy house, beware of exposing thyself to its baneful effect.

"Tybi 8.—Good, good, good.—That which thou seest on this day with thine eye, the divine cycle will grant thee. Consolidation of fragments.[169]

"Tybi 9.—Good, good, good.—The gods acclaim the goddess of the south on this day. Present festival cakes and fresh loaves, which rejoice the hearts of the gods and the manes.

"Tybi 10.—Evil, evil, evil.—Do not make a fire of rushes on this day. This day fire from the god Sop-ho went forth in the Delta, on this day.[170]

"Tybi 14.—Evil, evil, evil.—Do not approach the flame on this day; Ra, l. h. s., has directed it to annihilate all his foes, and whosoever approaches it on this day, he will not be well again all the time of his life."

The officer of high rank who on the 13th of Tybi braved a lion with all the assurance and pride of courage, or who engaged in a fight fearless of

---

that occur after each date in the *Sallier Calendar* applies to one of the sections. Usually the presage is the same for the whole day, and then one finds noted, good, good, good, or hostile, hostile, hostile. But it occasionally happened that one section was unlucky while the other two were favourable, and then we find the remark good, good, hostile, or an analogous notation corresponding to the quality of the presage. It will be observed that in this curious work there are no prognostications relating to the hours of the night. The fact explains itself when we consider the analogous superstitions that exist or have existed among other nations, either ancient or modern. In all of them the night is evil; it is the time when spirits, ghosts, and demons of all sorts and both of animal and human form attain their full power, and not having to fear the light, emerge from their hiding-places. There is therefore no scope for indicating the same divisions for the night as for the day.

166. I cannot say to what episode of the Osirian wars this passage alludes.

167. *Sallier Papyrus* IV., pl. xiii, l. 6–7.

168. The sun is intended here, or more probably the fire.

169. The last part of the phrase refers to the reconstruction of the mutilated body of Osiris by Isis. The legend relates in fact that Osiris, rent in pieces by Sîtu, collected bit by bit by Isis and Nephthys and placed on a funerary couch, was temporarily reconstituted and begat Horus.

170. I do not know who the god Sop-ho was, nor his reason for setting the Delta on fire.

the Syrian arrows,[171] on the 12th would be alarmed at the sight of a rat, and turn away his eyes, trembling.[172]

Each day had its influences, and the accumulated influences formed destiny. Destiny was born with the man, grew with him, guided him in youth and mature age, and, it may be said, cast his entire life in the unalterable mould that the doings of the gods had prepared from the beginning of time. Pharaoh and his nobles submitted to destiny, and so were the rulers of foreign nations.[173] Destiny followed a man even after death; with fortune it was present at the judgment of the soul,[174] either to render to the infernal jury the exact reckoning of his virtues or his crimes, or finally to arrange the conditions of his new life. There was nothing hideous in the guise under which it was figured. It was a goddess, Hâthor, or better still, seven young and beauteous goddesses,[175] the Hâthors of the rosy face and heifer's ears, always gracious, always smiling, who announced good fortune or predicted misery. Like the fairy godmothers of the Middle Ages, they clustered round a woman in childbed and awaited the arrival of the infant, either to enrich or to ruin it with their gifts. The sculptors of the temple of Luxor,[176] at Erment [177] and at Deîr el Baharî,[178] show us those that are acting as midwives to Mutemua, wife of Thûtmôsis IV, to Queen Ahmasi, and the celebrated Cleopatra. Some of them tenderly support the young mother, and aid her by their incantations, while the others perform the first services for the newly born, and prophesy all manner of happiness for the child. Khnumu having fashioned a wife for Baîti, they come to see her, examine her for a moment and exclaim with one voice that "she shall die by the sword!"[179] They appear at the cradle of the *doomed prince* and announce that he shall be slain by a serpent, a crocodile, or a dog.[180] In the

171. It was a lucky day. (*Papier Sallier* IV, pl. xvi, l. 4.)

172. For the 12th of Tybi there is the following note (*Papier Sallier* iv, pl. xiv, l. 3): "Tybi xii.—Evil, evil, evil.—Try to see no rat; do not approach one in thy house."

173. It is said of one of the princes of the Khâti that "his destiny" gave him his brother as successor (*Traité de Ramsis II avec le Prince de Khâti*, ll. 10–11).

174. See the picture of the judgment of the soul in chapter 125 of the *Book of the Dead*.

175. It is the number given in the *Tale of the Two Brothers*, pl. ix, l. 8, cf. p. 10 of the present volume, which is confirmed by the representations of Deîr-el-Medineh. In other documents, in the *Doomed Prince*, for instance (cf. p. 154 of this volume), their number is not limited.

176. Champollion, *Monuments de l'Égypte et de la Nubie*, pl. cccxl-cccxli. The text reproduced by Champollion indicates no name for the goddess. The Hâthors represented with the Queen in the birth scene are nine in number.

177. Champollion, *Monuments de l'Égypte et de la Nubie;* pl. clxv. 12.

178. Naville, *Deîr el Bahari*, vol. ii, pl. xlii-li.

179. *Papyrus d'Orbiney*, pl. ix, l. 5; cf. p. 10 of the present volume.

180. Cf. p. 154 of the present volume.

story of *Khufuî and the Magicians,* four of them, Isis, Nephthys, Maskhonuît, and Hiqaît, aided by Khnumu, disguise themselves as al-mehs to deliver the wife of the priest of Râ of the three infants who struggled within her. The point on which they differ from our fairy god-mothers is their inveterate love of punning. Each of the names they give the children is a play on words, difficult for a modern to understand, and yet more difficult to translate.[181] They are not alone in their preference, the Oriental has always been irresistibly attracted by this form of wit, and Arabia and Judæa in no way fell short of Egypt in the matter of strange etymologies for the names of their saints and heroes.

To see and hear the Hâthors at the moment when they pronounce their decrees was reserved for the great folk of the world. The common people were not usually in their confidence; they knew only by the experience of many generations that they assigned certain death for the men born on certain days.

"Paophi 4.—Hostile, good, good.—On no account go out of thy house on this day. Whosoever is born on this day dies of contagion on this day.

"Paophi 5.—Bad, bad, bad.—On no account go out of thy house on this day, approach not women; it is the day of offering offerings of things before the god, and Montu[182] rests on this day. Whosoever is born on this day, he will die of love.

"Paophi 6.—Good, good, good.—A joyous day in heaven. The gods rest in the presence of the god, and the divine cycle performs the rites in the presence of . . .[183] Whosoever is born on this day will die of drunkenness.

"Paophi 7.—Evil, evil, evil.—Do absolutely nothing on this day. Whosoever is born on this day shall die on the stone.[184]

"Paophi 9.—Mirth among the gods.—Men are keeping festival, for the enemy of Râ is cast down. Whosoever is born on this day will die of old age.

"Paophi 23.—Good, good, evil.—Whosoever is born on this day dies by the crocodile.

"Paophi 27.—Hostile, hostile, hostile.—Do not go out on this day; do not apply thyself to any manual work. Râ is at rest. Whosoever is born on this day shall die by the serpent.

181. Cf. pp. 29–31 of this volume.
182. Montu, god of Thebes and Hermonthis, is one of the principal gods of war.
183. The name of a divinity is missing here.
184. Perhaps "Whosoever is born on this day will die on foreign soil."

"Paophi 29.—Good, good, good.—Whosoever is born on this day shall die venerated by all people."

Not all the months were equally favourable to this kind of presage. Those who were born in the month of Paophi had eight chances out of thirty of knowing the manner of their death by the date of their birth. Athyr, which immediately follows Paophi, possesses only three fateful days.[185] The Egyptian who was born on the 9th or 29th of Paophi had nothing to do but to live, his good luck could not fail. The Egyptian born on the 7th or 27th of the same month had no need to disquiet himself unduly, the manner of his death was already fixed, but not the time: he was condemned, but he had power to retard the sentence almost at will. If, like the *Doomed Prince,* he were menaced with death by a crocodile or a serpent, he would not live long if he was not careful, or if as a child his parents did not take precautions for him; the first serpent or crocodile he met would execute the sentence. But he could arm himself with safeguards against his fate, keep at a distance from canals and from the river, never go for a sail on those days when the crocodiles were masters of the water,[186] and on other days he could safeguard his journeys by water by employing a crew skilful in averting danger by means of charms.[187] It was believed that at the slightest contact with the feather of an ibis, the most athletic crocodile with the sharpest of teeth would become motionless and harmless.[188] I would not myself rely on this; but the Egyptian who believed in the secret virtues of various objects would on no account omit to have several ibis feathers at hand, and imagined himself safeguarded thereby.

Divine precautions had also to be taken in addition to these human ones—incantations, amulets and ceremonies of ritual magic. The religious hymns, indeed, repeated in grand sonorous strophes that "the god is not shaped in stone—nor in the statues on which the double crown is placed; he is not seen—no service, no offering reaches him;—he cannot

185. The 14th, 20th, and 23rd. Whoever is born on the 14th will die by the stroke of a cutting weapon (*Sallier Pap.* iv, p. 8, l. 3). Whoever is born on the 20th will die of the annual contagion (*id.* p. 8, l. 9). Whoever is born on the 23rd will die on the river (*id,* p. 9, l. 12).

186. In the *Sallier Papyrus IV* the following note is placed, after the date Paophi 22: "Do not wash in any water this day; whosoever shall navigate the river, it is the day to be rent in pieces by the tongue of Sovku (the crocodile)."

187. See below, pp. 220, 221, what is said of the spells employed by the shepherds to prevent crocodiles attacking their flocks; those useful for animals were equally useful for men, and the charms of the Harris Magical Papyrus were as efficacious for one as for the other.

188. Horapollo, *Hieroglyphs,* II, lxxxi. The hieroglyph referred to in the text of the Greek author occurs frequently in the late periods.

be approached in the mysterious ceremonies; the place where he is, is not known—the sacred books are not found by force."[189] That was true of the gods considered each one as an ideal being, perfect, and absolute, but in the ordinary course of life Râ, Osiris, Shu and Amon were not inaccessible. Their royalty had left some traces of frailty and imperfection that constantly brought them down to earth. They were carved in stone, they were touched by services and offerings, they were approached in the sanctuaries and in the painted shrines. If their mortal past exerted an influence on the affairs of men, man in his turn exerted an influence on their divine present. There were words that pronounced with a certain intonation penetrated to the depths of the unknown, formulæ the sound of which acted irresistibly on the supernatural intelligences, and amulets which had secured some of the celestial power by their magical consecration. By their virtue, man had power over the gods; he enrolled Anubis, Thoth, Bastît, or Sîtu himself, in his service; he alternately annoyed and calmed them, he sent them forth and recalled them, he forced them to work or to fight for him. This formidable power that they believed themselves to possess was employed by some of them in advancing their fortunes, or gratifying their evil tempers and passions. It was not only in romance that Horus, son of the negress, armed himself with spells to persecute Pharaoh and humiliate Egypt in the eyes of Ethiopia.[190] During a plot aimed at Ramses III the conspirators were armed with books of incantations by which they might penetrate to the harem of Pharaoh.[191] The law punished with death those who thus transgressed, while their crime did not prevent it from making use of the services of the less turbulent of the confraternity and protecting those who exercised their art in a harmless or beneficial manner.

Henceforth the threatened man had not to watch alone. The gods watched with him, and supplemented his weak efforts with their unfailing vigilance. Take an amulet that represents "a figure of Amon with the four rams' heads, painted on clay, trampling on a crocodile with his feet, and eight gods adoring him, placed to right and left."[192] Pronounce over him this adjuration: "Behind, crocodile, son of Situ! Float not with thy tail;—Seize not with thy two arms. Open not thy mouth;—May the

189. *Sallier Papyrus* II, p. 12, ll. 6–8, and *Anastasi Papyrus* VII, p. 9, l. 13.

190. See p. 128 *et seq.*, of this volume, the *Veritable History of Satni-Khâmois*.

191. Chabas, *Papyrus magique Harris,* pp. 170–174, Dévéria, *Le Papyrus Judiciaire de Turin,* pp. 124–137.

192. *Harris' Magical Papyrus,* pl 6, ll. 8–9.

water become a sheet of fire before thee!—The charm of thirty-seven gods is in thine eye;—Thou art bound to the great crook of Râ.—Thou art bound to the four bronze pillars of the south—in front of the bark of Râ.—Stop, crocodile, son of Sîtu.—Protect me, Amon, husband of thy mother." The passage is obscure. It was necessarily so in order that it should work efficaciously. The gods understand at a word what is said to them; the allusions to events in their lives by which they are conjured, are sufficient to move them and there is no need to recall them in detail. Had you been born on the 22nd or 23rd of Paophi, Amon was bound to protect you against the crocodile and the perils of the water. Other incantations and other amulets protected from fire, scorpions, and from illness[193]; under whatever form destiny might disguise itself, it found the gods lying in ambush for the defence. Doubtless, nothing that was done could alter the sentence, and the gods themselves were powerless as to the issue of the struggle. The day must come when precautions, magic, and divine protection, would alike fail; destiny was more powerful. At any rate the man had succeeded in lasting perhaps to old age, perhaps even to that age of a hundred and ten years, the extreme limit of life to which the sages occasionally hoped to attain, and which no mortal born of mortal mother might surpass.[194]

After death, magic accompanied the man beyond the tomb and continued to dominate him. Our earth, such as the blind faith of the people and the superstitious science of the priests believed it to be, was like a theatre in two compartments. In one, the Egypt of the living was spread out in the light of day, the wind of the south wafted its delicious breath, the Nile rolled its abundant waters, the rich black earth produced its harvests of flowers, cereals, and fruit. Pharaoh, son of the Sun, lord of the diadems, lord of the two countries, reigned at Memphis or at Thebes, while his generals gained victories afar, and his sculptors toiled to carve the monuments of his piety in granite. It is there, in his kingdom or in the foreign countries dependent on him, that the action of most of the stories is placed. That of the romance of Satni takes place partly in the second division of our universe, the regions of tombs and of the night. The eternal waters, after having flowed during the day past the ramparts of the world, from east to south, and from south to west, arrived every

193. Papyrus I of Leyden, published by Pleyte (*Etudes égyptologiques*, vol. i, Leyden, 1866), is a collection of formulæ against various maladies.

194. For the age of one hundred and ten years see the curious memoir by Goodwin in Chabas, *Mélanges égyptologiques*, 2nd series, pp. 231–237.

evening at the Mouth of the Cleft[195] and were engulfed in the mountains that border the earth towards earth, carrying with them the bark of the sun and his cortege of luminous gods.[196] For twelve hours the divine equipage traversed the long dark corridors, where genii, some hostile, others friendly, either attempted to obstruct it, or assisted it in overcoming the dangers of the journey. From time to time a door guarded by a gigantic serpent opened before it and gave it access to an immense hall, full of monsters; then the narrow dark passages began once more, the blind course in the darkness, the struggles with hostile genii, and the joyous reception by friendly gods. In the morning the sun attained the extreme limit of the land of darkness, and issued forth from the mountain of the east to light up a new day.[197] It happened occasionally that living people by magic virtue penetrated these mysterious regions and emerged safe and sound. The Pharaoh Rhampsinitus carried away thence the gifts of the goddess Nuît,[198] and Satni, guided by his son Senosiris, was present at the judgment of souls.[199] But these were exceptions; in order to reach them in regular fashion, it was necessary to have first experienced the common lot of mortality.

The tombs of kings, princes, and distinguished people were often constructed on the plan of the underworld. They also had their shafts by which the dead men were lowered into the funerary chamber, their passages excavated far into the living rock, their great halls with many-coloured pillars, with round vaulted roofs,[200] and the walls themselves painted with the

---

195. The *Ro Pegaït* or *Ro Pegarît*, was situated in the *Wu Pegaït*, or *Wu Pegarît*, itself situated to the west of Abydos, behind that part of the Thinite necropolis now called by the Arabs Omm-el-Gaâb. The name signifies literally mouth of the tree, and refers to the tree that marked the cleft or fissure by which the sun entered the night world.

196. The description of the nocturnal course of the sun is found in the *Book of Knowing that which is in the Lower Hemisphere,* the text of which, recorded on papyrus, on sarcophagi, and on the walls of some tombs, can still be almost completely recovered. It gives hour by hour, with explanatory illustrations, the events of the journey of the sun, the names of the halls it traversed, of the genii and the gods it met with, illustrations of the punishment of the damned, and the discourse of the mystic parsonages who greet the sun. A complete translation and interpretation will be found in the memoir by Maspero on *les Hypogées Royaux de Thebes,* which is reproduced in vol. ii of *Mélanges de Mythologie et d'Archéologie égyptiennes,* pp. 1–181.

197. In the country of *Boqaït.* "Childbirth."

198. *Herodotus,* II, cxxii.; cf. p. 163 of this volume.

199. See the second tale of Satni, pp. 148–153 of this volume. Jules Baillet, reviewing these ideas, has concluded that they exercised an influence over the descent into the Inferno as described by Greek and Roman poets (*Descentes aux Enfers classiques et égyptiennes,* in the *Revue Universitaire* of March 15, 1902, published separately, 8vo, 7 pages).

200. What are called in the texts *Klil* (*Kerirt*), ovens, halls with circular vaulting.

demons and gods of Hades.[201] All the inhabitants of these "eternal homes"[202] were clothed in the livery of Egyptian death, in the bizarre splendour of its changing fashions—the wrappings of fine bandages, the coloured and gilt cartonnages, and the mask, with its great, ever-open, inlaid eyes. But beware of thinking that they were altogether dead. It may be said, speaking generally, that the Egyptians did not die as we die. The breath of life, with which the tissues were impregnated at the moment of birth, did not suddenly disappear with the final beatings of the heart—it persisted until decomposition was complete. However faint and obscure this life of the corpse might be, it was necessary to avoid its extinction. The early custom of drying the body, and later on of mummification, fixed the form and may be said to have petrified it. The usages of magic and religion maintained in it a kind of latent humanity, capable of developing and manifesting itself at some time. Also the embalmer was a magician and a priest as well as a surgeon. As he macerated the flesh, and rolled the bandages, he recited orisons, performed mysterious rites, and consecrated powerful amulets. Each limb in turn received from him the oil that rendered it incorruptible and the prayers that sustained the spark of life[203]; while towards the close of the Pharaonic period magic had invaded the corpse itself, and it was armed with amulets from head to foot. A disc of gilded cartonnage, covered with mystic legends and placed under the head, secured it some vestige of animal warmth.[204] The stone scarab set in gold, placed on the breast at the base of the throat, replaced the heart that had been rendered motionless by the stoppage of the blood or the absence of breath, and established artificial respiration.[205] Blades of grass, dried flowers, papyrus rolls, tiny figurines in glazed pottery hidden in the thickness of the bandages, bracelets, rings, plaques strewn with hieroglyphs, the thousand small objects which to-day crowd the cases of our museums, covered the trunk, the arms, and the legs like pieces of magic armour. The soul also did not venture defenceless into the life beyond the tomb. The chapters of the Book of the Dead and the other theological writings, of which a copy was placed in the coffin, were charms which opened up the roads of the under-

201. The tombs of Setuî I, of Mînephtah, and of Ramses IV and V, are painted thus.

202. The expression employed from the time of the earliest dynasties.

203. Cf. *Le Rituel de l'embaumement*, in Maspero, *Mémoire sur quelque papyrus du Louvre*, p. 14 *et seq.*

204. This is what is called the hypocephalus. The *Sacred Book* of the Mormons is a hypocephalus, taken to America and purchased by the prophet Joseph Smith (Devéria, *Mémoires et fragments*, vol. i. pp. 195–201).

205. *Book of the Dead*, chapters xxx, lxxii.

world for the soul and guarded it from danger. If it had taken the trouble during the time it dwelt in the body to learn these spells, all was well; but if poverty, ignorance, idleness, or incredulity had prevented its receiving the necessary instruction, even after death a charitable relation or friend might act as instructor. It was sufficient to recite each prayer near the mummy or over the amulets, and the knowledge would be imparted to the disincarnated soul by some subtle operation that I cannot explain.

This was the common fate. Some few escaped it by prestige and art magic, and for them return to this world was effected by actual rebirth from the womb of a woman. Thus it happened to Baîti in the *Tale of the Two Brothers,*[206] and to the sorcerer Horus, son of Panishi. The latter, knowing that Egypt was menaced by the incursions of an Ethiopian invader, insinuated himself into the body of the Princess Mahîtuaskhît, and was reborn into the world under the name of Senosiris and as the son of Satni-Khâmoîs. He traversed afresh all the stages of human existence, but he retained the acquirements and consciousness of his former life, and only returned to Hades after having victoriously accomplished the patriotic task he had imposed on himself.[207] Others, on the contrary, who only wished to produce some momentary effect, dispensed with so lengthy a procedure. They invaded our world abruptly and under the form that seemed to them most favourable for their projects, and only remained below for the number of hours that were absolutely indispensable. Such were the personages that Satni found collected in the tomb of Nenoferkephtah, and who were dead only in appearance and clothing. They were mummies; the blood no longer ran in their veins, their limbs were stiffened by the funerary bandages, their flesh was saturated and hardened by the perfumes of the embalmment, their skulls were empty. Nevertheless they thought, spoke, and moved; they behaved like living people; I am almost tempted to say that they lived. The Book of Thoth was in them, and supported them. Madame de Sévigné wrote of a treatise by M. Nicole that she "would much like to make broth of it and drink it." Nenoferkephtah had copied the formulæ of the magic book on a new papyrus; he had dissolved them in water and had then swallowed the brew.[208] Henceforth he was indestructible,

206. See p. 15 of this volume.

207. See the second tale of Satni, pp. 118–137 of this volume.

208. "The most approved mode of charming away sickness is to write certain passages of the Koran on the inner surface of an earthenware cup or bowl; then to pour in some water, and stir it until the writing is quite washed off; when the water, with the sacred words thus infused in it, is to be drunk by the patient" (Lane, *Modern Egyptians,* London, 1871, vol. i. 320–321).

death could change the conditions of his existence, it could not touch his actual existence. In the tomb he demands the doubles of his wife and son; he infuses them with the virtues of the book, and resumes with them the routine of family life, interrupted for a time by the formalities of embalmment. He can go in and out as he pleases, reappear by day, assume any form he pleases, and communicate with the living. He allows his power to remain dormant; but when Satni has despoiled him, he does not hesitate to rouse up and use it energetically. He sends his wife Ahuri to Memphis; escorted by pawns from a chessboard, who for the time have become so many servants,[209] she disguises herself as a hierodule to seduce the thief. When she has succeeded in her work of perdition, and he is helplessly at her mercy, Nenoferkephtah appears in his turn—at first in semblance of a king and secondly as an old man, and compels him to restore the precious manuscript. He could, if he desired, draw down vengeance on the impious being who had violated the secrecy of his tomb; but he contents himself with employing him to fulfil such of his wishes as could only be done by a living man. He forces him to take the mummies of Ahuri and Maîhêt, which were in exile in Coptos, back to Memphis, and to unite those who had been separated by the enmity of Thoth, in one tomb.

All this is Egyptian and purely Egyptian. If we persist in thinking that the original conception is foreign, we must at least confess that Egypt had appropriated it to the extent of rendering it entirely hers. Elsewhere we find mention of families of spectres or assemblies of the dead escaped from their coffins, but a family of mummies is only possible in the hypogea of the Nile Valley. After this no one will be astonished by the appearance of a ghost, in a fragment—which unfortunately is only too short—at the Florence Museum.[210] This ghost or, to call him by his Egyptian name, this *khu*, this *luminous*, faithful to the habits of his congenitors, related his story, how he was born under the King Rahotpu of the XVIIth dynasty, and what his life had been. His auditors do not appear to have been surprised to find him so loquacious; they knew that their time would soon come, when they would be such as he, and they understood the joy it must be to a poor spirit restricted for centuries to the conversation of spirits, once more to have a chat with the living.

209. See p. 111, note 52, of this volume.
210. Published by Golénischeff in the *Recueil de Travaux relatifs à l'Archéologie égyptienne et assyrienne*, 1881, vol. iii, p. 1 *et seq.;* cf. pp. 229–232 of this volume.

V

THIS IS sufficient to show the fidelity with which the popular narratives depict the customs and beliefs of the Egyptian in Egypt; it is interesting to extract from other stories the impressions gained by the Egyptian when travelling. I shall surprise many when I assert that, all things considered, the Egyptians were on the whole a nation of travellers. One is accustomed to regard them as a home-loving people, living by routine, so infatuated with the superiority of their race that they did not wish to mix with any other, and so devoted to their country as never to leave it unless forced to do so. This may have been true at the Græco-Roman period, notwithstanding that the presence of errant priests, necromancers, jugglers, and Egyptian sailors in different parts of the Empire of the Cæsars, and even as far away as Great Britain, shows that they manifested no reluctance to expatriate themselves, when they found it profitable to do so. But that which may have been the case in Egypt when aged and degenerated, may not have been equally so in Pharaonic Egypt.

The armies of Pharaoh when at war carried followers in their train—merchants, barterers, people of all sorts; their campaigns were undertaken almost every year, and almost every year thousands of Egyptians left their valley to follow the conqueror, and for the most part returned when the expedition terminated.[211] Thanks to this periodical exodus, the notion of travelling became so familar to the spirit of the nation, that the scribes did not hesitate to include this theme among their stylist exercises. One of them devoted twenty pages of small writing to tracing with considerable accuracy the itinerary of a circuitous journey undertaken across the Syrian provinces of the empire.[212] The ordinary incidents are briefly indicated: the hero penetrated forests peopled with bandits and wild animals, and encountered bad roads, hostile tribes, and mountain regions where his chariot was broken. Most of the towns he visited are merely mentioned in their geographical order, but picturesque details here and there interrupt the monotony of their enumeration; there is Tyre, an island with fish more

211. From the XIIth dynasty onward one finds allusions to the dangers of distant journeys (Maspero, *Du genre épistolaire*, pp. 59–60).

212. The text is found in the *Anastasi Papyrus No.* 1, pl. xviii, l. 3—pl. xxviii, l. 6. It was analysed by Hincks, translated and commented on by Chabas, *Le Voyage d'un Égyptien*, Paris, Maisonneuve, 4to, 1866, and published anew by A. H. Gardiner, *the Papyrus Anastasi 1 and the Papyrus Köller*, Leipzig, 4to, 1911. Chabas believed that the journey was actually undertaken. H. Brugsch has shown in an article in the *Revue Critique*, 1866, that the story is a mere practice in rhetoric.

numerous than the sands of the sea, boats that brought it water from the mainland; there is Byblos and its great goddess, Joppa and its numerous orchards of amorous seductions. "I will cause thee to know the road that passes by Magidi, for thou art a hero skilled in deeds of bravery: is there a hero to be found that charges like thee at the head of his soldiers, a lord who can hurl the arrow like thee? Thou art then on the edge of a gulf two thousand cubits deep, full of rocks and boulders; thou proceedest carrying thy bow and brandishing thy sword with the left hand; thou showest it to the excellent chiefs, and thou dost oblige their eyes to be lowered before thy hand. 'Thou art a destroyer like the god El, beloved hero.[213] Thou makest a name for thyself, hero, master of the cavaliers of Egypt. May thy name become like that of Kazarati, chief of the country of Asaru, when the hyenas met him in the midst of the thickets, in the sunken road, ferocious as the Beduîn who hide in the underwood, some of them as long as four or five cubits, their bodies as massive as that of a hippopotamus, ferocious of aspect, pitiless, deaf to prayers.' Nevertheless thou art alone, without a guide, without a troop following thee, and thou wilt not find a mountaineer to show thee the route thou shouldest follow; thus anguish will seize thee, thy hair will rise upon thy head, thy soul will pass wholly into thy hand, because the road is full of rocks and boulders, with no way marked out, obstructed by holly, brambles, aloes, dogs'-shoes,[214] the precipice on one side, the steep mountain on the other. Whilst thou dost travel there thy chariot jolts incessantly and thy horses are terrified at each bump; they leap to one side, they drag the chariot-pole, the reins are violently dashed away, and one falls. If while thou art pushing on straight before thee the horse drags away the pole at the narrowest part of the path there is no means of fastening it again, and as there is no means of re-adjusting it, the yoke remains in place and the horse wearies of carrying it. Thy heart yields at last; thou dost gallop, but the sky hath no clouds, thou art thirsty, the enemy is behind thee, thou art afeared, and when a branch of acacia crosses thy path thou throwest thyself to one side, thy horse is wounded at once, thou art thrown to the ground and art bruised with much pain. Entering into Joppa, thou findest an orchard in the prime of the season, thou makest a hole in the hedge in order to enter and eat; there thou findest the pretty girl who has charge of the orchards, she makes

213. Here the foreign chieftain begins to apostrophise the hero without any other indication in the text than the changes in the phrasing.

214. This is perhaps one of the thorny plants still called *Kelbiah* or *Omm-el-Kelb* by the Arabs of Egypt and Syria.

friends with thee, and yields the flower of her body to thee. Thou art seen, thou declarest who thou art, and thou art recognised as a hero."[215] All this might well form the geographical canvas of a Roman novelist, similar to certain Byzantine romances, the *Æthiopica* of Heliodorus, or the *Loves of Clitophon and Leucippus.*

We have therefore no reason to be surprised that the heroes of our stories travel far afield. Ramses II marries the daughter of the prince of Bahktan during the course of an expedition, and Khonsu does not hesitate to place his ark on a chariot and set forth in aid of Bintrashît.[216] In the *Doomed Prince,* a son of Pharaoh, weary of home, goes in search of adventures to Naharinna, in the north of Syria.[217] It is at Joppa, in Southern Syria, that Thutîyi finds an opportunity of displaying the qualities of a crafty soldier.[218] Exile carries Sinuhît to the Upper Tonu.[219] Any description of manners and customs is usually almost entirely absent, and there are no details to show that the author knew more than the mere name of the country to which he conducted his personages. The man who composed the memoirs of Sinuhît had, however, either explored the regions he describes, or had consulted those who had been there. He must have braved the desert and experienced its terrors to write as he does of the sufferings of his hero. "Then thirst rose upon me. I sank down. My throat rattled, and I already said to myself, 'This is the taste of death,' when suddenly I plucked up heart, and gathered up my limbs. I heard the loud voice of herds." The habits of the Beduîn are depicted to the life, and the singular combat between Sinuhît and the champion of Tonu is recorded with such fidelity that one might almost take it to be the story of a fight of Antar or Rebiâ.

To complete the series it only remained to discover a seafaring romance, and two of these were found by Golénischeff at Petrograd.[220] Greek and Latin authors repeatedly asserted that the sea was regarded by the Egyptians as impure, and that none of them would venture on it of

215. *Anastasi Papyrus* No. 1, pl. xxii, l. 1; pl. xxv, l. 5.

216. See pp. 143, 147 of this volume.

217. See p. 155 *et seq.* of this volume.

218. See p. 89 *et seq.* of this volume.

219. See p. 63 *et seq.* of this volume.

220. *Sur un ancien conte égyptien.*—Read at the Oriental Congress at Berlin by W. Golénischeff, 1881; see the complete bibliography on pp. 81–83 of this volume. The second was published for the first time, under the title *Papyrus hiératique de la collection W. Golénischeff, contenant la voyage de l'Égyptien Ounou-Amon en Phénicie,* in the *Recueil de Travaux,* vol. xxi, pp. 74–104; cf. p. 169 *et seq.* of this volume.

his free will. On the authority of the ancients moderns have long been accustomed to believe that Egypt never possessed either sailors or a navy; the expedition of Queen Hâtshopsuîtu, the naval victories of Ramses III were thought to have been achieved by Phœnicians fighting or sailing under the Egyptian banner. The Petrograd romances compel us to renounce this hypothesis. One of them, that of Unamunu, is the voyage of an officer sent by the high priest Hrihoru to buy wood on the coast of Syria in the twelfth century before our era.[221] The incidents are those which were of daily occurrence in the lives of merchants and ambassadors, and the whole document gives us an impression of maritime cruises similar to that conveyed by the *Anastasi Papyrus* with regard to journeys by land.[222] The misadventures are of the same kind as those of which one reads in accounts of the Levant in the sixteenth and seventeenth centuries, robbery on shore, ill-will from the port captains, threats from petty local tyrants, discussions and interminable palaver for permission to depart, and even for life. The second romance carries us back to a period more than twenty centuries earlier, when there was no question of Egypt conquering Syria. From the monuments we are already familiar with the maritime expeditions to the land of Puanît under the kings of the VIth and XIth dynasties.[223] The Petrograd romance shows us that the sailors whom the sovereigns of the XIIth dynasty commissioned to make long journeys to purchase the perfumes and produce of Arabia were Egyptians of good position and education.

Nothing could be more strange than the opening of the story. Some person sent on a mission has returned after an unlucky voyage in which he appears to have lost his vessel. One of his companions, perhaps the captain of the ship which has picked him up, encourages him to present himself boldly before the sovereign and to plead his own cause; to reassure him as to the result of the catastrophe he tells what happened to him under similar circumstances. The story is arranged on the model of the biographical notices that the great lords caused to be engraved on the walls of their rock tombs, or the reports they addressed to their sovereigns after the accomplishment of each mission. The phrases in it are precisely the same as those employed by the scribes when they had to report on an

221. See p. 169 *et seq.* of this volume.
222. See above, pp. cxlv–cxlvii of this *Introduction*.
223. Under Piupi II of the VIth dynasty (J. de Morgan, *De la frontière d'Égypte à Kom-Ombo*, pp. 175–176), and under Sankharîya Monthotpu of the XIth (Lepsius, *Denkm*, II, pl. clx).

affair of state. "I went to the mines of the sovereign, and I went to sea in a vessel a hundred and fifty cubits in length and forty in breadth, which carried a hundred and fifty sailors of the best of the land of Egypt, who had beheld the heavens, who had beheld the earth, and who were bolder of heart than lions."[224] The monarch Amoni-Amenemhaît, who lived about the time when this work was composed, speaks in the same style in the memoir that he has left us of his career. "I ascended the Nile in order to seek commodities of various sorts of gold for the majesty of the King Khopirkerîya; I ascended it with the hereditary prince, the eldest legitimate son of the king, Amoni, l. h, s.; I ascended it with the number of four hundred men of all the best of his soldiers."[225]

If it had chanced that the end of the manuscript had here been torn away and lost, a misfortune to which Egyptologists are well accustomed, we should almost have had the right to conclude that it contained a piece of actual history such as the Sallier papyrus No. 1 was long supposed to possess.[226] Happily, however, the manuscript is complete, and we can see clearly how the hero passed without any intermediate stages from the domain of reality into that of fable. A tempest sinks his vessel, and he is cast on an island. There is nothing unusual in the fact itself, but the island on which he lands, alone of all his comrades, is not an ordinary island. A gigantic serpent dwells there with his family, a serpent who welcomes the shipwrecked man, entertains and feeds him, predicts a happy return for him to his country, and loads him with gifts when he departs. Golénischeff has mentioned in this connection the adventures of Sindbad the sailor,[227] and the comparison made by him at once impresses itself on the reader. Only the serpents of Sindbad are not so accommodating in their temper as those of his Egyptian predecessor. They do not exert themselves to entertain the stranger with the charms of friendly conversation, they swallow him with pleasure, and if he eventually supplies himself with diamonds, rubies, and other precious stones, it is very much against their will, and only because, notwithstanding their variety they have failed to overcome the treasure seeker.

---

224. Cf. p. 83 of this volume.

225. *La Grande Inscription de Beni-Hassan,* in the *Recueil de Travaux relatifs à l'archéologie égyptienne et assyrienne,* vol. i, p. 172; cf. *Mélanges de Mythologie,* vol. iii, pp. 149–185; see Newberry, *Beni Hasan,* Egypt Exploration Fund, 1893, Part I, p. 25, pl. viii.

226. Cf. pp. 223–227 of this volume.

227. *Sur un ancien conte égyptien,* pp. 14–18.

I do not, however, conclude from this analogy that we have an Egyptian version of the story of Sindbad. Stories of marvellous voyages come easily from the lips of sailors, and they naturally present a certain number of incidents in common—storm, the shipwrecked man who is the only survivor of the crew, the island inhabited by monsters who talk, and the unhoped-for return with a wealthy cargo. The man who like Ulysses has accomplished a long voyage has a very feeble critical faculty and a lively imagination; he has barely got beyond the pale of ordinary life known to his auditors, before he plunges full sail into the sphere of miracles. The *Livre des merveilles de l'Inde*,[228] the *Relations des Marchands arabes*,[229] the *Prairies d'or* of Macondi inform those curious in such matters what was seen by travellers in good faith in Java, China, India and on the west coast of Africa only a few centuries ago. Many of the doings recorded in these works were inserted in the same manner as those in the adventures of Sindbad, or in the amazing journeys of Prince Seîf-el-Molûk; the *Arabian Nights* are in this respect no more untruthful than the serious narrations of the Mohammedan middle ages, and the Cairene who wrote the seven voyages of Sindbad had no reason to borrow his ideas from an earlier story. He had only to read the most serious authors or to listen to the tales of sailors and merchants returned from far-off countries, to collect a superabundance of material.

The ancient Egyptian was as well off in this respect as the modern Egyptian. The scribe to whom we owe the Petrograd story had the much-travelled captains of his time to guarantee the amazing rubbish that he set forth. At the time of the Vth dynasty, and even earlier, the Red Sea was navigated as far as the Land of Perfumes, and the Mediterranean as far as the islands of the Asiatic coast. The scanty geographical names in the narrative indicate that the hero directed his course towards the south. He arrived at the mines of Pharaoh, and the very authentic autobiography of Amoni-Amenemhaît proves that they were situated in Ethiopia in the region of the present Etbaye, and that they were reached by way of the Nile. The shipwrecked sailor is also at pains to tell us that, after having arrived at the far end of the country of Wawaît, at the south of Nubia, he

228. *Les merveilles de l'Inde,* an unpublished Arab work of the tenth century, translated for the first time, with introduction, notes, analytical and geographical index, by L. Marcel Devic: Paris, A. Lemerre, MDCCCLXXVIII, 12mo.

229. *Relation des voyages faits par les Arabes et les Persans dans l'Inde et à la Chine, dans le ixe siècle de l'ère chrétienne.* Arab text printed in 1811 by the exertions of the late M. Langlès, published by M. Reinaud, membre de l'Institut, Paris, Imprimerie royale, 1845, 2 vols. 18mo.

passed Sanmuît, that is to say the island of Bîgeh, at the first cataract. He went up the Nile, he reached the sea, where a long voyage brought him exactly to the neighbourhood of Puanît, and he then returned to the Thebaid by the same route.[230] The reader of to-day can make nothing of this mode of proceeding, but it is only necessary to consult some map of the xvith or xviith century to realise what the Egyptian scribe wished to convey. The centre of Africa is there occupied by a great lake whence the Congo and Zambesi flowed on one side and the Nile on the other.[231] The Alexandrian geographers never doubted that the Astapus and Astaboras, the Blue Nile and the Tacazzeh, threw out branches to the east that established communication with the Red Sea.[232] The Arab merchants of the Middle Ages believed that by following up the Nile one reached the country of the Zingis (Dinkas), and then passed out into the Indian Ocean.[233] Herodotus and his contemporaries derived the Nile from the Ocean river.[234] Neither Arabs nor Greeks invented this idea—they repeated the Egyptian tradition. This in turn may have had more solid foundations than would appear at first sight. The low marshy plain where the Bahr-el-Abiad at the present day unites with the Sabat and the Bahr-el-Ghazâl was formerly a lake larger than the Nyanza Kerouê of our time. The alluvial deposits have gradually filled it up with the exception of one basin deeper than the rest, now called the Birket-Nu and which is warping from day to day;[235] but in the sixteenth or seventeenth century B.C. it must have been sufficiently vast to give an impression to the Egyptian soldiers and river boatmen of an actual sea opening on to the Indian Ocean.

Had the island on which our hero landed any right to figure in a serious geography of the Egyptian world? It is described as a fantastic abode, the road to which is not given to every one to find. He who left it could not return; it resolved into waves—and sank beneath the surge. It is a

---

230. Erman (*Ægypten und Ægyptisches Leben,* p. 668) and Schäfer (*Kriegerauswanderung unter Psammetik und Sölderaufstand unter Apries,* in the *Beiträge zur Alten Geschichte,* vol. iv, pl. 162 and note 1) consider that the return alone was by way of the Nile, and that the hero started by the Red Sea.

231. Cf. the map of Odoardo Lopez reproduced by Maspero, in his *Histoire ancienne des peuples de l'Orient classique,* vol. i, p. 21.

232. Artemidorus, in Strabo, lxvii, p. 770. Cf. Vivien de Saint-Martin, *Le Nord de l'Afrique dans l'Antiquité,* pp. 226–268, 318.

233. Étienne Quatremère, *Mémoires géographiques et historiques sur l'Égypte et sur quelques centrées voisines,* vol. ii, pp. 181–182, from Maçoudi.

234. *Herodotus,* II, xxi.

235. Élisée Reclus, *Nouvelle Géographic universelle,* vol. ix, p. 67 *et seq.*

distant prototype of those enchanted lands—the island of St. Brandan, for example—that mariners of the Middle Ages frequently saw in the haze of the horizon, and which vanished when they attempted to approach them. The name borne by the island is very significant; it is called the *Island of the Double*.[236] I have so often explained what the double was[237] that I hesitate to refer to it again. The *double* was part of the human entity, that survived the body, and had to be clothed, lodged, and fed in the next world; an *island of the double* must be an island inhabited by the dead, a species of paradise similar to the Isles of the Blessed of classical antiquity. The geographers of the Alexandrian epoch knew of it, and it is in accordance with them that Pliny[238] indicates an *Island of the Dead* in the Red Sea, not far from the island Topazôn, which is concealed in mists[239] in the same way that the *Island of the Double* is lost to sight amidst the waves. It was the residue of a larger country, a *Land of the Doubles,* that the Egyptians of the Memphite Empire placed in the neighbourhood of Puanît, and the region of the Land of Perfumes.[240] The serpent that ruled there may himself have been a double, or the overseer of the dwelling of the doubles. I incline rather to the second explanation, because in all the sacred books, the *Book of the Dead,* and the *Book of Knowing that which is in the World of Night,* the guardianship of those places where the souls dwell is most frequently entrusted to serpents of various kinds. The doubles were too tenuous to be visible to the eye of an ordinary man, and therefore they do not come into the Petrograd story. The guardian was of more solid mould, and therefore the shipwrecked man could enter into relations with him. Lucian in his *True History* does not stand so much on ceremony. Almost as soon as he landed in the Elysian fields he entered into friendly relations with the manes, and kept company with the Homeric heroes. This was done to form a more complete satire on the maritime

236. Erman calls it the Island of Provisions (*Zeitschrift,* 1906, vol. xliii, pp. 14–15), and Golénischeff the Island of the Genii, the enchanted isle (*Recueil de Travaux,* vol. xxviii, p. 98).

237. Maspero, *Études égyptiennes,* vol. i, pp. 191–194.

238. Pliny, *H. Nat.* E. xxxvii, 9: "Insula Rubri maris ante Arabiam sita quæ Necron vocetur, et in eâ quæ juxta gemmam topazion ferat." Cf. *H. Nat.* vi, the mention of the island Topazôn, which is identical with the Ophiôdes of Artemidorus (in *Strabo,* l. xvi, p. 770), and Agatharchides (in *Diodorus of Sicily,* III, xxxix). Pliny probably borrowed the mention of this Island of the Dead from Juba.

239. Cf. Chassinat, *Ça et là,* § III, in the *Recueil de Travaux,* vol. xvii, p. 53, and Maspero, *Notes sur quelques points de grammaire et d'histoire* in the *Recueil de Travaux;* vol. xvii, pp. 76–78.

240. It is mentioned in the inscription of Hirkhûf (Schiaparelli, *Una tomba egiziana,* pp. 21, 33, 34; Maspero, *Histoire ancienne,* vol. i, pp. 19–20).

romances of the time; the Egyptian scribe who believed in the existence of the isles where dwelt the blessed ones brought the adventures of his hero into conformity with the details of his religion.

This journey of a simple sailor to the *Island of the Double* is, in fact, brought into the domain of theology. According to one of the most widely accepted theories, the Egyptian when dead could only reach the next world by means of a long voyage. He embarked on the Nile on the day of burial, and arrived at the west of Abydos, where the Osirian canal carried him out of this world.[241] The monuments show him steering his bark and making his way full sail on the mysterious sea of the west, but they do not tell us what was the object of his voyage. In a general way it was well understood that it ended by his landing in the *country that mingles men*,[242] and that he would there lead a life similar to his terrestrial existence. But with regard to the position of this land ideas were contradictory. Was the belief in a western sea a mere mythological conception, or may it not have been an indistinct recollection of a far-distant period when the waters of the Libyan desert, that which is now called the *Bahr-belâ-mâ, the rivers without water*, had not yet dried up, and formed a barrier of lakes and morasses in front of the valley? Whatever we may think of these questions, it seems to me certain that there is some indisputable connection between the journey of the shipwrecked sailor to the Island of the Double and the voyage of the dead on the sea of the west. The St. Petersburg story is little more than a theological idea transformed into a romance. It affords the earliest in date of those narratives where popular imagination was pleased to represent the living admitted with impunity among the dead, and thus it is a very remote ancestor of the *Divine Comedy*. We cannot say whether or not the original conception was Egyptian. If by chance it were not, we must at least admit that it is treated in a manner that in all points agrees with the manners and ideas of the Egyptians.

The future will no doubt bring us other fragments of this literature of romance. Several have emerged from the ground since the first edition of this book, and I know of others that are concealed in foreign museums or in private collections to which access has not been allowed me. New publications and discoveries may force us to reconsider the conclusions at which we have arrived by examination of the fragments already open to

241. Maspero, *Études égyptiennes,* vol i, p. 121 *et seq.*

242. This is the exact expression of the Egyptian texts (Maspero, *Études égyptiennes,* vol. i, p. 135.)

us. An Egyptologist speaking in favour of Egypt is always suspected of arguing in his own cause, but nevertheless there are several points that I think I may safely bring forward without incurring the charge of partiality. The first point which no one will contest is that some of the Egyptian versions are far more ancient than those of other nations. The manuscripts that contain the *Tale of the Two Brothers* and the *Quarrel of Apôpi and Saqnûnrîya* are of the fourteenth or thirteenth century B.C. The *Shipwrecked Sailor,* the *Fantastic Story* of Berlin, and the *Memoirs of Sinuhît* were written several centuries earlier. And these dates are only *a minima,* for the papyri we possess are copies of more ancient ones. India has nothing of equal antiquity, and Chaldæa, which alone among the countries of the classic world possesses monuments contemporaneous with those of Egypt, has not yielded a single romance. In the second place, the summary consideration of the subject I have given here will, I hope, be sufficient to convince the reader of the fidelity with which these stories depict the habits and customs of Egypt. Everything in them is Egyptian from beginning to end, and even the details that have been pointed out as being of foreign provenance appear to us to be entirely indigenous when closely examined. Not only the living, but also the dead, have the peculiar characteristics of the people of the Nile, and could not in any way be mistaken for the living or the dead of another nation. From these facts I consider that Egypt must he regarded, if not as the original home of folk tales, at least as one of those countries in which they were earliest naturalised, and where they earliest assumed the form of actual literature. I am convinced that those entitled to speak with most authority will agree with this conclusion.

THE STORY OF THE TWO BROTHERS [1]

(XIX*TH* DYNASTY)

THE MANUSCRIPT of this story, bought in Italy by Madame Elizabeth d'Orbiney, was sold by her to the British Museum in 1857, and was shortly afterwards reproduced by Samuel Birch in the *Select Papyri*, vol. ii, pl. ix-xix (1860), folio. A cursive edition of his facsimile occupies pp. 22-40 of *Ægyptische Chrestomathie* by Leo Reinisch, Vienna, 1875, small folio, and a very careful copy has been given by G. Möller, *Hieratische Lesestücke*, Leipzig, 1910, small folio, vol. ii, pp. 1-20. F. Ll. Griffith has carefully compared the text with the original, and has published his collation under the title *Notes on the Text of the d'Orbiney Papyrus*, in the *Proceedings of the Society of Biblical Archchæology*, vol. vii, 1888-9, pp. 161-172 and 414-416.

The text was translated and analysed for the first time by E. de Rougé, *Notice sur un manuscrit égyptien, en écriture hiératique, écrit sous le règne de Merienphtah, fils du grand Ramsès, vers le xve siècle avant l'ere chrétienne*, in the *Athénæum Français*, Saturday, October 30, 1852, pp. 280-284 (printed separately by Thunot, 1852, 12mo, 24 pp.), and in the *Revue archéologique*, 1st series, vol. viii, pp. 30 *et seq.* (printed separately by Leleu, 1852, 8vo, 16 pp. and 1 pl.); this memoir has been republished in the *Œuvres Diverses*, vol. ii, pp. 303-319.

Subsequently numerous analyses, transcriptions and translations have been given by:

C. W. Goodwin, *Hieratic Papyri*, in *Cambridge Essays*, 1858, pp. 232-239.

Mannhardt, *Das alteste Märchen*, in *Zeitschrift für Deutsche Mythologie und Sittenkunde*, 1859.

Birch, *Select Papyri*, part ii, London, 1860. Text, pp. 7-9.

Le Page Renouf, *On the Decypherment and Interpretation of Dead Languages*, London, 1863, 8vo; reproduced in *The Life Work of Sir Peter Le Page Renouf*, 1st series, vol. i, pp. 116-133.

Chabas, *étude analytique d'un texte difficile,* in the *Mélanges égyptologiques,* 2nd series, 1864, pp. 182-230.

Brugsch, *Aus dem Orient,* 1864, pp. 7 *et seq.*

Ebers, *Ægypten und die Bücker Moses,* 8vo, 1st ed., 1868, pp. 311-316.

Vladimir Stasow, *Drewnêjsaja powest w miré "Roman dwuch bratjew"* (*Le plus ancien conte du Monde, le Roman des deux Frères*), in the Review *Westnik Jewropi* (*les Messagers d'Europe*), 1868, vol. v, pp. 702-732.

Maspero, *Le Conte des deux Frères,* in the *Revue des Cours littéraires,* February 28, 1871, pp. 780 *et seq.*

Le Page Renouf, *The Tale of the Two Brothers,* in *Records of the Past,* 1st series, vol. ii, pp. 137-152; cf. his *Parallels in Folklore,* in the *Proceedings of the Society of Biblical Archæology,* vol. xi, pp. 177-189, reproduced in *The Life Work,* vol. iii, pp. 311-327.

Maspero, *Conte des deux Frères,* in the *Revue archéologique,* 2nd series, xixth year (March 1878). Printed separately by Didier, Paris, 8vo, 16 pp.; reproduced in *Mélanges de Mythologie et d'Archeologie Égyptiennes,* vol. iii, pp. 42-66.

Chabas, *Conte des deux Frères,* in the *Choix de textes égyptiens,* published after his death by M. de Horrack, Paris, 1883, 8vo, pp. 5 *et seq.,* reproduced in *Œuvres diverses,* vol. v, pp. 424-435.

E. M. Coemans, *Manuel de la langue égyptienne,* 1887, vol. i, pp. 95-120.

W. N. Groff, *Étude sur le Papyrus d'Orbiney,* Paris, Leroux, 4to, 84-iii pp., and *Quelques Observations sur mon étude sur le Papyrus d'Orbiney,* Leroux, 1889, 4to, viii pp.

Ch. E. Moldenke, *The Tale of the Two Brothers. A fairy tale of ancient Egypt, being the d'Orbiney Papyrus in hieratic character in the British Museum; to which is added the hieroglyphic transcription, a glossary, critical notes, etc.* New York, 1888-93, 8vo.

E. W. Budge, *Egyptian Reading Book,* 1st ed. London, Nutt, 1888, 8vo, pp. xi and 1-25, contains merely the transcription of the text into hieroglyphs; there have been several later editions.

W. Flinders Petrie, *Egyptian Tales,* 1895, vol. ii, pp. 36-86.

Ch. E. Moldenke, *The Oldest Fairy Tale translated from the Papyrus d'Orbiney, with Notes,* in the *Transactions of the Meriden Scientific Association,* Meriden, 1895, 8vo, vol. vii, pp. 33-81.

Karl Piehl, *En gammla Saga,* in *Kilder fran Egypten,* 1896, 8vo.

F. Ll. Griffith, *Egyptian Literature,* in *Specimen Pages of the World's Best Literature,* New York, 1898, 8vo, pp. 5253-5262.

D. A. Speransky, *Iz literatury Dpewnjago Jegygta,* Wipuski: *Razskaz o dwuch bratjach* (*Le Conte des deux Frères*), St. Petersburg, 1906, 8vo, 264 pp.

A. Wiedemann, *Altægyptische Sagen und Märchen,* Leipzig, 1906, small 8vo, pp. 58-77.

The manuscript includes nineteen pages of ten lines, of which the first five are considerably damaged. Several lacunæ have been filled in by one of its modern owners, and were pointed out on the facsimile. On the book in two places is the name of its ancient proprietor, Sêtûi Mainephtah, who reigned later under the name of Sêtûi II. On the verso of one of the leaves some contemporary person, perhaps Sêtûi himself, has traced the following memorandum (cf. W. Spiegelberg, *Rechnungen*, p. 41, n. 8):

Large loaves	17
Loaves of second quality	50
Temple loaves	68

The manuscript comes from the workshop of the scribe *Ennana,* to which we owe several other editions of classical works, among others the *Papyrus Anastasi IV;* and which was in full activity under the reigns of Ramses II., Menephtah, and Sêtûi II. It has been in existence over three thousand years.

There were once two brothers, who were sons of the same mother and of the same father[1]: Anupu[2] was the name of the elder, while Baîti[3] was the name of the younger. Now Anupu had a house and a wife, but his younger brother lived with him altogether as a junior. It was he who fashioned the stuffs even as he followed the cattle to the fields,[4] it was he who did the ploughing, it was he who beat out the grain, he who performed all the field work; for this younger brother was an excellent worker, and he had no equal in the Entire Land,[5] but the seed of every god was in him. And many

1. Polygamy was permitted, although it was not always practised by private individuals. A rich man, after having had children by a lawful wife or a concubine, would often give her in marriage to some subordinate, who would have children by her in his turn. It was not therefore unnecessary in naming two brothers, to say that they were "of the same mother and of the same father." The precedence here accorded to the mother over the father was the common right in Egypt; every one, whether noble or commoner, stated his maternal in preference to his paternal parentage. One would call himself "Sanûasrît, born of the lady Mankhuît," or another "Sesûsrîya, born of the lady Ta-Amon," and would most frequently omit to mention the name of his father.

2. Original form of the divine name, rendered Anubis by the Greeks and Romans.

3. Baîti, Bêti, Buti is the name of a very ancient god with a double bull's head (cf. *Introduction*, pp. cv–cvi) that the native chronicle transformed into a king of the time previous to Menes. The Greeks knew this mythical sovereign under the name of Bates or Butês, Bytis.

4. The fellahîn spin at the present day as they lead their flocks and herds to pasturage; it is to some custom of the kind that this passage alludes.

5. Egypt was divided into two halves (pashûï, into two lands (tauûï), each of which was regarded as forming a distinct country—that of the north (to-mûri), and that of the south (to-risi or to-shamâît). The union of these two lands was called sometimes *Qamaît,* the black land; sometimes *Torzerûf,* the Entire Land.

days after that,[6] when the younger brother was behind his cows, according to his daily custom, he came every evening to his house, laden with all the plants of the fields, as is done on returning from the fields. He laid them down before his elder brother, who was seated with his wife; he ate, he drank, he slept in his stable with the cows each day.[7] And when the earth lightened and it was a second day, as soon as the loaves were baked, he placed them before his elder brother, who gave him some loaves for the field. He drove his cows to feed in the fields, and while he walked behind his cows they said to him, "the grass is good in such a place," for, as to him, he listened to all that they said, and guided them to the good pasturage they desired. And they, the cows that were with him, they became fine, exceedingly, exceedingly, they multiplied their births, exceedingly, exceedingly.[8]

And on a time, at the season of tillage, his elder brother said to him, "Prepare for us our oxen, then we may set to work, for the land has emerged out of the water[9] and is good for tillage. Thou therefore, go thou to the field with the seed, for we will begin to work to-morrow morning." Thus he spake to him, and his younger brother did all the things that his elder brother had said to him, as many as they were. When the earth

6. This transition must not be taken literally. "Many days after that" does not necessarily imply a considerable lapse of time; it is a formula of uncertain value, employed to indicate that one event was posterior to another. To mark the passage of time from one day to the next the expression was used, "When the earth lightened and it was a second day"; while for an interval longer than the day following "Many days after that" was used.

7. In the pictures of agriculture one frequently sees the herdsman driving his cattle in front of him, whence the expression "To walk, to go behind the cattle" used instead of "to lead the cattle." On his shoulders he carries a sort of pack-saddle, similar to the shoulder strap of the French water-carriers, from which baskets filled with hay or grass are hanging, as in the case of Baîti, or cages containing a hare, a hedgehog, the fawn of a gazelle, a goose, or a creature of some kind caught during the day. On returning to the house, the herdsman deposited his load before his master, who is represented sometimes standing, sometimes seated on a chair beside his wife, like Anupu in our romance. The same expression and several others that occur in the course of the story are found word for word in the text on the paintings of El Kab, where scenes of field labour are represented (Lepsius, *Denkmäler*, III. pl. 10, and Maspero, *Notes sur différents points de Grammaire et d'Histoire, in Zeitschrift für Ægyptische Sprache 1879*, pp. 58-63).

8. All this part was not so incredible to the Egyptian as it is to us (cf. *Introduction*, pp. cxxxi-cxxxii). We shall see, in a fragment of a fantastic story given later on (pp. 219-222), that the good herdsman should be something of a magician in order to protect his beasts: the author of the *Story of the Two Brothers* has, however, permitted himself to endow Baîti with rather more knowledge than the ordinary drover possessed.

9. This is an allusion to the subsidence of the inundation.

lightened and it was a second day, they went to the fields with their team to begin work, and their heart was joyous, exceedingly, exceedingly, with their work, and they did not cease from work.

And many days after that, while they were in the fields and were hoeing, the elder brother sent his younger brother, saying, "Run, bring us the seed from the village." The younger brother found the wife of his elder brother, who was having her hair dressed.[10] He said to her, "Up! Give me the seed, that I may run to the fields, for my elder brother waits for me; do not cause me to delay!" She said to him, "Go, open the hutch,[11] and take what pleases thee, so that the dressing of my hair may not be left unfinished." The youth went into the stable, he fetched a large jar, for his intention was to take plenty of grain, he filled it with wheat and with barley, and he went out under the load. She said to him, "What is the quantity that is on thy shoulder?" He said to her, "Barley, three measures; wheat, two measures; five in all—that is what I have on my shoulder." Thus he said to her, but she, she addressed him saying, "There is great prowess in thee, and I observe thy strength each day."[12] And her heart went out to him as one desires a young man.[13] She arose, she laid hold on him, she said to him, "Come, let us lie together for the space of one hour. If thou wilt grant me this, in faith I will make thee two beauteous garments." The youth became like a cheetah of the south in hot rage, because of the evil suggestion she had made to him, and she was frightened exceedingly, exceedingly. He spake to her, saying, "But in truth thou art to me as a mother, and thy husband is to me as a father, and he who is my elder, it is he who enables me to live. Ah! this horrible thing that thou hast said to me, do not say it to me again, and for me I shall tell it to no one; I shall not let it escape from my mouth for any one." He took up his burden

10. The coiffure of the Egyptian women usually consisted of a great number of very small plaits; it required several hours to arrange, and once accomplished it would remain undisturbed for several days or even for several months, as with the Nubian women of to-day.

11. This refers, probably, to the hutches of beaten earth figured on the ancient tables of offerings in the form of peasant huts, and which are still in use throughout modern Egypt.

12. The five measures of grain represent 368 litres (647 pints) in capacity, weighing about 276 kilograms (608 lbs.). The market porters of France carry an average weight of 200 kilograms, and rarely attempt as much as 276 kilograms (Chabas, Recherches sur les poids, mesures et monnaies des anciens Egyptiens, pp. 9, 11). Baîti therefore possessed unusual strength, which justified the lady's admiration.

13. The text literally runs "Her heart knew him in recognition of a young man."

and went to the fields. When he reached his elder brother they set to work at their labour.

And after that, at the time of evening, when the elder brother returned to his house, and the younger brother was following his beasts, bearing all the things of the fields, and guiding his beasts before him to go to rest in their stables in the village,[14] as the wife of the elder brother was afraid concerning that she had said, she took some fat and a rag, and made herself appear as one who had been beaten by an evil-doer,[15] in order to say to her husband, "It is thy younger brother who has beaten me." When, therefore, her husband returned in the evening according to his daily habit, on arriving at his house, he found his wife lying down and as though mournful owing to violence; she poured no water over his hands according to her daily habit, she made no light before him, but his house was in darkness and she was lying down all soiled. Her husband said to her, "Who then hath spoken with thee?" She then said, "None hath spoken with me except, thy young brother. When he came to take the seed for thee, finding me seated quite alone, he said to me, 'Come, that we may lie together for the space of an hour; put on thy fine garments.' He spake thus to me and I did not listen to him. 'But am not I thy mother? for thy elder brother is he not to thee as a father?' Thus I spake to him. He was afraid, he beat me that I might not make any report to thee. If, therefore, thou permittest him to live, I shall kill myself, for behold when he returns this evening, as I have complained of his evil words, what he will do is evident."

The elder brother became like a cheetah of the south[16]; he sharpened his knife; he took it in his hand. The elder brother placed himself behind the door of his stable, in order to kill his younger brother, when he should come in the evening to bring his beasts to the stable. And when the sun set, and the younger brother carried up all the plants of the field according to his daily habit, and he came, the cow in front at

14. The elder brother, master of the farm, returned straight home when his work was finished. The younger brother, mere farm servant, must still carry up the grass and take the cattle to the stable; he would therefore walk more slowly and arrive at the house long after the other. The wife had thus ample time to tell the untrue story and excite her husband's wrath against her brother-in-law.

15. She rubbed herself with fat to imitate the shining marks and bruises caused by blows on human flesh.

16. This is the almost banal expression devoted to expressing anger on the part of a man or of a sovereign: Ramses II or the Ethiopian Paênekhi *conduct themselves like a cheetah* (the *guepard*) *of the south* neither more nor less than Baîti or Anupu.

the entrance to the stable said to her guardian, "Here is thy elder brother who stands before thee with his knife to kill thee; escape from him." When he had heard what the cow in front said, the second one said the same as she entered; he looked below the door of the stable, he perceived the feet of his elder brother who was standing behind the door, his knife in his hand,[17] he placed his load on the ground, he fled with all his might, and his elder brother started in pursuit with his knife. The younger brother cried to Phrâ-Harmakhis,[18] saying, "Good Master, it is thou that judgest iniquity justly!" And Phrâ heard all his lamentations, and Phrâ caused a large piece of water to appear between him and his elder brother; it was full of crocodiles, and one of them was on one side and one on the other, and the elder brother twice flung out his hand to strike him, but he did not kill him; this is what he did. His younger brother called to him on the bank, saying, "Remain there until the earth lightens. When the sun's disc rises, I will plead with thee before it, that I may re-establish the truth, for I shall never again be with thee, I shall never again be in the places where thou wilt be; I shall go to the Vale of the Acacia."[19]

When the earth lightened and it was a second day, Phrâ-Harmakhis having risen, each one perceived the other. The youth addressed his elder brother, saying to him, "Why dost thou come behind me to kill

17. The base of the Egyptian door very rarely touches the sill; in the greater number of paintings where the door is represented a considerable space can be seen between the door and the ground level.

18. The Egyptians named the sun Raîya, Rîya, from which we have made Râ, and with the masculine article, Prâ or Phrâ; Harmakhuîti was Horus, between the two horizons, that is to say the sun in its diurnal course, journeying from the morning horizon to the evening horizon. The two forms of Râ and of Harmakhuîti, distinct in origin, had been confused long before the period in which the *Story of the Two Brothers* was written, and the expression Phrâ-Harmakhuîti was employed as a simple variant of Phrâ or of Râ in the language of the period. The Greeks turned Harmakhuîti into Harmakhis; Harmakhis was personified in the great Sphinx of Gizeh, near the Pyramids.

19. The word I translate *acacia* has for a long time been translated *cedar*. Loret wished to render it *pine*, and Spiegelberg has more recently proposed *cypress* as its meaning (*Rechnungen*, pp. 54 *et seq*; and *die Bauinschrift Amenophis III*, in the *Recueil*, vol. xx, p. 52). The vale of the acacia, of the cedar, the pine or the cypress seems to correspond with the funerary valley where Amon the god of Thebes went for a visit every year to render homage to his father and mother, who were supposed to have been buried there; Virey indeed, generalising on the hypothesis (*La Religion de l'Ancienne Égypte*, pp. 194-197), believed that it was the other world, Amentît, which in fact communicated with Egypt by the Nile. Lefébure, misled by the current translation *Vale of the Cedar*, placed it in Phœnecia, the land of cedars (*Œuvres diverses*, vol. i, p. 163), which provided him with a new concordant detail between the history of Baîti and the Græco-Egyptian

me by craft without having heard what my mouth had to say? For me, I am truly thy younger brother, but thou, thou art like a father, and thy wife is to me as a mother, is it not so in truth? Yet when thou didst send me for the grain thy wife said to me, 'Come, let us pass an hour, lie with me,' and lo, this hath been perverted to thee to a different thing." He made known to him all that had passed between him and the woman; he swore by Phrâ-Harmakhis, saying, "Thou, to come behind me to kill me by craft, thy dagger in thy hand by treason, what infamy!" He took a bill-hook for cutting reeds, he severed his virile member, he cast it into the water, where the electric catfish devoured it,[20] he sank down, he fainted. The elder brother cursed his heart exceedingly, exceedingly, and he remained there and wept over him. He leapt, but he could not pass over to the bank where his younger brother was, because of the crocodiles. His younger brother called to him, saying, "Thus whilst thou didst imagine an evil action, thou didst not recall one of the good actions or even one of the things that I did for thee. Ah! go to thy house, and do thou thyself care for thy cattle, for I shall not live longer in the place where thou art—I go to the Vale of the Acacia. Yet here is what thou shalt do for me, when thou art returned to thy business, for know thou the things that will happen to me. I shall take out my heart by magic to place it on the top of the flower of the Acacia; and when the Acacia is cut down and my heart falls to the ground thou shalt come to seek for it. "When thou shalt have passed seven years in seeking for it, be not disheartened, but when once thou hast found it place it in a vase of fresh water[21]; without doubt I shall live anew, and recompense

---

legend of Osiris. In reality the Vale was situated, as we shall see later (p. 11), on the banks of the Nile (*iaûmâ*), no doubt near the spot where the river descended from heaven on to our world.

20. According to the legend, Osiris, after having been cut in pieces by Typhon, was thrown into the Nile; all the fish respected the remains of the god, except the oxyrrhynchus, which devoured the virile member. The scribe who wrote the *Story of the Two Brothers* substituted the name of another fish for that of the oxyrrhynchus, no doubt out of respect. This fish, which is represented several times on the walls of the tomb of Ti, was called *narû*. It can be easily recognised by the barbels with which the periphery of the mouth is furnished, and the convex form of its caudal fin. A comparison of the ancient drawings with the plates of the *Description de l'Égypts* (*Poissons du Nil,* pl. xii. figs 1-4) proves it to be the *Malapterus electricus* or electric catfish (*Description,* vol. xxiv. p. 299 *et seq.*).

21. The libation of fresh water is indispensable for the dead; without it they could not revive. As late as the Ptolemaic period the hellenised Egyptians stated in their epitaphs written in Greek that Osiris had "given them fresh water in the nether world."

the evil that shall have been done to me.[22] Now, thou wilt know that something is happening to me when a pitcher of beer is put into thy hand and it throws up froth; another of wine shall be given to thee, and it shall become thick. Do not delay, in truth, when that shall happen to thee." He departed to the Vale of the Acacia, and his elder brother returned to his house, his hand on his head, daubed with dust.[23] When he arrived at his house he killed his wife, he threw her to the dogs,[24] and he continued to mourn for his younger brother.

And many days after that, the younger brother being in the Vale of the Acacia without any one with him, employed the day in hunting the beasts of the desert, and he came to spend the night under the acacia, where his heart was placed on the top of its flower. And many days after that he constructed with his hand, in the Vale of the Acacia, an *ezbeh* filled with everything good, in order to form a house for himself. As he went out from his *ezbeh*, he met the Neuvaine of the gods[25] who were going forth to rule the affairs of the Entire Land.[26] The Neuvaine of the gods spake all together and said to him, "Oh, Baîti, bull of the Neuvaine of the gods,[27] art thou not here alone, for having left thy country before the wife of Anupu, thy elder brother? Lo! his wife is slain, and thou hast

22. Litt. "I will render reply to that which is transgressed."

23. One of the most frequent signs of sorrow in Egypt, as in the rest of the East; lumps of dust and of mud are collected to daub the face and head. A picture of a Theban tomb, reproduced by Wilkinson (*Manners and Customs,* 2nd edition, vol. iii. pl. lxviii.), shows the family and friends of the deceased daubing themselves in this way in presence of the mummy.

24. The same detail occurs in the *Story of Satnî-Khamoîs,* where Tbûbûî causes the children of the hero to be thrown "down from the window to the dogs and cats, and these ate their flesh" (cf. p. 114).

25. The cosmic gods of ancient Egypt formed a theoretic group of nine divine personages, which was called *psit* or *pauîtnutîru,* "the ennead, the neuvaine of the gods," or to employ a vaguer term the "cycle of the gods." This Ennead, each member of which was able to disintegrate into an infinite number of secondary forms, presided at the creation, and the duration of the universe, such as it was conceived to be by various sacerdotal schools. From other texts we learn that the gods descended at times to earth in order to walk about; on the 25th day of Paophi, for instance, one was liable to meet them under the form of a bull (Chabas, *Le Calendrier des Jours fastes et néfastes,* p. 43).

26. *i.e.* of Egypt: see above, p. 4, note 7.

27. The epithet "bull" is at least strange when applied to a eunuch. It must be remembered, however, that Baîti is a popular form of the god with the double bull's head (cf. *Introduction,* p. cvi, note 57); his misadventure, while depriving him on earth of his virile power, would not prevent him as a god from retaining his prolific faculties. In the same way Osiris in one of the variants of the legend, dead and mutilated as he was, revived to impregnate Isis and become the father of Horus.

rendered to him all that has been done of evil against thee." Their heart suffered for him exceedingly, exceedingly, and Phrâ Harmakhis said to Khnumu,[28] "Oh, fashion a wife for Baîti, in order that thou mayest not be alone."[29] Khnumu made him a companion to dwell with him who was beautiful in her members more than any woman in the Entire Land, for the seed of all the gods was in her. The Seven Hâthors[30] came to see her and they said with one voice: "Let her die by the sword." Baîti desired her exceedingly, exceedingly: as she dwelt in his house, while he passed the day hunting the beasts of the desert in order to lay them before her, he said to her, "Do not go out, for fear the river[31] should seize thee: thou knowest not how to escape it, for thou art merely a woman. As for me, my heart is placed at the top of the flower of the Acacia, and if another should find it, it would be necessary for me to fight him." He according-ly revealed to her all that concerned his heart.[32]

And many days after that, Baîti having gone hunting according to his habit of every day, as the girl had gone out to walk under the acacia which was near her house, lo! she perceived the river which drew its waves towards her, she fled before it, she entered into her house. The river cried to the Acacia, saying, "Let me take possession of her," and the Acacia delivered up a tress of her hair. The river carried it into

28. The name Khnumu signifies *the modeller*, and it was said that the god *modelled* the egg or the substance of the world on a potter's wheel. Khnumu, who was pre-eminently a local god of Elephantine, and of the first Cataract, was notwithstanding, a cosmic deity, and it is easy to understand why the divine Ennead should choose him to fashion a wife for Baîti; he kneaded her, and modelled her of the dust of the ground. We shall see later in the *Story of Khufuî* that he assisted at births, and the well-known pictures of the temples of Deir-el-Baharî and Luxor show that after the impregnation, it was he who formed the body and the double of the infant on his potter's wheel; he *modelled* it in the body of the mother, and also gave ifc the final form after birth.

29. This phrase includes a sudden change of person. In the first part Phrâ says to Khnu-mu, "Fashion a wife for Baîti"; in the second he says to Baîti, "in order that thou shalt not be alone."

30. The Seven Hâthors here play the same role as the fairy godmothers of our fairy tales. They appear also at the beginning of the story of the *Doomed Prince*, as will be seen later (p. 154).

31. There seems here an allusion to the *Bride of the Nile* and her immersion in the river. The ancient Egyptians called the Nile *the sea* (iaûmâ), like the modern Egyptians (*bahr*); the expression occurs again in the first story of Satni-Khâmoîs, p. 103, note 20 of the present volume.

32. Literally "he opened to her his heart in all its form."

Egypt and deposited it at the streamlet of the laundrymen of Pharaoh, l. h. s.[33] the scent of the ringlet penetrated the linen of Pharaoh, l. h. s., and they blamed the laundrymen of Pharaoh, l. h. s., saying, "Scent of pomade in the linen of Pharaoh, l. h. s.!" They scolded them every day, so much that they did not know what they were doing, and the chief of the washermen of Pharaoh, l. h. s., came to the streamlet, for his heart was annoyed exceedingly, exceedingly, with the scoldings he received every day. He stopped, he stayed at the rivulet just opposite the lock of hair which was in the water; he caused some one to go down, who brought it to him, finding that it smelt sweet, exceedingly, exceedingly, and he carried it to Pharaoh, l. h. s. They fetched the scribes, sorcerers of Pharaoh, l. h. s. They said to Pharaoh, l. h. s., "This lock of hair belongs to a daughter of Phrâ-Harmakhis who has in her the essence of all the gods.[34] Oh thou that receivest homage from foreign lands, cause messengers to go to all the foreign lands to find this damsel; and the messenger who shall go to the Vale of the Acacia, cause that plenty of men go with him to bring her back." Behold His Majesty, l. h. s., said, "It is perfect, perfect that which ye have said," and they sent away the messengers. And many days after that, the men who had gone to the foreign land came to report to His Majesty, l. h. s., but those who had gone to the Vale of the Acacia did not come: Baîti, having killed them, left one of them only to report to His Majesty, l. h. s. His Majesty, l. h. s., caused a number of men and archers, and some charioteers, to go to fetch the damsel; also a woman was with them who gave

---

33. Pharaoh is a form which was first Hebraised, then Hellenised, of the title Para-âûi, "the double great house," used to designate all the kings. That the sovereign was *the double great house* and not merely *the great house*, is because Egypt was divided from time immemorial into two countries (cf. p. 4, note 5); thus the king was a double king, king of Egypt of the North, and of Egypt of the South, and his house was a double house to correspond with each of the two personages of which he was composed. L. h. s. is an abbreviation of the formula, *Life, health, strength,* which always follows the name of a king or a royal title.

34. According to the beliefs of the Egyptians, as of many other nations, all parts of the body were so closely united by mutual sympathy, that they still exercised their influence one on another even when separated and removed to great distances. The sorcerer who possessed a limb, some morsels of flesh, nail clippings, and especially some hair, could impose his will on the man from whom they came. We need not, therefore, be surprised that the Nile asked for a lock of hair belonging to the Daughter of the Gods, nor that the magicians, on examining the lock, recognised immediately the nature of the person to whom it belonged.

into her hand[35] all the fine trinkets of a woman. This woman came to Egypt with her and they rejoiced over her in the Entire Land. His Majesty, l. h. s., loved her exceedingly, exceedingly, so well that One[36] proclaimed her as Principal Favourite. One spake to her to cause her to tell about her husband, and she said to His Majesty, l. h. s., "Let them cut down the Acacia and he will be destroyed." One sent men and archers to cut down the Acacia; they cut down the flower on which was the heart of Baîti, and in that evil hour he fell dead.

And when the earth lightened, and it was a second day, after the Acacia had been cut down, when Anupu, the elder brother of Baîti, had entered his house and was seated, having washed his hands, a jug of beer was given him, and it spurted out froth. Another of wine was given him, and it became thick with scum. He seized his staff and his sandals, and also his garments with his weapons, he started to walk to the Vale of the Acacia; he entered the villa of his younger brother, and he found his younger brother laid dead on his bed.[37] He wept when he perceived his younger brother lying down as though dead; he went to seek the heart of his younger brother under the Acacia, under the shelter of which his younger brother slept at night; he spent three years in the search without finding it. And he entered upon the fourth year, when, his heart desiring to come to Egypt, he said, "I will go to-morrow"; thus said he in his heart. And when the earth lightened and it was a second day, he went under the Acacia, he passed the day searching; when he returned in the evening and looked around him to search afresh, he found a seed, he returned with it, and lo! it was the heart of his younger brother. He brought a cup of fresh water, he threw it into it; he seated himself according to his habit of every day. And when it became night, the heart having absorbed the water, Baîti trembled in all his members, and he gazed fixedly at his elder brother, whilst his heart was in the cup.[38]

35. Piehl (*Zeitschrift*, 1886, pp. 80-81) preferred to translate this, "A woman was with them, she gave her all the sweet cakes of a woman." Cf. Max Müller, *Ueber einige Hieroglyphenzeichen* in the *Recueil de Travaux*, vol. ix, p. 170, and Piehl's reply, *Lettre à M. le Rédaoteur du Recueil,* 1888, pp. 1-3.

36. One, which corresponds to the form of the indefinite pronoun *emtutu*, followed by the determinative of divinity, appears to refer frequently to the Pharaoh. "One proclaimed her" would therefore be the equivalent of "Pharaoh proclaimed her."

37. This was the low rectangular bed, the *angareb* of the Berberines of to-day, the frame of which usually stands on four lions' feet.

38. Cf. Sethe's note, *zu d'Orbiney,* 14, 2-3, in *Zeitschrift,* vol. xxix, pp. 57-59.

Anupu, the elder brother, seized the cup of fresh water in which was the heart of his younger brother, who drank and his heart was in place, and he became as he was before. Each of them embraced the other, each spake with his companion, and then Baîti said to his elder brother, "Lo! I am about to become a great bull which will have all the right hairs, and of which the nature will not be known.[39] Seat thyself on my back when the sun arises, and when we are at the place where my wife is I will give some answers.[40] Thou therefore conduct me to the place where One is, and all good shall be done to thee, thou wilt be laden with silver and gold for having led me to Pharaoh, l. h. s., for I shall be a great miracle, and men will rejoice because of me in the Entire Land, and then thou shall go thence into thy city." And when the earth lightened and a second day was, Baîti changed into the form of which he had spoken to his elder brother. Anupu, his elder brother, seated himself on his back at daybreak, and he arrived at the place where One was.[41] It was made known to His Majesty, l. h. s., he looked at him, he became joyful exceedingly, exceedingly, he made him a great entertainment, saying, "It is a great miracle that has happened," and they rejoiced over him in the Entire Land.[42] They loaded his elder brother with silver and gold, and he settled himself in his city. They gave numerous attendants and numerous gifts to the bull, for Pharaoh, l. h. s., loved him exceedingly, exceedingly, more than all men in the Entire Land.

39. Our hero, being a form of the god with the double bull's head (cf. *Introduction*, pp. civ–cvi, note 57), changes easily into a bull, and also into Apis, the bull *par excellence*. Now Apis was required to have a certain number of mystic marks on his body, formed of hairs of various colours. He was black, with a triangular white tuft on his forehead, the figure of a vulture or of an eagle with outspread wings on his back, and the image of a scarab on his tongue; the hairs of his tail were double. "The scarab, the vulture, and all the other marks which were connected with the presence, and relative position of the tuft of hair over the forehead, did not exist in reality. No doubt the priests, initiated into the mysteries of Apis, were alone acquainted with them, and knew how to recognise in the divine animal the indispensable symbols, very much as astronomers recognised the outlines of a dragon, a lion, or a bear in certain arrangements of the stars." (Mariette, *Renseignements sur les Apis*, in the *Bulletin archéologique de l'Athénaeum français*, 1855, p. 54.)

40. Cf. The same expression, p. 9, note 22.

41. This is a survival of the very ancient tradition, according to which the dead "were conveyed to the domain and palace of Osiris by a sacred bull or by the cow Hâthor. On Theban coffins of the XXIst and following dynasties there may often be seen, on the yellow background, a scene representing the occupant in his living form riding astride the animal, or lying on its back in the form of a mummy.

42. During the time that elapsed between the death of an Apis and the discovery of a new Apis, the whole of Egypt was in mourning; the installation of the new Apis put an end to the

And many days after that the bull entered the harem,[43] and he stopped at the place where the favourite was, and he spake to her, saying, "Behold, I am alive nevertheless." She said to him, "Who art thou then?" He said to her, "I am Baîti. Thou knowest well when thou didst cause the Acacia to he hewn down by Pharaoh, l. h. s., that it would do me such an injury that I could live no longer; but behold I live nevertheless. I am a bull." The favourite was afeared exceedingly, exceedingly, on account of that which was spoken to her by her husband. He went out of the harem, and His Majesty, l. h. s., having come to spend a happy day with her, she was at the table of His Majesty, and One was kind to her exceedingly, exceedingly. She said to His Majesty, "Swear to me by God saying, 'that which thou shalt say to me I will listen to it for thee.'" He listened to all that she said. "Let there be given me the liver of that bull to eat, for he will do nothing worth doing." Thus she spake to him. One was grieved with that she said exceedingly, exceedingly, and the heart of Pharaoh was sick exceedingly, exceedingly. And when the earth lightened and a second day came, a great feast of offerings in honour of the bull was proclaimed, and one of the chief butchers of His Majesty, l. h. s., was sent to cut the throat of the bull. Then after his throat was cut, while he was on the shoulders of the men (who were carrying him), he twitched his neck, and let fall two drops of blood near the double flight of steps of His Majesty, l. h. s. One of them was on one side of the great doorway of Pharaoh, l. h. s., the other on the other side, and they sprang up into two great persea trees,[44] each of them of great beauty. They went to tell His Majesty, l. h. s., "Two great persea trees have grown as a great miracle for His Majesty, l. h. s., during the night, close to the great doorway of His Majesty, l. h. s.," and they rejoiced concerning them in the Entire Land, and One made offerings to them.[45]

mourning, and was celebrated with great festivities. Thus the romance here represents the actual customs of real life.

43. The sacred animals had free access to all parts of the temple where they dwelt. We know of the freedom enjoyed by the ram of Mendes, and the strange freaks in which he occasionally indulged (*Herodotus* II, 46; cf. Wiedemann, *Herodots Zweites Buch*, pp. 216-218). Baîti, in his character of sacred bull, could penetrate without hindrance into the parts of the palace closed to the public, and into the harem itself.

44. The persea, according to Schweinfurth the *Mimusops Schimperi*, was consecrated to Osiris. There was a persea tree on each side of the entrance to the temple of Deir el Baharî, and Naville has found the dried-up trunks of trees at places where Wilkinson marked on his plan the bases of obelisks; Spiegelberg has very ingeniously connected the fact with this passage in our romance. (Naville, *Un dernier mot sur la succession de Thoutmès*, in *Zeitschrift*, vol. xxxvii, pp. 48-52).

45. This is a result of the worship accorded to trees by the people (Maspero, *Histoire Ancienne*, vol. i, p. 121; cf. V. Scheil, *Cinq tombeaux thébains*, in the *Mémoires de la Mission française*,

And many days after that His Majesty, l. h. s., adorned himself with the diadem of lapis-lazuli, his neck hung with garlands of all manner of flowers, he mounted his chariot of vermilion, he went forth from the royal palace, l. h. s., in order to see the persea trees. The favourite went in a chariot with two horses, in the suite of Pharaoh, l. h. s. For His Majesty, l. h. s., seated himself under one of the persea trees,[46] the favourite seated herself under the other persea tree. When she was seated the persea spake to his wife, "Oh perfidious one! I am Baîti and I live, ill-treated by thee. Thou knewest well that to have the Acacia tree cut down by Pharaoh, l. h. s., was to do me an injury; I became a bull and thou hast caused me to be killed." And many days after that, when the favourite was at the table of His Majesty, l. h. s., and One was favourable to her, she said to His Majesty, l. h. s., "Grant me an oath by God saying, 'That which the favourite shall say to me, I will listen to it for her. Speak!'" He listened to all that she spake. She said, "Cause the two perseas to be hewn down and made into fine coffers."[47] One listened to all that she said. And many days after that His Majesty, l. h. s., sent skilful carpenters, they cut down the perseas of Pharaoh, l. h. s., and standing there, seeing it done, was the royal spouse, the favourite. A chip flew out, entered the mouth of the favourite and she perceived that she had conceived.[48] The coffers were made and One did with them all that she wished.

And many days after that, she brought a male child into the world, and they went to tell His Majesty, l. h. s., "A man child is born to thee." They brought him, they gave him wet-nurses and under nurses,[49] they rejoiced concerning him in the Entire Land. They began to make a feast day, they

---

vol. iv, pp. 578-579 and pl. iv), of which many traces exist at the present day in Mussulman Egypt (Maspero, *Mélanges de Mythologie*, vol. ii, pp. 224-227).

46. The Egyptian scribe has here missed an entire line : "His Majesty seated himself under one of the perseas, *the favourite seated herself under the other persea. When she was seated, the persea* spake to his wife." The scribe actually made an omission. In the original he had two consecutive lines ending in the word *persea,* and he omitted the second.

47. Cf. Chabas, *Œuvres diverses,* vol. v, p. 434, and K. Sethe, *Zu d'Orbiney,* 18. 1, in *Zeitschrift,* 1907, pp. 134-135.

48. This is an allusion to a mythological fact: every evening the sun entered the mouth of the goddess Nûît, who thereby conceived and the next morning brought into the world a new sun (Maspero, *Études de Mythologie et d'Archéologie égyptiennes,* vol. ii, pp. 25-26).

49. This office of "under nurse," or "cradle rocker," was at times filled by men: several high functionaries of the XVIIIth dynasty were invested with it. The word *khnumu,* by which it is designated, signifies properly *to sleep, to send to sleep;* the *khnumu,* therefore, is properly the person who puts the infant to sleep, the *monâit* is one who gives him the breast.

began to be in his name.[50] His Majesty, l. h. s., loved him exceedingly, exceedingly, forthwith, and he was proclaimed royal son of Kaûshû,[51] and many days after that His Majesty, l. h. s., made him hereditary prince of the Entire Land. And many days after that, when he had been many years hereditary prince of the Entire Land, His Majesty, l. h. s., took flight to the Sky.[52] One said, "Let the great officials of His Majesty, l. h. s., be brought, that I may cause them to know all that has happened with regard to me." They brought his wife to him, he judged her before them and they ratified his judgment. They brought his elder brother to him and he made him hereditary prince of his Entire Land. He was twenty years king of Egypt, then he passed from life and his elder brother was in his place on the day of the funeral.— This book is finished in peace, for the double of the scribe treasurer Qagabû, of the treasure of Pharaoh, l. h. s., of the scribe Haraûi, of the scribe Maîaemapît; the scribe Ennana, the owner of this book has made it. Whoever speaks against this book, may Thoth challenge him to single combat.[53]

50. This obscure phrase may be interpreted in various ways. It signifies either that the custom was then arising of giving the name of the youthful prince to children born after him, or, as Lefébure suggests (*L'importance du nom,* in *Sphinx,* vol. i, p. 97), that the prince having received a name, began to enter into full possession of his personality; the human person was in fact not complete until after receiving a name.

51. One of the titles of the princes of the royal family. The *royal son of Kaûshû,* to speak more accurately, was governor of the land of Kaûshû, that is to say of Ethiopia. As a matter of fact, the title may not have been entirely honorific; the young prince himself governed, and thus served the apprenticeship to his royal position, in the regions of the Upper Nile.

52. One of the ordinary euphemisms of the Egyptian official style, used to denote the king's death. An equivalent occurs at the beginning of the *Memoirs of Sinuhit;* cf. p. 62 of the present volume.

53. This formula appears to have been in current use, for it is found drawn, as a writing exercise, by a scribe who was getting his hand into practice, on the verso of the *Sallier Papyrus iv* pl. 21: "Done by the scribe Amânûâ, the master of this *teaching.* Whosoever shall speak against this *teaching* of the scribe Amânûâ, may Thoth slay him in single combat." the *Master of the book,* or of the *teaching,* was the person who had the exclusive right to its possession, whether he was the author, or merely the editor or the appointed reciter. The literal translation of the threat addressed to any one, whether reader or auditor, who should criticise it, runs thus: "may Thoth be made to him companion of combat." This expression is comprehensible when one finds scenes at Sakkara or Beni Hasan representing the gymnastic exercises executed by soldiers; each of them is matched—made companion—with another, like the wrestlers of Greece or the gladiators of Rome.

THE KING KHUFUÎ
AND THE MAGICIANS [2]

(XVIIITH DYNASTY)

THE PAPYRUS that has preserved this story was given to Lepsius, over fifty years ago, by an English lady, Miss Westcar, who had brought it from Egypt. Acquired by the Berlin Museum in 1886, it was first made known by a summary analysis of it published by A. Erman, *Ein neuer Papyrus des Berliner Museums,* in the *National-Zeitung* of Berlin (May 14, 1886), and has been reproduced by A. Erman, *Ægypten und Ægyptisches Leben im Altertum, 8vo,* Tubingen, 1885–7, pp. 498–502; Ed. Meyer, *Geschichte des alten Ægyptens, 8vo,* Berlin, 1887, pp. 129–131.

The translation given by me in the second edition of these tales was not so much a literal version as an adaptation, founded partly on a German translation, partly on a transcription in hieroglyphic characters communicated to me by Erman. Since then an English paraphrase has been inserted by W. M. Flinders Petrie in his *Egyptian Tales,* 1895, London, 12mo, vol. i, pp. 97–142, and the text itself has been published in facsimile and in a hieroglyph transcription, and also translated into German by A. Erman, *die Märchen des Papyrus Westcar* (forming vols. v-vi of the *Mittheilungen aus den Orientalischen Sammlungen*), 1890, Berlin, 4to, who has since reproduced his translation with various corrections in his pamphlet, *Aus den Papyrus der Königlichen Museen,* 1899, Berlin, 8vo, pp. 30–42, and has introduced several passages of his transcription into hieroglyphs in his *Ægyptische Chrestomathie,* 1904, Berlin, 12mo, pp. 20–27.

Finally a fresh German translation has been made by A. Wiedemann, *Altægyptische Sagen und Märchen,* Leipzig, 1906, small 8vo, pp. 1–24.

The tale would probably have been one of the longest known to us, if it had come down to us complete; unfortunately, however, the beginning has disappeared. It opened with several stories of marvels related one after another to their father by the sons of King Cheops. The first one of these that is found in our manuscript is almost entirely destroyed; only the final formula exists to show that the action occurred in the time of Pharaoh Zasiri probably that

Zasiri whom our lists of royal names place in the IIIrd dynasty. The pages that follow contain the account of a marvel performed by the sorcerer Ubaû-anir, under the reign of Nabka of the IIIrd dynasty. From the moment when Prince Baîufrîya opens his mouth, the story proceeds without any serious interruption to the end of the manuscript. It ends in the middle of a phrase, and we cannot conjecture with any certainty what is required to render it complete. The Egyptian romances have a disconcerting habit of breaking off abruptly when one least expects it, and of condensing into a few lines facts that we should consider it necessary to set out at length. It is possible that one or two more pages would have been enough to provide us with the sequel, or perhaps it required eight or ten more pages, and included incidents of which we have no suspicion.

It may be asked whether that portion of the romance that relates to the birth of the first three kings of the Vth dynasty rests on an historical basis. It is certain that a new family began to reign with Usirkaf; the Turin papyrus places a rubric before this king and thus separates him from the Pharaohs that preceded him. The monuments do not appear to admit of any interregnum between Shopsiskaf and Usirkaf, which inclines us to believe that the change of dynasty was effected without disturbance. If one were to believe the legend by which Usirkaf was the son of Râ and of a priestess, he was not of royal blood, and had no claim of kinship with the princes whom he succeeded. The parallel of the Theban theogamies, as we know them in the history of Queen Hatshopsuîtu, Amenôthes III, and Cleopatra, may still leave some doubt as to whether they were not connected with the great Pharaonic line through some ancestor. The idea that the three monarchs were born at the same time seems to have been fairly widespread in Egypt, for a text of the Ptolemaic period (Brugsch, *Dict. Hiér.*, vol. vii, p. 1093), speaking of the city of Pa-Sahurîya founded by one of them, asserts that it was also called the *City of the Triplets* (Piehl, *Quelques passages du Papyrus Westcar*, in *Sphinx*, vol. i, pp. 71–80); this nevertheless does not prove that we should ascribe an historic value to the statement. In fact, without further warrant it is safest to regard the story as purely imaginary.

Erman has shown that the writing of the Westcar papyrus closely resembles that of the Ebers papyrus; we may therefore ascribe the production of the manuscript at the earliest to the later reigns of the Hyksôs domination, or at the latest to the earlier reigns of the XVIIIth dynasty. It is, however, probable that the redaction is far more ancient than the execution; from the peculiarities of style, Erman is of opinion that it dates back perhaps to the XIIth dynasty. The story of Cheops and the magicians would then belong to very much the same time as the *Memoirs of Sinuhît* and the *Lamentations of the Fellah;* this would be a specimen of the popular romance of the period.

The commencement of the tale and its general setting may be restored with very tolerable certainty from the preamble of *Papyrus No. 1 of St. Petersburg.* "It happened at the time when Sanafruî was beneficent king over this Entire Land. One day when the privy councillors of the palace who had entered into the house of Pharaoh, l. h. s., to consult with him, had already retired after having consulted with him after their custom of every day, His Majesty said to the Chancellor who was near him, 'Run, bring to me the privy councillors of the palace who have gone out to depart, so that we may consult afresh, without delay." The councillors come back, and the king confesses to them that he had called them back to ask them whether they did not know a man who could amuse him by telling him stories: upon which, they recommend to him a priest of Bastît of the name of Neferhô."[1]

It is very probable that Cheops assembled his sons one day when he was depressed and dull, and asked them whether they knew of any marvel accomplished by the magicians either in the past or at the time then present. The first story is lost, but the part of the manuscript that is still preserved contains remains of the formula by which the amazed Pharaoh expressed his satisfaction.

His Majesty the King of the two Egypts Khufuî, true of voice, said, "Let them present to His Majesty the King Zasiri, true of voice, an offering of a thousand loaves, a hundred jugs of beer, an ox, two bowls of incense, and let a flat cake, a quart of beer, a ration of meat, a bowl of incense be given for the chief lector . . . , for I have seen the proof of his learning." And that was done which His Majesty commanded.[2]

Then, the royal son Khâfrîya rose to speak, and he said: "I am about to make known to Thy Majesty a marvel that happened in the time of thy father King Nabka,[3] true of voice, on a time when he resorted to the temple of Ptah, lord of Ankhutaûi."[4]

1 Golénischeff, *Papyrus No. 1 de Saint-Pétersbourg, Zeitschrift,* 1876, pp. 109-110.

2. This is the formula that ends the first story; the name of the magician is completely destroyed; Imhotep, son of Hapuî, was probably the missing chief lector.

3. King Nabka was not the actual father of Khufuî, but as he belonged to an earlier dynasty, and as all the Pharaohs were supposed to consist of one single family, the man telling the story, in speaking of one of them, calls him the *father* of Khufuî, the reigning sovereign.

4. Ankhutaûi, as Brugsch has pointed out, is the name of one of the quarters of Memphis. I have some cause to believe that the site may be fixed near the mound now called Kom el Azîz.

Thus, a day when His Majesty had gone to the temple of Ptah, lord of Ankhutaûi, and when His Majesty paid a visit to the house of the scribe, chief lector,[5] Ubaû-anir, with his suite, the wife of the first lector Ubaû-anir beheld a vassal[6] among those that were behind the king: from the hour that she beheld him, she no longer knew in what part of the world she was. She sent to him her serving-maid who was near her, to say to him, "Come, that we may lie together for the space of an hour; put on thy festival garments." She caused a coffer full of fine garments to be carried to him,[7] and he came with the serving-maid to the place where she was. And when the days had passed after this, as the chief lector Ubaû-anir had a kiosque at the lake of Ubaû-anir,[8] the vassal said to the wife of Ubaû-anir: "There is the kiosque at the lake of Ubaû-anir; if it pleases thee we will have a short time there." Then the wife of Ubaû-anir sent word to the major-domo who had charge of the lake, "Cause the kiosque which is at the lake to be made ready."

It was done as she had said, and she stayed there, drinking with the vassal until the sun set. And when the evening was come, he went down to the lake to bathe and the serving-maid was with him, and the major-domo knew what was occurring between the vassal and the wife of Ubaû-anir. And when the land was lightened and it was the second day, the major-domo went to seek the chief lector, Ubaû-anir, and told him these things that the vassal had done in the kiosque with his wife. When the chief

---

5. The expression *chief lector* is a more or less close translation of the title *Khri-habi. The khri-habi* was literally *the man of the roll,* he who, at a ceremony, directed the accessories and the performance, placed the performers, prompted them with the terms of the formula they had to utter, pointed out to them the gestures and the actions they had to perform, if needful recited the prayers for them, and was in fact an actual master of the ceremonies (cf. Maspero, *études égyptiennes,* vol. ii, p. 51 *et seq.*). The *khri-habi* or lector, whose business it was to know all the formulæ, had also to know the incantations and the magical formulæ as well as the religious formulæ; this is why all the sorcerers of our tale are *chief lectors, first lectors* (cf. Introduction, p. cxxxi). The title held by them in conjunction with this one, that of *writer of books,* shows that their learning was not confined to the reciting of charms; it extended to the copying, and if necessary, the composing of books of magic.

6. The Egyptian text gives *nozesu, a little one,* a man of humble position. The ancient word *vassal* appears to me to correspond exactly with the meaning of the Egyptian term.

7. Cf. in the *Tale of the Two Brothers,* p. 5 of the present volume, the two garments that the wife of Anupu promised to Baîti in order to tempt him.

8. The *Lake of Ubaû-anir* is the name of an estate formed of the name of an owner and of the word *she,* which signifies *pool, inundation basin,* the *birkeh* of Arabic Egypt. It is a method of construction frequently used in the geographical nomenclature of Egypt (cf. pp. 23, 59 of the present volume).

lector, Ubaû-anir, knew these things that had happened in his kiosque, he said to the major-domo "Bring me my ebony casket adorned with electrum that contains my book of magic."[9] When the major-domo had brought it, he modelled a crocodile in wax, seven inches long, he recited over it that which he recited from his book of magic; he said to it: "When that vassal comes to bathe in my lake, then drag him to the bottom of the water."[10] He gave the crocodile to the major-domo and said to him, "As soon as the vassal shall have gone down into the lake, according to his custom of every day, throw the wax crocodile into it behind him." The major-domo therefore went away and he took the wax crocodile with him. The wife of Ubaû-anir sent to the major-domo who had charge of the lake, and she said to him, "Cause the kiosque that is at the edge of the lake to be made ready, for behold, I come there to sojourn." The kiosque was furnished with all good things; one came and made diversion with the vassal. When it was the time of evening the vassal went according to his custom of every day, and the major-domo threw the wax crocodile into the water behind him; the crocodile changed into a crocodile of seven cubits; he seized the vassal, he dragged him under the water. Now the first lector, Ubaû-anir, dwelt seven days with His Majesty the King of Upper and Lower Egypt Nabka, true of voice, while the vassal was in the water without breathing. But after the seven days were accomplished, when the King of Upper and Lower Egypt Nabka, true of voice, went, and when he repaired to the temple, the first lector, Ubaû-anir, presented himself before him, and said to him, "May it please Thy Majesty to come and see the marvel that has occurred in the time of Thy Majesty in the matter of a vassal." His Majesty therefore went with the chief lector, Ubaû-anir. Ubaû-anir said to the crocodile, "Bring the vassal out of the water." The crocodile came forth and brought the vassal out of the water. The first lector, Ubaû-anir, said, "Let him stop," and he conjured him, he caused him to stop in front of the king. Then His Majesty, the King of Upper and of Lower Egypt Nabka, true of voice, said, "I pray you! this crocodile is terrifying." Ubaû-anir stooped, he seized the crocodile, and it became in his hands only a crocodile of wax. The first lector, Ubaû-anir, related to His Majesty the King of Upper and Lower Egypt Nabka, true of voice, that which the vassal had done in the house with his

9. In the first story of Satni-Khâmoîs, also, the miraculous book of Thoth is contained in a casket (cf. pp. 103, 105).

10. All the commencement is so much damaged that not one phrase is now complete. The restoration is founded on the admirable translation by Erman (*die Märchen des Papyrus Westcar;* pp. 22–26).

wife. His Majesty said to the crocodile, "Take thou that which is thine." The crocodile plunged to the bottom of the lake, and it is not known further what became of the vassal and of it. His Majesty the King of Upper and Lower Egypt, Nabka, true of voice, caused the wife of Ubaû-anir to be taken to the north side of the palace; she was burnt and her ashes thrown into the river.[11] Behold this is the marvel that happened in the time of thy father, the King of Upper and Lower Egypt Nabka, true of voice, and is one of those performed by the first lector, Ubaû-anir." His Majesty the King Khufuî, true of voice, said therefore, "Let there be presented to His Majesty the King Nabka, true of voice, an offering of a thousand loaves, a hundred jugs of beer, an ox, two bowls of incense, and also let a flat cake, a quart of beer, a bowl of incense be given for the first lector, Ubaû-anir, for I have beheld the proof of his learning." And that was done which His Majesty commanded.

Then the royal son Baîufrîya rose to speak, and he said: I am about to make known to Thy Majesty a marvel that happened in the time of thy father Sanafruî, true of voice, and which is one of those performed by the first lector Zazamânkhu.

One day when the king Sanafruî, true of voice, was feeling dull, His Majesty assembled the household of the king, l. h. s., in order to find something to lighten[12] his heart. As nothing was found, he said, "Hasten and let the first lector, Zazamânkhu, be brought to me," and he was brought to him immediately. His Majesty said to him, "Zazamânkhu, my

---

11. The way in which the climax is introduced in the text, without any comment, seems to prove that fire was the punishment appointed for adulterous wives. This supposition is confirmed by the story of Pheron, in which the King caused all the women to be burnt alive who, having had intercourse with a man other than their husband, could not provide him with the remedy necessary to restore his sight (Herodotus II, cxi.; cf. Introduction, pp. cxxix–cxxx). We were already aware that this punishment was accorded for a variety of crimes—parricide, sorcery, heresy, at any rate in Ethiopia (G. Maspero, *la Stèle de l'Excommunication*, in the *Revue archéologique*, 1871, vol. ii, p. 329 *et seq.*), for the robbery or destruction of temples, or of property in mortmain (Birch, *Inscriptions in the hieratic and demotic characters*, pl. 29, l. 8; cf. G. Möller, *Das Dekret des Amenophis, des Sohnes des Hapu*, in the *Sitzungsberichte* of the Berlin Academy, 1910, p. 936 i, note), for rebellion against the Pharaoh. It must have been the more dreaded, because in destroying the body it deprived the soul and the double of the support of which it had need in the other world. At the end of the *Tale of the Two Brothers* (p. 16 of the present volume) the author is careful to note the punishment of the *daughter of the gods*, without telling us of what it consisted; probably, according to custom, it was punishment by fire.

12. The Egyptian text gives here, as in all places where I have used the expression *"lighten,"* a verb signifying *refresh*. A literal translation would therefore be "something that *refreshed* his heart."

brother, I have assembled the household of the king, l. h. s., in order that something might be sought out that should lighten my heart, but I have found nothing." Zazamânkhu said to him, "Thy Majesty shall deign to go to the Lake of Pharaoh, l. h. s., and cause a bark to be equipped with all the beautiful damsels of the royal harem. The heart of Thy Majesty will lighten when thou shalt behold them go and come; and also when thou shalt contemplate the beauteous thickets of thy lake, when thou shalt gaze on the beauteous country that borders it and its beauteous banks, then the heart of Thy Majesty shall lighten. As for me, thus will I arrange the affair. Cause them to bring me twenty oars of ebony, adorned with gold, of which the blades shall be of maple wood adorned with electrum; twenty women also shall be brought to me of those who have beautiful bodies, beautiful bosoms, beautiful hair, and that have not yet borne a child; also twenty nets shall be brought and given to these women as clothing."[13] That was done which His Majesty had commanded. The women went and came, and the heart of His Majesty was rejoicing to see them row, when the oar of one of them struck her hair, and her fish of new malachite fell into the water.[14] Thereupon she became silent, she ceased to row, and her companions of the same band became silent and rowed no longer,[15] and His Majesty said, "You do not row any longer?" They said, "Our companion is silent, and she does not row any longer." His Majesty said to her, "Wherefore dost thou not row?" She said, "My fish of new malachite has fallen into the water." His Majesty said, "Only row on, I will replace it for thee." She said, "I wish for my own jewel, and not for another like it."

13. I have held that this refers to one of the fine bead fillets in faïence or glazed ware that one sees painted above the clothing of certain statues of the Memphite period or of the XIIth Dynasty—for instance on statue A 102 at the Louvre (cf. Perrot-Chipiez, *Histoire de l'Art*, vol.2 i, p. 143, and J. Capart, *l'Art égyptien*, vol. i, p. 42). Here, however, the twenty girls had no clothing made of any material, but were nude below their nets, as Piehl has admitted (*Sphinx*, vol. i, pp. 73–74; vol. iv, pp. 118–119). Borchardt confirms the meaning I have given by examples drawn from the statues at Cairo, but he believes that the girls had drawn the nets over their clothing (*Zeitschrift*, vol. xxxvii, p. 81). Petrie considers that it merely refers to a very fine material (*Deshasheh*, p. 32).

14. The text has here a word *nikhaû*, determined by a fish, and which is not found in any of the dictionaries published up to the present; I have translated it in general fashion by the word *fish*. It does not mean here a real fish, but one of the talismans in shape of a fish, to which the ancients, the Romans and Greeks, as well as the Eastern nations, attributed all sorts of marvellous virtues (F. de Mély, *le Poisson dans les Piérres gravées*, in the *Revue Archéologique*, 3ᵉ serie, vol. xii, pp. 319–332).

15. The girls sang as they rowed, to secure a rhythmic movement, according to Egyptian custom; the one who had lost her amulet became silent, the others also fell silent and the movement ceased.

Thereupon His Majesty said, "Very good; let the chief lector Zazamânkhu be brought to me." He was brought immediately, and His Majesty said, "Zazamânkhu, my brother, I have done as thou hast said, and the heart of His Majesty was lightened when he saw the women row, when behold, the fish of new malachite of one of the little ones has fallen into the water. Whereupon she has become silent, she has ceased to row and she has stopped her comrades. I said to her, 'Wherefore dost thou not row?' She said to me, 'The fish of new malachite is fallen into the water.' I said to her, 'Only row on, and I will replace it for thee.' She said, 'I wish for my own jewel and not for a jewel like it.'" Then the chief lector repeated that which he repeated of his book of magic; he raised a whole piece of water and laid it on the other; he found the fish lying on a lump of earth, he took it, he gave it to its owner. Now the water was twelve cubits deep in the centre, and now that it was piled up it was as much as twenty-four cubits. He repeated that which he repeated of his book of magic, and the water of the lake returned to its place. Thus His Majesty spent a happy hour with all the house of the king, l. h. s., and he rewarded the chief lector Zazamânkhu with all manner of good things. Behold this is the marvel that happened in the time of thy father, King Sanafruî, true of voice, and that was worked by the chief lector, Zazamânkhu, the magician.

His Majesty the King Khufuî, true of voice, then said, "Let these be presented to His Majesty the King Sanafruî, true of voice, an offering of a thousand loaves, one hundred jars of beer, an ox, two bowls of incense, also a flat cake, a quart of beer, a bowl of incense shall be given, for the chief lector Zazamânkhu, the magician, for I have seen the proof of his learning." And it was done as His Majesty had commanded.

Then the son of the king, Dadûfhoru,[16] arose to speak, and he said; "Until now Thy Majesty has heard the telling of marvels known only to people of other times, but of which the truth cannot be guaranteed. I can show to Thy Majesty a sorcerer who is of Thy time and whom Thy Majesty does not know." His Majesty said, "Who is that, Dadûfhoru?" The son of the king, Dadûfhoru, said, "There is a vassal who is called Didi, and who lives at Didusanafruî.[17] He is a vassal of a hundred and ten

16. Dadûfhoru is mentioned here as the son of Khufuî. Other documents make him his grandson, and the son of Menkaârîya (*Book of the Dead*, ch. lxiv, ll. 30–32).

17. The name of this locality is formed with that of King Sanafruî; its position is not known. We gather from the expressions employed in our text that from the place where Khufuî dwelt it was reached by going up the river. As this place was probably Memphis, the natural conclusion is that Didusanafruî was to the south of Memphis.

years[18] who still eats his five hundred loaves with a whole leg of beef, and to this day he drinks his hundred jars of beer. He knows how to put back in place a head that has been cut off; he knows how to make himself followed by a lion without a leash[19]; he knows the numbers of the caskets of books in the crypt of Thoth."[20] Now behold, His Majesty the King Khufuî, true of voice, had spent much time in seeking those caskets of books of the crypt of Thoth, in order to make a copy of them for his pyramid.[21] His Majesty said therefore: "Dadûfhoru my son, bring him to me thyself." Vessels were equipped for the son of the King, Dadûfhoru, and he set sail for Didusanafruî. When the vessels had arrived at the bank, he disembarked, and he placed himself on a chair of ebony wood, the shafts of which were of napeca wood[22] adorned with gold[23]; then

18. A hundred and ten years is the extreme limit of Egyptian life. Good wishes to people who are beloved or respected express a desire that they may live to the age of a hundred and ten. To exceed that is to pass the limits of human longevity: only certain privileged personages, such as Joseph, the husband of the Virgin, in Christian Egypt are so fortunate as to attain the age of a hundred and eleven years (cf. Goodwin in Chabas, *Mélanges égyptologiques*, 2ᵉ serie, p. 231 *et seq*). Later on a longer period was given, and Maçoudi speaks in the *Prairies d'Or* (trans. Barbier de Meynard, vol. ii, p. 372 *et seq*.) of a Coptic sage of a hundred and thirty years who was sent for by Ahmed-Ibn-Tulûn to be consulted.

19. Literally "leash on the ground"—*i.e.*, a lion that has been let loose and its leash thrown on the ground. In order to make it obey him, the magician had no need of a leash such as the lion tamers usually required; he managed the beast by means of eye and voice.

20. The Egyptians enclosed their books in wooden or stone boxes; the book boxes of the crypt of Thoth formed what we should call his *Library*. Thoth, the secretary of the gods, was the sage, and in consequence the magician, *par excellence*. It was he whom the superior deities—Ptah, Horus, Amon, Râ, and Osiris—commissioned to classify what they had created, and to set down in writing the names, the hierarchy, the qualities of things and of beings, and the formulæ binding on men and on gods. The usual work of the magician consisted of seeking out, reading, understanding, and copying the books of this library; he who knew and possessed them all, was as powerful as Thoth and became the real lord of the universe.

21. The Great Pyramid does not contain one line of writing, but the chambers in the pyramid of Unas and of the four first kings of the VIth dynasty are covered with hieroglyphs; they are the prayers and formulæ which insure a happy life in the other world for the *double* and the soul of the dead king. The author of our story, who knew the trouble taken by certain kings of antiquity to engrave extracts from the sacred books in their tombs, no doubt imagined that Khufuî had desired to do the same, but that he had not succeeded in securing them presumably on account of his legendary impiety. It is one method of explaining why there was no inscription in the Great Pyramid.

22. The napeca (*nabq*) is a species of jujube-tree—Zizyphus Spina Christi; the trunk and the branches are very straight and tough, and would form excellent shafts for a litter; the Arabs used them for lances and arrows.

23. See Wilkinson, *Manners and Customs*, vol. i, p. 287; also Lepsius, *Denkm.*, II, pl. 43a, pl. 121a, etc., representation of carrying chairs similar to that used by Dadûfhoru in our story.

when he had arrived at Didusanafruî, the chair was placed on the ground, he arose to salute the magician, and he found him laid on a low bed[24] at the threshold of his house, a female slave at his head who was scratching it, and another who was tickling his feet. The royal son, Dadûfhoru, said to him: "Thy condition is that of one who lives sheltered from old age. Old age is usually the arrival in port,[25] it is the putting on of bandages, it is the return to the earth; but to remain thus, well advanced in years, without infirmity of body, and without decrepitude of wisdom or of good judgment, is truly to be a fortunate one.[26] I have come hither in haste to invite thee, by a message from my father Khufuî, true of voice; thou shalt eat of the best that the king gives, and of the provisions which are such as they have who are among those who serve him, and thanks to him thou shalt attain in good condition of life to thy fathers who are in the tomb." This Didi said to him, "In peace, in peace,[27] Dadûfhoru, beloved royal son of thy father. May thy father Khufuî, true of voice, commend thee, and may he assure thee thy place before the aged! May thy *double* gain his suit against the enemies, and thy soul know the arduous roads that lead to the door of Hobs-bagaî,[28] for it is thou, son of the king, who art good of judgment!"[29] The son of the king, Dadûfhoru, held out his two hands to him; he raised him up, and as he went with him to the quay, he held him by the hand. Didi said

24. Probably an *angareb* like those found in the tombs, and similar to the *angarebs* of the Egyptians and Berberines of to-day; cf. p. 12, note 37. of the present volume.

25. *To land, to arrive in port, is* one of the numerous euphemisms employed by the Egyptians to express the idea of death. It is easily explained by the idea of the journey by boat that the dead were forced to make to reach the other world, and by the transport of the mummy in a bark across the river on the day of the funeral.

26. The compliment is so involved that I fear I may not have entirely understood it; I have been inspired in my translation by the observations of Piehl in *Sphinx*, vol. i, pp. 74, 75.

27. In the ancient language this is *me hatpu, me hatpu,* the equivalent of *bi-s-salamah,* the salutation so frequently heard to-day in Arab Egypt.

28. *Hobs-bagaî* is an important personage, under whose authority a part of the entrance gateways to the other world were placed (Erman, *die Märchen des Papyrus Westcar,* p. 49). He is a duplicate of one of the forms of Osiris; Osiris motionless in his mummy wrappings.

29. This phrase, very clear for ancient readers, is less so for moderns. According to the exigencies of the puerile and harmless civilities of the period, Didi was obliged to return compliment for compliment. He therefore states that Dadûfhoru, young as he is, has a position that places him above the aged, and he explains this excess of honour by the profound learning of the young man. Dadûfhoru had, in fact, a reputation for learning—*i.e.* as a sorcerer— which caused him to be quoted in the *Book of the Dead* as the originator of chapter lxiv., one of the most important in the collection, and in the *Anastasi Papyrus* i (pl. x, 1. 8), as one of the best accredited interpreters of those books which were least comprehensible to the vulgar.

to him: "Let a caïque be given me to bring me my children and my books"; they gave him two boats for his household, and Didi himself sailed in the bark in which was the king's son, Dadûfhoru. Now when they arrived at the Court, as soon as the king's son, Dadûfhoru, had entered to report to His Majesty the King of the two Egypts, Khufuî, true of voice, the king's son, Dadûfhoru, said, "Sire, l. h. s., my lord, I have brought Didi." His Majesty said, "Hasten, bring him to me," and when His Majesty had come into the audience chamber of Pharaoh, l. h. s., Didi was presented to him. His Majesty said: "How is it, Didi, that I have never yet seen thee?" Didi said to him: "Who is called comes, the sovereign, l. h. s., calls me, I am here, I have come." His Majesty said: "Is that true which is said, that thou knowest how to put back in place a head that has been cut off?" Didi said to him, "Yes, I know that, sire, l. h. s., my lord." His Majesty said: "Let a prisoner be brought me of those that are in prison, and who are condemned." Didi said to him: "No, no, not a man, sire, l. h. s., my lord; let there be no command to do such a thing to the noble cattle.[30] A goose was brought to him, its head was cut off, and the goose was put at the right-hand side of the chamber, and the head of the goose at the left-hand side of the chamber. Didi recited that which he recited of his book of magic; the goose rose up, it hopped, the head did the same, and when one had reunited with the other the goose began to cackle. He had a pelican (?) brought in; the same thing happened to it. His Majesty had a bull brought to him, they cast his head down on the ground, and Didi recited that which he recited of his book of magic; the bull placed himself behind him, but his halter remained on the ground.[31] King Khufuî, true of voice, said, "What is it they say, that thou knowest the numbers of the caskets of books of the crypt of Thoth?" Didi said to him, "Excuse me that I do not know the number, sire, l. h. s., my lord, but I know the place where they are." His Majesty said : "That place, where is it?" That Didi said to him, "There is a block of sandstone in what is called the room of the rolls at Onu,[32] and the caskets of books of the crypt of Thoth are in the block." The King said:

30. Piehl has shown that in this expression the author referred to humanity (*Sphinx*, vol. i, p. 75). In fact, the texts relating to the four human races call men the herds of Râ.

31. Cf. above, p. 67, note 27 of the present volume. When the neck of the bull was sundered the halter had fallen off; the head and the body reunited, but the leash remained where it had fallen.

32. Onu is Heliopolis, the City of the Sun. Each chamber of the temple had its special name, which was often inscribed over the principal door, and which was derived, sometimes from the appearance of the decoration, the *Golden Chamber*, sometimes from the class of

"Bring me the caskets that are in that block."[33] Didi said to him, "Sire, l. h. s., my lord, behold it is not I who shall bring them to thee." His Majesty said: "Who then will bring them to me?" Didi said to him: "The eldest of the three children who are in the womb of Rudîtdidît, he will bring them to thee." His Majesty said: "In faith! she of whom thou speakest, Rudîtdidît, who is she?" Didi said to him: "She is the wife of a priest of Râ, Lord of Sakhîbu. She hath conceived three infants by Râ, Lord of Sakhîbu, and the god has said to her that they will fulfil this beneficent function in the Entire Land,[34] and that the eldest of them will be great pontiff at Onu." The heart of His Majesty was troubled, but Didi said to him, "What are these thoughts, sire, l. h. s. my lord? Is it because of these three children? I say to thee: Thy son, his son, and one of hers."[35] His Majesty said: When will she give birth to them, this Rudîtdidît?" He said, "She will give birth to them on the 15th day of the month Tybi." His Majesty said, "If the shallow waters of the canal of the Two Fishes do not cut off the way, I will go myself, in order to see the temple of Râ, Lord of Sakhîbu." Didi said to him; "Then I will cause that there shall be four cubits of water on the shallows of the canal of the Two Fishes."[36] When the King had returned to his abode, His Majesty said, "Let Didi be put under the care of the house of the royal son Dadûfhoru, to dwell there with him, and let an allowance of a thou-

objects it contained, the *Chamber of Perfumes*, the *Chamber of Water*, or from the nature of the ceremonies performed in it. The block mentioned here was probably a movable block, like that in the *Story of Rhampsinitus* (cf. p. 164), and served to conceal the entrance to the crypt where Thoth had deposited his books.

33. The scribe has omitted here the end of Didi's reply and the beginning of a fresh question of the King's (Erman, *die Märchen des Papyrus Westcar*, p. 56); I have restored what was missing in the manuscript, according to the context.

34. Euphemism for designating royalty. For the meaning of the expression Entire-Land see above, p. 3, note 5.

35. This phrase is drawn up in oracular style, suitable to the reply of a magician. It appears to be intended to reassure the king, asserting that the accession of the three children is not immediate, but that his own son will reign and then his son's son before the destiny is accomplished. The royal lists place after Khufuî, first Didûfrîya, then Khafrîya, then Menkaurîya, then Shopsiskaf, before Usirkaf, the first of the three kings of the Vth dynasty for whom our story announces this great future. The author of our story has omitted Didûfrîya and Shopsïkaf, of whom the people had lost all recollection (Erman, *die Märchen des Papyrus Westcar*, p. 19).

36. The resolutions of the king are expressed in terms which do not appear clear to us, no doubt because we do not possess the end of the tale. After what the magician has said to him, the king no longer thinks of killing the children, but for all that he does not renounce the intention of struggling against destiny, and to begin with he asks which day Rudîtdidît will give birth to the children. Didi already knows the day, the 15th of Tybi, thanks to the amaz-

sand loaves, a hundred jars of beer, an ox, and a hundred bunches of eschalots be given to him." And it was done as His Majesty had commanded.

Then, one of those days, it came to pass that Rudîtdidît suffered the pains of childbirth. The Majesty of Râ, Lord of Sakhîbu, said to Isis, to Nephthys, to Maskhonuît,[37] to Hiqaît,[38] to Khnumu, "Hie! hasten to deliver Rudîtdidît of those three children who are in her womb, and who will fulfil that beneficent function in the Entire Land, building your temples for you, supplying your altars with offerings, provisioning your libation tables, increasing your possessions in mortmain." Then those gods departed; the goddesses changed themselves into musicians, and Khnumu went with them as porter.[39] They arrived at the house of Râusir, and they found him who dwelt there unfolding the linen.[40] They passed in front of him with their castanets and sistrums,[41] but he said to them, "Ladies, behold, there is a woman here suffering the pains of childbirth." They said, "Allow us to see her for, lo, we are skilled in midwifery." He said to them, "Come then," and

ing intuition so frequently possessed by the heroes of Egyptian tales (cf. p. 11, where the magicians appear to know at once that the *daughter of the gods* is in the Vale of the Acacia). The King asked this question, no doubt, in order to procure the horoscope of the children, and to discover whether the stars confirmed the prediction of the sorcerer. He considered for a moment whether he would not go to Sakhîbu to study what was occurring in the temple of Râ, but the state of the canal did not permit him to carry out his plan, although the magician promised to add four cubits of water at the shallows, that his bark might pass without difficulty. The canal of the Two Fish was the principal canal that crossed the Letopolite nome (Brugsch, *Dictionnaire Géographique*, p. 621).

37. Maskhonuît is the goddess of *Maskhonu, i.e.* of the cradle, and in this capacity she assists at the accouchement: she combines in herself Shaït and Ranênît, the goddess who controls destiny and the goddess who gives suck (*ranunu*) to the child, and gives him his name (*rinu*) and, in consequence, his personality. Cf. Maspero, *études égyptiennes,* vol. i, p. 27.

38. Hiqaît, who with Khnumu is called *one of the chief cradles of Abydos* (Louvre, C 3), *i.e.* one of the divinities who presided at the foundation of the city, is the goddess in form of a frog, or with a frog's head, one of the cosmic deities who acted at the birth of the world. Thus her presence is quite natural at an accouchement.

39. The text says, "as carrier of a coffer, a sack." Khnumu assumed the post of the domestic who accompanies the *almehs,* carrying their luggage, and, when necessary, taking part, vocal and instrumental, in the concert. One of the little wooden personages found at Meîr, who are in the Cairo Museum, carries a coffer, and seems to me to show clearly what a *hri-qani* may have been. (Maspero, *Guide du Visiteur* an *museé du Caire,* 1910, 5th English edition, p. 500, No. 155.)

40. He was unfolding the linen intended for the accouchement.

41. We shall see later in the *Memoirs of Sinuhît* (pp. 76, 77) a similar domestic scene, but where the actors are princes of the Pharaonic house.

they went in to Rudîtdidît, and then they closed the door on her and on themselves. Then Isis placed herself before her, Nephthys behind her, Hiqaît assisted the birth.[42] Isis said, "Oh, child, be not mighty in her womb, in thy name of Usirraf, he whose mouth is mighty!"[43] Thereupon this child came out upon her hands, a child of a cubit's length,[44] powerful of bone, with members the colour of gold and hair of true lapis-lazuli.[45] The goddesses washed him, they cut the umbilical cord, they laid him on a brick bed, and then Maskhonuît approached him and said to him, "This is a king who will exercise royalty in the Entire Land." Khnumu infused health into his members.[46] Isis then placed herself before Rudîtdidît, Nephthys behind her, Hiqaît assisted the birth. Isis said, "Child, do not journey longer in her

42. To understand the positions adopted by the goddesses in relation to the woman, it must be remembered that the Egyptian women in childbirth did not assume a horizontal position, as with us. Certain pictures show that they either crouched on a bed or a mat with their legs bent under them, or sat on a chair which appears to be in no way different from an ordinary chair. The women who assembled to help took different parts. One placed herself behind the patient and clasped her round the body with her arms during the pains, thus affording her a firm support and assisting expulsion; the other placed herself in front of her, kneeling or crouching, ready to receive the infant in her hands and prevent its falling roughly to the ground. The two goddesses, Isis and Nephthys, come to assist Rudîtdidît, acted like the ordinary midwives, and Hiqaît hastened the birth by massaging the womb, as is still done by the Egyptian midwives of to-day.

43. According to a custom usual not only in Egypt, but in the whole of the East, the midwife, when giving the infant his name, makes a pun, which is more or less intelligible, on the meaning of the words of which the name is composed. Here the child is called *Usir-rof, Usir-raf,* which by its meaning is a variant of the name *Usir-kaf,* which was borne by the first king of the Vth dynasty. *Usir-raf* signifies *he whose mouth is mighty. Usirkaf* is *he whose double is mighty,* and the goddess also employs the verb *usiru* in the first part of the phrase, "Be not mighty (*usiru*) in her womb,"—probably, do not bruise the womb of thy mother—"in the name of him whose mouth is mighty." The proceeding is the same as that by which the Hebrew historians explained the names of the sons of Jacob (Genesis xxix, 32-xxx, 24).

44. This is the normal height of newly born infants in Egyptian texts (Erman, *die Märchen des Papyrus Westcar,* p. 62).

45. The text states literally that "the colour of his limbs was of gold, and his wig of true lapis-lazuli," in other words that his limbs were precious as gold, his wig blue like lapis-lazuli. Can there be a pun here on *nubu,* gold, and *nubu,* to model, to cast, which is often used in the texts to express the creation of the limbs of a man by the gods? In any case the pictured wigs with which the mummy coffins are decorated are almost always coloured blue, so that the expression in our text answers exactly to a detail of Egyptian art or industry. Finally, the child described by our author is not a natural infant, but a statuette of a divinity, with its blue headdress and incrustations of gold on the body.

46. Maskhonuît being, as I have said (p. 29, note 37), human destiny, is called upon, to award the decree of life for the child. Khnumu, the modeller, completes the work of the goddesses: he massages the body of the new-born infant and infuses it with health (*cf.* p. 10, note 28).

womb, in thy name Sahurîya, he who is Râ journeying in heaven."[47]
Thereupon this child came out upon her hands, a child of a cubit's
length, powerful of bone, with members the colour of gold and hair of
true lapis-lazuli. The goddesses washed him, they cut the cord, they carried him on a brick bed, then Maskhonuît approached him and said,
"This is a king who will exercise royalty in this Entire Land." Khnumu
infused health into his members. Isis then placed herself before Rudîtdidît, Nephthys placed herself behind her, Hiqaît assisted the birth. Isis
said, "Child, do not tarry longer in the darkness of her womb, in thy
name of Kakauî, the dark one."[48] Then this child came out upon her
hands, a child of a cubit's length, powerful of bone, with members the
colour of gold and hair of true lapis-lazuli. The goddesses washed him,
they cut the cord, they laid him on a brick bed, then Maskhonuît
approached him and said, "This is a king who will exercise royalty in this
Entire Land." Khnumu infused health into his members.[49] When the
deities went out after having delivered Rudîtdidît of her three children
they said, "Rejoice, Râusir, for behold, three children are born to thee."
He said to them, "Ladies, what can I do for you? Ah, give this corn that
is here to your porter, that you may take it to the silos as payment!"[50] And
Khnumu took up the corn, and they returned to the place whence they
came. But Isis said to those deities, "What are we thinking of to have
come to Râusir without having performed some prodigy for these children whereby we can make known the event to their father who has sent
us?"[51] Then they fashioned three diadems of a sovereign lord, l. h. s.,[52] and
they placed them in the corn, they poured out storm and rain from the
height of the sky, they returned to the house, and then they said, "Place

47. The pun turns on the word *sâhu,* which forms part of the name of the king *Sâhurîya.*
Sâhu signifies to approach . . . , to journey to . . . . The goddess tells the child not to wander
longer in the womb of his mother, and that because his name is *Sâhurîya,* he who journeys to
heaven like the sun.

48. The third king of the Vth dynasty, Neferarkerîya, is also called Kakauî, and we do not
know the meaning of this name. To secure the pun on Kakauî, the scribe has been forced to
alter the traditional spelling.

49. The original manuscript here alters the sequence of the operations: I have placed each
one in the order adopted at the birth of the two first children.

50. Cf., for the meaning of the last part of the phrase, Bissing, *Zu Papyrus Westcar,* xi, 8, in
Zeitschrift, 1905, vol. xliv, p. 90.

51. *Their father* does not here mean Râusir, the husband of Rudîtdidît, who was not aware
of the divine origin of the three children, but the god Râ of Sakhîbu, the real father, who had
in fact sent the goddesses to the help of his mistress.

52. Cf. on this point the note by Sethe, *Zu Westcar,* 11, 13, in *Zeitschrift,* 1891, vol. xxix, p. 84.

this corn in a sealed chamber, until we return dancing northwards."[53] And the corn was placed in a sealed chamber.

Rudîtdidît purified herself with a purification of fourteen days, and then she said to her servant, "Is the house in good order?" The maid said to her, "It is furnished with all good things; nevertheless, the pots for the bouza, they have not been brought."[54] Then Rudîtdidît said to her, "Why have not the pots been brought?" The servant said, "They would have been ready to brew without delay, if the corn of those singers had not been in a chamber, sealed with their seal." Then Rudîtdidît said to her, "Go down,[55] bring us some of it; Râusir will give them some more in its place when they return." The servant went and she opened the chamber; she heard voices, music, singing, and dancing, zaggarit,[56] all that is done for a king, in the chamber.[57] She came back, she reported to Rudîtdidît all that she had heard. Rudîtdidît searched the chamber and did not discover the place from which the sound came. She placed her forehead against the bin, and she found that the sound was inside it. She therefore placed the bin in a wooden coffer, she placed on it another seal, she surrounded it with leather, she placed the whole in the chamber where the vases were, and this she closed with her seal.[58] When Râusir returned from the

53. It must not be forgotten that the goddesses were disguised as wandering musicians. They therefore requested the people of the house to keep the corn looked up, until they had finished their tour in the south country and should come north

54. The text runs "except the vases," and as Erman has clearly distinguished (*die Märchen, des Papyrus Westcar*, p. 67), the word vase should mean here a liquor: *vase* will have taken the same meaning as *cup, glass, pichet, litre*, in our modern languages, the name of the vessel being used for the liquid it contains. As the grain that had been given to the goddesses was necessary to prepare these vases, I imagine that *bouza* is here referred to, the sweet beer of the ancient Egyptians as of the modern Egyptians.

55. The women's apartment is on an upper floor. The servant had to go downstairs to fetch the corn.

56. This is the Arabic word used to designate the kind of shrill cry uttered in chorus by the women at festivals to show their joy. They produce it by placing the point of their tongue against their upper teeth and making it vibrate rapidly.

57. An Arabic author relates that in the Great Pyramid there was a closed chamber from whence issued a buzzing of incredible force (Carra de Vaux, *l'Abrégé des Merveilles*, p. 214); it was evidently what we call the serdab, that held the statues of the king. Our text explains the Arabic legend and shows that its origin was ancient; the visitors to the Great Pyramid believed they heard the same sounds of royal festival that Rudîtdidît and her servant heard in the bin that held the crowns of the three children.

58. The text is much involved here. I think I understand that Rudîtdidît took the clay bin in which the goddesses had put their wheat, and put it in a wooden case which she covered with leather and on which she placed a seal, and that she then shut it up in her cellar, to prevent any one hearing the mysterious sounds.

garden, Rudîtdidît related these things to him, and he was exceedingly pleased; they sat down and spent a day of happiness.

But lo, many days after this, Rudîtdidît disputed with her servant and caused her to be beaten. The servant said to the people who were in the house, "Is it thus that she treats me, she who has given birth to three kings? I shall go and tell it to the Majesty of the king Khufuî, true of voice." She went, therefore, and found her eldest brother by her mother, who was tying up the flax that had been stripped on the threshing-floor. He said to her, "Where art thou going, my little lady?" and she told him these things. Her brother said to her, "It is better to do what has to be done, than to come to me; I will teach thee to rebel." Thereupon he took up a bundle of flax against her, and administered punishment to her. The maid ran to fetch a little water, and the crocodile carried her off.[59] When her brother ran to Rudîtdidît to tell her that, he found Rudîtdidît seated, her head on her knees, her heart sad more than all things. He said to her, "Lady, why this heart?" She said, "It is because of that girl that was in the house; lo! she has gone saying, 'I will go and denounce.'" He prostrated himself with his face to the earth and said to her, "My lady, when she came to tell me that which had happened, and complained to me, lo! I gave her evil blows; then she went to draw herself a little water, and the crocodile carried her off. . . ."

The end of the romance may have contained, among other episodes, the journey to Sakhîbu, to which Cheops alluded towards the end of his interview with Didi. The king was powerless in his enterprises against the divine children; his successors, Chephren and Mykerinus, were not more fortunate than he, and the intrigue ended in the accession of Usirkaf. Possibly those last pages contained allusions to some of the traditions collected by the Greek writers. Cheops and Chephren avenged themselves for the enmity shown them by Râ, by closing his temple at Sakhîbu and in other towns. They thus justified one of the stories in which they are renowned for impiety. At all events the Westcar Papyrus is the first that has reached us with an original redaction of the romances of which the cycle of Cheops and the kings who built the pyramids is composed.

---

59. The crocodile or hippopotamus is often the minister of divine justice in Egypt. Menes is carried off by a hippopotamus, and Akhthoes, the first king of the IXth Dynasty, by a crocodile (Manetho, edit. Unger, pp. 78, 107 ward for the second time). The servant, beaten by her brother, runs to the nearest canal to procure a little water to wash with and refresh herself; the crocodile sent by Râ carries her off and drowns her.

THE LAMENTATIONS
OF THE FELLAH [3]

(XIIITH DYNASTY)

THIS tale seems to have been very popular throughout the period of the Theban Empire, as four manuscripts are known that contain it, three at Berlin and one in London. The three Berlin manuscripts have been published by Lepsius in the *Denkmäler aus Ægypten und Æthiopien,* Abtheilung VI, then in Vogelsang-Gardiner, *die Klagen, des Bauern* (forming vol. i of Erman's *Literarische Texten des Mittleren Reiches*) 1908, Leipzig, folio.

1ST. *The Berlin Papyrus No.* 2 (Berlin 3023), of pl. 108–110 of *Denkmäler* (cf. plates 5, 5a–17, 17a of *die Klagen*) consists of three hundred and twenty-five lines in a large script of the early part of the XIIIth dynasty; carefully written at first, it becomes increasingly careless towards the end. The beginning and the end of the narrative are missing.

2ND. *The Berlin Papyus No.* 4 (Berlin 3025), of pl. 113–114 of *Denkmäler* cf. pl. 18, 18a-24, 24a of *die Klagen*) comprises a hundred and forty-two lines of very rapid writing of the same period as that of the preceding manuscript. It seems to have been damaged by prolonged handling, and the lacunæ caused by usage combined with the lack of neatness in the writing, render it difficult to decipher. The parts which are preserved contain an additional fifty lines towards the end, but even so the end of the story is missing. Fragments of these two manuscripts, which had escaped Lepsius, were acquired by the late Lord Amherst of Hackney and formed part of his collection at Didlington Hall. The most important of these contain several of the missing fragments of pages of the *Berlin Papyrus No.* 4. Others belong to *Berlin Papyrus No.* 4, and have been published by Percy E. Newberry, *The Amherst Papyri,* 1901, vol. i, pl. I A-L and pp. 9, 10.

3RD. *The Ramesseum Papyrus* (Berlin 10499) formed part of a lot of papyri found during the winter of 1895–1896 near the Ramesseum during excavations by Quibell; handed over by Petrie to Alan H. Gardiner, he presented it to the Berlin Museum. On the obverse it contains the beginning of the *Lamentations of the*

Fellah, corresponding throughout with the *Butler Papyrus*, and with lines 1–87, 130–146 of the *Berlin Papyrus No.* 2. Its existence was noticed by Alan H. Gardiner, *Eine neue Handschrift des Sinuhegedichtes*, in the *Sitzugsberichte* of the Academy of Sciences of Berlin 1906, pp. 142, 143, pp. 1–2 of the separate publication.

It has been published in facsimile and in hieroglyphic transcription in Vogel-sang-Gardiner, *die Klagen des Bauern*, pl. 1, la–4bis *4bis.-a.*

4TH. *The Butler Papyrus No.* 527 (British Museum, 10274 reverse). It is in a large handwriting, sufficiently careful, and perhaps of the early part of the XVIIIth dynasty. It is more developed than the two ancient manuscripts of Berlin, and it has in addition fifteen lines of introduction, which however do not furnish us with the commencement of the story. Part of it has been published in cursive fac-simile by F. Ll. Griffith, *Fragments of Old Egyptian Stories*, in the *Proceedings of the Society of Biblical Archaeology*, 1891–1892, vol. xiv, plates i–iv. By combining the matter supplied us in these four manuscripts we are able to restore the text almost completely. Borchardt has shown (*Zeitschrift für Ægyptische Sprache*, vol. xxvii, p. 12), that sundry fragments, placed by Lepsius at the beginning of the *Berlin Papyrus No.* 4, should be inserted at the end of the same papyrus, when they provide almost the end of the story.

The subject of it was made out and published almost simultaneously by Chabas and Goodwin. Chabas gave a translation followed by the first few lines in his memoir *Les Papyrus hiératiques de Berlin, récits d'il y a quatre mille ans*, Paris, 1863, 8vo, pp. 5–36; cf. *Œuvres diverses*, vol. ii, pp. 292 *et seq.*

Goodwin merely published a very short analysis of the whole in an article entitled *The Story of Saneha, An Egyptian Tale of Four Thousand Years Ago*, in *Frazer's Magazine* (Feb. 15, 1865, pp. 185–202), p. 188. Chabas used only the Berlin papyri for his text, Goodwin was fortunate enough to discover the *Butler Papyrus* at the British Museum, and he inserted an analytical translation in Chabas' *Mélanges égyptologiques*, 2nd series, Paris, 1864, Benjamin Duprat, 8vo, pp. 249–266, which afforded Chabas an opportunity (pp. 266–272) of correcting certain details of his own translation as well as of the English version.

Since then the text has been repeatedly studied. In 1877 I transcribed and translated it at the Collège de France, and in 1893–4 at the École des Hautes-Études; and it was the beginning of this translation that appeared in the first three editions of these *Tales*. An English version covering those parts of the text on which I had already worked was published later by F. Ll. Griffith, *Fragments of Old Egyptian Stories*, in the *Proceedings of the Society of Biblical Archæology*, 1891–1892, vol. xiv, pp. 459–472.

A hieroglyphic transcription of some portions, and then a complete transla-tion of the whole, has been given in German by Erman, *Ægyptische Grammatik*,

1st Edition, 1899, pp. 28*–37*; Erman, *Aus den Papyrus der Königlichen Museen*, Berlin, Speeman, 1899, pp. 46–53; Erman, *Ægyptische Chrestomathie*, Berlin, Reuther and Richard, 1904, pp. 11–19 and 6*–10*.

A version somewhat freely translated will be found in Flinders Petrie, *Egyptian Tales*, 1895, vol. i, pp. 61–80.

Finally the transcription and translation of the whole was published in German in 1907 by Vogelsang-Gardiner, *die Klagen des Bauern*, pp. 8–15.

The name and quality of the two principal personages of this narrative have given rise to numerous researches. Pleyte read that of the persecutor as Sati, the hunter (*Sur quelques Groupes hiéroglyphiques* in *Zeitschrift*, 1869, p. 82), and his reading was long accepted. In 1891 Griffith deciphered it with hesitation as *Sûti* or *Sûtenti (Fragments of Old Egyptian Stories*, in the *Proceedings* 1891–1892, vol. xiv, p. 468, note 3), and soon after Max Müller rendered it as *hamuîti*, the carpenter, the artisan (*the Story of the Peasant*, in the *Proceedings* 1892–1893, vol. xv, pp. 343–344). Schäfer has demonstrated (*Eine kursive Form von Dhwti, in Zeitschrift* 1902–3, vol. xl, pp. 121–124) that it was not a term for a trade but a proper name, *Thotnakhuîti*. The term applied to the plaintiff, Sokhîti, has been rendered by common accord as *peasant, husbandman, fellah,* and it is undoubtedly the meaning it bears in ordinary texts. It appears to me that the context here indicates that it should be considered as an ethnic term. The *sokkhîti* of the tale is a man of the *Sokhît hamaît*, the *Oasis of natron*, and by way of abbreviation I translated it *le Saunier* in the preceding French edition of these stories. To avoid the confusion caused in the minds of my readers by this too-literal translation, I now revert to the old translation of *fellah.*

Like the preceding story, this one provides us with abundance of details concerning the habits, position, and sorrows of the poorer folk. The resemblance of ancient manners and customs with those of to-day is shown in a very remarkable degree; the man whom a petty village functionary has robbed of an ass or camel, his lamentations and futile recriminations, his prolonged waiting at the door of the police official or great lord whose duty it is supposed to be to render him justice, are daily experiences for any one who has lived outside Cairo or Alexandria. The interminable harangues of the ancient fellah are actually the same and with almost the same hyperboles as those of the fellah of to-day. The poor wretch considers himself obliged to make fine speeches in order to soften the judge, and he pours forth all the fine words and powerful imagery his imagination can suggest, often without pausing to think of their meaning or calculating the effect they will produce. The difficulties presented by his speeches no doubt arose from the same cause which prevents a European understanding a fellah when he lodges a complaint. The incoherence of his ideas and the obscurity of his language were due to the desire to speak well, and his want of practice in using fine language. It seems to me that the author of this story has succeeded only too well for our comprehension, in reproducing this somewhat comic and satirical side of the national character.

The name of the Pharaoh Nabkaûrîya, and the local setting of the story, show that the author placed his hero in the times of the Heracleopolitan dynasties, and more exactly under one of the Khatiû, probably the second of the name. I would therefore date the composition to the first Theban period, as has been done since Chabas, and rather to the centuries that followed the XIIth dynasty, than to the XIIth dynasty itself; a point that cannot be proved without long dissertation.

ﮌ

There was once a man, Khunianupu by name, who was a fellah of the Plain of Salt,[1] and he had a wife Nofrît by name.[2] This fellah said to this his wife, "Lo! I go down to Egypt to bring back bread[3] from thence for our children. Go, measure me the corn that is in the granary the remainder of [this year's] corn." Then he measured for her [eight] bushels of corn. This fellah said to this his wife, "Behold! here are these two bushels of corn for thee and thy children, but of these six bushels of corn make me bread and beer[4] for each day that I shall be on the journey." When this fellah went down into Egypt, he loaded his asses with reeds,[5] rushes, natron, salt, wood of Uît,[6] acacia from the Country

1. The Plain of Salt is the country of the Wady Natrûn, to the west of the Delta, and north-east of Hnes.

2. The name of the wife is damaged at the beginning: if the two signs that remain are an r and t, there is some probability that it may be read Nofrît or Nofrêt.

3. This must not be taken literally, and. we must not imagine that the man intended to return with a load of bread. The word *aîku* was used by the ancient Egyptians in the same way that *aish,* is employed by modern Egyptians, to express all kind of provisions required to feed a household.

4. This combination explains itself when we understand the Egyptian method of making beer. They used the crumb of stale bread in place of yeast. Scenes produced in bas-relief, or with wooden figures in the tombs of the first Theban empire and of the Memphite empire, always combine baking and brewing. It is therefore natural that the fellah should order his wife to make both bread and beer with the corn he gave her.

5. At the present time two kinds of reed are still exported from Wady Natrûn—*somâr* and *birdî,* which are used to make mats. Of these reeds the best quality come from the other side of Wady Natcûn, from Wady Maghara, also called Wady es-Sumàra.

6. This name is incomplete : I think I recognise traces of the name of the oasis of Uîti, preserved in that of the village of Bauîti, one of the villages of the Northern Oasis.

of the Oxen,[7] wolf skins, jackal hides,[8] sage, onyx, maize, colocynth, coriander, aniseed, talc, ollite, wild mint, grapes, pigeons, partridges, quails, anemones, narcissus, seed of the sun, *hairs of the earth*, and all-spice, complete with all the good products of the *Plain of Salt*.[9]

When therefore the fellah had gone south to Khininnsuît[10] and had arrived at the place called Pafifi to the north of the town of Madenît,[11] he met a man who was on the bank, Thotnakhuîti by name, son of a person Asari by name, both of them serfs of Rensi, son of Maru, mayor of the palace. This Thotnakhuîti, as soon as he beheld the asses of this fellah, being astonished at heart, said, "May every god favour me, that I may obtain the property of this fellah." Now the dwelling of this Thotnakhuîti was close to a riverside path, which was narrow, not ample, so much so that it was just the breadth of a piece of linen, with the water on one side and wheat on the other. This Thotnakhuîti said to his servant, "Hasten and bring me a piece of cloth from my house." It was brought him, and he spread it on the pathway, so that the edge touched the water and the fringe touched the wheat.[12] When therefore the fellah came on to the road which was for every one, this Thotnakhuîti said, "Be so good,[13] fellah, do not tread on my linen." This fellah said, "To do as thou shalt commend, my ways are good." As he

7. The Country of the Oxen is the Oasis of Farafrah.

8. Jackal skins appear to have been exported, in bunches of three, as one sees them in the hieroglyphic sign *mos*.

9. The names of these minerals and seeds are still very uncertainly identified with modern corresponding terms. I give a translation with all reserve.

10. Hâkhininnsuît, or Hâkhininnsuîti is the town called by the Assyrians Khininsu, by the Hebrews Khanes, and by the Copts Hnes; the modern *Henassieh* or *Ahnes el Medineh*.

11. The two towns of Pafifi and Madenît are otherwise unknown to us. They must be sought for between Wady Natrûn and Ahnes, but much nearer that town, probably at the entrance to the Fayûm.

12. The course of the story gives us the reason for these preparations. Thotnakhuîti, in barring the path, hoped to force the peasant to take the upper side of the way close to the field. In passing, the ass might snatch some blades of wheat; Thotnakhuîti could then accuse the delinquent and confiscate the animal. At the present day, the proprietor of a field is satisfied with cutting off an ear of the donkey; but the case is known where, like the man in the story, he seized the animal.

13. The words *Iri haru*, translated "be so good," form a polite phrase by which the Egyptians called the attention of their comrades or of passers-by to any work they were engaged on, or any matter of general interest. It is the equivalent of the *âmel maarûf* or *amelni el-maarûf* of modern Egyptians.

turned towards the higher part, Thotnakhuîti said, "Is my corn to serve as thy pathway, fellah?" This fellah said, "My ways are good, but the bank is high, the roads have wheat, thou hast barred the ways with thy linen, wilt thou not permit me to pass?" While he was speaking these words one of the asses took a mouthful of stalks of wheat. This Thotnakhuîti said, "Behold thou, since thine ass eats my wheat, I shall put him to labour on account of his strength." This fellah said, "My ways are good. To avoid trespass I led my ass aside, and now thou dost seize him because he has taken a mouthful of stalks of wheat. But assuredly I know the owner of this domain, who is the High Steward, Rensi, son of Maru; it is he of a certainty who drives away all robbery in this Entire Land,[14] and shall I he robbed in his domain?" This Thotnakhuîti said, "Is not that a true proverb that men use, 'The name of the poor wretch is quoted on account of his master.' It is I who speak to thee, and it is of the Mayor of the Palace, Rensi, son of Maru, that thou thinkest."[15] He thereupon seized a green branch of tamarisk and with it he beat all his limbs, and he then took away his asses and led them into his domain. This fellah wept very loud for grief at that which was done to him, and this Thotnakhuîti said, "Do not raise thy voice, fellah, or thou shalt. go to the city of the god, Lord of Silence."[16] This fellah said, "Thou hast beaten me, thou hast stolen my goods, and now thou wouldst take away lamentation from my mouth. Divine lord of silence, grant me my goods, in order that I may not call out thy fear."[17]

This fellah passed the whole of four days bewailing himself to Thotnakhuîti, but he did not lend him his face. When this fellah went to Khininnsuît in order to make complaint to the Mayor of the Palace, Rensi, son of Maru, he found him as he came out of the door of his house to enter the cange (Nile boat) of his office. This fellah said, "Oh, permit

---

14. As we have said, the *Entire-Land* is one of the names commonly given to Egypt by the Egyptians (cf. p. 4, note 5).

15. The sentence quoted translated literally runs thus, "Is pronounced the name of the poor wretch for his master." From the context it seems to signify that he who considers he has a grievance against a subordinate, is not satisfied with execrating him, but immediately attempts to appeal to his chief.

16. The reply of Thotnakhuîti is an actual threat of death. The *Lord of Silence* is Osiris, god of the other world; his city is the tomb. Osiris, in this role, had as an equivalent in Thebes a goddess who bore the significant name of Maruîtsakro, she who *loves silence*.

17. So far as I can see, this expression, too concise for us, seems as though it should be paraphrased, "for fear that I should go everywhere proclaiming that thou art a man to be feared."

me to refresh thy heart with my discourse.[18] It is an occasion to send me thy servant, the intimate one of thy heart, that I may send him back to thee instructed in my business." The Mayor of the Palace, Rensi, son of Maru, caused his servant to go, the intimate of his heart, the one first after himself, and this fellah sent him back, instructed in the whole of his business, such as it was. The Mayor of the Palace, Rensi, son of Maru, informed the burghers[19] who were near to him of this Thotnakhuîti, and they said to their lord, "Verily, this comes from his peasant to whom another has come, for behold what they do to their peasants when others come to them, behold this is just what they do.[20] Is it worth while to prosecute this Thotnakhuîti for the matter of a little natron and a little salt? Let him be told to give it back, and he will give it back."[21] The Mayor of the Palace, Rensi, son of Maru, kept silence; he did not reply to these burghers, he did not reply to this fellah.

When this fellah came to make his complaint for the first time before the High Steward, Rensi, son of Maru, he said: "Mayor of the Palace, my lord, great of the great, guide of that which is, and of that which is not, when thou descendest to the Pool of Justice[22] and thou dost sail there

18. The beginning of the discourse recalls the formula by which a man of lower degree begins letters addressed to his superior (Griffith, *Hieratic Papyri from Kahun*, p. 88).

19. Personages of high rank, royal functionaries or administrators of nomes and villages had a certain number of burghers associated with them who assisted them in carrying out their functions—the equivalent, it appears, of the *cohors* of young men who accompanied the Roman governors in their provinces. These officials, who were called *sâru*, the *mesheikh* of today, the burghers, occasionally had deputies, *nîti mâ sâru*, who are often mentioned on monuments of the XIIth dynasty (cf. Maspero, *Mélanges de Mythologie*, vol. iv, pp. 446, 447).

20. The construction of these phrases is somewhat elliptical in the original, and the meaning is not clear. The literal translation would be, "Behold, it is his fellah who comes to another besides to him; here is for thee that which they do to their fellahs who come to others instead of to them, here is for thee that which they do." The burghers appear to suppose that the *fellah* had regular dealings with Thotnakhuîti, that he was *the fellah of that one*, that he provided him with salt, natron, and other products, and that the fellah instead of coming straight to his patron according to custom had attempted to offer his wares to others. Hence arose this incident, which was merely an ordinary quarrel between merchant and customer.

21. Literally, "Is to be prosecuted (rejected) this Thotnakhuîti, for a little natron, a little salt? if he be commanded to repay him that, he will repay it!" It may be better to translate the verb *tuba* by the other meaning : "Let him be commanded to return it and he will return it."

22. The *Pool of Justice* is the name of one of the canals of the other world, and of the canal of this world that passed Khininnsuît. The fellah, playing on the double meaning of the expression, as Griffith has remarked (*Fragments of Old Egyptian Stories*, in the *Proceedings*, vol. xiv, p. 468), wishes a prosperous voyage for Rensi both on the terrestrial and the celestial waters. The remainder of this first appeal is not the logical development of this play on words nor of the metaphor on which it was founded.

with the right wind, may the sheet of thy sail not tear away, may thy skiff not drift away, may no ill happen to thy mast, may thy planks not be cut, mayest thou not be carried off, when thou dost arrive at the land; may the wave not seize thee, mayest thou not taste the shriekings of the river, mayest thou not behold the Terrible of Face (the crocodile), but may the most rebellious fish come to thee and mayest thou procure well-fatted birds. As it is thou who art the father of the weak, the husband of the widow, the brother of the divorced woman, the clothing of the mother-less, cause that I may proclaim thy name in this country as the head of all good law. Guide without caprice, great without pettiness, thou who destroyest falsehood, and makest truth to be, come to the voice of my mouth. I speak; listen, do justice, praiseworthy, whom the most praise-worthy praise, destroy my woes; behold I am laden with grief, lo! I am in despair, judge me, for behold I am in great need."

Now this fellah said these words in the time of the King of Upper and Lower Egypt, Nabkaûrîya, true of voice. The Mayor of the Palace, Rensi, son of Maru, went before His Majesty, and he said, "My lord, I have met one of these fellahs, who are in truth fine speakers, whose goods have been stolen from him by a man who depends on me: behold he comes to make his complaint to me." The king said, "Maruîtensi, if you desire to keep me contented, draw him out at full length; answer nothing at all to that he shall say. That which he shall please to say to thee, report it to us in writing that we may hear it. See to it that his wife and children live, send one of these fellahîn to banish want from his house, and cause also that this peasant lives in his members, but when thou makest him a gift of bread see that he does not know it is thou who givest it." Four loaves and two jars of beer were served to him each day; the Mayor of the Palace, Rensi, son of Maru, supplied them, but he gave them to one of his clients, and it was he who gave them to the other. Behold, the Mayor of the Palace, Rensi, son of Maru, sent to the castellan of the Oasis of Salt, so that bread was made for the wife of the peasant in the proportion of three measures each day.

This fellah came to make his complaint for the second time, saying: "Mayor of the Palace, my lord, great of the great, rich of the rich, thou who art greater than thy great ones, and richer than thy rich ones, rudder of heaven, support of the earth, cord that bears the heavy weights; rudder do not swerve,[23] support do not bend, cord do not break away. For the

---

23. Literally "rudder do not go behind." The rudder was a large oar, worked from fore to aft. If it were displaced by the current or by a mistake of the steerman, so that it turned from

great lord takes of her who has no lord,[24] he despoils him who is alone. Thy allowance in thy house is a jug of beer and three loaves [daily], and what dost thou give to feed thy clients? Who dies, does he die with his people? Art thou thyself eternal?[25] In fact it is an evil, a balance that bends, a lever balance that loses its steadiness, a just integrity that deviates. Oh thou, if the justice that moves beneath thee remove from its place, if the burgher commit errors, if he who keeps count of the speeches [spoken on both sides] incline to one side, the menials steal. He who is commissioned to seize the faithless one who does not keep the word [of the judge] in strictness, himself wanders far from it [the word], he who ought to give the breath [of life] is without it on earth, he who is calm pants [with wrath], he who divides into just portions is only a prepotent, he who represses the oppressor commands him to ill-use the city like an inundation, he who repels evil commits faults."

The Mayor of the Palace, Rensi, son of Maru, said, "Is it then so important a matter for thee and so close to thy heart that my servant[26] should be seized?"

This fellah said: "When the measurer of grain takes by violence for himself, he causes another to lose his property. He who guides [to the observance of] the law, if he command that one shall rob, who then will repel crime? He who should crush error, if he himself wander from equity, has another the right to give way? If another is approved for misdeeds, how shalt thou find the means to subdue the misdeeds [of others]? When the wealthy man comes to the place that he occupied yesterday, it is an order to do to others as they have caused to be done, to honour others for what they have done, it is to administer riches wisely instead of squandering them, it is to assign property to those who already possess wealth.[27] Oh the

---

aft to fore, it would lose control of the ship's course; hence the metaphor in the text. *Swerve* is more or less free translation.

24. The widow or the rejected woman who had no man to protect her.

25. This development, which appears to us slightly disconnected, seems to signify that the master is wrong to despoil the defenceless, for his needs are so small, and he spends so little on feeding his clients, that it is not necessary for him to accumulate riches at the expense of others. Also when he dies, does he carefully take with him all the attendants he has to provide for? and does the master consider himself eternal, that he should perpetually plan to increase his wealth?

26. The servant of whom Rensi, son of Maru, speaks is Thotnakhuîti, whose punishment is demanded by the fellah.

27. The jingle of words with which this sentence begins merely signifies that if a wealthy man is reinstated in the position he had vacated, it is to encourage him to continue to act as

moment that destroys, when all shall be destroyed in thy vineyards, when thy poultry yard shall be destroyed and thy water-fowl shall be decimated, when he who sees shall become blind, and he who hears becomes deaf, when he who leads the way shall become him who misleads! . . . Art thou indeed sound? Act for thyself, for thou art very powerful, thine arm is valiant, thy heart is bold, indulgence is far from thee, the prayer of the wretched is thy destruction, thou seemest the messenger of the crocodile god. Thou art the travelling companion of the *Lady of Pestilence:* if thou art not, she is not; if she is not, thou art not; that which she does not do, thou dost not do.[28] When a rich strong man with lawful revenues is against a beggar, he who is firmly in possession of his spoils against one who has no possessions; if the beggar is despoiled of his property it is an evil business for him who is not deprived of all, he has no means of complaining of it, for he has sought it (his fate). But thou, thou art satiated with thy bread, thou art drunken with thy beer, thou art richer than all the living. When the face of the steersman is turned backward[29] the boat wanders where it pleases. When the king is in the harem, and the rudder (of state) is in thy hand, and there are abuses around thee, lamentation is abundant, ruin is heavy. "What matter?" they say. Make places of refuge, for thy embankment is sound, and behold, thy city is well surrounded with walls;[30] thou whose tongue is right, do not err, for the worm, destroyer of man, is but his own members![31] Speak not falsehood, heed well the burghers, the vassals and the servants, to speak lies is their hay (perquisite) and a tradition that is very near their hearts. Thou who knowest the property of all people, art

---

well as he had done during his previous period of office. It is hoped, in fact, that being rich already, he will have no need to pillage the country to enrich himself, and that he will administer the public wealth honestly. Thus he considers that Rensi, honest himself, did not know how to insist on honesty in his subordinates, and would end by being their victim and coming to ruin, as is said in the sentence that follows.

28. The crocodile god is either Sovku or Set-Typhon, and the lady of pestilence is Sokhît-Sakhmit. I gather that the fellah points out to Rensi that he is powerful and should deal rigorously with those who commit injustice under his protection, after the fashion of those two divinities.

29. Instead of observing the river and the direction of the currents and wind.

30. Rensi, son of Maru, in justice, desired that the poor should have an asylum in him against violence; the dyke he had metaphorically constructed to oppose the torrent of injustice was in good condition, but is it possible that the man of righteous judgments should at last swerve and become an oppressor?

31. The *members* of a great lord are his vassals and attendants, as the *members* of Râ are the lesser gods; the great lord is destroyed by the faults of his *members* rather than by his own.

thou ignorant of my fortune? Oh thou who reducest to nought all accident by water, I am here where there is no landing! Oh thou who leadest back to earth whosoever is drowning and who savest the shipwrecked, I am oppressed by order of thine."

This fellah came to make his complaint for the third time, saying; "Mayor of the Palace, my lord, thou art Râ, lord of heaven, with thy court, and it is the interest of all the world. Thou art like a wave of inundation, thou art the Nile which makes the fields green, that seizes the isles and cultivated lands. Repress robbery, protect the wretched, be not as a flood to those who complain [to thee], but beware that eternity approaches, and let it please thee that there be [for thee] that which is spoken, 'It is breath to the nose to do justice.'[32] Punish him who has punished, and that will not be placed to thy account. Does the spring bend, does the balance turn to one side, is not Thoth indulgent? If thou dost commit errors, thou makest thyself equal with those three.[33] If those three are indulgent, be thou also indulgent and do not reward good as though it were evil, or put the last in the place of the first. The word grows more than living herbage, more than a smell; do not reply to it, for when the water comes that clothes the fields, let it do so.[34] When thou art steering with the sail up, work with the current; in order to do this rightly, beware that thou manœuvrest well the tiller when thou art facing the land.[35] Do not lie, thou art greatness; be not light, thou art weightiness; do not lie; thou art the steel-yard, do not lose equilibrium; thou art the accurate reckoning; oh thou, thou art in accord with the lever, so that if it yields, thou also dost yield. Do not swerve when thou art steering, but manœuvre well the rope. Take nothing when thou shalt

32. Transcribed from Egyptian phraseology into modern expressions, this sentence signifies that to be just assures life in the presence of the king and the gods; to do to the evil-doer the same as he himself has done, is not recorded as a crime on the part of those who administer the punishment.

33. Literally "Thou art placed the second of these three;" in other words, "thou dost become a spring badly balanced, a false balance, a Thoth indulgent when he should not be."

34. As far as I can understand it, the word, that is the sentence or equitable command given by the superior, is efficacious in proportion to the rigour of those who respond, that is, who are responsible for its execution. It is like the water that imparts vigour to the vestments of the just word, *i.e.* that renders them clean and intact during the whole of the time that it acts in such a manner as to obtain this result.

35. This figure is borrowed from incidents in the navigation of the Nile. When the wind is contrary, the pilot steers almost in zigzags, going from one side to the other and making a little way each time. In this manœuvre there is a dangerous moment, when the prow of the boat is near one of the banks, *âqaît níti taû,* "facing the land," as the text says, and the direction has to be altered. If the helm is not put over at the right instant, the boat runs the risk of being shattered on the bank.

go against him who takes, for he is not a great one, that great one who is rapacious. Thy tongue is the spring of a balance and thy heart is the weight and thy two lips are its arms. If thou veilest thy face from him whose countenance is hard,[36] who then will subdue evil? Oh thou, thou art like a wicked rapacious launderer who treats a friend with harshness and rejects a client who is poor, but who holds as a brother him who comes and brings him [what is due]. Oh thou, thou art the ferryman who ferries him only who possesses the amount of the toll, and of whom the toll is the ruin [of others]. Oh thou, thou art the chief of the granary, who dost not permit him to go free who comes with empty hands. Oh thou, thou art for men a bird of prey who lives on the miserable little birds. Oh thou, thou art the cook whose joy it is to kill and from whom there is no escape. Oh thou, thou art the shepherd who troubles himself not at all; thou hast not reckoned how many [of thy beasts] thou dost lose by the crocodile, that violator of places of refuge, who attacks the district of the Entire Land.[37] Oh, auditor who hast not heard, why wilt thou not hear, since here I have repelled a furious one with whom there is a crocodile? When shall that be done? He who hides the truth is always discovered, and the lie is hurled to the ground. Do not rely on the morrow which is not yet come; it is not known what ills there are in it."

After the fellah had made this oration to the Mayor of the Palace, Rensi, son of Maru, on the esplanade which is before the gate, he dispatched two men of his clan to him with kurbashes, and they beat all his limbs.

This fellah said: "The son of Maru, he deviates indeed; his face is blind to that which he sees, he is deaf to that which he hears, he passes regardless of that of which he is reminded. Oh thou, thou art like a city that has no commander, like a community that has no chief, like a boat that has no captain, like a caravan without a leader. Oh thou, thou art like a ghafir who steals, like a sheikh-el-Beled that takes, like the chief of a district appointed to punish brigandage, and who puts himself at the head of those who commit it."

36. In other words, "If thou settlest thyself complacently so as not to see what the powerful do to the weak."

37. The fellah here alludes to an incident of rural life that is often represented in tombs of the Memphite age—the crossing of a ford by a herd of cattle (cf. pp. 219-222 of this volume) menaced by crocodiles; the careless herdsman, instead of watching over his animals, lets them go, and on coming out of the water does not trouble to find out whether the number of the cattle is still intact or whether the crocodiles have reduced it.

When the peasant came to make his complaint for the fourth time, he found the Mayor of the Palace as he was coming out of the gate of the temple of Harshafi, and he said: "Oh blessed one, mayest thou be the blessed of Harshafi, who comes from his temple, when good perishes and there is none to boast that he hath destroyed falsehood on the earth. And in truth the ferry-boat which you are made to enter and on which you cross the river, when the season of low water comes, to cross the river on foot, is it not a good way to cross? And who sleeps in full daylight? He destroys [by that means], going [in safety] during the night, and travelling [without danger] by day, and [the possibility that] the individual may verily profit by his good fortune. Oh thou, one must not cease from telling thee if indulgence departs from thee, the prayer of the wretched is thy destruction.[38] Thou art like a huntsman, light of heart, bold to do that which pleases thee, to harpoon the hippopotamus, to transfix wild bulls with arrows, to strike fish [with the bident],[39] to net birds. Oh thou who hast not the ready mouth, and who art without a flow of words, thou who hast not a light heart, but whose bosom is heavy with projects, apply thou thy heart to know the truth, subdue thy [evil] inclination until the silent one arrives.[40] Be not the [unskilful] inquisitor who destroys perfection, nor a rapid heart [which fails] when truth is brought to it, but cause that thy two eyes perceive, that thine heart is satisfied, and trouble not thyself doubting of thy power[41] for fear that misfortune overtake thee; he who passes by his fortune [without seizing it] will be [always] in the second rank. The man who eats, tastes; he who is questioned, replies; he who is in bed, dreams; but make no opposition to the judge at the gate[42] when he is at the head of the malefactors; [for thanks to him] if imbecile, thou dost prosper, if ignorant of everything, thou art consulted, if thou art like a flow of water that diverges, thou canst enter. Oh helmsman, misdirect

38. See the same remark on p.44.

39. Only the fishermen by profession and the peasants fished with a line, an eel-pot or a net; as one sees them on the pictures of the Theban and Memphite tombs, nobles caught fish with a single- or double-pronged harpoon. Fishing carried on thus required considerable strength and skill, comparable with hunting the hippopotamus.

40. Here I believe *the silent one* is Osiris, god of the dead, or some other divinity (cf. p. 40, note 16 of this volume).

41. Literally, "Do not trouble thyself on account of power." He who doubts his power, and fears he is not sufficiently strong, accomplishes nothing.

42. It must not be forgotten that in Egypt, as in the whole of the ancient East, the prince and notables administered justice *at the gate* of thair house or of the city.

not thy boat; thou who grantest life, cause not to die; thou who canst destroy, cause not that one should be destroyed. Luminous one, be not as a shadow; place of refuge, permit not the crocodile to carry off [his victims, on account of thee]. These four times I have lamented to thee: has not time enough been spent over that?"

This fellah went to make his complaint the fifth time, saying : "Mayor of the Palace, Rensi, son of Maru, my lord, the fisherman with the eel-pot cages his fish, the fisherman with the knife cuts the throat of the eel, the fisherman with the trident harpoons the bayyâds, the fishermen with the sweep nets take the châls,[43] in short the fishermen depopulate the river. Oh thou, thou art of their kind; do not ravish his property from a poor wretch, for thou knowest the weak. His goods are the vital air of the poor man, to ravish them from him is to stop up his nose. Thou hast been commissioned to listen to speech, to judge between two parties, to repress robbery; and lo! the malefactor is with thee, it is a heavy burden of robberies, which thou dost bear. One has made thee a favourite,[44] and thou art become a criminal; thou hast been given as a dyke to the wretched to prevent his drowning, and lo! thou art a man similar to a pool that fills rapidly."[45]

This fellah came to make his complaint the sixth time, saying: "Mayor of the Palace, Rensi, son of Maru, my lord, silent lord,[46] who punishes lies and causes justice to be, makes good to be; destroys evil, as satiety that ends hunger, clothing that ends nakedness, as the sky clears after the north wind and its heat warms all those who were cold, as fire cooks what is raw, as water quenches thirst. Oh thou who beholdest do not [turn away] thy face;[47] thou who dost distribute equitably, be not rapacious[48] thou who consolest, do not cause rancour; thou who healest, do not cause maladies; for the delinquent diminishes truth; he who well

43. The names of fish given here are all uncertain equivalents of the Egyptian names, of which we do not know the exact value; the *bayyâd* and the *châl* are two Nile fish that are excellent to eat, especially the first.

44. *One* here means Pharaoh who has Rensi, son of Maru, for his mayor of the palace.

45. The water in consequence washes away the dyke, ruining the field that the dyke was intended to protect.

46. Rensi is called son of Maru, "silent lord," because he does not reply to the lamentations of the fellah.

47. The scribe has here missed a word owing to its assonance; *me haru haru-k.* The fellah implores Rensi son of Maru who, seeing all, can remedy all, not to turn his face from him and leave him in misery.

48. Rensi being just, divides the goods of his subordinates exactly into two halves, and only takes the moiety due to him. The fellah implores him not to show himself rapacious and not to keep the whole.

fulfils [his duties] does not injure, does not overpower truth. If thou hast revenues, give of them to thy brother, that he may share them without legal proceedings [brought against him], for he who has rancour is a guide to discord, and he who relates his griefs in a whisper leads to schisms, without its having been known what was in his heart.[49] Therefore be not inactive in proclaiming thy intention; for who restrains the emission of water? Lo, the water gates are open, the water must flow; if the bark enter therein it is seized [by the current], its cargo perishes on the ground [scattered] on all the banks.[50] Thou art instructed, thou art well set up, thou art established solidly and not by violence; but while thou dost establish regulations for all men, those that are about thee wander from the straight road. Equitable [at times] and culpable towards the Entire Land, gardener of misery, who irrigates his land with villainies that his land may become a land of falsehood, to disseminate crimes on the soil."

This fellah went to make his complaint for the seventh time, saying: "Mayor of the Palace, my lord, thou art the rudder of the Entire Land, who navigates the world at thy pleasure; thou art the second Thoth,[51] who when he judges inclines not to one side. Oh my lord, may it please thee to permit an individual to appeal [at the tribunal] for the rights to which he is entitled. Restrain not thy heart; it is not in thy nature that from greatness of spirit thou shouldst become narrow of heart.[52] Be not preoccupied with that which does not yet happen, and rejoice not at that which has not yet come. As the impartial man is great in friendship, he regards as nothing the deed that is done by one who knew not what was the

49. The comparison here is between gain acquired by illegal means, and legitimate gains, those which are brought—*anu*—to the owner, or which the owner himself procures. The fellah counsels Rensi to give "his brother," that is to say his neighbour, that which he procures from his domains, part of his legitimate revenues, because to keep them for himself, to eat them—*uagait*—as the text says is incorrect, inappropriate, impolitic; the poor man to whom nothing is given becomes rancorous—*ahu*—and he "leads to separate," he conduces to discord, and he who tells his woes in a whisper, "he who makes known"—*sarkhi*—causes schisms without his sentiments being suspected.

50. The sequence of ideas is not easy to follow; this is how I read it. After having pointed out how dangerous it is for a man in the position of Rensi to arouse concealed rancour, the fellah, reverting to his own business, implores him to repress injustice. If he wished to do so, who would dare to resist him openly? His action would be like that of a current of water formed by a breach in a dyke, when the inundation is at its height; boats caught in the current are wrecked and their crews scattered along the banks.

51. Literally: "Thou art the second of Thoth," or perhaps "Thou art the brother of Thoth," the god who acts the part of scribe at the judgment of souls.

52. Literally: "It is not to thee that, to become the wide of face, a narrow of heart."

intention at the bottom of his heart.[53] He who diminishes the law, and destroys the reckoning [of human actions], he is a miserable wretch who lives when he has robbed, and truth no longer answers him.[54] But my bosom is full, my heart is charged, and that which issues from my bosom in consequence is like the breaking of a dyke from which water flows; my mouth opens to speech, I have striven [to stop up] my breach, I have thrown out my current, I have cast forth that which was in my bosom, I have washed my rags, my speech has come forth and my misery is complete before thee. What is thy final opinion? Thy inertia will injure thee, thy rapacity will render thee imbecile, thy avidity will make thee enemies. But where wilt thou find another fellah such as I? Would he not be an idler who, bringing his complaint, should stand at the door of his house?[55] There will be no silent one whom thou hast made to speak, there will be no slumberer whom thou hast awakened, there will be no timid one whom thou hast made bold,[56] there will be no dumb man whose mouth thou hast opened, there will be no ignorant one whom thou hast changed to a learned one, there will be no stupid one whom thou hast instructed. These are destroyers of evil, the notables [who surround thee] these are lords of good, these are artisans who produce [all] that exists, replacers of severed heads."[57]

This fellah came to make his complaint for the eighth time, saying: "Mayor of the palace, my lord, since one falls by deed of violence, since rapacity has no fortune [or rather] that its fortune is useless, since thou art violent when it is not thy nature to be so, and since thou robbest when it is useless to thee, leave people in possession of their good fortune. Thou hast what is needful for thee in thy house, thy belly is full, but the shock of wheat overflows,[58] and that which comes out of it perishes on the soil, for the notables pillage, ravishing by force; they who are set to repulse crime,

53. Literally: "Being the impartial, he makes himself wide in friendship, he destroys action which is produced, it not being known that which was in the heart."

54. The virtues we regard as abstractions, truth and justice, were goddesses of the Egyptians; and it is therefore not surprising to find that the terms applied to them are those employed for living people. We should say here, "Truth is no longer known to him."

55. Instead of coming daily to the gate of the palace, as our fellah does.

56. Literally: "There will be no restraint of face that thou hast provided [with face]."

57. Cf. above, p. 27, the story of the magician Didi, who replaced several heads. The expression *replacers of severed heads* appears to be the stock phrase to designate the most learned of the learned.

58. Literally, "it dances." The word used is employed to designate the various kinds of dances depicted on the walls of Memphite mastabas.

and who are the protection of the persecuted, the cruel ones who are set to repulse falsehood. Fear of thee has prevented me from supplicating thee [rightly], and thou hast not understood my heart. Oh, silent one,[59] he who turns to make his objurgations to thee, he fears not to present them, and it is not his brother who brings them to thee in thy private dwelling. Thou hast portions of land in the country, thou hast revenues in the town, thou hast thy bread at the storehouses,[60] the notables bring thee gifts, and thou takest [more?]. Art thou not a robber, because when one presents himself with his rent for thee, there are pillagers with thee to deduct half of the rentage-in-kind of the lands?[61] Do truth to the lord of truth, whose truth is the [real] truth.[62] Thou the calamus, the papyrus roll, the palette, the god Thoth, beware of making errors [of justice]; good, be good, truly good, be good! because truth is for eternity, it descends into Hades with him who practises it. When he has been placed in the coffin and laid in the ground, his name has not been effaced from the earth, and he is remembered for his goodness, in consequence of the word of the god.[63] It is in truth that the lever has not bent, the balance has not inclined to one side. And yet when I come to thee, when another comes, do not answer as if it were a silent one whom thou dost answer, do not attack one who does not attack thee, for thou hast not been injured, thou hast not suffered, thou hast not fled, thou hast not suppressed [evil], thou hast not shown on my behalf the conduct that corresponds with that excellent saying that issued from the mouth of Râ himself:[64] 'Speak the truth, do the truth, do that which conforms to

59. Here again Rensi is referred to by this epithet for the same reason given above, p. 48, note 46.

60. The word *faqaû* designates the revenues drawn by Rensi from his city property, houses, shops or factories; *âqaû,* literally loaves, includes in itself the emoluments in kind that he received from the royal storehouses as a state official.

61. Literally: "for the halves of the rented lands." It seems, according to the custom of Ancient Egypt, that the state, the towns, or the wealthy proprietors rented the lands belonging to them to the peasants for a rental of half the products of the soil.

62. The lord of truth or of justice is Thoth; the truth of the lord of truth is verity and justice, such as Thoth exercises, and *the truth of truth* and *the justice of justice* we should call the *quintessence* of truth and justice.

63. Literally, "reckoning of the speech of the god." Thoth, scribe of the Osirian tribunal (cf. above, p. 49, note 51), noted down the indications of the balance at the weighing of deeds, and proclaimed the result in a speech; according to his report the dead man was either admitted to Paradise or excluded, and his name remained either of good or evil savour on earth."

64. Literally: "Thou hast not given me the equivalents of saying." The peasant wished by this to say that Rensi had not acted towards hima as he would have done had he taken ino consideration the aphorism placed by tradition in the mouth of Rá.

truth, because truth is powerful, because it is great, because it is lasting, and when its parts are found it leads to a blessed state of existence.' If the balance bend not, if its scales carry objects [at the same level] the results of the true reckoning will not be felt [against me]. Shame will not come behind me in the city and will not land."

This fellah came to make his complaint for the ninth time, saying, "Mayor of the palace, my lord, the balance of people is their tongue, and it is the balance that verifies reckonings.[65] When therefore thou dost punish those who have done wrong the reckoning is audited in thy favour.[66] [On the contrary, he who makes a compact with] falsehood, his portion [henceforth] is that truth turns away from him, for then his good is falsehood, and truth does not concern itself for him.[67] But when the lie goes out it loses its way; it does not cross the water in the ferry-boat; it is not [received].[68] If he be wealthy he has no children; he has no posterity on earth.[69] If he travels he does not reach the land, and his boat does not come into port at his city.[70] Therefore do not make thyself heavy, for already thou art no small weight; do not rush, for already thou art not light in running[71]; do not cry aloud, be not an egoist,[72] veil not

65. It is by their tongue that the value of men is judged, and, on the other hand, it is by weighing their words that one ascertains whether the judgment that has been formed of them is correct.

66. Literally "the reckoning is equalised to thee." In other words, at the judgment of the dead the punishment inflicted by Rensi on a criminal will not be imputed to him as a sin, or rather it will not appear in the list of evil actions.

67. The beginning of this sentence translates literally "his portion becomes that truth turns away in front of him." The end of it is difficult to read, and I have confined myself to giving the general meaning as I take it to be, without attempting an exact translation.

68. This, I believe, is an allusion to the ferry-boat which carried over the doubles from this world to the domain of Osiris. He who does not exercise justice and truth will not be admitted, after death, to dwell with the god.

69. Having no posterity, no one will trouble to perform the funerary cult for him; his soul will be consigned to oblivion, and will in consequence cease to exist.

70. The term *saqdudu,* here employed for navigation, is that applied to the journey of the Sun round the world during the day and night; the dead man will not be admitted to follow the god, and his boat will perish before arriving at the celestial port where he desires to land.

71. Literally, "be not heavy, thou art not light, walk not heavily, thou dost not run." If I understand this sentence aright, it means that the peasant recommends Rensi not to treat his subordinates brutally. He has no need to press them, or to use force with them; he already presses them down, and his personality is so weighty that there is no need for him to aggravate the harm he unconsciously causes them by the exercise of his natural course of action.

72. Literally, "do not listen to thy heart." *To listen to the heart* both in Coptic and in the ancient language means *to obey;* here I think we must give it a slightly different meaning—*to listen to oneself, to listen only to oneself, to be egoistic.*

thy face from that thou knowest, close not thine eyes to that thou hast seen, turn not away from him who begs of thee. If thou fallest into idleness, use is made of thy conduct against thee.[73] Act therefore against him who has acted against thee. Hearken not to every one, but sentence a man only for the deed that he has verily committed. There is no yesterday for the idle[74]; there is no friend for him who is deaf to the truth; there is no happiness for the violent. [On the other hand], he who protests becomes wretched, and the wretched man passes into a condition of [perpetual] plaintiff, [and the plaintiff] is slain. Oh thou, I have made complaint to thee, and thou hast not listened to my pleading; I go to complain of thee to Anubis."[75]

The mayor of the palace, Rensi, son of Maru, sent two men of his clan to cause the fellah to return. This fellah therefore feared that the mayor did thus in order to punish him for this speech he had made, and this fellah said, "To repel the thirsty from the water, to remove the mouth of the babe from the milk, to intercept him who wishes to see Him [the god] all that causes his death to come to him slowly . . ."[76] The mayor of the palace, Rensi, son of Maru, said, "Fear nothing, fellah. I will act towards thee as thou dost act towards me." This fellah said, "Oh that I might live, eating thy bread and drinking thy beer, eternally!" The mayor of the palace, Rensi, son of Maru, said, "Come then, that thou mayest hear thy complaints." He then caused to be set down on a sheet of new papyrus all the lamentations of the fellah unto this day. The mayor of the palace, Rensi, son of Maru, sent them to His Majesty the King of the two Egypts, Nabkaûrîya, true of voice, and this was agreeable to him more than all things that are in this Entire Land, and His Majesty said, "Judge for thyself, son of Maru." The mayor of the palace, Rensi, son of Maru, forthwith commanded two men of his clan to fetch the clerk of the records, and he sent a message to the

73. Literally, "If thou fallest into idleness, report is made of thy concept, of thy conduct."

74. From the context this phrase appears to me to signify that the idle—it might perhaps be better translated indifferent—man cannot expect gratitude, because he has done no good to others in the past, *yesterday,* as the text says.

75. As Vogelsang has truly observed, the fellah in desperation now thinks of carrying his appeal into the other world, to the gods of the dead (*die Klagen des Bauern,* p. 15, note 2). Can this mean that he will kill himself? The word *samamu* employed above applies rather to assassination or execution. The fellah evidently fears that Rensi, annoyed and wearied with his appeals, will rid himself of him by one or other of these methods.

76. The reply of the fellah is so frequently interrupted by lacunæ that it is impossible for me to be sure of the meaning.

Natron Oasis, that his people to the number of six should be brought to him, over and above the slaves [he possessed already], with corn of the south, dûrah, asses, with [good things of all sorts. He commanded] Thotnakhuîti [to restore] to this peasant [his asses with] all his goods that he had taken from him. . . .

The end is missing, and it is difficult to say whether the fine speeches to which the fellah was addicted were not continued at some considerable length, this time to extol Pharaoh and to thank Rensi, son of Maru, for his justice. The fellah of to-day never ceases to speak when his interest is involved or his cupidity is satisfied. The man we have just disposed of was fully as long-winded, and would have no difficulty in evolving as many more fine speeches as he had already uttered. I fear that my readers, if they have had the patience to read to the end of his harangues, have experienced no more pleasure in perusing them than I have had in setting forth the translation. Have they always been able to appreciate the details? The conceptions of the Egyptians rarely correspond with ours, and they would combine several in one expression that we are unable to disentangle. They had only one word for truth and for justice, for falsehood and for evil, for personal idleness and for indifference to the acts and interests of others; while on the contrary the author renders the variety of physical and moral ills by a variety of terms for which I have not succeeded in finding equivalents. I have been forced to paraphrase rigorously those passages that a modern, unversed in Egyptology, would not have understood had I transcribed them literally. The general meaning is there; it remains for others to scrutinise the several phrases minutely and extract from them the subtle shades of thought and of language by which they charmed the Egyptians.

THE MEMOIRS OF SINUHÎT [4]

THE memoirs of Sinuhît appear to have been held in high estimation in the literary circles of Pharaonic Egypt, for they were frequently copied either in whole or in part, and we still possess the remains of three manuscripts which contained them complete—the *Berlin Papyrus No.* 1, to which the fragments of the *Amherst Papyrus* belong, the *Golénsfcheff Papyrus* and the *Ramesseum Papyrus No.* 1 at Berlin (Berlin 3022).

The *Berlin Papyrus No.* 1, bought by Lepsius in Egypt, and inserted by him in the *Denkmäler au Ægypten und Æthiopien,* vi, pl. 104–107, is imperfect at the beginning. It has been published in photographic facsimile with a hieroglyphic transcription by Alan H. Gardiner, *die Ezrälung des Sinuhe und die Hirtengeschichte,* in Erman, *Hieratische Texte des Mittleren Reichies,* 8vo, Leipzig, 1909, vol. ii, pl. 5–15. In its present state it contains three hundred and eleven lines of text. The hundred and seventy-nine lines of the commencement are vertical; followed immediately by ninety-six horizontal lines (180–276); but from line two hundred and seventy-seven to the end the scribe has reverted to the system of vertical columns. The first forty lines of the part that has survived have suffered more or less from wear and tear; some of them (lines 1, 13, 15, 38) have lacunæ that I should have been unable to fill in, had I not been fortunate enough to discover another copy at Thebes. The end is intact and closes with the well-known formula: *It has come from its beginning to its end, as it has been found in the book.* The writing, which is very good and bold in the vertical portions, becomes thick and confused in the horizontal lines, and full of ligatures and cursive forms, which in places render decipherment difficult. Some scraps of the parts that are missing at the beginning have been found among fragments belonging to the collection of the late Lord Amherst of Hackney. They have been published in hieroglyphic transcription by F. Ll. Griffith, *Fragments of Old Egyptian Stories* in the *Proceedings of the Society of Biblical Archœology,* 1891–1892, vol. xiv, pp. 452–454, and later in facsimile by P. Newberry in *Amherst Papyri,* 1901, vol. i, pl. i, MQ, and pp. 9, 10. According to G. Möller, *Hieratische Palœographie,* part I, pp. 14, 15, and also according to Alan H. Gardiner, *die Klagen des Bauern*, pp. 5, 6, and *die Erzählung des Sinuhe*, p. 5, it was written during the second half of the XIIth dynasty or the first half of the XIIIth; certain details, among others the corruption of the royal name, appear to me to indicate a somewhat later period of the XIIIth dynasty.

The *Golénischeff Papyrus* consists of the very mutilated remains of four pages. The first thirteen lines of p. 1 contained the beginning of the text, which is missing from the *Berlin Papyrus No. 1*. The fragments that still remain of this page and of the pages following belonged to that portion of the narrative that extends from line 1 to line 66 of the *Berlin Papyrus*. It has not been edited, but M. Golénischeff was good enough to send me photographs and a hieroglyphic transcription, that I published in G. Maspero, *Les Mémoires de Sinouhît* (forming vol. i of the *Bibliothèque d' Étude* 1906, pp. 32, 33, and which helped me to reconstitute the text. The script is the good hieratic of the XIXth and XXth dynasties.

The *Berlin Papyrus* has been analysed and translated into French by Chabas, *Les Papyrus de Berlin, récits d'il y a quatre mille ans*, pp. 37–51, and *Bibliothèque Universelle*, 1870, vol. ii, p. 174 in part only (cf. *Œuvres diverses,* vol. iv, pp. 254–255).

Mr. Goodwin gave an English version of the whole in *Frazer's Magazine,* 1865, under the title *The Story of Saneha*, pp. 185–202, then in a pamphlet, *The Story of Saneha, an Egyptian Tale of Four Thousand Years ago, translated from the Hieratic text* by Charles Wycliffe Goodwin, M.A. (Reprinted from *Frazer's Magazine*, London, Williams & Norgate, 1866, 8vo, 46 pp.). This translation was corrected by the author himself in *Zeitschrift*, 1872, pp. 10–24, and reproduced in full in the *Records of the Past,* first series, vol. vi, pp. 131–150, with a rather arbitrary division of the lines.

A second French translation is one given under the title *Le Papyrus de Berlin No. 1*, transcribed, translated, and commented on, by G. Maspero (Cours au Collège de France, 1874–1876), in *Mélanges d'Archéologie égyptienne et assyrienne,* vol. iii, pp. 68–82, 140 *et seq.;* reproduced partly, with corrections, in *Histoire ancienne des peuples de l' Orient,* sixth edition, pp. 115–116, 121–124.

Finally Henry Daniel Haigh examined the historical and geographical bearings of this document in a special article of *Zeitschrift*, 1875, pp. 78–107, and Erman inserted a short German analysis of it in his book *Ægypten und Ægyptisches Leben in Altertum,* 1885–1888, pp. 494–497. The *Ramesseum Papyrus No. 1* contained obverse a complete copy of the *Memoirs of Sinuhît,* but we only possess about twenty pages more or less damaged. The first represent a hundred and four horizontal lines, which correspond with the complete text of the *Cairo Ostracon,* 27419, of which we shall speak later, to the *Golénischeff Papyrus,* to the fragments of the *Amherst Papyrus,* and to lines 1–77 of the *Berlin Papyrus No. 1*.

After this beginning there remains only one page which is almost intact, with the ends of the lines that belonged to two pages on the right and the left; there, with many lacunæ, can be read the story of the duel between Sinuhît and the brave man of Tonu, of lines 131–145 of *Berlin Papyrus No. 1*. The discovery of this was announced by Alan H. Gardiner, *Eine neue Handschrift des Sinuhegedichtes*, in the *Sitzungsberichte* of the Academy of Sciences of Berlin, 1907, pp. 142–150, published separately in an octavo of nine pages. The text of it has been published in facsimile, with a hieroglyphic transcription, by Alan H. Gardiner, *die Erzählung des Sinuhe und die Hirtenengeschichte*, pl. 1–4.

Beside the editions on papyrus we possess copies of two considerable portions from the beginning and the end of the narrative on ostraca two of which were recently published by A. H. Gardiner in *Recueil de Travaux*, 1892. The earliest known of them is at the British Museum with the number 5629. It was first mentioned by Birch in his *Memoir on the Abbott Papyrus* (French translation by Chabas in *Revue archéologique*, 1858, p. 264; cf. *Œuvres diverses*, vol. i, p. 284); and published in facsimile in *Inscriptions in the Hieratic and Demotic Characters, from the Collections of the British Museum*, folio, London, MDCCCLXVIII, pl. xxiii, and p. 8.

Lauth translated it in *Die zweiälteste Landkarte nebst Gräberplänen* (extract from the *Sitzungsberichte* of the Academy of Munich, 1871, pp. 233–236), but the identity of the text it contains with the text of lines 300–310 of the *Berlin Papyrus No. 1*, was discovered by Goodwin, *On a Hieratic Inscription upon a Stone in the British Museum*, in *Zeitschrift*, 1872, pp. 20–24, where the text is given at full length. The writing is of the XIXth and XXth dynasties, the same as that of the *Golénischeff Papyrus*. As the version it bears differs in certain details from that of the Berlin Papyrus, it is worth while to give a complete translation of it here.

[A pyramid was] constructed [for me] in stone—in the circle of the pyramids,—the dressers of stone dressed the tomb—and devised the walls of it;—the draughtsmen drew there—the chief of the sculptors carved there,—the chief of the works which are done at the necropolis travelled the country [for] all the furnishing—with which I beautified the tomb.—I assigned peasants to it,—and it had domains and fields in the neighbourhood of the city—as is done with Friends *of the first rank.—[There was] a statue of gold with a loincloth of silver gilt,—which the* sons of the King *made for me, rejoicing to do that for me;—for I was in favour with the King—until the day arrived that I landed on the other bank.*

It is happily finished in peace.

Another ostracon which is at the Cairo Museum was found on February 6, 1886, in the tomb of Sannozmu, at Thebes. It is a piece of limestone, broken in two, one metre in length, with a medium height of twenty centimetres, covered with rather large hieratic characters punctuated with red ink, and divided into paragraphs, as is the case with most manuscripts of the Ramesside period. On the back two lines, which unfortunately are almost illegible, contain a name I have not succeeded in deciphering—probably the name of the scribe who wrote the text. The break is not a recent one. The limestone was broken when it was placed in the tomb, and the breakage was not accomplished without damage; several chips of the stone have disappeared, and have carried off fragments of words with them. Most of the lacunæ can be filled in without difficulty. The text is very incorrect, like most works intended for the use of the dead. Many variants on it arise from imperfect reading of the original manuscript; the scribe was unable to read accurately the archaic writing and transcribed it by guesswork. The ostracon was published for the first time with a hieroglyphic transcription and French translation by G. Maspero, *Les premières lignes des Mémoires de Sinouhit, restituées d'après l'Ostracan 27419 du Musée de Boulaq,* with two plates, of facsimile, in *Mémoires de l'Institut égyptien,* 4to, vol. ii, pp. 1–23; published separately, 4to, with special title and mention, Bulak, 1886, reproduced in *Études de Mythologie et d'Archéologie égyptiennes,* vol. iv, pp. 281–305.

Since then it has been described and published in facsimile in the *Catalogue Général du Musée du Caire,* by G. Daressy, *Ostraca,* 4to, 1901, pl. xli, pp. 46, 47, where it bears the new number 25218.

The complete text of the *Mémoires,* reconstituted for the first time twenty years ago in the second edition of these *Stories,* has since been translated into English. See:

W. M. Flinders Petrie, *Egyptian Tales,* 1895, London, 12mo, vol. i, pp. 97–142.

F. Ll. Griffith, *Egyptian Literature* in *Specimen Pages of a Library of the World's Best Literature,* 1898, New York, 4to, pp. 5238–5249.

Translated into German by:

A. Erman, *Aus den Papyrus den Königlichen, Museen,* 1899, Berlin, 8vo, pp. 14–29, who has also introduced a hieroglyph transcription of several passages into his *Ægyptische Grammatik,* 1st edition, 1894, pp. 17, 18, and in his *Ægyptische Chrestomathie,* 1904, pp. 1–11.

A. Wiedemann, *Altägyptische Sagen und Märchen,* 8vo, Leipzig, 1906, pp. 34–57.

Alan H. Gardiner, *die Erzählung des Silnuhe und die Hirtengeschichte,* folio, Leipzig, 1909, pp. 9–15.

Almost at the same time as the appearance of this volume, Gardiner made a translation into English with critical notes, running commentary and text of the new ostraca, contributed by him to the *Receiil des Travaux* (1910, vol. xxxii, pp. 1–28, 214–230; 1911, vol. xxxiii.pp. 67–94, etc.), with the title *Notes on the Story of Sinuhe,* and published separately by Champion, 4to, Paris.

Finally a critical edition of the text with introduction and glossary has been attempted by G. Maspero, *Les Mémoires de Sinuhît* (forms vol. i of the *Bibliothèque d'études*), 1908, 4to, Cairo, pp. 51-184.

The discovery of the first lines has enabled us to reconstitute the route taken by Sinuhît in his flight. He left the camp established in the Libyan region in the country of the Timihu, or in other words, he started from some point on the western desert, crossed the canal Maûti, the canal of the two Truths, *i.e.* that part of the Bahr Yusûf which crosses the entrance to the Fayûm and rejoins the Nile near Terraneh, passing the foot of the mountain. He reached the valley near a locality called Nuhît, *The sycamore* According to Brugsch (*Dictionnaire géographique,* p. 53), Nuhît should be the Panaho of the Copts, the Athribis of the Greeks, and Benha-el-Assal of to-day. This identification fails *a priori,* as Nuhît is mentioned at the beginning of the journey, *i.e.* on the west side of the Nile, while Benha is on the east bank. At first I considered *The sycamore* as an appellation intended for the whole of Egypt, but for a long time a Nuhît or Pa-nabît-nuhît has been known, which appears at first to have been a village in the vicinity of Memphis, but the name of which was at last attached to Memphis itself (Brugsch, *Dictionnaire géographique,* pp. 330–332). *The sycamore* is probably that *Quarter of the Sycamore* consecrated to Hathor in all localities where a sacred sycamore existed; it is possible that the name of the hero, *Sinuhît,* signified the *son of the goddess Sycamore,* analogous with *Sihathor* the son of Hathor. From Nuhît the story of the flight leads him to Shi-Sanafruî or Aî-Sanafruî. The lake Sanafruî or the island Sanafruî is not known elsewhere, but Brugsch connects it with the nome Myekphoris of Herodotus (iii, clxvi), on the strength of the pronunciation *Muî-hik-Snofru,* which, he says, is borne by the signs of which the name is composed (*Dict. géog.,* p. 54). The position in the itinerary occupied by this place leads me to look for it between the Libyan desert, Memphis, and the Nile, about a day's march from the town of Nagaû, perhaps in the vicinity of the pyramids of Gizeh or Abu-Roâsh. In the evening Sinuhît crossed the Nile near Nagaû, probably at Embabeh, and resumed his route, passing the district of Iaûku on the east. This is the country of stone-cutters, the region of the quarries that extend from Turah to the desert, along the Gebel Ahmar, the *red mountain,* and we may perhaps take it that the place called Haruît-nabît-Duû-doshir, *"the goddess Firmament, lady of the Red Mountain,"* is more especially the point of the Gebel-Giyuchi. From there Sinuhît proceeded on foot to one of the fortified posts that protected Egypt on that side, between Abu-Zabel and Belbeis, but farther on he only mentions Puteni and Qamuêri. Brugsch identifies Puteni with a country of Pâ, which he met with on a monument of the Saite period, and of which the town of Belbeis indicates the centre (*Dict. géog.,* pp. 54, 55). The great Ptolemaic stela discovered by M. Naville at Tell-el-Maskhuta furnished several points that aid in determining the exact position of Qamuêri. A name Qamuêr occurs on it, which has been identified by M. Naville, not unreasonably, with the Qamuêri of the Memoirs of Sinuhît (*The Store-City of Pithom* and the *Route of the Exodus*, pp. 21, 22). Here Ptolemy Philadelphus constructed the town that he called Arsinoe after his sister, and which became one of the store-cities of the commerce of Egypt with the Red Sea. M. Naville places Arsinoe, and in consequence Qamuêri, near El-Maghfâr, at the base of the ancient Gulf of Suez. This site fits in well with the narrative; after leaving Puteni, Sinuhît would plunge into the desert, towards the north-east, and would lose himself among the sand, in attempting to reach Qamuêri.

From this point, the localities he crossed and those in which he dwelt have been studied by Maspero (*Notes sur quelques points de Grammaire et d'Histoire*, in the *Recueil*, vol. xvii, p. 142), and by Isidore Lévy (*Lotanu-Lotân*, in *Sphinx*, vol. ix, pp. 76–86), who agree in placing them in the Sinaitic desert. To begin with, Sinuhît enters two countries the names of which have been differently interpreted and have given rise to numerous discussions. The first, read by me with hesitation as *Suanu*, has been transcribed *Kapuna* by Gardiner (*Eine neue Handschrift des Sinuhegedichtes*, pp. 7, 8, and *Notes on the Story of Sinuhe*, in *Recueil*, vol. xxxii, pp. 21–23), and then identified by him with the town of Byblos: I have stated (*Mémoires de Sinuhît*, pp. xlii-xliv) the reasons that prevent my accepting this proposed reading and identification. The second name, read *Edimâ, Edumâ*, by Chabas, has been identified with Idumea (*Les Papyrus de Berlin*, pp. 39, 75–76). To-day it is read *Kadimâ, Kedem*. The author states that it is a district of the Upper Tonu, and a scribe who was contemporary with Thothmes III has placed it near Megiddo (Max Müller, *Egyptological Researches*, vol. ii, pp. 81, 82). The Tonu should at least include the space between the Dead Sea and the Sinaitic Peninsula, but it would not be necessary to seek farther towards the north of Syria, if the version Tonu is an error for Ratonu-Latonu; the Latonu, as Max Müller was the first to observe (*Asien und Europa*, p. 211; cf. Isidore Lévy, *Lotanu-Lotân*, p. 72 *et seq.*), and as Alan Gardiner strongly maintains (*Eine neue Handschrift des Sinuhegedichtes*, p. 8; *die Erzählung des Sinuhe*, p. 10, n. 4), may have been originally a district contiguous to that of the Kharu, the Horites. The Prince of Tonu or of Lotanu gives the Egyptian hero a district, Aaa, or rather Aîa, the name of which designates a species of plant, the *Arundo-Isiaca*, according to Loret (*Saccharum Ægyptiacum*, in *Sphinx*, vol. viii, pp. 157–8). Max Müller has found it after Megiddo and before Qadimâ in the list of Thûtmôsis III (*Egyptological Researches*, vol. ii, pp. 81, 82). Is this the Ajah of Genesis (xxxvi, 24), nephew of Lotantu-Lotân, and eventually a province of Sinai (Maspero,

Notes sur quelques points, in the *Recueil,* vol. xvii, p. 142)? Sinuhît remained there some years in friendly intercourse with the nomad archers, the *Saatiu;* on his return he was received by the Egyptian garrison of a frontier station, *Hariu-Horu, the roads of Horus.* Erman (*die Horuswege,* in *Zeitschrift,* vol. xliii, pp. 72, 73) has shown that in the Ptolemaic period this name was given to the eastern border of the Delta—*Khont-abti*—and that it was a mythological designation of the locality that in political geography was called Zaru. It is borrowed from the Horus myth; Horus, pursuing after Set-Typhon, must have passed by Wady Tumilât, and left his name there. Sinuhît therefore went by boat from near Ismailia to near Dahchûr or Lisht, where the Court then resided.

An English novelist, Guy Boothby, has made the flight of Sinuhît the starting-point of a novel of theosophical tendencies, entitled *A Professor of Egyptology.*

⁂

The hereditary prince, the King's man, the unique friend,[1] the jackal, administrator of the domains of the sovereign and his lieutenant among the Beduîn, he who is known of the king in truth and who loves him, the servant Sinuhît[2] saith:

I am the follower who follows his master, the servant of the royal harem of the hereditary princess, supreme favourite, royal spouse of Sanuosrît in Khnumisuîtu, the royal daughter of Amenemhaît in Qanofir, Nofrît[3] Lady

---

1. The *friends* occupied the highest positions at the Court of Pharaoh; in the *Hood Papyrus* of the British Museum the hierarchy places them in the seventh rank after the king. They were divided into several categories: the *unique friends,* the *friends of the seraglio,* the *gilded friends,* the *juniors,* whose positions it is not possible to gauge exactly. The title continued to exist at the Ptolemaic Court, and spread through the Macedonian world (cf. Maspero, *Études égyptiennes,* vol. ii, pp. 20, 21).

2. Sinuhît's protocol, beside the ordinary Egyptian dignities, includes a title which unfortunately is damaged, and which we are not accustomed to find on the monuments, but which connects it with the Beduîn of Asia. Sinuhît had been in fact chief of a tribe of the Saatiû, and something of this remained with him after his return to Egypt and the Court of Pharaoh. It is a new fact, and one not unworthy of being called to the notice of Egyptologists.

3. The Sanuosrît and Amenemhaît, of whom the princess was the wife and daughter, are here distinguished by the name of the pyramids in which they were buried, Khnumisuîtu and Qanofir. The Cairo Museum possesses two statues of Princess Nofrît, discovered by Mariette at Sân, the ancient Tanis (Maspero, *Guide to the Cairo Museum,* 5th Edition, 1910, pp. 93, 94, Nos. 200 and 201).

of fealty. The year xxx, the third month of Iakhuît,[4] the seventh day, the god entered his double horizon, the king Sahotpiaburîya sprang to heaven,[5] uniting himself with the solar disc, and the limbs of the god were absorbed in him who had created them. Now the palace was in silence, hearts were in mourning, the great double gate was sealed up, the courtiers remained crouched down with their heads on their knees, and the people also lamented him. Now, His Majesty, l. h, s., had sent a numerous army to the country of the Timihu,[6] and his eldest son, the good god Sanuosrît, l. h. s., was chief of it. He had been sent to strike the foreign countries and to reduce the Tihonu to slavery, and now he was returning, he was conducting the living prisoners taken from among the Timihu, and all sorts of cattle without number. The Friends of the Seraglio, l. h. s., commanded the people of the western side to inform the son of the king of the matters that had chanced in the palace, l. h. s.[7] The messengers found him on the way, they reached him in the night; never did he make less delay, the falcon took wing with his servants[8] without making anything known to his army. One commanded the royal sons who were with the army to tell no one of those who were there but as for me, I was there; I heard his voice as he was speaking, and when I went away, my heart melted, my arms sank down, fear settled on all my limbs, I crept away, winding and turning to seek a place to hide myself[9]; crawling between two bushes in order to get off the beaten path,[10] I journeyed toward the south, but I did not think of returning to the palace, because

4. One of the texts, that of the Cairo ostracon, mentions here the *second* month of Iakhuît.

5. In other words *the king Amenemhaït 1st died*. On p. 16 of this volume we have another example of this euphemism.

6. The Timihu are tribes of Berbers that inhabited the Libyan desert, to the west of Egypt.

7. At the king's death the *friends of the Seraglio* would assume the regency in the absence of the heir.

8. The *falcon who takes wing*, according to Egyptian usage, is the new king, identified either with Haruêri, Horus the elder, or with Harsiesît, Horus son of Isis.

9. Sinuhît omits to tell us by what accident he was in a position, when all were excluded, to overhear the news brought by the messenger to the new king. We do not know whether the Egyptian law, in such a case, required the death of the unfortunate man, who involuntarily committed such an indiscretion. There is no doubt that Sinuhît feared for his life and decided to fly.

10. Sinuhît hid among the bushes while the royal procession passed in secret before him. He then struck out a way for himself among the thickets, avoiding the route taken by Pharaoh.

I imagined that war had already broken out.[11] Without saying a good wish for life for that palace, I crossed the canal Mauîti at the place called of The sycamore.[12] I reached the island of Sanafruî, and I passed the day there in a field; then I departed at daybreak and travelled. A man who was standing at the side of the road craved mercy of me, for he was afeared. Towards the time of supper, I approached the town of Nagau; I crossed the water on a punt without a rudder, owing to the west wind, and I crossed to the east, by the district of the quarries in the place called Haruît-nabît-duû-doshir; then, making way on foot towards the north, I gained the Wall of the Prince, which was constructed to repel the Saatiu and to crush the Nomiu-Shâiu; I remained crouched in a bush, for fear of being seen by the guard who watches on the curtain of the wall in his day. I started again at night, and the next day at sunrise I reached Puteni, and rested at the island Qamuêri. Then thirst descended and assailed me; I failed, my throat rattled, and I then said to myself, 'This is the taste of death'; when I uplifted my heart and gathered my limbs together, for I heard the loud voice of a herd. The Beduîn perceived me, and one of their sheikhs,[13] who had sojourned in Egypt, recognised me; lo, he gave me water and caused milk to be boiled for me, then I went with him with his tribe, and he rendered me the service of passing me from country to country.

I set forth for Suânu. I arrived at the Kadimâi, and I remained there a year and a half.

Ammûianashi, who is the prince of the Upper Tonu,[14] summoned me and said to me, "Thou findest thyself at ease with me, because thou hearest talk of Egypt." He said this because he knew who I was and had heard of my ability; some Egyptians who were in the country with me had borne witness of me to him.[15] This is then what he said to me: "What is the reason wherefore thou art come hither? What is it? Is it caused by a journey to the horizon in the palace of the King of the two Egypts,

11. This passage can scarcely allude to anything but civil war. In Egypt, as in all Oriental countries, a change of reign often led to a revolt; the princes who had not been chosen to succeed their father took up arms against their more fortunate brother.

12. For this geographical name, and the following ones, see the introduction to this story, pp. 59, 60.

13. Cf. L. Borchardt, *zu Sinuhe* 35 ff., in *Zeitschrift*, 1891, vol. xxix, p. 63.

14. The Ramesseum papyrus gives here a variant, the *Upper Lotanu*. Cf. introduction to this story, above, p. 60.

15. Probably refugees escaped from Egypt under similar circumstances to those that caused Sinuhît's flight.

Sahotpiaburîya,[16] without its being known what happened on that occasion?"

I replied to him with guile, "Yes verily, when I returned from the expedition to the land of the Timihu, a certain matter was repeated to me. My heart was stirred, my heart was no longer in my bosom, but it led me out on to the desert ways. I had not been blamed, no one had spat in my face, I had heard no villainy, and my name had not been heard in the mouth of the heralds! I know not what it was that led me to this country; it was as though designed by God!" "How will it be then in that land of Egypt without the beneficent god whose terror is spread abroad among foreign nations, as Sokhît[17] in a year of pestilence?"

I told him my belief, and I replied to him:[18]"God preserve us! his son as entered into the palace and has taken the heritage of his father. He is a god who verily has no second; no one is before him. He is a lord of wisdom, prudent in his schemes, beneficent in his decrees, by order of which one comes and goes. It is he who has already subdued foreign regions, while his father remained within his palace, and he reported to him (his father) that which he had decided that he should do. He is the strong man that verily toils with the sword, a valiant man who has no equal, when one sees him flinging himself against the barbarians, and joining the fight. He is one who tosses with the horn, and makes feeble the hands of his enemies; the enemy cannot restore order in their ranks. He is the chastiser who breaks heads; nothing can stand before him. He is the rapid runner who destroys the fugitive; there is no refuge to be reached by him who has shown him the back. He is firm of heart at the moment

16. The question of the prince of Tonu, intentionally somewhat obscure, is simpler when we know from other documents (*Sallier Papyrus* II, p. 1, last line; p. 2, lines 1, 2) that there had been a conspiracy against Amenemhaît. Ammûianashi asks whether Sinuhît had not been implicated in some attempt of that kind, and if he had not been forced to make his escape with the assassin of the king.

17. Sokhît or Sakhmît, for a long time confounded with *Pahhûit*, was one of the principal goddesses of the Egyptian Pantheon. She belonged to the triad of Memphis, and had the title *Great friend of Ptah*. She was a lioness or a lion-headed goddess; with a cat's head she was called Bastît or Ubastît, and was worshipped at Bubastis in the Delta.

18. Sinuhît replies to the question of the chief of Tonu, who asked him whether his exile was not occasioned by some complicity in an attempt directed against the life of the sovereign. His flight is by the will of God, and like a fatality; in fact, as we have seen above (p. 62), it was by chance and not by his wish that he heard of the death of Amenemhaît. In order to show that he had never taken part in any plot, nor would ever do so, he launches forth into emphatic praises of the new Pharaoh, Sanuosrît I; the exaggerated compliments are here a proof of loyalty and innocence.

of attack. He it is who returns without ceasing to the charge, and has never turned the back. He is the strong heart, who when he sees the multitudes does not let weariness enter his heart. He is the brave one, who dashes forward when he beholds resistance. He it is who rejoices when he pounces upon the barbarians; he seizes his buckler, he overthrows the adversary, he never gives a second blow when he slays, but there is no one who can turn away his lance, no one who can draw his bow; the barbarians flee, for his two arms are as strong as the souls of the great goddess.[19] When fighting he knows no cessation, he heeds nothing, he leaves nothing remaining. He is the well-beloved, the very delightsome, who has conquered love, and his city loves him more than itself; it rejoices in him more than in its own god, and men and women go exulting because of him. He is a king who has governed from the egg,[20] and he has worn diadems since his birth; he it is who has caused his contemporaries to multiply,[21] and he is one whom the gods have granted us, and by whom that land rejoices to be governed. He it is who enlarges frontiers; he will take the lands of the South and regards not the lands of the North. He was created to smite the Saatiu and to crush the Nomiu-Shâiu.[22] If he sends an expedition here, may he know thy name for good, and may no evil word of thee reach His Majesty. For he never ceases to do good for the land that submits to him."

The chief of the Tonu replied, "Verily, Egypt is happy in that she knows the vigour of her prince! As to thee, since thou art here, stay with me and I will do well for thee." He placed me before his children, he married me to his eldest daughter, and he gave me what I chose for myself in his country, of the best that he possessed on the frontier of a neighbouring country. It is an excellent land, Aîa[23] by name. There are figs in it and grapes; wine is more abundant there than water; honey abounds there; there is oil in plenty, and all sorts of fruits upon its trees;

19. One of the titles given to Sokhît (see p. 64 note 17) and to her warlike forms.

20. This is the Egyptian formula to indicate that royal power belonged to the being from the moment he was conceived in his mother's womb.

21. According to Gardiner (*Notes on the Story of Sinuhe*, in *Recueil*, vol. xxxii, p. 224), this passage signifies that he left Egypt more populous than it was at the time of his birth. In this connection it recalls the names of Horus, *he who renews births* for Amenemhaît I, and *he who is the life of births* for Sanuosrît I.

22. The nomad population that inhabit the desert to the east of Egypt. Elsewhere they are called *Harûiû-Shâiu*, the *lords of the sands;* the variant Nomiû-Shâiu appears to signify *those who rule the sands.*

23. see on p. 60–61 in the introduction to this story the identification proposed for this locality.

barley and wheat are there without limit, and all breeds of cattle. Also great privileges were conferred on me when the prince came on my account, and he installed me prince of a tribe of the best of his country. I had bread daily and wine daily, boiled meat, poultry for roasting, and the game of the country, for it was chased for me and presented to me, beside what my own hunting dogs brought me. Plenty of cakes[24] were made for me, and milk was cooked in all ways. I passed many years, my children became mighty ones, each ruling his tribe. The messenger who went north, or returned southward to Egypt, tarried at my house, for I received every one; I gave water to the thirsty, I put back into the way the traveller who had lost his road; I rescued the pillaged. The Beduîn[25] who dared to resist the princes of the land, I directed their movements, for the prince of Tonu granted me for long years to be general of his soldiers. All countries against which I marched, when I flung myself on them, trembled because of me in the pastures on the borders of their water springs. I took their cattle, I led away their vassals, and I carried off their slaves. I slew their men.[26] By my sword, by my bow, by my marches, by my well-laid plans, I won the heart of my prince, and he loved me when he knew my valour; he made me the chief of his children when he beheld the vigour of my arms.

A strong man of Tonu came, he defied me in my tent; he was a hero who had no second, for he had vanquished the whole of Tonu. He said he would fight me, he proposed to despoil me, he said aloud he would take my cattle at the instigation of his tribe. This prince deliberated with me, and I said, "I do not know him. Verily, I am not his ally who has free access to his tent; have I ever opened his door or entered his enclosures? It is pure jealousy, because he sees me to be one who does his business. God preserve us, I am as the bull in the midst of his cows when a young bull from without descends on him to take possession of them. Does a suppliant please when he becomes a master? There is no nomad who associates willingly with a fellah of the Delta, for how

24. This word has been left blank in the Berlin manuscript. Very probably it was illegible in the original papyrus from which the copy we possess of the story of Sinuhît was made. The scribe preferred to write nothing rather than fill up the gap on his own authority.

25. Literally *the archers*. It is the generic name given by the Egyptians to the nomad population of Syria in opposition to Monatiu, which was applied to the agricultural peoples.

26. Those are the expressions used in official reports describing the ravages of wars conducted by the Pharaohs. Sanuosrît III says the same: "I took their women. I carried off their subordinates appearing at their wells, driving their cattle before me, spoiling their houses and setting them on fire." Lepsius, *Denkm.* ii, pl. 136, h, lines 14–16.

should a jungle of bulrushes be transplanted on a mountain? Is he a bull in love with battle, a bull of the best who delights in giving blow for blow, and who fears to meet one who equals him? Then, if he has the heart to fight, let him utter the intention of his heart. Is God ignorant of what is decreed with regard to him? or if it is thus, how shall it be known?"[27] I passed the night tightening my bow, loosing my arrows, practising my poniard, furbishing my weapons. At daybreak the country of Tonu assembled; they had collected their tribes and convoked all the neighbouring countries, for they had foreseen the combat. When the strong man came, I stood up, I placed myself opposite him; all hearts burned for me, men and women uttered cries, every heart was anxious on my account, and it was said, "Is there in truth another champion strong enough to be able to fight with him?" Behold, he took his buckler, his lance, his armful of javelins. When I had caused him to use his arms in vain, and had avoided his shafts so that they struck the ground and not one of them fell near me, he fell upon me, then I discharged my bow against him, and when my shaft buried itself in his neck, he cried out and fell on his nose. I slew him with his own battle-axe, I uttered my cry of victory on his back, and all the Asiatics shouted for joy; I uttered thanksgivings to Montu[28] while his people lamented over him, and the prince, Ammûianashi,[29] folded me in his arms. Behold, then, I took possession of the goods of the vanquished. I seized his cattle; that which he had desired to do to me, I did to him; I took what he had in his tent, I pillaged his encampment and enriched myself, I enlarged my treasure and increased the number of my cattle.

Thus the god showed himself gracious to him who had been reproached with having fled to a strange land, and who was to-day joyous of heart. A fugitive had fled in his time, and now good report of me

27. The whole of this passage is difficult to interpret. On the whole I have adopted Gardiner's latest translation (*Notes on the Story of Sinuhe*, in *Recueil*, vol. xxxiii, pp. 68–72). Sinuhît appears to think that his foreign origin is the cause of the provocation of which he could not otherwise understand the motives. He accepts it, however, and refers it to the judgment of God.

28. The god of war at Thebes. He was worshipped at Hermonthis, in the immediate vicinity of the great city. The Greeks identified him with Apollo; he was in fact a solar deity, and the monuments often confuse him with Râ, the sun.

29. The vocalisation with an i is given in this name by the manuscript where it is not given earlier, or should it be read *Amu si Anashi*, Anashi son of Amu? The Egyptians, with their imperfect system of writing, found it exceedingly difficult to render foreign vowel sounds, and thence arose the variations one finds in spelling.

was carried to the Egyptian court. A wanderer had wandered painfully, dying of hunger, and now I gave bread to my neighbour. A poor wretch had quitted his country naked, and I was gorgeous in vestments of fine linen. There was one who did his errands himself, having no one to send, and I possessed many serfs. My house was fine, my domain wide, I was remembered in the king's palace. "Oh, all ye gods who predestined that I should flee, be gracious to me, bring me back to the palace, perchance grant me to see again the place where my heart dwells. What happiness if my body should one day rest in the country where I was born.[30] Oh that henceforth my good fortune may endure, that the god may grant me peace, that he may act in a manner expedient for the man he has grieved, that he may be compassionate to him whom he has forced to live in a strange land. Is he not now appeased? Oh that he may listen to him who prays from afar, and turn to the man he has cast down and to the place from which he has taken him;[31] may the king of Egypt be favourable to me, and may I live on his gifts, and may I administer the goods of the Regent of the Earth[32] who is in her palace, and may I hear the messages of her children. Oh that my limbs may grow young, for now that old age approaches, weakness hath seized me, my two eyes are heavy, my arms hang down, my limbs refuse their service, my heart stops. Death approaches me, and soon I shall betake myself to the eternal cities[33] to follow the *Lady of All*.[34] Oh, may she tell me of the beauties of her children and spend eternity by my side!"[35]

30. Cf. The same wish expressed on behalf of the shipwrecked man by the serpent who received him in his island, p. 85.

31. So far as I can understand, Sinuhît implores the king to consider the disgrace he has incurred, and the land from which he has been banished, and then, considering the want of proportion between his offence and its punishment, to recall him, Sinuhît, to Egypt.

32. This is one of the titles of the Queen. As we have seen above (p. 61), Sinuhît was administrator of the harem, and therefore of the possessions of the Queen. He asks to be restored to his former function.

33. The *eternal cities* or the *eternal house* is the name given by Egyptians to the tomb.

34. The *Lady of All*, like the *Master of All*, is a divinity of the dead. Erman (*Aus den Papyrus der Königlichen Museen*, p. 22, note 2), and Gardiner (*Notes on the Story of Sinuhe*, in *Recueil*, vol. xxxiii, pp. 85, 86), think rather that it refers to the Queen; Sinuhît would hope to serve her through eternity in the other world as he served her in this.

35. One knows the dread felt by the Egyptians of dying, and yet more of being buried in a foreign country. They believed they could only enjoy life beyond the tomb if their mummy was laid in the land of Egypt. It is to avoid the opprobrium and misfortune of a tomb in Syria that Sinuhît, now grown old, requests to be allowed to return home. He insists so much on his funerary ideas, because, more than any other consideration, they would arouse the pity of Pharaoh.

When therefore one had spoken to His Majesty the King Khopirk-erîya,[36] true of voice,[37] of those matters that concerned me, His Majesty deigned to send me a messenger with presents from the King to put into joy the servant who speaks to you[38] such as those that are given to the princes of all foreign lands, and the Infants[39] who are in the palace caused me to receive their messages.

Copy of the Command brought to the Servant here Present on the Subject of his Recall to Egypt

"Horus, life of births, lord of the diadems of the North and the South, life of births, King of Upper and Lower Egypt, Khopirkerîya, son of the Sun, Amenemhaît[40] living for ever and ever.

"Command of the King to the servant Sinuhît. Behold, this command of the King is brought thee to instruct thee as to his will.[41]

"Thou hast traversed foreign lands, going from Kadimâ to Tonu, and from each land thou hast passed to another, and that only by the advice of thine own heart. What hast thou obtained there that is done for

36. The prenomen of King Sanuosrît 1st, son and successor to Amenemhaît 1st with a variant on the word *Ka*.

37. The Egyptians, like all Oriental people, attached great importance not only to the words of their religious formulæ, but also to the intonation given to each of them. For a prayer to be effective, and to have its full effect with the gods, it must be recited with the traditional melopeia. Thus the highest praise that could be given to a person obliged to recite prayers was to call him *Mâ-khrôu, true of voice*, to say that he had a correct voice and knew the accent that must be given to each sentence. The king or priest who performed the office of lector (*khri-habi*, see p. 24, note 2) during sacrifices was called *mâ-khrôu*. The gods triumphed over evil by the *correctness of their voice* when they pronounced the words intended to render evil spirits powerless. The dead man who spent all the time of his funerary existence in uttering incantations, was above all things the *mâ-khrôu*. The expression thus employed eventually becomes an actual laudatory epithet, applied to all the dead and personages of a bygone time when spoken of not unfavourably.

38. L. Borchardt, *der Ausdruch Bk'im*, in *Zeitschrift*, 1889, vol. xxvii, pp. 122–124.

39. The *Infants* are either the children of the reigning king, or the children of one of the preceding kings; in the Egyptian hierarchy they rank immediately after the reigning King, the Queen and the Queen-mother. (Cf. Maspero, *Études égyptiennes*, vol. ii, pp. 14, 16.)

40. The style of this King is formed of the prenomen *Khopirkerîya* of Sanuosrît 1st and of the name of Amenemhaît II. For the import of this combination see the Introduction, p. cxvii.

41. This is the reply to the indirect appeal that Sinuhît had addressed to the Queen (see above, p. 68, note 32), one of whose principal officials we know him to have been (see p. 61), as well as of the children of Pharaoh by that princess. From this passage it appears that their intercession was efficacious and that Sinuhît owed his pardon to the intercession of Nofrît and of the Infants.

thee? Thou canst no longer curse,[42] for no account is made of thy words; thou canst no longer speak in the council of the notables, for thy speech is put aside. And yet this position that thine heart has taken is not due to ill-will on my part toward thee. For that Queen, thy heaven, who is in the palace, she yet remains flourishing, her head is exalted among the royalties of the land, and her children are in the reserved part of the palace.[43] Thou shalt enjoy the riches they will give thee, and thou shalt live on their bounty.

"When thou art come to Egypt and seest the residence where thou didst dwell, prostrate thyself face to earth before the Sublime Porte, and join thyself to the Friends.[44] For now, behold thou dost begin to grow old, thou hast lost virile power and thou hast thought of the day of burial of the crossing to eternal beatitude. Nights among the embalming oils and bandages are assigned to thee by the hand of the goddess Tat.[45] Thît convoy on the day of burial is made, a sheathing of gold, the head painted blue,[46] a canopy above thee;[47] placed in the hearse, oxen will

42. Gardiner has determined the general bearing of this sentence with great ingenuity, but it appears to me that he has missed the meaning of the detail (*Notes on the Story of Sinuhe* in *Recueil*, vol. xxxiii, pp. 87–89). *To curse*, in other words to utter imprecations against an individual or an object which obliged the gods invoked to destroy them, was a faculty that belonged only to persons in full possession of their civil rights, such as being placed among the Notables; by voluntarily exiling himself Sinuhît had renounced these faculties, his malediction had no longer any weight and was no longer regarded. If he wished to prevent theft and pronounced the imprecations usual in such circumstances, no one would fear them and could rob him with impunity. This is only one example to indicate the meaning I attribute to the passage; it would take too long to quote others.

43. It must be remembered (see pp. 61, 68, note 32) that Sinuhît has been attached to the harem of the Queen. While he was in exile she had undertaken his defence, and had gained the good will of Pharaoh on his behalf.

44. See above, p. 61, note 1, on the *Royal Friends*.

45. The name of the goddess Taît signifies literally *linen, bandages;* she is the goddess who presides at the swaddling of the new-born or newly dead. The ceremonies alluded to in this passage are set forth in a special book, which I have had an opportunity of translating and publishing under the title *Rituel de l'embaumement* (Maspero, *Mémoire sur quelques papyrus du Louvre*).

46. The mummy coffins of the XIth dynasty and of the following epochs, such for instance as we have in the Louvre, are completely gilded, with the exception of the human face, which is painted red, and the head-dress, which is painted blue.

47. During the funeral ceremonies the mummy was deposited on a funerary bed surmounted by a wooden canopy. One of these was found by Rhind at Thebes (Rhind, *Thebes, its Tombs and their Tenants*, pp. 88–90), and is now in the Edinburgh Museum. Since then I have discovered three; the first at Thebes, of the XIIIth dynasty; the second also at Thebes, of the XXth; the third at Akhmlm, of the Ptolemaic period. They are all in the Cairo Museum (Maspero, *Manual of Egyptian Archæology*, Grevel, 1914, p. 328, and *Guide to the Cairo*

draw thee, the singers shall go before thee, dances of mountebanks shall be performed for thee,[48] to the sound of thy syrinx; the invocations of the tables of offerings will be recited for thee,[49] victims will be slain for thee at thy funerary stelæ, and thy pyramid will be built of white stone within the circle of the royal Infants.[50] Thou shalt not die in a strange land, nor shall the Asiatics carry thee to the tomb, nor shalt thou be laid in a sheepskin when thy vault is constructed,[51] but when thou art come hither there will be compensation for the oppression of thy body to which thou hast been subjected."[52]

Museum, 5th edition, pp. 496, 511, 512). The Cairo Museum also possesses two sledges with canopies, we might say two hearses, of the XXth dynasty (Maspero, *op. cit.*, pp. 327–329, and *Guide to the Cairo Museum*, 5th edition, pp. 487, 488), exhumed at Thebes in 1886 in the tomb of Sannozmu. They are of the kind to which oxen were harnessed to drag the mummy to its last dwelling-place.

48. In the tombs of the Theban period, especially in those of the XVIIIth dynasty, in places I know, one sees two or three men clothed in a short loin-cloth, and wearing a tall head-dress, probably a wig of long hair or their own hair allowed to grow long, raised up in a sugarloaf form and tied above their heads. These are the mountebanks who performed funerary dances during the burial ceremonies and amused the crowd in the intervals of lamentation and tears by their tricks and contortions.

49. At the time of the funeral, and at all subsequent offices performed in honour of the dead, the man of the roll (cf. p. 20, note 5, p. 69, note 37, and Introduction, p. cxxxi) summoned (*naîs*) the objects necessary for the well-being and support of a human being, one after another, and placed them on the table of offerings. From there, by virtue of the formulæ, they passed at once on to the table of the dead person.

50. This is an exact description of Egyptian funerals, as the details are shown us on the monuments (cf. Maspero, *Études égyptiennes*, vol. i, pp. 81–194).

51. We know from Herodotus that the Egyptians disliked to have wool placed with the dead; we also know that, notwithstanding their dislike of it, sheepskin was occasionally made use of in burials; one of the mummies of Deir-el-Bahari (No. 5289) was wrapped in a white skin with the fleece attached (Maspero, *Les Momies royales*, in the *Mémoires présentés par les membres de la Mission permanente*, vol. i, p. 548). As this mummy is that of a nameless prince who appears to have died of poison, it may be asked whether the sheepskin was not reserved for people of a certain class, prisoners or executed criminals who were condemned to be impure, even in the tomb. If this were the case, it would explain the position occupied by the mention of a sheepskin in the royal rescript. Pharaoh, in promising to Sinuhît that he should be carried to the tomb with the solemn dignity of princes or of the wealthy, and that his mummy should not be wrapped in the sheepskin of condemned persons, assured him of complete pardon even in the future life.

52. This final part of the sentence appears to have been altered in the only manuscript we have for this passage. The long description terminated by it is a reply to the request made earlier by Sinuhît (p. 68), to be allowed to return and be laid to rest in his native land, and it shows that the appeal made by him to the compassion of the king had been successful. He would have all the rites necessary for the survival of his *double*, and his future in the tomb was assured to him by the royal clemency.

When this command reached me, I was in the midst of my tribe. As soon as I had read it, I threw myself on my belly, I dragged myself in the dust,[53] I scattered it on my head, I went round my *dûar* (encampment) rejoicing and saying "How is it that such a thing has been done for the servant here present, whose heart has led him to strange barbarous lands? And verily how beauteous is the compassion that delivers me from death. For thy double allows me to end my existence at the court."

Copy of the Acknowledgment of the Receipt of this Command

"The servant of the Harem, Sinuhît, saith: In peace, more excellent than anything! That flight taken by the servant in his ignorance, thy double knows it, good god, lord of the two Egypts, friend of Râ, favourite of Montu, Lord of Thebes. May Amon, Lord of Karnak, Sovku,[54] Râ, Horus, Hâthor, Tumu,[55] and the Ennead of the gods,[56] Sûpdu the god of the beauteous souls, Horus of the land of the East, the royal Uræus that envelops thy head,[57] the chiefs who preside at the inundation, Minu-Horus who dwells in foreign countries,[58] Uarurît, lady of Puanît,[59] Nuît,[60]

---

53. The Egyptians called this ceremony *san-taû*, to smell the earth; it was the enforced accompaniment of all royal audiences and of all divine offerings; cf. p. 215, note 77.

54. Sovku is the crocodile god worshipped at Ombo, Esneh, and in the towns of the Fayûm.

55. Tumu, Atumu, is the god of Heliopolis, the chief of the divine Ennead which created and has maintained the world from the first day. For the *Neuvaine of the gods* and the Neuvaine or Ennead in general, cf. p. 9, note 25.

56. Sûpdu, who bears these various epithets, was the god adored in the Arabian nome of Egypt. At times he is figured as a man carrying the solar disc on his head, and has the title *of the most noble of the spirits of Heliopolis.* He must not be confused with the goddess Sopdît, the Greek Sothis, who represents the most celebrated constellation of the Egyptian sky, that which corresponds with our Sirius.

57. The royal uræus is the serpent that the king wears attached to his crown, and which is supposed to protect him against his enemies.

58. Minu, the Horus of foreign lands, is the god of the Arabian desert, and in a general way of all the countries that immediately surround Egypt, both on the east and west.

59. Uarurît is scarcely known to me except in this passage. Her title, *Lady of Puanît,* appears to show that she is a secondary form of Hâthor, whom several very ancient traditions state to have come from this country. Can Uarurît be the Alilat of classical writers?

60. Nuît is the shy goddess. With *Sibu-Gabu* the earth-god she forms a divine couple, one of the most ancient of the divine couples of Egypt; one of those that could not be included

Haroêris-Râ,[61] the gods, lords of Egypt and of the islands of the Very Green,[62] give life and strength to thy nostril; may they supply thee with their gifts, may they give thee time without limit, eternity without measure, so that one may repeat the fear that thou inspirest over all the countries of the plain and the mountain, and that thou mayest subdue all that the disc of the sun encircles in its course. This is the prayer that the servant here present makes for his lord, who delivers him from the tomb.

"The lord of wisdom who knows men knew it in His Majesty the Sovereign, when the servant here present feared to say it, so serious a matter was it to utter.[63] But the great god, the image of Râ, makes him who labours for himself skilful, and the servant here present is submissive to Him who takes counsel concerning him, and is at His command; for thy Majesty is Horus,[64] and the might of thy arms extends over all countries.

"Now therefore let thy Majesty give command to bring in Mâki of Kadimâ, Khentiâush of Khonti-Kaûshu,[65] Menûs of the two subjugated lands,[66] princes whose name is without blame and who love thee, who have never been reproached for any matter, for Tonu is thine as are thy hounds. For this flight made by thy servant here present, he did not make it knowingly, it was not my intention to do so; it was not premeditated and I know not what tore me from the place where I was. It was as a

in the solar type by the theologians of the great Theban school of the time of Ramses. Pictures represent Nuît bending over her spouse, and by the outline of her figure representing the starry firmament.

61. Horus the elder, Haruêri, of which the Greeks made Aroîres, is a solar god with the same title as Râ, which explains why he is connected with him in this passage. He must not be confused with Horus the younger, the son of Isis and Osiris.

62. The Egyptians gave the name *Very Green*, Uaz-uêrît, to the sea. This name occasionally applies to the Red Sea, but more often to the Mediterranean; it is the latter sea that is alluded to here.

63. The matter that was serious to utter, and that was known to the sovereign in his wisdom, was the petition of Sinuhît to be permitted to return to Egypt.

64. The kings of primitive Egypt believed themselves to be descended directly from Horus, the divine falcon, and in consequence they called themselves *the Horus, the living Horus, the life of Horus,* as is set forth in official protocols.

65. *Khonti-Kaûshu* signifies *he who is imprisoned in Kaûshu,* and in consequence appears to indicate some personage of Ethiopian origin. Nevertheless the neighbourhood of Kadimâ appears rather to indicate a Syrian locality, and I do not know where to place it exactly.

66. The words I render by *the subjugated lands* have been rendered by Brugsch and others *The Country of the Phœnecians.* Without entering into the question as to whether the ethnic name Fonkhu lends itself to identification with Phœnecia, it is sufficient to say that the orthography of this manuscript does not permit us to recognise it in this passage. I do not know from other sources what region was called by the Egyptians *the subjugated land* or more exactly *the ravaged land.*

dream, as when a man of Athu beholds himself at Iabu[67] or a man of the marshes in the desert of Nubia.[68] I had nothing to fear, nobody pursued me. I had heard no villainy, and my name had never been in the mouth of the herald, and yet my flesh trembled, my limbs impelled me, my heart guided me, the god who predestinated me to this flight drew me, for I am not one who hardens his back, and the man is afeared who knows his own country well. Now Râ has granted that thy fear should reign over the land of Egypt, that thy terror should be on all foreign lands. For me, whether I am in the palace, or whether I am here, it is thou who canst veil my horizon; the sun arises at thy pleasure, the water of the river which it pleaseth thee to drink, the breeze of heaven which thou art pleased to breathe. I, the servant here present, will leave the functions that I, the servant here present, have had in this place. May Thy Majesty do as it pleaseth thee, for one lives on the air thou givest, it is the love of Râ, of Horus, and of Hâthor that refreshes thy nostril, and it is the gift of Montu, lord of Thebes, that it lives eternally."

When they had come to fetch me, the servant[69] here present, I celebrated a day of festival in Aîa to hand over my goods to my children; my eldest son became chief of my tribe, so that my tribe and all my possessions became his, my serfs, all my cattle, all my plantations, all my date-palms. Then I, the servant here present, I travelled southwards, and when I stopped at Hariu-Horu[70] the general who is there with the frontier guards sent a messenger to the palace to tell them. His Majesty sent an excellent super-

67. Iabu is the Egyptian name of Elephantine, Athu that of a province of the Delta; these two localities which are situated, one at the extreme south, the other at the extreme north of Egypt, like Dan to Beersheba of the Hebrews, were used proverbially to express the entire extent of the country. A man of Iabu who sees himself at Athu is an Egyptian of the north transported to the south and completely on foreign ground; the difference, not only of manners and customs but also of dialect, is so great that one might compare the unintelligible language of a bad scribe to the speech of a man of Iabu who finds himself at Athu.

68. The exact translation would be the *land of Khonti*. This land of Khonti, by comparison with the cultivated plain of Egypt, should refer to *Khato*, Nubia or the dry and sterile heights that border the valley on the east and west. (Cf. Brugsch, *Dictionnaire géographique,* pp. 1281–1284.)

69. Gardiner transfers here, and I think correctly, that part of the sentence which is placed two lines higher in the only manuscript we possess (*die Erzählung des Sinuhe*, p. 13). It appears that the scribe, having arrived at the bottom of this page, placed all the peroration of his document after *I shall leave;* and that he observed his mistake before having written anything more than the misplaced sentence. All that was missing he put in after that, without troubling to place the words he had here inserted by mistake, on the top of the following page, where they belonged.

70. See the introduction to this story, p. 61.

intendent of the farmers of the King's house, and with him cargo boats full of presents from the King for the Beduîn who had come with me to Hariu-Horu. I said good-bye to each of them by name; then as there were serving-men there of all sorts, each assigned to his own duties, I cast off, set sail, and bread was kneaded and beer was brewed for me[71] until I arrived at the royal city Taîtu-taûi.[72]

The following morning when the earth brightened they came to summon me: ten men came and ten men went to lead me to the palace. I touched the ground with my forehead between the sphinxes,[73] then the royal Infants who were standing in the guard-room came to meet me, the Friends who are charged with ushering into the hypostyle hall led me to the reception room of the King.[74] I found His Majesty on the great raised dais in the *Embrasure of Silver Gilt*.[75] I threw myself on my belly, and I lost consciousness before him. The god addressed me with kindly words, but I was like one caught by the dusk; my soul failed, my limbs sank, my heart was no longer in my bosom, so that I knew the difference there is between life and death. His Majesty said to one of the Friends, "Raise him, and let him speak to me." His Majesty said, "So, thou art come, after thou hast been in foreign lands, and hast taken flight. Age has attacked thee, thou hast attained old age; it is no small matter that henceforth thy body may be laid to rest without being buried by barbarians. Do not again offend by not speaking when thou art questioned." I feared punishment, and I answered with the reply of a frightened man, "What has my lord said to me? Lo, I reply thus: 'It was not my doing, it was the hand of God; the fear now in my breast may be

71. Beer was made daily at the same time as the bread, which was employed as yeast to ferment the brew.

72. The name of this locality is written Taîtu, lit. *the dominatrix*. Griffith has very ingeniously recognised in it an equivalent to the expression *the dominatrix of the two lands*, which designates the royal city of the earlier kings of the XIIth dynasty, in the neighbourhood of the pyramids of Lisht.

73. This refers to the colossi or the sphinxes which were usually erected on each side of the gate of a temple or palace.

74. See above, pp. 27–29 in the story of Khufuî, the description of a royal audience, less developed, but similar to this in the terms employed.

75. The Egyptians used a great deal of gold and precious metal in the decoration of their temples and houses; there is frequent mention of doors, columns, and obelisks covered with gold leaf, silver, or electrum, which latter is a mixture of gold and silver containing at least twenty per cent. of silver. The *Embrasure of Silver Gilt,* the golden gate where the Pharaohs sat in audience, acquired its name from its decoration. The great hall of the Theban royal tombs, corresponding to the throne-room of the palaces, was called the *Hall of Gold,* although it was not gilded. No doubt it had been decorated with gold leaf at some time, and had retained the name.

said to have caused the fateful flight.[76] Here am I before thee; thou art life, may thy Majesty do according to thy pleasure.'"

The royal Infants were made to pass before him, and His Majesty said to the Queen, "Here is Sinuhît who comes, resembling an Asiatic, or a Beduîn that he has become." She uttered a great peal of laughter, and the royal Infants shouted all together. They said before His Majesty, "No, that is not so in truth, oh sovereign, my lord." His Majesty said, "It is so in truth." Then they took their castanets,[77] their sceptres,[78] their sistra, and then, lo, they said to His Majesty, "Place thy two hands upon the good ones, oh long-lived King, for they are the ornaments of the Lady of Heaven[79]; the *Golden goddess* gives life to thy nostril, the *Lady of the Stars* unites with thee, the diadem of the South sails down and the diadem of the North sails up the river, united firmly by the mouth of Thy Majesty, and the uræus is on thy forehead. Thou hast warded off evil from thy subjects, for Râ is favourable to thee, oh lord of the Two Lands, Thou art

76. Sinuhît once more asserts his innocence. We have seen (pp. 62, 63, 64, 73, 74) under what circumstances he had fled, and this precipitate flight might well give rise to a belief that he had been involved in a plot against Amenemhaît, or especially against Sanuosrît. Most of the clauses of the treaty between Ramses II and the prince of Khati relative to an exchange of fugitives show with what care Pharaoh attempted to arrest such of his subjects as had fled to foreign countries. This is why Sinuhît reverts with such insistence to the motive of his flight, and the fatality of which he had been the victim.

77. According to Loret (*les Cymbales égyptiennes*, in *Sphinx*, vol. v, pp. 93–96), the kind of necklace to which I give the name of castanet was the cymbal. The ceremonial of Pharaonic audiences, like that of the Byzantines, admitted of songs arranged beforehand. The Infants, after having saluted the King, commenced this part of the ceremony; they resumed their insignia, which they had laid aside before defiling before the King and offering their adoration, and also the sistrum, which would supply the rhythm for their chant.

78. *Sceptre* does not exactly correspond to the term used here, and which reads *sakhmu*. The *sakhmu* was originally a weapon of war and of hunting composed of a kind of flat blade of hard wood, sharpened on both sides, shaped square at the upper end and set into a round handle. It served both as a sabre and a mace, stunning rather than cutting. In primitive times it was so associated with the idea of a strong man that it served as an emblem of him, and was deposited in the tomb as a support or an emblem of survival; the *sakhmu*, the wooden sword animated by the spirit of its ancient terrestrial owner, is a form of the soul like the *double* and the *luminous*. As with us the sword has become a mere mark of rank when worn at court, the *sakhmu* was no more than an honorific emblem among Egyptians of the historic age. People of good family and officials carried it in ceremonies. A variety of it, the *kharpu*, and sometimes the *sakhmu* itself, played a part in sacrifices; whereas at one time it had been used actually to slay the animal, the personage officiating now raised it above the head of the victim as a signal to the butcher to cut its throat.

79. The expression *to touch the adornments of the Lady of Heaven*, meaning the castanets, seems to express an idea of clemency. Several divinities bear the title *Lady of Heaven*; the

acclaimed as the Mistress of All[80] is acclaimed: string thy bow, loose thy arrow; cause that he who is oppressed may breathe. Grant to us this signal favour that we ask of thee for this sheikh Simihît,[81] the Beduîn who was born in Tomuri. If he fled, and left this land, it was for fear of thee; what face does not whiten that sees thy face, and what eye does not fear that contemplates thee?" His Majesty said, "He need fear no more, nor call out in terror. He shall be a Friend of those who are among the arbitrators, and be placed among the people of the royal circle.[82] Go with him to the royal dressing hall to give him that which is his due."

When I went out of the royal residence, the Infants gave me the hand, and we went together at once to the great double gate.[83] The house of a Royal Son was assigned me, with its wealth, its bath-room, with its celestial decorations and its furniture brought from the double white house, clothes from the royal wardrobe, and choice perfumes in every room, of the kinds used by the King and the nobles, and serving-men of every sort, each carrying on his business.[84] Removing the years from my flesh, I shaved myself, I combed my

mention of Nubuît, *the lady of gold*, in the following line shows that it is Hâthor who is referred to here.

80. Here as above (cf. p. 68, note 34) this expression designates either a goddess, Hâthor in her funerary character, or as Gardiner considers (*Notes on the story of Sinuhe* in *Recueil*, vol. xxxiii, pp. 85, 86) the queen, Nofrît.

81. This variant of the name of Sinuhît signifies literally *the son of the north*; Gardiner (*die Erzählung des Sinuhe*, p. 14, note 5) translates it *the son of the north wind*. Sinuhe is called the Sîti, because of his long sojourn among the Beduîns, which had caused him to lose the fine appearance of a courtier. The King had already remarked (p. 76) that he comes *like a rustic with the appearance of a Sîti*. The *Tomuri, the land of canals*, is a name for the Delta that also applied to the whole of Egypt.

82. Personages attached to the court of Pharaoh received two collective qualifications, that of Shanûatiu, the *people of the circle*, those who are in the circle round the sovereign, and that of Qanbûatiu, the *people of the corner*, perhaps those who remained in the corners of the audience chamber.

83. Ruîti, or with the article Pruîti, is like Paruî-âu, Pharaoh, a topographical term at first used to denote the palace of the sovereign, and then the sovereign himself. In the *Introduction* (p. cxiv) we have seen that it was from this title Greek legend derived the name of Proteus, King of Egypt, who entertained Helen, Paris, and Menelaus, at his court (Herodotus II, cxii-cxvi). Here the term may be taken in its etymological meaning, and the double gateway recognised that gave access to the palace and under which the Pharaohs gave audience or administered justice. Sinuhît is conducted by the Infants to the great double gates to receive legally the grant accorded him by the sovereign (Spiegelberg, *Über zwei Stelle der Sinuhe-Novell*, in *Sphinx*, vol. iv, pp. 140–141).

84. Every royal palace and every mansion of the wealthy and great had attached to them what were called *houses* or *chambers*, *ait*, where all the necessities of life were manufactured, and where the slaves or artisans employed in making them were lodged. Then there were

hair,[85] I left squalor to the foreign lands, and their garments to the Nomiû-Shâïu[86]; then I clad myself in fine linen, I perfumed myself with delicate essences, I slept in a bed, and I left the sand to those who dwell there, the oil of the tree to those who rub themselves with it.[87] A house was given me suitable to a landed proprietor, such as a Friend possesses. Many brickmakers toiled to build it, all the woodwork of it was made new, and victuals were brought me from the palace three times, four times daily, in addition to that which the Infants gave me without ceasing for a moment. A pyramid of stone was built for me in the midst of the funerary pyramids,[88] the chief of the stone-masons of His Majesty marked out the site, the chief of the draughtsmen designed the decoration, the chief of the sculptors carved it, the chiefs of the works that are carried on in the necropolis traversed the land of Egypt on this account.[89] All kinds of furnishing were placed in the storehouses and all that was needful was placed there. I appointed priests of the double,[90] I made a tomb garden in it in front of its town. I gave the furniture, making the necessary arrangements in the pyramid itself. Then I gave lands and

houses of bread, beer, meat, stuffs and so forth. The scenes figured with little wooden models that are found in tombs of the first Theban period or at the close of the Memphite age show us some of these houses in full activity (Maspero, *Guide to the Cairo Museum*, 1910, 5th ed., pp. 501–503).

85. This confirms a statement of Diodorus of Sicily (i, 18) where it says that the Egyptians kept their hair long and matted when they lived abroad, and only cut it on their return (Spiegelberg, *op. cit.*, vol. iv, pp. 140–141).

86. For the geographical import and the meaning of this word, see above, p. 65, note 22.

87. The oil of the tree is olive oil, which is produced in Asia, in distinction to oil of *kiki*, castor oil, which is used in Egypt.

88. These are the statements often found on funerary inscriptions, here placed in the usual order in the narrative. Sinuhît receives a supreme favour from Sanuosrît—a tomb built and endowed at the expense of Pharaoh, *khir hosu nite sutonu*, "by the King's favour." The site itself is given gratuitously, then, when the pyramid is built, the funerary feasts are instituted, the revenues and landed property intended to supply the sacrifices are taken from the royal domain; and finally the statue itself, which has to serve as a support to Sinuhît's *double*, is of precious metal.

89. See at the beginning of this story (p. 57) the version of this passage that occurs on ostracon 5629 of the British Museum. The journeys across Egypt made by these personages were in order to provide the sarcophagus, the tables of offerings, the coffers and the stone statues which were placed in the tombs.

90. The *servants* or *priests of the double* were personages whose duty it was to keep the tomb in order, and to perform all the acts and ceremonies required to assume the existence and comfort of the *double*.

instituted a funerary domain[91] with the lands in front of the city,[92] as is done for Friends of the first rank; my statue was overlaid with gold with a skirt of electrum, and it was His Majesty who caused it to be made. It is no common man for whom so much has been done, but I was in favour with the King until the day of death arrived for me.—This is finished from beginning to end, as it was found in the book.

91. This might be rigorously translated "a lake." The lake, or rather the piece of water surrounded by a stone margin, was in fact the indispensable ornament of every house of any pretensions to comfort (cf. pp. 23–24 in the *Story of Khufuî*, the lake of the palace of Sanafruî, and later that of the palace of Amasis in the *Story of the Mariner*, pp. 234, 236). The ideal tomb being above all a figure of a terrestrial house, care was taken to place a lake there similar to that of the houses. The dead man would come there to sail in his boat drawn by slaves, or to sit on its banks in the shade of the sycamores. The kiosk, like the lake, was one of the indispensable ornaments of a garden. The bas-reliefs of Thebes show them amidst the trees, sometimes by the side of the regulation piece of water. The dead resorted there, like the living, to take a siesta, to chat with his wife, to read stories, or to sport with women.

92. The fields of the funerary domain were the property of the dead, and provided him with all he needed. Each of them produced some special object, or the revenue from it was devoted to providing the dead man with some special article of food or clothing, and it bore the name of that article. For instance, the field from which Ti procured his figs or dates was called *the figs of Ti, the dates of Ti*. This property was administered by the *priests of the double* or of the funerary statue, who were often themselves priests of the principal temple of the locality where the tomb was situated; the family made a contract with them by the terms of which they engaged to celebrate the sacrifices necessary for the well-being of the dead in exchange for certain rents levied on the bequeathed domains.

THE SHIPWRECKED SAILOR [5]

(XIITH DYNASTY)

THE Papyrus that contains this story belongs to the Imperial Egyptian Museum of the Hermitage, St. Petersburg. It was discovered in 1880 by W, Golénischeff, and by him brought to the notice of the scholars who took part in the fifth International Congress of Orientalists, at Berlin in 1881. He did not then edit the text, but he has published a translation in French; *Sur un ancien conte égyptien. Notice lue au Congrès des Orientalistes à Berlin,* per W. Golénischeff, 1881, without publisher's name, large 8vo, 21 pp. Breitkopf and Härtel, Leipzig. It was inserted in the *Verhandlungen des* 5ten *Internationalen Orientalisten-Congresses,* Berlin, 1882, 2tes Theil, Erste Hälfte, *Africanische Section,* pp. 100–122. This is the version I reproduced in the two first editions of this work, modifying it slightly on certain points, and it was from it that a Russian translation was made by Wladimir Stasow: *Jegipetskajaskarka otkrytaja w Petersburgskom Ermitaze (An Egyptian tale discovered at the Hermitage of St. Petersburg)* in the review *Westnik Jewropy (the Messengers of Europe),* 1882, vol. i, pp. 580–602, and the two English translations given by Griffith in W. Flinders Petrie, *Egyptian Tales,* 1895, London, 12mo, vol. i, pp. 81–96, and F. Ll. Griffith, *Egyptian Literature,* in *Specimen Pages of a Library of the World's Best Literature,* 1898, New York, 4to, pp. 5233–5236.

Since then, Golénischeff inserted a translation of it in his *Catalogue du Musée de l'Ermitage,* 1891, St. Petersburg, 8vo, pp. 177–182.

A Portuguese translation was sketched out, with a study of the text, by Francisco Maria Estevez Pereira, *O Naufrago Conte Egipcio,* extract from the review *O Instituto,* vol. xlviii, 4to, Coimbre, Imprensa da Universidade, 23 pp.

Finally Golénischeff himself has given a complete hieroglyphic transcription of the text with a French translation and commentary: W. Golénischeff, *Le Papyrus hiératique de Saint Pétersbourg,* in the *Recueil de Travaux,* 1906, vol. xxviii, pp. 73–112; published separately in a quarto of 40 pages, Champion, 1906, and a critical edition in hieroglyphs with introduction and glossary, in *Bibliothèque d'étude* of the Institut français d'Archéologie Orientale du Caire, under the title *Le Conte du Naufragé,* 4to, Caire, 1911.

From Golénischeff's transcription, collated with photographs of the original, a hieroglyphic transcription and German translation was produced by Adolf Erman, *die Geschichte des Schiffbrüchigen* in *Zeitschrift*, 1906, vol. xliii, pp. 1–26, and a German translation only by A. Wiedemann, *Altägyptische Sagen und Märchen*, 1906, Leipzig, 8vo, pp. 25–33.

An examination of some difficult passages has been made, and hypotheses regarding the origin of the story have been issued by Maspero, *Notes sur le Conte du Naufragé*, in the *Recueil*, 1907, vol. xxix, pp. 106–109; by Kurt Sethe, *Bemerkungen zur Geschichte des Schiffbrüchigen*, in *Zeitschrift*, 1907, vol. xliv, pp. 80–88; and by Alan H. Gardiner, *Notes on the Tale of the Shipwrecked Sailor*, 1908, vol. xlv, pp. 60–66.

It is not known where the manuscript was found, how it found its way to Russia, or at what time it became the property of the Hermitage Museum. It was not opened until 1880, and had it not been for the interest shown by M. Golénischeff it would still have been lying in a drawer waiting for some one to unroll it. The writing is the same as that of the Berlin Papyri 1–4, and like them it dates back to a period previous to the XVIIIth dynasty. It contains a hundred and eighty-nine vertical columns and horizontal lines of text, it is complete from beginning to end, and almost every word is intact. The language is clear and well expressed, the script neat and well formed. It is only very occasionally that one finds some terms that are difficult to decipher, or ambiguous grammatical forms. It is worthy to be regarded as the classical Egyptian of its period as completely as the *Tale of Two Brothers* is of that of the XIXth dynasty.

The author has arranged his romance in the form of a report such as Egyptian officials addressed to their lord, of which several were reproduced in the tombs of the princes of Elephantine of the VIth dynasty, and elsewhere. One of the subordinates of the explorer, perhaps the man who is supposed to have written the report, comes to announce to his master that the vessel has arrived in Egypt, close to the place where the Court resides, and he invites him to take precautions before presenting himself to Pharaoh. As the ship on which the expedition sailed had been lost on the way, the master, rescued by the ship that brought him to Egypt, would certainly be closely examined, and condemned if it should be found that the disaster was due to some serious mistake on his part; as in a similar case our naval officers are tried by court martial. The scribe, in order to reassure him as to the result of the enquiry, tells him how he himself had been able to escape from a similar position with advantage to himself. Sethe thinks that the scene is laid in Elephantine, and that therefore the Court resided, there (*Bemerkungen* in *Zeitschrift*, 1908, vol. xliv, pp. 81, 82), which led Gardiner to question whether in this narrative we had not a survival of a cycle of Elephantine tales (*Notes on the Tale of the Shipwrecked Sailor*, in *Zeitschrift*, 1908, vol. xliv, pp. 60, 899).

⌒

The wise servant said: "May thy heart be sound, my lord, for behold we have arrived at the country. One has taken the mallet and driven in the stake, the rope has been fixed ashore, the acclamation has been shouted, the god has been adored[1]; and each one embraces his comrade, and the crowd of us shout 'Good arrival.' None of our soldiers are missing, although we reached the farthest parts of the country of Wawaît; we have passed Sanmuît,[2] and now behold we have returned in peace, and arrive here at our country. Hearken, my prince, for I exaggerate in nothing. Wash thyself, pour water over thy fingers, then answer when thou art invited to speak. Speak to the King with all thy heart, reply without being disconcerted, for though the mouth of man saves him, yet his speech may cause veiling of the face.[3] Do according to the movements of thy heart and let that which thou sayest be a pacification.[4]

"Now I will relate to thee an account of a similar adventure that happened to me myself, when I went to the mines of the Sovereign, and went down to the sea in a ship a hundred and fifty cubits long, and forty cubits broad. It carried five hundred sailors of the best of the land of Egypt, who had seen the sky, who had seen the earth, and who were bolder of heart than lions.[5] They were persuaded that the wind would not come, that disaster would not be produced, but the wind arose while we were in the open, and before we had reached the land itself the gale increased and

1. Cf. Maspero, *Note sur le Conte du Naufragé*, in the *Recueil de Travaux*, vol. xxix. pp. 106–108.

2. The country of Wawaît is the part of Nubia situated beyond the second cataract; San-muît is the name attributed by the monuments to the island of Bigeh, opposite Philæ, at the entrance to the first cataract. From this passage it appears that the Egyptian sailor boasted of having reached the southern frontier of Egypt by passing from the Red Sea into the Nile (cf. Introduction, p. cli).

3. There is here, I think, an allusion to the custom of covering the face of criminals when led to execution. The order "*let his face be covered*" was equivalent to condemnation.

4. In other words, his speech should be framed in such a manner as to appease the wrath of the King and lead to the acquittal of the shipwrecked man.

5. If we admit that the royal cubit of 52 centimetres is here referred to, the vessel must have measured about 78 metres in length and 21 in breadth, which even when taking into account the fact that these Egyptian ships were very large must still give us very exaggerated dimen-

raised a wave of eight cubits. I seized a plank; as to the ship, it perished, and of those on board not one was left. For me, I landed on an island, and that was thanks to a wave of the sea. I spent three days alone, with no other companion than my heart, and at night I lay in the hollow of a tree and embraced the shade, then [by day] I stretched my limbs to seek something to put in my mouth. I found there figs and grapes, magnificent leeks, berries and seeds, melons at will, fish, and birds; there is nothing that was not there. I satisfied my hunger, and I left on the ground the superfluity of that with which my hands were filled; I made a fire-striker, I lighted a fire,[6] and I offered a burnt offering to the gods.[7]

"Lo, I heard a voice like thunder, and I thought, 'it is a wave of the sea.' the trees creaked, the earth trembled.[8] I uncovered my face, and I knew that it was a serpent that came, thirty cubits long, with a great tail of two cubits; his body was inlaid with gold, his two eyebrows were of real lapis, and he was yet more perfect on the side than in front. He opened his mouth against me; while I lay on my belly before him he said to me, 'Who has brought thee, who has brought thee, vassal, who has brought thee? If thou dost delay to tell me who has brought thee to this island, I shall make thee to know how, reduced to ashes, it is possible to become invisible.' 'Thou speakest to me, and I do not hear thee; I am before thee without consciousness.'[9] He then took me in his mouth, he carried me to his lair and laid me down there without my receiving any injury; I was safe and sound, and none [of my limbs] had been taken away.

sions. The ships of Queen Hâtshopsuîtu built for the expedition were not more than 22 metres in length, and they must have carried a crew of about fifty men (Maspero, *De quelques navigations des Égyptiens*, pp. 11, 16, 17). Thus the vessel of our story belongs, both in size and the number of the sailors, to the class of fictitious ships of which there are plenty of examples in the popular literature of all countries.

6. Cf. Ungnad, *der Fuerbohrer*, in *Zeitschrift*, 1906, vol. xliii, pp. 161, 162.

7. The appearance of the lord of the island occurs after the fire is lighted. Invocations only produce their effect if a perfume is burnt, or any substance which is prepared according to regulations. The passage which Golénischeff regards as referring merely to a sacrifice should perhaps be taken in this sense, and the ceremony indicated in the text considered as an actual invocation; or we may confine ourselves to admitting that among the mass of plants used by the shipwrecked sailor for lighting his sacrificial fire there may have been some that acted as a summons to the genius of the island, while he himself had no intention of performing a magic rite.

8. Cf. Golénischeff's commentary on this thunderous arrival of the king of the island (*Le Papyrus No. 1115*, in *Recueil*, vol. xxviii, pp. 93–95).

9. The shipwrecked man here abruptly begins to speak, to excuse himself for not having replied to the inquiries of the serpent. Fear had deprived him of the use of his senses, and he could not hear what was said to him. Cf. a similar passage in *Sinuhit*, p. 75.

"Then, after he had opened his mouth while I lay on my belly before him, behold he said to me, 'Who has brought thee, who has brought thee, vassal, to this island of the sea, the two shores of which are bathed in the waves?'[10] I answered him thus, my hands hanging down before him,[11] and I said to him, 'I am one who was going down to the mines, on a mission from my sovereign, on a vessel a hundred and fifty cubits long and forty broad; it carried five hundred sailors of the best of the land of Egypt, who had seen the sky, who had seen the earth, and who were bolder of heart than lions. They were persuaded that the wind would not come, that disaster would not be produced; each of them was bolder of heart and more powerful of arm than his companions, and there were no cowards among them. But the wind arose while we were in the open, and before we had reached the land the gale increased—it raised a wave of eight cubits. A plank I seized; as to the vessel, it perished, and of those who were on board not one was left except myself alone, and now I am here near to thee. For me, I landed on this island, and it was thanks to a wave of the sea.'

"He said to me, 'Fear not, fear not, vassal; fear not, and be not sad of visage. If thou comest to me it is because God has permitted thee to survive, and he has led thee to this Isle of the Double,[12] where there is nothing that is not found here, and which is full of all good things. Behold, thou wilt pass month after month until thou wilt have sojourned four months in this island, and then a vessel shall come from the country with sailors whom thou knowest; thou shall go with them to the land, and thou shalt die in thy city.[13] When sorrows are passed, it is delight to tell of what one has tasted; I will give thee an exact account of what is in this island. I am here with my brothers and my children,

10. Sethe (*Bemerkungen zur Geschichte des Schiffbrüchigen*, in *Zeitschrift*, 1908, vol. xliv, pp. 83–84) suggests that a floating island should be recognised as "that island of the sea half of which turns into surge."

11. This is the posture in which suppliants or inferiors are depicted on the monuments before their lords.

12. The *double* is the Egyptian soul. The Island of the Double is therefore an island inhabited by happy souls, one of those Fortunate Isles mentioned in the *Introduction*, pp. clii, cliii. Golénischeff declines to regard the term *ka*, as meaning anything else than *spirit, genius,* and translates it "this *enchanted* island, this isle of the genius" (*Le Papyrus No.* 1115 in Recueil, vol. xxviii, p. 98), but the *ka* is not a genius. Erman prefers to regard it as the word *kaû,* viands, provisions, and translates it "this island of provisions" (*die Geschichte des Schiffbrüchigen,* in *Zeitschrift*, 1906, vol. xliii, p. 1).

13. Golénischeff considers that it may be concluded from this passage that at the time this story was written there were regular services between Egypt and the land of Puanît, "maintained by an Egyptian fleet that conveyed commercial expeditions to Puanît *three times in the*

in the midst of them; we are of the number of seventy-five serpents, my children and my brothers, and still I do not mention a girl who was brought to me by art magic.[14] For a star having fallen,[15] those who were in the fire with her came out of it, and the young girl appeared without my being with the beings of the flame, without my being in the midst of them; without which I should have been dead by their deed, but I found her afterwards, alone, among the corpses.[16] If thou art courageous and thy heart is strong thou shalt press thy children to thy bosom, thou shalt embrace thy wife,[17] thou shalt see thy house, and that which is of more value than all, thou shalt reach thy country and thou shall be among thy brethren.' Then I stretched myself on my belly, I touched the ground before him, and I said to him, 'I shall describe thy souls[18] to the Sovereign, I shall cause him to know thy greatness, and I

year. It is to this fleet, no doubt well known to his fellow citizens, that the narrator alludes, and very probably the hero is supposed to await their periodic return" (*Le Papyrus No.* 1115, in *Receuil*, vol. xxviii, p. 96). It is very possible, but, considering the marvellous character of the story, it is better to regard this as another case of the prescience I have called attention to above, p. 11, note 34.

14. Golénischeff supposes, with very good reason, that the episode of the girl is a very much shortened and unintelligible redaction of a different, story in which she played the principal part (*Le Papyrus No.* 1115, in *Recueil*, vol. xxviii, p. 100). This hypothesis has been adopted by Erman (*die Geschichte des Schiffbrüchigen*, in *Zeitschrift*, 1906, vol. xliii; pp. 106, 107).

15. This is the only mention of a falling star that has yet been found in the texts. It shows the idea held by the Egyptians of this phenomenon. They considered the mass as inhabited by genii, who came out of it as it fell to earth and were consumed in their own flames. The incident of the young girl appears to show that they believed that certain of these genii could survive and acclimatise themselves on our earth. Golénischeff compares this episode with the Arab legend of the *Burnt Island*, situated in the sea of the Zingis (Dinkas), which is reduced to ashes about every thirty years by a maleficent comet (*Le Papyrus No.* 1115, in *Receuil*, vol. xxviii, pp. 101, 102).

16. The text is too concise to be clear, and various explanations have been proposed for it, especially by Sethe (*Bemerkungen*, in *Zeitschrift*, vol. xliv, pp. 85, 86), and by Gardiner (*Notes*, in *Zeitschrift*, vol. xlv, p. 65). Golénischeff thinks the girl no longer existed when the serpent- was describing her birth, and that she had been reduced to ashes by the flames of the falling star (*Le Papyrus No.* 1115, in *Recueil*, vol. xxviii, p. 101). It appears to me, on the contrary, that she was still living, but that the serpent was apologising for not being able to describe the manner of her birth. He could not approach the spot where the star had fallen until the fire caused by it had died out, when he found the girl alone among the corpses, and did not himself see the manner of her entry into the world.

17. The text says: "Thou shalt smell thy wife." The bas-reliefs (*Guide to the Cairo Museum*, 5th edition, 1910, p. 88) show us the action that took the place of the kiss among the Egyptians; the king and the deity place themselves nose to nose and breathe one another's breath.

18. The gods and the kings of Egypt had several souls. Râ the Sun had seven, it is said. The shipwrecked man treats the serpent as an Egyptian divinity, and speaks of his souls out

shall present to thee cosmetics, *perfume of acclamation,*[19] pomade, cassia, and the incense of the temples, by which one acquires the favour of every god. I shall tell also what has befallen me, and that which I have seen of thy souls, and thou wilt be adorned in thy city in presence of all the arbitrators of the Entire Land, I will slay bulls for thee, to be put to the fire, I will throttle birds for thee, and I will cause vessels to be brought to thee laden with all the riches of Egypt, as is done for a god, friend of men in a distant land that men know not.' He laughed at me for that I said, and because of that he had in his heart, he said to me, 'Hast thou not [here before thine, eyes] abundance of myrrh, and everything here is of incense, for I am the king of the land of Puanît,[20] and I have myrrh; that *perfume of acclamation* that thou speakest of sending me, that alone is not abundant in this island. But it will chance that as soon as thou art departed from this place thou wilt never behold this island again—it will transform itself into waves.'[21]

"And lo! the vessel came as he had predicted beforehand I went therefore, I perched myself on a high tree, and I recognised those who were there.[22] I went at once to tell him the news, and he said to me, 'Good luck, good luck, vassal, to thy home, see thy children, and may thy name be good in thy city; those are my good wishes for thee.' Then I lay down on my belly, my hands hanging down, before him, and he gave me gifts of myrrh, *perfume of acclamation,* pomade, cassia, pepper, cosmetics, powder of antimony, cypress, a quantity of incense, *hippopotamus tails,*

of compliment to him. Each of the souls corresponds to some quality or sense, and to describe the souls of a personage was to portray him physically and morally.

19. The *perfume of acclamation, Hakanu,* was one of the seven ritual oils offered to the gods and the dead during sacrifices. Its composition is not known; the name is probably derived from the invocations that attended its manufacture or presentation.

20. Puanît is the name of districts situated to the south-west of Egypt, first as far up as Sauakîn and Massâwah, and later on the two banks of Bab-el-Mandeb, in the country of the Somalis, and in Yemen. It was from there that the Egyptians early obtained the most highly esteemed of the perfumes employed in their cult.

21. The opposition of the serpent to the proposal of the shipwrecked man to give him gifts was only natural. Even had the gifts been to his liking he could not have accepted them, for as the isle was to disappear the messengers to be sent would be unable to find it.

22. Evidently the narrator was aware that the sailors were those with whom he had started from Egypt, and who had perished in the shipwreck (cf. pp. 83–84, 85). It is an additional miracle, but not surprising when it occurs in a story so replete with marvels. We shall see later, in the first story of Satni (pp. 114, 115), that the children of the hero, slain and cast to the dogs, reappear, living, at Memphis.

elephants' teeth, greyhounds, cynocephali, giraffes, and all excellent riches.[23] I loaded the whole on that ship; I then stretched myself on my belly, and I worshipped the serpent. He said to me, 'Behold, thou shalt arrive at the country in two months, thou shalt press thy infants to thy bosom, and in due time thou shalt go to renew thy youth in thy tomb.' And lo! I went down to the shore at the place where the vessel was, and I called the soldiers who were in that vessel, I offered thanksgiving on the shore to the lord of that island, and they of the vessel did likewise.

"We returned to the north, to the residence of the Sovereign; we arrived at the palace in the second month, according to all that the serpent had said. I entered before the Sovereign, and I presented to him the gifts I had brought from that island, and he made much of me in the presence of the nobility of the Entire Land. Lo, he made of me a servant, and I had fine slaves as recompense. Bend thy regard on me, now that I have returned to the land of Egypt after I have seen and tasted those trials. Listen to me, for behold, it is good for men to listen."[24] The prince said to me, 'Do not be malicious, my friend. Who gives water to a goose on the morning of the day it is to be killed?'"—This is finished from beginning to end, as it was found in writing. He who has written it is the scribe of the skilful fingers Amâuni-Amanâu, l. h. s.

23. This enumeration, strange as it appears to us, contains nothing that is not authentic. Almost exactly the same is found at an interval of over a thousand years, on the monument where Queen Hatshopsuîtu of the XVIIIth dynasty represents the voyage of discovery made by an expedition sent by her to the land of Puanît. Unfortunately the greater number of the substances are unknown to us, and we can only transcribe the ancient names or give the conjectural values that seem most suitable to each term.

24. Here the story told by the scribe to encourage his hero comes to an end; and his auditor, who appears to be far from confident as to the fate that awaits him, replies with a proverb applicable to his position.

HOW THUTÎYI TOOK THE
CITY OF JOPPA [6]

(XXTH DYNASTY)

THE FRAGMENTS of this story cover the first three pages that exist of the Harris Papyrus No. 500, where they immediately precede the *Story of the Doomed Prince*. Like the latter, it was discovered in 1874 by Goodwin, who took it for fragments of a historical narrative, and announced his discovery at a meeting of the Society of Biblical Archæology, March 3, 1874: Goodwin, *Translation of a fragment of an historical Narrative relating to the reign of Thotmes the Third*, in the *Transactions of the Society of Biblical Archæology*, 1874, vol. iii, pp. 340–348.

It was subsequently published with facsimile hieroglyphic transcription and translation by Maspero, *Comment Thoutii prit la ville de Joppé* (*Journal asiatique*, 1878, without the three plates of hieratic text), and in *études égyptiennes* 1879, vol. i. pp. 49–72, with the plates of facsimile. An English translation is to be found in Flinders Petrie, *Egyptian Tales*, vol. ii, pp. 1–12, and a German translation in A. Wiedemann, *Altägyptische Sagen und Märchen*, small 8vo, Leipzig, 1906, pp. 112–117.

The beginning is lost. At the point where we take up the story, there are three personages in the scene: an Egyptian officer named Thutîyi, the prince of a Syrian town and his equerry. The name of the country where the action is laid in that part of the story which is still preserved was read by Goodwin as Imu, and identified by him with the Emîm of the Bible (Genesis xiv, 5, Deut. ii, 10, 11). The real form is Jôpu, or according to Greek orthography Joppa. This reading has been objected to in its turn (Wiedemann, *Ægyptische Geschichte*, pp. 69–70); it is however certain, notwithstanding the lacunæ in the papyrus and the cursive form of the writing (Maspero, *Notes sur quelques points de Grammaire*, in *Zeitschrift*, 1883, p. 90).

Birch, without entirely rejecting the authenticity of the narrative, suggested that it might be only a fragment of a tale (*Egypt from the earliest times to B.C. 300*, pp. 103, 104). I have reconstructed the beginning by assuming that the trick employed by Thutîyi, with the exception of the episode of the jars, which recalls the history of Ali Baba in the *Arabian Nights,* is a variant of the stratagem attributed by Persian legend to Zopyre (cf. *Introduction,* p. cxiii–cxiv). Here, as in the earlier reconstructions, I have confined myself to using no expressions except those borrowed from other stones or from monuments of a good period. I make no pretensions to having restored the lost portion of the work. I have simply attempted to sketch out a probable introduction that will enable readers who are not acquainted with Egyptology to understand the meaning of the fragment with greater ease.

There was once in the land of Egypt a general of infantry, Thutîyi was his name. He followed the king Manakhpirîya,[1] l. h, s., on all his marches to the lands of the South and the North,[2] he fought at the head of his soldiers, he knew all the stratagems that are employed in war, and he received every day the gold of valour,[3] for he was an excellent general of infantry, and he had not his equal in the Entire Land; this is what he did.

And many days after that a messenger came from the country of Kharu,[4] and he was conducted into the presence of His Majesty, l. h. s., and His Majesty said to him, "Who hath sent thee to My Majesty? wherefore hast thou journeyed?" The messenger replied to His Majesty, l. h. s., "It is the Governor of the land of the North who sent me to thee, saying, the vanquished of Jôpu[5] has revolted against His Majesty, l. h. s.,

---

1. Manakhpirrîya is the royal prenomen of the Pharaoh Thutmôsis III of the XVIIIth dynasty. The pronunciation I attribute to it is justified by the abridged transcription Manakhbîya, which occurs in the El-Amarna letters.

2. This is a frequent formula on Egyptian monuments of the time, "he who followed his lord in all his expeditions," to which the variants add, "in all his expeditions to the south and to the north."

3. The autobiographies of Ahmasi-si-Abna and of Amenemhabi tell of the rewards given by the Egyptian kings to those of their generals who had distinguished themselves in warfare. Slaves, male and female, were given them, objects taken as booty, or gold in rings, which was called *gold of valour.*

4. The land of Kharu corresponds to Palestine, or at least to that part of Palestine which is situated between Jordan and the sea.

5. In the official language of Egypt all strangers received the title of *Pa khiri,* the *falling,* the *overthrown; Pa khiri ni Khati,* the *overthrown of Khati; Pa khiri ni Tunipu,* the *overthrown, of Tunipu; Pa khiri ni Jôpu,* the *overthrown of Joppa,* or *the vanquished of Joppa.* Cf. *Introduction,* p. cxii–cxiii.

and he has massacred the foot-soldiers of His Majesty, l. h. s., also his charioteers, and no one can stand against him."

When the king Manakhpirrîya, l. h. s., heard all the words that the messenger had said to him, he fell into a rage like a cheetah of the south.[6] "By my life, by the favour of Râ, by the love borne for me by my father Amon, I will destroy the city of the vanquished of Jôpu, I will make him feel the weight of my arm."

He called his nobles, his captains of war, also his magician-scribes, and repeated to them the message that the Governor of the land of the North had sent him. Lo! they were all silent with one mouth, they knew not what to reply, either good or evil. But Thutîyi said to His Majesty, l. h. s.: "Oh thou to whom the Entire Land pays homage, command that there be given me the great staff of the King Manakhpirrîya, l. h. s., the name of which is . . . tiutnofrît.[7] Command also that there be given me foot-soldiers of His Majesty, l. h. s., also charioteers of the flower of the brave ones of the land of Egypt, and I will slay the vanquished of Jôpu, I will take his city." His Majesty, l. h. s., said, "It is excellent, excellent, that which thou hast spoken." And the great staff of the King Manakhpirrîya, l. h. s., was given to him, and foot-soldiers were given to him and the charioteers which he had asked for.

And many days after that, Thutîyi was in the country of Kharu with his men. He caused a great sack of skin to be made which would hold a man, he had iron shackles forged for feet and hands, he had a great pair of shackles with four rings, and many wooden fetters and collars, and five hundred large jars. When all was ready he sent word to the vanquished of Jôpu: "I am Thutîyi, the general of infantry of the land of Egypt, and I have followed His Majesty, l. h. s., in all his marches to the lands of the North and the lands of the South. But lo! now, the King Manakhpirrîya, l. h, s., has been jealous of me because I am a hero, and wished to kill me,

6. This is one of the formulæ used to denote the impression produced on the king by some disastrous event. Cf. The *Stela of Paênekhi*, i. 27, etc., and also above, the *Tale of Two Brothers*, pp. 5, 6, note 16.

7. The first words that formed the name of this staff are destroyed. Not only the king's walking-stick, but also those of ordinary folk had each its special name. This is shown by the inscriptions borne by various staffs found in the tombs and preserved in our museums. It appears that the Egyptians accorded a real personality, and a kind of *double,* to the natural and manufactured objects by which they were surrounded; at any rate a proper name was assigned to each of them. This custom was carried so far that the various parts of one object occasionally received each a distinct name; for instance, the cover of a sarcophagus would have a surname different from that of the sarcophagus itself.

but I fled before him, and I have brought the great staff of the King Manakhpirrîya, l. h. s., and I have hidden it in the baskets of forage for my horses, and if thou wilt, I will give it thee, and I will be with thee, I and the people who are with me of the flower of the brave ones of the army of Egypt." When the vanquished of Jôpu heard this he rejoiced greatly, greatly, for the words that Thutîyi had spoken, for he knew that Thutîyi was a hero who had not his equal in the Entire Land. He sent to Thutîyi saying, "Come with me, and I will be to thee as a brother, and I will give thee a piece of land chosen from what is the best of the country of Jôpu."[8]

The vanquished of Jôpu came out of his city with his equerry, and with the women and children of the city, and he came before Thutîyi. He took him by the hand and embraced him and caused him to come into his camp, but he did not cause the companions of Thutîyi and their horses to enter with him. He gave him bread, he ate, he drank with him, and he said to him in the way of conversation, "the great staff of the king Manakhpirrîya,[9] what is it?" Now Thutîyi, before entering the camp of the city of Jôpu, had taken the great staff of the king Manakhpirrîya, l. h. s.; he had hidden it in the forage which he had placed in[10] the baskets, and he had arranged them as the baskets of forage are arranged for the chariotry of Egypt. Now while the vanquished of Jôpu drank with Thutîyi, the people who were with him were amusing themselves with the foot-soldiers of Pharaoh, l. h. s., and were drinking with them. And after they had passed their hour of drinking, Thutîyi said to the vanquished of Jôpu, "If it please thee, while I remain here with the women and children of thy city, allow my companions to enter with their horses to give them provender, or that an Âpuriu[11] may hasten to the place where they are." They were made to enter, the horses were hobbled, their provender was given them, and the great staff of King Manakhpirrîya, l. h. s., was found, and one went to tell Thutîyi.

And after that the vanquished of Jôpu said to Thutîyi: "My desire is to behold the great staff of the King Manakhpirrîya, l. h. s., the name of

---

8. To reconstruct this part of the text, I have made use of the analogous position that occurs in the story of Sinuhît. We have seen (pp. 63–64, 66) the manner in which the prince of Kadimâ received the hero of the story, and in a general way the welcome given to Egyptians, whether exiles or refugees, by the petty Asiatic chiefs.

9. It is probable that the staff had some magic virtue. That would explain the desire shown by the prince to possess it, no doubt in the hope that it would render him invincible.

10. It is at this point that the fragment of the manuscript commences.

11. M. Chabas believed that he recognised in this name that of the Hebrews. Various circumstances prevent my accepting this hypothesis and the conclusions too hastily drawn from it.

which is . . . tiût-nofrît. By the *double*[12] of the King Manakhpirrîya, l. h. s., since it is with thee this day, that great excellent staff, bring it to me." Thutîyi did as he said, he brought the staff of the King Manakhpirrîya, l. h. s., he seized the vanquished of Jôpu by his raiment and flung him down, saying, "Behold, oh vanquished of Jôpu, the great staff of the King Manakhpirrîya, l. h. s., the, redoubtable lion, the son of Sokhît,[13] to whom Amon his father gives strength and power." He raised his hand, he struck the temple of the vanquished of Jôpu, who fell unconscious before him. He put him in the great sack he had prepared with the skins, he seized the men who were with him, he had the pair of iron shackles brought that he had prepared, with them he fastened the hands of the vanquished of Jôpu, and on his feet were placed the pair of iron shackles of four rings.[14] He had the five hundred jars brought that he had caused to be made, he put two hundred soldiers into them; he then filled the belly of the other three hundred with cords and wooden fetters. They sealed them with a seal, they covered them with their covering and the cordage necessary to carry them, and placed them on as many strong soldiers, five hundred men in all, and one said to them, "When you shall enter the city, you shall open the jars of your companions, you shall seize all the inhabitants who are in the town, and you shall put the fetters on them immediately." One went out to say to the equerry of the vanquished of Jôpu, "Thy master has fallen! Go, say to thy sovereign lady,[15] 'Rejoice, for Sutekhu[16] has delivered Thutîyi to us, with his wife and his children.' Behold, under the name of booty

12. The *double* of the king is represented as an emblem formed of two upraised arms, between which are placed the titles that compose *the name of the double* of the king. This is inaccurately called *the royal banner*, It is placed upright on a flagstaff, and figures in the bas-reliefs behind the person of Pharaoh himself.

13. Sokhît (p. 64, note 17) is represented under the form or with the head of a lioness, and this peculiarity explains why King Thutmosîs III, regarded as her son, is called in this text a *redoubtable lion*.

14. It appears to me that the stratagem consisted, after having killed the prince of Jôpu, of passing him off as Thutîyi himself. The body was placed in a sack prepared beforehand, so that no one could recognise his features or limbs and detect the deception, and the corpse when thus concealed was loaded with chains, as was done with the bodies of the vanquished. It is this corpse that the equerry of the prince shows later to the inhabitants of the city, saying to them, "We are masters of Thutîyi."

15. The wife of the prince, who was not in camp with her husband, but, had remained in Joppa.

16. *Sutekhu, Sutekh,* was the name given by the Egyptians to the principal gods of the Asiatic and Libyan peoples. This appellation goes back to the time of the Hyksôs, and probably owes its existence to the attempts made to assimilate the god of the Hyksôs with the gods of

taken from them two hundred jars are disguised, which are full of men, wooden collars and fetters.[17]

The equerry went at the head of these people to rejoice the heart of his sovereign lady by saying, "We are masters of Thutîyi!" The fastenings of the city were opened to give passage to the porters; they entered into the city, they opened the jars of their companions, they took possession of the whole city, small and great; they placed the fetters and collars at once on the people who lived there. When the army of Pharaoh, l.h.s., had taken possession of the city, Thutîyi reposed himself, and sent a message to Egypt to the King Manakhpirrîya, l. h. s., his lord, to say, "Rejoice thou! Amon, thy father, has given thee the vanquished of Jôpu with all his subjects, and also the city. Let men come to take them into captivity, that thou mayest fill the house of thy father, Amonrâ, king of the gods, with slaves and maid-servants, who shall be beneath thy two feet for ever and ever."—Is happily finished this narration, by the office of the scribe instructed in narrations, the scribe . . . .

Egypt. Baal was identified with Sît, Suti, and under this mixed form he became *Sutekhu*. The word *Sutekhu* appears to be a grammatical form of the radical *sît, suti;* it would appear to be Egyptian, and not foreign, in its origin.

17. The number *two hundred* appears to be contradictory witli that of *five hundred* which is indicated previously. We must suppose that the scribe had the two hundred jars that contained the men in his mind, and gave this partial number without remembering the total number of five hundred.

❧

THE CYCLE OF
SATNI-KHAMOÎS

I

❧ *The Adventure of Satni-Khamoîs*
with the Mummies [7] ❧

THE LAST leaf of this story bears a date of year XV of a king whose name has never been written, but who must have been one of the Ptolemies. Two manuscripts of it, at least, exist, the fragments of which are now in the Cairo Museum. The first was discovered and published by Mariette, *Les Papyrus du Musée de Boulaq,* 1871, vol. i, pl. 29–32, after a facsimile by Emile Brugsch, and then by Krall, *Demotische Lesestücke* 1897, folio, pl. 29–32, from Mariette's edition, collated with the original. It was composed of six pages numbered from 1 to 6: the first two are lost and the beginnings of all the lines of the third are missing. The second manuscript was discovered by Spiegelberg among detached sheets brought from the Fayûm, and was published by him in the Catalogue of the Cairo Museum, *Demotische Denkmäler,* 2nd part, *die Demotische Papyri,* 4°, 1906, Texts pp. 112–115. It is greatly damaged, and it is rarely that we can distinguish a single consecutive sentence referring to the incidents of Satni's descent into the tomb of Nenoferkephtah. The text of the first manuscript has been translated by:

H. Brugsch, *Le Roman de Setnau contenu dans un papyrus démotique du Musée égyptien à Boulaq,* in the *Revue archéologique,* 2nd series, vol. xvi (Sept. 1867), pp. 161–179.

Lepage-Renouf, *The Tale of Setnau* (from the version of Dr. Heinrich Brugsch-Bey) in *Records of the Past,* 1875, 1st series, vol. iv, pp. 129–148.

E. Révillout, *Le Roman de Setna, étude philologique et critique, avec traduction mot à mot du texte démotique, introduction historique et commentaire grammatical,* Paris, Leroux, 1877–1880, 45, 48, 224 pp., 8vo.

G. Maspero, *Une page du Roman de Satni, transcrite en hiéroglyphes*, in *Zeitschrift für Ægyptische Sprache und Alterthumskunde*, 1877, pp. 132 146, 1878, pp. 15–22.

G. Maspero, translation of the whole story, with the exception of the first eight lines of the first existing sheet, in the *Nouveau Fragment de commentaire sur le second livre d'Hérodote*, Paris, Chamerot 1879, 8vo, pp. 22–46. Read at the *Association pour l'encouragement des études grecques en France*, May-June 1878. Published in *Annuaire* for 1878.

H. Brugsch, *Setna, ein Altägyptische Roman, von H. Brugsch Bey, Kairo Sendschreiben an D. Heinrichs Sachs-Bey zu Kairo* in *Deutsche Revue* III (Nov. 1, 1878) pp. 1–21.

E. Révillout, *Le Roman de Setna*, in *Revue archéologique*, 1879. Published separately by Didier, 8vo, 24 pp. and 1 pl.

Jean-Jacques Hess, *Der demotische Roman von Stne Ha-m-us*, Text, translation, commentary and glossary, 1888, Leipzig, J. C. Hinrichs, pp. 18–205.

Flinders Petrie, *Egyptian Tales*, 1895, London, 12mo, vol. ii, pp. 87–141.

F. Ll. Griffith, *The Story of Setna* in *Specimen Pages of the World's Best Literature*, 1898, New York, 4to, pp. 5262–5274.

F. Ll. Griffith, *Stories of the High Priests of Memphis, the Sethon of Herodotus, and the Demotic Tales of Khamuas*, 1900, Oxford, Clarendon Press, 8vo, pp. x–208.

A. Wiedemann, *Altägyptische Sagen und Märchen*, small 8vo, 1906, Leipzig, pp. 118–146.

Révillout, *Le Roman dit du Satme Khaemouas*, in the *Revue égyptologique*, vol. xii, pp. 110, 112, vol xiii, pp. 38–43, etc.

The first translation by Révillout was popularised by Rosny, *Taboubou*, 1892, Paris, 32mo, in the small Guillaume collection. One of the principal points in the story, the return to earth of an Egyptian princess, to avenge herself on an enemy, has been utilised by Marie Corelli in one of her strangest books, *Ziska Charmezel*.

The name of the scribe who wrote this manuscript has been commented on by J. Krall, *Der Name des Schreibers der Chamois-Sage* in the volume of *études dédiées à M. le professeur Leemans*, Leyden, Brill, 1886, folio, and read by him Ziharpto, but this reading is still uncertain; the name is known to us from Ptolemaic monuments.

The beginning, up to the point where the still extant text of the first manuscript commences, has been reconstructed by me as far as possible from the formulæ employed in the rest of the narrative. I have also made use of the analysis of details that Spiegelberg succeeded in extracting from the second manuscript. A note indicates where the restitution ends and all that remains of the original story commences.

At one time there was a king named Usimares, l. h. s.,[1] and this king had a son named Satni-Khamoîs, and the foster-brother[2] of Satni-Khamoîs was called Inarôs by name. And Satni-Khamoîs was well instructed in all things. He passed his time wandering about the necropolis of Memphis, to read there the books of the sacred writings and the books of the *double House of Life*,[3] and the writings that are carved on the stelæ and on the walls of the temples; he knew the virtues of amulets and talismans, he understood how to compose them and to draw up powerful writings, for he was a magician who had no equal in the land of Egypt.[4]

Now, one day, when he was walking in the open court of the temple of Ptah, reading the inscriptions, behold, a man of noble bearing who was there began to laugh. Satni said to him, "Wherefore dost thou laugh at me?" The noble said, "I do not laugh at thee, but can I refrain from laughing when thou dost decipher the writings here which possess no power? If thou desirest truly to read an efficacious writing, come with me. I will cause thee to go to the place where the book is that Thoth wrote with his own hand, and which will put thee immediately below the gods. The two formulæ that are written there, if thou recitest the first of them, thou shalt charm the heaven, the earth, the world of the night, the mountains, the

---

1. I remind the reader once more that this is a restitution, and that the original text of the first two pages is destroyed. Uasimarîya is the prenomen of Ramses II, which the Greeks transcribed Usimares, from the pronunciation current at the time of the Ptolemies.

2. Brugsch read the Egyptian name *An-ha-hor-rau* (1867) or *An-ha-hor-ru* (1878), which is a mere difference in transcription; Griffith proposed Anukh-harerôu (*Stories of the High Priests of Memphis,* pp. 31, 118). Spiegelberg has shown (*Demotischen Miscellen,* in *Recueil de Travaux,* vol. xxviii, p. 198; cf. *die Demotische Papyri,* text, p. 114, note 6, that Eiernharerôu or Einharôu was the prototype of the name that was translated Inarôs by the Greeks.

3. That is to say, the magic books of the sacerdotal library. We have direct evidence of the activity of the Egyptian scholars and sorcerers in the text published by Daressy, *Note sur une inscription hiératique d'un mastaba d'Abousir,* extract from the *Bulletin de l'Institut égyptien,* 1894.

4. The author of the romance did not invent the character of his hero Khâmuasît, Khamoîs. He found it ready to hand. In one of the Louvre Papyri (No. 3248) there is a series of magic formulæ the invention of which is attributed to this prince. The note giving this attribution states that he found the original manuscript under the head of a mummy in the necropolis of Memphis, probably during one of those deciphering expeditions spoken of in our text.

waters; thou shalt understand what all the birds of heaven and the reptiles say, as many as there are. Thou shalt behold the fish, for a divine power will bring them to the surface of the water. If thou readest the second formula, even when thou art in the tomb, thou shalt resume the form thou hadst on earth; thou shalt also behold the sun rising in the heavens, and his cycle of gods, also the moon in the form that she has when she appears." Satni said, "By my life! let it be told me what thou dost wish for, and I will do it for thee; but lead me to the place where the book is." The noble said to Satni, "The book in question is not mine, it is in the midst of the necropolis, in the tomb of Nenoferkephtah, son of the King Merenephthis,[5] l. h. s. Beware indeed of taking this book from him, for he will make thee bring it back, a forked stick and a staff in thy hand, a lighted brazier on thy head." From the hour when the noble spake to Satni, he knew no longer in what part of the world he was; he went before the king, and he said before the king all the words that the noble had said to him. The king said to him, "What dost thou desire?" He said to the king, "Permit me to go down into the tomb of Nenoferkephtah, son of the King Merenephthis, l. h. s.; I will take Inarôs, my foster-brother, with me, and I shall bring back that book." He went to the necropolis of Memphis with Inarôs, his foster-brother. He spent three days and three nights searching among the tombs which are in the necropolis of Memphis, reading the stelæ of the *Double House of Life,* reciting the inscriptions they bore. On the third day he recognised the place where Nenoferkephtah was laid. When they had recognised the place where Nenoferkephtah was laid, Satni recited a writing over him; a gap opened in the ground, and Satni went down to the place where the book was.[6]

[What he first saw we do not know. From the fragment discovered by Spiegelberg it appears that the man met in the forecourt of the temple of Ptah was Nenoferkephtah himself, who only kept his wife and son with him in his tomb temporarily, and desired to have them there permanently,

5. Brugsch finally read the king's name *Mer–kheper–ptah.* His first reading, *Mer–neb–phtah,* or *Minebptah,* has proved to be correct. Spiegelberg has pointed out (*Demotische Papyrus aus der Insel Elephantine,* p. 9) the Greek transcriptions, Berenebthis, Berenebtis, Perenebthis, Pernebthis, were in accordance with a phenomenon fairly frequent in Egyptian—the initial M has become a B-P.

6. Some of the Hermetic books were supposed to have been taken in this way from the tomb of the sage who had written them, and as early as the Græco-Roman period this conception had reached the West. The celebrated romance of Antonius Diogenes was put together in this way. According to the testimony of Pliny (xxx. 2), the philosopher Democritus of Abdera acquired his knowledge of magic from Apollobêchis of Coptos, and from Dar-

and that he reckoned on making use of Satni to transfer their mummies from Coptos, where they had been buried, to the Memphite necropolis. Satni, in too much haste to go down into the tomb, had not fulfilled all the necessary rites, and could not open the door. Nenofer-kephtah appeared to him and pointed out to him the expiatory sacrifices demanded by the Manes. Crows and vultures conducted him in safety to the appointed place, and at the spot on which they settled there was a stone that Satni raised immediately and which masked the entrance to the tomb.[7]]

When he entered, behold, it was as light as if the sun shone there, for the light came from the book and lighted all around.[8] And Nenofer-kephtah was not alone in the tomb, but his wife Ahuri, and Maîhêt[9] his son, were with him; for though their bodies reposed at Coptos, their double[10] was with him by virtue of the book of Thoth. And when Satni entered the tomb, Ahuri stood up and said to him, "Thou, who art thou?" He said, "I am Satni-Khamoîs, son of the King Usimares, l. h. s.; I am come to have that book of Thoth, that I perceive between thee and Nenoferkephtah. Give it me, for if not I will take it from thee by force." Ahuri said, "I pray thee, be not in haste, but listen first to all the misfor-tunes that came to me because of this book of which thou sayest, 'Let it be given to me.' Do not say that, for on account of it we were deprived of the time we had to remain on earth.

"I am named Ahuri, daughter of the King Merenephthis, l. h. s., and he whom thou seest here with me is my brother Nenoferkephtah. "We were born of the same father and the same mother, and our parents had no other children than ourselves. When I was of age to marry, I was taken

danus the Phœnician, *voluminibus Dardani in sepulchrum ejus petitis;* he owed his chemical knowledge to the works of Ostanes, which he discovered in one of the columns of the tem-ple at Memphis.

7. It is thus that I interpret the fragments that can be read on the sheet of papyrus dis-covered by Spiegelberg (cf. introduction to this story, p. 95).

8. Cf. the passage (p. 110) where Satni carries off the book, and where the tomb becomes darkened, and again (p. 116) where the light reappears when the book is brought back.

9. Brugsch read *Merhu*, then *Mer-ho-nefer,* Maspero *Mikhonsu,* Hess and Griffith *Mer-ab,* as the name of the child. The decipherment by Hess is very good and his reading would be irreproachable if it were based on a text of the early period; for Egyptians of the Ptolemaic age, the reading should be *Mihêt, Maîhêt,* or *Meîhêt.*

10. The *ka* or double was born with the child, grew up with the man, and still subsisting after death, dwelt in the tomb. It was necessary to feed, clothe, and amuse it; and it was to it that the funerary offerings were presented. As this story shows, it could leave the place where its corpse was, and dwell in the tomb of some other member of the family.

before the king at the time of diversion with the king;[11] I was much adorned and I was considered beautiful. The king said, 'Behold, Ahuri, our daughter, is already grown, and the time has come to marry her. To whom shall we marry Ahuri, our daughter?' Now I loved Nenoferkephtah, my brother, exceedingly, and I desired no other husband than he.[12] I told this to my mother; she went to find the King Merenephthis, she said to him, 'Ahuri, our daughter, loves Nenoferkephtah, her eldest brother; let us marry them one to the other according to custom.' When the King had heard all the words that my mother had said, he said, 'Thou hast had but two children, and wouldest thou marry them one to the other? Would it not be better to marry Ahuri to the son of a general of infantry, and Nenoferkephtah to the daughter of another general of infantry?' She said, 'Dost thou wrangle with me?[13] Even if I have no children after those two children, is it not the law to marry them one to the other?—I shall marry Nenoferkephtah to the daughter of a commander of troops, and Ahuri to the son of another commander of troops, and may this turn to good for our family.' As this was the time to make festival before Pharaoh, behold, one came to fetch me, one led me to the festival; I was very troubled, and I had no longer the manner of the previous day. Now Pharaoh said to me, 'Is it not thou who didst send me those foolish words, "Marry me to Nenoferkephtah my eldest brother"?' I said to him, 'Well! let me be married to the son of a general of infantry, and let Nenoferkephtah be married to the daughter of another general of infantry, and may this turn to good for our family.'—I laughed, Pharaoh laughed. Pharaoh said to the major-domo of the royal house, 'Let Ahuri be taken to the house of Nenoferkephtah this very night; let all manner of fine presents be taken with her.' They took me as spouse to the house of Nenoferkephtah, and Pharaoh commanded that a great dowry of gold

11. One sees, from the pictures on the *Pavilion* of Medinet Habu, that the king went every day to the harem to amuse himself there with his wives; it was probably that part of the day that this story speaks of as *the time of diversion with the king*.

12. The universal custom in Egypt was for the brother to marry one of his sisters. The gods and the kings themselves set the example, and the custom of these marriages, which to us appear incestuous, was so firmly seated, that the Ptolemies eventually complied with it. The celebrated Cleopatra had her two brothers in succession as husbands.

13. The part of the text that is preserved commences here. In the restitution that precedes it I have attempted, as far as possible, to use expressions and ideas borrowed from the remaining pages. It must therefore be understood that the preceding pages do not by any means represent the contents of the two lost leaves of demotic. Without developing the events in detail I have confined myself to reconstructing a general beginning that will enable readers to understand the story.

and silver should be taken to me, and all the servants of the royal house presented them to me. Nenoferkephtah spent a happy day with me; he received all the servants of the royal house, and he slept with me that very night, and he found me a virgin, and he knew me again and again, for each of us loved the other. And when the time of my monthly purifications was come, lo, I had no purifications to make. One went to announce it to Pharaoh, and his heart rejoiced greatly thereat, and he had all manner of precious things of the property of the royal house taken, and he had very beautiful gifts of gold, of silver, of fine linen, brought to me. And when the time came that I should be delivered, I brought forth this little child who is before thee. The name of Maîhêt was given him, and it was inscribed on the register of the *Double House of Life*.[14]

And many days after that, Nenoferkephtah, my brother, seemed only to be on earth to walk about in the necropolis of Memphis, reading the writings that are in the tombs of the Pharaohs, and the stelæ of the scribes of the Double House of Life,[15] as well as the writings that are inscribed on them, for he was greatly interested in writings. After that there was a procession in honour of the god Ptah, and Nenoferkephtah entered the temple to pray. Now while he walked behind the procession, deciphering the writings that are on the chapels of the gods, an old man

14. The *double house of life* was, as E. de Rougé has shown (*Stèle de la Bibliothèque imperiale*, pp. 71–99) the college of hierogrammarians versed in the knowledge of the sacred books, each of the great Egyptian temples had its *double house of life*. This passage of the story might lead one to think that the scribes belonging to it held some sort of civil position, but this was not the case. The scribes of the *double house of life*, like all the learned men of Egypt, were astrologers, diviners and magicians. The children of kings, princes, and nobles were brought to them; they drew the horoscope, they predicted the future of the new-born babe, they indicated the best names, the special amulets, the precautions to be taken according to circumstances, to circumvent as far as possible the indications of ill-fortune. All the information given by them was inscribed on registers which probably served to draw up calendars of propitious and unpropitious days, similar to the fragment preserved in the *Sallier Papyrus* (Chabas, *Le Calendrier des jours fastes et néfastes de l'anée égyptienne*, 1868) of which I have spoken in the *Introduction*, pp. cxxxiv–cxxxviii.

15. It is not easy to understand at once what *the stelæ of the scribes of the double house of life* can have been to which Satni and Nenoferkephtah attached so great importance. I think we must take them to be the talisman-stelæ of which the Pseudo-Callisthenes, the Hermetic writers and after them the Arab authors of Egypt, told so many marvels. The only ones that have come down to us, such as the *Metternich Stela*, contain charms against the bite of venomous creatures, serpents, scorpions, spiders, centipedes, and against savage animals. It would be supposed that such a student of magic as Nenoferkephtah would pore over monuments of this kind in hopes of discovering some ancient powerful formula forgotten by his contemporaries.

saw him and laughed. Nenoferkephtah said to him, 'Wherefore dost thou laugh at me?' The priest said, 'I am not laughing at thee; but can I refrain from laughing when thou readest here writings that have no power? If thou verily desirest to read a writing, come to me. I will cause thee to go to a place where the book is that Thoth wrote with his hand[16] himself, when he came here below with the gods. The two formulæ that are written there, if thou recitest the first thou shalt charm the heavens, the earth, the world of the night, the mountains, the waters; thou shalt understand that which the birds of the heaven and the reptiles say, as many as they are; thou shalt see the fish of the deep, for a divine power will rest on the water above them. If thou readest the second formula, even after thou art in the tomb, thou shalt resume the form that thou hadst on earth; also thou shalt see the sun rising in the heavens, with his cycle of gods, and the moon in the form she has when she appears.'[17] Nenoferkephtah said to the priest, 'By the life of the King, let me be told what good thing thou dost wish for and I will cause it to be given to thee if thou wilt lead me to the place where the book is.' The priest said to Nenoferkephtah, 'If thou desirest that I should send thee to the place where the book is thou shalt give me a hundred pieces of silver[18] for my burial, and thou shalt cause the two coffins[19] of a wealthy priest to be made for me.' Nenofer-

16. Cf. p. 25, note 20, and p. 27–28, in the story of Khufuî and the magicians, what is said about the books of Thoth. The *Hermetic books* which have reached us in a Greek redaction are the remains of this sacred library that was considered to be the work of the god.

17. The powers accorded to its possessor by the second part of the book of Thoth are the same as those assured by knowledge of the prayers in the *Funerary Ritual;* chapter xviii gives the power of passing unharmed through fire; chapter xxiii possesses the charms necessary for the personal security of the man who knows them by heart; and so forth. The book of Thoth secured for the dead the power of animating his mummified body and using it as he pleased; and for the living the sight not of the solar orb, but of the god himself concealed in the orb, and the gods who accompanied him.

18. The text mentions one hundred *tabonu*. The *tabonu* weighed on an average 89 to 91 grammes. One hundred *tabonu* would therefore represent between 8 kil. 900 gr. and 9 kil. 100 gr. of silver, which in *weight* would exceed 1,800 francs.

19. The Egyptian word is illegible. There is nothing surprising in the priest's request, for those who know something of the customs of the country. It is merely the expression of a good wish for a good burial—*qaîse nofre*—which is found on funerary stelæ of all periods; at the time when this romance was written so much stress was laid on the importance of good mummification and of a good tomb (ταφὴ ἀγαθή), that it is several times mentioned in papyri among the gifts which accrued to humanity from the beneficent influence of the stars, riches, excellent posterity, good fortune. The kings and great nobles usually began the excavation of their tombs as soon as they entered into possession of their inheritance. Uni was presented by the Pharaoh Piupi I, and the physician Sokhîtniânukhu by Usirkaf, with the principal furnishing of their funerary chambers. As in China, it is quite possible that the gift

kephtah called a page and commanded him that the hundred pieces of silver should be given to the priest, also he caused the two coffins to be made that he desired, in short, he did all that the priest had said. The priest said to Nenoferkephtah, 'The book in question is in the midst of the sea of Coptos[20] in an iron coffer. The iron coffer is in a bronze coffer; the bronze coffer is in a coffer of cinnamon wood[21]; the coffer of cinnamon wood is in a coffer of ivory and ebony; the coffer of ivory and ebony is in a coffer of silver; the coffer of silver is in a coffer of gold, and the book is in that.[22] And there is a schene[23] of reptiles round the coffer in which is the book, and there is an immortal serpent[24] rolled round the coffer in question.

"From the hour that the priest spoke to Nenoferkephteh he knew not in what part of the world he was. He came out of the temple, he spake with me of all that had happened to him; he said to me, 'I go to Coptos, I will bring back that book, and after that I will not again leave the country of the north.' But I rose up against the priest, saying, 'Beware of Amon for thyself, because of that which thou hast said to Nenoferkephtah; for thou hast brought me disputing, thou hast brought me war; and the country of the Thebaid, I find it hostile to my happiness.[25] I raised my hand to Nenoferkephtah that he should not go to Coptos, but he did not listen to me; he went before Pharaoh, and he spake

of a coffin would be highly esteemed. The *two coffins* of the priest were necessary for a wealthy interment. In addition to the cartonnage every mummy of distinction had two wooden coffins, one inside the other, as can be seen in our museums.

20. The word employed here is *iaûmâ*, the sea. Reitzenstein (*Hellenistische Wünderzählungen*, pp. 114–115) interprets this by *the sea near Coptos, i.e.* the Red Sea which is reached from Coptos. Here, as in the *Tale of the Two Brothers* (see above, p. 10, note 31), it means the Nile. Where it crosses the nome the Nile bore a special name. The *river of Coptos* is that part of the Nile that traverses the nome of Coptos.

21. Loret has given good reasons for recognising in this word *qad, qod,* our cinnamon tree (*Recueil de Travaux,* vol. iv, p. 21, vol. vii, p. 112).

22. On comparing this passage with that where Nenoferkephtah finds the book it will be seen that the order of the coffers differs. The scribe here made a mistake in his method of enumeration. He should have said "the iron coffer *contains* a bronze coffer, the bronze coffer *contains* a cinnamon-wood coffer," etc., instead of "the iron coffer *is in* a bronze coffer, the bronze coffer is in a cinnamon-wood coffer," etc.

23. The schene at the Ptolemaic period measured about 12,000 royal cubits of 52 centimetres each.

24. The immortal serpent is perhaps the great serpent that is still supposed to live in the Nile, and of which the fellahîn tell strange stories (Maspero, *Mélanges de Mythologie,* vol. ii, pp. 411–414).

25. The district of the Thebaid and the city of Thebes are represented under the form of a goddess. It is therefore possible that the *hostility of the country of the Thebaid* was not the

before Pharaoh all the words that the priest had said to him. Pharaoh said to him, 'What is the desire of thy heart?' He said to him, 'Let the royal cange be given to me fully equipped. I shall take Ahuri, my sister, and Maîhêt, her little child, to the south with me; I shall bring back the book, and I shall not leave this place again.' The cange fully equipped was given to him; we embarked on it, we made the voyage, we arrived at Coptos. When this was told to the priests of Isis of Coptos. and to the superior of the priests of Isis, behold they came down to us; they came without delay before Nenoferkephtah, and their wives came down before me.[26] We disembarked, and we went to the temple of Isis, and of Harpocrates. Nenoferkephtah caused a bull to be brought, a goose, and wine; he presented an offering and a libation before Isis of Coptos, and Harpocrates. We were then conducted to a house which was very beautiful, and full of all manner of good things. Nenoferkephtah spent five days diverting himself with the priests of Isis of Coptos, while the wives of the priests of Isis of Coptos diverted themselves with me.[27] When the morning of the following day came Nenoferkephtah caused a large quantity of pure wax to be brought before him; he made of it a bark[28] filled with its rowers and sailors, he recited a spell over them, he brought them to life, he gave them breath, he threw them into the

---

hostility of the inhabitants, who received the visitors cordially when they landed at Coptos, but the hostility of the goddess in whom the country of the Thebaid was incarnate, and who would be unwilling to see the book removed that had been placed under her charge by Thoth.

26. The canal which passes to the west of the ruins of Coptos is not navigable at all times, and the Nile is about half an hour from the town. This explains the remarks in the text. Nenoferkephtah probably came to land at the same place, which is still the stopping-place for those who wish to go to Kuft or to the hamlet of Barûd. The priests and priestesses of Isis, informed, of his arrival, came to him along the embankment that unites Kuft and Barûd, and which from remote antiquity has delimited one of the most important irrigation basins of the Theban plain.

27. The actual expression for *diversion* is to *make a happy day.*

28. *Roms, Romes* is a raft built of papyrus stems, the name of which is transcribed as Rhômpsis and Rhôps in certain papyri of the Græco-Roman period (cf. p. 240, note 2 of the present volume). In the Greek romance of Alexander there is a description of a magic bark, constructed by the royal sorcerer Nectanebo, and in the romances of Alexander derived from Greek romance there is the mention of a glass bell by means of which the hero descends to the bottom of the sea. The work-people and their tools are magic figures to which the formula pronounced by Nenoferkephtah *gives life and breath,* as chapter vi of the *Book of the Dead* did for the funerary figures that are so numerous in our museums. These figures were also servants intended to work for the dead men in the fields of the next world; they hoed, laboured, and reaped for him, as the magic labourers rowed and dived for Nenoferkephtah.

water,[29] he filled the royal cange with sand, he said farewell to me,[30] he embarked, and I placed myself on the sea of Coptos, saying, 'I know what will happen to him.'

"He said, 'Rowers, row for me, to the place where the book is,' and they rowed for him, by night, as by day. When he had arrived there in three days, he threw sand in front of him, and a chasm opened in the river. When he had found a schene of serpents, of scorpions, and of all manner of reptiles round the coffer where the book was, and when he had beheld an eternal serpent round the coffer itself, he recited a spell over the schene of serpents, scorpions, and reptiles who were round the coffer, and it rendered them motionless.[31] He came to the place where the eternal serpent was; he attacked him, he slew him. The serpent came to life, and took his form again. He attacked the serpent a second time; he slew him. The serpent came to life again. He attacked the serpent a third time; he cut him in two pieces, he put sand between piece and piece; the serpent died, and he did not again take his previous form.[32] Nenoferkephtah went to the place where the coffer was, and he recognised that it was an iron coffer. He opened it and he found a bronze coffer. He opened it and found a cinnamon-wood coffer. He opened it and found an ivory and ebony coffer. He opened it and found a silver coffer. He opened it and found a gold coffer. He opened it and found that the book was inside. He drew the book in question out of the gold coffer, and recited a formula of that which was

29. Cf. above, p. 21, in the same range of ideas, the wax crocodile made by Ubaûanir, which when thrown into the water came to life, and grew so large as to become an actual crocodile.

30. This phrase is a probable restitution, but not certain.

31. Literally: "They did not carry themselves off." It is the same expression used in the *Story of the Doomed Prince* (cf. p. 155, note 5) to mark the magic proceeding employed by the princes to reach the window of the daughter of the chief of Naharinna. One of the Leyden papyri and a papyrus in the Louvre, *The Harris Magic Papyrus*, contain spells against scorpions and reptiles, of the kind placed by the author in the mouth of Nenoferkephtah.

32. This struggle with serpents, guardians of a book or of a place, is based on a religious idea. At Denderah, for instance (Mariette, *Denderah*, vol. iii, pl. 14 *a, b*), the guardians of the doorways and crypts are always figured under the form of vipers, as are also the guardians of the twelve regions of the lower world. The serpent goddess Maruitsakro was guardian of part of the funerary mountain of Thebes, between Assasîf and Qurnah, and especially of the pyramidal-shaped summit which dominates the whole chain, and which is called *Ta-tehnit*, the *forehead*. In the romance of Alexander, on the subject of the foundation of Alexandria, there is an account of a fight similar to that of Nenoferkephtah (*Pseudo Callisthenes*, pp. 34, 35), but the order is reversed; the small fry of the serpents only appear after the death of the *eternal serpent*. On the persistency of this superstition of a guardian snake, see Lane, *Modern Egyptians*, London, 1871, vol. i, pp. 286, 287, where it is said that every quarter of Cairo "has its peculiar guardian genius . . . which has the form of a serpent."

written in it; he enchanted the heaven, the earth, the world of the night, the mountains, the waters; he understood all that was spoken by the birds of the heaven, the fish of the waters, the beasts of the mountain. He recited the other formula of the writing, and he beheld the sun as it mounted the sky with his cycle of gods, the moon rising, the stars in their form; he beheld the fishes of the deep, for a divine force rested on the water above them. He recited a spell over the water, and it made it return to its former shape, he re-embarked; he said to the rowers, 'Row for me to the place where Ahuri is.' They rowed for him, by night as by day. When he arrived at the place where I was, in three days, he found me sitting near the sea of Coptos. I was not drinking nor eating; I was doing nothing in the world; I was like a person arrived at the *Good Dwelling*.[33] I said to Nenoferkephtah, 'By the life of the King! Grant that I see this book for which you have taken all this trouble.' He put the book in my hand, I read one formula of the writing which was there; I enchanted the heaven, the earth, the world of the night, the mountains, the waters; I understood all that was spoken by the birds of the heaven, the fish of the deep, and the quadrupeds. I recited the other formula of the writing. I beheld the sun which appeared in the heaven with his cycle of gods, I beheld the moon rising, and all the stars of heaven in their form; I beheld the fish of the water, for there was a divine force which rested on the water above them. As I could not write, I said so to Nenoferkephtah, my eldest brother, who was an accomplished scribe and a very learned man; he caused a piece of virgin papyrus to be brought, he wrote therein all the words that were in the book, he soaked it in beer, he dissolved the whole in water. When he saw that it had all dissolved, he drank, and he knew all that was in the writing.[34]

"We returned to Coptos the same day, and we made merry before Isis of Coptos and Harpocrates. We embarked, we set off. We reached the north of Coptos, the distance of a schene. Now behold, Thoth had learnt all that had happened to Nenoferkephtah with regard to this book, and Thoth did not delay to plead before Râ, saying, 'Know that my right and

33. This is one of the euphemisms employed in Egypt to designate the workshop of the embalmers, and also the tomb.

34. This proceeding of Nenoferkephtah has been employed at all periods in the East. In ancient Babylon, as now at Bagdad and Cairo, bowls of unglazed pottery were made on which magic formulæ against various maladies were written in ink. Into them water was poured, which partially removed the ink, and which was swallowed by the patient. However much the ink remained at the bottom of the bowl, the cure was certain. (Lane, *Modern Egyptians*, 1871, vol. i, pp. 320–321.) Did not Mme. de Sévigné wish that she could make broth of the works of M. Nicole, and thus assimilate their virtues?

my law are with Nenoferkephtah, son of the King Merenephthis, l. h. s. He has penetrated into my abode, he has pillaged it, he has taken my coffer with my book of incantations, he has slain my guardian who watched over the coffer.' One[35] said to him, 'He is thine, he and all his, all of them.' One sent down a divine force from heaven saying, 'Nenoferkephtah shall not arrive safe and sound at Memphis, he and whoever is with him.' At this same hour Maîhêt, the young child, came out from under the awning of the cange of Pharaoh.[36] He fell in the river, and while he praised Râ,[37] all who were on board uttered a cry. Nenoferkephtah came out from below the cabin; he recited a spell over the child, and brought him up again, for there was a divine force which rested on the water above him. He recited a spell over him, he made him tell all that had happened to him, and the accusation that Thoth had brought before Râ. We returned to Coptos with him, we had him carried to the *Good Dwelling*, we waited to see that care was taken of him, we had him embalmed as beseemed a great one, we laid him in his coffin in the cemetery of Coptos. Nenoferkephtah, my brother, said, 'Let us go; do not let us delay to return until the king has heard what has happened to us, and his heart is troubled on this account.' We embarked, we parted, we were not long in arriving at the north of Coptos, the distance of a schene. At the place where the little child Maîhêt had tumbled into the river, I came out from below the awning of the cange of Pharaoh, I fell into the river, and while I praised Râ all who were on board uttered a cry. It was told to Nenoferkephtah, and he came out from below the awning of the cange of Pharaoh. He recited a spell over me, and he brought me up again, for there was a divine force which rested on the water above me. He took me out of the river, he read a spell over me, he made me tell all that had happened to me, and the accusation that Thoth had brought before Râ. He returned to Coptos with me, he had me carried to the *Good Dwelling*, he waited to see that care was taken of me, he had me embalmed as beseemed a very great personage, he had

35. In the *Story of the Two Brothers* (p. 12, note 36) *One* was Pharaoh. Here it is Râ, king of the gods, and at the beginning of time the Pharaoh of Egypt.

36. On the meaning of this expression cf. E. Lefébure, *Rites égyptiens*, p. 87.

37. The term *hasi*, the praiser, the singer of the god, is applied to the dead in a manner that is almost constant from the time of the second Theban empire: *To praise Râ* is a euphemism for the act of dying, more especially that of dying by drowning. In the Ptolemaic period *hasi* means *drowned*, and it is much used for Osiris, whose body Typhon had thrown into the Nile (Griffith-Thompson, *The Demotic Magical Papyrus*, p. 38; and *Apotheosis by drowning* in *Zeitschrift*, 1910, vol. xlvi, pp. 132–134). Thus *he was praising Râ* is here equivalent to *he was drowning*.

me laid in the tomb where Maîhêt, the little child, was already laid. He embarked, he set out, he was not long in arriving at the north of Coptos, the distance of a schene, at the place where we had fallen into the river. He communed with his heart, saying, 'Would it not be better to go to Coptos, and take up my abode with them? If, on the contrary, I return at once to Memphis, and Pharaoh questions me on the subject of his children, what could I say to him? Could I say thus to him: 'I took thy children with me to the nome of Thebes; I have killed them, and I live. I returned to Memphis still living.' He caused a piece of royal fine linen that belonged to him to be brought, he made of it a magic band, he tied the book with it, he put it on his breast, and fixed it there firmly.[38] Nenoferkephtah came out from below the awning of the cange of Pharaoh, he fell into the water, and while he praised Râ all who were on board uttered a cry, saying, 'Oh, what great mourning, what lamentable mourning! Is he not gone, the excellent scribe, the learned man who had no equal!'

"The cange of Pharaoh went on its way, before any one in the world knew in what place Nenoferkephtah was. When it arrived at Memphis one informed Pharaoh, and Pharaoh came down in front of the cange. He was wearing a mourning cloak, and all the garrison of Memphis wore mourning cloaks, as well as the priests of Ptah, the high priest of Ptah, and all the people who surround Pharaoh.[39] And lo! they beheld Nenoferkephtah, who was fixed on to the rudder-oars of the cange of Pharaoh by his knowledge as an excellent scribe.[40] They raised him, they saw the book on his breast, and Pharaoh said, 'Let the book that is on his breast be taken away.' The courtiers of Pharaoh, as well as the priests of Ptah and the high-priest of Ptah, said before the king, 'Oh, our great lord—may he have the duration of Râ!—he is an excellent scribe and a very learned man,

38. One of the magic books of the Leyden Museum professes to be a copy from the original "discovered at the neck of King Usimares, in the tomb" (Pleyte, *Chapitres supplémentaires du Livre des Morts*, pp. 50 *et seq.*). Another copy of the same work, which belongs to the Cairo Museum, was found in the coffin of Tatumaut, priestess of Amon, placed at the base of the neck. (Daressy, *Inscriptions sur les objects accompagnant la momie de Tadumaut*, in the *Annales du service des Antiquités*, vol. iii, pp. 156-157.)

39. *Qanbûatiu, the people of the corner,* those who stand at the four sides of the king and of the hall in which he gave audience (cf. p. 77, note 82).

40. Nenoferkephtah having disappeared beneath the river, *no one knew in what place he was;* at Memphis he is found attached to the rudder-oars of the royal bark, and the text is careful to add that it was *in his quality of excellent scribe.* This prodigy was due to the precaution he had taken in fixing the book of Thoth to his breast; its magic virtue had raised the corpse and attached it to the oars without human intervention.

this Nenoferkephtah!"[41] Pharaoh had him placed in the *Good Dwelling*[42] for the space of sixteen days, clothed with stuffs for the space of thirty-five days, laid out for the space of seventy days, and then he was laid in his tomb among the *Dwellings of Repose*.

"I have told thee all the sorrows that came to us on account of this book, of which thou sayest, 'Let it be given me.' Thou hast no right to it; for, on account of it, the time we had to remain on the earth was taken from us."

Satni said, "Ahuri, give me that book that I see between thee and Nenoferkephtah; if not, I will take it from thee by force." Nenofer-kephtah raised himself on the bed and said, "Art thou not Satni, to whom that woman has told all those misfortunes that thou hast not yet experienced? Art thou capable of obtaining this book by the power of an excellent scribe,[43] or by thy skill in playing against me? Let us two play for it."[44] Satni said, "Agreed." Then they brought the *board* before them,[45] with its *dogs*, and they two played. Nenoferkephtah won a game

41. The exclamation of the priests of Ptah, which at first nothing appears to justify, is an indirect reply to the order of the king. The king commands them to take the book of Thoth, which had already caused the death of three persons. The priests did not dare to disobey him openly, but by remarking that Nenoferkephtah was a great magician, they intimated to him that all the science in the world could not protect men against the vengeance of God. By what misfortunes would not the assistant be menaced who took the book without the knowledge of sorcery possessed by Nenoferkephtah! The event proves that this somewhat subtle inter-pretation of the text is correct. The king comprehended the fears of his courtiers, and revoked the imprudent order given by him; for the book of Thoth was still on the mummy of Nenoferkephtah when Satni came to take it.

42. Cf. p. 106, note 33, for the *Good Dwelling*.

43. In other words, by a trial of magic skill between magicians of equal power (cf. p. 108, note 40).

44. For the meaning of this passage, cf. Spiegelberg, *der Sagenkreis des Königs Petubastis*, p. 56, note 9. The game of draughts was the favourite amusement of the dead; there was often deposit-ed in the tomb with them a draughtsboard, draughtsmen, and some small knuckle-bones to reg-ulate the movement of the pieces. A certain vignette of the *Funerary Ritual* shows the owner playing thus in the other world, in a small pavilion or under the vault of a hypogeum (Naville, *Todtenbuch*, vol. i. pl. xxvii). The modern Egyptians have at least two games, the *munkalah* and the *tab*, which should present analogies with Satni's games against Nenoferkephtah. They are to be found explained at full length in Lane, *An Account of the Manners and Customs of the Modern Egyptians*, 5th edit., London, 1871, vol. ii, p. 46 *et seq*. The *munkalah* is played with sixteen points. We may add that in the Turin Museum there are fragments of a papyrus, unfortunately dam-aged, in which are given the rules of several games of draughts, which have been studied by Devéria, then by Wiedemann. I have searched in vain for an explanation of the game played by the two heroes of the story; in the present state of our knowledge the connection is impossible to follow, and the translation of this passage remains conjectural.

45. The playing pieces were called *dogs;* in the museums there are some examples with the head or a dog or jackal (Birch, *Rhampsinitus and the Game of Draughts*, pp. 4, 14). It is the same

from Satni[46]; he recited his magic over him, he placed over him the playing-board which was before him, and he caused him to sink into the ground up to the legs. He did the same with the second game; he won from Satni, and he caused him to sink into the ground up to the waist. He did the same with the third game, and he caused Satni to sink into the ground up to the ears. After that, Satni attacked Nenofer-kephtah with his hand; Satni called Inarôs, his foster-brother, saying, "Do not delay to go up on to the earth; tell all that has happened to me before Pharaoh; bring me the talismans of my father Ptah,[47] as well as my books of magic." He went up without delay on to the ground; he recounted before Pharaoh all that had happened to Satni, and Pharaoh said, "Take him the talismans of his father as well as his books of incantations." Inarôs went down without delay into the tomb; he placed the talismans on the body of Satni, and he at once rose to the earth. Satni stretched out his hand towards the book and seized it; and when Satni came up out of the tomb, the light went before him and darkness came behind him.[48] Ahuri wept after him, saying, "Glory to thee, oh darkness! Glory to thee, oh light! All of it is departed, all that was in our tomb."[49] Nenoferkephtah said to Ahuri, "Do not afflict thyself. I shall make him bring back this book in due time, a forked stick in his hand,

name given them by the Greeks, and also the same (*kelb,* plural *kilâb*) by which those of the game of *tab* are known at the present time in Egypt. I use the word *board* to render the Egyptian term, for want of a more appropriate expression; it is the small board, divided into compartments, on which the dogs are moved. There are two in the Louvre, one of which bears the cartouche of Queen Hâtshopsuîtu, XVIIIth dynasty.

46. Nenoferkephtah has won a game; this advantage allows him to recite his book uf magic, which results in depriving Satni of part of his magic power. Nenoferkephtah puts the board in front of him over his adversary, which action has the same virtue as that of the magic hammer, and causes his feet to sink into the ground. The apocryphal Acts of St. Philip recount a similar adventure which happened to the saint: at each point that he lost, his adversary, a pagan priest, forced him first into the ground up to the knees, then to the waist, and finally to the neck (Reitzenstein *Hellenistische Wundererzählungen,* pp. 132–133).

47. The title of *father* is that which the king, descendant and actually *son* of the Sun, confers on all the gods; here the special reason for it was the fact that Khamoîs was high priest of the Memphite Ptah. The talismans of Ptah are not otherwise known to us; it is interesting to ascertain from this passage that their virtue was considered superior to the talismans of Thoth that Nenoferkephtah possessed.

48. The book of Thoth (cf. above, p. 99); Satni, when carrying it off, takes away the light and leaves darkness.

49. Thus, in the *Book of Hades,* every time that the sun, having traversed one of the hours of the night, departs to enter the following hour, the manes and the gods that he leaves plunged into darkness for twenty-three hours, till he returns, utter exclamations in his honour, and lament their return to darkness.

a lighted brazier on his head."[50] Satni went up out of the tomb, and he closed it behind him as it was before. Satni went before Pharaoh, and he recounted to Pharaoh all that had happened to him on account of the book. Pharaoh said to Satni, "Replace this book in the tomb of Nenoferkephtah, like a wise man; if not, he will force thee to take it back, a forked stick in thy hand, a lighted brazier on thy head." But Satni did not listen to him; he had no other occupation in the world than to spread out the roll and to read it, it mattered not to whom.[51]

After that it happened one day, when Satni was walking on the forecourt of the temple of Ptah, he saw a woman, very beautiful, for there was no woman who equalled her in beauty[52], she had much gold upon her, and there were young girls who walked behind her, and with her were servants to the number of fifty-two.[53] From the hour that Satni beheld her, he no longer knew the part of the world in which he was. Satni called his page,[54]

50. In all magic rites the fire or the sword, or, in default of the sword, a metal weapon pointed or forked, is necessary for the invocation and expulsion of spirits. On the lead rolls found in African cemeteries, Typhon and the evil Egyptian genii summoned by the sorcerer are at times figured lance in hand and with a flame on the head. Krall has thought that this represents a courier (*Papyrus Erzherzog Rainer, Führer durch die Ausstellung*, p. 53, No. 166) in this story.

51. This kind of overpowering obsession produced by a magic writing is forcibly described in other texts. It was thus that Prince Didûfhoru, son of Mykerinus, one of the heroes of the *Story of Khufuî and the Magicians* (cf. p. 24 *et seq.*), having discovered chapter xliv of the *Book of the Dead*, "saw no more, heard no more, so much did he recite this pure and holy chapter; he did not approach women, he ate neither flesh nor fish." Abstinence and chastity were in fact indispensable conditions for the exercise of those superhuman powers that books of magic conferred on their possessors, as will be seen in the course of this romance (cf. p. 115, note 67). It is by the incontinence of Satni that Nenoferkephtah hopes to recover his talisman.

52. The part played by Tbubui in this episode is in conformity with the universal ideas of demonology, and shows us the nature of the personage. She is no other than Ahuri returned to earth to seduce Satni and render him incapable of making use of his magic powers; when she has accomplished this, Nenoferkephtah will come in his turn and force him to return the book of Thoth. For this conception, cf. *Introduction*, pp. cxliii–cxliv.

53. Thus, as Wiedemann has very ingeniously observed (*Altägyptische Sagen und Märchen*, p. 136, note 1), the fifty-two pages who accompany Tbubui are the fifty-two playing pieces of the magic chess-board, animated and incarnated to serve as escort to the princess Ahuri in her excursion into the world of the living; cf. *Introduction*, p. cxliv.

54. The word *page* is a more or less accurate equivalent that I use for want of a better. The Egyptian term *sôtm âshu* signifies literally *he who hears the call*; it is found abbreviated into *sôtmu* in the *Doomed Prince*. On the monuments there is a numerous series of *sôtmu âshu m isît mâit*, or *pages in the true place*, that is to say, domestics attached to those parts of the Theban Necropolis which adjoin Drah Abu'l Neggah, Deîr el Baharî, el Assassîf, Sheikh Abd el Gurnah, Deîr el Medineh, especially this last locality.

saying, "Do not delay to go to the place where that woman is and learn who she is." The young page made no delay in going to the place where the woman was. He addressed the maid-servant who walked behind her, and he questioned her, saying, "What person is that?" She said to, him, "She is Tbubui, daughter of the prophet of Bastît, lady of Ankhutaûi,[55] who now goes to make her prayer before Ptah, the great god." When the young man had returned to Satni, he recounted all the words that she had said to him without exception. Satni said to the young man, "Go and say thus to the maid-servant, 'Satni-Khamoîs, son of the Pharaoh Usimares, it is who sends me, saying, "I will give thee ten pieces of gold that thou mayest pass an hour with me.[56] If there is necessity to have recourse to violence, he will do it, and he will take thee to a hidden place, where no one in the world will find thee." When the young man had returned to the place where Tbubui was, he addressed the maid-servant, and spake with her, but she exclaimed against his words, as though it were an insult to speak them. Tbubui said to the young man, "Cease to speak to that wretched girl; come and speak to me." The young man approached the place where Tbubui was; he said to her, "I will give thee ten pieces of gold if thou wilt pass an hour with Satni-Khamoîs, the son of Pharaoh-Usimares. If there is necessity to have recourse to violence, he will do so, and will take thee to a hidden place where no one in the world will find thee." Tbubui said; "Go, say to Satni, 'I am a hierodule, I am no mean person; if thou dost desire to have thy pleasure of me, thou shalt come to Bubastis[57] into my house. All will be ready there, and thou shalt have thy pleasure of me, and no one in the world shall know it, and I shall not have acted like a woman of the streets.'" When the page had returned to Satni, he repeated to him all the words that she had said without exception, and he said, "Lo, I am satisfied." But all who were with Satni began to curse.

55. For the quarter Ankhutaûi see above, p. 19, note 4.

56. Ten *tabonu* in gold (cf. p. 102, note 18) made between 890 and 910 grammes of gold, or about 3,000 francs *in weight*, but far more in actual value.

57. Now Tell Basta, near Zagazig. Brugsch has separated the two parts of the word, and has translated it *to the temple of Bastît*. The orthography of the Egyptian text does not admit of this interpretation. It does not concern either a temple of Bastît situated in one of the quarters of Memphis, nor a part of Memphis called *Pubastît*, but *the house of Bastît*, Bubastis. The journey would not necessitate long preparation; it would only occupy a few hours—a contrast to the journey to Coptos that was successively undertaken by Nenoferkephtah and by Satni himself.

Satni caused a boat to be fetched, he embarked, and delayed not to arrive at Bubastis. He went to the west of the town, until he came to a house that was very high; it had a wall all round it, it had a garden on the north side, there was a flight of steps in front of it. Satni inquired, saying, "Whose is this house?" They said to him, "It is the house of Tbubui." Satni entered the grounds, and he marvelled at the pavilion situated in the garden[58] while they told Tbubui; she came down, she took the hand of Satni, and she said to him, "By my life! the journey to the house of the priest of Bastît, lady of Ankhutaûi, at which thou art arrived, is very pleasant to me. Come up with me." Satni went up by the stairway of the house with Tbubui. He found the upper story of the house sanded and powdered with sand and powder of real lapis-lazuli and real turquoise.[59] There were several beds there, spread with stuffs of royal linen, and also many cups of gold on a stand. They filled a golden cup with wine, and placed it in the hand of Satni, and Tbubui said to him, "Will it please thee to rest thyself?" He said to her, "That is not what I wish to do." They put scented wood on the fire, they brought perfumes of the kind that are supplied to Pharaoh, and Satni made a happy day with Tbubui, for he had never before seen her equal. Then Satni said to Tbubui, "Let us accomplish that for which we have come here." She said to him, "Thou shalt arrive at thy house, that where thou art. But for me, I am a hierodule,[60] I am no mean person. If thou desirest to have thy pleasure of me, thou shall make me a contract of sustenance, and a contract of money on all the things and on all the goods that are thine."[61] He said to her, "Let the scribe of the school be brought." He was brought immediately, and Satni caused to be made in favour of Tbubui a contract for maintenance, and he made her in writing a dowry of all his things, all the goods that were his. An hour passed; one came to

58. This description corresponds very exactly with various plans of Egyptian houses that are figured in the pictures in the Theban tombs. To take one that I have figured in *Egyptian Archæology* (6th English edition, 1914, Grevel, London, fig. 14, p. 15), one sees the high wall, the doorway, the flight of steps, the great garden, and the house of two storeys in the garden.

59. *Mâfkaît* is a name common to all green minerals, or such as verge on green, sulphate of copper, emerald, turquoise, etc., known to the Egyptians.

60. For the meaning of this word cf. Maspero, *Mélanges de Mythologie et d'Archéologie égyptiennes*, vol. iv, pp. 431–432.

61. Tbubui here conforms to the jurisprudence of the Ptolemaic period, according to which the existence of two transactions, one of "sustenance" and the other of "money," is necessary to assure a legal basis for the union of a man and a woman, and to raise it to the semblance of concubinage; cf. Spiegelberg, *Demotische Miscellen*, § 32 in *Recueil de Travaux*, vol. xxviii, pp. 190–195.

say this to Satni, "Thy children are below." He said, "Let them be brought up." Tbubui arose, she put on a robe of fine linen[62] and Satni beheld all her limbs through it, and his desire increased yet more than before. Satni said to Tbubui, "Let us accomplish now that for which I came." She said to him, "Thou shalt arrive at thy house, that where thou art. But for me, I am a hierodule, I am no mean person. If thou desirest to have thy pleasure of me, thou wilt cause thy children to subscribe to my writing, that they may not seek a quarrel with my children on the subject of thy possessions." Satni had his children fetched and made them subscribe to the writing. Satni said to Tbubui, "Let me now accomplish that for which I came." She said to him, "Thou shalt arrive at thy house, that where thou art. But for me, I am a hierodule, I am no mean person. If thou dost desire to have thy pleasure of me, thou shalt cause thy children to lie slain, so that they may not seek a quarrel with my children on account of thy possessions." Satni said, "Let the crime be committed on them of which the desire has entered thy heart." She caused the children of Satni to be slain before him, she had them thrown out below the window, to the dogs and cats,[63] and they ate their flesh, and he heard them while he was drinking with Tbubui. Satni said to Tbubui, "Let us accomplish that for which we have come here, for all that thou hast said before me has been done for thee." She said to him, "Come into this chamber." Satni entered the chamber, he lay down on a bed of ivory and ebony, in order that his love might be rewarded, and Tbubui lay down by the side of Satni. He stretched out his hand to touch her; she opened her mouth widely and uttered a loud cry.[64]

62. This is the great robe of transparent linen, sometimes supple and falling in soft folds, sometimes stiff and starched, which the women are wearing in pictures of the interior of the second Theban period. The whole body was visible through this transparent veiling, and the Egyptian artists have not failed to indicate the details that show the extent to which the garment left the body visible. Several of the mummies found at Deîr el Bahari, among others those of Thût-môsis III. and Ramses II., had bandages of this linen next to their skin, of which specimens can be seen in the Cairo Museum; it has yellowed, with time and by the perfumes with which it was soaked at the time of the embalmment, but the ancient paintings have not exaggerated when they represented the ladies clothed in it as almost nude. Examining them, one understands what the gauzes of Cos must have been that the classical writers called *woven air*.

63. In the same way, according to Egyptian tradition, the eunuch Bagoas, having murdered the Persian king Okhos, threw his body to the cats (*Diodorus of Sicily*, xvii, v, § 3, and Élien, *Histoires variées*, vi, 8). In the *Tale of Two Brothers* (p. 9 of this book) Anupu kills his wife and throws her to the dogs, as a punishment for having tempted and calumniated Baîti.

64. Examples of these transformations at the moment of amorous indulgences, are not rare in popular literature. Generally they are produced by the intervention of a good genius, a thaumaturgus or a saint who comes to rescue the hero from the bonds of the succubus. Else-

When Satni came to himself he was in a place of a furnace without
any clothing on his back.[65] After an hour Satni perceived a very big
man[66] standing on a platform, with quite a number of attendants
beneath his feet, for he had the semblance of a Pharaoh. Satni was
about to raise himself, but he could not arise for shame, for he had no
clothing on his back. This Pharaoh said, "Satni, what is the state in
which you are?" He said, "It is Nenoferkephtah who has had all this
done to me." This Pharaoh said, "Go to Memphis; thy children, lo! they
wish for thee. Lo! they are standing before Pharaoh." Satni spake
before this Pharaoh, "My great lord the king—mayest thou have the
duration of Râ—how can I arrive at Memphis if I have no raiment in
the world on my back?" This Pharaoh called a page who was standing
near him and commanded him to give a garment to Satni. This
Pharaoh said, "Satni, go to Memphis. Thy children, behold they live,
behold they are standing before the king."[67] Satni went to Memphis; he
embraced his children with joy, because they were in life.[68] Pharaoh
said, "Is it not drunkenness that has caused thee to do all that?" Satni

where it is the succubus herself who affords herself the malicious pleasure of terrifying her
lover by a sudden metamorphosis. This last conception has often been made use of by European writers, and particularly by Cazotte, in his *Diable amoureux*. An obscene detail, which
occurs several lines farther on, and which I have not translated, proves that here, as in all tales
of the kind, Tbubui was forced to yield herself entirely in order to get her enemy into her
power. As soon as she had done so, she opened an enormous mouth and emitted a gale of
wind: Satni lost consciousness, and during his fainting fit he was carried far away from the
house.

65. The text here contains a phrase, *aû qunef hi-khen n uât shakki,* which I omit, and of
which the sense will be clear to any one who would wish to refer to the original.

66. A figure of more than human size was at that period the mark by which one recognised gods or genii when they manifested themselves to mankind; thus Hermes-Thoth in the
Poimander, § 1.

67. One sees from the *king's* remarks that he is Nenoferkephtah, and that all the preceding scene of coquetry and murder was merely a magical deed; Satni, rendered impure and a
criminal, loses his supernatural power. As I have already remarked (p. 111, note 51), connection
with women has always the effect of suspending the power of the sorcerer, until he has been
able to accomplish the prescribed ablutions and again become pure. Thus amorous seduction
is always a method much resorted to when there is any question of the supernatural. Only to
quote one example among hundreds, in the *Arabian Nights* (fourteenth night) the enchanter
Shahabeddin, after having had connection with a woman, could not use his formulæ with any
success until he had accomplished the purifications prescribed by the Koran to be adopted
under such circumstances, and had been cleansed from his impurity.

68. Cf. above, p. 87, n. 22, an analogous instance of resurrection in the case of the companions of the *shipwrecked sailor.*

related all that had happened to him with Tbubui and Nenoferkephtah. Pharaoh said, "Satni, I have before come to thine aid, saying, 'They will slay thee, if thou dost not return that book to the place where thou didst take it for thyself, but thou hast not listened to me up to this hour.' Now take back the book to Nenoferkephtah, a forked staff in thy hand and a lighted brazier on thy head." Satni went out before Pharaoh, a fork and a staff in his hand and a lighted brazier on his head, and he descended into the tomb where Nenoferkephtah was. Ahuri said to him, "Satni, it is Ptah the great god who brings thee here safe and sound."[69] Nenoferkephtah laughed, saying, "This is what I said to thee before." Satni began to talk with Nenoferkephtah, and he perceived that while they talked the sun was altogether in the tomb.[70] Ahuri and Nenoferkephtah talked much with Satni. Satni said, "Nenoferkephtah, is it not something humiliating that thou askest?" Nenoferkephtah said, "Thou knowest this by knowledge, that Ahuri and Maîhêt, her child, are at Coptos, and also in this tomb, by the art of a skilful scribe. Let it be commanded to thee to take the trouble to go to Coptos and bring them hither."[71]

Satni went up out of the tomb; he went before Pharaoh, he related before Pharaoh all that Nenoferkephtah had said to him. Pharaoh said, "Satni, go to Coptos and bring back Ahuri and Maîhêt her child." He said before Pharaoh, "Let the cange of Pharaoh and its crew be given me." The cange of Pharaoh and its crew were given him; he embarked, he started, he did not delay to arrive at Coptos. One told the priests of Isis, of Coptos, and the High-priest of Isis; behold, they came down to him, they came down to the bank. He disembarked, he went to the temple of Isis of Coptos, and Harpocrates. He caused a bull, a goose, and some wine to be brought; he made a burnt offering and a libation before Isis of Coptos and Harpocrates. He went to the cemetery of Coptos with

69. Satni was high-priest of Ptah; the protection of the god had saved him from the magicians, and it is this that Ahuri avows, probably not without some vexation.

70. In returning the magic book, Satni had brought back light into the tomb, of which he had deprived it when he carried off the talisman (see above, p. 110, n. 48).

71. The *double* ought to live where the body is buried. Nenoferkephtah had screened the *double* of Ahuri and Maîhêt from that law by *the art of an able scribe,* that is, by magic, and had given them hospitality in his own tomb; but this was a precarious position that might be changed at any moment. Satni, defeated in the struggle for the possession of the book of Thoth, owed some indemnity to the conqueror, who imposed on him the obligation to go to Coptos to find Ahuri and Maîhêt and bring them to Memphis. The union of the three mummies would ensure the union of the three *doubles* for all time.

the priests of Isis and the High-priest of Isis. They spent three days and three nights searching among the tombs that are in the necropolis of Coptos, moving the stelæ of the scribes of the Double House of Life, deciphering the inscriptions on them; they did not find the chambers where Ahuri and Maîhêt her child reposed. Nenoferkephtah knew that they did not find the chambers where Ahuri and Maîhêt her child reposed. He manifested himself under the form of an old man, a priest very advanced in years, he presented himself before Satni.[72]

Satni saw him; Satni said, "Thou seemest to be a man advanced in years, dost thou not know the house where Ahuri and Maîhêt her child repose?" The old man said to Satni, "The father of the father of my father said to the father of my father, 'the chambers where Ahuri and Maîhêt her child repose are below the southern corner of the house of the priest...."[73] Satni said to the old man, "Perchance the priest... hath injured thee, and therefore it is that thou wouldest destroy his house."[74] The old man said to Satni, "Let a good watch be kept on me while the house of the priest... is destroyed, and if it happens that Ahuri and Maîhêt her child are not found under the southern corner of the house of the priest... let me be treated as a criminal." A good watch was kept over the old man; the chamber where Ahuri and Maîhêt her child reposed was found below the southern angle of the house of the priest.... Satni caused these great personages to be carried to the cange of Pharaoh, and he then had the house of the priest... rebuilt as it was before.[75] Nenoferkephtah made known to Satni that it was he who had

72. This is at least the second transformation performed by Nenoferkephtah in that part of the story that has been preserved. The ordinary manes had the right to assume all the forms they wished, but they could only render themselves visible in very rare cases. Nenoferkephtah owes to his quality of magician the power to do with ease what was forbidden to them, and to appear at one time as a king, at another as an old man (cf. *Introduction* pp. cliii, cxliv).

73. The text is too much damaged in this place to allow of the restitution being regarded as certain.

74. By destroying the *house*, i.e. the tomb of an individual, his funerary cult was rendered impossible, the *double* was starved and ran the risk of perishing, thus arousing the wrath of the double, which showed itself in apparitions, attacks, possessions by spirits and maladies from which the living suffered. The law was very severe on those who, by demolishing a tomb, risked the letting loose of various ills. Nevertheless it happened at times that people who cherished hatred against some deceased persons would ran the risk. Satni feared that his informant might profit by his researches to satisfy his hatred and render him an involuntary accomplice in his crime.

75. The restorations of tombs, and in consequence the transport of mummies, was not unusual in Ancient Egypt. The most striking example was afforded at Thebes by the find at Deîr el Baharî. In 1881 about forty royal corpses were found there, including the most cele-

come to Coptos, to discover for him the chamber where Ahuri and Maîhêt her child reposed.

Satni embarked on the cange of Pharaoh. He made the voyage, he did not delay to arrive at Memphis, and all the escort who were with him. One told Pharaoh, and Pharaoh came down before the cange of Pharaoh. He caused the great personages to be carried to the tomb where Nenoferkephtah was, and he had the upper chamber all sealed as before.—This complete writing, wherein is related the history of Satnî Khamoîs and Nenoferkephtah, also of Ahuri his wife and Maîhêt his son, has been written by the scribe Ziharpto, the year 35, in the month of Tybi.

II

ᴕ The Veritable History of Satni-Khamoîs and His Son Senosiris [8] ᴕ

THE Veritable History of Satni-Khâmoîs and his son Senosiris was discovered on Papyrus DCIV of the British Museum, and published, transcribed, and translated into English by F. Ll. Griffith, *Stories of the High Priests of Memphis, the Sethon of Herodotus, and the Demotic Tales of Khamuas,* Oxford, Clarendon Press, 1909, 8vo, pp. 41–66, 142–207, and Atlas of xiv plates, folio, since analysed, commented on, and partially translated into French by G. Maspero, *Contes relatifs aux grands-prêtres de Memphis,* in the *Journal des Savants,* 1911, pp. 473–504, finally transcribed into hieroglyphs and translated by Revillout, *Le Roman de Satme, Second Roman du Satme Khaemouas,* in *Revue égyptologique,* vol. xii, pp. 107–109, vol. xiii, pp. 29–38.

It is found on the reverse of two collections of official writings written in Greek, and dated the year vii of Claudius Cæsar, 46–47 A.D. The two rolls of papyri, treated as old paper, were fixed to each other end to end, and this story

brated of the Pharaohs of the XVIIIth, XIXth, and XXth dynasties—Ahmôsis I, Amenôthes I, Thûtmosis II, and Thûtmosis III, Sêtui I, Ramses II, and Ramses III. Their mummies, inspected and repaired at different times, had finally been deposited, under Sheshonq I, in one pit, where it was easy to protect them from the attempts of robbers. The hero of our story acts in the same way as Sheshonq, but with a different object; he obeys an order from the dead themselves, and endeavours rather to please them than to give them protection, which their magic power enables them to dispense with.

was transcribed on such parts of the verso as were unused; in its present condition it is incomplete on the right-hand side for some length which we cannot determine, and the beginning of the narrative has disappeared. The writing appears to indicate for the date of the copy the latter half of the second century A.D. It is large and feeble, careful and yet clumsy; but notwithstanding its peculiarities it is easy to decipher. The language is simple, clear, and poorer than that of the preceding narrative. The whole of the first page is missing and a long fragment of the second page, but the explanation of the subject can be restored with fair certainty. The remainder of the text is interrupted with serious lacunæ that render it difficult to follow the narrative. The minute and patient study Mr. Griffith has bestowed on the whole of the work enables us to grasp the general meaning, and also to restore the detail with accuracy in many places. According to my usual custom, I have summarily filled in the missing portions, taking care to indicate the exact point where the authentic text commences.

There was at one time a king named Usimares, l. h. s., and among his children he had one called Satmi[76] who was a scribe, skilled with his fingers and very learned in all matters. He was more expert than any man in the world in the arts in which the scribes of Egypt excel, and there was no sage to compare with him in the Entire Land. And after that, it chanced that the chiefs of the foreign lands sent a messenger to Pharaoh to say to him: "This is what my lord saith: 'Who is there here who could do such and such a thing that my lord has devised, under such and such conditions? If he does it as it should be done, I will proclaim the inferiority of my country to Egypt. But if it happens that there is no good scribe nor learned man in Egypt who can do it, I will proclaim the inferiority of Egypt to my country.'" Now, when he had spoken thus, King Usimares, l. h. s., called his son Satmi and repeated to him all the things that the messenger had said to him, and his son Satmi at once gave him the right reply that the chief of the foreign country had devised, and the

76. The text of this story gives the variant *Satmi* for the name of *Satni*, which might raise a doubt as to whether the same person was intended. The addition of the surname of *Khâmois* in several places proves that *Satmi* is really identical with *Satni*. *Satmi* is elsewhere the title of the priest of Ptah, which accords perfectly with our hero, who was High-priest of Ptah at Memphis (cf. p. 116, note 69 of this volume).

messenger was obliged to proclaim the inferiority of his country to the land of Egypt. And none of the chiefs who had sent messengers could triumph over him, for the wisdom of Satmi was great, so that there was no ruler in the world who dared to send messengers to Pharaoh.[77]

And after that it chanced that Satmi had no man child by his wife Mahîtuaskhît, and it afflicted him greatly in his heart, and his wife Mahîtuaskhît was greatly afflicted with him. Now one day when he was more sad than usual, his wife Mahîtuaskhît went to the temple of Imûthes, son of Ptah, and she prayed before him, saying: "Turn thy face towards me, my lord Imûthes, son of Ptah, it is thou who dost work miracles, and who art beneficent in all thy deeds; it is thou who givest a son to her who has none. Listen to my lamentation and give me conception of a man-child."[78] Mahîtuaskhît, the wife of Satmi, slept in the temple and she dreamed a dream that same night.[79] One spake with her, saying: "Art thou not Mahîtuaskhît, the wife of Satmi, who dost sleep in the temple to receive a remedy for thy sterility from the hands of the god? When to-morrow morning comes, go to the bath-room of Satmi[80] thy husband, and thou wilt find a root of colocasia that is growing there. The colocasia that thou meetest with thou shall gather with its leaves, thou shalt make of it a remedy that thou shalt give to thy husband, then thou shall lie by his side, and thou shalt conceive by him the same night." When Mahîtuaskhît awoke from her dream after having seen these things she did everything according to that which had been told her in her dream; then she lay by the side of Satmi her husband, and she conceived by him. When the time came she had the signs of pregnant women, and Satmi announced it to Pharaoh, for his heart rejoiced greatly thereat; he bound an amulet upon her, and recited a

77. The theme of this opening was suggested to me by the passage that will be read farther on, pp. 153 *et seq.* I have spoken in the *Introduction,* pp. xxix-xxx, of the idea of a challenge between kings as a theme current in Egypt.

78. I have restored this passage from a scene that occurs later (p. 131), where the sorcerer Horus the Egyptian passes the night in the temple of Thoth, to obtain a prophetic dream (cf. Maspero, *Le début du second Conte de Satni-Khâmoîs,* in *Mélanges Nicole,* pp. 349–355). A stela of the time of Augustus, slightly anterior to the redaction of our papyrus, provides us with a good example of a dream, followed by the birth of a child (Prisse d'Avenne, *Monuments,* pl. xxvi *bis*).

79. It is here that the part of the text that is preserved commences.

80. Griffith considers, but not without some doubt, that this refers to the latrines in Satmi's house. I think rather that it refers to a fountain, a bath-room, or a kind of artificial reservoir, such as we found in front of the temple of Denderah during the winter of 1904–5.

spell over her. Now, Satmi slept one night and he dreamed a dream. One spoke to him, saying: "Mahîtuaskhît thy wife, who has conceived by thee, the infant that she shall bear shall be called Senosiris, and many will be the wonders that he will perform in the land of Egypt." When Satmi awoke from his dream after having seen these things, his heart rejoiced greatly. When the months of pregnancy were fulfilled, when the time for the birth was come, Mahîtuaskhît brought into the world a man-child. They told this to Satmi, and he called the child Senosiris, according to that which was told him in his dream. He was put to the breast of Mahîtuaskhît, his mother, as soon as she was delivered of the remains of her pregnancy, and he was fed by her. And it came to pass, when the little child Senosiris was one year old, one would have said, "He is two years old"; when he was two, one would have said, "He is three years old," so vigorous was he in all his limbs. It came to pass, however, that Satmi could not live an hour without seeing the little child Senosiris, so great was the love that he bore him. When he became big and strong he was sent to school; in a little time he knew more than the scribe who had been given him as master. The little child Senosiris began to read the books of magic with the scribes of the Double House of Life of the Temple of Ptah,[81] and all who heard him were lost in astonishment. Satmi delighted in taking him to the festival before Pharaoh, so that all the magicians of Pharaoh should compete with him, and he remained head of them all.

And after that it came to pass, one day when Satmi was washing himself for the festival on the roof of his apartments, and the little boy Senosiris was washing with him to go also to the festival, at that hour, behold Satmi heard a voice of lamentation which was very loud. He looked out from the roof of his dwelling, and lo! he saw a rich man being carried to his burial in the mountain with much lamentation and plenitude of honours. He looked down a second time at his feet, and behold a poor man was being carried out of Memphis, rolled in a mat, alone, and without a man in the world who walked behind him. Satmi said, "By the life of Osiris, lord of Amentît, let there be done for me in Amentît, as for these rich ones who have great lamentation, and not as these poor ones who are carried to the mountain without pomp or honours." Senosiris, his little child, said to him, "Let there be done to thee in Amentît that which is done for that poor man in Amentît, and may that not be done to thee in Amentît that is done to

81. For the *double House of Life* see what is said above, p. 101, note 14.

that rich man in Amentît." When Satmi heard these words that Senosiris, his little child, had said to him, his heart was greatly afflicted, and he said, "Is that which I hear the voice of a son who loves his father?" Senosiris, his little child, said to him, "If it please thee, I will show thee, each in his place, the poor man who was not wept for, and the rich man over whom there was lamentation." Satmi asked, "And how wilt thou do that, my son Senosiris?" And after that Senosiris, the little child, recited his books of magic. He took his father Satmi by the hand and led him to a place that he did not know of in the mountain of Memphis. It contained seven large halls,[82] and in them were men of all conditions. They crossed three of the halls, the first three without any one stopping them.[83] On entering the fourth, Satmi perceived persons who ran and moved about while the asses ate behind them[84]; others had their food, water and bread, hung above them, and they leapt up to pull it down, while others dug holes under their feet to prevent their reaching it. When they arrived at the fifth hall, Satmi perceived the venerable manes who were each in their proper place, but those who were guilty of crimes stood at the door as suppliants; and the pivot of the door of the fifth hall was fixed on the single right eye of a man who prayed and uttered great cries.[85] When they arrived at the sixth hall, Satmi perceived the gods of the council of the men of the people of Amentît, who were each in their proper place, while the doorkeepers of Amentît called the cases. When they arrived at the seventh hall, Satmi perceived the image of Osiris, the great god, seated on his throne of fine gold, and crowned with a diadem with two feathers,[86] Anuibis the great god on his

82. The seven great halls of the lower world described here are those referred to in chapters cxliv and cxlvii of the *Book of the Dead*. The same number has passed (from a descent into the lower world now lost) into the Hermetic books (Zosymus, § v, in Berthelot, *Les Alchimistes Grecs*, vol. i, pp. 115–118, and vol. ii, pp. 125–127; *cf.* Reitzenstein, *Poimandrés*, pp. 8–11).

83. From the place where it is said that Satmi was grieved by his son's words, as far as where we find him entering the fourth hall, only a few words remain of each line, and even their places are uncertain. It is probable that the description of the first three halls contained nothing of interest. In any case it was very short, and at most covered only four or five lines.

84. As will be seen later (p. 124), *the asses who eat behind* are the women who devoured the substance of individuals during their life. Cf. the Greek legend of Ocnos and the ass, who devoured all his labour behind him (Pausanias, *Hellenica*, x, 24).

85. The idea of this punishment was very ancient in Egypt. As early as the Thinite period, at Hieraconpolis, on the threshold of one of the gates of the temple, there are figures of human beings lying face downwards, over which the leaf of the door passed when opening and shutting (Quibell, *Hieraconpolis*, vol. i, pl. 1). They were the enemies of the god, whom the faithful trod underfoot every time they came to worship him.

86. This diadem, called by the Egyptians *iatef, iôtef,* was formed of the white crown of Upper Egypt, and the two ostrich feathers set right and left.

left, the great god Thoth on his right, the gods of the council of the people of Amentît on his left and on his right, the balance set up in the middle in front of them, where they weighed misdeeds against good deeds, while Thoth the great god performed the part of scribe and Anubis addressed them.[87] Him whose misdeeds they found more numerous than his good deeds they delivered to Amaît, the bitch belonging to the lord of Amentît;[88] they destroyed his soul and his body, and did not permit him to breathe any more. Him whose good deeds they found more numerous than his evil deeds, they lead him among the gods of the council of the lord of Amentît, and his soul goes to heaven among the venerable names. Him whose merits they find equal with his faults, him they place among the manes furnished with amulets who serve Sokarosiris.

Then Satmi perceived a personage of distinction, clad in materials of fine linen, and who was near the place where Osiris was, in a very lofty rank. While Satmi marvelled at all that he saw in Amentît, Senosiris placed himself before him, saying, "My father, Satmi, dost thou not see that high personage clad in raiment of fine linen, and who is near the place where Osiris is? It is that poor man whom thou sawest who was carried out of Memphis, with no one accompanying him, and rolled in a mat. He was taken to Hades, his misdeeds were weighed against the merits he had while on earth; the merits were found more numerous than the misdeeds. As there was no total of happiness while he was on earth sufficient to correspond with the length of life inscribed to his account by Thoth, an order was given on the part of Osiris to transfer the funerary outfit of the rich man thou sawest carried out of Memphis with many honours to this poor man, beside placing him among the venerable manes, fief of Sokarosiris, near the place where Osiris is. That rich man thou sawest, he was taken to Hades, his misdeeds were weighed against his merits, the misdeeds were found more numerous than his merits that he had on earth, and command was given that he should be punished in Amentît, and he it is whom thou sawest, the pivot of the door of Amentît planted on his right eye and revolving on that eye, whether it be closed or open, while his mouth utters loud cries. By the life of Osiris, the great god, lord of Amentît, if I said to thee on earth, "May it be done to thee as to that

---

87. This is an exact description of the scene of the *judgment of the soul*, as it is represented in some instances on wooden coffins and stone sarcophagi of the Ptolemaic period, and as it is figured at the head of chapter cxxv of the *Book of the Dead*.

88. Amaît is usually represented as a female hippopotamus, seated in front of Osiris near the balance, with open mouth, waiting for any of the dead who shall be pronounced guilty.

poor man, but may it not be done to thee as to that rich man, it was because I knew what was about to happen to him." Satmi said, "My son, Senosiris, many are the marvels that I have seen in Amentît! Now, therefore, cause me to know who are those persons who run and move about while asses eat behind them; also about those others who have their food, bread and water, hung above them, and who leap in order to pull it down, while others dig holes at their feet to prevent their reaching it." Senosiris replied, "Verily, I say to thee, my father Satmi, those men that thou sawest who run and move about while asses eat behind them, are the figure of the men of this world who are under the curse of God, who work night and day for their food, but because their wives steal what is theirs from behind, they have not bread to eat. When they appear in Amentît, it is found that their misdeeds are more numerous than their merits, and they find that what happened to them on earth happens to them again in Amentît. With them also, as with those thou sawest, their food, water and bread, hung above them, and who leapt to draw it down, while others dug holes at their feet to prevent their reaching it: these are the figure of the people of this world who have their food before them, but the god digs out holes before them to prevent their finding it. When they appear in Amentît, lo! that which happened to them on earth happens to them again in Amentît. For having received their soul in Amentît, they find, if it please thee, my father Satmi, that he who does good on earth, good is done to him in Amentît, but he who does evil, evil is done to him. They have been established for ever, and these things that thou seest in the Hades of Memphis will never change, and they are produced in the forty-two nomes where are the gods of the council of Osiris.[89]

When Senosiris had finished these words that he spake before Satmi his father, he went up to the mountain of Memphis, holding his father embraced, and his hand in his hand. Satmi asked him, saying, "My son Senosiris, is the place where one descends different to that by which we came up?" Senosiris did not reply to Satmi any word in the world, and Satmi marvelled at the discourse he had made, saying, "He will be capable of becoming one of the actual manes and a servant of the god, and I shall go to Hades with him saying 'This is my son.'[90] Satmi repeated a

89. The jury of the Inferno, before whom the dead are tried, were composed of as many members as there were nomes in Upper and Lower Egypt. Each of them was competent for a special sin, and judged the dead on that sin.

90. In other words, Senosiris, when he died, would be registered among the elect, and his father would be admitted to Paradise by the virtues of the son.

formula of the book to exorcise the manes, and he remained in the greatest amazement in the world because of the things he had seen in Amentît, but they weighed greatly on his heart, because he could not reveal
them to any man in the world. When the little boy Senosiris was twelve
years old, there was no scribe or magician in Memphis who equalled him
in reading books of magic.

After that it happened one day that Pharaoh Usimares was seated in the
court of audience of the palace of Pharaoh at Memphis, while the assembly of the princes, the military chieftains of the chief ones of Egypt, were
standing before him, each one according to his rank at court, one came to
say to his Majesty, "This is the speech made by a plague of Ethiopia;[91] to
wit, that he brings a sealed letter on him." As soon as this had been told
to Pharaoh, they brought the man into the court. He saluted, saying,
"Who is there here who can read the letter I bring for Egypt to Pharaoh
without breaking the seal, by reading the writing that is in it without
opening it? If it chances that there is no good scribe, nor learned man in
Egypt who can read it without opening it, I shall report the inferiority of
Egypt to my country, the land of the Negroes." When Pharaoh and his
princes heard these words they no longer knew the part of the world
where they were, and they said "By the life of Ptah, the great god, is it in
the power of a good scribe or a magician, skilled in reading the writings
of which he sees the tenor, to read a letter without opening it?" Pharaoh
said, "Let Satmi-Khamoîs, my son, be called." They hastened, he was
brought immediately; he bowed himself to the earth, he adored Pharaoh,
then he raised himself and stood up, blessing and acclaiming Pharaoh.
Pharaoh said to him, "My son Satmi, hast thou heard the words that this
plague, the Ethiopian, has spoken before me, saying, 'Is there a good scribe
or a learned man in Egypt who can read the letter which is in my hand
without breaking the seal, and who knows that which is written in it without opening it?'" The instant that Satmi heard these words, he no longer
knew the part of the world in which he was, he said, "My great lord, who
is there who would be capable of reading a letter without opening it? Now,
however, let me be given ten days' respite, to let me see what I can do to
prevent the inferiority of Egypt being reported in the country of the

91. The term applied by the author to the Ethiopians, and more especially to the magician
Horus, son of Tnahsît, *atu, iatu,* lit. *the scourge, the plague,* is the same that the *Sallier Papyrus
No.* 1 bestows on the Hyksôs of Asiatic origin (cf. p. 224, note 11), and which was rendered in
Greek by Manetho and his contemporaries by the epithet we translate *impure.*

Negroes, those eaters of gum."⁹² Pharaoh said, "They are granted to my son Satmi." A lodgment to which he could retire was assigned to the Ethiopian, they prepared for him various filth after the fashion of Ethiopia,⁹³ then Pharaoh rose up in the court, his heart extremely sad, and lay down without eating or drinking.

Satmi returned to his apartments still without knowing the part of the world in which he was. He wrapped himself in his garments from head to foot, and he lay down still without knowing the part of the world in which he was. They informed Mahîtuaskhît, his wife; she came to the place where Satmi was, she passed her hand below his garments. She said to him, "My brother Satmi, no fever of the body, suppleness of the limbs: ailment, sadness of heart."⁹⁴ He said to her, "Leave me, my sister Mahîtuaskhît! The matter about which my heart is troubled is not a matter that it would be well to disclose to a woman." The little boy Senosiris then entered, he bent over Satmi his father, and said to him, "My father Satmi, wherefore art thou lying down, thy heart troubled? The matters that thou hast within thy heart, tell them to me, that I may drive them from thee." He replied, "Leave me, my child Senosiris! The matters which are in my heart, thou art not of age to concern thyself with them." Senosiris said, "Tell them me, that I may calm thy heart with regard to them." Satmi said to him, "My son Senosiris, it is a plague of Ethiopia, who is come to Egypt, bringing on his body a sealed letter, and saying, 'Is there one here who will read it without opening it? If it chances that there is neither good scribe nor sage in Egypt capable of reading it, I shall report the inferiority of Egypt to the land of the Negroes, my country.' I laid me down, my heart troubled concerning this, my son Senosiris." When Senosiris heard these words, he laughed long. Satmi said to him, ""Why dost thou laugh?" He said, "I laugh to see thee thus laid down, thy heart troubled, for so

92. This is an insult intended for the negroes, that the poverty of their country forced them to obtain food by collecting gums of various kinds from their forest trees. Some further examples of this will be found in another writing of the same period, *the High Emprise for the Throne* (cf. p. 186, note 11).

93. The *filth after the fashion of Ethiopia* merely means food as usually prepared by the Ethiopians. The hatred that the Egyptians of Lower Egypt professed for the inhabitants of the Kingdom of Napata was felt not only for the people, but for all that they used, even for their food.

94. The wife of Satmi having tested and examined him after the manner of the doctors, sums up the result of her observations in the form of a short diagnosis also copied from medical diagnoses. It is not his body that is ill, but his spirit; sorrow is the malady he is suffering from.

small a matter. Rise, my father Satmi, for I will read the letter that has been brought to Egypt, without opening it, and also I will find what is written in it without breaking the seal." When Satmi heard these words, he rose up suddenly and said, "What is the guarantee for the words that thou hast spoken, my child Senosiris?" He said to him, "My father Satmi, go to the chambers on the ground floor of thy dwelling, and every book that thou shalt draw from its vase,[95] I will tell thee what book it is, I will read it without seeing it, standing before thee in the chambers of the ground floor." Satmi arose, he stood upright, and all that Senosiris had said, Senosiris did it to the full; Senosiris read all the books that Satmi his father took before him without opening them. Satmi went up from the chambers of the ground floor more joyful than anybody in the world; he did not delay to go to the place where Pharaoh was, he related before him all the things that the child Senosiris had said to him in their entirety, and the heart of Pharaoh rejoiced thereat extremely. Pharaoh arose to make festival in his time with Satmi, and he caused Senosiris to be brought to the feast before him; they drank, they passed a happy day. When the next morning arrived, Pharaoh went out into the court of audience in the midst of his nobles; Pharaoh sent to fetch the plague of Ethiopia, and he was fetched into the court with the sealed letter on his body; he stood upright in the midst of the court. The child Senosiris also came into the middle; he stood by the side of the plague, the Ethiopian, he spake against him, saying: "Malediction, Ethiopian, foe against whom Amon, thy god, is pro-voked.[96] Thou it is who art come up to Egypt, the pleasant fruit-garden of Osiris, the seat of Râ-Harmakhis, the beautiful horizon of the Agatho-demon,[97] saying, 'I shall report the inferiority of Egypt to the land of the Negroes;' the enmity of Amon, thy god, fall upon thee! The words that I shall make pass before thee and which are written on this letter, say noth-

95. The books were enclosed in pottery or stone vases; we have the mention of rolls thus protected in a catalogue of judicial writings (Brugsch, *Hieratischer Papyrus zu Wien,* in *Zeitschrift,* 1876, pp. 2, 3).

96. The author of the story is not mistaken in regarding Amon as the protecting divinity of the plague of Ethiopia. The kingdom of Napata, to which had succeeded the kingdom of Meroë, that which is here called the country of the Negroes, was founded by a member of the family of the high priest of the Theban Amon, and it had Amon as its principal god. It seems that the people of the Delta and of Middle Egypt had not forgiven the Ethiopians for the division of the ancient Theban empire into two independent states. The little that is known of their writings shows real hostility against the Ethiopians and their god Amon.

97. *Shaî is* the name of the great serpent that represented the Agatho-demon, the protect-ing deity of Egypt, chiefly called Knûphis or Kneph after the beginning of the Roman period.

ing that is false of them before Pharaoh, thy sovereign!" As soon as the plague of Ethiopia saw the little boy Senosiris standing in the court, he touched the earth with his head, and he spake, saying, "All the words that thou shalt speak, I will say nothing of them that is false."

Beginning of the tales told by Senosiris, speaking them in the middle of the court before Pharaoh and before his nobles, the people of Egypt listening to his voice, while he read the writing on the letter of the plague of Ethiopia, who stood upright in the middle of the court, to wit:

"It happened one day in the time of Pharaoh Manakhphrê Siamânu,[98] —he was a beneficent king of the Entire Land, Egypt abounded in all good things in his time, and his gifts and his works were many in the great temples of Egypt,—it happened one day that while the king of the land of the Negroes was taking his siesta in the pleasure-kiosk of Amon, he heard the voice of three plagues of Ethiopia who talked in the house behind him. One of them spake aloud, saying among other things, 'If it pleased Amon to protect me from harm, so that the king of Egypt could not injure me, I would cast my spells over Egypt so that I would cause the people of Egypt to pass three days and three nights without seeing the light after the darkness.' The second said among other things, 'If it pleased Amon to protect me from harm, so that the king of Egypt could not injure me, I would cast my spells over Egypt so that I should cause the Pharaoh of Egypt to be transported to the land of the Negroes, then give him a beating with the kurbash, five hundred strokes in public before the king, and finally to bring him back to Egypt within six hours of time, no more.' The third said among other things,[99] 'If it pleased Amon to protect me from harm, so that the king of Egypt could not injure me, I would cast my spells over Egypt so that I should prevent the fields from producing during three years.' "When the king of Ethiopia heard the words and the voice of the three plagues of Ethiopia he had them brought before him, and he said to them, 'Which of you has said, "I will cast my spells over Egypt and I will not allow the Egyptians to see the light for three days and three nights"?' They said, 'It is Horus, the son of Trirît.'[100] He said, 'Which of you has said, "I

---

98. For this Pharaoh, whose prenomen recalls that of Thûtmôsis III and is almost identical with that of a Thûtmôsis and a Psammetichus of fiction, discovered at Karnak and Asfûn in 1905 (Maspero, *Ruines et Paysages d'égypte*, pp. 225–233). Cf. *Introduction*, p. cxvii, of this volume.

99. The speech of the third sorcerer has been omitted by the scribe, but it occurs later, and from that passage I have been able to reconstruct it.

100. *Trirît, Trêret*, signifies the *sow* or *female hippopotamus*.

will cast my spells over Egypt, I will bring Pharaoh to the land of the Negroes, and I will have a beating administered to him with the kurbash, five hundred blows in public before the king, then I will cause him to be taken back to Egypt in six hours of time, no more"?' They said, 'It is Horus, the son of Tnahsît.'[101] He said, 'Which of you has said, "I will cast my spells over Egypt and I will prevent the fields producing during three years"?' They said, 'It is Horus, the son of Triphît.'[102] The King said to Horus, the son of Tnahsît, 'Execute thy magic deed by thy book of magic, and as Amon lives, the bull of Meroë, my god, if thy hand accomplishes that which is pleasing, I will do thee good in abundance.'

"Horus, the son of Tnahsît, fashioned a litter for four bearers, of wax, he recited a magic writing over them, he breathed on them violently, he gave them life, he commanded them saying, 'You shall go up to Egypt, you shall bring the Pharaoh of Egypt to the place where the king is; a beating of the kurbash shall be given him, five hundred blows in public before the king, then you shall take him back to Egypt, the whole in six hours of time, no more.' They said, 'Truly, we will omit nothing.' The sorceries of the Ethiopian therefore went into Egypt, they made themselves mistresses of the night,[103] they made themselves mistresses of Pharaoh Manakhphrê Siamânu, they carried him to the land of the Negroes where the king was, they administered a beating to him with the kurbash, five hundred blows in public before the king, then they carried him back to Egypt, the whole in six hours of time, no more."

Thus Senosiris told these tales, relating them in the middle of the court before Pharaoh and before his nobles, and the people of Egypt listened to his voice while he said, "The enmity of Amon, thy god, fall upon thee! The words that I have made to pass before thee, are they indeed those that are written in the letter that thou hast in thy hand?" The plague of the Ethiopians said, "Continue to read, for all the words are true words, so many as they are."

Senosiris said before Pharaoh: "Then after these things had come to pass, Pharaoh Siamânu was brought back to Egypt, his loins exceeding bruised with blows, and he lay down in the chapel of the city of

---

101. *Tnahsît, Tnehset,* signifies *the negress.*

102. *Triphît* signifies *the girl, the young woman,* and is one of the surnames of Isis, transcribed. *Triphis* in Greek.

103. The night is peopled with beings, some evil, others good, which latter protect sleeping men and women. The magic personages sent by Horus the Ethiopian, by making themselves *masters of the night,* prevent the good genii opposing the execution of their malicious schemes.

Horus,[104] his loins exceedingly bruised with blows. When the next morning arrived, Pharaoh said to his courtiers, 'What has happened in Egypt, that I should be made to leave it?' Ashamed of their thoughts, the courtiers said to themselves, 'Perhaps the mind of Pharaoh is darkened.'[105] Then they said, 'Thou art whole, thou art whole, Pharaoh, our great lord, and Isis the great goddess will calm thy afflictions; but what is the meaning of the words that thou has spoken to us, Pharaoh, our great lord? Since thou dost sleep in the chapel of the city of Horus, the gods protect thee.' Pharaoh arose, he showed the courtiers his back exceeding bruised with blows, saying, 'By the life of Ptah, the great god, I was carried to the country of the Negroes during the night; a beating was administered to me with the kurbash, five hundred blows in public before the king, then I was brought back to Egypt, the whole in six hours of time, no more.' When they saw the loins of Pharaoh greatly bruised with blows, they opened their mouths for great cries. Now Manakhphrê Siamânu had a master of the mystery of the books, his name Horus, the son of Panishi, who was extremely learned. When he came to the place where the king was, he uttered a loud cry, saying, 'My lord, those are the sorceries of the Ethiopians. By the life of thy house, I will cause them to come to thy house of torture and execution.' Pharaoh said to him, 'Do it quickly, that I may not be carried to the country of the Negroes another night.'

"The master of the mystery, Horus, son of Panishi, went at once; he took his books with his amulets to the place where Pharaoh was, he read a formula to him, he bound an amulet on him to prevent the sorceries of the Ethiopians taking possession of him; he then went out from before Pharaoh, he took his bowls of perfumes and libation vases, he embarked on a boat, and he went without delay to Khmunu.[106] He entered the temple of Khmunu, he offered incense and water before Thoth, nine times

---

104. *The city* or *the castle of Horus is* the royal palace in the official phraseology of Egypt, and the *chapel* of this *city* is the sleeping chamber of Horus, *i.e.* of Pharaoh.

105. The courtiers, who as yet knew nothing of the events of the night, are disconcerted by the King's question, and imagine that he is drunk to the point of losing his reason, or that he has been smitten with sudden madness. In any case they are ashamed of their thought, and before expressing it aloud, they ask the sovereign for an explanation of the words he has just uttered.

106. Khmunu is the Ashmuneîn of the Arabs, the Hermopolis of the Greeks, the city of Thoth, Hermes Trismegistus, the god who is lord of magic and incantations. It is natural that the magician Horus should go there to consult his patron deity.

great,[107] Lord of Hermopolis, the great god, and he prayed before him, saying 'Turn thy face to me, my lord Thoth, so that the Ethiopians may not report the inferiority of Egypt to the land of the Negroes. It is thou who didst create magic by spells, thou who didst suspend the heavens, establish the earth and Hades, and placed the gods with the stars; let me know the way to save Pharaoh from the sorceries of the Ethiopians.' Horus, the son of Panishi, slept in the temple and he dreamed a dream that same night. The figure of the great god Thoth spake with him, saying, "Art thou not Horus, son of Panishi, the master of the mystery of Pharaoh Manakhphrê Siamânu? Then on the morrow, in the morning, go into the hall of the books of the temple of Khmunu; thou wilt there discover a naos, closed and sealed, thou shalt open it, and thou shalt find there a box containing a book, one that I wrote with my own hand. Take it out, take a copy of it, then put it back in its place, for it is the same book of magic that protects me against the wicked, and it is that which shall protect Pharaoh, it is that which shall save him from the sorceries of the Ethiopians.'

"When therefore Horus, the son of Panishi, awoke from his dream after having seen these things, he found that which had chanced to him had chanced to him by a divine act, and he acted in everything as it had been said to him in his dream.[108] He did not delay to go to the place where Pharaoh was, and he made him a charm written against sorcery. When it was the second day, the sorceries of Horus, son of Tnahsît, returned to Egypt during the night to the place where Pharaoh was, then they went back to the place where the king was in the same hour, for they could not overmaster Pharaoh, because of the charms and sorceries that the master of the mystery, Horus, the son of Panishi, had bound upon him. The next morning Pharaoh told the master of the mystery, Horus, the son of Panishi, all that he had seen during the night, and how the sorceries of the Ethiopians had gone away without being able to master him. Horus, the son of Panishi, caused a quantity of pure wax to be brought, he made of it a litter with four bearers, he recited a written formula over them, he breathed violently on them, he caused them to live, he commanded them, saying, 'You shall go to the country of the Negroes this

107. Thoth is called *the twice great*, which is like the comparative, and *the thrice great*, which is the superlative *megistos;* the epithet *Trismegistus,* which is given him especially at the Græco-Roman period, is therefore the superlative of a superlative, and properly speaking, signifies *the three times three the greatest,* the equivalent of the *nine times great* of the text.

108. See at beginning of this story, pp. 120, 121, another example of incubation and a prophetic dream.

night, you shall bring the king to Egypt to the place where Pharaoh is: a beating with a kurbash shall be given him, five hundred blows, in public, before Pharaoh, then you shall take him back to the land of the Negroes, all in six hours of time, no more.' They said, 'Verily we will omit nothing.' The sorceries of Horus, the son of Panishi, sped away on the clouds of heaven, they did not delay to go to the land of the Negroes during the night. They seized the king, they brought him to Egypt; a beating with the kurbash was given him, five hundred blows in public before the king, they then carried him back to the land of the Negroes, the whole in six hours of time, no more."

These tales then were told by Senosiris, relating them in the middle of the court, before Pharaoh and before his nobles, the people of Egypt listening to his voice, while he said "The enmity of Amon, thy god, fall on thee, wicked Ethiopian! The words that I speak are they those that are written in thy letter?" The Ethiopian said, his head bent to the ground, "Continue to read, for all the words thou sayest are those that are written in this letter."

Senosiris said: "Then after these things had happened, that the king of the land of the Negroes had been taken back in six hours, no more, and had been set down in his place, he lay down, and he rose next morning exceedingly bruised by the blows that had been given him in Egypt. He said to his courtiers, 'That which my sorceries did to Pharaoh, the sorceries of Pharaoh have done to me in my turn. They carried me into Egypt during the night[109]: a beating with the kurbash was given me, five hundred blows, before Pharaoh of Egypt, and they then brought me back into the country of the Negroes.' He turned his back to the courtiers, and they opened their mouths for great cries. The King caused Horus, son of Tnahsît, to be fetched, and said, 'Beware for thyself of Amon, the bull of Meroë, my god! As it is thou who didst go to the people of Egypt, let us see how thou canst save me from the sorceries of Horus, son of Panishi.' He made some sorceries, he bound them on the king, to save him from the sorceries of Horus, son of Panishi. When it was the night of the second day the sorceries of Horus, son of Panishi, transported themselves to the country of the Negroes, and carried off the king to Egypt. A beating was given him with a kurbash, five hundred blows in public before Pharaoh, then they carried him back to the country of the Negroes, the whole in six hours of time, no more. This treatment happened to the king

109. The whole of this passage is almost completely destroyed. I have reconstructed it according to the parallel development that occurs earlier, p. 129.

for three days, while the sorceries of the Ethiopians were not able to save the king from the hand of Horus, son of Panishi, and the king was extremely afflicted, and he caused Horus, son of Tnahsît, to be brought, and said to him, 'Sorrow to thee, enemy of Ethiopia, after having humiliated me by the hand of the Egyptians, thou hast not been able to save me from their hands! By the life of Amon, the bull of Meroë, my god, if it happens that thou knowest not how to save me from the magic barks of the Egyptians, I will deliver thee to an evil death, and it shall be slow for thee.' He said, 'My lord the king, let me be sent to Egypt that I may see that one of the Egyptians who makes the enchantments, that I may work magic against him, and inflict on him the punishment I meditate against his hands.' Horus, the son of Tnahsît, was sent therefore, on behalf of the king, and he went first to the place where his mother Tnahsît was. She said to him, 'What is thy purpose, my son Horus?' He said to her, 'The sorceries of Horus, son of Panishi, have overmastered my sorceries. Three times they have transported the king to Egypt, to the place where Pharaoh is, a beating has been given him with the kurbash, five hundred blows in public before Pharaoh, then they have brought him back to the country of the Negroes, the whole in six hours of time, no more, and my sorceries have not been able to save him from their hands. And now the King is exceedingly angry with me, and to avoid his delivering me to a slow and evil death, I wish to go to Egypt to see him who makes these sorceries and to inflict on him the punishment that I meditate against his hands.' She said, "Be wise, oh my son Horus, and do not go to the place where Horus, son of Panishi, is.[110] If thou goest to Egypt to conjure there, beware of the men of Egypt, for thou canst not strive with them, nor conquer them, so that thou wilt not return to the country of the Negroes, ever.' He said to her, 'This is nothing to me, that which thou sayest; I cannot but go to Egypt, to cast my spells there.' Tnahsît, his mother, said to him, 'If then thou must go to Egypt, arrange some signs between thee and me; if it chances that thou art vanquished, I will come to thee to see if I can save thee.' He said to her, 'If I am vanquished, when thou drinkest or when thou eatest, the water will become the colour of blood before thee, the provisions will become the colour of blood before thee, the sky will become the colour of blood before thee."[111]

110. The scribe has omitted the sorcerer's speech and the beginning of the mother's reply owing to dittography, as Griffith has observed (*Stories of the High Priests of Memphis*, p. 193, note). I have filled in this lacuna with sentences borrowed from preceding passages.

111. See above (pp. 8–9), the intersigns arranged between Anupu and Baîti.

"When Horus, son of Tnahsît, had arranged these signs between him and his mother, he made his way to Egypt; having eaten his sorceries[112] he journeyed from that which Amon made[113] as far as Memphis and to the place where Pharaoh was, tracking out[114] who made magic of written spells in Egypt. When he arrived in the court of audience before Pharaoh, he spoke with a loud voice, saying 'Hullo! who is he who will perform sorceries against me in the court of audience, in the place where Pharaoh abides, in the sight of the people of Egypt? The two scribes of the House of Life, or only the scribe, of the House of Life who has enchanted the king, bringing him to Egypt notwithstanding me?' After that he had spoken on this wise, Horus, the son of Panishi, who was standing in the court of audience before Pharaoh, said 'Hullo! Ethiopian foe, art thou not Horus, son of Tnahsît? Art thou not he who in order to charm me in the orchards of Râ, having with thee thy Ethiopian companion, didst plunge with him into the water, and didst let thyself float with him below the mountain, to the east of Heliopolis?[115] Is it not thou who hast been pleased to cause Pharaoh, thy master, to travel, and who hast bruised him with blows at the place where the king of Ethiopia was, and who dost now come to Egypt, saying, "Is there not some one here to make sorceries against me?" By the life of Atumu, the master of Heliopolis, the gods of Egypt have brought thee here to repay thee in their country. Take courage, for I come to thee!' When Horus, son of Panishi, said these words, Horus, the son of Tnahsît, answered him, saying, 'Art thou not he to whom I taught the saying of the jackal[116] who makes enchantment against me?' The Ethiopian plague performed a deed of magic by

112. Horus, the son of Tnahsît, *eats his magic*, as in the first story of Satni-Khamoîs, Satni *drank* the book of Thoth (p. 106). Here it is not to assimilate it, but to conceal it from all eyes, and to prevent its being stolen from him on the road.

113. Ethiopia, which, as we have seen (cf. p. 127, note 96), is considered in the romance as being the creation and the domain of Amon, in apposition to Memphis and Egypt of the North, which belongs to Ptah.

114. This is literally *smelling*. He discovered by the scent, the smell peculiar to sorcerers, all such who were among those he met by the way and who might either stop him, or give notice of his presence before the time.

115. There is an allusion here to another romance of which the two Horus were the heroes, and which must have been sufficiently well known at this time for the readers of this story to know to what it refers. The *water* is evidently the *Nile of the North*, the stream that rises near Gebel-Ahmar, at Aîn-Musa, and was supposed to be the source of those branches of the Nile that water the provinces on the east of the Delta.

116. Is this an allusion to the propositions of the jackal mentioned in one of the Leyden demotic papyri?

his book of magic; he caused a flame to burst forth in the court of audi-ence, and Pharaoh, as well as the great ones of Egypt, uttered a great cry, saying, 'Hasten to us, chief of the writings, Horus, son of Panishi!' Horus, the son of Panishi, did a formula of magic; he produced from the sky a rain of the south[117] above the flame, and it was extinguished in a moment. The Ethiopian performed another deed of magic by his book of magic; he caused an immense cloud to appear over the court of audience, so that no one perceived any longer his brother or his companion. Horus, the son of Panishi, recited a writing to the sky which dispersed it, so that it stilled the evil wind that breathed in it. Horus, the son of Tnahsît, performed another deed of magic by his book of magic; he caused an enormous roof of stone, two hundred cubits long and fifty wide, to appear above Pharaoh and his princes, and that in order to separate Egypt from its king, the land from its sovereign. Pharaoh looked up, he perceived the roof of stone above him, he opened his mouth with a great cry, he and the people who were in the court of audience. Horus, the son of Panishi, recited a written formula, he caused a papyrus barge to appear, he caused the stone roof to be placed on it, and the barge went away with it to the immense haven,[118] the great lake of Egypt.

"The Ethiopian plague knew that he was incapable of combating the sorcerer of Egypt; he performed a deed of magic by written spells, so that no one saw him any more in the court of audience, and that with the intention of going to the land of the Negroes, his country. But Horus, the son of Panishi, recited a writing over him, he unveiled the enchantments of the Ethiopian, he caused Pharaoh to see him, as well as the people of Egypt who were in the court of audience, so that he appeared as a wretched gosling ready to start. Horus, the son of Panishi, recited a writing over him, he turned him over on his back with a fowler standing over him, a pointed knife in his hand, on the point of doing him an evil turn. "While all this was being done the signs which Horus, the son of Tnah-sît, had arranged between him and his mother[119] occurred all of them

117. It is from the south, more exactly the south-west, that the torrential rains usually come by which Cairo is occasionally deluged; the expression *rain of the south is* therefore here the equivalent of *storm* or *waterspout.* On the other hand the word *southern* is often employed with an aggravative shade of meaning, as in the expression *cheetah of the south,* which we have already met with several times (pp. 5, 6, note 16).

118. The *Immense Haven, Sh-oêri,* is one of the names borne by Lake Mœris; the boat that carries the stone roof is probably the same that is seen on the *Fûm Papyrus,* bearing the sun god over the waters of Lake Mœris.

119. See above, p. 133, the enumeration of these signs.

before her; she did not delay to go up to Egypt in the form of a goose, and she stopped above the palace of Pharaoh; she called with all her voice to her son, who had the form of a wretched bird menaced by the fowler. Horus, son of Panishi, looked up to the sky; he saw Tnahsît under the form in which she was, and he recognised that she was Tnahsît, the Ethiopian; he recited a writing against her, he turned her over on her back with a fowler standing over her with a knife ready to deal death. She cast off the form in which she was, she assumed the form of an Ethiopian woman, and she prayed him, saying, 'Do not come against us, Horus, son of Panishi, but forgive us this criminal deed! If thou wilt but give us a boat, we will never come back to Egypt again.' Horus, the son of Panishi, swore by Pharaoh, as well as by the gods of Egypt, to wit, 'I will not stay my work of magic by written spells if you will not swear to me never to return to Egypt under any pretext.' Tnahsît raised her hand as witness that she would not come to Egypt for ever and ever. Horus, the son of Tnahsît, swore, saying, 'I will not come back to Egypt for fifteen hundred years.' Horus, the son of Panishi, reversed his deed of magic, he gave a boat to Horus, son of Tnahsît, as well as to Tnahsît, his mother, and they departed to the land of the Negroes, their country."

This discourse Senosiris uttered before Pharaoh while the people listened to his voice, and Satmi, his father, beheld all, the Ethiopian plague being prostrated with his forehead to the ground; then he said, "By the life of thy countenance, my great lord, the man here before thee is Horus, the son of Tnahsît, the same whose doings I recount, who has not repented of that he did before, but who has come back to Egypt after fifteen hundred years to cast his enchantments over it. By the life of Osiris, the great god, lord of the Amentît, before whom I go to rest, I am Horus, son of Panishi, I who stand here before Pharaoh. When I learnt in Amentît that this Ethiopian enemy was going to hurl sacrilege against Egypt, as there was no longer a good scribe or a sage in Egypt who could contend with him, I implored Osiris in Amentît to allow me to appear again on earth to prevent his reporting the inferiority of Egypt to the land of the Negroes. Command was given on the part of Osiris to return me to earth, I came back as a seed until I met with Satmi, the son of Pharaoh, on the mountain of Heliopolis or Memphis. I grew in that plant of colocasia in order to enter a body and be born again on earth to make enchantments against that Ethiopian enemy who is there in the court of audience." Horus, son of Panishi, performed a deed of magic by written spells in the form of Senosiris against the plague of Ethiopia; he surrounded him with a fire, which consumed him in the midst of the court, in the sight of Pharaoh, as well as of his nobles and the people of Egypt, then Senosiris vanished as a shadow from before Pharaoh and his father Satmi, so that they saw him no more.

Pharaoh marvelled more than anything in the world, as well as his nobles, at the things that he had seen in the court of audience, saying, "There has never been a good scribe, nor a sage, equal to Horus, son of Panishi, and there will never again be another of his like after him." Satmi opened his mouth with a great cry, because that Senosiris had vanished like a shadow, and he saw him no longer. Pharaoh rose from the court of audience, his heart very afflicted with that which he had seen; Pharaoh commanded that preparations should be made in the presence of Satmi to entertain him well on account of his son Senosiris and to comfort his heart. When the evening came Satmi went to his lodging, his heart greatly troubled, and his wife Mahîtuaskhît lay down by his side, she conceived of him that same night, she did not delay to bring into the world a man child, who was named Usimanthor. Nevertheless, it happened that Satmi never omitted to make offerings and libations before the genius of Horus, son of Panishi, at all times. Here is the end of this book written by. . . .

III

๛ How Satni-Khamoîs Triumphed over the Assyrians [9] ๛

FOR a long time the romantic character of the narrative told us by Herodotus in the second book, chapter cxli, of his history has been recognised. It is the story of Sethon, priest of Vulcan, who triumphed over the Assyrians and their king Sennacherib. One would gladly agree that it is an Egyptian version of the facts recorded in the Bible in *The Second Book of Kings* (xix, 35, 36), but we do not know who the Sethon was to whom popular imagination ascribed this miracle. King Zet, whom Africanus adds to the lists of Manetho at the end of the XXIIIrd dynasty, is perhaps only a slightly altered double of the Sethon of Herodotus, and up to the present the monuments of the Assyrian or Ethiopian epochs have given us the name of no sovereign that corresponds exactly with the Greek name.

Krall was the first to connect Sethon with Satni, son of Ramses II, who is the hero of the two preceding stories (*Ein neuer historischer Roman,* in the *Mitteilungen aus den Sammlungen der Papyrus des Erzherzogs Rainer,* vol. vi, p. 1, note 3), but he only suggested it without insisting on it, and his opinion found little acceptance among Egyptologists. It was taken up and developed at full length by Griffith, in the preface of his edition of the two tales (*Stories of the High Priests of Memphis,* pp. 1–12), and after having weighed the question carefully, it appears to me difficult not to admit, at any rate, that he is probably right. If so, Herodotus has preserved to us the principal theme of one of the stories relating to Satni-Khamoîs, the most ancient of those that have come down to us. Satni had here no occasion to exercise the supernatural powers with which later tradition endowed him in superabundance. It is his piety that assures him the victory, and the story does not belong to a cycle of magic. It is one of a collection of tales intended to justify the opposition felt by the sacerdotal class against the military class after the downfall of the Ramessides, and to show the superiority of theocratic government over other governments. The feudal aristocracy might well refuse its aid to a priest-king; the protection of the god would be sufficient to assure victory to a chance levy of devout middle-class people or artisans over a professional army, and it was that alone that delivered Egypt from invasion.

After Anysis reigned the priest of Hephæstos named Sethon. This monarch despised and neglected the Egyptian warriors, thinking he did not need their services. Among other indignities which he offered them, he took away their fiefs composed of twelve arures of land that previous kings had granted to each of them.

Now, after a time, Sanacharibus, king of the Arabs and of the Assyrians, led a great army against Egypt; but when the Egyptian men-at-arms refused to march, the priest, rendered powerless, entered the temple and lamented himself before the statue at the thought of the misfortunes that menaced him. While he thus lamented he was overtaken by sleep; it seemed to him that the god appeared to him, exhorting him to take courage, and assuring him that nothing untoward should happen to him during his campaign against the Arab army, for that he himself would send him help.[120]

120. See above, pp. 120, 121 and 131, 132, examples of incubation and prophetic dreams.

Placing his confidence in this dream, he assembled such of the Egyptians as consented to follow him, and he went to camp at Pelusium, for that is where Egypt is entered. None of the men-at-arms followed him, but only merchants, artisans, and market people. When, however, the foe presented themselves to besiege the town the field mice during the night flocked to their camp, and gnawed all their quivers, their bows, and also the thongs of their bucklers, so that the next day they had to fly disarmed, and many of them perished.

And now the stone figure of this king is standing in the temple of Hephæstos. He is holding a mouse in his hand, and the inscription on it says, "Whosoever looks at me, let him reverence the god."

THE CYCLE OF RAMSES II
I

The Daughter of the Prince of Bakhtan and the Possessing Spirit [10]

THE monument on which this strange narrative is preserved is a stela discovered by Champollion in the temple of Khonsu at Thebes, removed in 1846 by Prisse d'Avenne and given by him to the Bibliothèque Nationale of Paris. It has been published by:

Prisse d'Avenne, *Choix de monuments égyptiens,* folio, Paris, 1847, pl. xxiv and p. 5.

Champollion, *Monuments de l'égypte et de la Nubie,* 4to, Paris, 1846–1874. Text, vol. ii, pp. 280–290.

Champollion studied this inscription and several sentences of it are quoted in his works. It was translated and reproduced elaborately on a separate sheet of paper, composed at the Imperial Printing Press for the Universal Exhibition of 1855, under the superintendence of Emmanuel de Rougé. Two translations appeared almost simultaneously:

Birch, *Notes upon an Egyptian Inscription in the Bibliothèque Impériale of Paris* (from *The Transactions of the Royal Society of Literature, New Series,* vol. iv), London, 8vo, 46 pp.

E. de Rougé, *étude sur une stèle égyptienne appartenant à la Bibliothèque Impériale* (extrait du *Journal Asiatique,* cahiers d'Août 1856, Août 1857, Juin et Août-Septembre 1858), Paris, 8vo, 222 pp., and the plate composed for the Exhibition of 1855.

Later work at first did not add much to the results obtained by E. de Rougé. They were accepted entirely by:

H. Brugsch, *Histoire d'égypte,* 4to, Leipzig, 1859, pp. 206–210.

H. Brugsch, *Geschichte Ægyptens,* 8vo, Leipzig, Hinrichs, 1877, pp. 627–641.

The narrative has throughout the appearance of an official document. It begins with a royal protocol of the name of a sovereign who has the same name and prenomen as Ramses II—Sesostris. Dates then follow, arranged at intervals throughout the text; the details of the Pharaonic cult and ceremonial are set forth with scrupulous care, and the whole presents such a character of reality that for a long time the inscription was regarded as being an historic document. The Ramses named in it was placed in the XXth dynasty, the twelfth in order, and the map was diligently searched to find the country of Bakhtan that had provided Egypt with a queen. Erman recognised with much insight that this was an actual forgery, perpetrated by the priests of Khonsu, with the intention of enhancing the glory of the god, and ensuring the possession of certain material advantages for the temple (A. Erman, *Die Bentreschstele*, in the *Zeitschrift für Ægyptische Sprache*, 1883, pp. 54–60).

He has shown that the forgers intended to connect this story of the possession by a spirit with Ramses II, and he has rendered us the service of relieving us from an imaginary Pharaoh. He has brought the date of the redaction down to about the Ptolemaic times; I think it may be attributed to the middle period of the Ethiopian invasions. It was composed at the time when the office of High Priest of Amon had just fallen into abeyance, and when the priesthoods that remained must have tried by every means in their power to secure the immense influence that had been exercised by the vanished sacerdotal power.

Since then the text has been translated into English by Breasted, *Ancient Records of Egypt*, vol. iii, pp. 439–447; into German by A. Wiedemann, *Altägyptische Sagen und Märchen*, 8vo, Leipzig, 1906, pp. 86–93.

The narrative contains a theme frequently found in popular literature; a spirit having taken up its abode in the body of a princess, contends successfully with the exorcists charged to expel it, and will only leave it under certain conditions. The Egyptian redaction furnishes us with the simplest and most ancient form of the story. A different redaction adapted to Christian beliefs has been notified by O. de Leimm, *Die Geschichte von der Prinzessin Bentresch und die Geschichte von Kaiser Zeno und seinen zwei Töchtern*, in *Mélanges Asiatiques tirés du Bulletin de l'Académie des Sciences de Saint-Pétersbourg*, vol. ii, pp. 599–603, and in the *Bulletin*, vol. xxxii, pp. 473–476.

A modern Egyptologist has borrowed the idea of our text to make it the subject of a story: H. Brugsch-Bey, *Des Priesters Rache, eine historisch beglaubigte Erzählung aus der ägyptischen Geschichte des zwölften Jahrhunderts vor Chr.*, in the *Deutsche Revue*, vol. v, pp. 15–41.

Erman has observed an attempt at archaism, and somewhat serious mistakes of grammar in this document. One understands that the priests of Khonsu would attempt to imitate the language of the period to which they attributed the stela, and one understands also that they would not be able to maintain the ancient style with equal success throughout, and that at times they mistook what was incorrect for archaism. Their propositions are awkwardly constructed, the expression of their ideas is halting, their phraseology is curt and monotonous. Also they have credited a king of the XIXth dynasty with methods of government that essentially belonged to the sovereigns of the XXth. Ramses II, pious as he was, did not consider himself obliged to submit all affairs of state to the approval of the gods. It was the latest successors of Ramses III who introduced the custom of consulting the statue of Amon under all circumstances. With these exceptions it may be said that the interpretation of this text presents no other difficulties, and that with a little care we can translate it with considerable ease; like the *Tale of the Two Brothers,* it may advantageously be placed in the hands of beginners in Egyptology.

The stela is surmounted by a representation in which one of the scenes in the story is placed before our eyes. On the left the bark of Khonsu, the good counsellor, arrives carried on the shoulders of eight personages, and followed by two priests who are reading some prayers; the king standing before it is offering incense. On the right, the bark of Khonsu, who regulates the destinies in Thebes, is figured supported by four men only, as it is smaller than the other; the priest who is offering incense to it is Khonsuhânu-tirnabît, the prophet of Khonsu, who rules destinies in Thebes. It is probably the return of the second god to Thebes that is illustrated in this manner; Khonsu the first comes to receive Khonsu the second, and the priest and king render similar homage, each to his divinity.

꒰ꙟ꒱

Horus, mighty bull, crowned with diadems, and established as firmly in his royalties as the god Atumu; Horus triumphant over Nubîtî, mighty with the sword, destroyer of the barbarians, the king of both Egypts, Uasimarîya-Satapanrîya, son of the Sun, Rîyamasasu Maîamânu, beloved of Amonrâ lord of Karnak and of the cycle of the gods lords of Thebes; the good god, son of Amon, born of Maût, begotten by Harmakhis, the glorious child of the universal Lord, begotten by the god, husband of his own mother, king of Egypt, prince of the desert tribes, sovereign who rules the barbarians, when scarcely issued from his mother's womb he directed wars, and he commanded valour while still in the egg like a bull who thrusts before—for this king is a bull, a god who comes out on the day of fighting, like Montu, and who is very valiant like the son of

Nuît.[1] Now, when His Majesty was in Naharaina,[2] according to his rule of every year, the princes of every land came, bending beneath the weight of offerings that they brought to the souls of His Majesty,[3] and the fortresses brought their tribute, gold, silver, lapis lazuli, malachite[4] and all the scented woods of Arabia on their back, and marching in file one behind the other; behold the prince of Bakhtan caused his tribute to be brought, and put his eldest daughter at the head of the train, to salute His Majesty, and to ask life of him. Because she was a very beautiful woman, pleasing to His Majesty more than anything, behold, he gave her the title of Great Royal Spouse, Nafrurîya, and when he returned to Egypt, she accomplished all the rites of a royal spouse.[5]

And it happened in the year XV, the 22nd of the month Payni, that His Majesty was at Thebes the mighty, the queen of cities, engaged in doing that whereby he praised his father Amonrâ, lord of Karnak, at his fine festival of southern Thebes,[6] his favourite dwelling, where the god has been since the creation; behold, one came to say to His Majesty, "There is a messenger from the prince of Bakhtan, who comes with many gifts for the Royal Spouse." Brought before His Majesty with his gifts, he said, while saluting His Majesty, "Glory to thee, Sun of foreign nations, thou by whom we live," and when he had said his adoration before His Majesty, he began again to speak to His Majesty. "I come to thee, Sire my lord, on account of Bintrashît,[7] the youngest sister of the royal spouse, Nafrurîya, for a malady pervades her limbs. Let Thy Majesty send a sage to see her." Then the king said, "Bring me the scribes of the Double

1. The son of Nuît is the god Set-Typhon.

2. This is a different spelling of the name written Naharinna in the *Tale of the Doomed Prince,* p. 155, note 4. Naharinna is the country placed astride on the Euphrates between the Orontes and the Balikh.

3. As has been remarked already, p. 86, note 18, Pharaoh, son of the Sun, and the Sun himself, had several souls, *baû.* Conquered nations hoped to gain their favour by their gifts.

4. On the stone called *mafkaît* by the Egyptians, see p. 113, note 59.

5. The daughter of Kbattusîl II, prince of Khati, on her arrival in Egypt, also received the title of *Great Royal Spouse* and an Egyptian name, Maûrnafrurîya, of which that of our princess is probably only a familiar abbreviation.

6. Southern Thebes is the modern Luxor; it was therefore the patronal festival of the temple of Luxor that the king was celebrating when the arrival of the Syrian messenger was announced to him, and during which the statue of Amon and its bark were transported from Luxor to Karnak, and then taken back to Luxor, three weeks later.

7. The name of this princess seems to be compounded of the Semitic word *bint,* girl, daughter, and the Egyptian word *rashît,* joy. It signifies *daughter of joy.*

House of Life who are attached to the palace."[8] As soon as they had come, His Majesty said, "Behold, I have sent for you that you may hear this saying: Send me from among you one who is skilled in his heart, a scribe learned with his fingers." When the royal scribe, Thotemhabi, had come into the presence of His Majesty, His Majesty commanded him to repair to Bakhtan with the messenger. As soon as the sage had arrived at Bakhtan, he found Bintrashît in the state of one possessed, and he found the ghost that possessed her an enemy hard to fight.[9] The prince of Bakhtan therefore sent a second message to His Majesty, saying, "Sire my lord, let Thy Majesty command a god to be brought to fight the spirit."

When the messenger arrived in the presence of His Majesty, in year XXIII, the 1st of Pakhons, the day of the feast of Amon, while His Majesty was at Thebes, behold, His Majesty spake again, in the presence of Khonsu in Thebes, god of good counsel,[10] saying, "Excellent lord, I am again before thee on account of the daughter of the prince of Bakhtan." Then Khonsu in Thebes, god of good counsel, was transported to Khonsu who rules destinies, the great god who drives away foreigners, and His Majesty said, facing Khonsu in Thebes, god of good counsel, "Excellent lord, may it please thee to turn thy face to Khonsu who rules destinies, great god who drives away foreigners; he will be taken to Bakhtan." And the god nodded with his head greatly twice.[11] Then His Majesty said, "Give him thy virtue, that I may cause the majesty of this god to go to Bakhtan to deliver the

8. See p. 101, note 14, what is said of the *Scribes of the Double House of Life.*

9. E. de Rougé and most scholars who have studied this stela have thought that a demon was referred to. Krall has shown that the possessing spirit was the ghost of a dead person (*Tacitus und der Orient,* i, pp. 41–12).

10. In order to understand this passage, it must be remembered that according to Egyptian beliefs, each divine statue contained a double detached from the actual person of the god that it represented, and that the statue was a real incarnation of the god, differing from other incarnations of the same kind. Now Khonsu possessed, in his temple at Karnak, at least two statues, each of which was animated by an independent *double* whom the rites of consecration had made into a god. One of these represented Khonsu, unchangeable in his perfection, calm in his grandeur, and not mingling directly in the affairs of mankind; that was Khonsu Nafhotpu, whose translated name I have paraphrased *god of good counsel.* The other statue represented a more active Khonsu, who ruled the affairs of men, and drove foreigners, *i.e.* enemies, far from Egypt, *Khonsu pa iri sokhru m uasit, nutir âu, saharu shemaû.* The first Khonsu regarded as the most powerful, we know not for what reason, does not condescend to go to Bakhtan himself; he sends the second Khonsu, after having transmitted his powers to him (E. de Rougé, *étude sur une Stèle,* pp. 15–19). We shall meet later, in the *Voyage of Unamunu* (pp. 173, 180), an *Amon of the Road* who emanates from Amon of Karnak in the same way that the second Khonsu here proceeds from the first, and who accompanies the hero on his expedition to Syria.

11. The statues animated by a *double* expressed their wishes sometimes with the voice, sometimes by cadenced movements. We know that Queen Hatshopsuîtu *heard* the god Amon

daughter of the prince of Bakhtan." And Khonsu in Thebes, god of good counsel, nodded with his head greatly, twice, and he made the transmission of magic virtue to Khonsu who rules destinies in Thebes, four times.[12] His Majesty commanded that Khonsu who rules destinies in Thebes should be sent on a great bark escorted by five smaller boats, by chariots, and many horses marching on the right and on the left. When this god arrived at Bakhtan, in the space of a year and five months, behold the prince of Bakhtan came with his soldiers and his generals before Khonsu who rules destinies, and threw himself on his belly, saying, "Thou comest to us, thou dost join with us, according to the orders of the king of the two Egypts, Uasimarîya-Satapanrîya." Behold as soon as the god had gone to the place where Bintrashît was, and had made the magic passes for the daughter of the prince of Bakhtan, she became well immediately, and the spirit who was with her said in presence of Khonsu who rules destinies in Thebes, "Come in peace, great god who drives away foreigners, Bakhtan is thy town, its people are thy slaves, and I myself, I am thy slave. I will go, therefore, to the place from whence I came, in order to give satisfaction to thy heart on account of the matter which brings thee, but let Thy Majesty command that a feast day be celebrated for me and for the prince of Bakhtan." The god made an approving nod of the head to his prophet, to say, "Let the prince of Bakhtan make a great offering before this ghost."

command her to send a fleet to the *Ports of Incense* to bring back the perfumes required for the cult. The kings of the XXth and XXIst dynasties, less fortunate, usually obtained only movements, always of the same kind; when they asked a question of a god, the statue remained motionless if the reply was in the negative, but it nodded its head twice vigorously if favourable, as was the case here. These consultations were carried on according to a strictly regulated ceremonial, of which contemporary texts have preserved the principal details (Maspero, *Notes sur différents points,* in *Recueil de Travaux,* vol. i. pp. 158–159).

12. The innate virtue or power of the gods, the *sa,* seems to have been regarded by the Egyptians as a sort of fluid, similar to that which we call by different names—magnetic fluid, *aura,* etc. It was transmitted by imposition of hands and by actual passes, performed on the neck or spine of the recipient. This was called Satapu-sa, and may be translated more or less closely as *practising passes.* The ceremony by which the first Khonsu transmitted his virtue to the second is rather frequently represented on the monuments, in scenes where the statue of a god is represented making passes on a king. The statue, usually a wooden one, had movable limbs; it embraced the king, and passed its hand over his neck while he knelt before it with his back turned to it. Each statue had at its consecration acquired not only a *double,* but also some part of the magic virtue of the god it represented; the *sa of his life* was *behind it,* animating and permeating it, in proportion as the statue made use of some part of what it possessed for transmission. The god himself, whom this perpetual outflow of *sa* might have exhausted, could supply himself from a mysterious reservoir of *sa* contained in the other world; it is not stated by what means this lake of *sa* was itself supplied (Maspero, *Mélanges de Mythologie et d'Archéologie égyptiennes,* vol. i, p. 308).

Now, while this was happening between Khonsu, who rules destinies in Thebes, and the spirit, the prince of Bakhtan was there with his army stricken with terror. And when they had made a great offering before Khonsu who rules destinies in Thebes, and before the ghost, from the prince of Bakhtan, while celebrating a feast day in their honour, the spirit departed in peace whithersoever it pleased him, according to the command of Khonsu who rules destinies in Thebes.

The prince of Bakhtan rejoiced greatly, as well as all the people of Bakhtan, and he communed with his heart, saying, "Since this god has been given to Bakhtan, I will not send him back to Egypt." Now after this god had remained three years and nine months at Bakhtan, when the prince of Bakhtan was laid down on his bed, he saw in a dream this god issuing from his shrine in the form of a sparrow-hawk of gold which flew towards Egypt; when he awoke he was shivering greatly. He then said to the prophet of Khonsu who rules destinies in Thebes, "This god who has dwelt with us, he wills to return to Egypt, let his chariot go to Egypt." The prince of Bakhtan granted that this god should depart for Egypt, and he gave him numerous presents of all good things, and also a strong escort of soldiers and horses. When they had arrived at Thebes, Khonsu who rules destinies in Thebes repaired to the temple of Khonsu in Thebes, the good counsellor; he placed the gifts that the prince of Bakhtan had given him of all good things in the presence of Khonsu in Thebes, the good coun-sellor, he kept nothing for himself. Now, Khonsu the good counsellor in Thebes returned to his temple in peace, in the year XXIII, the 19th Mechir, of the King Uasimarîya-Satapanrîya, living for ever, like the Sun.

II

ᴗ *The Exploits of Sesôstris* [II] ᴗ
(Persian Period)

As HAS been said in the general *Introduction* to these tales (pp. cxxii, cxxiii), Ram-ses II was divided by tradition and gave birth to two different personages, one named Sesôstris, after his popular name, Sesusrîya, which is found on several of the monuments, while the other was called Osimanduas, or Osimandyas, from the prenomen Uasimarîya. The form Sesôstris and the legend attached to it is of Memphite origin, as I have had occasion to show elsewhere (*La Geste de Sesôstris,* in the *Journal des Savants,* 1901, pp. 599–600, 603). It arose, or at least it was localised round a group of six statues standing in front of the temple of Ptah at

Memphis, which the sacristans called on Herodotus to admire, assuring him that they represented the Egyptian conqueror, his wife, and four sons (II, cx). When inserting it in his history, he merely transcribed it without any suspicion of its being a popular romance, and that the themes which were of apparent authenticity merely served to introduce a certain number of purely imaginary episodes. In fact, if we try to discover the proportion of the different parts in the *Exploits* when the commentaries added by Herodotus are eliminated, we find that the most developed are those which speak of the treatment of conquered nations, and of the way in which the hero, on his return to Egypt, escaped death near Pelusium; the first occupies more than half of chapter cii, and the latter the whole of chapter cvii. The way in which the return home is set forth, as well as the accompanying circumstances, almost leads us to believe that this is the principal theme. Without insisting too much on this point, I would say that the proportions of the various parts in the original Egyptian must have been the same in the main as in the Greek summary; Herodotus did not repeat all the details he had heard, but the abridged version he wrote of the whole gives us a sufficient insight into the action and general lines. The first idea seems to have been to account for the origin of the canals, and of the legislation with regard to landed property in force in the country; and the people, incapable of following the long evolution that had led matters up to the point at which they then were, had recourse to the simplifying conception of a sovereign who, by himself, and in a few years, had accomplished the work of many centuries. As war alone could provide him with the necessary workmen, be was sent to conquer the world, and themes that already existed were added to the medley, such as the description of commemorative stelæ, and the treacherous fire at Daphnæ. The theme of the perilous banquet was an idea familiar to Egyptian imagination, and up to the present we know of two other examples—that in which Set-Typhon murdered his brother Osiris, when like Sesôstris he had returned from his conquests, and that given by Nitocris to the murderers of her brother (*Herodotus* II, c). Here, then, are the elements of many tales that the imagination of the dragomans united in one story for the benefit of visitors to the temple of Ptah.

The King Sesôstris, in the first place, sailed out of the Arabian Gulf with lofty vessels, and reduced the people who dwelt on the shore of the Erythræn Sea, until, as he pushed on, he arrived at a point where the shallows rendered the sea impracticable. After that he returned to Egypt, and taking with him a numerous army, he traversed the solid land, subduing all the nations he encountered. Those of them who proved to be brave, and who fought determinedly for their freedom, he raised stelæ for them in their lands, on which were inscribed their name, that of their country, and how he had subdued them to his power; those on the contrary, whose towns he had taken without difficulty or fighting, he wrote on their stelæ the same information as for the people who had given proof of courage, but he added in addition an emblem of femininity, to show to all that they had been cowardly. In this way he traversed the solid land until, having crossed from Asia into Europe, he subdued both the Scythians and the Thracians.[13] Then, having retraced his steps, he came back.[14]

Now, this Sesôstris, who returned to his country and who brought with him many men of the nations he had subdued, when he was returning to Daphnæ, in the neighbourhood of Pelusium, his brother, to whom he had committed the government of Egypt, invited him to a feast, and his children with him, surrounded the house outside with wood, and then after having surrounded it, set fire to it. As soon as he knew of it, he conferred hurriedly with his wife—for he had brought his wife with him—and she advised him, of the six sons they had, to lay two of them across the furnace, and to cross it on their bodies, and thus to escape. Sesôstris did this, and two of his children were burnt in this way, but the others were saved with their father. Sesôstris having entered Egypt and revenged himself on his brother, employed the crowd of prisoners he had brought from the countries he had subdued for the following tasks: they dragged the blocks of enormous size that the king transported for the temple of Hephæstus, they dug out perforce all the canals that are now in Egypt. By these means and against their will they rendered the whole of Egypt, that previously had been practicable for horses and chariots, impracticable, so that since that time Egypt has had neither horses nor chariots. He divided the land between all the Egyptians, giving to each one by lot a quadrangular piece of equal extent, and it was according to this that he established the assessment of the tax, commanding the tax to be paid annually. And if the river carried off a part of his lot from any one, that man, coming before the king, gave notice of the accident; he then sent officials charged to examine and measure the loss which the property had sustained, so that the taxpayer

---

13. *Herodotus* II, cii-ciii.
14. *Ibid.*, ciii.

should not pay more on what was left him, than the due proportion of the original tax.[15]

This king was the only one of the kings of Egypt who reigned over Ethiopia.[16]

Diodorus of Sicily (I, liii-lviii) has given a version of the story recorded by Herodotus, but augmented and rendered less childish by the successive historians who repeated the fable of Sesôstris. Thus, in the episode of the banquet at Pelusium, he suppresses, probably as too barbarous, the sacrifice of two of the sons, made by the conqueror to save himself and the rest of his family; the king "then raising his hands implored the gods for the safety of his children and his wife, and crossed the flames" (I, lvii). Diodorus, or rather the Alexandrian writer whom he copied, has substituted for the form Sesusrîya-Sesôstris of the dragomans of Herodotus, the abbreviated form Sesusi-Sesoôsis.

III

ᘒ *The Exploits of Osimandyas* [12] ᘒ
(Ptolemaic Period)

THE THEBAN versions of the legend of Ramses II were attached to the funerary temple that this prince had built on the left bank at the Ramesseum, and as one of the names of this temple was *ta haît Uasimarîya Maîamanu*, "the castle of Uasimarîya Maîamanu," and, as an abbreviation, "the castle of Uasimarîya," the prenomen Uasimarîya caused his proper name Ramses to be forgotten; transcribed *Osimanduas* in Greek, as I have said in the *Introduction* (p. cxv, note 87), it passed into the writings of Hecatæus of Abdera and Artemidorus, and thence into Diodorus as the name of a king other than Sesôstris-Sesoôsis. That which now remains of his *Exploits* is merely the description of the Ramesseum and of the sculpture which decorated the different parts. Nevertheless, one recognises that, like the *Exploits of Sesôstris*, it included an important account of battles in Asia against the Bactrians. Osimanduas besieged a fortress surrounded by a river, and he exposed himself to the blows of the enemy, accompanied by a lion, who afforded him powerful assistance in the fight. The dragomans of the Ptolemaic age did not agree on this last point: some said that the animal figured on the walls was an actual lion tamed and fed by the hands of the king, who by his strength put the

15. *Herodotus* II, cvii-cix.
16. *Ibid.*, cx.

enemy to flight; the others, taking it in a metaphorical sense, asserted that the king, being exceedingly valiant and powerful, wished to indicate these qualities by the figure of a lion. Only half of the building now exists of which the Greeks and Romans admired the arrangement, and in consequence a certain number of those sculptures have disappeared, the subject of which was summarily indicated by Diodorus of Sicily; but we know that Ramses III almost servilely copied the plans of his great ancestor, and, as his temple at Medinet-Habu suffered less, we have in it what we may call a second edition of scenes copied from the Ramesseum. Here we find the procession of prisoners, the trophies of phalli and of hands which testified to the prowess of the Egyptian soldiers, the sacrifice of the ox, and the procession of the god Mînu, which the dragomans interpreted as the triumphal return of Pharaoh. The famous library, *A Pharmacy of the Soul*, was without doubt the workshop from which, under the XIXth and XXth Dynasties, a quantity of books issued, the classics of the Theban age. The halls and accessory chapels are probably identical with one or other of those of which the ruins have been brought to light by the recent excavation of the town and magazines.

It would be rash to attempt to re-establish the *Exploits of Osimandyas* in its primitive form with the help of the extracts that Diodorus has given us at third or fourth hand. One can only guess that it was very probably similar in its development to that of Sesoôsis-Sesôstris. Doubtless it began with an account of the victories of the king, which furnished him with the necessary resources to construct what the Greeks believed to be his tomb, but which is in reality the chapel of the tomb that was cut out in the funerary valley. The description of the marvels that this building contained occupied the second half, and we may judge of its tone by the version, still current, of the inscription graved on the base of the colossus of rose granite : "I am Osimanduas, king of kings, and he who would know who I am and where I repose, let him surpass one of my deeds."

An abbreviated version of the war against the Khâti should be found, treated in the way in which the authors of the *High Emprise for the Throne* and *the Cuirass* arranged the quarrels of the Egyptian barons among themselves at the Assyrian epoch. It is disappointing that the Alexandrian authors, to whom we are indebted for our knowledge of it, have not transmitted it more or less complete, as Herodotus did for *The Exploits of Sesôstris*.

THE DOOMED PRINCE [13]

(XXTH DYNASTY)

THE TALE of *The Doomed Prince* is one of the works contained in the *Harris Papyrus No.* 500, of the British Museum. It was discovered and translated into English by Goodwin, in the *Transactions of the Society of Biblical Archæology*, vol. iii, pp. 349–356, and in *Records of the Past*, vol. ii, pp. 153–160, then rapidly analysed by Chabas from Goodwin's translation, *Sur quelques Contes égyptiens*, in *Comptes rendus de l'Académie des Inscriptions et Belles-lettres*, 1875, pp. 118–120. The Egyptian text has been published, transcribed and translated into French by Maspero in the *Journal Asiatique*, 1877–8, and in *études égyptiennes*, vol. i, pp. 1–47. It has been collated with the original by H. O. Lange, *Notes sur le texte du Conte prédestiné*, in *Recueil de Travaux*, vol. xxi, pp. 23–24, and has since been reproduced in hieratic only by G. Möller, *Hieratische Lesestücke*, small folio, Leipzig, 1910, pp. 21–24. Ebers rendered it in German, and completed it with his usual ability, *Das alte Ægyptische Märchen vom verwunschenen Prinzen, nacherzählt und zu Ende geführt*, in the number of October 1881 of *Westermann's Monatshefte*, pp. 96–103. Since then it has been rendered in English by W. M. Flinders Petrie, *Egyptian Tales*, 1895, London, 12mo, vol. ii, pp. 13–35, and translated by F. Ll. Griffith, in *Specimen Pages of the World's Best Literature*, 1898, New York, 4to, pp. 5250–5253; into German by A. Wiedemann, *Altägyptische Sagen und Märchen*, small 8vo, Leipzig, 1906, pp. 78–85.

It is said that the manuscript was intact when it was found, and that it was injured in Egypt, several years later, by the explosion of a powder magazine, which partially destroyed the house in Alexandria in which it was. It is supposed that a copy, made by Mr. Harris before the disaster, contains the destroyed portions of the original; but at present no one knows where the copy is to be found. In its present state the *Story of the Doomed Prince* covers four and a half pages. The last line of the first, the second, and the third pages, and the first line of the second, the third, and the fourth pages, have disappeared. The whole of the right-hand half of the fourth page, from line 8 to line 14, is defaced or almost entirely destroyed. The fifth page, in addition to several tears of small importance, has lost on the left side about a third of every line. Nevertheless the style is so simple, and the sequence of ideas so easy to follow, that it is possible to fill in the gaps and restore actually the letter of the text. The end may be guessed, thanks to indications afforded by stories of a similar nature found in other countries.

It is difficult to determine accurately the period to which this narrative should be assigned. The scene is placed alternately in Egypt and Northern Syria, of which the name is spelt Naharinna, as in the *Anastasi Papyrus No. IV,* pl. xv, l. 4. One cannot therefore place the redaction of the fragment earlier than the XVIIIth dynasty, that is to say, than the seventeenth century B.C., and Möller (*Hieratische Lesestücke,* vol. ii, p. 21) thinks our copy was made at the beginning of the XIXth dynasty. In my opinion, however, the form of the letters, the use of certain ligatures, the presence of certain new grammatical forms, recall unquestionably the Theban papyri contemporary with the later Ramessides. I am inclined therefore to place, if not the first redaction of the story, at least the version we possess in the Harris papyrus and the writing of the manuscript, at the end or the middle of the XXth dynasty at the very earliest.

There was once a king[1] to whom no man child was born. His heart was very sad thereat; he asked for a boy from the gods of his time, and they decreed that one should be born to him. He lay with his wife during the night, and she conceived; when the months of the birth were accomplished, lo, a man-child was born. When the Hâthors[2] came to decree him a destiny, they said, 'He shall die by the crocodile, or by the serpent, or indeed by the dog.' When the people who were with the child heard this, they went to tell His Majesty, l. h. s., and His Majesty, l. h. s., was sad at heart thereat. His Majesty, l. h. s, had a stone house built for him on the mountain, furnished with men and all good things of the dwelling of the king, l. h. s., for the child did not go out of it. And when the child was grown, he went up on to the terrace[3] of his house, and he perceived

1. The author does not state explicitly the country to which he refers, but to designate the father of our hero, he employs the word *nsut,* the official title of the kings of Egypt. It is therefore in Egypt that all the events occur that are recounted at the beginning of the story.

2. For the Hâthors see p. 10, note 30, and *Introduction,* pp. cxxxvi–cxxxvii.

3. The roof of Egyptian houses is flat, and like that of the temples, formed terraces on which the open air could be enjoyed. Slight kiosks were built on them, and sometimes, as at the temple of Denderah, actual ediculæ of worked stone, which served as chapels and observatories.

a greyhound who ran behind a man walking on the road. He said to his page who was with him: "What is it that runs behind the man passing along the road?" The page said to him, "It is a greyhound." The child said to him, "Let one be brought to me exactly like it." The page went to repeat this to His Majesty, l. h. s., and His Majesty, l. h. s., said, "Let a young running dog be taken to him, for fear his heart should be saddened." And lo, the greyhound was taken to him.

And after the days had passed in this manner, when the child had acquired age in all his limbs, he sent a message to his father, saying, "Come! why be like the sluggards? Although I am doomed to three grievous destinies, yet I will act according to my will. God will not do less than he has at heart." One listened to that which he spake, one gave him all kinds of weapons, and also his greyhound to follow him, and transported him to the eastern coast.[4] One said to him, "Go where thou desirest." His greyhound was with him; he went therefore as he fancied across the country, living on the best of all the game of the country. Having arrived to fly[5] to the prince of Naharinna,[6] behold there was no son born to the prince of Naharinna, only a daughter. Now, he had built a house with seventy windows which were seventy cubits above the ground. He caused all the sons of the princes of the country of Kharu[7] to be brought, and he said to them, "To him who shall reach the window of my daughter, she shall be given him for wife."

---

4. The eastern coast of Syria is compared with Egypt. We find, in fact, that the prince arrives at the country of Naharinna. *Naharinna* is known also as *Naharaîna* (p. 144, note 2): marriages of Egyptian princes with Syrian princesses are numerous in real history.

5. The word *pui*, employed several times in our text to define the action of princes, really means *to fly, to fly away*, and it is solely by error that it has been translated *to climb*. Is it possible that the prince of Naharinna imposed a magic test on the suitors? I am disposed to believe this, because further on the son of the king of Egypt *conjured his limbs* before entering into the competition. In the first *Story of Satni-Khâmois*, we have met with a personage who came out of the ground, literally, *who flew upwards*, by means of the talismans of the god Ptah (cf. p. 110).

6. It may be thought strange that this prince, unknowing of the history of the princess of Naharinna, should arrive in the country where she was with the intention of flying to acquire her. But then the Egyptian author merely intended to acquaint his reader beforehand with what was about to happen. Thus, in the *Story of the Two Brothers*, the magicians of Pharaoh, without knowing precisely where the woman was of whom Pharaoh was in search, sent messengers to all countries, and specially recommended that an escort should be sent with the messenger who went to the Vale of the Acacia, as though they already knew that the daughter of the gods was living there (p. 11).

7. Cf. p. 90, note 4, what the Egyptians meant by the name *Country of Kharu*.

Now, many days after these things were accomplished, while the princes of Syria were engaged in their occupation of every day, the prince of Egypt, having come to pass into the place where they were, they conducted the prince to their house, they brought him to the bath, they gave provender to his horses, they did all manner of things for the prince, they perfumed him, they anointed his feet, they gave him of their loaves, they said to him, by way of conversation, "Whence comest thou, goodly youth?" He said to them, "I am the son of a soldier of the chariots[8] of the land of Egypt. My mother died, my father took another wife. When children arrived she hated me, and I fled before her." They pressed him in their arms, they covered him with kisses. Now, after many days had passed in this way, he said to the princes, "What are you doing here?" They said to him, "We pass our time doing this: we fly, and he who shall reach the window of the daughter of the prince of Naharinna, she shall be given him for wife." He said to them, "If it please you, I will conjure my limbs, and I will go and fly with you." They went to fly, as was their occupation of every day, and the prince stood afar off to behold, and the face of the daughter of the prince of Naharinna was turned to him. Now, after the days had passed in this manner, the prince went to fly with the sons of the rulers, and he flew, and he reached the window of the daughter of the chief of Naharinna; she kissed him, and she embraced him in all his limbs.

They went to rejoice the heart of the father of the princess, and said to him, "A man has reached the window of thy daughter." The prince questioned the messenger, saying, "The son of which of the princes?" They said to him, "The son of a soldier of chariots who comes as a fugitive from the country of Egypt to escape his step-mother when she had children." The prince of Naharinna became very angry; he said, "Shall I give my daughter to a fugitive from the land of Egypt? Let him return there!" They went to say to the prince, "Return to the place from whence thou art come." But the princess seized him, and she sware by God, saying, "By the life of Phrâ Harmakhis[9]! if he is taken from me, I will not eat, I will not drink, I will die immediately." The messenger went to repeat all that

---

8. The Egyptian war-chariot carried two men—the charioteer, *kazana,* who drove, and the other, *sinni,* who fought; it is a *sinni* whom the prince claims as his father. The texts show that these two persons were of equal importance, and ranked as officers (Maspero, *études égyptiennes,* vol. ii, p. 41).

9. One would expect to find a Syrian princess swear by Baal or Astarte; the author, not considering the matter closely, twice puts in her mouth the Egyptian form of oath by Phrâ-Harmakhis and by Phrâ.

she had said to her father, and the prince sent men to slay the young man while he was in her house. The princess said to them, "By the life of Phrâ! if he is killed, by sundown I shall be dead, I will not spend one hour of life apart from him." They went to tell her father. The prince caused the young man to be brought with the princess. The young man was seized with terror when he came before the prince, but the prince embraced him, he covered him with kisses, he said to him, "Tell me who thou art, for behold, thou art to me as a son." The young man said, "I am the son of a soldier of chariots of the country of Egypt. My mother died, and my father took another wife. She hated me, and I fled before her." The chief gave him his daughter to wife; he gave him a house, vassals, fields, also cattle, and all manner of good things.[10]

Now, when the days had passed thus, the young man said to his wife, "I am doomed to three destinies, the crocodile, the serpent, the dog." She said to him, "Let the dog be killed that runs before thee." He said to her, "If it please thee, I will not kill my dog that I brought up when it was little." She feared for her husband greatly, greatly, and she did not let him go out alone. Now it happened that one desired to travel; the prince was escorted to the land of Egypt, to wander about the country.[11] Now behold, the crocodile of the river came out of the river,[12] and he came into the midst of the town where the prince was; they shut him up in a dwelling where there was a giant. The giant did not let the crocodile go out, but when the crocodile slept the giant went out for a stroll; then when the sun arose, the giant returned every day, for an interval of two months of days.[13] And after that the days had passed in this manner, the prince remained to divert himself in his house. When the night came, the prince lay down on his bed, and sleep took possession of his limbs. His wife filled a vase with milk, and placed it by her side. When a serpent came out of its hole

10. See above, pp. 65–66, the enumeration of the possessions settled by the prince of Tonu on Sinuhît when he gave him his daughter in marriage.

11. Possibly to *hunt* in that country; as at the beginning of this story, p. 155.

12. As in the *Tale of the Two Brothers* (p. 10, note 31), the author does not name the river to which he refers. He uses the word *iaûmâ, iôm, the sea, the river,* and that is sufficient. Egypt had, in fact, no other river than the Nile. The reader would immediately realise that the Nile was intended by *iaûmâ,* as the fellah of to-day understands when the word *bahr* is used without the epithet *malkhah,* salt; *bahr el malkhah* signifies *the sea.*

13. The giant and the crocodile are two astronomical personages, the emblems of two important constellations which are seen figured, among others, on the roof of the Ramesseum. It seems that the god had sent them down to earth to accomplish the destiny predicted by the seven Hathors.

to bite the prince, behold, his wife watched over her husband with close attention. Then the maid-servants gave milk to the serpent;[14] it drank of it, it became drunk, it lay on its back, and the wife cut it in pieces with blows of her hatchet. Her husband was awakened, who was seized with astonishment, and she said to him, "Behold, thy god has given one of thy fates into thy hand; he will give thee the others." He presented offerings to the god, he adored him, and exalted his power all the days of his life.

And after the days had passed in this manner, the prince came out to walk near his domain, and as he never came out alone, behold, his dog was behind him. His dog started in pursuit of the game, and he ran after the dog. When he readied the river, be went down the bank of the river behind his dog, and the crocodile came out and dragged him to the place where the giant was. He came out and saved the prince; then the crocodile said to the prince, "Lo, I am thy destiny that pursues thee; whatever thou mayest do, thou wilt be brought back on to my path (?) to me, thou and the giant. Now, behold, I am about to let thee go, if the . . . thou wilt know that my enchantments have triumphed, and that the giant is slain; and when thou seest that the giant is slain, thou seest thy death."[15] And when the earth lightened, and the second day was, then came . . .

[The prophecy of the crocodile is so much mutilated that I cannot guarantee its exact meaning; we can only guess that the monster set some kind of fatal dilemma before his adversary or that the prince fulfilled a certain condition, and succeeded in overcoming the crocodile, or that he did not fulfil it, and that *he saw his death*. Ebers has restored this episode in a different way.[16] He has supposed that the giant was not able to save the prince, but that the crocodile proposed to him to spare the prince under certain conditions.]

"Thou wilt swear to me to slay the giant; if thou dost refuse this, thou shalt see death." And when the earth lightened, and a second day was, the dog came up and saw that his master was in the power of the crocodile. The crocodile said again, "Wilt thou swear to slay the giant?" The prince

14. Cf. on the method by which the Egyptians attracted serpents the passage of Phylarchus, *Fragment* 26, in Möller-Didot, *Fragmenta Historicorum Græcorum*, vol. i, p. 340.

15. There is here the indication of an intersign similar to those I have already remarked on in the *Tale of the Two Brothers* (pp. 8–9) and in the second story of *Satni-Khamoîs* (p. 133). Unfortunately a lacuna prevents our recognising its nature.

16. Ebers, *Das alte Ægyptische Märchen vom verwunschenen Prinzen*, in the number for October 1881 of *Westermann's Monatschefte*, pp. 99–102.

replied, "Why should I slay him who has watched over me?" The crocodile said to him, "Then shall thy destiny be accomplished. If, at sundown, thou wilt not make the oath that I demand, thou shalt see thy death." The dog, having heard these words, ran to the house, and found the daughter of the prince of Naharinna in tears, for her husband had not reappeared since the day before. When she saw the dog alone, without its master, she wept aloud, and she tore her breast; but the dog seized her by her robe, and drew her to the door, as asking her to come out. She arose, she took the hatchet with which she had killed the serpent, and she followed the dog to that part of the shore where the giant was. She then hid herself in the reeds, and she neither drank nor ate; she did nothing but pray the gods for her husband. When evening arrived the crocodile said again, "Wilt thou swear to slay the giant? if not, I will take thee to the shore, and thou shalt see thy death." And he replied, "Why should I slay him who has watched over me?" Then the crocodile took him to the place where the woman was, and she came out of the reeds, and, behold, as the crocodile opened its jaws, she struck it with her hatchet, and the giant threw himself on it and killed it. Then she embraced the prince, and she said to him, "Behold, thy god has given the second of thy fates into thy hands; he will give thee the third." He presented offerings to the god, he adored him, and exalted his might all the days of his life.

And after this enemies entered the country. For the sons of the princes of the country of Kharu, furious at seeing the princess in the hands of an adventurer, had assembled their foot-soldiers and their chariots, they had destroyed the army of the chief of Naharinna, and they had taken him prisoner. When they did not find the princess and her husband, they said to the old chief: "Where is thy daughter and that son of a soldier of chariots from the land of Egypt, to whom thou hast given her as wife?" He answered them: "He is gone with her to hunt the beasts of the country—how should I know where they are?" Then they deliberated, and they said one to another: "Let us divide into small bands, and go hither and thither over the whole world, and he who shall find them, let him slay the young man, and let him do as pleases him with the woman." And they departed, some to the east, and some to the west, to the north, to the south; and those who had gone to the south reached the land of Egypt, at the same time that the young man was with the daughter of the chief of Naharinna. But the giant saw them; he hastened to the young man, and said to him: "Behold, seven sons of the princes of the country of Kharu come to seek thee. If they find thee, they will slay thee, and will do with thy wife as it pleases them. They are too many for thee to resist; flee from them, and for me, I will return to my brothers." Then the prince called his wife, he took his dog with him, and they all hid themselves in a cave of the mountain. They had been there two days and two nights when the sons of the princes of Kharu arrived with many soldiers, and they passed before the mouth of the cave without any of them perceiving the prince; but as the last of them came near, the dog went out against him and began to bark. The sons of the princes of Kharu recognised him, and they came back and went into the cave. The wife threw herself before her husband to protect him, but, behold, a lance struck her, and she fell dead before him. And the young man slew one of the princes with his sword, and the dog killed another with his teeth, but the rest struck them with their lances, and they fell to the ground unconscious. Then the princes dragged the bodies out of the cave, and left them stretched on the ground to be devoured by wild beasts and birds of prey, and they departed to rejoin their companions and divide with them the lands of the chief of Naharinna.

And behold, when the last of the princes had departed, the young man opened his eyes, and he saw his wife stretched on the ground by his side, as dead, and the dead body of his dog. Then he trembled, and he said: "In truth, the gods fulfil immutably that which they have decreed beforehand. The Hâthors have decided, from my infancy, that I should perish by the dog, and behold, their sentence has been executed, for it is the dog which has betrayed me to mine enemies. I am ready to die, because, without these two beings, who lie beside me, life is intolerable to me." And he raised his hands to the sky, and cried: "I have not sinned against you, O ye gods! Therefore grant me a happy burial in this world, and to be true of voice before the judges of Amentît." He sank down as dead, but the gods had heard his voice, the Ennead of the gods came to him, and Râ-Harmakhis said to his companions: "The doom is fulfilled; now let us give a new life to these two wedded people, for it is good to reward worthily the devotion which they have shown one to the other." And the mother of the gods approved with her head the words of Râ-Harmakhis, and she said: "Such devotion deserves very great reward." The other gods said the same; then the seven Hâthors came forward, and they said: "The doom is fulfilled; now they shall return to life." And they returned to life immediately.

In his conclusion, Ebers relates that the prince reveals to the daughter of the chief of Naharinna his real origin, and that he returns to Egypt, where his father receives him with joy. He speedily returns to Naharinna, defeats his murderers, and replaces the old chief on his throne. On his return, he consecrates the booty to Amonrâ, and passes the remainder of his days in complete happiness.

Nothing could be better conceived than this ending; I do not, however, believe that the ancient Egyptian writer had the compassion for his heroes that is so ingeniously shown by the modern author. Destiny does not allow itself to be set aside in the ancient East, and does not permit its decrees to be evaded. At times it suspends their execution, but never annuls them. If Cambyses is condemned to die near Ecbatana, it is in vain for him to fly from Ecbatana in Media on the appointed day—he finds in Syria the Ecbatana with which the gods threatened him. When a child is doomed to perish violently in his twentieth year, his father may shut him in a subterranean abode; to that place Sindbad the sailor is led by fate, and by mischance will slay the doomed victim. I do not believe that the hero of this story escaped this law; he triumphed over the crocodile, but the dog, in the ardour of battle, mortally wounded his master, and fulfilled, without intending it, the prediction of the Hâthors.

THE STORY
OF RHAMPSINITUS[14]

(Saite Period)

THE earliest known form of this story was transmitted to us by Herodotus (II, cxxi). It is found among most nations, both of the East and the West, and the question of its origin has often been discussed. In the *Introduction* to this volume I have given my reasons for believing that if it was not invented in Egypt it had been Egyptianised long before Herodotus wrote it down. I will add here that the name of Rhampsinitus was given in Egypt to the hero of many marvellous adventures. "The priests say that this king descended alive into the region that the Greeks call Hades, that he played at dice with the goddess Demeter, sometimes beating her, sometimes beaten by her, and that he returned, bringing with him as a present from the goddess a golden napkin" (*Herodotus* II, cxxii). These lines contain a brief summary of an Egyptian tale, the two principal scenes of which recall in a remarkable manner the game played by Satni and Nenoferkephtah in the first place (pp. 109–110), the descent of Satni into Hades with the aid of Senosiris in the second place (pp. 122–125).

The French translation adopted here was that of Pierre Saliat, slightly touched up; by a singular coincidence, it has served to re-introduce the story into the popular literature of Southern Egypt. In 1884 I gave a copy of the first edition of this book to M. Nicholas Odescalchi, then master of the school at Thebes, who died in 1892. He related the principal points to some of his pupils, who told them to others. Since 1885 I have acquired two transcriptions of this new version, one of which was published in the *Journal Asiatique,* 1885, vol. vi, pp. 149–159, the text in Arabic with a French translation, but reproduced in *Études égyptiennes,* vol. i, pp. 301–311. The narrative has not been much altered; although one of the episodes has disappeared—that in which Rhampsinitus prostitutes his daughter. One can understand that a schoolmaster, speaking to children, would not relate the story in all its native crudity.

King Rhampsinitus[1] possessed a treasure so great that his successors, far from surpassing, could never even approach it. To keep it in safety, he caused a small chamber of hewn stone to be built, and desired that one of the walls should project beyond the work and beyond the enclosure of his palace; but the mason cut and set a stone so accurately that two men, and even one alone, could draw it and move it from its place.[2] When the chamber was finished, the king placed all his treasures in it; some time afterwards, the mason-architect, feeling the end of his life approaching, called his children, who were two sons, and declared how he had provided for them, and the artifice which he had used within the chamber of the king, in order that they might live luxuriously. And after having made them clearly understand the means of withdrawing the stone, he gave them certain measurements, telling them that if they guarded them carefully they would be the custodians of the king's treasury; thereupon he departed from life to death.

After this his sons barely waited to commence work; they came by night to the palace of the king, and having easily found the stone, they drew it from its place and took away a large sum in silver. But when fortune decreed that the king should open his chamber, he was greatly astonished, seeing his coffers much diminished, and not knowing whom to accuse or suspect, although he found the marks he had placed there whole and entire, and the chamber very well closed and sealed. And after he had returned two or three times to see whether his coffers still diminished, in order to secure that the robbers no longer returned home so freely, he commanded certain traps to be made and placed near the coffers in which were the treasures. The robbers returned according to their custom, and one went into the chamber; but, as soon as he went near a coffer, he found himself caught in a trap. Knowing the danger that threatened him, he speedily called his brother, and showed him the position in which he was, recommending him to come to him and cut off his head, in order that if he were recognised both might not perish. His brother thought that he spoke wisely, and thereupon did that which

1. This name is merely Ramses augmented by the addition of a syllable *nitos* to differentiate it (see *Introduction*, p. cxv).

2. See in the *Introduction*, pp. cxxvi–cxxvii, the commentary on this passage. It is possible that in the *Story of Khufui* we have another instance of a movable block (cf. p. 27–28).

he had suggested. Having replaced the stone, he returned with his brother's head.

When it was day the king went into his chamber, but seeing the body of the thief caught in the trap, and without a head, he was greatly afraid, as there was no appearance of a way in or out, and being in doubt how he could act in such a circumstance, he adopted the expedient of hanging the body of the dead man on the wall of the town,[3] and charging certain guards to apprehend and bring to him any one they saw weeping and bewailing the suspended body. The body being thus promptly hung up, his mother, in the great grief she felt, spoke to her other son, and commanded him, however it was done, to have the body of his brother brought to her, threatening, if he refused to do so, to go to the king and tell him who had his treasure. The son, seeing that his mother took these matters thus to heart, and that he profited nothing by the remonstrance that he made, invented this trick. He had pack-saddles placed on certain asses, loaded them with goat-skins full of wine,[4] and drove them in front of him. When he arrived at the place where the guards were, that is to say, near the dead body, he untied two or three of his goat-skins, and seeing the wine running out, began to beat his head while making loud exclamations, as though he did not know which of his asses he should turn to first. The guards, seeing what a large quantity of wine was being spilt, ran to the place with vessels, considering it so much gain to themselves if they could collect the wasted wine. The merchant began to abuse them, and pretended to be very infuriated with them. However, the guards were civil, and after a time he quieted down and moderated

3. This exposing of a corpse on the wall of the city has been quoted to show that the origin of the story was not Egyptian. The Egyptians, it has been said, had religious scruples that would prevent their civil law allowing such an exhibition, and that after execution the body was handed over to the relatives to be mummified. Against this objection I will only quote a passage of a stela of Amenothes II, where the king states that after having captured several Syrian chieftains he exposed their bodies on the walls of Thebes and Napata, in order to deter the rebels by such a terrible example. That which was done by a real Pharaoh may well have been done by the Pharaoh of a romance, even if it were exceptional.

4. The Egyptians did not usually make use of skins to contain wine, but almost invariably employed small pointed jars. The slaves carried them to the workshops or the fields, and it is not unusual in the paintings that represent farm work to see a harvester with his reaping-hook under his arm drinking out of a jar. The use of goat-skins was, however, not unknown, and among other instances I can quote a picture of gardening found in a Theban tomb, reproduced by Wilkinson (*A Popular Account of the Ancient Egyptians,* vol. i, p. 35, fig. 29); one sees there three goat-skins of water placed on the edge of a pool as a refreshment. The detail given by Herodotus is therefore consistent at all points with the customs of ancient Egypt.

his wrath. Finally he turned his asses out of the road to re-saddle and reload them, while making various small remarks of one sort and another, so that one of the guards made a jest to the merchant, at which he only laughed, at the same time giving them in addition another skin of wine. And when they were minded to sit down as they were, and drink more, asking the merchant to stay and keep them company in drinking, he consented, and seeing that they treated him well in the matter of drinking, he gave them the remainder of his skins of wine. When they had drunk so much that they were dead drunk, sleep came upon them, and they slept in that same place. The merchant waited well into the night, then went to take down the body of his brother, and laughing at the guards, cut off all their beards[5] on the right side. He placed the body of his brother on the asses, and drove them back to his dwelling, having carried out the command of his mother.

The next day, when the king was told that the body of the robber had been taken away by subtlety, he was greatly grieved, and wishing by any means to discover who had used such ingenuity, he did a thing which, for my part, I cannot believe. He opened the house of his daughter, he enjoined her to receive indiscriminately whosoever might come to her to take his pleasure, but always, before allowing him to touch her, to force each one to tell her the cleverest and the most wicked thing he had done in his life; and that he who told this escapade of the thief was to be seized by her, and not allowed to leave her room.[6] The daughter obeyed her father's order, but the thief, understanding the object with which this was done, wished to outdo the ingenuity of the king, and counteracted it in this fashion. He cut off the arm of a man newly dead, and hiding it under his robe, he made his way to the girl. When he had entered she questioned him as to his doings, and he told her that the most enormous crime he had committed was when he cut off the head of his brother, caught in a trap in the king's treasury. Also, that the cleverest thing that he had done was when he took down that same brother after having made the guards drunk. When she heard it she did not fail to seize him, but the thief, with the aid of the darkness in her chamber, held out the

5. For the appreciation of this detail I refer readers to the *Introduction*, p. cxxvii, for what is said as to the beards of Egyptian soldiers.

6. However strange this proceeding may appear to us, we must believe that it seemed natural to the Egyptians, since the daughter of Cheops was ordered by her father to open her house to all comers for the sake of money (*Herodotus* II, cxxvi), and Tbubuî invited Satni to her house in order to force him to give up the book of Thoth (see above, pp. 112–115).

dead hand which he had hidden, which she seized, believing that this was the hand of him who spoke to her; but she found herself mistaken, for the thief had time to get out and escape.

When the thing was reported to the king he marvelled greatly at the astuteness and boldness of that man. Finally he commanded that it should be proclaimed in all the towns of his kingdom that he pardoned this person, and that if he would come and present himself to him, he would confer great benefits on him. The thief placed faith in this proclamation made by the king, and he came to him. When the king saw him he made much of him; he gave him his daughter in marriage, as the most clever of men, who had outwitted the Egyptians, who themselves outwit all nations.

THE VOYAGE OF UNAMUNU
TO THE COASTS OF SYRIA [15]

THE manuscript that contains this story was found in the autumn of 1891 near the village of El-Hibeh, almost opposite Fechn, and the principal part of the fragments of which it consists were acquired shortly afterwards by Golénischeff. They comprise the first quarter and the last half of the first page, the second page almost complete, and several lines much mutilated that Golénischeff attributed to the third page. In 1892 Henri Brugsch discovered in a quantity of papyrus just acquired by him, a fragment that completed the second page. Since then no other fragment has been recovered, and it is to be feared that the manuscript will always remain incomplete.

In 1898 Golénischeff inserted a Russian translation, accompanied by a phototype of the first twenty-one lines, in the *Recueil de Mémoires* presented to M. de Rosen by his pupils of the University of Petrograd on the occasion of his jubilee. The following year he published the text transcribed into hieroglyphs, and a complete translation, extremely good as a whole: Golénischeff, *Papyrus hiératique de la collection W. Golénischeff, contenant la description du Voyage de l'égyptien Ounou-Amon en Phénicie*, in the *Recueil de Travaux*, 1899, vol. xxi, pp. 74–104 (published separately by Bouillon, 1899, 24 pp. 4to.).

The text was almost immediately worked through and translated into German by W. Max Möller, *Studien zur vorderasiatischen Geschichte. Die Urheimat der Philister, Der Papyrus Golénischeff, Die Chronologie der Philistereinwanderung* (in the *Mittheilungen der Vorderasiatischen, Gesellschaft*, 1900, I), Berlin, 8vo, pp. 14–29; then by A. Erman, *Eine Reise nach Phönizien in XI. Jahrhundert vor Christ*, in *Zeitschrift*, 1900, vol. xxxviii, pp. 1–14.

Erman recognised that the fragment supposed by Golénischeff to belong to page iii of the manuscript belonged in reality to the first page, and he restored the sequence of events more accurately than had been done before; he admitted on the other hand that the document was historic. Lange immediately contributed a Danish translation, in which he followed the order adopted by Erman: H. O. Lange, *Wen-Amons beretning om hans rejse tel Phönizien*, in *Nordisk Tidskrift*, 1902, pp. 515–526 (printed separately 11 pp. 8vo, without special pagination).

Finally there is a fresh German translation in the charming little work by A. Wiedemann, *Altägyptische Sagen und Märchen*, 8vo, Leipzig, 1906, pp. 94–113, as well as a short analysis with English translation in Breasted, *Ancient Records of Egypt*, vol. iv, pp. 274–287, which still maintains the historical nature of the fragment.

All the scholars who have worked at this papyrus have admitted, more or less frankly, that the writing it contains is an official report addressed to Hrihoru by Unamunu on his return from his mission to Phœnecia. The general form of the fragment, the emphatic tone that predominates it, the importance attributed all through it to the statue of *Amon of the Road*, leads me to believe, and Wiedemann is equally of my opinion, that it is a document of the same kind as that on the *Stela of Bakhtan* (p. 142). Without doubt it is an attempt to bring into prominence a form of Amon that bore that title, which was supposed to protect travellers in foreign countries. The narrative of Unamunu tells how it saved the Egyptian envoy at Byblos, and probably also in Alasia. It formed part of the official charter of this Amon, and the redactor has borrowed the historical mannerisms necessary to give an appearance of probability to documents of this nature. Perhaps they had authentic deeds in their hands that enabled them to date their story with accuracy. If one could rely on it with certainty, important conclusions might be drawn from it for the history of the Ramessides. One might, in fact, note that after the fifth year of his reign, the last of them retained a mere semblance of power; and that the High-priest Hrihoru exercised power in the south, Smendes in the north, and other princes flourished elsewhere. Smendes had a wife Tantamânu, whose name connects her with the Theban family, whose rights were equal to his own, since he is scarcely referred to without a mention of her; it was perhaps owing to her that he succeeded to the throne.

The information given in the manuscript as to the condition of affairs on the Syrian coast is by no means less valuable. A century later than Ramses III, the Zakkala, those allies of the Philistines who had established themselves between Carmel and Egypt, still formed a distinct population that kept its ancient name; one of their princes lived at Dora, their sailors swarmed in numbers over the Syrian sea, and threatened such cities as Byblos. They were still under the influence of Egypt, but they were no longer directly dependent on it, and the prince of Dora did not hesitate to make a parade of his independence before Unamunu. The Phœnician coast from Tyre to Byblos also remained in communication with

Egypt; Egyptian was understood there commonly, at least by persons of high rank, and the princes of every city entertained feelings of respect, almost of awe, for Pharaoh. This was a survival of the long domination of four or five centuries exercised by the Theban kings, but it was not always sufficient to procure a pacific reception for Egyptian envoys. This story speaks of the legates of Khamoîs, who had been retained as prisoners by Zikarbal, Prince of Byblos, and who, having died after seventeen years of captivity, had been buried in the vicinity of the city. Two of the Pharaohs of the XXth dynasty bore the prenomen of Khamoîs, and the mummy of one of them is now in the Cairo Museum (No. 1196); as the expedition of Unamunu dates from the fifth year of the second of these, Ramses XI, the Khamoîs who sent those poor wretches to their destruction must necessarily be the first Ramses IX. Nevertheless, the name of Thebes still carried weight to a surprising extent with the ancient vassals of Egypt. The prince of Byblos maintained that he was no servant of Pharaoh's, and denied that his forefathers had ever been. He even searched his archives to prove that they had always exchanged their wood for gifts of equal value, and that it had never been given for nothing. When he had given vent to his bad temper in violent talk, he caused the cedars of Lebanon to be cut down for Amon, and parted with them, while contenting himself with very mediocre presents. Every one must notice the resemblance that exists between this story and that which the Bible tells of the negotiations of David and Solomon with the King of Tyre, to obtain from the latter the wood necessary for the palace and temple at Jerusalem. Like our Zikarbal of Byblos, Hiram the Tyrian was not satisfied with the price that he received for his supplies. He lamented the poverty of the villages and territory which Solomon taxed as suzerain, but he accepted the payment, and did not run the risk of pushing his claim too far.

After leaving Byblos, Unamunu was cast by the winds on to Alasia, and there he found himself outside the influence of Egypt. Whether Alasia was, as I think, the mountainous country at the mouth of the Orontes, or if it was, as others regard it, the great island of Cyprus, matters little; it had never submitted to Egypt for any length of time, and Egyptian was not commonly understood by the people, as it was in the cities of Phœnicia. Unamunu incurred many perils there, from which he was rescued by the sacred virtue of Amon-of-the-Road— how, we do not know. The story breaks off at the critical moment, and there is little chance that we shall ever recover the leaves that contain the end of it. I have not attempted to guess with what vicissitudes it ended, nor to restore the incidents that filled the very long gap of the first page. I have introduced a few sentences between the fragments that unite them to some extent. In my translation I have attempted to reproduce the halting and diffuse style of the narrator, which at times is very involved, and to convey as clearly as possible the meaning of the high-flown periods that he puts into the mouths of his personages. Here and there we find touches of picturesque description and felicitous imagery. The author, whoever he may have been, was what we may call well-educated, and he excelled in the presentment of his story.

In the year v, the 16th day of the third month of *the Harvest,* on that day, Unamunu, the senior member of the hall[1] of the temple of Amonrâ, king of the gods, lord of Karnak, started to procure wood for the very august bark of Amonrâ, king of the gods, which is on the Nile, Amânusihaît.[2]

The day that I arrived at Tanis, the place where Smendes and Tanta-mânu were, I placed in their hands the rescripts of Amonrâ, king of the gods.[3] They caused them to be read in their presence, and they said, "Let it be done, let it be done, according to that which Amonrâ, king of the gods, our master, has said." I remained till the fourth month of *the Harvest* in Tanis, then Smendes and Tantamânu sent me with the ship's captain, Mângabuti, and I embarked on the great sea of Syria on the first of the fourth month of *the Harvest. I* arrived at Dora, a city of Zakkala, and Badîlu, its prince, caused ten thousand loaves to be brought to me, an amphora of wine, a haunch of beef. A man of my vessel deserted, taking a gold vase five *tabonu*[4] in weight, five silver vases of twenty *tabonu,* and a small bag of silver of eleven *tabonu,* which made a total of five *tabonu* of gold and thirty-one *tabonu* of silver. I arose early in the morning, I went to the place where the king was, I said to him, "I have been robbed

1. The title *Samsu hai* is best known to us by the representations in the tombs of the Memphite and first Theban Empires, but it continued, at least in the temples, up to the end of the pagan civilisation of Egypt. The persons who bear it are seen superintending carpenters' work, and that is perhaps why Unamanu was chosen as the ambassador of the god in the expedition to procure wood. The translation given by me renders the Egyptian term word for word, but does not give the meaning. I retain it, however, for want of a better.

2. This is the official name of the great bark of Amon of Karnak. (Cf. Brugsch, *Dict. géographique,* p. 165.)

3. Amonrâ was supposed to reign over Thebes, and the High-priest was merely the official who executed his commands on earth. Official acts therefore frequently took the form of decrees issued by the god, and this was the case in this instance.

4. For the value of the *tabonu* see above, p. 102, note 18.

in thy port. Now, it is thou, the prince of this country, who art its inquisitor; seek my gold! Alack, this silver, it belongs to Amonrâ, king of the gods, lord of the countries, it belongs to Smendes, it belongs to Hrihoru, my lord, and to other nobles of Egypt, it is thine, it belongs to Waradi, it belongs to Makamaru, it belongs to Zikarbal, prince of Byblos."[5] He said to me, "To thy wrath, and to thy kindness![6] But, behold, I know nothing of this tale that thou tellest me. If the thief is of my country, and has gone down into thy vessel and stolen thy silver, I will repay thee from my treasure, until the thief himself is found; but if the thief who has robbed thee is thine, and if he belongs to thy vessel, remain several days near me, that I may seek for him."

I was nine days ashore in this port, then I went to him, and I said to him, "So! thou findest not my silver. I will go, as well as the ship's captain, with those who go *to the port of Tyre. If thou findest my money, keep it by thee, and when I return to Egypt I will stop here and take it.*" He consented to this, *and on the 20th of the fourth month of the Harvest, I embarked again on the great sea of Syria. I arrived at the port of Tyre, I told my story to the prince of Tyre and I complained of the prince of Dora who had not found the thieves and who had not returned me my money, but the prince of Tyre was a friend of him of Dora.* He said to me, "Be silent, *or misfortune will happen to thee.*" I departed from Tyre with the morning, *and I went down on the great sea of Syria to go to the place where was* Zikarbal, prince of Byblos. *Now there were some Zakkala with a coffer on the vessel; I opened the coffer,* I found the silver in it, thirty *tabonu,* I took possession of them. I *said to them, "Behold, I take* your silver and it will remain with me until you have found *my own money. If you say, 'We do not know him who* has stolen it, we have not taken it,' I shall take it nevertheless." *When they saw that I was decided,* they went away, and I arrived at the port of Byblos. *I disembarked, I took the naos which contained the statue* of Amon, god of the Road,[7] I placed inside it the

---

5. The meaning of this long enumeration appears to be: the stolen money was the property both of those who had entrusted it to Unamunu, Hrihoru and Amon of whom Hrihoru was high-priest, Smendes, Tantamânu, and the other Egyptian princes; and also of the foreigners for whom it was intended, whether as a gift, or as price for the required wood. One of these latter, Zikarbal, is the prince of Byblos whom we shall meet with later; we know nothing of the other two, Waradi and Makamaru. Zikarbal is the real form of the name Acerbas, Sychas, Sicheus, that was borne by the husband of the famous Dido.

6. This is a polite form of address, both Syrian and Egyptian: "I submit beforehand to thy wrath or to thy kindness, according as my explanations please or displease thee."

7. This is the image that Hrihoru had given to Unamunu to protect him on his expedition. Golénischeff remarked from the first (*Recueil de Travaux,* vol. xxi, p. 94, note 1) that it

equipment of the god. The prince of Byblos caused to be said to me, "Depart from my port." I sent to him, saying, "*Why dost thou drive me away? Have the Zakkala told thee that I have taken their money? But, behold, the money that they had was my own money, which was stolen from me while I was in the port of Dora. Now behold, I am the messenger of Amon, whom Hrihoru, my lord, has sent to thee to procure the necessary wood for the bark of Amon, and the vessel that Smendes and Tantamânu gave me has already returned. If thou desirest that I depart from thy port, give an order to one of the captains of thy vessels that,* when one goes to sea, I may be taken to Egypt." I passed nineteen days in his port, and he spent the time in sending every day to say to me, "Depart from my port."[8]

Now, as he sacrificed to his gods, the god seized one of the chief pages from among the pages, and caused him to fall into convulsions.[9] He said: "Bring the god into the light! Bring the messenger of Amon who is with him! Send him away, cause him to depart." While the convulsed man was in convulsions, that night, I had found a vessel destined for Egypt, I had placed all that was mine upon it, and I regarded the darkness, saying: "Let it descend, that I may embark the god so that no eye beholds him except mine own," when the commandant of the port came to me. He said to me: "Stay till to-morrow, by desire of the prince." I said to him: "Art thou not he who spent the time in coming to me every day saying, 'Depart from my port'? And dost thou not say to me now, 'Remain here,' so that the vessel that I have found may depart, after which thou wilt come to me and wilt say again, 'Depart quickly'?" He turned his back, he went, he told this to

stood in the same relation to Amon of Karnak that in the Stela of Bakhtan (see above p. 145, note 10) the Khonsu sent to Bakhtan stood in to the Khonsu who remained at Thebes, an actual ambassador of Amon to the foreign princes and gods.

8. The restorations that I have inserted in this paragraph are printed in italics; they give only a very summary account of the events that occurred between Dora and Byblos. The original text must have contained two or three episodes which I have not mentioned, but to which allusion is made later on: the departure of the vessel that had brought Unamunu from Egypt, the introduction of the image *Amon of the Road,* and the reasons for which the prince of Byblos refused to receive Unamunu.

9. This is a scene of prophetic mania of the sort that occurred among the Israelites. The page, seized by the god, falls into a kind of epileptic ecstasy, during which he feels the presence of the image *Amon of the Road;* he gives the prince a command from above which obliges him to receive Unamunu, and to do what he requests. Frazer (*Adonis, Attis, Osiris,* p. 67) refuses to believe with Wiedemann (*Altägyptische Sagen und Märchen,* p. 99) that the god by whom he is possessed is Amon; he thinks rather that it is Adonis, because Adonis is the city god, and the privilege of possession over one of the officials of the country belonged rather to him than to a foreign god. The example of Balaam shows that a national god could even take possession of the prophet of a foreign god, and justifies our interpretation.

the prince, and the prince sent to tell the captain of the vessel, "Stay till to-morrow morning, by desire of the prince." When it was morning, he sent to have me brought up, while the sacrifice was taking place, into the castle where he dwells on the sea-coast. I found him seated in his upper chamber, his back leaning against the balcony, while the waves of the great Syrian sea beat behind him. I said to him, "By the favour of Amon!" He said to me, "How long is it up to to-day since you left the place where Amon is?" I replied, "Five months and a day up to to-day." He said to me, "Come, be true. Where are the rescripts of Amon that should be in thy hands? Where is the letter of that high-priest of Amon which should be in thy hand?" I said to him, "I gave them to Smendes and Tantamânu." He became very angry, he said to me, "Then there are no longer rescripts nor letters in thy hands? And where is that vessel of acacia-wood that Smendes gave thee? Where is thy crew of Syrians? Did he not hand thee over to this ship's captain, at the time of departure, to slay thee and throw thee into the sea? It this is so, who will seek for the god? and thou also, who will seek for thee?"[10] Thus he spake to me. I said to him, "Was it not an Egyptian vessel, and was it not an Egyptian crew, which sailed by order of Smendes? For there are not with him any Syrian crews." He said to me, "Are there not twenty vessels lying in my port in communication with Smendes? And that Sidon, that other town thou wishest to reach, are there not there ten thousand other vessels which are in communication with Warakatîlu,[11] and which sail to his house?"[12]

I was silent at this serious moment. He resumed; he said to me, "What commission art thou come here to fulfil?" I said to him, "I am come for

10. The prince of Byblos, learning that Uuamunu had not the letters of credence with him that he should have had, says openly that he suspects him of being an adventurer. Hrihoru and Smendes may have sent him with an order to the captain to throw him overboard at sea. In that case he might be treated without pity; for if any misfortune happened to him and to his statue of *Amon of the Road*, who would trouble themselves as to his fate? Further on (p. 180) it will be seen that Unamunu insists on the fact that if he should disappear, he would be sought for to the end of time to avenge his death. It is to some speech of this kind, now lost with the missing portions of the text, that the prince of Byblos replies here.

11. Warakatîlu is a dialectic form of a name which would be in Hebrew Berkatel or Berekôtel.

12. Unamunu, as a reply to the suspicions of Zikarbal, reminds him that he duly arrived in an Egyptian vessel manned with an Egyptian and not a Syrian crew. By this he means to infer that the Egyptian princes would not commission Syrians to make away with an Egyptian. Zikarbal does not hesitate to silence him and remind him that most of the vessels employed in the Egyptian coasting trade were Syrian vessels, and in consequence would not scruple to execute any orders with regard to an Egyptian that the princes of Egypt might give them.

the woodwork of the very august bark of Amonrâ, king of the gods. That which thy father did, that which the father of thy father did, do thou likewise." Thus I spake to him. He said to me, "That which they did, and thou givest me to do, I will do it. Formerly my ancestors fulfilled this commission because Pharaoh, l. h. s., caused six vessels, filled with the merchandise of Egypt, to be brought, which were unloaded into their warehouses. Thou, therefore, cause them to be brought to me likewise." He had the records of his fathers brought and read in my presence, and he found that in all a thousand *tabonu* of silver[13] was inscribed on his register. He said to me, "If the sovereign of Egypt were my lord, and I were his servant, he would not have to cause silver and gold to be brought, saying, 'Fulfil the commission of Amon.' It was not a royal order that was brought to my father. Now I, in faith, I myself am not thy servant; I am not, I myself, the servant of him who sent thee. I cry with a loud voice to the trees of Lebanon, and the heaven opens, and the wood lies stretched on the ground by the sea-coast;[14] but let the sails be shown me that thou bringest to take thy boats laden with thy wood to Egypt. Let the cords be shown me that thou bringest to bind the beams that I will cut for thee as *gifts. If I do not make the cords for thee,* if I do not make the sails of thy vessels, the fashioning of the bows and stern are heavy, they will be broken,[15] and thou wilt die in the midst of the sea;[16] for Amon thunders, and

13. The ancient value reckoned in modern values represents 92 kilograms of silver (cf. p. 102 note 18).

14. It appears that we should regard this part of the sentence as an emphatic expression of the confidence placed by the prince of Byblos in his own powers. He is no servant of Egypt, and in consequence he is not a servant of Amon, and Amon has no power over the territory occupied by him. If he calls to the cedars of Lebanon to come to the sea, the heaven opens, and the trees, uprooted by the god of the country, fall of themselves on to the sea-shore.

15. The Egyptian sea-going vessels had two points that curved inwards, one at the prow and one at the stern. These were raised above the water, and were generally adorned with the heads of divinities, men, or animals. These two extremities were supported by cords which, attached to the prow, passed over spars fixed along the axis of the bridge and were fastened to the poop at the height of the rudder. The force of the wind and waves greatly strained these outlying portions, and continually threatened to carry them off; should they succeed in doing so the vessel would inevitably founder.

16. The lacunæ that occur in lines 16 and 17 of the text render the meaning uncertain; this, however, is how I understand it. After having said to Unamunu that he was independent of him and of Amon, Zikarbal wished to show that he could do more for Unamunu than Unamunu could do for him. He demands of Unamunu to show him the sails and cordage of the vessels that are to carry the wood, and he finds them insufficient; if he, Zikarbal, does not give him stronger ones, the vessels of Unamunu will not be able to withstand storms and will founder at sea.

he unchains Sutekhu in his time.[17] Now, Amon watches over all countries. Above all, he rules the land of Egypt, whence thou comest, and perfection issues thence to reach the country where I am. What are then these mad journeys they have caused thee to take?"[18]

I said to him, "A lie! There are no mad journeys for those to whom I belong. There are no vessels on the Nile which do not belong to Amon; the sea is his, and the trees of Lebanon are his, of which thou sayest, "They are mine," but which are the property of the bark Amânusihaît, queen of barks. Alack! Amonrâ, king of the gods, spake, saying to Hrihoru, my lord, 'Send me.'[19] And he sent me with this great god. Now behold, thou hast caused this great god to dwell for twenty-nine days since he arrived at thy port, without knowing whether he was there or not; and is it not he who is there, whilst thou dost bargain about the cedars of Lebanon with Amon, their owner? And when thou sayest, 'The kings of former times sent silver and gold,' in truth, if they had sent life and health, they would not have sent material presents; but they sent material presents, instead of life and health, to thy fathers. But Amonrâ, king of the gods, it is he who is lord of life and health, it is he who was the lord of thy fathers, and they passed their lifetime in sacrificing to Amon. Thou thyself, thou art a good follower of Amon. If thou sayest, 'I will do it, I will do it,' to Amon, and thou dost execute his order, thou wilt live, thou wilt be safe, thou wilt be in health, thou wilt be a blessing to the whole of thy country and to thy people. But covet not the things of Amonrâ, king of the gods, for the lion loves his own.[20]

17. Sutekhu, cf. p. 93, note 16.

18. The connection between the end of this speech and the beginning of the next one is not evident at first sight. The transition occurs after the passage where Zikarbal points out the danger of death that threatens Unamunu during his return: "Thy vessel, badly rigged, will founder, and thou wilt perish in the sea, for after all the weather is not always fine, but at frequent intervals Amon makes it to thunder, and gives free course to Sutekhu, the storm god. For Amon, if he watches over all countries, watches principally over Egypt, and he has given more wisdom to it than to other nations. How does it happen that the sovereign of so wise a country commanded such a foolish journey for Unamunu as that which had brought him to Byblos?"

19. *I.e.* Send a statue of Amon with Unamunu, which would contain some of the power of Amon, and would be the divine ambassador by the side of the human ambassador. It is the statue of *Amon of the Road* who is referred to immediately afterwards, when Unamunu says, "Hrihoru sent me with this great god" (cf. p. 145, note 10, the two Khonsus, and the envoy to Bakhtan that one of them makes of the animated statue of the other).

20. In other words, "Give the wood to Amon gratuitously and do not ask him to pay thee, for Amon is a lion, and the lion likes not to be deprived of his prey." The sentence is probably a well-known proverb.

And now, cause my scribe to come to me, that I may send him to Smendes and Tantamânu, the protectors whom Amon has placed in the north of his country, that they may cause to be brought all of which I say, 'Let it be brought,' before I return to the south and despatch thy miserable remnants, all, all." Thus I spake to him. I gave my letter to his messenger, he placed on a vessel the bridge, the head of the bows, the head of the stern,[21] and four other beams shaped with a hatchet, seven pieces in all, and he sent them to Egypt.

His messenger went to Egypt, and he returned to me in Syria in the first month of winter. Smendes and Tantamânu sent four jugs and a basin of gold, five jugs of silver, ten pieces of royal linen for ten cloaks, five hundred rolls of fine papyrus, five hundred ox-hides, five hundred cords, twenty sacks of lentils, and thirty bales of dried fish; and Tantamânu sent me five pieces of royal linen for five cloaks, a sack of lentils, five bales of dried fish. The prince rejoiced, he levied three hundred men and three hundred oxen, he put officers at their head to cut down the trees; they felled them, and the trees lay on the ground all the winter; then in the third month of *the Harvest* they were brought to the sea-coast. The prince came out, he stood near them, he said to me, "Come." As I came near him, the shadow of his umbrella[22] fell on me, and Penamânu, one of the familiar friends who were with him, placed himself between the prince and me, saying, "the shadow of Pharaoh, l. h. s., thy master, falls on thee."[23] But the prince was angry with him, and said to him, "Let be!" I went up to him, and he spake to me, saying, "Lo, the commission that my father executed of old, I have executed myself also, even though thou hast not done for me what thy fathers did. Now do thou behold! Thy wood has arrived to the last piece, and it is there; do now according to thy heart and come to lade it, for is it not to thee that it is given? Neverthe-

21. The bark of Amon had rams' heads at the prow and stern; it is the baulks of wood intended for these two heads that Zikarbal sends as a preliminary present, to arouse the generosity of Hrihoru and Smendes.

22. This is an umbrella similar to that one sees figured in Assyrian bas-reliefs, and which is held above the head of the king by a eunuch or an officer standing behind him.

23. The meaning of this remark, which was clear to an Egyptian, is not clear to us. I think it is founded on the idea prevalent in the East, that every person on whom the shadow of a powerful being falls, whether of a god, a genius, or a king, is under the protection and also under the authority of that being. Penamânu, seeing the shadow of the umbrella of the prince of Byblos fall on Unamunu, said to him jeeringly that *the shadow of his Pharaoh falls on him*— that is, in other words, that henceforth his Pharaoh and his master will be no other than the prince of Byblos, whose shadow falls on him.

less do not come to contemplate the terrors of the sea, or if thou dost contemplate the terrors of the sea, contemplate also mine own.[24] Alas! I have not had done to thee that which was done to the envoys of Khamoîs,[25] who dwelt seventeen years in this country and died here." He said to his intimate, "Take him to see their tomb in which they are laid." I said, "Do not cause me to see it. Khamoîs, the men he sent as ambassadors were only people of his household; there was not *a god* as one of his ambassadors. Notwithstanding thou sayest to me 'Hasten, see thy peers.'[26] Why dost thou not rather rejoice, and cause a stela to be erected on which thou shalt say, 'AMONRÂ, KING OF THE GODS, SENT AMON-OF-THE-ROAD TO ME AS HIS DIVINE AMBASSADOR, WITH UNAMUNU AS HIS HUMAN AMBASSADOR FOR WOOD FOR THE VERY AUGUST BARK OF AMONRÂ, KING OF THE GODS. I FELLED IT, I LOADED IT, I SUPPLIED MY VESSELS AND MY CREWS AND I SENT IT TO EGYPT, TO OBTAIN TEN THOUSAND YEARS OF LIFE FROM AMON MORE THAN THOSE ORDAINED FOR ME: MAY IT BE THUS!' When, after other times, a messenger shall come from the land of Egypt who shall understand the writing, when he reads thy name on thy stela, thou shalt receive the water of Amentît, like the gods who dwell there."[27] He said, "That which thou hast said is a great theme for discourse." I said to him, "The many words thou hast said to me, when I shall have arrived at the place where the chief prophet of Amon is, and when he shall have seen how thou hast executed his commission, he will cause gifts to be brought thee."

I went to the sea-shore where the wood lay, and I perceived eleven vessels that had come in from the sea, and that belonged to the Zakkala with this mission, "Let him be imprisoned, and let there be no boat of his that goes to the land of Egypt." I sat down, I wept. The secretary of the prince

24. I think this passage must be taken thus. After having handed over the wood to Unamunu, the prince of Byblos, who had not yet forgiven the inadequate nature of the gifts he had received, adds, "And now depart quickly, even if the weather is bad; and if thou dost allow thyself to consider the rage of the sea when thou art starting, think that my wrath may be still worse than that of the sea, and that thou mayest run the risk of meeting with the same fate as the envoys of Khâmoîs, whom I kept prisoners here till their death."

25. This Khamoîs is the Pharaoh Ramses IX, as I have already said above, p. 171.

26. Unamunu here develops the theme already indicated above (p. 177), that his embassy is not an ordinary one, but that it includes a god *Amon of the Road*. He complains therefore that the prince should think of comparing him with the merely human envoys of Khâmoîs, and representing them as on the same footing with himself.

27. As a recompense for the service rendered by the prince, his *double* shall have the libations of fresh water that the blessed enjoy in Hades. Cf. p. 8, note 21.

came; he said to me, "What is the matter?" I said to him, "Dost thou not see the herons that go down to Egypt? Behold then, they return to fresh waters; but alas! how long shall I remain abandoned? For seest thou not yonder those who come to imprison me again?" He went, he spake to the prince; the prince wept because of the woeful words that were spoken to him. He sent his secretary, who brought me two amphoræ of wine and a sheep, and he caused Tantanuît, a girl-singer of Egypt who was with him, to be brought to me, saying, "Sing to him, that his heart may make pleasant fancies." And he sent to me, saying, "Eat, drink, that thy heart may not make fancies. Thou shalt hear all that I have to say to-morrow morning." When it was morning, he sent for his people to the mooring-place; he stood in the midst of them, and he said to the Zakkala, "What is your manner of coming?" They said to him, "We are come in pursuit of those broken vessels that thou art sending to Egypt with thy accursed comrades." He said to them, "I cannot hold the messenger of Amon captive in my country. Let me send him off and then hasten after him to take him prisoner."

He let me embark, he sent me off; I left the seaport, and the wind drove me on to Alasia.[28] They of the city came out against me to kill me, and I was dragged in the midst of them to the place where was Hatibi, the princess of the city. I found her coming out of one of her dwellings and entering another. I implored her, saying to the people standing near her, "Is there not one among you who understands the language of Egypt?" One of them said, "I understand it." I said to him, "Say to the Lady, 'I have heard it said even in the city of Thebes and in the place where Amon is, "If injustice is done in every city, justice is done in the country of Alasia," yet behold injustice is done here every day.'" She said, "Alas! what is it thou sayest?" I said to her, "Now that the sea has become furious, and the wind has thrown me on the land where thou art, dost thou not permit me to be brought before thee to be slain? Now I am a messenger of Amon. Verily, behold, I shall be sought for to the end of time.[29] And as to this crew of the prince of Byblos which they seek to slay, if their lord finds afterwards ten of thy crews, will he not slay them as a reprisal?" She caused her people to be assembled; they were arrested, and she said to me, "Go rest. . . ."

28. For the site of the country of Alasia see above, p. 171.

29. It is the same argument already employed by Unamunu before the prince. Cf. above, p. 175.

THE CYCLE OF PETUBASTIS

I

⤙ The High Emprise for the Cuirass [16] ⤙

As I HAVE said in the *Introduction* (pp. cxx-cxxi), we now possess two romances that belong to the cycle of Petubastis. The first of the two, which I have called *The High Emprise for the Cuirass,* is contained in one of the manuscripts of the Archduke Régnier; the fragments of it were among a mass of scraps bought at Dimeh, in the Fayûm, at the north-eastern point of the Birket Karûn. Scattered among several hundred original documents of that locality, covering a period of about three hundred years, from the second century b.c. to the second century a.d., were forty-four pieces of varying sizes that belonged to one demotic papyrus. Krall at once recognised that they formed part of a literary composition—an historical romance as it then appeared—and he applied himself to studying it, putting other things aside. Many of the pieces declined to fit into place, but the greater number were finally arranged into three large pieces, the first of which measured 1 m. 88 in length, the second 79 centimetres, and the third 66 centimetres and 28 centimetres high. The first of these pieces, which is composed of eight fragments, contained the remains of eight columns, of 32, 33, 34, 36, and 38 lines apiece; the second and the third contained five and four columns, more or less mutilated. The twenty-three smaller fragments appeared to arrange themselves into five different columns, so that the entire volume must originally have consisted of twenty-two columns at least, containing more than seven hundred lines, and extending to a length of about six metres. None of the stories known up to the present have attained such dimensions, and yet the work is incomplete. We possess the second half without gaps of any importance, but a large part of the commencement is still missing. When Krall arrived at this point he considered the time had come to announce his discovery. He did so at Geneva in September 1894, at a meeting of the Congress of

Orientalists; but three years passed before a published memoir appeared to confirm the hopes that his verbal communication had raised. He published it under the title *Ein neuer historischer Roman in Demotischer Schrift,* von Jakob Krall, in the *Mitteilungen aus der Sammlung der Papyrus Erzherzog Rainer,* 1897, 4to, vol. vi, pp. 19–80. (Published separately, 62 pp.)

Properly speaking, this was only a detailed analysis of the text, accompanied by numerous notes, in which sentences difficult of translation were reproduced. Such as it was, this first memoir was sufficient to show us the original character of the book. It was a real *chanson de geste,* a song of heroic achievements, the exploits of Pemu the Small, which presents us with a vivid picture of the customs of the Egyptian feudal lords at the time of the Assyrian invasions. The principal points in it were discussed by G. Maspero, *Un Nouveau Conte égyptien,* in the *Journal des Savants,* 1898, pp. 649–659 and 717–731.

Meanwhile, in sorting out the smallest fragments of the Archduke's collection, Krall discovered a number of other minute pieces that had become detached from the original manuscript, which finally brought up the number of small fragments to eighty-two. He then decided to publish the large pieces (J. Krall, *Demotische Lesestücke,* part 2, 1903, plates 10–22): and then to give a translation of all the fragments, large and small, provisional on some points, but complete: J. Krall, *Der demotische Roman aus der Zeit des Königs Petubastis,* in the *Wiener Zeitschrift für die Kunde des Morgenlandes,* 1902, 8vo, vol. xvii. (Published separately, 38 pp. 8vo.)

The discovery of the small fragments has not seriously modified the first restoration that Krall made for the whole of the romance. The order of the three large pieces has been exactly verified, but the smaller pieces have had to be divided between nine columns instead of five, and rather a large number of them come from the first pages; many are unpublished. Krall's text, the only one we have at our disposal, furnished Révillout with a reading for beginners, and a partial translation: E. Révillout, *Le Roi Petibastît II et le roman qui porte son nom,* in the *Revue égyptologique,* 1905, vol. xi, pp. 115–173, and 1908, vol. xii, pp. 8–59.

A transcription into Roman characters and a German translation will be found in: W. Spiegelberg, *der Sagenkreis des Königs Petubastis,* 4to, Leipzig, 1910, pp. 43–75.

The translation I give here has been made from the actual text where it has been published, and from Krall's second translation for the unpublished portions. The author's language is simple, clear, and very similar to that of the first romance of Satni Khamoîs, formed generally of short sentences: a good work to put into the hands of beginners. A certain movement and warmth of style can be recognised in it—a noticeable feeling for description and ability to depict some features in the character of the principal heroes. The beginning is missing, but the general bearing of it can be restored without difficulty. At the time when the Pharaoh Petubastis reigned at Tanis, the whole country was divided between two rival factions, one of which had as leader the great lord of Amon in Thebes—perhaps in this case the Thebes of the Delta, now Ibshân, with which the author has confused the Thebes of the Saîd either involuntarily or intentionally—while the other obeyed the King-priest of Heliopolis, Eiernharerôu-Inarôs, and his ally Pakrûr, prince of Pisapdi, the great chieftain of the East. The great lord of Amon in Thebes was only supported by four nomes in the centre of the Delta, but the four most *weighty* nomes, as the text says (p. 199), those of Tanis, Mendes, Tahaît, and Sebennytos. Inarôs, on the contrary, had succeeded in establishing his children or his relations in most of the other nomes, and also he possessed a sort of talisman, a cuirass which he valued greatly, perhaps one of those iron or brass cuirasses which play a part in the Saite and Memphite legend of the Dodecarchy (*Herodotus* II, clii). When he died the great lord of Amon in Thebes profited by the unrest among the Heliopolitans caused by their mourning to take possession of the cuirass, and to place it in one of his fortresses. When Prince Pemu, the heir of Inarôs, heard of this he despatched a messenger to the robber to summon him to return the talisman. The great lord of Amon in Thebes refused, and the part of the romance still preserved begins with the scene of the refusal.

I have followed the text as closely as was possible for me to do in the mutilated condition in which it has reached us. When the restitution of missing words or parts of sentences came naturally, I did not hesitate to accept them; but frequently, when the gaps were serious, I compressed into two or three sentences the subject of several lines. It is therefore less a translation than a free adaptation, and in many places the reader will find the general sense rather than the actual letter of the Egyptian narrative. At present I can do no more than this.

"*I am not* the first who has come to him on this subject. It is he who carried it off to the fortress of Zaûîphrê,[1] his city, at first, after he had taken the armour out of their hands, and had taken it out of their houses without any one in the world perceiving it. He has taken it to his own city, that I gave him in the district near the superintendent of the flocks of

---

1. The reading of this name is uncertain, although it often occurs in the text. Translated it means *the city of the twins of the Sun*, Shu and Tafnît, and it is the name of a place situated on an island in the nome of Mendes (cf. pp. 185–186, 189).

Sakhmi."[2] All the words that his young servant spake before him he repeated to Pharaoh, and he spent two days in telling them to Petubastis without missing any word in the world. Pemu said to him, "Sorrow of heart be to Zaûîphrê! Hast thou not carried off that cuirass to thy place? Hast thou not stretched out thine hand to the cuirass of the prince Inarôs,[3] to carry it away to Zaûîphrê, thy city, and hast thou not concealed it in order not to restore it to its former place? Hast thou not acted in this manner because of thy confidence in thy strength or because thy family is well versed in the teaching of the soldier?"[4] The great lord of Amon in Thebes said to him, "By Horus! I will not give thee back this cuirass without a fight. Does not my family know the teaching of the soldier?" They went away to prepare for war, each to his own place,[5] then Pemu the Small embarked in his yacht, and having sailed on the river during the night, he arrived at Tanis to notify to the king that which the great lord of Amon in Thebes had done.

Pharaoh Petubastis summoned them before him—the prince of the East, Pakrûr, and Pemu the Small, saying, "Let them prostrate themselves on their bellies in our presence, and let them drag themselves thus before us." The sergeants, the heralds, and the masters of ceremonies said, "Let them come to the Pavilion of audience." The prince of the East, Pakrûr, said: "Is that indeed good that the great lord of Amon of Thebes hath done in covering the prince Inarôs with insults while he had his face turned towards his servants?" When Pharaoh had heard his voice, Pharaoh said, "Chiefs of the East, Pakrûr and Pemu the Small, be not grieved in your hearts on account of the words he has uttered. By the life of Amonrâ, lord of Diospolis, king of the gods, the great god of Tanis, I say to thee again, I will give a great and fine burial for prince Inarôs." As soon as Pemu heard these words, he said, "Pharaoh, my great Lord, the words thou hast pronounced are as balm for the people of Mendes who will escape my vengeance. By Atumu, lord of Heliopolis, by Râ-

2. Sakhmi is the name of the ancient city of Latopolis, now Ussîm, some distance to the north-west of Cairo.

3. For the reading of the Egyptian name Inarôs, see what is said above, *Introduction,* cxvii, note 91, and p. 97, note 2.

4. This expression *the teaching of the soldier,* which occurs several times in the text, appears to mean ability for the military profession, either in the management of weapons in fencing, or in leading troops, in strategy. Elsewhere (p. 198), *to do the teaching of the soldier* signifies to fight according to rules, or simply to fight, to make a thrust.

5. This sentence corresponds to fifteen lines of text, which are too much damaged to permit of restoration.

Horus-Khoprûi-Maruîti, the great god, my god, let him assemble the men of Egypt who are subject to him, and I will return him the blow he has dealt me."[6] Pharaoh said: "My son Pemu, do not leave the paths of wisdom, so that disasters may arise in my time in Egypt." Pemu bowed his head and his face became sad. The king said: "Oh scribe, let messengers be sent to all the nomes of Egypt, from Elephantine to Suânu,[7] to say to the princes of the nomes, "Bring your lectors,[8] and your tarichutes of the Divine House, your funerary bandages, your perfumes of the city of Busiris-Mendes, in order that all that is prescribed for Hapis, for Mnevis, for Pharaoh the king of the gods, may be done, celebrating all the rites in honour of Prince Inarôs, according to that which His Majesty has commanded." And when the time was accomplished, the country of the South was forward, the country of the North hastened, the West and the East ran, and they all assembled at Busiris-Mendes. Then the great chief of the East, Pakrûr, said, "My son Pemu, see the people of the nomes of the east, how they prepare their funerary bandages, their perfumes, their tarichutes of the Divine House, their chief magicians and their assistants who come to the laboratory. How they assemble at Busiris, how they take the body of the dead king Inarôs into the hall of embalmment, how they embalm him and wrap him in the most sumptuous and beautiful wrappings, such as is done for Hapis and for Pharaoh, king of the gods. Let him be served thus and laid in his tomb on the parvise of Busiris-Mendes."[9] After that, Pharaoh sent away the host of Egypt to their nomes and their cities.

Then Pemu said to the great prince of the East, Pakrûr, "My father, can I return to Heliopolis, my nome, and there celebrate a festival, while the cuirass of my father Inarôs remains on the island of Mendes, at

6. Pemu, realising that Pharaoh's intentions are pacific, becomes indignant, and demands that the quarrel shall be settled by combat.

7. The name Suânu is that borne by Assuan in antiquity, but here it is applied to a city of the Delta, and Spiegelberg, identifying it with the Biblical name Sin (Ezekiel xxx. 15), conjectures that it signifies Pelusium. To express the same idea, the Egyptians of the Pharaonic age used the expression, *from Elephantine to Nathô*. Perhaps Suânu, which takes the place of Nathô, should rather be sought in the same latitudes as the latter.

8. For *lectors* see above, p. 20 note 5.

9. This passage appears to show that at Busiris-Mendes the princes were interred in the town itself, in the temple of Osiris. At Sais also (*Herodotus* II, clxix), they were buried in the temple of Neith. This may have been the case throughout the Delta; the distance from the two chains of mountains would not admit of cemeteries being established on the edge of the desert, as was done in the valley.

Zaûîphrê?" The great prince of the East, Pakrûr, said, "These were great words of thine, oh Sûpdîti, god of the East,[10] when thou saidst, 'Thou goest contrary to the will of my prophet, Inarôs, if thou canst return to Heliopolis without our bringing the cuirass with us.'" The two lords embarked on a yacht, they sailed until they arrived at Tanis, they hastened to the pavilion of audience before the king. When the king perceived the princes of the East, Pakrûr and Pemu and their host, his heart was troubled, and he said to them, "What is this, my lords? Did I not send you to your nomes, to your cities, and to your noble men, to celebrate a great and fine funeral in honour of my prophet Inarôs? What then is this troublesome conduct of yours?" The great chief of the East, Pakrûr, said, "My great lord, can we then return to Heliopolis without taking back with us, into our nomes and into our cities, the cuirass of the prince Inarôs, that which is a disgrace for us in the whole of Egypt? Can we celebrate the funerary feasts for him while his cuirass is in the fortress of Zaûîphrê, and we have not brought it back to its former place in Heliopolis?" Pharaoh said, "Oh scribe, write the message of my command to the fortress of Zaûîphrê, to the great lord of Amon in Thebes, saying, 'Do not delay to come to Tanis for a certain matter that I desire thee to do.'" The scribe closed up the letter, he sealed it, he placed it in the hands of a man of colour, who did not delay to go to Zaûîphrê; he gave the despatch into the hands of the great lord of Amon in Thebes, who read it and did not delay to go to Tanis, to the place where Pharaoh was. Pharaoh said, "Great lord of Amon in Thebes, behold the cuirass of the Osiris, the King Inarôs, let it be returned to its former place, let it be taken back to Heliopolis, into the house of Pemu, to the places whence thou hast taken it." As soon as the great lord of Amon in Thebes heard this, he bowed his head and his face became darkened; Pharaoh spake to him three times, but he did not reply.

Then Pemu advanced before Pharaoh and said, "Negro, Ethiopian, eater of gum,[11] is it thy intention, trusting in thy power, to fight with me before Pharaoh?" When the army of Egypt heard these words it said, "The great lord of Amon in Thebes desires war." Pemu said, "By Atumu, lord of Heliopolis, the great god, my god, were not the command

---

10. Sûpdîti, otherwise Sûpdu (cf. p. 72, note 56) the god of the East, is Pakrûr's god. He is usually represented as a sparrow-hawk, crouching, and with a headdress of two feathers.

11. See on this point p. 126, note 92. This insult to the great lord of Amon is the result of hatred of Thebes and its colonies.

issued[12] and did not the respect due to the king protect thee, I would at once inflict on thee the evil colour."[13] The great, lord of Amon in Thebes said, "By the life of Mendes, the great god, the struggle that will break out in the nome, the war that will burst forth in the city, will raise clan against clan, will cause man to march against man, on account of the cuirass, before it will be carried off from the fortress of Zaûîphrê." The great chief of the East, Pakrûr, said to Pharaoh, "Is that well that the great lord of Amon in Thebes has done and the words that he has spoken, 'Pharaoh will see which of us is the stronger'? I will cause the shame of their deeds and their words to recoil on the great lord of Amon in Thebes and on the nome of Mendes, the words that they have spoken, speaking of civil wars; I will restrain them from war, and I will take measures that battle and war may not prevail in Egypt in the days of Pharaoh. But if I am authorised to do so, I will show to Pharaoh war between men of two escutcheons.[14] Thou shalt then be witness of what shall happen. Thou shalt see the mountain leap up to the sky which stretches above the earth and the earth tremble; thou shalt see the bulls of Pisapdi, the lions of Metelis, and their manner of fighting, the sword become drenched after we have warmed it in blood." Pharaoh said, "Nay, oh our father, great chief of the East, Pakrûr, be patient, and do not disquiet thyself farther. And now go each of you to your nomes and your cities, and I will cause the cuirass of the deceased king Inarôs to be taken and brought back to Heliopolis to the place whence it was taken, joy before it, love behind it. If thou dost doubt [this] a great war will break out; [therefore] act that there may be no war in our country. If it pleases you, grant me five days, and by the life of Amonrâ, the lord, king of the gods, my great god, after you have returned to your nomes and your cities, I will cause the cuirass to be returned to its former place." Pharaoh ceased to speak, he arose, he advanced, and Pemu the Small went before Pharaoh and said, "My great lord, by Atumu the great god, if the cuirass is given me and I take it to Heliopolis, without having car-

12. The king had forbidden (p. 185) that there should be any fighting in his time.

13. Krall considers (*Der Demotische Roman*, p. 14) that the evil colour is the colour of death, the livid hue that overspreads the body when life is extinct.

14. Pakrûr entering into the good intentions of Pharaoh, and yet wishing to give satisfaction to Pemu, proposes a duel between the "two escutcheons," *i.e.* between the two rival factions, each represented by the arms of the nome of which their leader was a native; in order to prevent civil war spreading over the whole of Egypt. The rest of the narrative shows that this "suggestion" was not accepted. A combat in the lists was decided upon, which brought the forces of the whole country into action.

ried it off by force, then the lances will be at rest in Egypt, on that account. But if the army of the Entire land returns to its hearths, I shall march in the name of my prophet Inarôs and I will take the cuirass away to Heliopolis."

The great lord of Amon in Thebes said, "Pharaoh our great lord— mayest thou attain the long life of Râ!—may Pharaoh command a scribe to carry my voice into my nomes and into my cities, to my brothers, my companions, my charioteers, who are of my clan, that they may hear me." Pharaoh said: "Come, let a scribe be brought." When he had come, by order of Pharaoh, he wrote to the people of Mendes,[15] as well as to Takhôs, the chief of the militia of the nome, and to Phrâmoonî, the son of Ankhhoru, saying, "Make your preparations, you and your men. Let them be given food, clothing, and money from the king's house, and let them receive command to depart. And to him who has no weapons and no accoutrements, let money be given from my treasury, so that he may come with me to the lake of the Gazelle,[16] which will be the landing-place of the princes, the archons, the chiefs of militia in readiness for the strife of town against town, nome against nome, clan against clan which is about to begin. Also that one is sent to the houses of Ankhhoru, son of Harbîsa, prince of the canton of Palakhîtit. Also that one is sent to the houses of Teniponî, son of Uzakau, prince of . . ." Then the princes of Tanis, those of Mendes, those of Tahaît, those of Sebennytos sent to fetch their armies, and Ankhhoru, son of Pharaoh, sent to his cities and his children, the children of Pharaoh, and they ranged themselves before the pavilion of Pharaoh, each according his nomes and his cities. Thus was it done. When Pemu the Small heard the names of the princes and the armies of the nomes, and the cities to which the great lord of Amon in Thebes had sent, he wept like a little child. The great chief of the East, Pakrûr, looked at him, and he saw that his visage was troubled, and that he was sad in his heart, and he said, "My son, chief of the militia, Pemu

15. This part of the sentence represents two lines of text which are too much damaged to be translated. The following ten lines are in somewhat better condition. Still Spiegelberg has not restored the context perfectly (*Der Sagenkreis des Königs Petubastis,* pp. 52–53), and I am not sure that I have recovered the meaning correctly.

16. The expression employed to designate this locality is rather long—"the lake of the Gazelle, which is the *birkeh* of the city of the goddess Uotît, the lady of the city of Amît," possibly Tell-Mokdam of the present day, "which is the Didu of Hathor of Mafkît," a small village situated in the xixth nome of the Delta (cf. Spiegelbeig, *Der Sagenkreis des Königs Petubastis,* p. 52, note 2). To avoid undue length, I shall translate it everywhere as "the lake of the Gazelle," suppressing the epithets.

the Small, be not troubled. When they hear what has happened, thy allies will join thee also." The great chief of the East, Pakrûr, said to Pharaoh, "Cause Sunisi, the son of Uazhor, the scribe, to be brought, that he may write an order to our nomes and our cities, to our brothers, to our men." Pharaoh said, "Scribe, do all that thou art commanded." The great chief of the East, Pakrûr, said, "Scribe." He replied, "At thy command, my great lord." The great chief of the East, Pakrûr, said, "Make a dispatch for Haruî, son of Petekhonsu, the keeper of the records of the quarters of my city and of the affairs of the people who dwell there, saying, 'Make thy preparations with the host of the nome of the East. That provisions and clothing may be given them, and to him who has no arms or accoutrements let them be given him out of my treasury,[17] and let them set forth on campaign, but let them abstain from all acts of violence, until I anchor in the lake of the Gazelle for the conflict which is about to take place nome against nome, and clan against clan, on account of Pemu the Small, the son of Inarôs, and of the cuirass of the prophet, the deceased prince Inarôs, for Pemu the Small is about to fight with the great lord of Amon in Thebes, about the cuirass of Inarôs that he has carried off to his fortress of Zaûîphrê, which is in the island of the nome of Mendes.'

"Make another dispatch for the nome of the East, for the city of Pisapdi, for the chief of the soldiers, Petekhonsu, saying, 'Make thy preparations as well as thy host, thy horses, thy cattle, thy yacht, and all the men of the East who are bound to follow thee, and this on account of the cuirass of the prophet, the deceased prince Inarôs, that the great lord of Amon in Thebes has carried away into the fortress of Zaûîphrê. I will meet thee at the lake of the Gazelle on account of the quarrel which is about to break forth.'

"Make another dispatch for Phrâmoonî, the son of Zinufi, prince of Pimankhi,[18] in the terms indicated above.

"Make another dispatch for the prince Mînnemêî, the son of Inarôs, of Elephantine, also for his thirty-three men-at-arms, his esquires, his chaplains, his Ethiopian mercenaries, his foot-soldiers, his horses, his cattle.

"Make another dispatch to Pemu, the son of Inarôs, the Small, with the strong hand, saying, 'Make thy preparations with thy host, thy men-at-arms, thy seven chaplains,' in the terms indicated above.

17. It appears the scribe has omitted a line. I give the whole of the formula as it occurs on p. 188.

18. Perhaps this town is identical with one of the same name mentioned on a stela in the quarries of Masara (Spiegelberg, *Der Sagenkreis des Königs Petubastis*, p. 54, note 10).

"Make another dispatch to Busiris, for Baklulu, the son of Inarôs, saying, 'Make thy preparations with thy host,' in the terms mentioned above.

"Make another dispatch to the island of Heracleopolis, to Ankhhoru of the one arm, saying, 'Make thy preparations with thy host as well as thy men-at-arms,' and make another order for Mendes, the son of Petekhonsu and his chaplains in the terms indicated above.

"Make another dispatch to Athribis for Sukhôtês, the son of Zinufi, saying, 'Make thy preparations with thy host and thy men-at-arms.'

"Make another dispatch for Uiluhni, the son of Ankhhoru, the prince of the fortress of Meitûm, saying, 'Make thy preparations with thy host, thy mercenaries, thy horses, thy cattle.'

"And finally make another dispatch to the great chief of the East, Pakrûr, to his nomes and to his cities, saying, 'Make thy preparations for the lake of the Gazelle.'"

Now, after that, the great chief of the East, Pakrûr, said, "My son Pemu, listen to the words that the scribe hath said for thee in thy dispatches to thy nomes and thy cities. Go there speedily, be beforehand with the great lord of Amon in Thebes, and be the first with thy forces at the place, at the head of thy brethren who are of thy clan, so that they may all find thee waiting; for if they do not find thee, they will go back to their nomes and their cities. I myself will go to Pisapdi and I will encourage the host, so that they may not fail, and I will make them go to the place where thou wilt be." Pemu the Small said, "My heart is satisfied with that thou hast said." After that the exalted personages repaired to their nomes and their cities. Pemu the Small set forth, he went up on a new galley furnished with all good things; the galley descended the river, and, after a certain time, Pemu arrived at the lake of the Gazelle, and a place was shown him where he could instal himself in privacy.

Now, while all this was happening, one came to make announcement to the chief of the militia, the great lord of Amon in Thebes, saying, "Pemu the Small has arrived at the lake of the Gazelle, he is established there in privacy, and he is there alone with Zinufi, his young esquire. Make, therefore, thy preparations with thy host, and let it hasten to arm itself. Let the men of Tanis, of Mendes, of Tahaît, and of Sebennytos depart with thee, and let them arrange well with thee to give battle to Pemu the Small. For he has preceded thee, and there are only two feeble ones there. The nomes and the cities that are with thee, command them to repair to the field of battle, and to attack him on the south, on the north, on the east, on the west. They shall not cease their attacks till they have taken his life. When his brethren come and hear of his tragic death, their hearts will be broken within them and their strength will be lessened; they will return to their cities and their nomes, nothing will hold back their feet, and the cuirass of Inarôs will never go forth from thy dwellings." He said, "By the life of Mendes, the great god, it is good that for this cause I have summoned Mendes and the four nomes that are with me. Let a galley be armed for me." It was armed immediately, and the great lord of Amon in Thebes embarked with his host and his men-at-arms. Now it chanced that the host and the men-at-arms of his city were ready, and they departed with the bands of the host of the four nomes. In a short time the great lord of Amon in Thebes arrived at the lake of the Gazelle; he inquired immediately and heard that Pemu the Small had arrived before him.

When the great lord of Amon in Thebes had brought his people to the place where Pemu was, at the lake of the Gazelle, he said, "Let us fight a duel for the space of an hour until one of us has conquered the other." When Pemu heard these words, his heart was troubled immediately, and he thought, "I said to myself that there would be no battle until my brethren had joined me, for my defeat would discourage the host of the nomes of Egypt when they arrive here." But the reply of Pemu was, "I am ready for the combat." Zinufi, his young esquire, wept and said, "May my god protect thee, may thy arm be fortunate, and may God be merciful to thee. Thou knowest well that one man alone among a multitude is in an evil situation, and that a nome is lost if he is alone. Shall I name to thee the bands that are here with the great lord of Amon in Thebes, those of Tanis, of Mendes, of Tahaît, and of Sebennytos, as well as the exalted personages that are with him? Lo! thou enterest the lists with him, without a single one of thy clan with thee. Alas, if he attacks thee, without one of the men-at-arms with thee! By Atumu, an entire army draws nigh to the field of battle for thee, and they will save thy life, a great life; do not fling thyself to destruction by thy temerity." Pemu said, "My brother Zinufi, all the words thou hast said, I have thought them myself. But since matters are such that it is not possible not to have battle before my brothers join me, I will smite down the men of Mendes, I will humiliate Tanis, Tahaît, and Sebennytos, who do not reckon me among the valiant. As it is thus, my brother Zinufi, have good courage, and let my armour of a hoplite be brought me." It was brought to him immediately and was handed to him on a mat of fresh rushes. Pemu stretched forth his hand and grasped a shirt made of byssus of many colours, and on the front of it was embroidered figures in silver, and twelve palms in silver and gold adorned the back. He again stretched forth his hand to a second shirt of linen of Byblos and of byssus from the city of Panamhu, figured in gold, and he put it on. He then stretched forth his hand to a dyed coat, three and a half cubits long of fine wool, with a lining of byssus of Zalchel, and he put it on. He again stretched forth his hand to his corselet of brass, which was decorated with spikes of gold and the four male figures and the four female figures representing the gods of combat, and he put it on. He stretched forth his hand to a greave of smelted gold and fitted it on his leg, he then grasped with his hand the second greave of gold and fitted it on his leg. He fastened the straps, he then placed his helmet on his head, and he went to the place where the great lord of Amon in Thebes was.[19]

This one said to his esquire, "By Mendes, my young squire, bring me my armour." It was brought to him immediately, he put it on, and he delayed not to go to the place where the contest should be. He said to Pemu, "If thou art ready, let us fight one against the other." Pemu accepted and the contest began, but soon the great lord of Amon in Thebes had the advantage.[20] When Pemu perceived this his heart was troubled. He signed with his hand to Zinufi, his young esquire, "Do not delay to go to the port, and see if our friends and comrades have not arrived with their host." Zinufi started off,[21] and delayed not to run to the port; he waited an hour, during that time he watched the top of the bank. At last he raised his face and perceived a yacht painted black with a white border, equipped with seamen and rowers, loaded with armed men, and he saw that they had bucklers of gold on their planks, that there was a lofty spur of gold at the prow, that there was a figure of gold at the poop, and that the squads of seamen worked the tackle. Behind there followed two galleys, five hundred transport-boats, forty *bari* and sixty small boats with their rowers, so that the river was too narrow for the vessels that were there, and the banks were too narrow for the cavalry, for the chariots, for the engines of war, for the foot-soldiers. A chief was standing on the yacht. Zinufi called with a loud voice and he cried aloud, saying, "Oh ye men of the white fleet, men of the green fleet, men of the many-coloured fleet, which of your boats will aid the race

19. The text here describes in twenty-seven lines the shape, material, metal, and decoration of each piece of armour; unfortunately it is much mutilated and the details cannot be made out with certainty. I have been obliged to content myself with giving the general meaning.

20. Here, again, the text is too much damaged to be translated completely. I have been obliged to compress into a few words the probable contents of about eighteen lines.

21. Lit. "Zinufi found [his legs]."

of Pemu the Small, son of Inarôs? Hasten to him in the lists, for he is alone in the conflict. There are neither calasîries,[22] foot-soldiers, horsemen, nor chariots with him, against the great lord of Amon in Thebes. The people of Tanis, of Mendes, of Tahaît, of Sebennytos are aiding the great lord of Amon in Thebes, their god, who dwells in the fortress of Zaûîphrê. His brethren, his allies, his armed men are all supporting him." When the men of the yacht heard him, a calasîries arose on the prow, saying, "A terrible misfortune it is that thou dost announce with thy lips, that Pemu and his clan are fighting against the great lord of Amon in Thebes." Zinufi returned to carry the news. He turned his steps to the place where Pemu was, and he found him engaged against the great lord of Amon in Thebes; his horse had been slain and lay on the ground. Zinufi cried, "Fight, my god Pemu; thy brethren, the children of Inarôs, hasten to thee."

When the great lord of Amon in Thebes saw that Zinufi came back, he commanded the people of Tanis, of Mendes, of Tahaît, and of Sebennytos to redouble their efforts against Pemu.[23] Zinufi, the young esquire, found Pemu, his heart grieved, his face covered with tears, by reason of his horse, saying, "Have they then slain thee, my good beast?" When he heard Zinufi, he lifted up his face and he beheld a yacht furnished with seamen and oarsmen, loaded with armed men, and sailors who sang to the breeze and hastened to the battle. He cried with a loud voice to his little squire Zinufi, "Brother, who are those men?" "It is the clan of Inarôs, who hasten to the aid of Pemu the Small, son of Inarôs." Petekhonsu, the brother of Pemu, who was at their head, defied Ankhho-ru, the son of Pharaoh; then the general fighting was stopped by common accord, and they armed themselves for single combat. Then a messenger did not delay to go to the place where Pharaoh Petubastis was, to tell him all that had passed between Petekhonsu and Ankhhoru, the child of the king. When His Majesty heard it, he became furious. "What is this wicked deed? was it not against my commands, that Ankhhoru, child of Pharaoh, should fight against this dangerous bull, the people of the East? By Amonrâ, king of the gods, my great god, misfortune to the host of Pisapdi! Shame to the men of Athribis, to the host of the nome of Mendes, who bear down the bands of Sebennytos in conflict on account

22. This is the name given by Herodotus (II, cxliv-clxvi) to one of the classes from which the army was recruited. See also p. 215.

23. Once more I am obliged to condense into a few words the meaning of several lines, about twelve, that are half destroyed.

of the clan of high personages, princes, sons of the prophet Inarôs. The banner of the Prince Inarôs is laid down until their allies arrive.[24] Let them prepare for the lists, for the circle of the tilt-yard. Some lies have been repeated to the prince Petekhonsu that he may not joust with Ankhhoru, the royal child, my son, and that he may not raise his flag before all the bands have disembarked and have raised their standards[25] before Pharaoh for the circle of the tilt-yard." The host of the two sceptres and the men of the two bucklers[26] then started on their way. When Pharaoh arrived at the place where Petekhonsu was he perceived the pages of Petekhonsu, and Petekhonsu himself, who was wearing a cuirass of solid iron. Pharaoh advanced and said, "Have not the evil eye, my child, chief of the militia, Petekhonsu; do not engage in war, do not fight, until thy brethren have arrived; do not raise thy banner until thy clan has come." Petekhonsu saw that the Pharaoh Petubastis was wearing the crown on his head; Petekhonsu praised him and addressed the usual prayer to him, and did not engage in battle that day. Pharaoh caused a rescript in honour of Prince Petekhonsu to be inscribed on a stela.[27]

Now while all this was happening, the yacht of the great chief of the East, Pakrûr, arrived at the lake of the Gazelle, and the transports of Petekhonsu and the people of Athribis pushed farther to the north. A wharf was assigned for their transports, and a wharf was assigned for the transports of Ankhhoru, the son of Panemka. A wharf was assigned for the transports of the people of Heliopolis and for the transports of the people of Sais. A wharf was assigned for the transports of Mînnemêî, prince of Elephantine. A wharf was assigned for the transports of Phrâmoonî, the son of Zinufi, and for the host of Pimankhi. A wharf was assigned to Pebrekhaf, the son of Inarôs, and to the host of the nome of Sais. A wharf was assigned to the yacht of the chief, Baklulu, the son of

24. Into this one sentence I condense the meaning of the whole of a long mutilated passage of forty-seven lines which contained the defiance of Petekhonsu, the reply of Ankhhoru, the preparations for the combat, and the beginning of Pharaoh's speech. I have tried to render the general meaning rather than to give its exact tenor.

25. It seems that at the moment of engaging in combat, two troops or two individuals planted a small flag in the ground at each end of the lists or of the field of battle, to which they retired after each bout; towards the end of the day, if neither of the standards had been carried off by force, which was an assurance of defeat, they were laid down to mark the suspension of hostilities. The expression *to suppress the flag* in our text corresponds with *to proclaim a truce, an armistice.* Cf. below, p. 214.

26. In other words, the troops of Pharaoh, his royal guards.

27. This was to record for ever Petekhonsu's act of obedience towards his suzerain.

Inarôs, and to the host of the nome of Busiris. A wharf was assigned to the yacht of Uiluhni, the son of Ankhhoru, and to the host of Meitûm. A wharf was assigned to Uohsunefgamûl, son of Inarôs. A wharf was assigned to the yacht of Pemu the Small, of the strong hand, and to other sons of the prince Inarôs, as well as to the brothers of the chief of the soldiers, Petekhonsu, and to those of the clan of the prophet Inarôs. He who beholds the pool and its waterfowl, the river and its fish, he beholds the lake of the Gazelle with the faction of Inarôs! They roared after the fashion of bulls, they were imbued with power like lions, they raged like lionesses. One came therefore to tell Pharaoh, saying, "The two factions have arrived; they resemble lions in their cuirasses and bulls in their weapons." A high platform was then set up for the king, Petubastis, and another platform was set up for the great chief of the East, Pakrûr, opposite it. A platform was set up for Takhôs, the son of Ankhhoru, and another was set up for Petekhonsu opposite it. A platform was set up for Uiluhni, the commandant of the soldiers of Meitûm, and another was set up for the royal son Ankhhoru, the son of the Pharaoh Petubastis, opposite it. A platform was set up for Psintalês, the son of Zauîranamhaî, the prince of the great circle of Hanufi, and another was set up for Phrâmoonî, son of Zinufi, prince of Pimankhi, opposite it. A platform was set up for Ankhhoru, the son of Harbîsa, the prince of the province of Pilakhîti, and another was set up for Petekhonsu of Mendes opposite it. A platform was set up for Ankhhophis, the son of Phrâmoonî, the prince of Pzoeis, and another was set up for Sukhôtes, the son of Tafnakhti of Athribis, opposite it. The host of the four nomes were ranged behind the great lord of Amon in Thebes, and the host of Heliopolis behind Pemu the Small.

Then Pharaoh said, "Oh great chief of the East, Pakrûr, I see there is no one who can prevent the two bucklers meeting, nome against nome, and every city against its neighbour." The great chief of the East, Pakrûr, went forth clothed in a coat spangled with good iron and cast bronze, belted with a sword of good cast iron, and his dagger in the fashion of the people of the East, cast in one single piece from the handle to the sharpened point. He grasped a lance of Arabian wood for one third, and of gold for another third, and of which one third was of iron, and he took in his hand a buckler of gold. The great chief of the East, Pakrûr, stood in the midst of the bands of Egypt, between the two sceptres and the two bucklers, and he addressed the chieftains in a loud voice, saying, "Know thou, chief of the militia, great lord of Amon in Thebes; it belongs to thee to fight Pemu, chief of the soldiers, the Small, the son of Inarôs, with whom march the seven armed men who were in the camp of the divine son, of the prince Inarôs, and you, men of the nome of Heliopolis, place yourselves in front of the numerous bands of the nome of Mendes. Know thou, chief of the soldiers, Petekhonsu: it belongs to thee to fight Ankhhoru, the royal son, the son of Pharaoh Petubastis. Know ye, Ps ituêris, son of Pakrûr, Phrâ-moonî, son of Ankhhoru, Petekhonsu, son of Bocchoris, and know thou, host of Pisapdi: it belongs to you to fight the host of the nome of Seben-nytos. Know ye, Phrâmoonî, son of Zinufi, and the host of Pimankhi: it belongs to you to fight the host of the nome of Tanis. Know thou, Sûkhôtes, son of Zinufi, chief of the host of the nome of Athribis: it belongs to thee, and also to Ankhhoru, the son of Harbisa, to fight the prince of Tiôme, the chief of the herds of Sakhmi." He placed them man against man, and great was their prowess, great their murderous zeal.

Now after that, it happened that the great chief of the East, Pakrûr, turned in the midst of the fray, and he perceived a calasîris, tall and of fine carriage, who was standing up in a new and well-decorated chariot. He was covered with his armour, and with all his weapons, and he had forty men-at-arms with him, firm and straight on their forty horses, and four thousand foot-soldiers marched behind him, armed from head to foot, and four thousand soldiers well equipped were behind him. He raised his hand[28] before the great chief of the East, Pakrûr, saying, "Be favourable to me, oh Baal, great god, my god! Wherefore hast thou not given me a place in the fight, that I may place myself among my brethren, the sons of the prince Inarôs, my father." The prince of the East, Pakrûr, said to him, "Which art thou of the men of our clan?" The calasîris said to him, "In truth, my father, prince of the East, Pakrûr, I am Montubaal, the son of Inarôs, who was sent against the country of Khoîris.[29] By thy prowess, my father, prince of the East, Pakrûr, I was uneasy, and I could not sleep in my chamber, when I dreamed a dream. A [female] singer of divine words was near me,[30] and said to me, 'Montubaal, son of Inarôs, my son,

28. This is the attitude of adoration with which the gods, Pharaoh, and people of high degree were saluted.

29. This is the Kharu of earlier texts (see p. 90, note 4). The vocalisation Khoîri of the Greek and Baltic period is supplied by the Greek transcription Pkhoîris of the name of Pkhairi, the Syrian.

30. As Spiegelberg has remarked, the word I have here translated *singer* is in the feminine (*Der Sayenkreis des Königs Petubastis*, p. 67, note 10). As it is usually divinities who appear to the slumbering heroes, I think the *singer* is a goddess, probably an Ishtar or an Astarte. Mon-tubaal, having lived in Syria, would see a Semitic goddess in his dream, as naturally as he swears by a Semitic god (cf. below, p. 200, note 36).

hasten as greatly as thou canst hasten! Delay no longer, but go up to Egypt, for I will go with thee to the lake of the Gazelle, on account of the battle and the war that the host of Mendes, and the clan of Har-makhuîti, the son of Smendes, wage against thy brethren and against thy clan, because of the cuirass that they have carried off into the fortress of Zaûîphrê.' Oh my father, prince of the East, Pakrûr, let me be given a place in the lists; for if one is not given me, what will become of me, my father, prince of the East, Pakrûr?" The prince of the East, Pakrûr, said to him, "Hail to thee, hail to thee, Montubaal! Thou dost arrive with thy bands when all is arranged, yet since thou dost demand an order of me this is the order that I give thee. Remain on thy yacht and send none of thy men to the battle, for I will not give thee the signal to fight until the bands of the nomes attack our vessels; then let them not make havoc on the river." Montubaal said to him: "Oh my father, prince of the East, Pakrûr, I will remain on my yacht." Pakrûr showed him the position where he should place himself, and he mounted his platform to follow the vicissitudes of the battle.[31]

The two factions fought from the fourth hour of the morning to the ninth hour of the evening, while the men-at-arms did not cease to strike one against another. At last Ankhhoru, son of Harbisa, the prince of Tiôme, raised himself to rescue another hero of the bands of Seben-nytos, and they ran towards the river. Now Montubaal was on the river on his yacht; he heard the loud cry that arose from the host and the neighings of the horses, and one said to him: "It is the host of the nome of Sebennytos that flies before thy brethren." He said, "Be with me, oh Baal, the great god, my god! Behold it is already the ninth hour, and my heart is troubled because I have taken no part in the battle and the war." He put on his coat and he seized his weapons of war, and hastened to encounter the host of the nome of Sebennytos, the bands of Mendes, and of the fortress of Zaûîphrê, of Tahaît, of the forces of the great lord of Amon in Thebes. He spread defeat and carnage among them, like Sokhît in her hour of fury, when her wrath is inflamed in dry grass. The host dispersed before him, and defeat was spread out beneath their eyes, carnage among them. There was no ceasing from sowing death among them. It was reported to Pharaoh Petubastis, and he opened his

---

31. These few lines represent a summary of the probable meaning of two entire pages, which are so much mutilated that I cannot venture to restore them as a consecutive whole.

mouth with a great cry, he flung himself down from his high platform. Pharaoh said, "Great chief of the East, Pakrûr, go among the soldiers. It is reported to me that Montubaal, the son of Inarôs, is spreading defeat and carnage among the host of the four nomes. Make him cease from destroying my army." The great chief of the East said, "May it please Pharaoh to go with me to the place where Moutubaal is; I will make him cease from slaying the host of Egypt. Pakrûr put on his coat, he mounted a litter with Pharaoh Petubastis. They met with Montubaal, the son of Inarôs, on the field of battle, and the great chief of the East, Pakrûr, said, "My son Montubaal, retire from the lists of the fight. Is it well to spread defeat and ruin among thy brethren, the host of Egypt?" Montubaal said, "Is that well which those men have done; to carry off the cuirass of my father Inarôs into the fortress of Zaûîphrê by guile, and that thou hast not done all that was needed to make them return it to us?" The king said, "Hold thy hand, oh my son Montubaal, and that which thou demandest shall be done forthwith. I will have the cuirass taken back to Heliopolis to the place where it was before, and joy will go before it, jubilation after it." Montubaal had the clarion sounded in his army. They retired from the lists, and it was as though no one had fought.

They then returned, Pharaoh and Pakrûr, with Montubaal, to the battle, to the place where Pemu was, and they found him engaged with the great lord of Amon in Thebes. Pemu had half overthrown his adversary beneath his buckler of plaited rushes; he gave a kick, he caused the buckler to fall on the ground, and he raised his hand and his sword as though to slay him. Montubaal said, "No, my brother Pemu, do not push thy hand to the point of taking revenge on those men, for man is not like a reed that grows again when it is cut. Since Pakrûr, my father, and Pharaoh Petubastis have commanded that there shall not be war, let all be done that Pharaoh has said in the matter of the cuirass, to bring it back to its first place, and let the great lord of Amon in Thebes go, and return to his house." They then separated the one from the other; but it happened immediately that the captain of the troops, Petekhonsu, engaged Ankhhoru, the royal son, and he made a thrust at him in jest. Petekhonsu leapt behind him at one bound, and struck Ankhhoru, the royal son, a blow more hard than stone, more burning than fire, lighter than a breath of air, swifter than the wind. Ankhhoru could not stay the deed nor parry it, and Petekhonsu held him half overthrown before him beneath his buckler of plaited reeds; Petekhonsu flung him to the ground, he raised his arm, he brandished his harpâ[32] and a loud wail like a profound lamentation rose in the army of Egypt, on account of Ankhhoru, the royal son. The tidings were not long concealed from the place where Pharaoh was, to wit, "Petekhonsu has overthrown Ankhhoru, thy son, to the ground, and he raises his arm and his harpâ to destroy him." The king Pharaoh was greatly anguished. He said, "Be merciful to me, Amonrâ, lord king of Diospolis, the great god, my god. I have done my best to prevent fighting and war, but they have not listened to me." When he had said these things, he hasted, and he seized the arm of Petekhonsu. The king said, "My son Petekhonsu, preserve his life, turn away thine arm from my son, for fear if thou slayest him that the hour of my revenge will come. You have had your revenge, you have conquered in your war, and your arm is strong throughout Egypt." The great chief of the East, Pakrûr, said, "Turn away thine arm from Ankhhoru, by reason of Pharaoh, his father, for he is his life."[33] He parted therefore from Ankhhoru, the royal son. Pharaoh said, "By Amonrâ, king of Diospolis, the great god, my god, it is done that the host of the nome of Mendes, and the great lord of Amon in Thebes, he is overthrown, and Petekhonsu has conquered him as well as the host of the four nomes which were the most weighty of Egypt; it only remains to stop the carnage."[34]

Now, while this was happening, Mînnemêi advanced on the river with his forty sergeants-at-arms, his nine thousand Ethiopians of Meroë, with his esquires of Syene, with his chaplains, with his hounds of Khaziru,[35] and the armed men of the nome of Thebes behind him, and the river was too narrow for the people of the yachts, and the bank was too narrow for the cavalry. When he arrived at the lake of the Gazelle, a wharf was assigned to the bull of the militia, Mînnemêi, the son of Inarôs, the prince of the militia of Elephantine, near the yacht of Takhôs, chief of the soldiers of the nome of Mendes, near his fighting galley, and it happened that the cuirass of prince Inarôs was found on

32. The *harpâ* is the sword, with a curved blade shaped like a reaping-hook, which from the earliest times was the characteristic weapon of the Egyptian troops. It is still in use among the Masai, the Chilluks, and many other tribes of equatorial Africa.

33. The text says in the Egyptian, *his respiration, his breath.*

34. The king's speech is so broken by lacunæ that it cannot be translated accurately. I have summarised in a few words the meaning gleaned from fragments of sentences.

35. It may be asked whether these are war-dogs, such as the Asiatic Greeks took with them into battle, in their wars against the Cimmerians; cf. Maspero, *Passing of the Empires,* p. 429, note 1.

this galley. Mînnemêî exclaimed, "By Khnumu,[36] lord of Elephantine, the great god, my god. Lo, here is that for which I have invoked thee, to behold the cuirass of my father, the Osiris Inarôs, in order that I might become the instrument to avenge him." Mînnemêî donned his coat and his weapons of war, and the host that was with him followed him. He went to the galley of Takhôs, the son of Ankhhoru, and he encountered nine thousand armed men who guarded the cuirass of the Osiris Inarôs. Mînnemêî flung himself into the midst of them. He who was there, ready for battle, his place of combat became for him a place of slumber, he who was there, ready for the struggle, he encountered his contest at his post, and he who loved carnage, he had his fill of it, for Mînnemêî dealt defeat and carnage among them. Then he stationed his sergeants-at-arms on board the galley of Takhôs, son of Ankhhoru, to prevent any man in the world mounting thereon. Takhôs resisted as well as he could, but at last he gave way, and Mînnemêî pursued him with his Ethiopians and his hounds of Khaziru. The children of Inarôs hastened with him, and they seized the cuirass.[37]

After that, they brought the cuirass of the Osiris, prince Inarôs, to Heliopolis, and they deposited it in the place where it was before. And the sons of prince Inarôs rejoiced greatly, as well as the host of the nome Heliopolis, and they went to the king, and said to him, "Our great lord, take the calamus and write the history of the great war which was in Egypt on account of the cuirass of the Osiris, the prince Inarôs, as well as the combats fought by Pemu the Small to reconquer it, that which he did in Egypt, with the princes and the host who are in the nomes and in the cities; then cause it to be engraved on a stela of stone and erect it in the temple of Heliopolis." And the king Petubastis did that which they had said.

36. I have already explained the part played by Khnumu (p. 10, note 28, and p. 29, note 38): as he is the god of Elephantine, it is by him that Mînnemêî swears, himself prince of Elephantine. It is also well to notice that all through this story the author has taken care to place in the mouth of each of his heroes the local oath belonging to the fief he governs: Pemu, prince of Heliopolis, swears by the god of Heliopolis, Atumu (cf, p. 186); Petubastis, who reigns at Tanis, swears by Amonrâ, the great god of Tanis (cf. pp. 184, 193); Montubaal, who lives in Syria, swears by Baal (pp. 196, 197); the great lord of Amon by the gods of the Mendesian nome (cf, pp. 184, 187).

37. The three last sentences comprise the substance of about twenty-seven lines of text that are too damaged to be completely reconstructed.

II

The High Emprise for the Throne of Amon [17]

THE second romance has come down to us in a Theban manuscript, which dates from the first half of the first century A.D. The fragments of it were bought from a dealer at Gizeh in 1904 by Borchardt and Rubensohn, and in 1905 by Seymour de Ricci. The larger part, which was acquired by Borchardt and Rubensohn, has gone to the University of Strasburg, where Spiegelberg discovered the subject of it. It has been published, as well as the pieces recovered by Ricci in W. Spiegelberg, *Der Sagenkreis des Königs Petubastis, nach dem Strassburger Demotischen Papyrus sowie den Wiener und Pariser Bruckstücken,* 4to, Leipzig, 1910, 80 and 102 pages, and 22 plates in phototype.

So far as it is possible to judge at present, it contains the Theban version of the theme dealt with in the first romance. The cuirass is replaced by the throne of Amon, probably, as I have said in the *Introduction* (p. cxxiii), by the sacred throne on which the priests placed the strangely shaped emblem, representing one of the types of the god of the Græco-Roman period. The personages that surround Pharaoh in the narrative are many of them the same as those of the previous story—Pakrûr prince of the East, Pemu son of Eienharerôu-Inarôs prince of Heliopolis, Ankhhoru son of Pharaoh and his son Takhôs, and Mînnebmêî prince of Elephantine; and yet, as Spiegelberg has justly observed (*Der Sagenkreis,* p. 8), years have passed since the affair of the cuirass, and new personages have arisen—Pesnufi, the son of Pakrûr, and a young prophet of Horus of Bûto who is not named anywhere, but whose auxiliaries are named generally as the Amêu. This name, which Spiegelberg translates literally as *the Shepherds,* and interprets as *the Asiatics,* affords the basis for a very ingenious comparison with the legend of Osarsûph, the priest of Heliopolis, the Moses of Jewish tradition, and his companions the shepherds or the Impure of Asia; here, however, the term Amêu may have been applied in a vague and inaccurate manner to the Assyrians, the actual masters of Egypt at the time when the Petubastis and Pakrûr of the narrative were living (*Der Sagenkreis,* pp. 8–9). A passage in this romance (p. 249) speaks of these people as being natives of the *country of the papyrus,* and Spiegelberg, following up this idea, recognises in this term an expression analogous with that of the *sea of rushes* by which the Hebrew books designate the bitter lakes of the isthmus of Suez (*Der Sagenkreis,* p. 86, No. 582). It seems to me that this identification, by placing them beyond the Arab nome, the country of the East, over which Pakrûr reigned, assigns them a situation too far from that city of Bûto, where their master, the priest of Horus, exercised his sacerdotal authority. I should prefer to apply the term *country of the papyrus* to those marshes on the north coast of the Delta where, after Isis and Horus, several kings of popular legend or of history had taken refuge. These districts, almost inaccessible, were inhabited by fishermen and half-savage herdsmen, whose bravery and strength struck terror to the hearts of the fellahîn of the cultivated plain and their masters. I have mentioned the Bucolics in the *Introduction* (p. cxxiii), and I consider the word *Amê,* plural *Amêu,* which in Coptic signifies *the drover,* to be similar to the Egyptian original of the Greek *Boukolos* and the Arab *Biamu*—the Coptic *Amê* with the masculine article—by which the chroniclers of the Middle Ages designated the inhabitants of these quarters.

The fragments obtained by de Ricci are for the greater part so short that I have disregarded them. For those of Strasburg, I have followed Spiegelberg's excellent translation, except on some points of minor importance. I have summarily restored the beginning of the narrative, but without attempting to find a place for several incidents to which the author alludes in various parts of his work, especially for those which refer to Petubastis, Pemu, and Pesnufi (cf. pp. 206–207, 210, 212–213), and which inspired the latter with so many picturesque insults to hurl at his suzerain. Like the *High Emprise for the Cuirass,* the *High Emprise for the Throne* is written in a simple style, which occasionally verges on platitude. The romantic interest is only mediocre in the eyes of a literary public, but the information it affords us on certain religious or military usages, and on many points of etiquette among the Egyptians of the Græco-Roman period is sufficiently valuable to merit close study by archæologists.

∽

There was once a high-priest of Amon of Thebes, in the time of the Pharaoh Petubastis, who possessed much land, much cattle, and many slaves, and he had in his mansion a throne of Amon more beautiful than anything else in the world. When he died his beasts and his slaves passed into the hands of his children, but Ankhhoru, son of Pharaoh Petubastis, took possession of the throne. Now it chanced that the eldest son of the high-priest, who himself was priest of Horus at Bûto, desired to have it. He assembled his thirteen men-at-arms, who were herdsmen of the Bucolics, and he sent a message to Pharaoh saying, "If thy son Ankhhoru does not restore to me the throne of Amon which belonged to my father, the high-priest of Amon, I will make war on thee to take it from him." When this message arrived at Thebes, Pharaoh assembled his princes, his military chiefs, the principal ones of Egypt, and he demand-ed of them what he should do; they counselled him to refuse the demand. As soon as the priest of Horus heard this he embarked with his thirteen men-at-arms, and he went up the river until he reached Thebes. He arrived there when they were celebrating the great annual festival of Amon of Karnak, and, falling unexpectedly on the crowd, he seized the sacred bark that carried the statue of the god. Pharaoh Petubastis was very angry, and he summoned the priest of Horus to return the bark; but the priest declared to him that he would keep it as long as the throne was not returned to him; and, no doubt to show yet more the importance he attached to the object he demanded, he boasted of the qualities of the bark, and described it piece by piece.[38] He then added, "And now,[39] is there a man who has more right to the throne than I, a prophet of Horus of Paî in Bûto,[40] the son of Isis in Khemmis? It is to me that this throne belongs, and verily my father, verily my father,[41] who is now first prophet of Amon, and the priests of Amon, have no right to it."

Pharaoh looked at the face of the priest; he said, "Have you heard that which the young priest has said?" The priest said to Pharaoh, "We have not heard these same words before this day, and letters about it have not hitherto reached us." Now, while the young priest said these words Amon, the great god, had appeared, listening to his voice.[42] The

38. This description, which occupies the first page that is preserved of the *Spiegelberg Papyrus,* is too much damaged to permit of a consecutive translation. As Spiegelberg has stat-ed (*Der Sagenkreis des Königs Petubastis,* p. 13), it is composed on the model of mystic descrip-tions of barks in the world of the dead; every part of the hulk and of the rigging is compared to a god or goddess who protects it.

39. Here begins that part of the text that I have thought possible to translate.

40. Pai, Pi, Pu is the name of one of the twin cities that formed the city of Bûto, the Tell Abtu of to-day. The second was called Dupu.

41. Although the position occupied by these words at the end of the fourth line, repeated at the beginning of the next, might make one suspect them of being an unconscious dittog-raphy on the part of the scribe, I regard the reduplication as a voluntary one. The priest would utter it to give greater force to his claim.

42. This must not be regarded as an actual theophany of the god himself, appearing at the king's council, but, according to Egyptian custom, as the arrival, on priests' shoulders, of the ark that contained the statue of Amon (cf. Maspero, *Causeries d'Egypte,* pp. 167, 173, 293, 298, and *Au temps de Ramsès et d'Assourbanipal,* pp. 66–69).

lector[43] said therefore, "If it please Pharaoh, let Pharaoh question Amon, the great god, saying, 'Is the young priest he who has a right to the said throne?'" Pharaoh said, "That thou sayest is just." Pharaoh then questioned Amon, saying, "Is the young priest he who has a right to the said throne?" Amon then advanced with rapid steps,[44] saying, "It is he." Pharaoh said, "Young priest, as these matters were known to thee in thy heart, wherefore didst thou not come yesterday to raise thy voice as to these same matters, before I gave a brief with regard to them to the first prophet of Amon? For I should have forced Ankhhoru, the royal son, to cede thee the throne itself." The young priest said to Pharaoh, "My great lord, I came to Pharaoh to speak of it with the priests of Amon.[45] As Amon, the great god, was he who found the things for Horus, before he had avenged his father Osiris, I came to receive the charm of Amon, the great god, even that which he made when Horus, son of Isis, son of Osiris, was sent to the Saîd to avenge his father Osiris, I spoke with him about the vengeance obtained by Horus [with his aid]." Takhôs, the son of Ankhhoru, said, "If then thou spakest with him yesterday, do not come back to-day, and do not hold evil discourse. Ankhhru, the royal son, was armed before the diadem of Amon, the great god; he has returned to the Saîd, and he has been calmed as in the day when he arrived at Thebes."[46] The young priest said, "Cease speaking to me with thy mouth, Takhôs, son of Ankhhoru, and when I question thee on those matters of the chief

43. For the meaning of this title and the function of the priest who bears it, see above, p. 20, note 5.

44. Naturally it is the priests who advance at a rapid pace, bearing the ark of the god.

45. The text is damaged and the sequence of ideas is not clear. The priest here gives the reason why he had not presented himself the previous day, while before he claimed the return of the throne Pharaoh Petubastis had adjudged it in legal form to Ankhhoru. The reason he gives for his delay, and which appears to justify his action, is drawn, so far as I can judge, from the myth of the god. It seems that Horus before entering on a campaign to *refresh—qabhu—* the wrath of his father Osiris, in other words to appease him by avenging him, was sent by his mother Isis to Amon at Thebes, that the god might provide him with the necessary charms to triumph over Typhon; the most powerful of these charms was provided by the crown of the god, *i.e.* by the uræus that adorns the crown, the flame of which destroys enemies. The priest, starting for the Saîd, to win back his property, acts as the god had done, and he goes first of all to request Amon for the magic power of his crown, which has assured victory to Horus. It was while he was reporting—*sami, semme*—his intentions to Amon that the throne was given to Ankhhoru.

46. These words of Takhôs evidently contain a threat which is only half expressed. If I understand them aright, they suggest that Ankhhoru also is provided with the charm that dwells in the crown of Amon. He has been calmed—*talko*—with much difficulty; but if the priest insists, he will give rein to his anger.

of militia which concern thee, attend to them. The thrones of the temple, where hast thou put them? By the life of Horus of Paî in Bûto, my god, Amon shall not return to Thebes, in the usual manner, until Ankhhoru, the royal son, has given me the throne which is in his hands." Ankhhoru, the royal son, said to him, "Art thou come to take the said throne by an action in law, or art thou come to take it by battle?" The young priest said, "If my voice is listened to, I consent that it is decided by action in law; if my voice is not listened to, I consent that it is decided by battle."[47]

When he had spoken thus, Ankhhoru, the royal son, gave way to wrath like the sea, his eyes flashed fire, his heart darkened with dust like the mountain of the East;[48] he said, "By the life of Amonrâ, lord of Sebennytos, my god, the throne that thou claimest, thou shalt not have; I will return it to the first prophet of Amon, to whom it belonged from the beginning." Ankhhoru, the royal son, turned his face to the dais,[49] he flung on the ground the vestments of fine linen that were upon him, and also the ornaments of gold with which he was adorned; he caused his harness to be brought, he sent for his talismans of the lists,[50] he went to the forecourt of Amon. When the young priest had turned his face to the dais, behold, there was a page in front of him, who was hidden in the crowd, and who had a cuirass of fine workmanship in his hands; the young priest went to him, and took the cuirass from his hands, he put it on, he went to the forecourt of Amon, he marched to encounter Ankhhoru, the royal son, he struck him, he fought with him. Then Takhôs, son of Ankhhoru, opened his mouth to protest, and the men of battle were indignant against the host, saying, "Are you going to remain there near Amon, while a herdsman fights with the son of Pharaoh, without placing your arms on his side with him?" The host of

47. Lit. "I grant that he take it by judgment. . . . I grant that he take it by battle." The young priest here addresses the king and the auditors in general, and he designates his adversary by the pronoun *he;* he declares himself ready to accept either an action in law or a duel to decide the question of proprietorship.

48. Lit. "His heart gave birth for him of dust like the mountain of the East." The effect of his wrath is here compared to the effect of the storm-wind, the Khamsîn.

49. The word *tuôt,* employed here, seems to me to be the latest form of the word *zadu, zatu,* of the Ramesside age, which denotes a platform surmounted by a dais, on which the Pharaoh gave audience. The two champions one after the other turn to the sovereign to salute him before putting on their armour.

50. These were the talismans that the soldiers took with them to protect them during the fight; they will be referred to later (pp. 207–208).

Egypt hastened from every side, those of Tanis, those of Mendes, those of Tahaît, those of Sebennytos, the host of the four weighty nomes of Egypt;[51] they came, they repaired to the lists to join themselves to Ankhhoru, the royal son. [On their side], the thirteen herdsmen of the Bucolics[52] fell on the host, enclosed in their harness, the helm with a bull's face on their head,[53] a buckler on their arm, and the harpâ in their hand; they ranged themselves to right and left of the young priest, and their voices resounded, saying, "Receive our oath that we make before Amon, the great god, present here to-day: if one among you shall cause the prophet of Horus of Pu, in Bûto, to hear a word that displeases him we will water the ground with his blood." The fame of the strength of the priest, the fear in which they held the thirteen herdsmen for Pharaoh was so great in the host, that no one in the world ventured to speak. The young priest arose against Ankhhoru, the royal son, as a lion against a wild ass, as a nurse against her nursling when he is naughty: he seized him below his cuirass, he threw him on the ground, he bound him firmly, he pushed him on the road before him. The thirteen herdsmen walked behind him, and not a person in the world attacked them, so great was the fear that they imposed. They made their way to the bark of Amon, they went on board, they laid down their harness, they pushed Ankhhoru, the royal son, into the hold of the bark of Amon, bound with a strap from Gattani,[54] and they let down the trap-door over him. The seamen and the rowers went down on to the bank; they placed their bucklers by their side, they washed themselves for a festival, they brought the bread, the meat, and the wine which they had on board, they placed it before them, they drank, they made a happy day.

Now, while they turned their faces to the bank, in the direction of the diadems of Amon, the great god, while they purified themselves with salt and incense before him, Pharaoh opened his mouth for a great cry, saying, "By Amon, the great god, mourning for Pemu is finished, lamenta-

51. Probably those in which the contingents were most numerous, and weighed most heavily in the fight; cf. above, p. 199.

52. Lit. *The district of the Papyrus*, the Bucolics of the Roman period; see above, pp. cxxiii, 201.

53. The helmet, with the bull's face is probably the helmet with the bull's horns that is seen, worn for instance by the Pharaohs at the time of Ramses III; cf. Champollion, *Monuments de l'égypte*, pl. xxviii, cxxi, cccxxvii, and Rosellini, *Monumenti Storici*, pl. 101, 106, 129, 131.

54. Gattani, or Gatatani, is a country unknown up to the present. If it should really be read Gattani or Kattani, one might consider Cataonia.

tions for Pesnufi have ceased;[55] more mourning! My heart is now all pre-occupied by these herdsmen, who have come on board the bark of Amon enclosed in their harness, and have made it their hall of festival." Takhôs, son of Ankhhoru, said, "My great lord, Amon, the great god, has shown himself; let Pharaoh consult him, saying, 'Is it thy excellent command that I cause the host of Egypt to arm against these herdsmen, to deliver Ankhhoru from their hands?'" Pharaoh therefore consulted the diadems of Amon, saying, "Is it thy excellent command that I cause the host of Egypt to arm to fight against these herdsmen?" Amon made the sign of refusal, saying, "No." Pharaoh said, "Is it thy excellent order, that I cause a carrying-chair to be brought, on which to place thee, and that I cover thee with a veil of byssus, that thou mayest be with us until the affair is ended between us and these herdsmen?" Amon advanced with rapid steps,[56] and he said, "Let one be brought." Pharaoh therefore caused a carrying-chair to be brought, he placed Amon therein, he covered him with a veil of byssus.

And then after that, Pharaoh Petubastis was with the army in the western region of the Saîd opposite Thebes, and Amon, the great god, reposed under an awning of byssus, while the host of Egypt donned its armour, and the thirteen herdsmen remained on board the bark of Amon, keeping Ankhhoru, the royal son, bound in the hold of the bark of Amon, because they had no fear of Pharaoh in their hearts, nor yet of the diadems. Pharaoh raised his face, and he saw them on the bark of Amon. Pharaoh said to Pakrûr, son of Pesnufi, "What shall we do about those herdsmen who are on board the bark of Amon, and who incite revolt and battle before Amon, on account of the throne which accrued to the first prophet of Horus, and which now belongs to Ankhhoru, the royal son? Go, say to the young priest, arm thyself, put on a vestment of byssus, go in before the talismans of Amon, and become the first prophet before Amon, when he comes to Thebes." Pakrûr did not delay to go and place himself in front of the bark of Amon, and when he was in the presence of the herdsmen he told them all the words that Pharaoh said to him. The young priest said, "By Horus! I have taken Ankhhoru, the royal

55. Petubastis no doubt alludes here to the same incidents that he, Pesnufi and Pemu refer to later (cf. pp. 210–211, 212–213), and which are related either in the missing part of this story, or in some other story, now lost. Faced by this new grief that falls on him by the action of the drovers, he will think no longer of the sorrow caused him by the affair of Pesnufi and Pemu.

56. Cf, above, p. 204, note 44, for the meaning of this expression.

son, prisoner, and thou comest to speak to me in the name of his father.[57] Go, and carry my reply to Pharaoh, saying, 'Hast thou not said; come to the bank, put on byssus, and let thy hand put away the weapons of war; if not, I will turn against thee the host of Egypt, and I will cause them to inflict on thee very great injury, very great?' If Pharaoh will adjudge me the throne, let them also bring me the veil of byssus, with the talismans of gold here on the bark of Amon; then I will come near to them, and I will lay down my harness of battle. Therefore let them bring me the diadems of Amon on board; I will take the pole of the bark[58] and I will take Amon to Thebes, being alone on board with him and the thirteen drovers, for I have not allowed any man in the world to come on board with us." Pakrûr went to the place where Pharaoh was, and he told him the words that the young priest had spoken to him. Pharaoh said to him, "Life of Amon! as to that which the young priest spake, saying, 'I have taken Ankhhoru, the royal son, thy son, therefore let them give me the diadems of Amon, I will take them on board, and the next day I will depart for the north with them, and I will take them to Buto, my city.' If it were gold, silver, or precious stones that the young priest asked of me, I would have caused them to be given him; but I will not give him the diadems for him to carry to Buto, his city, and for him to make a great concert in Thebes."[59]

And after that, the general, the great lord of Amon in Thebes, went to the south of Thebes to honour Monturâ, and when the ceremonies were finished in presence of Pharaoh,[60] the general, great lord of Amon in Thebes, rose in front of him and said, "My great lord, the talismans are on me on their account, and thanks to that, I am about to captivate thy heart by that which is about to happen to these drovers. They shall not reach here, on account of the heritage of the prophet of Amon, but if they

57. Spiegelberg has remarked that there was a gap in the narrative at this point, and supposed that the scribe had carelessly omitted the speech of Pakrûr to the priest of Horus, as well as the beginning of the priest's reply (*Der Sagenkreis des Königs Petubastis*, p. 21, note 15). The analogy with lines 19–21 of the same page leads me to think that the author had not placed the speech directly in the mouth of Pakrûr, and that only the first words of the priest's reply are missing. I have given the probable meaning in a few words.

58. According to Egyptian custom, there are two pilots on each vessel: one at the stern who works the rudder-oars, and one in the bows with a long pole in his hand, who sounds the channel and gives directions to his comrade in the stern. Here the priest of Horus takes the part of the pilot in the bows in order to ensure the safe arrival at Thebes of the bark of Amon.

59. In other words, "that he may celebrate his victory over us by singing thanksgivings at Thebes itself."

60. These few words condense what I believe to be the meaning of three lines of text too much damaged to be read with certainty.

wish that there should be battle between them and Pharaoh, I will give battle." He put on his harness, he went to place himself before the bark of Amon, he addressed himself to the young priest, saying, "Bethink thee well of the guilty acts which have been done by thee and by thy men who have gone up on board the bark of Amon, you who have put on your harness, and have allowed the bark of Amon to become the property of the priest of another god. If thou art come here on account of the heritage of the priest of Amon, come on shore and take it; if thou art here greedy of battle, come on shore and I will give thee thy fill." The young priest said to him, "I know thee, general, great lord of Amon in Thebes; thou art a man of the great land of the North as much as we, and thy name has often reached us for the long speeches that thou hast made. I will send one of the herdsmen ashore with thee, that thou mayest pass an hour talking with him."[61] The young priest cast a glance over the thirteen herdsmen who were on board with him; he arose, he put on his harness, he went down to the bank, he encountered the general, great lord of Amon in Thebes, he rose up against him as a nurse rises against her nursling when he is naughty, he threw himself on the chief of the militia, the great lord of Thebes, he seized him under his cuirass, he flung him to the ground, he bound him, he put him on his feet, he led him on board the bark of Amon, he thrust him into the hold where Ankhhoru, the royal son, was already, he shut down the trap-door on him, he took off his harness in order to wash himself for the feast with the priests, his companions. The crew went to pour out the libation of wine; they drank, and they celebrated a festival in the presence of Amon, under the eyes of Pharaoh, and in the sight of the host of Egypt.

Then Pharaoh opened his mouth with a great cry, and he said, "When I sailed towards the south, the galley of Ankhhoru, the royal son, sailed at the head of the fleet that bore Pharaoh with the host of Egypt, a golden buckler hoisted at the top of his mast, for, said he, 'I am the first buckler of Egypt.' And the great galley of the great lord of Amon in Thebes sailed at the rear of the fleet of Pharaoh, for, said he, 'I am the great vessel of Egypt.' And now a young herdsman is come to the south, who has taken the first buckler of Egypt and the great vessel of Egypt; he makes Egypt to tremble like a disabled vessel that no pilot steers, and he is stronger than all these men, as well as Amon, the great god who is on the west of the Saîd, opposite Karnak; he has not allowed him to

61. This must be taken ironically, as mocking the general.

return to Karnak." Takhôs said, "Beware, my great master. If the host of Egypt does not arm against these herdsmen, they will remain as they now are; let the men of Pharaoh be called together against them." Pakrûr spake to Takhôs, saying, "Is not that which thou sayest madness, and have not those yielded who provoked the herdsmen, who have taken Ankhhoru, the royal son, and the general, the great lord of Amon of Thebes. The host could not rescue even one of them. That which thou hast spoken, saying, 'Let the host of Egypt arm themselves against them,' will not this cause the drovers to make a great carnage? and since Amon, the great god, is here with us, has it ever happened to us to undertake anything whatsoever in the world without consulting him? Let Pharaoh consult him, and if he says to us, 'Battle,' we will fight; but if he commands otherwise, we will act in accordance." Pharaoh said, "The advice is good which comes from the prince of the East, Pakrûr."

When Pharaoh had commanded that Amon should appear, Pharaoh went to meet him. Orisons and prayers he made, saying, "My great lord, Amon, great god, is it thy excellent command that I cause the host of Egypt to arm against these herdsmen, to do battle with them?" Amon made the gesture of refusal, saying, "No." Pharaoh said, "My great lord, Amon, great god, is it thy excellent command that, if I abandon the throne which was in the heritage of the prophet of Amon to the young priest, he shall restore their liberty to Ankhhoru, the royal son, and the great lord of Amon of Thebes?" Amon made the gesture of refusal, saying, "No." Pharaoh said, "My great lord, Amon, great god, shall these herdsmen take Egypt out of my hands in the position they now hold?" Amon made the gesture of refusal, saying, "No." Pharaoh said, "My great lord, wilt thou give me victory over these herdsmen, that they may abandon the bark of Amon?" Amon advanced with rapid steps,[62] and behold, he said, "Yes." Pharaoh recited before Amon, the great god, the names of the chieftains, the generals of the host, the princes, the commandants of chariots, the officers of the militia, the captains of the militia, and the chiefs of the reserve of the men of Egypt, and Amon, the great god, approved of none of them, Amon approved only of the prince Pesnufi, and the captain of militia, Pemu, saying, "These are they whom I take to chase away the herdsmen in whose hands is the bark of Amon; these are they who shall deliver Ankhhoru, the royal son, and the general, the great

62. For the meaning of this expression see p. 204, note 44.

lord of Amon in Thebes; these are they who shall lead to battle the young troops of Thebes."

When Pharaoh had designated by Amon the chiefs of the appropriation, Pharaoh cast a glance at Pakrûr, the chief of the East; he spake to him, and he laid before Amon the questions that he asked. The chief of the East said, "If it please Pharaoh, let some one be sent to the young troops of Thebes, who shall come south, and then they will do all that Pharaoh shall command them." Pharaoh said, "Amon preserve me from that! It matters not whom I send to them to the south, they will not come because of the affront that I put upon them when I went south to Thebes, and when I did not invite them to the feast of Amon, the great god, my father.[63] Chief of the East, Pakrûr, it falls to thee to send them a message in case some one must send them a message; but they will not come south for me." The chief of the East, Pakrûr said, "My great lord, the affronts that thou hast put on the young troops are great; one time after another thou hast not thought of the men of war until thou hast caused them to be rejoiced by thy misfortunes." Pharaoh said, "Amon, the great god, protect me! It is not I who have affronted them, but is it not the evil intrigues of Takhôs, the son of Ankhhoru? It is he who has caused me to leave them, so that I did not bring them with me; for he said, 'Dissension and quarrels should not be spread abroad among the host of Egypt.'[64] And after that, he who spreads his nets, they will catch him; he who digs a perfidious pit, he will fall into it; he who sharpens a sword, it will cut his throat. Now behold, the brothers-at-arms of Takhôs, the son of Ankhhoru, are in the bonds of the herdsmen, and no man can be found to fight for them. And after that, dispute not about words,[65] but act."

The chief of the East, Pakrûr, sent a message to the young warriors, saying, "Come south, for thy glory and thy power, for they are demanded in the host of Egypt." The chief of the East, Pakrûr, said, "Let Higa, the son of Mînnebmêî, my scribe, be called." One ran and returned, and he was brought immediately, and the chief of the East, Pakrûr, said to

63. The episode to which Petubastis alludes is probably recorded in the first pages of the papyrus, that are now lost.

64. It appears that these Theban bands had the reputation of being turbulent and quarrelsome; Takhôs advised Pharaoh to let them return home, alleging as a reason that they were an element of discord in the army.

65. Lit. "do not set one word against its companion."

him, "Make a letter, and let it be carried to Pisapdi,[66] to the place where prince Pesnufi is." Here is the copy: "The chief of the East, Pakrûr, son of Pesnufi, father of the bulls of Egypt, good shepherd of the calasîries,[67] salutes Prince Pesnufi, his son, the powerful bull of those of Pisapdi, the lion of those of the East, the wall of brass which Isis has given me, the iron stake of the lady of Tasonût, the beautiful bark of Egypt, in which the host of Egypt has placed its heart. If it please thee, my son Pesnufi, when this letter reaches thee, if thou art eating, lay down the bread, if thou art drinking, put down the jug that makes drunk, come, come, hasten, hasten, and embark with thy brothers-at-arms, thy fifty-six men of the East, thy brother-at-arms, Pemu, the son of Inarôs, with his new bark, the *Star*,[68] and his four chaplains. Come to the south of Thebes, on account of certain herdsmen of the Bucolics, who are here at Thebes, fighting each day with Pharaoh. They allow no one to attain to Amon nor to Karnak; Amon dwells exiled on the west of Thebes beneath the veil of byssus, and the host of Egypt trembles before his violence and bloodshed. Ankhhoru, the royal son, the son of Pharaoh Petubastis, and the general, the great lord of Amon in Thebes, are prisoners of the herdsmen; they are on board the bark of Amon. Come to the south, give battle, and let the host of Egypt learn to know the fear and the terror that thou inspirest." The letter was closed, it was sealed with the seal of the chief of the East, Pakrûr, it was placed in the hands of Hakôris, and he hastened to the north by night as by day. After several days, he arrived at Pisapdi; he went without delay to the place where Pesnufi was. He gave him the letter. Pesnufi read it, he heard every word it contained, he growled like the sea, he boiled like resin [which is burning], he said: "This fisher of eels of Tanis, this trap hidden in the reeds of Bûto, Petubastis, son of Ankhhoru, whom I have never called Pharaoh, when he does honour to me, it is because he needs me against injury done to him, but when he goes to celebrate the festival of his god, and there is neither war nor battle against him, he sends me no message. I swear here, this is what I will do in the name of Sapdi, chief of the East, my god. Since the chief of the East, Pakrûr, my father, has written to me in this

66. Pisapdi is the Saft-el-Hineh of to-day.

67. For this word, which designates certain troops of the Egyptian army, cf. *Herodotus* II, clxiv, clxvi, clxviii; cf. above, pp. 204, 208.

68. The royal bark from the earliest times was called *the Star*, or at full length *the Star of the gods*.

letter, saying, "Amon, the great god, in the west part of the Saîd, which is opposite Karnak, is not allowed to return to Thebes, because no one will fight for the children of Tahuris, the daughter of Patenefi.[69] And after that, neither I nor my brothers-at-arms, the fifty-six men of the East, we will no longer remember the injury that Amon has done me. Our eight chaplains have embarked, and they have put on their harness, to repair to the south of Thebes. Depart, running hound of Sapdi, servant of the throne,[70] do not delay, go to Heliopolis. Speak to Pemu, the son of Inarôs, saying, 'Put on thy harness, arm thy new vessel of cedar and thy four chaplains. I will meet with thee and thy crew at Pinebôthes, the port of Heliopolis.'"[71] The servant of the throne did not delay to repair to Heliopolis; he stood before Pemu, and he repeated all that Pesnufi had said to him, "Do thus." Pesnufi put on his harness, and so did his fifty-six men of the East, and his eight chaplains; he embarked, he delayed not to repair to Pinebôthes, and he there met with Pemu, who was on his galley, with his new vessel named the *Star*, and his four chaplains, and they sailed for the south of Thebes.

And after that, when Pharaoh Petubastis was with the army on the western bank of the Saîd, opposite Thebes, and that the host of Egypt was all armed, Pharaoh went up on to the bark of Amon, looking at the side opposite to that by which Pesnufi and Pemu, the son of Inarôs, should arrive. At the end of an hour Pharaoh perceived a new galley of cedar which descended the stream. When it had reached the quay of Amon of Thebes, a man-at-arms leapt on to it, his cuirass on his back, and crossed in it to the west side of the Saîd, to the south of the vessel of Pharaoh. The man came off it on to the bank, armed from head to foot, like a horned bull. He went up with great strides farther up stream than the bark of Amon without going as far as the place where Pharaoh was, and he spake in front of the host, saying, "Oh, may the good Genius[72]

69. Tahuris is probably the mother of Petubastis.

70. The messenger, acting for Petubastis and Amon, might in fact be called a servant of the throne.

71. Lit. "My mooring stake with thee and thy [crew is] at Pinebôthes, the port of landing for Heliopolis." The stake Pesnufi speaks of is that which Egyptian sailors thrust into the bank and tie their boat to (cf. above, p. 212), "the iron stake of the lady of Tasonût." The Egyptian expression, which is obscure to us, seems to be capable of being paraphrased as I have rendered it in the text.

72. *Pshaï*, the Agathodemon, often represented under the form of a round-faced serpent crowned with the pschent. He is the ancient Shaî, *destiny*: his cult, secondary in Pharaonic times, developed considerably under the Ptolemies and Cæsars.

grant life to Pharaoh! I know the crime you have committed in going on board the bark of Amon, cuirass on back, and giving it over to a priest who is not his." The prophet of Horus of Paî said to him, ""Who art thou who speakest thus? Art thou a man of Tanis, or art thou a man of Mendes?" The armed man said to him, "I was not born in that land of the North of which thou speakest. I am Mînnebmêî, son of Inarôs, the great prince of Elephantine, the chief of the south of Egypt." The herds-man[73] said to him, "Since thou art not a man of the land of the North, why has Pharaoh put the bark of Amon under thy charge? Now! come on board with us and make a happy day before Amon, and that which happens to us concerning it will happen also to thee." And after that, Mînnebmêî said to him, "May Khnumu the great lord of Elephantine, protect me! You cannot atone for the crime you have committed. If I allowed myself to embark and pass a happy day with you, it would be a declaration of war against Pharaoh. Now, that which I speak, I do it to you: open the road to Amon that he may go to Thebes; if not, that which you do, I will make you do it by force, notwithstanding your unwilling-ness." One of the thirteen herdsmen rose up and said, "I come to thee, negro, Ethiopian, eater of gums,[74] man of Elephantine." He put on his armour, he hastened to the bank, he struck, he fought with Mînnebmêî up-stream from the bark of Amon, from the moment of the first hour of the morning till the moment of the eighth hour of the day, under the eyes of Pharaoh and in the sight of the host of Egypt, each of them showing the other a knowledge of weapons, and neither one of them could tri-umph over the other. Pharaoh said to the chief of the East, Pakrûr, and to Takhôs, the son of Ankhhoru, "Life of Amon! There is a combat that endures in the lists, but afterwards I do not know how our fortune will be maintained[75] to the moment of the tenth hour of evening." The herds-man spake to Mînnebmêî, saying, "To-day we have fought; let us end the combat and fight between us, let us each lay down our flag.[76] He who does not return here will be disgraced." Mînnebmêî assented to the words

---

73. The herdsman here is not one of the thirteen who accompanied the priest of Bûto; it is the priest himself.

74. Cf. for this expression, p. 126, note 92, and p. 186, note 11 above.

75. Lit. "the foot of this combat is stable on the lists, but afterwards I do not know what our luck will do to them." I have been forced to paraphrase this paragraph very considerably to make it intelligible to modern readers.

76. For this expression, p. 194, note 25.

that he had spoken; they each of them laid down their flags, they went out of the lists, and the drover went on board the bark of Amon.

And after that, when Mînnebmêî returned on board his galley, Pharaoh betook himself to meet him with the chief of the East, Pakrûr, and with Takhôs, the son of Ankhhoru. They said to him, "Is there a man who goes into the lists, and comes out, without going immediately to the place where Pharaoh is, that the reward of his combat may be given him?" The calasîris went to the place where Pharaoh was; he took off his helmet from his head, he bowed himself to the ground, he uttered the salutation, and he then kissed the ground.[77] Pharaoh perceived him, and when he had recognised him, he advanced to the place where he was, he folded him in his arms, he placed his mouth on his mouth, he kissed him at length in the manner in which a man salutes his betrothed.[78] Pharaoh said to him, "Hail to thee, hail to thee, Mînnebmêî, son of Inarôs, chief of the south of Egypt. It was that which I asked of Amon, the great god, that he would grant me to see thee without injury to thy excellent strength and health.[79] Life of Amon! the great god, at the hour that I beheld thee in the lists I said, "No man will do battle for me, if he is not a bull, son of a bull, and a lion, son of a lion, like myself." Pakrûr, the son of Pesnufi, and Takhôs, the son of Ankhhoru, and the great ones of Egypt seized his hand, and spake words to him; and Pharaoh came with him under the hangings of his tent. And after that, Mînnebmêî went up on to his galley, and Pharaoh caused perfumes and provisions to be given

77. Here for the first time we find all the moments of the Egyptian proscynema enumerated: 1st, the hero prostrates himself on his hands and knees, the spine bent, but the head slightly raised; 2nd, he repeats the ordinary formula of salutation; 3rd, he bows his head and kisses the ground between his hands. Sinuhît saluted in somewhat the same fashion, but he meanwhile threw dust over his body (cf. p. 72, note 53). That was no doubt to express his humility; the ordinary proscynema did not include this supplementary proceeding. Another point of etiquette forbade Pharaoh to appear to notice the presence of any person; he only recognised him after a certain interval, probably indicated by one of his officials, and it was then only that he addressed him, or on great occasions made a few steps towards him to raise him up, to embrace and receive him.

78. Lit. "he kissed him many hours"—one of those exaggerated formulæ of which I have given an example (p. 4, note 6). The kiss on the mouth had replaced the ancient greeting of placing the noses together (cf. p. 86, note 17), perhaps under Greek influence, at least in official ceremonies.

79. *I.e.,* if I understand it correctly, come safe and sound out of the fight against the drover. The word I have translated *strength* is the same used in the *Voyage of Unamunu* to designate the condition of epileptic ecstasy into which the page of the king of Byblos falls (cf. p. 174). Here it marks the mysterious power that animates Mînnebmêî by the Inspiration of Amon, and which up to this moment enables him to withstand the herdsman.

him in plenty, and the great ones of Egypt loaded him with gifts. Mînnebmêî fought three days. When the three days were accomplished in the lists, during which he went to fight with the herdsman, and he came out safe and sound, without one being able to do anything to him, the host of Egypt spake among themselves, saying, "There is no clan of men-at-arms in Egypt who equal the clan of the Osiris King Inarôs, for Ankhhoru, the royal son, and the general, great lord of Amon in Thebes, they could not stand a single day of fighting against those herdsmen; while throughout three days, Mînnebmêî has been constantly in the lists while no one could do anything to him."

Now, while it was thus, Pesnufi and Pemu arrived at the South; they arrived with their galleys at the south of the vessel of Pharaoh, they flew to the bank, cuirass on back. When it was announced to Pharaoh and to the chief of the East, Pakrûr, as well as to Takhôs, son of Ankhhoru, Pharaoh betook himself to meeting with them, and he seized the hand of Prince Pesnufi. . . .

After several lines which are too much damaged for me to attempt to translate them, the manuscript breaks off, and there is no indication as to how many more pages there were. One guesses that as soon as Pesnufi and Pemu arrive, fortune will turn in favour of Petubastis; the thirteen herdsmen will be slain or made prisoners as well as their chief, the bark of Amon will return into the possession of the Theban priesthood, and the throne of Amon, the subject of the quarrel, will remain in the hands of Prince Ankhhoru.[80]

80. Spiegelberg, *Der Sagenkreis des Königs Petubastis*, pp. 7, 35.

FRAGMENTS

THE foregoing stories are sufficient to give the general public an idea of the romantic literature of the Egyptians. I might without inconvenience have stopped after the *High Emprise for the Throne of Amon;* none of my readers would have demanded the publication of the fragments that follow. I have thought, however, that there was some interest that should not be neglected in these poor remains; if those of literary tastes see nothing of importance in them, scholars will perhaps find it worth while not to ignore them entirely.

In the first place, their very number clearly proves how many of the kind to which they belong were popular in the valley of the Nile; it provides one more argument in favour of the hypothesis that places the origin of some of our folk tales in Egypt. Also, some of them are not so mutilated that it is impossible to find anything of interest in them. No doubt twelve or fifteen lines of text can never be interesting to read as a mere matter of curiosity; a specialist may perhaps gather from them some detail in which he will recognise an incident known to him otherwise, or the hieroglyph version of a narrative still possessed by different nationalities. The benefit would be a double one; Egyptologists would thus gain material to enable them to reconstitute, at least approximately, certain works that without it would remain incomprehensible to them; and the others would have the satisfaction of proving the existence, at the remote period of the manuscript, of a story of which they had only much later redactions.

I have therefore collected in the following pages the remains of six stories of various periods.

1. A fantastic story, the composition of which is anterior to the eighteenth dynasty;
2. The quarrel of Apôpi and Saqnûnrîya;
3. Some scraps of a ghost story;
4. The story of a mariner;
5. A small Greek fragment relating to the King Nectanebo II;

6. Several scattered pages of a Coptic version of the romance
   of Alexander.

I regret that I have been unable to add either the romance of the Cairo
Museum, or the first story of St. Petersburg; the Cairo manuscript is so mutilated that nothing can be made out consecutively, and the St. Petersburg text
is not yet edited. I may perhaps succeed in filling up this gap if at some future
time I am permitted to undertake a fifth edition of this book.

FRAGMENT OF A FANTASTIC STORY, ANTERIOR TO THE EIGHTEENTH DYNASTY [18]

THE Berlin Papyrus No. 3 includes the fragments of two works: a philosophical dialogue between an Egyptian and his soul,[1] and a fantastic story. It appears that the story began at line 156, and it occupied the last thirty-six lines of the manuscript as it exists at present (ll. 156–191); it is impossible to estimate exactly what is missing from the end; all that can be said now is that the lines with which the narrative opens were anciently effaced. A second edition of the text has been given in phototype by Alan H. Gardiner, *Die Erzählung des Sinuhe und die Hirtengischichte*, in vol. iv. of *Hieratische Texten des Mittleren Reiches* by Erman, folio, Leipzig, 1909, pl. xvi, xvii. It was translated for the first time into French by Maspero, *études égyptiennes*, vol. i, p. 73 *et seq.*, then into German by Erman, *Aus den Papyrus der Königlichen Museen*, 1899, pp. 20–30, and by Alan H. Gardiner, *Die Erzählung des Sinuhe und die Hirtengeschichte*, pp. 14, 15.

Now behold, as I went down to the marsh which adjoins that wadi, I saw there a woman who had not the appearance of a mortal; my hair rose up when I perceived her tresses, by the variety of their colour. I could make nothing of that which she spake to me, so much had the terror of her penetrated my limbs.

---

1. Erman, after giving a short analysis of it in his *Ægypten*, pp. 393–394, published, transcribed, and translated it in a special memoir, entitled *Gesprach eines Müdenlebens mit seiner Seele*, which was inserted in the *Abhandlungen der Berliner Akademie*, 1896; he has given a new analysis and long fragments of it in the volume entitled *Aus den Papyrus der Königlichen Museen*, 1889, pp. 54–59, and in his *Ægyptische Chrestomathie*, 1904, pp. 33–55 and 16*–17*.

I say to you, "Oh bulls let us pass the ford! oh that the calves had crossed, and that the small cattle were resting at the opening of the marsh, the shepherds behind them, while our canoe in which we take the bulls and the cows across, remained behind, and that those of the shepherds who are skilful in magic things recite a charm over the water in these words: 'My double exults, oh shepherds, oh men, I do not avoid this marsh during this year of the great Nile in which the god decrees his decrees concerning the earth, and in which one cannot distinguish the pool from the river. Return to thy house, while the cows remain in their place! Come, for thy fear perishes and thy terror is about to perish, the fury of the goddess Uasrît and the fear of the *Lady of the two lands.*'"

The next day at daybreak, while that was being done as he had said, this goddess met him when he went to the pool; she went to him, denuded of her vestments, her hair dishevelled. . . .

THE STORY the existence of which is proved by this fragment was written before the XVIIIth dynasty, perhaps in the XIIth, if, as is the case in the dialogue contained in the first lines of the manuscript, the text we now possess is a copy executed from a more ancient manuscript. The country and the scenes described are borrowed from nature and from Egyptian customs. We are on the borders of one of those sheets of water, half marsh, half pool, on which the nobles of the Ancient Empire loved to hunt birds, the crocodile, and the hippopotamus. The shepherds are chatting, and one of them tells the other that he has met with a mysterious creature who inhabits an inaccessible retreat in the middle of the water. In the tomb of Ti, the shepherds are seen driving the bulls and their heifers across a canal. Men and beasts are in the water half way up their legs, and one of the drovers is carrying an unfortunate calf on his back to save it from the force of the current. Farther on, other shepherds, in light reed boats, are convoying a second herd of oxen across another canal which is deeper. Two crocodiles, placed on each side of the picture, are present at this procession, but are unable to profit by the occasion; incantations have rendered them motionless. As the accompanying legend points out, the face of the shepherd is all-powerful on the canals, "and those who are in the water are struck with blindness."[2] Our story shows us the drovers who understood their business walking behind their herds and reciting the formulæ intended to conjure away the perils of the river. The Harris magical papyrus contains several charms directed against the crocodile and, more generally, against all dangerous animals that live in the

2. Maspero, *Études égyptiennes*, vol. ii, pp. 106–110.

water.[3] They are too long and too complicated to have served for daily use; ordinary charms were short, and easy to remember.

It is not easy to guess with any certainty what was the theme here developed. The Arab authors who have written on Egypt are full of marvellous stories, where a woman corresponding to the description in our story plays the principal part. "It is said that the spirit of the Southern Pyramid never appears outside except in the form of a nude woman, beautiful, and whose ways are such that when she wishes to inspire some one with love, and cause him to lose his reason, she smiles at him, and, incontinently, he approaches her, and she draws him to her, and makes him distracted with love, so that he immediately loses his reason and runs wild about the country. Several persons have seen her circling around the Pyramid at midday and at sunset."[4] The author of this fragment certainly affirms that the being with whom he places his hero in communication is a goddess,—*nutrît*—, but this is a statement which we need not take literally; she is a goddess, if we please, such as are her cousins, the nymphs of the Greek and Roman religions, but she has no claim to an official cult such as is practised in the temples.[5] Let us say, then, that she is a nymph, nude, and with hair of a changeable colour: was it rose-coloured, like that of Nitocris whom tradition of the Greek period located in the Pyramid of Mykerinus? Another legend, that I find in the Arab historians of Egypt, also presents some analogy with the episode recorded in this fragment.[6] The Arabs frequently attribute the foundation of Alexandria to a king, Gebire, and a queen, Charobe, of whom Western historians have never heard. While Gebire was endeavouring to build the city, his shepherd drove the herds that provided milk for the royal kitchen to pasture by the seashore. "One evening, as he was giving his beasts into the charge of the shepherds who were his subordinates, he, who was handsome, of good bearing and fine figure, beheld a beautiful young woman come out of the sea, who came to him, and having approached him very closely, saluted him. He returned her salute, and she began to speak to him with all possible courtesy and civility, and said to him, "Oh, young man, will you wrestle with me for a certain matter that

3. Chabas, *Le Papyrus magique Harris*, Châlons-sur-Saône, 1860, pp. 20 *et seq.*, 92 *et seq.*

4. L'ÉGYPTE DE MVRTADI FILS DV GAPHIPHE, où il est traité des Pyramides, du débordement du Nil, et des autres merueilles de cette Prouince, selon les opinions et traditions des Arabes. *De la traduction de M. Pierre Vattier, Docteur en Médicine, Lecteur et professeur du Roy en Langue Arabique.* Sur un manuscrit Arabe tiré de la Bibliothèque de feu Monseigneur le Cardinal Mazarin. A Paris, chez lovys billaine, au second pillier de la grande Salle du Palais, à la Palme et au grand Cesar, m.d.c. lxvi. *Avec Privilège du Roy*, 12mo, pp. 65 *et seq.*

5. Cf. Virey, *La Religion de l'Ancienne Égypte*, 1910, p. 60.

6. *L'Égypte de Murtadi, fils du Gaphiphe*, pp. 143 *et seq.*

I will stake on it?" "What do you wish to stake?" replied the shepherd. "If you overthrow me," said the young lady, "I will be yours, and you shall do what you please with me, but if I overthrow you, I will have an animal from your flock." The struggle ended in the defeat of the shepherd. The young lady returned the next day and the days following. How she again overcame the shepherd, how the king Gebire, seeing his sheep disappear, undertook to wrestle with her, and overcame her in his turn, is not all this written in the *Egypt* of Murtadi, son of Gaphiphe, in the translation of M. Pierre Vattier, Doctor of Medicine, Lecturer and King's Professor of the Arabic language? I think that this beautiful woman of the Egyptian author made some proposition to our shepherd of the same kind as that which the young lady of the Arab author made to his. The story of the *Shipwrecked Sailor* has already introduced us to a serpent endowed with speech, and lord of an enchanted isle[7]; the fragment of Berlin presents us with a nymph, the Lady of a pool. If chance favours our researches, we may hope to find in Egyptian literature all the fantastic beings of the Arab literature of the Middle Ages.

7. Cf. above, pp. 84 *et seq.*

THE QUARREL OF APÔPI AND SAQNÛNRÎYA [19]

(XIXTH DYNASTY)

THIS narrative covers all that remains of the first pages of the *Sallier Papyrus No. 1*. For a long time it was regarded as an historical document; the style, the expressions employed, and the actual groundwork of the subject all indicate a romance in which the principal parts are played by personages borrowed from history, but of which the ideas are almost entirely those of popular imagination.

Champollion twice saw the papyrus at the house of its first proprietor, M. Sallier, of Aix in Provence—a few days before his departure for Egypt in 1828, and again on his return in 1830. The notes published by Salvolini show that he recognised, if not the actual nature of the narrative, at any rate the historical significance of the royal names in it. The manuscript, bought in 1839 by the British Museum, was published in facsimile as early as 1841 in *Select Papyri*.[1] Hawkins' notice, evidently drawn up on indications given him by Birch, read the name of the antagonist of Apôphis that Champollion had not read, but attributes the cartouche of Apôphis to king Phiôps of the Vth dynasty. E. de Rougé was the first who actually discerned what was contained in those pages of the papyrus. In 1847 he accorded Saqnûnrîya his proper place in the list of the Pharaohs; in 1854 he pointed out the name Hâuâru in the fragment, and contributed to the *Athénæum Français*[2] a somewhat detailed analysis of the document. The discovery was popularised in Germany by Brugsch, who attempted to establish a word-for-word translation of the first lines,[3] then in England by Goodwin, who thought it possible to risk a complete translation.[4] Since then the text has been

---

1. *Select Papyri*, vol. i, pl. i *et seq.*

2. *Athénæum Français*, 1854, p. 532; cf. *Œuvres diverses*, vol. ii, pp. 412–413.

3. Brugsch, *Ægyptische Studien*, ii, *Ein Ægyptisches Datum über die Hyksoszeit*, pp. 8–21, 8vo, Leipzig, 1854, Extract from *Zeitschrift der Deutschen Morganländischen Gesellschaft*, vol. ix.

4. Goodwin, *Hieratic Papyri*, in *Cambridge Essays*, 1858, pp. 243–245.

frequently studied: by Chabas,[5] Lushington,[6] Brugsch,[7] and Ebers.[8] Goodwin, after mature examination, cautiously expressed his opinion that it might well prove to be not an accurate narrative, but a romantic version of historic facts.[9] It is an opinion with which I am in agreement and which appears to prevail among scholars. The transcription, translation, and commentary on the text are given at full length in my *Études égyptiennes.*[10]

It seems to me that the extant remains enable us to reconstitute the two first pages almost completely. Perhaps the attempt at restitution that I propose may seem bold, even to Egyptologists. It will at least be seen that I have not undertaken it lightly. A minute analysis of the text has led me to the results I submit to criticism.

჻

It happened that the land of Egypt belonged to the Impure,[11] and, as they had no lord, l. h. s., king at that time, it happened that the king Saqnûn-rîya,[12] l. h. s., was sovereign, l. h. s., of the land of the South, and that the scourge of the towns, Râ-Apôpi, l. h. s., was chief of the North in Hâuâru;[13] the Entire Land paid him tribute of manufactured products, and supplied him also with all the good things of Tomuri.[14] Lo, the king Râ-Apôpi, l. h. s., took Sutekhu for his lord, and he served no other god

5. Chabas, *Les Pasteurs en Egypte,* Amsterdam, 1868, 4to, pp. 16–18.

6. Lushington, *Fragment of the first Sallier Papyrus,* in *Transactions of the Society of Biblical Archæology,* vol. iv, pp. 263–266, reproduced in *Records of the Past.* 1st series, vol. viii. pp. 1–4.

7. Brugsch, *Histoire d'Égypte,* 4to, 1859, pp. 78 *et seq.;* and *Geschichte Ægyptens,* 8vo, 1878, pp. 222–226; cf. *Tanis und Avaris* in *Zeitschrift für allgemeinen Erdkunde,* new series, vol. xiv, pp. 81 *et seq.*

8. Ebers, *Ægypten und die Bücher Moses,* 1868, pp. 204 *et seq.*

9. Bunsen, *Egypt's Place,* vol. iv, p. 671.

10. Maspero, *Études égyptiennes,* vol. i, pp. 195–216.

11. This is one of the insulting epithets that the resentment of the scribes expended on the Shepherds and other foreign nations who had occupied Egypt; see p. 125, note 91.

12. This is the most probable pronunciation of the prenomen usually transcribed *Râskenen.* Three kings of Egypt bore this prenomen, two of the name of Tiuâu one of the name of Tiuâqen, who reigned several years before Ahmôsis.

13. Hâuâru, the Avaris of Manetho, was the fortress of the shepherd kings in Egypt. E. de Rougé has proved that Hâuâru was one of the names of Tanis, that most commonly in use in ancient times.

14. Lower Egypt, the Land of Canals, the country of the North; cf. p. 4, note 6.

in the Entire land but Sutekhu, and constructed a temple of excellent and eternal work at the gate of the king, Râ-Apôpi, l. h. s., and he arose each day to sacrifice the daily victims to Sutekhu, and the chiefs, vassals of the sovereign, l. h. s., were there with garlands of flowers, exactly as was done for the temple of Phrâ Harmakhis. And the king Râ-Apôpi, l. h. s., intended to send a message to the king, to announce it to the king Saqnûnrîya, l. h. s., prince of the city of the South.[15] And many days after that, the king Râ-Apôpi, l. h. s., caused his great chieftains to be called . . .

The text breaks off here, and does not commence again till the beginning of page 2; where it recommences, after a lacuna, which is almost complete, of five and a half lines, we find phrases that evidently belong to the message of king Apôpi. Now, many examples taken from romantic as well as historic texts, show us that a message, confided to some person, is invariably repeated by him almost word for word; we may therefore rest assured that the two lines in page 2, placed in the mouth of the envoy, must have occurred in the missing lines of page 1, and, in fact, the small isolated fragment that appears at the foot of the facsimile shows remains of signs which correspond exactly with one of the passages in the message. This first version was then spoken by the king's counsellors; but who were those counsellors? Were they the *great princes that he caused to be called* at the point where the text breaks off? No, for in the fragments that remain of line 7, one finds the term *learned scribes,* and at line 2 of page 2 it is expressly asserted that Apôpi sent to Saqnûnrîya the message *that had been spoken to him by his learned scribes.* We must therefore admit that Apôpi, having consulted his civil and military chiefs, they advised him to apply to his scribes; their remarks begin at the end of line 7 with the obligatory expression, *Oh suzerain, our lord.* In fact, for the whole of the first part of this lacuna we have a consultation very similar to that which we meet with later on at the court of Saqnûnrîya, and in the *Story of the Two Brothers,* when Pharaoh wished to know to whom the lock of hair belonged that perfumed his linen.[16] Therefore resume thus:

And many days after that, the king Râ-Apôpi, l. h. s., caused his great chiefs to be called, as well as his captains and his general advisers, but they did not know how to give him a good speech to send to the king

15. The *City of the South* is Thebes.
16. See above, p 11.

Saqnûnrîya, l. h. s., chief of the country of the South. the king Apôpi, l. h. s., therefore caused his magician-scribes to be called. They said to him, "Suzerain, l. h. s., our master, . . ."[17] and they gave to the king Râ-Apôpi, l. h. s., the speech he desired. "Let a messenger go to the city of the South, to say to him, the king Râ-Apôpi, l. h. s., sends to thee, saying, 'Let the hippopotami which are in the canals of the country be hunted on the pool, in order that they may let sleep come to me by night and by day. . . .'"

Here we have a portion of the gap filled up with certainty, at least as regards the sense; but at the bottom of the page there remains a good line and a half, perhaps, even two lines or more, to be filled up. Here, also, the remainder of the narrative enables us to re-establish the exact meaning, if not the letter, of what is missing from the text. It is seen, in fact, that having received the message given above, King Saqnûnrîya assembles his counsellors, who are perplexed, and can discover no reply; upon which King Apôpi sends a second ambassador. It is obvious that the embarrassment of the Thebans, and their silence, was foreseen by the scribes of Apôpi, and that that part of their discourse which is preserved at the top of page 2 contained the end of the second message that Apôpi intended to send, if the first received no reply. In analogous stories, which turn on some extraordinary deed to be accomplished by one of two kings, the penalty he will have to submit to, in case he is unsuccessful, is always set forth. It must certainly have been the same with this story, and I propose to restore it as follows:

He will not know what to reply, neither well nor ill. Then thou wilt send him another message, "The king Râ-Apôpi, l. h. s., sends to thee, saying, 'If the chief of the South is not able to reply to my message, let him serve no other god than Sutekhu.' But if he replies, and if he does that which I tell him to do,[18] then I will take nothing from him, and also I will bow myself before no other god of the country of Egypt than Amonrâ, king of the gods."

And many days after that, the king Râ-Apôpi, l. h. s., sent to the prince of the country of the South the message that his magician-scribes had given him; and the messenger of the King Râ-Apôpi, l. h. s., arrived before the prince of the country of the South. He said to the messenger of the King Râ-Apôpi, l. h. s., "What message dost thou bring to the

17. This line must have contained a compliment paid to the king.
18. The part of the text still extant begins here.

country of the South? wherefore hast thou taken this journey?" The messenger said to him, "The King Râ-Apôpi, l. h. s., sends to thee, saying, "Let them hunt on the pool the hippopotami that are in the canals of the country, that sleep may come to me by day as by night . . ." The chief of the country of the South was seized with stupor, and he knew not what to reply to the messenger of the king Râ-Apôpi, l. h. s. The chief of the country of the South said therefore to the messenger, "Behold, that which thy master, l. h. s., sends for . . . the chief of the country of the South . . . the words that he has sent to me . . . his possessions. . . ." The chief of the country of the South caused all sorts of good things, of meat, of cake, of . . ., of wine, to be given to the messenger, then he said to him, "Return, and say to thy lord, . . . 'All that thou hast said, I approve. . . .'" The messenger of the king Râ-Apôpi, l. h. s., set out for the place where his lord, l. h. s., was. Behold, the chief of the country of the South caused his great chiefs to be called, as well as his wise captains and generals, and he repeated to them all the message that the king Râ-Apôpi, l. h. s., had sent him. Behold, they were silent with one mouth for a long time, and they knew not what to reply either of good or of bad.

The king Râ-Apôpi, l. h. s., sent to the chief of the country of the South the other message that the magician-scribes had given him. . . .

It is disappointing that the text breaks off just at this point. The three Pharaohs who bore the name of Saqnûnrîya reigned at a troublous time, and must have left vivid memories among the Theban population. They were restless and warlike princes, the last of whom perished by a violent death—perhaps while fighting against the Hyksôs, perhaps by the hand of an assassin. His beard had been shaved the same morning, "adorning himself for battle like the god Montu," as the Egyptian scribes say. A blow with an axe carried off part of his left cheek, laying his teeth bare, splitting the jawbone, and laying him senseless on the ground; a second blow penetrated deep into the skull; a dagger or short lance cut into the forehead on the right, slightly above the eye. The body was hastily embalmed, in the position into which it had stiffened at death. The features still express the rage and fury of the fight, a great whitish patch of exuded brain covers the forehead, the lips are drawn back showing the jawbone, and the tongue bitten between his teeth.[19] Did the author of our story bring up the narrative to the tragic death of his hero? The scribe to whom we owe the *Sallier*

19. Maspero, *Les Momies royales d'Égypte récemment mises au jour,* pp. 14, 15.

Papyrus No. 1 certainly intended to finish his story; he had copied the last lines on the verso of one of the pages, and was preparing to go on with it when he was interrupted by some accident unknown to us. Perhaps the professor from whose dictation he appears to have been writing was not acquainted with the final events. In the *Introduction*, pp. cxi–cxii, I have already indicated the probable ending: King Saqnûnrîya, after long hesitation, succeeded in extricating himself from the embarrassing dilemma in which his powerful rival had attempted to involve him. It may be supposed that his reply would be no less strange than Apôpi's message, but we have no means of conjecturing what it was.

FRAGMENTS OF A GHOST STORY [20]

(XXᵀᴴ DYNASTY)

THESE fragments have come down to us on four potsherds, one of which is now at the Louvre, and another at the Vienna Museum; the two others are in the Egyptian Museum in Florence.

The Paris ostracon is formed of two pieces joined together, which bear the remains of eleven lines. It has been translated, but not published, by Devéria, *Catalogue des manuscrits égyptiens du Musée du Louvre,* Paris, 1872, p. 208, and the cartouche it contains has been studied by Lincke, *über einem noch nicht erklärten Königsnamen auf einem Ostracon des Louvre* in *Recueil de Travaux relatifs à la philologie et à l'archéologie égyptienne et Assyrienne,* 1880, vol. ii. pp. 85–89. Five lines of the text have been published in cursive facsimile by Lauth, who read the royal name Râ-Hap-Amh, and places it in the IVth dynasty (*Manetho und der Turiner Königspapyrus,* p. 187). Finally the whole has been given by Spiegelberg, *Varia,* in *Recueil de Travaux,* vol. xvi, pp. 31, 32. The two fragments at Florence in Migliarini's Catalogue are numbered 2616 and 2617. They were photographed in 1876 by Golénischeff, then incompletely transcribed by Erman in *Zeitschrift* (1880, 3rd fasc.), finally published in facsimile, transcribed, and translated, by Golénischeff, *Notice sur Un Ostracon hiératique du Musée de Florence* (*avec deux planches*), in *Recueil,* 1881, vol. iii. pp. 3–7. I added a note to Golénischeff's memoir (*Recueil,* vol. iii, p. 7) which contains some corrections of no great importance. The two fragments at Florence in reality only contribute one text, for ostracon 2617 appears to be only a copy of ostracon 2616. The Vienna ostracon was discovered, published, and translated by E. de Bergmann, in his *Hieratische und Hieratisch-Demotische Texte der Sammlung Ægyptischer Alterthümer des Allerhöchsten Kaiserhauses,* Vienna, 1886, pl. iv, p. vi. It is broken across the middle, and half of each line has disappeared.

It is impossible to discover what the leading idea of the story may have been. Several personages appear in it: a Theban high-priest of Amon, Khonsûmhabi, three unnamed men, and a ghost who employs very good language to tell the story of his former life. The Paris ostracon seems to have preserved a fragment of the commencement. The high-priest, Khonsûmhabi, appears to be entirely occupied with finding a suitable site for his tomb.

༄

He sent one of his subordinates to the place of the tomb of the king of Upper and Lower Egypt Râhotpu, l. h. s.,[1] and with him the men under the orders of the high-priest of Amonrâ, king of the gods, three men, four men in all; he embarked with them, he steered, he led them to the place indicated, near the tomb of the king Râhotpu, l. h. s. They went to it with her, and they went inside; she adored twenty-five . . . in the royal . . . country, then they came to the river-bank, and they sailed to Khonsûmhabi, the high-priest of Amonrâ, king of the gods, and they found him who sang the praises of the god in the temple of the city of Amon.

He said to them, "Let us rejoice, for I have come, and I have found the place favourable for establishing my dwelling to perpetuity." The three men said to him with one mouth, "It is found, the place favourable for establishing thy dwelling to perpetuity," and they seated themselves before her, and she passed a happy day, and her heart was given to joy. Then he said to them, "Be ready to-morrow morning when the solar disc issues from the two horizons." He commanded the lieutenant of the temple of Amon to find lodgment for those people, he told each of them what he had to do, and he caused them to return to sleep in the city in the evening. He established . . .

In the fragments at Florence, the high-priest found himself face to face chatting with the ghost, and perhaps this was while digging out the more ancient tomb, the owners of which entered into conversation with him, as the mummies of Nenoferkephtah talked with Prince Satni-Khamoîs.[2] At the point where we

---

1. The name of Râhotpu was borne by an obscure king of the XVIth or XVIIth dynasty, whose tomb was apparently situated at Thebes, in the same quarter of the necropolis as the pyramids of the sovereigns of the XIth, XIIIth and XIVth and following dynasties, towards Drah-Abu'l-Neggah. He is probably the Râhotpu of this text (cf. H. Gauthier, *Le Livre des Rois d'Égypte,* vol. ii, pp. 88, 89).

2. See above, pp. 99 *et seq.*

take up the text again, one of the mummies seems to he relating the story of his earthly life to the first prophet of Amon.

I grew, and I did not see the rays of the sun, I did not breathe the air, but darkness was before me every day, and no one came to find me." The spirit said to him, "For me, when I was still living on earth, I was the treasurer of king Râhotpu, l. h. s., I was also his infantry lieutenant. Then I passed before men and behind the gods,[3] and I died in the year XIV, during the months of Shomu,[4] of the king Manhapurîya,[5] l. h. s. He gave me my four casings, and my sarcophagus of alabaster; he caused to be done for me all that is done for a man of quality, he gave me offerings . . ."

All that follows is very obscure. The ghost seems to complain of some accident that has happened to himself or to his tomb, but I cannot clearly make out what is the subject of his dissatisfaction. Perhaps, like Nenoferkephtah in the story of Satni-Khamoîs, he simply wished to have his wife, his children, or some one whom he had loved, to dwell with him. When he has finished his speech, his visitor speaks in his turn.

The first prophet of Amonrâ, king of the gods, Khonsûmhabi said to him, "Oh, give me excellent counsel as to what I should do, and I will have it done for thee, or at least grant that five men and five slaves may be given me, in all ten persons, to bring me water, and then I will give corn every day, and that will enrich me, and a libation of water shall be brought me every day." The spirit, Nuîtbusokhnu,[6] said to him, "What hast thou done? If the wood is not left in the sun, it will not remain dried, it is not a stone worn with age that is brought . . ."

The prophet of Amon appears to ask some favour from the ghost; which, on his part, the ghost does not appear disposed to grant him, notwithstanding the promises made by his visitor. The conversation on this theme lasted a consider-

---

3. *To pass in front of men and behind the gods* is to die. The dead man preceded to the other world those who remained on earth and went to join those who followed Râ, Osiris, Sokaris or some other or the funerary gods.

4. The Egyptian year was divided into three seasons of four mouths each; *Shomu* was the season of harvest.

5. For this king, who was yet more obscure than Rahotpu, see H. Gauthier, *Le Livre des Rois d'Egypte*, vol. ii, p. 95.

6. This name signifies *the dwelling does not contain it*. Perhaps, instead of being the name of the dead man, it is a generic name used to denote ghosts.

able time, and I think we find it continued on the Vienna ostracon. Khonsûm-habi enquires to which family one of his interlocutors belonged, and his very natural curiosity was amply satisfied.

The spirit said to him, "X . . . is the name of my father, X . . . the name of the father of my father, and X . . . the name of my mother." The high-priest Khonsûmhabi said to him, "But then I know thee well. This eternal house in which thou art, it is I who had it made for thee; it is I who caused thee to be buried, in the day when thou didst return to earth; it is I who had done for thee that which should be done for him who is of high rank. But behold, I am in poverty, an evil wind of winter has breathed famine over the country, and I am no longer happy. My heart does not touch (joy), because the Nile. . . ." Thus said Khonsûmhabi, and after that Khonsûmhabi remained there, weeping, for a long time, not eating, not drinking, not . . .

The text is so interrupted by lacunæ that I cannot hope to have interpreted it correctly throughout. Even had it been complete, the difficulty would have been scarcely less great. I do not know whether the fashion among Egyptian ghosts was to render their language obscure at pleasure; this one does not seem to have attempted to make himself clear. His remarks are brusquely broken off in the middle of a phrase, and unless Golénischeff discovers some other fragments on a potsherd in a museum, I see scarcely any chance that we shall ever know the remainder of the story.

STORY OF A MARINER [21]

(Ptolemaic Period)

THIS fragment is taken from the great Demotic Papyrus of the Bibliothèque Nationale of Paris. The document, brought to France at the beginning of the nineteenth century by one of the members of the expedition to Egypt, until 1873 remained forgotten among a mass of family papers. Offered by the Maisonneuve library to the Bibliothéque Nationale, it was purchased by it, on my representations, for the moderate sum of a thousand francs.

It is written on both sides, and contains several compositions of a special character—Messianic prophecies, semi-religious dialogues, and apologues. The only fragment that is clearly marked out for insertion in this collection is this one of which I give a translation in the following pages. The credit for having discovered and published the text belongs to Eugène Révillout, who was then co-conservator of the Egyptian Museum at the Louvre:

Premier Extrait de la Chronique Démotique de Paris: le roi Amasis et les Mercenaires, selon les données d'Hérodote et les renseignements de la Chronique in the *Revue égyptologique,* vol. i, pp. 49–82, and pl. II, 4to, Paris, 1880, E. Leroux.

Since then Révillout has given a more complete translation of it in French: E. Révillout, *Hérodote et les oracles égyptiens,* in the *Revue égyptologique,* vol. ix, 1900, pp. 2, 3: then a hieroglyphic transcription with a new French translation: E. Révillout, *Amasis sur le lac et le Conte du Nautonnier,* in *Revue égyptologique,* 1908, vol. xii, pp. 113–116.

It seems as though King Amasis was privileged to act as an inspiration to Egyptian story-tellers. His humble origin, the caustic quality of his wit, and the boldness of his policy with regard to the Greeks, raised enduring hatred against him from some, while they were the passionate admiration of others. Herodotus collected very contradictory statements about him, and *The Story of the Mariner* gives us in its original form one of the anecdotes related about him. The author supposes that King Amasis, having become intoxicated one evening, awoke next morning with a very muddled head; and not feeling inclined to deal with serious matters, he enquired of his courtiers whether one of them did not know some amusing story. One of those standing by seized the moment to tell him the story of a mariner. The narrative is interrupted too soon to enable us to judge of the form it took. There is nothing to prevent our supposing that the narrator drew a moral from it applicable to the king. At any rate, it seems to me most probable that the episode at the beginning is only a pretended piece of history. Not to speak of the passage in the book of Esther where Ahasuerus, suffering from insomnia, had the annals of his reign read to him, the first Egyptian romance of St. Petersburg begins in very much the same manner; King Sanafruî assembles his counsellors and demands a story from them.[1] I may therefore be forgiven if I attach no more historical importance to this tale than I accorded to the stories of Sinuhît or Thutîyi.

It happened one day, in the time of the king Ahmasi, that the king said to his grandees, "It pleases me to drink the brandy of Egypt." They said, "Our great lord, it is hard to drink the brandy of Egypt." He said to them: "Do you intend to object to what I have said?"[2] They said: "Our great master, that which pleases the king, let him do it." The king said: "Let them bring some brandy of Egypt on to the lake." They did according to the order of the king. The king washed himself with his sons, and he had no wine in the world with them except the brandy of Egypt; now the king delighted himself with his sons, he drank of the wine in very great quantities, by reason of the greediness shown by the king for the brandy of Egypt; then the king went to sleep on the lake, the evening of that day, for he had caused the sailors to bring a bed under a bower on the border of the lake. When the morning arrived, the king could not rise, on account of the greatness of the drunkenness in which he was sunk. When an hour had passed and he still could not rise, the courtiers complained, saying, "Is it possible that, if it happens to the king to be drunk more than any man in the world, no man in the world can approach the king for business?"[3] The courtiers therefore came into the place where the king was, and said to him, "Our great lord, what desire possesses the king?" The king said, "It pleases me to be very drunk. . . . Is there no one among you who can tell me a story, so that I may

1. See on this subject p. 18 of this volume.
2. Lit.: "Has that which I say to thee *an evil smell*?"
3. Lit.: "Is it a thing that may happen that, if the king makes drunkenness of man of all the world, the man of all the world does not make entrance for business to the king?"

keep awake with it?" Now there was a *Royal Brother*[4] among the courtiers whose name was Peûn,[5] and he knew many stories, he approached the king, he said, "Our great lord, does the king not know the adventure that happened to a young pilot to whom was given the name . . ."

It chanced in the time of the king Psamatiku[6] that there was a married pilot; another pilot, to whom was given the name . . . fell in love with the wife of the first, to whom was given the name Taônkh.[7] She loved him, and he loved her. It happened one day the king caused him to come in the bark named . . . that day. After the feast a great desire seized him . . . which the king had given him; he said, ". . . .," and they caused him to enter the presence of the king. He arrived at his house, he washed himself with his wife, he could not drink as usual. When the time arrived for the two to go to bed, he could not know her, owing to the excess of suffering in which he was. She said to him, "What happened to thee on the river?"

The publication of an accurate facsimile may perhaps some day enable us to translate the last lines completely. I will attempt in the meantime to comment on the little episode at the commencement, that served as a framework to the history of the mariner. King Ahmasi, the Amasis of the Greeks, wished to drink some kind of liquor which is always called *kolobi of Egypt* in the text, no doubt in distinction to the foreign liquors that were imported in large quantities. Révillout conjectured that *kolobi of Egypt* might be the heavy wine of the Fayûm, or of Marea.[8] One might imagine that kolobi was not made with grapes, in which case it might be possible to compare it with the kind of beer that the Greeks called *kumi.*[9] I am disposed to believe that this concoction which was so severe a drink, and rendered the king incapable of work after his drunken bout, was not a natural wine. Perhaps we may regard it as the strange wine spoken of

4. The reading is doubtful. The title of *Royal Brother,* somewhat unusual in Egypt, marks a high degree of nobility in the hierarchy.

5. The reading of the name is uncertain. Révillout read it *Pentsate,* Petesêtis. I have taken from the known signs that one which is most similar in appearance to the formula he gives in his facsimile.

6. The name fills in the end of a line and is much mutilated. I think I recognise a P in the first sign, as it is in the facsimile, and this reading suggested to me the name Psamatiku. Révillout transcribed it *Oudja-Hor.*

7. Lit.: "Took love for herself, one calling her Taônkh (?) or Sônkh, her name, another pilot was of his name. . . ." Révillout simply read Ankh as the name of the wife.

8. *Revue égyptologique,* vol. i, p. 65, note 1; in his article in vol. x, p. 2. he decides for the wine of the Fayûm.

9. Dioscorides, *Materia Medica,* vol. ii, ch. 109 and 110.

by Pliny,[10] with the Greek name *ekbolas* which may have some distant assonance with the Egyptian term *kolobi*. Or, again, it may be one of those wines so charged with alcohol, as to affect the drinker in the same way as brandy. On this second hypothesis I elected to use the inexact term *brandy* for *kolobi*.[11]

The scene is enacted on a lake, but I do not think on Lake Maræotis,[12] nor on any of the natural lakes of the Delta. The term *shi*, lake, is perpetually applied in Egyptian writings to the pieces of artificial water that adorned the gardens of the great and wealthy.[13] A pious wish frequently expressed for the dead was that, as a supreme favour, they should wander in peace on the borders of the pool of water excavated in their garden, and there is no need to have lived long in Egypt to understand such a wish. The paintings on the Theban tombs show the deceased seated on the edge of his pool, and many paintings also prove that the pools were often placed close to vines and fruit trees. One of the tales of magic in the Cheops story shows us that the royal palace had its *shi*, like the houses of private persons. They were usually of very moderate dimensions, although that of Sanafruî was bordered by flowery country, and was of sufficiently large extent to admit of the evolutions of a bark containing twenty women and a pilot.[14] The author of the demotic narrative therefore merely mentions a small fact of daily life when he describes Ahmasi as drinking wine on the lake of his villa palace, and passing the night under a bower by the side of the water.[15] A passage of Plutarch which states that Psammetichus was the first to drink wine[16] appears to show that Ahmasi was not the only one who yielded to habits of this kind. Perhaps the same stories of intoxication were told of Psammetichus that were attributed here to one of his successors; the author from whom Plutarch borrowed his information must have known the *Story of the Mariner* or a story of the same kind, in which Psammetichus played the part of the intoxicated Pharaoh. The tales told by Herodotus at least show that at the Persian period Amasis was that Saite king to whom the most ignoble actions were attributed. I regard these stories as the natural consequence of the hatred felt for him by the sacerdotal class, and the adherents of the ancient Saite family. Had these

10. Pliny, *Historia Naturalis*, xiv. 18.

11. M. Groff has expressed his opinion that the *kolobi* was a boiled wine of superior quality (*Note sur le mot Kaloui du Papyrus Égypto-Araméen du Louvre* in the *Journal Asiatique*, viii[th] series, vol. xi, pp. 305, 306).

12. Révillout, *Premier extrait de la Chronique* in *Revue Égyptologique*, vol. i. p. 65, note 2.

13. Cf. pp. 20–22, and p. 79, note 91, of this volume.

14. See above, pp. 23, 24.

15. Wilkinson, *A Popular Account of the Anceint Egyptians*, vol. i, pp. 25, 38, 42.

16. Plutarch *de Iside et Osiride*, § 6.

rumours any foundation in fact, or were the stories related by Herodotus merely the malicious exaggeration of royal weaknesses? Egyptian scribes waxed eloquent when they discoursed on drunkenness, and they would voluntarily warn their pupils and subordinates against the houses of almehs, and places where beer was drunk.[7] Drunkenness was no rare vice among people of rank, and even among women; the painters who decorated the tombs of Upper Egypt did not hesitate to depict its effects with closest fidelity. Thus, while there is nothing to prevent our accepting the possibility of a Pharaoh such as Ahmasi having a taste for wine, there is also nothing known from the monuments to show that he was guilty of drunkenness. Without further information, I shall be content to regard the indications as to his character given in the demotic story and in the stories collected by Herodotus as no more authentic than those as to the character of Khufuî or Ramses II provided by the stories of Sesôstris or Cheops.

17. *Anastasi Papyrus,* No. iv, pl. xi, l. 8 *et seq.;* and *Papyrus de Boulaq,* vol. i, pl. xvii, ll. 6–11; cf. Chabas, *L'Égyptologie,* vol. i, p. 101 *et seq.*

THE ADVENTURE OF THE SCULPTOR PETÊSIS AND KING NECTONABO [22]

(Ptolemaic Period)

THE GREEK Papyrus that contains this story at one time formed part of the Anastasi collection. Acquired by the Leyden Museum in 1829, it was unrolled and analysed by Reuvens, *Lettres à M. Letronne sur les Papyrus bilingues et grecs et sur quelques autres monuments gréco-égyptiens du Musée d'Antiquités de Leyde,* Leyden, 1830, 4to, pp. 76–79.

It was afterwards completely published, translated, and commented on by Leemans, *Papyri Graeci Musaei antiquari publici Lugduni Batavi,* Lugduni Batavorum CIƆIƆCCCXXXVIII, pp. 122–129. Since then it has been studied by U. Wilcken, *Der Traum des Königs Nektonabos* (extract from *Mélanges Nicole,* pp. 579–596, 8vo), Geneva, 1906, 18 pp., and by St. Witkowski, *In Somnium Nectanebi (Pap. Leid. U.), observationes aliquot scripsit* (extract from *Eos,* vol. xiv, pp. 11–18), 8vo, Leopold, 1908, 8 pp.

The form of the characters and the texture of the papyrus determined Leemans to assign the writing of the fragment to the second half of the second century B.C.; Wilcken placed it in the first half of the same century, and attributed it to a personage who formed one of the company of *recluses* of the Serapeum. The part that has survived is composed of five columns unequal in length. The first, which is very narrow, contains twelve lines, of which only a few words are legible; but these enable us to restore conjecturally the title of the story "the sculptor Petêsis and the King Nectonabo." The second and fourth columns each contain twenty-one lines; the third twenty-four. The fifth only consists of four lines, after which the story breaks off suddenly in the middle of a sentence, like the *Quarrel of Apôpi and Saqnûnrîya* in the *Sallier Papyrus No. 1.* The scribe amused himself by drawing a comic figure of a man below the writing, and left his story unfinished.

The writer of this fragment did not draw it up himself from some tale told him by a professional story-teller; the errors, of which the text is full, show that it was copied, and from a poor manuscript. The Egyptian words found in the redaction we possess indicate that the prototype was written in Egyptian. The sculptor Petêsis is unknown to us. King Nectanebo—whose name is here vocalised as Nectonabo—was celebrated among the Greeks of the Alexandrian period as a magician and astrologer; he was therefore marked out as the recipient of such a dream as that accorded to him in the story. The demotic papyrus from which I have taken the *Story of the Mariner* contains lengthy imprecations against him. The romance of Alexander, written much later by the Pseudo-Callisthenes, represents him, instead of Philip of Macedonia, as the father of Alexander the Great. The Leyden story, transcribed perhaps two hundred years after his death, is, up to the present, the earliest known of the more or less imaginative stories about him that were in circulation in ancient times and during the Middle Ages.

In the year XVI, the 21st day of Pharmuti, in the night of the full moon which falls on the 22nd, King Nectonabo, who ruled at Memphis, had made a sacrifice and prayed to the gods to show him the future;[1] he imagined that he beheld in a dream the papyrus boat, called Rhôps[2] in Egyptian, arrive at Memphis; on the boat there was a great throne, and on the throne was seated the glorious one, the beneficent distributor of the fruits of the earth, queen of the gods, Isis, and all the gods of Egypt were standing around her, on her right and on her left.[3] One of them, whose height the king reckoned to be twenty cubits, advanced into the midst of the assembly—he who is called Onûris in Egyptian,[4] Ares in Greek—and,

1. The opening is the same as in the story utilised by the Egyptians to explain the exodus of the Jews, which Manetho sets forth in his work. Amenophis desired to behold the gods, as Horus had done before him (Josephus. *Contra Apionem*, i, 26), and the gods, offended at his wish, predicted his ruin.

2. In the preceding edition of this book (p. 255, note 2), I conjectured that the original Egyptian of this word was *romes, rames*, which is the name for a kind of bark (cf. p. 104, note 28 of this volume); Wilcken has since discovered, in a Paris papyrus, a form Rhômpsis, which is nearer the Egyptian term than Rhôps (*der Traum des Königs Nectonabos*, p. 587), and that which was only conjecture has proved to be reality. The Egyptian word is preserved in the term *ramûs*, used in Nubia and Upper Egypt (Burckhardt, *Travels in Nubia*, p. 247) to denote a canoe made of rushes (cf. Maspero, *Notes d'inspection*, § 11, in *Annales du Service des Antiquités*, vol. x, pp. 138–141.

3. This is an exact description of certain scenes that occur not infrequently in temples of the Ptolemaic and Roman periods.

4. The transcription adopted at the present day for this name is Anhûr, Anhûri, Onhûri. Anhûri is one of the numerous variants of the sun-god; he was one of the gods worshipped

prostrating himself, he spake thus: "Come to me, goddess of the gods, thou who hast the greatest power on earth, who commandest all that is in the universe, and who preservest all the gods; oh, Isis, be merciful and listen to me. As thou hast commanded, I have guarded the country without fail, and although up to the present I have concerned myself greatly for the king Nectonabo, Samaûs,[5] into whose hands thou hast given authority, has neglected my temple, and has shown himself opposed to my laws. I am out of my own temple, and the works in the sanctuary that is called Phersô[6] are left half undone owing to the perversity of the king." The queen of the gods having listened to what was said to her, answered nothing.

Having seen this in his dream, the king awoke, and he commanded in haste that one should be sent to Sebennytos inland[7] to summon the high-priest and the prophet of Onûris. When they arrived at the hall of audience the king asked them, "What are the works that are suspended in the sanctuary called Phersô?" When they said, "Everything is finished, except the carving of the hieroglyphic texts on the stone walls," he commanded in haste that letters should be sent to the principal temples of Egypt to summon the sacred sculptors. When they arrived according to this command, the king asked which of them was the most skilful, and could soonest finish the works that were suspended in the sanctuary called Phersô. When he had said this, he of the city of Aphrodite, of the Aphroditopolite nome, he who is named Petêsis, son of Ergeus, arose,

in the Thinite nome and at Sebennytos. He is represented in human form, with a crown of high feathers on his head, and transfixing a fallen enemy with his lance. The XXXth dynasty was Sebennytic in origin, and Anhûri was its titular patron; Nectanebo I, in his cartouche, styled himself Mêionhûri, *the beloved of Onûris.*

5. The hieroglyphic equivalent of this name has not yet been found in the texts. Wilcken (*Der Traum des Königs Nectonabos,* pp. 586–589) thinks it may be recognised as a transcription of the banner-name of Nectanebo *Tamaû,* and therefore of the sovereign himself. But the banner-name is not merely *Tamaû,* it is *Hor-tamaû,* and it seems to me improbable that the writer would omit to transcribe so important an element as the name of Horus. Witkowski, on the contrary (*In Somnium Nectanebi,* pp. 14–15), as Leemans had done previously, regards Samaûs as the name of the governor of the city.

6. Wilcken (*Der Traum des Königs Nectonabos,* pp. 589, 590) has here restored a part of the sentence that is missing in the original. According to inscriptions recovered from the ruins of Sebennytos, the name of one of the principal sanctuaries of this town was Per-Shôû, "the house of the god Shôû, Shû" (Ahmed bey Kemal, *Sébennytos et son temple,* in *Annales du Service des Antiquités,* 1906, vol. vii, p, 90); possibly this corresponds with Phersô.

7. Sebennytos is here called *inland* to distinguish it from the other town of the same name, which was situated near the *sea* (Wilcken, *Der Traum des Königs Nectonabos,* p. 590).

and said he could finish the work in a few days.[8] The king questioned all the others after the same manner, and they affirmed that Petêsis spake the truth, and that there was not a man in the whole country that approached him in skill. For this reason the king committed the work in question to him, and also entrusted him with large sums of money and recommended him to arrange to finish the work within a few days, according to what he had told him of the will of the god. Petêsis, having received much money, repaired to Sebennytos, and, as he was by nature a notorious wine-bibber, he made up his mind to have a good time before beginning his work.

Now it chanced that, as he was walking in the southern part of the temple, he met the daughter of a maker of perfumes,[9] who was the most beautiful of those who were distinguished for their beauty in that place. . . .

The narrative ends at the very point at which the action begins. Petêsis' encounter in the southern part of the temple reminds us of Satni's adventure in the forecourt of the temple of Ptah.[10] We may conclude, if we wish, that the author is here introducing a heroine of the same kind as Tbubui. Possibly the plot centred wholly in the architect's somewhat bragging promise to finish the work at Phersô in a few days. The god Onûris, annoyed at seeing Petêsis begin a sacred work with a bout of indulgence, or merely desiring to teach him a lesson, sent a temptress to make him lose his time and money. There is here an opportunity for a variety of conjectures. The safest plan is to decide on none of them, but confess that there is nothing in the fragment to guide us as to the events or the conclusion of the drama.

8. Queen Hatshopsuîtu boasts of having had the two great obelisks of rose granite at the entrance of the sanctuary of the temple at Karnak, one of which is still standing, quarried near Assuan, transported to Thebes, carved, polished, and set up all in seven months. The rapidity with which such work was carried out was a mark of skill greatly boasted of by those who possessed it. The author of our story is therefore entirely following the Egyptian tradition in representing his architect as undertaking to finish his work in a very short space of time.

9. I have here followed Wilcken's reading and correction; Witkowski (*In Somnium Nectanebi*, p. 17) regarded the Greek word as the name of the girl.

10. See above, pp. III *et seq.*

FRAGMENTS OF THE THEBAN=COPTIC VERSION OF THE ROMANCE OF ALEXANDER [23]

(Arab Period)

THE remains of a romance of Alexander were discovered among the manuscripts of Deîr Amba Shenoudah, acquired through me in 1885–8 for the Bibliothèque Nationale at Paris. Three leaves of it were first published by U. Bouriant, *Fragments d'un roman d'Alexandre en dialecte thébain,* in the *Journal asiatique,* 1887, viiith series, vol. ix, pp. 1–38, with one plate; printed separately in 8vo, 36 pp.

Then three more leaves, a few months later, by U. Bouriant, *Fragments d'un roman d'Alexandre en dialecte thébain (Nouveau Mémoire)* in the *Journal asiatique,* viiith series, vol. x, pp. 340–349; printed separately, 8vo, 12 pp.

Several leaves of the same manuscript were found soon afterwards in different European libraries. In 1891 a single one was found at the British Museum, and published by W. E. Crum, *Another fragment of the Story of Alexander,* in *Proceedings of the Society of Biblical Archæology,* 1892, vol. xix, pp. 473–482; printed separately, 8vo, 10 pp. Two at Berlin, which were noticed as early as 1888 by L. Stern (*Zeitschrift,* vol. xxvi, p. 56), but not published till fifteen years later by O. de Lemm, *Der Alexanderroman bei der Kopten, ein Beitrag zur Geschichte der Alexandersage im Orient,* large 8vo, St. Petersburg, 1903, vol. xix, 161 pp. and two plates.

The whole of the fragments and their arrangement, the nature of the episodes, and the constitution of the text were studied almost simultaneously by O. de Lemm in the work just mentioned, and by R. Pietschmann, *Zu den Ueberbleibseln des Koptischen Alexanderbuches,* in *Beiträge zur Bücherskunde und Philologie, August Wilmanns zum 25 Mars 1903 gewidmet,* 8vo, Leipzig, 1903, pp. 304–312; printed separately, 12 pp.

The manuscript was written on a thin, flexible cotton paper, and measured about 18 centimetres in height by 125 millimetres in breadth. The writing is scratchy, small, and rapid, the letters badly formed, the spelling corrupt, and the grammar faulty at times. It seems to me improbable that the writing is earlier than the thirteenth century, but the redaction of the work may go back as far as the tenth or eleventh century A.D.

As far as we can judge from the small number of fragments that are preserved, the story is a reproduction, pure and simple, of the life of Alexander by the Pseudo-Callisthenes. That which remains of the chapters dealing with the poisoning of Alexander is so closely allied to the Greek that one is inclined to regard it as a translation. On the other hand, the fragments that relate to the old man Eleazar and his connection with Alexander, to the dream of Menander, and the unexpected return of the Macedonian hero to his camp, do not correspond with those versions of the Pseudo-Callisthenes that have been published up to the present. I have come to the conclusion that between the time when the redactions of the Pseudo-Callisthenes that we possess were composed, and when our Theban redaction was made, various new episodes, belonging no doubt to Egypt or Syria, were added to the romance; and that it is this recension, so far unknown to us, which our fragments have transmitted in part. Was it in Coptic, in Greek, or in Arabic? I believe an examination of the text allows us to reply easily to this question. The Coptic remains have all the appearance of a translation, thus, in the account of the plot against Alexander, the Coptic phrase so exactly follows the Greek construction that it is impossible to regard it otherwise than as a translation. Until further information, I shall therefore take for granted that our Theban-Coptic text is a direct translation from the Greek, and also that we may hope some day to recover one or more Greek versions more complete than those we now possess. They must no doubt have been confined to Egypt, and that is the reason that in Western recensions no trace is found of several incidents that are partly recorded in these stray Coptic fragments.

The order of the fragments given in the following pages is that which was given them by O. de Lemm, and my translation is founded on the text established by him.

The first fragments refer to an adventure which is not related in any of the versions known to me, either Eastern or Western. Alexander disguises himself as a messenger, as on the day when he went to visit the Queen of Ethiopia,[1] and went to a town under the rule of one of her enemies, probably the King of the Lamites.[2] There, having laid his business before him, he meets with an aged Per-

1. In Pseudo-Callisthenes (ii, 14) he disguises himself as Hermes to go to the court of Darius.

2. This is at least a very probable conjecture, suggested to Lemm by the remainder of the text (*Der Alexanderroman*, p. 20).

sian[3] of the name of Eleazar, who takes him away with him, and tells him that the king never allows the messengers of foreign countries to return, but retains them as prisoners till their death. The messengers are there, impatient to see the new-comer. At the point where the story commences, Alexander has just been introduced to them, and Eleazar has told him of the fate awaiting him.

He said to Alexander, "Ask each of these, How long hast thou been in these parts?" The first of them said, "Listen to me, my brother. I belong to the country of Thrace, and lo! forty years ago I came here; for I was sent with letters to this country." The second said, "As to me, my brother, lo! I have spent twenty-two years since I came to the land of the Lektumenos."[4] The third said to him, "Lo! sixty-six years ago I came to this place, for I was sent with letters from my lord the king . . .ês. Now, console thyself." Eleazar said to Alexander, " . . . I have heard that it is the son of the king, who is now king. As to thee, my brother, thou wilt never see thy lord, thy king, again for ever." Alexander wept bitterly. All who beheld him marvelled at him, and some of them said, "He has only now arrived, and his heart is still hot within him." Eleazar, the old Persian, took hold of Alexander; he took him to his house. The messengers followed them, and seated themselves; each of them talked of his country and lamented over his family, and they wept over Alexander. As he wept . . . my lord . . . Eleazar said . . .

I do not exactly know what happened after this. It may be said that Alexander succeeded in taking the city of the Lamites and setting the prisoners free. One of the existing leaves tells us what he did on this occasion.

He took command of the troops; he sent them with the men who were crucified, while the women were chained together in groups. Alexander commanded his troops to hold the gate of the city and to let

3. According to a very ingenious hypothesis suggested by Lemm (*Der Alexanderroman,* pp. 22, 23) the word *old man* in Coptic is a literal translation from the original Greek πρεσβύς; Eleazar was in reality the Persian ambassador to the king of the Lamites.

4. If this is not an invented word made up of scraps, it must at least be admitted that the Coptic copyist has strangely disfigured the name of the people of that neighbourhood from the original Greek. *Lektumenos,* pronounced *Lekdumenos,* comprises nearly all the elements of the Greek *Lake-dæmonios.* I believe this refers to an envoy of Lacedemonia.

no one go out. Now when it was daybreak the old man Eleazar caused a royal garment to be brought, and all the messengers who were there he loaded in this manner, with gold, silver, and all the precious stones that had been found in that palace—sardonyx, topaz, jasper, onyx, agate, amber, chrysolite, chrysoprase, and amethyst;—now, that stone which is the amethyst, is that with which gold is tested. Then they despoiled the Lamites,[5] and they went away from their city, and he established Iôdaê as its governor.[6] Alexander said . . .

Alexander's speech is lost. It was not long, but its loss is annoying, as it finished the episode. On the *verso* of the sheet, we are already in the midst of a new adventure of which the hero is a certain Antipater. This Antipater seems to be the son of one of the messengers who were with the Lamites, and the messenger himself had been king of a town over which Antipater was now reigning. The father, who had been set free by Alexander, suspecting that his long captivity would have caused him to be forgotten, did not wish to return openly to his domains.

He took the garments of a beggar, and he said "I will prove all the notables[7] who are in the city, and I will know what they are doing." He therefore entered into the city and seated himself in front of the king's house. The king had never seen him, he only knew that for seventy-seven years his father had been with the Lamites. Therefore he did not speak to the old man, for he did not know that he was his son, and for his part the old man did not know that he was his father, the man who was there wrapt in a mantle. But, behold, a woman addressed him, and said to him, "Antipater, why dost thou not go to search for thy father? for I have heard it said of the Lamites that Alexander is their lord, and that he has sent

5. The Lamites are mentioned in the martyrdom of St. John of Phanizoît (Amélineau, *Un document copte du xiiie siècle, Martyre de Jean de Phanidjoît*, pp. 20, 52, 65), where the word is an abbreviation for *Islamites*, Mohammedan (Lemm, *Der Alexanderroman*, p. 41). Here we may recognise it as an abbreviation of *Elamites*, as Bouriant realised, and as Lemm has shown after him (*Der Alexanderroman*, pp. 38–42). Susa, the residence of the kings of Persia, was in Elam, and it would not be surprising if the name of the Elamites played an important part in the traditions about Alexander that were current among the people.

6. The name Iôdaê is uncertain. If it may really be read thus in this place, the propinquity of Eleazar would enable us to recognise a name, Iadoue identical with that of the high-priest of Jerusalem, whom legend places in direct connection with Alexander.

7. Here the text gives the word *apa*, pronounced *amba*, which is applied in Coptic to the professed religious. It is another proof, in conjunction with those we have already, of the Egyptian and Christian origin of this episode.

back all the messengers." The young man said, "My father is dead, and certainly over forty years ago. . . . As my father went away before I came into the world, and my mother told me the story of my father. . . ."

The three following sheets transport us to Gedrosia. Alexander has fallen, we do not know by what misadventure, into the hands of the king of the country, who has condemned him to be flung into Chaos,[8] the chasm into which criminals were cast. One of the Gedrosian counsellors, Antilochos, vainly attempted to commute the sentence; charged with its execution, he negotiates with Alexander, and tries to find some means of saving him. From the first lines of the fragment, it appears that this was the result of Alexander lamenting his fate and exclaiming, "What would I not do for any one who would save me!" which was overheard by Antilochos as he entered the prison.

When Antilochos heard him, he immediately went to Alexander, and said to him, "If I speak to the king to release thee, what will thou do for me?" Alexander said to him, "Shall I ever see thee when I go free in my city? If it is thus, the half of my kingdom, take it from me, from to-day." Antilochos gave him ink and paper, and he wrote as follows: "By the throne of my royalty and by my personal safety, if thou savest me, all that thou askest of me I shall give thee." Antilochos therefore sent in haste, to the guardian of Chaos, and said to him, "Take of me three hundred-weight of gold, on a condition that I am about to tell thee. Alexander the king has commanded to throw him into Chaos, but, when he is brought to thee, hide him in thy hiding-place, and throw a stone of his shape into Chaos, that we may hear it, we and those who are with us. If thou actest thus, thou shalt live, and thou shalt find favour with me, and when that man shall come to thee, thou shalt find plenty of baskets and he will give thee numerous presents." They promised each other, and Antilochos returned home. When it was daybreak, Antilochos bound Alexander. Alexander followed Antilochos until they arrived at the edge of Chaos, and he beheld it with his eyes. Alexander, whose power was exhausted, and whose strength had failed, raised his eyes to heaven, and spake to those who were holding him, "Allow me, my brothers, to behold the sun." Alexander wept, saying, "Oh sun, which givest light, shall I see thee again to-morrow morning?" He was brought inside, and Antilochos said to

8. The text sometimes gives *Chaos*, sometimes *Chaosm*. It is an erroneous reading by the Coptic translator. The original Greek must evidently have been *khasma*, "a gulf," which under the pen of an ignorant scribe has become a proper noun.

him, "Take some wine and bread, and eat, before thou beholdest Chaos." Alexander said, "If it is the last bread that I shall eat, I will not eat it." But Antilochos spake to him in a low voice, and said to him, "Eat and drink. Thy soul, I will save it. For we have already agreed on this method; when they seize the stone and throw it down, cry with a loud voice, so that it is thou whom we hear." Antilochos went out with ten soldiers; Antilochos said, "Let us go out that our eyes may not behold his misery." They seized the stone, Alexander cried with a loud voice. Antilochos said, weeping, to those who were with him, "Oh, the misery of King Alexander, and the poverty of the glories of this world!" Then Alexander, the guardian of Chaos, led him back to the city.

The lacuna that separates this fragment from the following fragment cannot be large. The guardian of Chaos, after having taken Alexander back to the city, shuts him up in a hiding-place, as had been arranged; on his side, Antilochos hastens to the king, to give an account of his mission, and the report that Alexander is dead spreads everywhere. The effect produced by the news is such that the king himself is alarmed, and regrets that he has slain the hero.

" . . . Alexander has died in Chaos," all those who heard it exclaimed; on hearing them, the king was greatly distressed, and he bewailed himself, with the queen and with Antilochos, and he said, "I repent me at having thrown that great king into Chaos, and I fear that his army may march against us." Antilochos said to him, "I was wearied with praying thee, 'Let him go.' And thou wouldst not let thyself be persuaded to listen to me, and thou didst not incline thy face to me." The king said, "Why didst thou not find some means of sending him away?" Now, during the night Alexander was taken to the house of Antilochos, he was received, and he was let down into a hole, and all that was necessary was given him. The tidings spread over the whole country, "Alexander is dead," and all those who heard it became congealed like stone on account of that which had happened.

After that, Menander saw a dream of this kind, and he perceived a vision in this manner: he beheld a lion loaded with irons that one was throwing into a fosse. And behold, a man said to him, "Menander, why dost thou not go down with this lion, since his purple is fallen? arise now, and take him by the collar of his purple." In haste he arose, and he spake to Selpharios, as well as to Diatrophê, saying, "Are you asleep?" They said,

"What is the matter, oh first of the philosophers,[9] Menander?" He said, weeping, "the dream that I have seen will turn out against the enemies of Alexander, for the vision of those who hate him has passed before me in a dream, and I have been petrified with grief." Menander said to them, "The lion I saw is the king." While they exchanged these words till the morning, behold, a messenger came to Selpharios, Menander, and Diatrophê, crying and weeping, and he said to them, "Who will hear those words that I have heard and keep silence? It is a terror to speak them, it is an infamy to pronounce them." Menander said, "What is this speech, my son? I know already what has happened to King Alexander." The messenger said to them, "Men worthy of death have raised their hand on our lord the king, in Gedrosia, and they have slain him." Menander took his vestment of purple and tore it; Selpharios and Diatrophê tore their chlamydes, they bewailed themselves, and they all did as though there was an earthquake. Diatrophê said, "I will go, and I will bring back tidings of my lord." He took with him a khiliarch[10] and three soldiers, and they went to Gedrosia, they heard the tidings, they knew all that had happened, and they returned to the camp, and they told Menander, they repeated it to him with groans and tears, saying, " . . .

The three personages introduced here do not usually figure among Alexander's companions. Two of them, Selpharios and Diatrophê—a man, notwithstanding the feminine form of his name—are entirely unknown. It appears to me that Menander is the comic poet of that name, whose moral maxims, taken from his comedies, acquired so great a reputation in the Christian world; the title borne by him, First of Philosophers or First of Friends, shows us that tradition assigned him a high rank among the crowd of learned men and scribes that accompanied Alexander to the East. He seems, in fact, to exercise considerable authority over those around him, for it is he, in conjunction with Selpharios, who takes the measures necessary under these circumstances; in two or three pages, now lost, he announces to the troops the tidings of Alexander's death, he orders mourning, and he goes to besiege the town where the crime has

9. I have restored the text thus, by analogy with the Byzantine titles, protospatharios, protostrator, protovestarchos, protonosocomos, and proto notary. M. de Lemm prefers to restore the title *protophilos,* the first friend (*Der Alexanderroman,* pp. 68–69, 132–133), which is no less probable.

10. A damaged word which I think I can recognise as khiliarch, the term for a commandant of 1,000 men.

been committed, in order to obtain vengeance. In the meantime, Antilochos, taking advantage of the king's remorse, has told him that Alexander still lives, and the adventure ends with an agreement by which the Macedonian recovers his liberty, on condition of forgetting the injury received by him. Knowing that his army believed him to be dead, he desired to test the fidelity of his subordinates, and he disguised himself, so that he might mix with them freely.

When the evening came, Alexander took the outfit of a plain soldier, and went out to go to the camp. Now Selpharios had forbidden in his proclamation that any one should drink wine or clothe themselves in fine garments, during the forty days of mourning in honour of King Alexander. Alexander came, therefore, and he beheld Agricolaos, king of the Persians, stretched on his bed, who spake to his people: "Arise now, ye men of heart, eat and drink, for a yoke is fallen off you, this Alexander, who has been slain. What is it, then, that you have in your hearts? I will not allow you to remain thus, slaves of Macedonia and of Egypt."[11] Alexander said to himself aside, "No, in faith, it will not be to-day that thou eatest and that thou drinkest, excellent man, who art so pleased with thyself." He arose therefore, and he said to them, "Why dost thou not eat and drink? For he is dead, who made you to die in these wars; now that he himself has been made to die, rejoice, be full of happiness." They said to him, "Thou art mad." And when they had said that, they began to throw stones at him. Alexander remained hidden until the middle of the night; he then went to the house of Antilochos, he mounted on Chiron,[12] and he went to the place where Menander was, for his eyes were heavy with sleep. He said to Menander, to Selpharios, and to Diatrophê, "It is you who are my strength." Menander said, "My father, what is it? Is it then an untruth that I have heard about thee?" When they were silent, he began to speak: "I am indeed Alexander, who was slain by them of Gedrosia, but Antilochos has given me back my life; Chiron, tell them what has chanced to me." When it was dawn, he seated himself on the throne of his royalty. Alexander thereupon caused the herald to proclaim, saying, "King Alexander has

11. It must not be forgotten that, according to the romance, Alexander is the son of Nectanebo, that is to say, of an Egyptian king. To obey him is therefore to obey Egypt as well as Macedonia.

12. This must be the centaur Chiron, for later on Alexander says, "Chiron, tell them what happened to me." This would only be said to a being possessed of a human voice, as the centaur was. The substitution of Chiron for Bucephalus is in itself an indication of a bad period; such confusion could only have occurred at a time and in a country where ancient tradition was already much obliterated.

arrived." And thereupon the multitude came. Agricolaos himself came, and he said, "We have seen thy face, and we live." King Alexander said to him, "Thou hast, then, awaked from thy drunkenness of last night, when thou saidst, 'The yoke of Alexander has been taken from us; eat, drink.'" The king thereupon commanded to cut off his head with a sword; the king said, "Take now vinegar in place of the wine that thou hast drunk, until thou art drunken with it." Then King Alexander said, "Bring me the ilarchs,"[13] and they were brought to him . . .

Selpharios is the hero of the fragment that follows, but I see nothing in the Pseudo-Callisthenes which resembles that which we find in the Coptic text. Defeated in a first expedition against the Persians, and on the point of again starting for war, he dictates his will.

"Then they went away. They heard the name of . . . Jeremiah . . . thy health . . . the king, behold that which thou shalt do; he who brings thee my letter, be merciful to him, and deliver him, so that he may go away with all that is his. I salute . . . the general; I salute Jeremiah and Dracontios, I salute Sergios and Philea. My son, who shall place thy mouth on my mouth, thy eyes on my eyes, my hands on thy hair? The birds of the air who fly, they fill their beaks with the fruits of the fields, and they bring them in their beaks to their little ones; and they, the fledglings, they rejoice in the presence of their parents, by reason of the provision that they have made for them, and they beat their little wings, and it is thus that the little birds show their kindliness. Thou thyself, Philea, mine own son, remember the hour when I went forth from . . . In a dream he has seen the ruin of our great lord Alexander. . . . May Alexander, our king, rest a moment; consider . . . my power for thee. I have fought . . . Okianos, and I have overthrown him, but I have not been able to overcome the valour of the Persians; they have been the most powerful, and they have conquered me. I, Selpharios, I have written this with mine own hand; when thou art grown, look at it, and take notice of it, read it and recite it, with tears and lamentations. I have written the lines of my will with the tears of my eyes for ink, for the places where I used to drink are become solitudes, and the places where I refreshed myself are become deserts. I salute you one by one, my brethren; fare ye well, my beloved, and remember me."

13. I had regarded the word *Alarichos* which occurs in the text as the name of a man. Lemm (*Der Alexanderroman*, p. 86) has taken it as the title ilarchos, the commandants of the Macedonian cavalry.

When he had written this, he gave the paper to Alexander, and Alexander wept, and turned away his eyes, that Selpharios might not see him. Alexander said, . . .

The episode that follows recalls one of the most curious passages of the Pseudo-Callisthenes, where Alexander, arrived at the confines of the country of the dead, wishes to enter and plunge into the darkness which separates it from the land of the living.

He marvelled at the beauty of the garden, from which four rivers flowed, which are the Pisôn, the Gihon, the Tigris, and the Euphrates; they drank the waters, and rejoiced, for they were sweet. Thereupon they perceived the thick darkness, and they said, "We cannot enter there." Menander said, "Let us take brood-mares, let us mount them, and let their foals be kept back, while we plunge into the darkness." They marvelled, for it was very dark, so that they could not see the faces of their comrades. Alexander said, "Come with me, thou Menander, as well as Selpharios and Diatrophê." They mounted four brood-mares, while their foals remained in the light, so that each heard the voice of the other, and they plunged into the darkness. But they heard a voice which said, "Alexander and Menander, as well as Selpharios and Diatrophê, consider yourselves happy to have penetrated thus far." Alexander said, "I shall not consider myself happy until I find that which I seek." He pushed forward a little, and he stopped with his mare. The voice said to him a second time, "Consider thyself happy, oh Alexander." But Alexander would not stop; he looked beneath the feet of his horses, and he perceived some lights. Alexander said, "Let us take these lights, for they are precious stones." Selpharios stretched out his hand and took four, Menander three, Diatrophê two; as to Alexander, he stretched out his left hand and filled it, and he took three stones with his right hand, and immediately his left hand became as his right hand, and when he went to war, from that hour he fought with his two hands. Alexander smelt a strong perfume, but the voice reached the ears of Alexander for the third time, "Consider thyself satisfied, oh Alexander. When a horse hastens too much in running, he stumbles and falls." And the voice spake again. "I ask thee, what dost thou desire?" Alexander said, "Give me power over the entire earth, and let my foes submit to me." The voice said to him, "Since thou hast not asked a long life, but merely power over the whole world, behold the whole world, thou shalt see it with thine eyes, and thou shalt be its lord; but when morning sheds its light, then . . ."

The voice probably announced immediate death, but either by stratagem or prayer Alexander succeeded in obtaining a prolongation of life, which he made use of to visit the Brachmânes in their country. A leaf which we possess contains a description of their costumes, manners, and customs; but the lines are all so damaged that no consecutive text can be constructed from it. All that can be made out shows that it deals with the country of the Homerites, with Kalanos, of which the name is changed to Kalynas, with India, the beds of leaves used by the Gymnophistes, and their nudity; but the connection between these scanty gleanings is not traceable.

The last of the fragments we found belongs to the end of the work. It relates, in terms that forcibly recall those employed by the Pseudo-Callisthenes, the intrigues that preceded the death of Alexander, and the method by which Antipater prepared and poured out the poison by which the hero died.

He calmed the rage of Olympias and its anger with Antipater, by sending Krateros into Macedonia and Thessaly. When Antipater knew of the wrath of Alexander—for he learnt it from the men who had been licensed for military service—Antipater conspired to slay Alexander, in order that he might escape great tortures; for he had heard and he knew what Alexander intended against him, on account of his arrogancy and his intrigues. Now, Alexander sent for the troop of archers, who were in considerable numbers, to come to Babylon. Among them there was a son of Antipater, named Julios, who waited on Alexander. Antipater prepared a fatal potion, of which no vase, either of bronze or of pottery, could endure the strength, but all fell to pieces as soon as it touched them. When therefore he had prepared it, he put it in an iron receptacle, and gave it Casandra, his son, whom he sent as page to Alexander. When Casandra came to Babylon, he found Alexander engaged in offering a sacrifice, and receiving those who came to him. He spake to Julios, his brother, for he was the first cup-bearer of Alexander. Now, it had chanced, a few days before, that Alexander had struck the servitor Julios on the head with a staff, while he was seated, for a reason that arose from a want of care; for this the young man was furious, and willingly declared himself ready to commit the crime. He took with him Mesios the Thessalonian, a friend of Alexander, and one of his judges whom he had punished for prevarication, and they agreed between them to cause Alexander to drink the poison.

ON THOSE WHO CAUSED ALEXANDER TO DRINK THE DEATH POTION [24]

WHO LOOKS at a table that does not belong to him, his existence is not life.

The commencement of this chapter does not belong to the romance; as Lemm[1] has recognised, it is a simple epigraph borrowed from one of the books of the Old Testament, that of Jesus, son of Sirach.[2] Nothing of the narrative itself remains. What I have to say about the Theban version of the romance of Alexander ends here; it may still be hoped that fresh fragments may be found to enrich our collection, and they will enable us some day to recognise with more accuracy their connection with the versions known at the present time. The special value that is now attached to them arises from the fact that, with the fragments of the *Romance of Cambyses* recently discovered by Schäfer, they form the sole evidence that remains to us of the existence of those Coptic manuscripts to which Arab authors so often refer, and from which they assert that they acquired their fabulous history of Ancient Egypt.

1. O. de Lemm, *Der Alexanderroman*, pp. 129–131.
2. *Jesus, son of Sirach*, xi, 29.

INDEX
OF PROPER NAMES

Aaa, 60

Aarne, Antti, xiv

Abdemon, cxi

Abu-Roâsh, 59

Abu-zabel, 59

Abydos, cxli *n.* 195, cliii

Acerbas, 173 *n.* 5

Aesop, cxi

Africanus, 137

Agricolas, 250

Ahasuerus, 232

Ahmasi, cxxvi, cxxxvi, 232

Ahmasi-si-Abna, 90 *n.* 3

Ahmed, cxxx

Ahmed-ibn-Tulûn, 25 *n.* 18

Ahmôsis, 224 *n.* 12

Ahnes el Medineh, 39 *n.* 10

Ahuri, cxvi, cxxx, cxlvi, 98 *seq.*

Aia, 60

Aîn-Musa, 134 *n.* 16

Aî-Sanafruî, 59

Ajah, 60

Akhthoes, 33 *n.* 59

Alasia, 170, 171

Alexander, cxv, 218, 240, 243

Alexandria, 221

Ali Baba, xcv, cxiv, 90

Amaît, 123

Amânûa, 16 *n.* 53

Amânusihaît, 172, 177

Amasis, 233

Amâuni-Amanâu, 88

Amê, 202

Amenemhabi, 90 *n.* 3

Amenemhaît, cvii, 61, 64 *n.* 16, 64 *n.* 18, 69

Amenophis, 240 *n.* 1

Amenothes, cx *n.* 76

Amenothes II, cx *n.* 76, 165 *n.* 3

Amentît, 7 *n.* 19, 121, 122, 123, 136, 179

Amêu, 202

Amgiâd, cii, ciii

Amît, 188 *n.* 16

Ammûianashi, 63, 67

Amon, cxxxix, 72, 127, 128, 170, 171, 183, 202, 203, 204 *n.* 45

—of the Road, cx *n.* 75, 171, 173, 179

Amoni, cvii, cxlix

Amoni-Amenemhaît, cxlix

Amonrâ, 143, 172, 193

Anhur (Anhuri), 240 *n.* 4

Ani, cxxviii

Ankh, 235, *n.* 7

Ankhhophis, 195

Ankhhoru, 188, 193, 194, 202

Ankhutaûi, 19 *n.* 4, 112 *n.* 55

Antar, cxlvii

Anteia, ci

Antilochos, 247

Antipater, 246 *seq.*, 253

Antipatridas, cxiii

Anubis, cvi *n.* 59, cxxxix, 53, 122, 123

Anupu, xcix, cv, cxxiii, cxxiv, 3

Anupuî, cvii *n.* 62

Anysis, cxv, 138 *et seq.*

Aphrodite, 241

Aphroditopolite-nome, 241

Apis, 13 *n.* 39

Apollobechis, 15

Apôphis, 223

Apôpi, xcvi, cxi, 217, 224 *et seq.*

Apuriu, 92

Arabian nights, xciii, cii, ciii *n.* 36, cxiv, cxix, cxxx, 90

Ares, 240

Arinar, civ

Aroîris, 73 *n.* 61

Arsinoë, 60

Artemidorus, clii *n.* 238

Asari, 39

Asaru, cxlvi

Asfûn, 128 *n.* 98

Ashmunein, 130 *n.* 106

Ashukhîtu, cxvii *n.* 94

Assâd, cii, ciii

Assasîf, 105 *n.* 32

Assuan, 185 *n.* 7, 242 *n.* 8

Assyrians, 137, 201

Asukhis, cxvii *n.* 94

Asychis, cxv, cxvii *n.* 94

Athribis, cxx, 59, 195

Athu, 74

Athyr, cxxxiv, cxxxviii

Atumu, 72 *n.* 55, 134, 184, 191

Atys, cv

Avaris, 224 *n.* 13

Baal, 93 *n.* 16, 196, 200 *n.* 36

Babylon, cxi, 253

Bactrians, 150

Badîlu, 172

Badûr, cii

Bahr-belâ-mâ, cliii

Bahr Yusûf, 59

Baîti, xcix, c, cvi *n.* 57, cxxiii, cxxxii, 3 *n.* 3 *seq.*

Baîufrîya, 18, 22

Bakhtan, cix, cx, 144 *et seq.*

Baklulu, 194

Balikh, 144 *n.* 2

Bastît, cxxxix, 19, 64 *n.* 17

Beduîn, cxlvi, 61, 63, 66

Belbeis, 59

Bellerophon, ci

Benfey, Theodor, xxiii

Benha-el-Assal, 59

Beni-Hasan, 16 *n.* 53

Bêti, 3 *n.* 3

Biamu, 202

Bîgeh, cli, 83 *n.* 2

Bintrashît, cx, cxlvii, 144 *n.* 7, *seq.*

Birkatil, 175

Birket Karûn, 181

—Nu, cli

Bocchoris, cviii

Bonaparte, cxv

Boqaît, cxli *n.* 197

Boukolos, 202

Boulaq, 95

Boutes, cvi *n.* 61

Brachmânes, 253

Bubastis, 64 *n.* 17, 112, 113

Bucolics, cxxiii, 202

Busiris, cxx, 185, 202

Butes, 3 *n.* 3

Butês, cvi *n.* 60, 3 *n.* 3

Buti, 3 *n.* 3

Bûto, cviii *n.* 71, cxxiii, 201, 202, 203
  n. 40, 212

Byblos, cxlvi, 60, 170, 173, 192

Bytis, cvi *n.* 60, 3 *n.* 3

Cambyses, cxv, 161, 255

Casandra, 253

Cataonia, 206 *n.* 54

Chaos, 247 *n.* 8

Charlemagne, cviii, cix

Charobe, 221

Cheops (*cf.* Khufuî), xcv, xcvii, xcvii,
  xcviii, cix, cxv–cxix, 17, 19, 33, 237

Chephren, cxv, 33

Chilluk, 199 *n.* 32

Chimaera, ci

Chiron, 250 *n.* 12

Cimmerians, 199 *n.* 35

Cleopatra, civ, cxxv, cxxxvi

Clitophon, cxlvii

Combabos, cv *n.* 55

Coptos, cxliv, 103 *seq.*

Cosquin, E., xxiii

Cybele, cv

Cynopolite nome, cvi

Cyprus, 171

Dadûfhoru, cxvii, 24, 26, 27

Dahchûr, 61

Daphnae, 148, 149

Dardanus, 98 *n.* 6

Darius, 244 *n.* 1

David, 171

Deîr Amba Shenoudah, 243

Deîr el Baharî, cxxv, cxxxvi

Deîr el Medineh, xciv, cx *n.* 76,
  cxxvi *n.* 124, cxxxvi. *n.* 175

Delta, cxxiii, cxxxv *n.* 170

Demeter, 163

Democritus, 98 *n.* 6

Denderah, cxxvi, cxxvii, 105 *n.* 32

Diatrophê, 248 *seq.*

Didi, cxxxii, 25 *seq.*

Dido, 173 *n.* 5

Didu, xcvii, 188 *n.* 16

Didûfhoru, 24, 111 *n.* 51

Didusanafruî, 25

Dimeh, 181

Dinkas, cli

Dio Cassius, cxxiii *n.* 111

Diodorus, cxx *n.* 105

Diospolis, cxx, cxxi, 184, 199

Dodecharchy, cviii *n.* 71, 183

Dora, 170, 172

Dracontios, 251

Drah-Abu'l-Neggah, 230 *n.* 1

Dupu, 203 *n.* 40

Ecbatana, 161

Edessa, cxiii

Edimâ, 60

Eiernharerôu, cxvii *n.* 91, 97 *n.* 2,
  183, 201

El, cxlvi

El Amarna, 90 *n.* 1

Elamites, 246 *n.* 5

Eleazar, 244 *seq.*

Elephantine, cxx, 74 *n.* 67, 82, 83,
  185, 189, 194, 214

El-Hibeh, 169

El-Kab, 4 *n.* 7

El-Maghfâr, 60

Embabeh, 59

Emîm, 89

Ennana, 3, 16

Ergeus, 241

Erment, cxxv, cxxxvi

Erythræan Sea, 148

Esneh, 72 *n.* 54

Etbaye, cl

Ethiopia, cxvi, cxxxii *n.* 153, cl, 150, 244

Euphrates, 252

Fayûm, 235

Fechn, 169

Fonkhu, 73 *n.* 66

Gatatani, 206 *n.* 54

Gattani, 206 *n.* 54

Gebel Ahmar, 59, 134 *n.* 115

Gebel Giyuchi, 59

Gebire, 221, 222

Gedrosia, 247

Germain, civ

Gihon, 252

Gizeh, cxvii, 201

Glaucus, ci

Greek mercenaries, cxxvii

Grimm, Wilhelm, xxiii

Gurneh, cvii

Gymnophistes, 253

Haïat-en-nafûs, cii

Hakhininnsuîti, 39 *n.* 10

Hakôris, 212

Hanufi, 195

Hapis, 185 (See Apis)

Hapuî, cx *n.* 76

Haraûi, 16

Harbisa, 188 *et seq.*

Hariu-Horu, 61, 74, 75

Harmakhis, 7 *n.* 18, 143 *seq*

Harmakhuîti, 7 *n.* 18, 197

Harmhabi, cxxiv *n.* 116

Haroêris-Râ, 73

Harshafi, 47

Harsiesît, 62 *n.* 8

Haruêri, 62 *n.* 8, 73 *n.* 61

Haruî, 189

Haruît-nabît-duû-doshir, 59, 63

Harûiû-Shâiu, 65 *n.* 22

Harûn-ar-rashid, cxix

Hassan, Salîm, xxvii–xxviii

Hâthor, lv, 59, 76 *n.* 79, 188 *n.* 16

Hatibi, 180

Hatshopsuitu, cxlviii, 88 *n.* 23, 145 *n.* 11, 155 *n.* 7

Hâuâru, 223, 224 *n.* 13

Hecatæus, cxx *n.* 105

Helen, cxiv, 77 *n.* 83

Heliodorus, cxxii, cxlvii

Heliopolis, cxx, cxxi, 72 *n.* 55, 194, 213

Henassieh, 39 *n.* 10

Hephæstion, c *n.* 31

Hephæstus, 138, 139, 149

Hermes, 244 *n.* 1

Hermes Trismegistus, 130 *n.* 106

Hermonthis, cxxxvii *n.* 182

Hermopolis, 130 *n.* 106

Herodotus, cxxiii, cxxvi, cxxvii, cxxix, 137, 138, 148

Hieraconpolis, 122 *n.* 85

Higa, 211

Hippolytus, ci

Hiqaît, cxxxvii, 29 *seq.*

Hiram, cxi, 171

Hobs-bagai, 26 *n.* 28

Homerites, 253

Horapollo, cxxxviii *n.* 188

Horites, 60

Horus, the child, cxxxiv

—the elder, 62 *n.* 8, 72, 73 *n.* 61

—in the two horizons, 7 *n.* 18

—king as, 69, 73 *n.* 64, 143

—son of Isis, cxxvi, 61, 62 *n.* 8, 203, 240

—son of Panishi, cxliii, 130, 131, 132, 134, 135 *et seq.*

—son of Tnahsit the negress, cxxxii, cxxxix, 125, 129 *n.* 101, 132, 134, 135

—son of Triphrît, 129 *n.* 102

—son of Trirît, 128 *n.* 100

Hrihoru, cxlviii, 170, 178 *n.* 21

Hu-Sau, cxxxv

Hyksôs, 18, 93 *n.* 16, 125 *n.* 91

Iabu, 74 *n.* 67

Iadoue, 246 *n.* 6

Iakhuit, 62

Iaûku, 59

Iaumâ, name of Nile, 7 *n.* 19

Ibshân, 183

Idumea, 60

Imu, 89

Inarôs, cxvii, cxxi, 97, 110, 183, 198 *et seq.*

India, 253

Inferno, xcvi

Iôdaê, 246 *n.* 6

Isis, cxxxiii, cxxxv, *n.* 169, cxxxvii, 9 *n.* 25, 29, 104, 203

Ismailia, 61

Ivan, civ

Jacob, 30 *n.* 43

Jeremiah, 251

Jesus, son of Sirach, 255

Johns, Mrs. C. H. W., ix–x, xvi, xxii, xxxii

Joppa, cxii–cxiii, cxlvi, 89

Jôpu, cxii, 89

Juba, clii *n.* 238

Julios, 253 *seq.*

Jupiter Amon, cviii *n.* 71

Kadimâ, 60, 63, 69

Kakauî, 31 *n.* 48

Kalanos, Kalynas, 253

Kamaralzaman, cii, ciii

Kapuna, 60

Karnak, xx, 128 *n.* 98, 143, 242 *n.* 8

Kaûshû, 16

Kazareti, cxlvi

Kedem, 60

Khâfrîya, cvii, 19

Khamoîs (*cf.* Satni), cxv, cxvi, cxxxii, 171, 179

Khamsîn, 205 *n.* 48

Khanes, 39 *n.* 10

Kharu, 60, 90, 155, 196 *n.* 29

Khati, cx, cxxxvi *n.* 173, 38, 144 *n.* 5

Khato, 74 *n.* 68

Khattusil II, cx, 144 *n.* 5

Khaziru, 199

Khemmis, 203

Khininnsuît, 39, 41 *n.* 22

Khmunu, 130, 131

Khnumisuîtu, 61

Khnumu, c *n.* 31, cxxxvi, cxxxvii, 10, 29, 200 *n.* 36, 214

Khoïak, cxxxiv

Khoîris, 196

Khonshotpu, cxxix

Khonsu, cx, 142, 145, 10

Khonsuhânutirnabît, 143

Khonsumhâbi, 229, 230

Khonti, 74 *n.* 68

Khonti-Kaushu, 73 *n.* 65

Khopirkerîya, cvii, cxlix, 69 *n.* 40

Khoprûi-maruîti, 185

Khufuî, cvii–cix, cxix, 17 *seq.*, 19, 237

Khunianupu, 38

Kneph, 127 *n.* 97

Knuphis, 127 *n.* 97

Kodshu, cxiii

Krateros, 253

Lacedemonia, 245 *n.* 4

Lamites, 244, 245 *n.* 3, 246 *n.* 5

Latopolis, 184

Lektumenos, 245 *n.* 4

Leucippus, cxlvii

Libyans, cxxvii

Lisht, 75 *n.* 72

Loiseleur-Deslongchamp, A., xxiii

Lotanu-Lotan, 60, 63 *n.* 14

Luxor, cvii, cxxv, cxxxvi

Lycerus, cxi

Lycia, ci

Macedonia, 253

Madenît, 39 *n.* 11

Mafkit, 188 *n.* 16

Magidi, cxlvi

Mahîtuaskhît, cxxviii, cxxxi *n.* 143,
        cxliii, 120 *seq.*, 126

Maîaemapît, 16

Maîhet, cxvi, cxliv, 99 *et seq.*

Makamaru, 173

Mâki, 73

Makrizî, cxxxi *n.* 145

Maluli, cxv *n.* 87

Manahkbîya, 90 *n.* 1

Manakhphrê, cviii *n.* 68, cxviii *n.* 97,
        128, 129, 131

Manakhpirrîya, 90 *n.* 1

Mandulis, cxv *n.* 87

Manetho, cxxii *n.* 108, 125 *n.* 91, 240
        n. 1

Mângabuti, 172

Manhapurîya, cviii, 231

Mankhuît, 3 *n.* 1

Maræotis, 236

Marea, 235

Mariette, Auguste, vii

Maru, 39 *seq.*

Maruîtsakro, 105 *n.* 32

Maruli, cxv *n.* 87

Maruri, cxv *n.* 87

Masai, 199 *n.* 32

Masara, 189 *n.* 18

Maskhonuît, cxxxvii, 29 *n.* 37 *seq.*, 31

Maspero, Gaston Camille Charles

—avoidance of conjecture, xviii

—biographical sketch, vii–viii

—and folk songs and folktales,
        xxviii–xxx

—hope that stories would be
        reintroduced into Egyptian
        culture, xxxi–xxxii

—text analysis tools (terminology),
        xi–xii

—theoretical orientation, xii–xiv

—translation approach, xvii–xviii

Mauiti, 59, 63

Maût, 143

Maximilian, cxxxii *n.* 147

Mazaiu, cxxvii

Medinet Habu, cvii, 151

Megiddo, 60

Mêionhûri, 240 *n.* 4

Meîtum, cxx, 195

Memphis, xcvii, cvii, cxviii, cxx, cxxxix–cxxx, cxliv, 19 *n.* 4, 24, 17 *n.* 59, 97, 240

Menander, 244 *seq.*

Mendes, cxx, 183, 190, 191, 195

Menelaus, cxiv, 77

Menes, cvi *n.* 60, cxv, cxxxiii, 3 *n.* 3, 33 *n.* 59

Menkaûrîya, 24 *n.* 16

Menûs, 73

Merenephthis, 98 *n.* 5

Meroë, 127 *n.* 96, 199

Mesios, 253

Metelis, 187

Mînephtah, xciii, cxvi, cxlii *n.* 201

Mînibphtah, cviii, cxvi, cxvi, cxvii *seq.*

Minnebonêî, 211

Mînnemêî, 189, 194, 199, 200

Minu, 72 *n.* 58

Mnevis, 185

Moeris, 135 *n.* 118

Mohammed Ali, cxix, cxx

Moiris, cxv

Monatiu, 66 *n.* 25

Monthotpu, cxlviii *n.* 223

Montu, cxxxvii, 67, 143, 227

Montubaal, 196 *seq.*

Monturâ, 208

Moses, cxxxi *n.* 145, 201

Muî-hik-Snofru, 59

Mutemua, cxxv, cxxxvi

Myekphoris, 59

Mykerinus, cxv, 33, 221

Nabka, 18, 19, 21, 22

Nabkaûrîya, cviii, 38, 42

Nafhotpu, 145 *n.* 10

Nafrurîya, 144

Nagaû, 59, 63

Naharaina, 144

Naharinna, cxxviii, cxlvii, 105, 144 *n.* 2, 154 *et seq.*

Napata, 127 *n.* 96

Nathô, 185 *n.* 7

Nearchus, cxiii

Nectanebo, cxi, 217, 240, 241 *n.* 5

Nectonabo, 239, 240 *seq.*

Neferarkerîya, 31 *n.* 48

Neferhô, 19

Neith, 185 *n.* 9

Nenoferkephtah, xcvi, cxvi, cxxxii *n.* 149, cxliii, cxliv, 101, 163, 230, 231

Nephthys, cxxxv *n.* 169, cxxxvii, 29 *seq.*

Nitocris, 148, 221

Nofrît, 38 *n.* 2, 61 *n.* 3

Nomiu-shâiu, 63, 65 *n.* 22, 78

North Syria, 154

Noureddin, cxxx

Nubîti, 143

Nubuît, 76 *n.* 79

Nuhît, 59

Nuît, cxli, 72, 144

Nyanza Kerouê, cli

Oasis of Salt, 42

Oenos, 122 *n.* 84

Okianos, 251

Olympias, 253

Ombo, 72 *n.* 54

Omm-el-gaâb, cxli *n.* 195

Onhûri, 240 *n.* 4

Onu, 27

Onuris, 240 *n.* 4

Ophiôdes, clii, *n.* 238

Orontes, 144 *n.* 2

Osarsûph, 201

Osimanduas, cviii, cxv, 150, 151

Osimandyas, 147

Osiris, cvi, cxxxiv, cxxxv, cxxxix, 8 *n.* 20, 9 *n.* 27, 107 *n.* 37, 121, 122, 148, 185 n. 9

—lord of silence, 40

Ostanes, 98 *n.* 6

Oudja-Hor, 235 *n.* 6

Paênekhi, 6 *n.* 16, 91 *n.* 6

Pafifi, 39 *n.* 11

Pai, 203 *n.* 40

Pakhons, 145

Pakhuît, 64 *n.* 17

Pakrûr, cix, cxx, 183, 201, 202

Palakhîtit, 188

Pa-nabît-nuhît, 59

Panaho, 59

Panamhu, 192

Pandora, c *n.* 31

Panishi, cxxxii, *n.* 153 *seq.*

Panshatantra, cv *n.* 53

Paophi, cxxxvii, cxxxviii, 9 *n.* 25

Para-âûi, 11 *n.* 33

Paris, 77 *n.* 83

Pa-Sahurîya, 18

Pât, 59

Patenefi, 213

Payni, 144

Pebrekhaf, 194

Peleus, ci

Pelusium, 139, 148, 149, 185 *n.* 7

Pemu, cxx, 182 *seq.*, 190, 191, 201, 213

Penamânu, 178

Pentsate, 235 *n.* 5

Per-Shôû, 241 *n.* 6

Pesnufi, 201, 207, 212

Petekhonsu, cxx, 189, 193, 194

Petesêtis, 235 *n.* 5

Petêsis, 239 *seq.*

Petrie, William Matthew Flinders, viii

Petubastis, xcv, cviii, cxx, 183, 201, 202, 212

Peûn, 235

Pharaoh, 11 *n.* 33, 77 *n.* 83

Pharmuti, 240

Pheron, cxiv, cxv, cxviii

Phersô, 241 *n.* 6

Philae, 83 *n.* 2

Philea, 251

Philip of Macedonia, 240

Phineus, ci

Phiôps, 223

Phœnicia, 73 *n.* 66

Phrâ, 7 *n.* 18

Phrâ Harmakhis, 7, 156, 157, 225

Phrâmoonî, 188, 189, 194

Phtahhotpu, cxxviii

Pi, 203 *n.* 40

Pilakhîti, 195

Pimankhi, 189, 194

Pinebôthes, 213

Pisapdi, 183, 187, 212

Pisôn, 252

Piupi, cxlviii *n.* 223

Plain of Salt, cxxiv, 38, 39

Pliny, clii *n.* 238

Plutarch, cxxxiv *n.* 163

Polyænus, cxiii

Potiphar, ci

Prâ, 7 *n.* 18

Proetus, ci

Proteus, cxiv, cxviii, 77 *n.* 83

Pruîti, 77 *n.* 83

Psamatiku, 235 *n.* 6

Psammenetos, cxv

Psammetichus, cviii *n.* 71, cxiv, cxv,
    128 *n.* 98, 236

Psammis, cxv

Pseudo-Callisthenes, cxv, 240, 244

Psintalês, 195

Psituêris, 196

Ptah, cxxxv, 19, 20, 64 *n.* 17, 97, 116

Ptahhotpu, cxxviii

Ptolemy Philadelphus, 60

Pu, 203 *n.* 40

Puanît, clii, 72 *n.* 59, 87 *n.* 20

Puteni, 59, 63

Pzoeis, 195

Qadimâ, 60

Qagabû, 16

Qamâit, 3 *n.* 5

Qamuêri, 59, 60, 63

Qanofir, 61

Qurnah, 105 *n.* 32

Râ, xcvii, xcviii, cxxxiii, cxxxv,
    cxxxvii, cxxxix, 7 *n.* 18, 18, 28, 51,
    87 *n.* 18

—Apôpi, 224

—Harmakhis, 127

Râhotpu, cviii, cxliv, 230

Raîya, 7 *n.* 18

Ramesseum, 35, 150, 151

Ramses II, cix, cxvi–cxvii, cxxii,
    cxlvii, 6 *n.* 16, 143, 147, 150, 237

—III, cxlviii, 143, 151

—IV, cxlii *n.* 201

—V, cxlii *n.* 201

—IX, 171, 179 *n.* 25

—XI, 171

Râskenen, 224 *n.* 12

Ratonu-Latonu, 60

Râusir, 29

Rebîa, cxlvii

Rensi, 39 *seq.*

Rhampsinitus, cxv, cxvii, cxviii,
    cxxviii, 163, 164 *seq.*

Rhamses, cxv

Rîya, 7 *n.* 18

Riyamasâsu Maîamânu, 143

Ro Pegaît, cxli *n.* 195

Ro Pegarît, cxli *n.* 195

Rougé, Emmanuel de, ix

Ruditdidît, cxxv, 28 *seq.*

Ruîti, 77 *n.* 83

Saatiu, 61, 63, 65

Sabaco, cxv

Saft-el-Hineh, 212 *n.* 66

Sahotpiaburîya, 62, 63–64

Sahurîya, 31

Saîd, the, 183, 204

Sais, cxx, 185 *n.* 9, 194

Saka, cvi

Sakhîbu, cix, 28–33

Sakhmi, 184, 196

Sakhmît, 44 *n.* 28, 64 *n.* 17

Sakkara, 16 *n.* 53

Samaûs, 241

Sanacharibus, 138

Sanafruî, cvii, cxix, cxx, 19, 22, 59,
    63, 234

—island, 59, 63

—lake, 59

Sankharîya, cxlviii *n.* 223

Sanmuît, cli, 83

Sannozmu, 70 *n.* 47

Sanuosrît, cvii, cxxii *n.* 108, 61, 62,
    64 *n.* 18, 66 *n.* 26

Sapdi, 212, 213

Saqnûnrîya, cxi, 217, 223 *seq.*

Satapanrîya, 143

Sati, 37

Satmi (cf. Satni), 119 *seq.*

Satni, cxii, cxxviii, cxxx, cxli, cxliv, 95, 163, 242

—Khamôis, xciv, xcvi, xcviii, xcix, cxvi–cxvii, 97, 182, 230, 231

Satu, xciii *n.* 2

Sauakîn, 87 *n.* 20

Scythians, 149

Sea = Nile, 10, 103

—of Syria, 172

Sebonnytos, cxx, 183, 190, 239, 241

Selpharios, 248 *seq.*

Sennacherib, cxvii, 137

Senosiris, xcix, cxxxii, cxli, cxliii, 121 *seq.*,128

Serapeum, 239

Sergios, 251

Sesôstris, xciii, cviii, cxiv, cxv, cxxii *n.* 108, 147–151, 284

Sesusi-Sesoôsis, cxv, cxxii, 150, 151

Sesûsrîya, cxv, cxxii, 3 *n.* 1, 147–150

Sethon, cxviii, 137, 138

Set-Typhon, 44, 61, 148

Setûi Mainephtah, 3

—I, cxlii *n.* 201

—II, xciii, 3

Shaî, 127 *n.* 97

Shi-Sanafruî, 59

Shomu, 231 *n.* 4

Shopsiskaf, 18, 28 *n.* 35

Shôû, 241 *n.* 6

Shu, cxxxv, cxxxix, 183, 241 *n.* 6

Shubra, cxix

Siamânu, xcix, cviii, cxviii *n.* 97

Sibu-Gabu, 72 *n.* 60

Sicheus, 173 *n.* 5

Sidon, 175

Sihathor, 59

Simihît, cxlvii, 77

Sindbad, cxlix

Sinuhît, cvii, cxlvii, 55, 215 *n.* 77

Sît, 93 *n.* 16

Sîti, 77 *n.* 81

Sîtu, cxxxiv, cxxxv *n.* 169, cxxxix

Smendes, 170, 172, 178 *n.* 21

Sokarosiris, 123

Sokhît, cxxxv, 44, 64 *n.* 17, 65 *n.* 20, 93, 197

—hamaît, 37

—sakhmît, 44 *n.* 28

Sokhîti, 37

Solomon, cxi, 171

Sonkh, 235 *n.* 7

Sopdît, 72 *n.* 56

Sop-hô, cxxxv *n.* 170

Sothis, 72 *n.* 56

Sovku, cxxxviii *n.* 186, 44 *n.* 28, 72

Strabo, cxxvi

Suânu, 60, 63, 185

Sukhôtes, 195

Sunisi, 189

Sûpdîti, Sûpdu, 72 *n.* 56, 186 *n.* 10

Susa, 246 *n.* 5

Sutekhu, cxi, 93 *n.* 16, 177, 224, 225

Sûtenti, 37

Suti, 37, 93

Sychas, 173 *n.* 5

Syene, 199

Syria, 170, 175

Ta Amon, 3 *n.* 1

Tafnakhti, 195

Tafnît, 183 *n.* 1

Tahaît, 183, 190

Tahuris, 213

Taît, 70

Taîtu-tauî, 75

Takhôs, 188 *seq.*

Tanis, cxx, 172, 183, 190

Tantamânu, 170, 172, 178

Tantanuît, 180

Taônkh, 235 *n.* 7

Tasonût, 212

Tatumaut, 108 *n.* 38

Tbubui, xcvi, cxxviii, cxxix, cxxx, cxxxii, 111 *seq.*, 242

Tell Abtu, 203 *n.* 40

—Basta, 112 *n.* 57

—el-Maskhuta, 60

—Mokdam, 188 *n.* 16

Telmissus, cxiii

Temanthes, cviii *n.* 71

Teniponî, 188

Terraneh, 59

Thebaid, 103

Thebes, cvii, cxxx, cxxxvii *n.* 182, 171

Thessaly, 253

Thompson, Stith, xiv–xv, xxvii

Thotemhabi, cx, 145

Thoth, cxxii, cxxxiv, cxxxv, cxxxix, cxliv, 16, 25, 27, 28, 49, 51, 106, 123

Thotnakhuîti, cviii *n.* 66, 39

Thracians, Thrace, 149, 245

Thutîyi, cxi, cxii, cxiii, cxlvii, 90 *seq.*

Thûtmôsis I, cxii, cxviii

—II, cviii

—III, cviii, cxii, cxvii, 60, 128 *n.* 982

—IV, cxxxvi

Ti, 8 *n.* 20, 220

Tigris, 252

Tihonu, 62

Timihu, 59, 62 *n.* 6

Tiôme, 196

Tiuâqen, 224 *n.* 12

Tiuâu, 224 *n.* 12

Tnahsît, cxxxii *n.* 153, 129 *n.* 101

Tonu, cxlvii, 57, 60

Topazôn, cliii

Torzerûf, 3 *n.* 5

Tréménéazour, cv

Triphît, 129 *n.* 102

Trîrît, 128 *n.* 100

Trismegistus, 131 *n.* 107

Tumu, 72 *n.* 55

Tunipu, cxiii

Turah, 59

Tybi, cxxxiv, cxxxv, 28, 118

Typhon, 8 *n.* 20, 204 *n.* 45

Tyre, cxlv, 170, 173

Uarurît, 72

Uasimarîya, cviii, cxv–cxvii, 147 *seq.*

—Satapanrîya, 143, 146, 147

Uazhor, 189

Uaz-uêrit, 73 *n.* 62

Ubastît, 64

Ubaû-anir, cxxvii, 132 *n.* 150, 18, 20

Uchoreus, cxv

Uiluhni, 195 *seq.*

Uîti, 38 *n.* 6

Ulysses, cl

Unamunu, xcvi, cx *n.* 75, cxlviii, 170 *seq.*

Uohsunefgamûl, 195

Uotît, 188 *n.* 16

Upper Tonu, 60, 63

Usimanthor, 137

Usimares, cxii, 97

Usirkaf, 18, 30 *n.* 43

Usirraf, 30 *n.* 43

Ussîm, 184 *n.* 2
Uzakau, 188

Wady Natrûn, 38 *n.* 1, *n.* 5
—Tumilât, cxx, 61
Waradi, 173
Warakatîlu, 175 *n.* 11
Wawaît, cl, 83 *n.* 2
Wu Pegaît, Pegarît, cxli, *n.* 195

Zagazig, 112 *n.* 57
Zaggerit, 32
Zakkala, 170, 172, 173, 174, 179, 180

Zalchel, 192
Zaru, 61
Zasiri, 17, 18, 19
Zaûîphrê, 183, 186, 189, 193
Zauîranamhaî, 195
Zazamânkhu, cxxxi, 22
Zet, 137
Ziharpto, 96, 118
Zikarbal, 171, 173 *seq.*, 178 *n.* 21
Zingis, cli
Zinufi, 189
Zobeïde, cxxx
Zopyre, 90

Index
of General Subjects

Abstinence, iii *n.* 51, 115 *n.* 67

Acacia, 7

Académie des inscriptions et belles lettres, viii

"The Adventure of Satni-Khamoîs," xvi–xvii

Agathodemon, 127

Agricultural life, 4 *n.* 7

Almehs, cxxxvii, 237

Amulets, 23, 97

Angarebs, 12 *n.* 38, 26

Animals speaking: cows, 7

—serpent, 84 *seq.*, 222

The Arabian Nights, xiii–xiv, xxvi–xxvii

Arabic vernacular, xxviii–xxix

Asses, 39, 54, 163

Ba (soul), 144 *n.* 3

Baking, cxxiv, 38 *n.* 4, 75

Bark of Amon, 172, 178 *n.* 21

—of Khonsu, 143

—of wax, 104

Beards of soldiers, cxxvii, 166 *n.* 5

Beds, 26, 30, 31, 114

Bin for corn, 32

Birth customs, 29–30

—scenes, cxxv–cxxvi

Book of magic, 21, 23

—of the Dead, cxlii

—of Thoth, xcviii, cxxxii, cxliii, 25, 27, 97, 102 *seq.*, 108 *n.* 40, 110 *n.* 49

—caskets, 21, 25, 27

—vases, 127 *n.* 95

Bouza, 32

Brandy, 234 *seq.*

Brazier, 98, 111, 116

Brewing, 32, 38, 75

Bride of the Nile, c, 10 *n.* 31

Burghers, 41

Burial customs, 70–71, 108–109

Burnt offering, 84, 116

Byssus, 191, 207

Cairo Catalogue of Antiquities, viii

Calasîris, 193, 196, 212

Canals, 148, 149

—of two fishes, 28

—of two truths, 59

Cange, cxix, 41, 104, 107

Cartulary, xciv

Casket, 21, 25, 27

Castanets, 76

Cat, cxi–cxii

Cedars, 171 *seq.*

Cermonial prostrations, 71, 215

Challenges to kings, cxi–cxii, 119–120

Chansons populaires recueillies dans la

Haute-Égypte de 1900 à 1914 pendant les inspections du Service des antiquités, xxviii

Chariot, 156

Chasm in water, 105

Chastity, III *n.* 51, 115 *n.* 67

Cheetah, 6 *n.* 16, 91 oft.

City of Horus, 130 *n.* 104

Coffer, 103

Coiffure, 5 *n.* 10

Colocasia, 120

Composition of stories, xcvi *seq.*

Concubine, cxxiv

"The Contendings of Horus and Seth," xxvii, xxviii

Contes populaires de l'Égypte ancienne. See Popular Stories of Ancient Egypt

Contract of maintenance, 113

Convulsions, 174

Coptic fragments, 218

Corn payment, 31

Country of oxen, 39

—of papyrus, 201–202

Covering of the face, 83

Cradle rockers, 15 *n.* 49

Crocodile, 33, 46, 154, 157

—god, 44 *n.* 28

—wax, 21 *seq.*

Crow, 99

Crypts, cxxvi

Curses, 70 n.42

Days lucky or unlucky, cxxxiv

Death, euphemism for, 26 *n.* 25

Deir el-Bahari, viii

Delineation of Pharaoh, cix

Demotic, xcivx

—papyri, 95, 107 *n.* 37, 233

Destiny, cxxxvi, 161

Diadems, magic, 31

Dice, 163

Dog, 154, 157, 199

—deity, xxiii

—playing piece, 110 *n.* 45

"The Doomed Prince," xviii

Doorpost, 122 *n.* 85

Double (or ka), clii, 26, 78, 93, 99, 117 *n.* 74

—of gods, cx

—house of life, 97, 98, 101, 117, 121

——scribe of, 101 *n.* 14, 145 *n.* 8

Draughts, 109 *n.* 44

Dreams, cxxx–cxxxi, 120, 131, 138–139

Drinking magic, 106 *n.* 34

Duration of life, 25

Dust on the head, 72

Eaters of gum, 126, 186

Eating magic, 133–134

Ebony, 21, 23, 25

Egyptian astuteness, 167

—civilisation, cxxv

—doors, 7 *n.* 17

—expressions, 54

—house, 112–113

—language, 171

—vessels, 176–177

Electrum, 21, 23, 75 *n.* 75, 79

Elementargedanke (primitive theme), xxiv–xxv

Embalming, cxlii

Ennead of gods, 9

Entire land, 3 *n.* 5, 19

Escutcheons, 187

Euphemisms, 16, 28, 62, 64

Evil colour, 187 *n.* 13

Exodus, 240 *n.* I

Exposure of corpse, 165
External soul, xcix–c

Fables, xxii
Fairy tales, xxii
Falcon, 62
Falling star, 86
Fellah, cxxiii, cxxiv, 38
Ferry boat, 52
Fillets, 23 *n.* 13
Fine linen, 114
Fire making, 84, 113
Fish amulet, 23
Fishing, 47, 48
Flying, 62, 155
Forged inscription, 142
Friends, 61, 70
—of Seraglio, 62
Funeral ceremonies, 70, 108–109
Funerary outfit, 78, 79, 102–103

Game of chess, 109
Gap opening in ground, 98
Garments as bribe, 5, 20
Genii, cxli, 115 *n.* 65
Ghost, 145
Giant, 157, 158
Gold, 23, 26
Good dwelling, 106, 107
Good god, cxix
Goose, 27
Gospel of S. Luke, xcviii
Great pyramid, cxxvi, 25 *n.* 20
—royal spouse, 144 *n.* 5
Guepard, 6 *n.* 16

Hades, 163
Harpâ, 199 *n.* 32, 206
Head replaced, 25, 27

Heart on a flower, xcix, 8, 10
Herdsmen, cxxiii, 202 *seq.*
Hermetic books, 98 *n.* 6
Hieratic, xciv, *n.* 5
Hierodule, 112
Hippopotamus, 33 *n.* 59
Historical legends, xxii
Hutches for grain, 5 *n.* 11
Hypocephalus, cxlii *n.* 204

Imprecations, 70
Impure, the, 43 *n.* 27, 201, 224 *n.* 11
Incubation, cxxx *seq.*, 120, 131 *n.* 108,
    138 *n.* 120
Infants, 69 *n.* 39, 71, 75 *seq.*
Inheritance, cxxiv
Inshâ-style, xxv–xxvi
Institute Français d'Archaeologie
    Orientale, vii
Intersigns, cv *n.* 54, cxxxi–cxxxii,
    133–134, 158 *n.* 15
Invocations, 71
Island of the blessed, clii
—of the dead, clii
—of the double, clii, 85

Jars containing men, cxiv, 93
Journey of Sun, cxli, 52 *n.* 70
Judgment of soul, cxli, 123
Jurisprudence, 113 *n.* 61

Ka or double, 85 *n.* 12, 99 *n.* 10
Khu or luminous, cxliv
King as god, 62
"King Khufuî and the Magicians,"
    xvi, xix–xx, xxiv
Kissing, 86 *n.* 17, 215 *n.* 78
Kolobi, 235–236
Kurbash, 46, 128, 129

Lady of all, 68
—pestilence, 44, 44 *n.* 28
Lake, 20, 21, 23, 79 *n.* 91
—divided by magic, 24
—of the Gazelle, 188 *seq.*
"The Lamentations of the Fellah,"
    xxi, xxv
Land tax, 149–150
—tenure, 51 *n.* 61
Lapis lazuli, 113
—hair, 30, 31
Last Egyptian scholar, xciv
Leather, 32
Lector, cxxxi, 19 *n.* 2, 20, 185, 204
—chief, 22
L.h.s. explained, 11 *n.* 33, 22
Libation, 104, 116
Light due to magic, 99, 110, 116
Limit of life, cxl
Lion, 150–151
Lord of Silence, 40
Luminous, cxliv

Magic, books of, xciv, 21, 23, 97
—charms, cxxxviii *seq.*, 101*n.* 15
—formulæ, cxxxiii, cxxxviii–cxl, 97
—island, 84 *seq.*
—rites, 111 *n.* 50
Magicians, chastity of, 111 *n.* 51, 115
    n. 67
Malachite, 23, 113 *n.* 59, 144
Male-bound themes, xxvi–xxvii
Man of the roll, cxxxi, 19, 20 *n.* 5, 69
    n. 37, 71 *n.* 49
Mannhardt, W., ix
Maple wood, 23
Märchen, ix, xii–xiii, xxvi, xxxi
Marks on Apis, 13 *n.* 39

Marriage of brother and sister, 100
Masterless man, cxxv
Masters of the night, 129
Mediæval maps, cli
Mines of Pharaoh, cl
Miracles, cxxxi
Mistresses of the night, 129
Morals, cxxxvii–cxxxviii
Motif-Index of Folk Literature,
    xiv–xv
Mouth of the tree, cxli
Movable stone, cxxvi–cxxvii, 27–28,
    164
Mummification, cxlii
Musée de Boulaq, vii
Musicians, 29

Napeca wood, 25 *n.* 22
Narû, 8 *n.* 20
Nets as clothing, 23
Nine times great, 131 *n.* 107
Nocturnal course of sun, cxli *n.* 196
Nubian Temple volumes, viii

Obsession by magic writings, 111
Offerings, 104
One (periphrasis), 12 *n.* 36, 107 *n.* 35
Ostraca, xcv
Ostracon, British Museum, 57
—Cairo, 57
—Paris, 229

Papyrus Anastasi, No. 4, cxxxix,
    cxlv, cxlvii, 3, 154, 239
—Berlin, No. 1, 55
——No. 2, cxxiv, 35, 36
——No. 3, 219
——No. 4, 35

—Boulaq, xciv, xcv, 95

—British Museum, DCIV, 118

—Butler, 36

—Demotic, 95

—D'Orbiney, xciii, xciv, cii

—Ebers, 18

Papyrus Fayûm, 135 *n.* 118

—Golénischeff, 19 *n.* 1, 55

—Harris, xcv, cxxxix *n.* 192, 89, 153, 221

—Hieratic, xciv *n.* 5, 81, 127, 169

—Hood, 61 *n.* 1

—Leyden, cxl, *n.* 193

—Ramesseum, 35, 55, 150

—Sallier, xcvi *n.* 20, cxxxiv *n.* 164, cxxxv *n.* 167, cxxxviii *n.* 185, cxxxxix *n.* 189, 16 *n.* 53, 125 *n.* 91, 223

—Turin, xcv, 18

—Westcar, cviii, cix *n.* 73, 17, 18, 33

Patron, cxxv

People of the circle, 77

—of the corner, 77 *n.* 82, 108

Perfume of acclamation, 86, 87

Persea tree, c, cv, 14, 15

Personal experience narratives, xxii

Pharmacy of the soul, 151

Pictoral illustrations, cxxv

Pilots, 208 *n.* 58

Playing board, 109

—pieces, 109

Polygamy, 3 *n.* 1

Pool of Justice, 41

Popular Stories of Ancient Egypt, ix–x

—authorship of, xxiii–xxvi, xxvi

—contents and structure, x, x *n.* 11–xii *n.* 13

—contextual notes, xviii–xx

—cultural comparisons, xx–xxi

—ethnographic comparisons, xxi

—ethnological comparisons, xx–xxi

—explanations of actions, xix

—in folklore indexes, xiv–xv

—genres, xxii

—languages and writing systems of texts, xv

—narrative sources, xv–xvii

—notes on social practices, xix

—popular stories rather than folktales, xxii

—verbal lore and material culture in, xix–xx

Position of Pharaoh, cxx

Possession and exorcism, 142

Prayer for hours of the night, xciv

Presages, cxxxiv *seq.*

Prescience, 85

Priests of the double, 78

Primogeniture, cxxiv

Princess of Bakhtan, xcvi, 144 *seq.*

Prophetic frenzy, 174

Prostration, 86–87

Punishment by fire, 22

Punning names, cxxxvii, 30

Pyramid, Dahchûr, cxxvi *n.* 123

—Great, cxxvi, 25 *n.* 20

—of Senuhît, 57

Ram of Medes, 14 *n.* 43

Rebirth, xcviii, xcix, cxliii

Recapitation, 25, 27

Recluses of the Serapeum, 239

Regent of the earth, 68

Rise of romance, xcvi

Roads of Horus, 61

Romances, xciv

Roof of house, 121, 154

Sacred book of the Mormons, cxlii
Sallier calendar, cxxxiv *n.* 165
Salutation, 86 *n.* 17
Sceptre, 76
Schene, 103
Sea faring, cxlvii
Seal, 32
Season, harvest, 178
Self-mutilation, cv
Senior member of the Hall, 172
Serpent, cxli, cxlix, 84 *seq.*, 103, 105,
    154, 158
Service des antiquités de l'Égypte,
    vii–viii
Seven halls of Hades, 122
Share, cxxiv
"The Shipwrecked Sailor," xxii,
    xxvii
Silo, 31
Silver gilt, 75
Sinking into earth, 110
Sistrum, 76
Slaves, 54, 88
Sliding stone, cxxvi, cxxvii *n.* 124, *n.*
    127, 27–28, 164
Solar disc, 62
Sorcery, cxxxi
Souls of gods and kings, 87
Sparrowhawk, 147
Sphinx, 7 *n.* 18, 75
Spinning, cxxiv
Staff, 91
Stela, cxxiv *n.* 116, 60, 101, 149
Step-brother, 33

Tabonu, 102, 176

"The Tale of the Two Brothers," ix,
    xiv, xv, xxii, xxiv–xxv
Talisman, 208
Talking animals, 7
—mummies, cxliii
—serpent, 84–85 *seq.*, 222
Tarichutes, 185
Temple sculptures, 150–151
Terrace, 154
Text analysis tools (terminology),
    xi–xii
The impure, 43 *n.* 27, 201, 224 *n.* 11
Theocracy, 138
The subjucated land, 73
The sycamore, 59
The vanquished, cxii–cxiii, 90 *n.* 5
The very green, 73
Throne, cxxiii
Tilt yard, 194
To praise Râ, 107
Tourney, cxxii
Transformation, 114, 117
Travel, cxlv
Treasure chamber, 164
Triplets, xcvii, 18, 28
True of voice, 19, 69 *n.* 37
Turquoise, 113
The Types of the Folktale, xiv, xv

Umbrella, 178
Underworld, cxl–cxli
Uræus, 72 *n.* 57, 204 *n.* 45

Vale of the acacia, xcix, 7
Vanquished, cxii–cxiii, 90 *n.* 5
Vassal, cxxv, 20
Vendetta, cxxii
Voyage of the dead, cliii

Vulture as guide, 99

War dogs, 199 *n.* 35
Wax, boat, 104

—crocodile, 21
—litter, 129
Weaving, cxxiv
Wine skins, 165

About the Volume Editor

Hasan El-Shamy is Professor of Folklore, Near Eastern Languages and Cultures, and African Studies at Indiana University, Bloomington, Indiana. He is the author of several books, including *Tales Arab Women Tell, and the Behavioral Patterns They Portray* (1999); *Folk Traditions of the Arab World: A Guide to Motif Classifications* (1995); and *Folktales of Egypt: Collected, Translated, and Edited with Middle Eastern and [Sub-Saharan] African Parallels* (1980).